INTER-AMERICAN DEVELOPMENT BANK

FACING UP TO INEQUALITY IN LATIN AMERICA

ECONOMIC AND SOCIAL PROGRESS IN LATIN AMERICA • 1998-1999 REPORT

Distributed by the Johns Hopkins University Press for
the Inter-American Development Bank

Washington, D.C.

ECONOMIC AND SOCIAL PROGRESS IN LATIN AMERICA

© Copyright 1998 by the Inter-American Development Bank
   1300 New York Avenue, N.W.
   Washington, D.C. 20577

Distributed by
The Johns Hopkins University Press
2715 North Charles Street
Baltimore, Maryland 21218-4319

Library of Congress Card No.: 98-75411
ISBN: 1-886938-36-9
ISSN: 0095-2850

PREFACE

A window of opportunity has opened for Latin America. Thanks to its changing demographics, the region has a chance to accelerate its development and attack one of its greatest socioeconomic ills: inequality. With the right policies, right now, there would be no tradeoff between development and equity in what has become the most unequal region in the world.

Most of Latin America stands at an opportune moment in its demographic transition. Fertility rates are falling and a large cohort of children is entering the workforce. With fewer children to care for and still relatively few old people to pay for, the present generation of Latin Americans is in a position to be a motor for economic growth and an agent for social change.

How long will this opportunity last? For the next two decades, most countries will enjoy a declining ratio of children to workers before a rising ratio of retired to active workers begins to represent a much heavier financial burden. This leaves two decades to accelerate the development process, put people to work, finance educational improvements and save for the future. If policies are enacted to further these goals, Latin America could open up its growth potential while it closes its income gap.

Clearly, economic growth and income redistribution are not new goals in Latin America. What is new is the demographic moment and the urgency to get the policies right or waste an historic opportunity. For this reason, we dedicated the 1998-1999 edition of *Economic and Social Progress in Latin America* to the study of inequality. With a better understanding of the problem, better policy responses are possible.

We begin by measuring the magnitude of the problem. How skewed is income distribution in Latin America? How does it vary within and across countries? We then paint a portrait of Latin America's rich and poor. Who are they? What are their families like? How do they make decisions about whether to go to school or to work, or to have children? With this description of individuals and families along the income spectrum, we ask why Latin America is the most unequal region in the world. We un-

cover a complicated, multidimensional story that attributes the region's poor income distribution to a complex set of factors ranging from Latin America's stage of development to its natural endowments and geography. Latin America's inequality has less to do with political exclusion—as populist diatribe would have us believe—and more to do with where these countries are placed on the map, what resources they have, and how far they are along the development time line.

Armed with this information, we look at what can be done to improve income distribution. There are a variety of policy options available to promote both development and equity and capitalize on this period of favorable demographics: labor law reforms to welcome new entrants to the workforce; improvements in public services to free up more women for gainful employment; fully-funded pension systems to generate savings; collateral, group lending and other mechanisms to deepen the credit market and make capital available to previously excluded groups; decentralized school systems to improve the quality of education; and direct subsidies for school supplies and food to keep low-income children in school. All of these policies would not only help economies grow, but allow more and more people to benefit from that growth.

In this report, we have tried to face up to the inequality that has long plagued Latin America, understand its causes, and offer policies that will make a difference. In doing so, our research and findings speak to a number of audiences: to the institutions both within and outside the region whose priorities include promoting social development and reducing poverty; to Latin American governments, fearful of the political consequences of socioeconomic stratification; to the region's policymakers, ready to translate years of good intentions into measurable results; and to the millions of Latin Americans who are anxious to share in the region's development.

Ricardo Hausmann
Chief Economist

ACKNOWLEDGMENTS

Research Team

The research team of the Office of the Chief Economist was responsible for this report under the direction of Ricardo Hausmann and the coordination of Eduardo Lora. The principal coauthors were Michael Gavin (Chapters 4 and 7), Ricardo Hausmann (Introduction and Chapter 3), Eduardo Lora (Chapters 1, 2, 6 and 8), Carmen Pagés (Chapter 6), William Savedoff (Chapters 3, 5 and 8), Miguel Székely (Chapters 1 and 3) and Glenn Westley (Chapter 7). Suzanne Duryea and Miguel Székely were responsible for the processing of household surveys and for econometric analyses based on those surveys. Ricardo Paes de Barros provided technical support for that processing and analytical material based on the surveys. Background material was contributed by Mónica Barbosa, Mymon Dahan, Ruthanne Deutsch, Suzanne Duryea, Edward Leamer, Juan Luis Londoño, Nora Lusting, Gustavo Márquez, Rosane Mendoça, Phillipe George Pereira, Claudia Piras and Antonio Spilimbergo. Martín Cumpa, Marianne Hilgert, Marie Claude Jean, Mauricio Olivera, and Naoko Shinkai were research assistants. José Antonio Mejía supported the organization of the household surveys.

Data Bases

The principal source of information for this report was the household surveys generously provided by the Governments of Argentina, Bolivia, Brazil, Chile, Costa Rica, Ecuador, El Salvador, Honduras, Mexico, Panama, Paraguay, Peru, Uruguay and Venezuela. The "Improvement of Surveys and Measurement of Living Standards Program" (Mecovi) contributed to the gathering and organization of surveys. The World Bank, ECLAC, the International Monetary Fund and the Harvard Institute for International Development provided international data bases used in the report.

Comments

The study was enriched by comments and suggestions from Nelson Avila, Gregorio Arévalo, Neville Beharie, Nancy Birdsall, Euric Bobb, Luis Rene Cáceres, Xavier Comas, Ciro de Falco, Ruthanne Deutsch, Luis Fierro, Carol Graham, Carlos Alberto Herrán, Enrique Iglesias, Bernardo Kliksberg, Arianna Legovini, Ruth Levine, Nora Lustig, Miguel Martínez, Bertus Meins, Alberto Melo, Samuel Morley, Carlos Oliva, Andrew Powell, Alberto Pico, Stephen Quick, Nohra Rey de Marulanda, Inder Ruprah, Ricardo Santiago, Graciela Schamis, Carlos Eduardo Velez, and Waldemar Wirsig.

Statistical Appendix

The Statistical Appendix was prepared under the direction of Michael McPeak and the coordination of Rajindra Lalchan, with participation by Nathalie Carcenac, Augusto Clavijo, Cleary Haines and Rafael Salas.

Translation, Editing and Administrative Support

Larry Hanlon and Carlos Trípodi were in charge of the translation for the respective English and Spanish versions. Rita Funaro, Marie Claude Jean, Mauricio Olivera, and Graciela Thomen collaborated in the compilation process. Rafael Cruz, David Einhorn, and Gerardo Giannoni were responsible for the editorial revision. The cover was designed by Alejandra Luzardo. Cecilia Coder, Leticia Cuevas, and Graciela Thomen provided administrative support throughout the entire process

TABLE OF CONTENTS

Introduction

FACING UP
TO INEQUALITY

It was a difficult year for Latin America and the Caribbean. The East Asian economic crisis and the financial rumblings in Russia generated unsettling aftershocks in emerging financial markets. The bottom fell out of prices for key commodities such as oil and metals, and even nature dealt its blow in the form of El Niño. Volatility has hit again. But thanks to a decade of structural reforms, the region has been better able to cope with economic disruption. Macroeconomic stability may have been at risk in some countries, but the prospects of growth and price stability remain strong.

Beyond these recent and hopefully transitory concerns, however, Latin America has a very sad tale to tell. And this is where we have cast our eyes this year. Instead of applauding recent advances, we once again have chosen to address a pressing regional issue. This year's Report on *Economic and Social Progress in Latin America* focuses on income distribution, an area where there has been much less progress and where the region still appears to under-perform significantly.

On average, the countries of the region suffer from the greatest income inequality in the world. True, there are some countries, such as Costa Rica, Jamaica and Uruguay, where inequality is relatively low by regional standards. But the region also has the countries with the widest income gaps in the world: in Brazil and Guatemala, the top 10 percent of the population amass almost 50 percent of national income, while the bottom 50 percent scrape up little more than 10 percent. More importantly, the problem shows no obvious signs of improvement. Our best measures indicate that income distribution improved in the 1970s, worsened considerably in the 1980s and has remained stagnant at high levels in the 1990s. Even these variations are small relative to the high overall level of income inequality. Thus, income inequality appears to be an enduring phenomenon with deep long-run causes.

Addressing income inequality in the region is important for social and political as well as economic reasons. Inequality contributes not only to high rates of poverty, but also to social tension and political disaffection.

When only a few can feast on the fruits of economic progress, social stress tears at the fabric of society and political support wanes for the policies that underpin that progress. The issue is on the table in most countries of the region. Despite relatively little evidence, and many unsatisfactory explanations, income distribution is an issue impassioned by strong opinions. This study attempts to assemble the available evidence on inequality, expand it with special statistical information, and use it systematically to test a wide range of potential explanations and remedies.

SURVEYING THE EVIDENCE

Much of the region's inequality is associated with large wage differentials. In other words, it results not only from differences between owners of capital and workers, but from a divergence of incomes among workers. Large wage differentials reflect, among other factors, unequal distribution of the quantity and quality of schooling. The inequality in wages also reflects gender differences, gaps between formal and informal employment and between rural and urban incomes, and other forms of labor market segmentation that are exacerbated by current labor legislation.

The evidence does not support the notion that high inequality in Latin America is simply a matter of a few rich families owning a disproportionate share of each country. If this were the case, it would be impossible to measure the high levels of inequality, given that the very rich are under-represented in the household surveys on which measures of inequality are based. But it is precisely these same surveys that point to Latin America as unequal relative to other parts of the world. According to these surveys, inequality primarily results not from the existence of a few people at the top but from a much more widespread social phenomenon.

In fact, much of Latin America's inequality relates to the difference between the top 10 percent of the population and the rest. While in the United States families in the top decile have an average per capita income about 60 percent higher than those in the ninth decile, in Latin America they earn about 160 percent more. The top earners in Latin America are mainly employees and professionals who receive very high returns for their education and experience. Only 14 percent of them are employers. Why are the returns so concentrated at the top? After all, it is a full 10 percent of the population, a very large group of people who on average have barely completed 12 years of education.

Nonetheless, much of this gap between the top 10 percent and the rest reflects the region's slow and unequal progress in improving the level and quality of schooling. The second richest 10 percent of the population has three fewer years of education, and those in the bottom 30 percent have almost seven years less. Moreover, differences in schooling are transmitted from one generation to the next through the family. Human capital is, after all, a family affair. It involves an inter-generational transfer of resources, as parents limit their own consumption to pay for the education of their children, who go on to enjoy the benefits of their accumulated human capital in the future labor market. This transfer of educational attainment from one generation to the next has led many to fault the educational systems, which do carry part of the blame. But families also make decisions and choices that affect the educational attainment and welfare of their children.

Families play many roles in the complex relationships that sustain income inequality. They mitigate the effects of high inequality by sharing resources, often across generations. They also play a role in determining how many of their members should try to find work, how many children to have, and how much education to give them. Many of these decisions are influenced by relative prices in the economy, particularly wages.

A very important relative price in these choices is the return to a woman's work in the market. As this expected wage rises, more women tend to participate in the labor force. Under these circumstances, families also tend to have fewer children, and the children they do have complete more years of school. But this wage is not the same for everyone. Unskilled women can expect much lower earnings than their counterparts from higher-income families, since they have less education and because they are more likely to find informal than formal sector jobs. Furthermore, these wages will vary across countries, depending on the structure of each economy and trends in its particular labor market. Each country's particular economic structure generates differences— some large, some small—in the relative prices faced by different families, which in turn cause variations in the amount of human capital each family will accumulate.

From this point of view, educational attainment is not only the consequence of education policy but also reflects wage patterns in the labor market, family choices about working and having children, and other factors that vary across countries. Two couples with similar characteristics who live in different countries of the region can be expected to make very different choices about education, work and children. Furthermore, the income inequality they and their children will face varies by about a factor of three from one country to the next. Hence, inequality only partially reflects personal characteristics and family choices; it also reflects important elements of the economic environment where people live.

It is precisely this economic environment that we have tried to piece together in this study—a task made more difficult by the confluence of temporary and permanent phenomena. Our tentative diagnosis is that the malady of income inequality in Latin America reflects both growing pains typical of developing societies and congenital features peculiar to the region. This combination has exacted a high toll from the socioeconomic health of many countries in recent years. But there is hope. Latin America is expected to eventually outgrow the transitional income inequality that often accompanies the early stages of development. And countries can choose policy remedies capable of turning their inherent liabilities into important assets.

MORE THAN A TRANSITION

Economic development is a long process whose fruits may seem forbidden for large segments of developing societies. In fact, the somewhat perverse relationship between income distribution and the initial stages of development is at once unsettling and accepted. It has long been suspected that economic development worsens income distribution, at least in its early stages. After all, societies do not move as a whole along the development curve. On the contrary, certain development trends—education, for instance—give some individuals and groups an advantage over others, advancing them more quickly along the curve and introducing a source of inequality. After a certain point, the relationship between development and equality is a win-win situation, but until then, results can be frustrating at best.

Stage of Development

We have identified five development trends in particular whose effects on inequality follow just such a tortuous path: capital accumulation, urbanization, formalization of the workforce, education, and the demographic transition. In each case, Latin American countries are either close to or on the crest of the development wave, suffering the transitional effects of greater inequality but poised for the long-term rewards.

Economic development is, to a large extent, the story of accumulating capital. In its early stages, capital tends to be very scarce, so its returns are very high. Initially, at low levels of capital accumulation, the share of national income going to profits is high. However, when enough capital has eventually been accumulated, the returns and the profit shares tend to decline. As a middle income region, Latin America is probably at a point in terms of capital accumulation where profit shares are still very high and will tend to decline as the development process continues and expands the capital stock.

A second characteristic of development is increasing urbanization. In underdeveloped societies, most people live in rural areas and most people are poor. Weak product and labor markets, lack of infrastructure and inadequate health and education services are just a few of the factors affecting poverty in rural areas. From this poor but generally equal baseline, a country urbanizes. But since incomes are higher and grow faster in the cities, the urbanization process will contribute to gradually increasing inequality. Near the end of the process, when most workers have made the transition to the urban sector, the rural-urban earnings gap will affect only a small fraction of the population, and its effect on the country's income inequality will thus be small. In Latin America, the rapid urbanization of the past four decades has, in most countries, contributed to rising inequality. But now that most Latin Americans are already city dwellers, the natural increase in the share of the population in urban areas will tend to reduce inequality in the future.

As an economy develops, it also becomes more formalized. Incomes in the formal sector tend to outstrip those of the informal sector, introducing a similar source of inequality in the initial stages of this process. But differences in hourly income among formal sector workers of similar characteristics are much narrower than those among workers in the informal sector. This means that, once a large share of the workforce is incorporated into the formal sector, inequality tends to decline.

A more educated society is also a more developed one. However, at low levels of development, most people have little or no education, and the absence of educational differences keeps income inequality low. As countries establish and expand their educational systems, new cohorts attain higher levels of education and earning potential, while uneducated cohorts are left behind. This inter-cohort inequality is accompanied by unequal attainment within each cohort; those in areas (generally urban) with more schools enjoy more and better education than individuals of the same age in less privileged areas. Once again, Latin America is at a stage where inter-cohort educational inequality is still very high, while intra-cohort inequality has been falling. Over time, this should lead to less inequality overall.

Finally, the development process is marked by a demographic transition. As countries move from high to low fertility and mortality rates, a very powerful set of changes is unleashed. In the first phase, mortality declines but fertility remains high. More children survive to adulthood, the average age of the population is low, and much of the potential labor force is engaged in caring and raising children. In this context, educational progress is hampered by the large number of children relative to the low number of working adults. Families frequently need to depend on a single wage earner, limiting resources to improve the education of children. However, in almost every Latin American country today, fertility rates are on the decline, families are having fewer children, and women, in particular, are participating in the labor market in growing numbers. With more earners and fewer children, families can concentrate their resources on fewer children, helping them attain ever higher levels of education. Rates of population growth are still very high in some Latin American countries, but as this pressure recedes, income concentration will decline.

We will show how these five trends are closely inter-related. A large factor in diminishing family size is related to a rise in women's earning potential in the labor market. As women become more educated, they tend to have fewer children, participate more in the job market, and demand more education for their children. More education also means better access to those types of employment that offer higher wages and more security. More capital per worker means a higher value for women's work in the labor force. In urban areas, this process proceeds more quickly than in rural areas. Hence, the five trends interact in a reinforcing manner. They are not specific to Latin America, but clearly they are at work in the region and explain a substantial part of its high level of income inequality. Although it may be little solace for those riding in the last cars of the development train, most of Latin America appears to be turning the corner; as these trends continue, they should provide a basis to reduce income inequality in the future, as long as the adequate economic and social policies are in place.

However, our analysis suggests that inequality in Latin America is only partially explained as a hapless moment on the development time line. Only about one-third of the gap in income inequality between Latin America and the industrial countries can be attributed to the region's stage of development vis-à-vis these five trends. Obviously, there is more to the story than a simple transition.

Endowments

Having found only part of the answer in the process, we turned to the characteristics and location of the region itself. What is it in the make-up of Latin America or in its particular history that makes it more unequal than other regions of the world? Important clues can be found in the region's geography and in its endowments of land and natural resources. Overall, tropical countries, especially when their economies are intensive in land and mineral resources, tend to be more unequal. The strong statistical relationship reflects a combination of factors whose relative importance is still under discussion. In more land-intensive countries, more of national income accrues to land, an asset whose ownership tends to be more concentrated than other assets such as human capital. At the same time, tropical land and the crops it supports offer larger economies of scale under more adverse climatic conditions with less technological innovation than temperate lands. The result has been relatively low labor productivity in tropical areas, which has depressed the wage level for unskilled labor across sectors and over time. All told, while temperate lands historically have promoted family-run farms and institutions aimed at fostering cooperation, the larger economies of scale and harsh labor conditions typical of tropical lands have generated plantation agriculture and promoted slavery. This in turn has promoted vertical relationships, hierarchies and class divisions rather than the horizontal linkages that build social capital and contribute to development and equity. Hence, while part of Latin America's inequality may have been inherited from its colonial past, this past itself may have been shaped by its geography and resource endowments.

Another intervening factor is the capital-intensive nature of the region's natural resources. Mineral resources and agricultural crops are capital intensive and act as capital sinks. They suck up scarce capital in the economy while offering few employment opportunities, thus making capital more scarce and labor more abundant for other activities. The low return to labor in tropical farming is thus reinforced by the region's exploitation of its natural resources.

Another factor that contributes to inequality is Latin America's history of volatility. Economic instability is strongly related to inequality. It slows the development process by limiting the accumulation of capital, interfering in the ability of families to educate their children, and adversely affecting productivity. Moreover, weaker groups in society are less able to cope with volatility and become even worse off.

Hence, natural resources and volatility make inequality a more serious problem. The transitional stories are played out against this permanent backdrop, adding another layer of complications. If natural resources keep the wages of unskilled workers low, demographic and educational transitions are slowed. Inequality may increase distrust and make political agreement more difficult, preventing societies from reigning in the distributive pressures that interfere with fiscal prudence, which is the key to overcoming volatility.

Globalization can also affect the process of becoming more equitable societies. It has been argued that globalization drives down the price of unskilled labor, as populous countries such as China and India supply increasing proportions of goods that are labor-intensive. Globalization increases the relative price of Latin America's abundant natural resources to the detriment of labor, promotes technological changes that increase the returns to skilled workers, and limits the ability of governments to tax the now more mobile capital.

These challenges, to whatever extent they exist, provide even further justification for a development strategy that emphasizes the accumulation of skills and the use of the natural resource base in order to avoid competing in sectors dependent only on low wages for unskilled labor.

IT TAKES MORE THAN TIME

Many of the forces that keep inequality high will prove temporary, especially if the development process deepens. Over the long term, there are no tradeoffs between development and equality. Still, neither development nor equality are matters of destiny. It takes more than time to overcome income inequality and to advance a country along the development curve. This is particularly true in Latin America, where transitional concerns are superimposed on very special regional handicaps. For this reason, the third part of this study looks at policies aimed at furthering the five key development trends, promoting their mutual reinforcement, and converting the region's characteristic impediments to equitable growth into viable assets for reconciling development and equality.

The Demographic Window of Opportunity

Latin America is peeking through a unique window of opportunity in its demographic transition. Since fertility is falling, the proportion of people of working age is rising faster than the number of children. The decline in fertility also means that more adult women will be working. Thus, there will be fewer students per worker, making it easier to finance a better educational system. But while this trend will persist for many decades, eventually it will be overtaken by the rise in the proportion of elderly people. Still, in most of Latin America over the next two decades, the declining ratio of children to workers will be more important financially than the rising ratio of retired to active workers. This leaves two decades to accelerate the development process. Not only should this allow Latin America to finance improvements in education, but it should also allow it to raise its savings ratio, as today's workers make provisions for their old age. Therefore, it is of the utmost importance that the region adopt fully funded pension systems. This will make it clear for the present generation how much must be set aside to provide for old age. If they simply pay as they go, they will be transferring the costs of old age onto the generation of their children, who will face far less favorable demographic trends. A fully funded pension system would generate over the next few decades a major stock of savings that could be used to accelerate the development process, so that pensions could be paid out of increased wealth and not increased taxation of the next generation. If, in addition, the social security system generates claims not only on the government but also on the broader economy, as the Bolivian capitalization program does, it will expand the constituency with a vested interest in market-oriented policies.

A Social Context for Human Capital Accumulation

The demographic and educational transition must also be hastened so that families gradually become smaller and more educated. To this end, female participation in the labor force must be facilitated to provide the incentives for smaller families and generate the resources for higher educational attainment. One line of action is to increase the productivity of housework by improving access to water, electricity and telecommunications so that appliances and information can be used in order to save time. Better urban transport will allow easier access to jobs and more time at home. More child care and longer school days and school years, although basically aimed at improving the quality of education, will also cut down on the need for women to be at home taking care of the children. Better preventive health will make for fewer days lost to children's illness. More flexible labor codes will allow women to overcome many of the limitations that currently prevent them from entering the formal sector.

It is also important to reduce the cost and increase the benefits of sending children to school and keeping them there, especially through the secondary level. In this respect, school lunch programs and subsidies for books, uniforms and transportation can reduce the out-of-pocket expenses of keeping children in school. Better quality education will raise the returns to schooling and hence the incentives to forgo work.

Educating Everyone

Educational inequality within each income level is coming down as educational attainment improves. Overall inequality is still high because of the widening gap between the educational attainment of more-educated younger cohorts and older ones. This process will continue to cause a significant amount of measured inequality. However, this can be seen as a positive trend, since it ultimately means that children are becoming more educated than the previous generation.

For most countries in the region, universalizing elementary education is a fait accomplis. In a few, such as Brazil, Honduras and Guatemala, it remains a problem. For the others, the challenge now is to improve the quality of primary education and to universalize secondary education. This would increase returns to education and reduce the inefficiency of school repetition and dropouts. Better quality education may mean lengthening the school day and year, and therefore have the secondary effect of increasing female labor force participation.

The biggest educational differences today are related to secondary education. The poor drop out soon after primary school while the rich go on to higher education. Moving quickly in the direction of universal secondary education would upgrade the labor force, increase the incomes of the great majority, enlarge the pool of potential university students, and promote a different, more humanistic and capital-intensive kind of development process.

Inequality in Latin America is unusually concentrated in the top decile, which in part reflects the relatively high returns to higher education and the fact that relatively few people get that far. Moreover, returns to higher education in most countries have been rising in recent years with the recovery of growth. The market is giving clear signals that it needs more of this type of education. Consequently, any changes in higher education policy should not imply a reduction in the supply of graduates. Rather, policies should support better targeting of subsidies to higher education so as to use the resources to increase overall supply.

Finally, the governance structure of educational systems must be improved in order to align what societies seek from those systems with the incentives that providers have. This implies moving away from centralized monopoly provisioning by increasing school autonomy, empowering citizens with information, voice and choice, and making budgetary resources follow outputs, and not inputs.

Opening up the Labor Market

There is significant labor market segmentation in Latin America and it is an important contributor to inequality. Controlling for other observable factors such as education, experience and hours worked, rural workers make nearly 30 percent less than urban workers, urban formal workers make about 20 percent more than their informal counterparts, and within the informal sector women make a quarter less than men. In part, this reflects imperfections in the markets for products and for capital, as well as women's need for greater flexibility. But there is also increasing evidence that these income differentials reflect the rigidities caused by regulations regarding formal employment. These regulations were designed to protect workers from the greater power of employers and from labor market risks. They include restrictions to temporary or part-time work, extra hours, and high costs of firing. However, current legislation tends to protect prime-age urban formal male workers but restrict opportunities to other groups. Hence, initiatives to make labor market protection less discriminatory must be considered. These may include a more socialized solution to unemployment risk by substituting current severance payment schemes with contributory individual savings and credit accounts. Also worth considering is greater flexibility in the working day, fewer restrictions on temporary or part-time contracts, and a socialization of the cost of maternal leave to facilitate formal female employment.

In order to expand the social security system to workers outside the formal sector, a basic noncontributory pillar paid for by general taxation is needed. This will expand the system and reduce the current reliance on payroll taxes, which negatively impact on formal employment.

Expanding Financial Markets

A poor functioning capital market tends to generate high returns to the lucky few with access to capital, but opportunities lost for those with abilities and ideas but no access to financing. Taxi drivers need not have enough capital to cover the full value of a car—they simply need to have access to credit at a reasonable rate. The same goes for many other activities. However, financial markets are underdeveloped in Latin America and the blame goes beyond the region's history of inflation and financial instability. Weak institutions to support the credit market are also at fault. Credit is a relationship based not only on an assessment of the borrower's ability to repay, but also on his or her willingness to do so. It is efficient for markets to price credit according to the borrower's ability to repay because this ability reflects the economic risks involved. Willingness to repay is different because it essentially reflects the availability of institutional arrangements that allow a person to commit to repay. Such arrangements must be provided by society and cannot be created by individuals. If these arrangements are not present, lenders will inefficiently restrict worthy customers from credit because they are unsure about their intentions to repay. Collateral, credit bureaus, creditor rights and group lending are mechanisms to deal with this problem that are sorely lacking in much of the region. Inadequate land titling is also an obstacle that limits not only access to credit but also mobilization of savings. In particular, rural land tenure and informal urban dwellings are assets that could be used as collateral but lack proper legal titles. A deeper credit market would increase the availability of capital to both the formal and informal sector, causing productivity to increase and boosting the incomes of the groups currently excluded.

Managing Natural Resources

Latin America's natural resource endowment of minerals and (especially tropical) land is strongly associated with its inequality, although there are policies that could alter this relationship. In general, restricting the development of natural resource-intensive sectors seems inefficient—there must be something better to do than to blame one's own good fortune. However, it can also be argued that tax exemptions and other incentives to exploit scarce natural resources are inefficient because they imply giving away, at below its opportunity cost, resources that are scarce and often nonrenewable. This would accentuate the capital sink characteristics of the natural resource sector with its negative distributive implications. Also, the natural resource sector tends to produce unstable revenues. Tax structures should not transfer all these risks onto the government so that the perceived risk by private investors is artificially lowered. The government should also adequately manage the risks involved in the revenues generated by this sector so that they do not increase the overall volatility of the economy.

Using the Distributive Power of Fiscal Policy

Given Latin America's high level of inequality, how much can fiscal policy contribute to redistributing unequal revenues generated by the economy? If the government were to appropriate a larger share of national income and distribute it more equally, would that not improve income distribution? Latin America has a long history of attempting to make the tax structure more progressive. In doing so, it has severely limited its tax capacity, cutting down the resources the government can appropriate to promote its social agenda and maintain macroeconomic balance. It is much easier to achieve progressive spending than progressive taxation. After all, the top decile of the population uses neither the health nor basic education services provided by the government. Latin America has been able to collect more revenue from a relatively flat income tax than it used to collect from rapidly rising marginal tax rates. Value-added taxes with a broad base and few exceptions perform far better than those that exclude goods in order to make them more progressive. In this context, tax systems in the region would be far more progressive if collection were improved. The best way to improve the distributive power of fiscal policy would be to make tax administration more efficient and evasion more difficult by adopting simple tax structures.

CONCLUSIONS

Latin America is very unequal in its distribution of income and wealth. While this report helps us to understand why, there is still much to be learned about the underlying causes of inequality. The complicated multidimensional story of the region's stage of development, plus a discussion of its bittersweet natural endowments, suggests that the causes of inequality are deep and complex. They are not simply the consequence of denying political representation to the majority and therefore ignoring the issue. On the contrary, Latin America has in fact been largely democratic for most of this century, and in keeping with the democratic tradition its governments have tried to cater to the median voter. This voter is far from the top of the income scale and, contrary to rhetoric, far from ignored. Government after government in Latin America has tried to appeal to this majority with policies they promised would achieve redistribution.

And that's the irony of it all. Latin American governments have tried hard to mitigate the unequal outcomes that economies tend to generate. They have long committed their countries to universal education and health care. Often their policy repertoire has been cluttered with large public enterprises, massive subsidy schemes, unmanageable progressive taxation, restrictive labor legislation, multiple exchange rates and price controls. This is the stuff of which Latin American populism has been made—populism directed not to the elite but to the vast majority of the people, the median voter. All these efforts were conceived as means of spreading the wealth and protecting the poor; most achieved very much the opposite. Clearly, the problem is less related to a lack of trying and more to a lack of effectiveness in the strategies and instruments adopted.

To break the stalemate in progress in this area, a deeper understanding is needed of the processes that have made Latin America unequal and of the dynamics that may usher in a more equitable region. Not only should equity be a goal in itself, but without it the region will fail to achieve sustainable development. To further the development process, broad support is needed for successful policies, yet this will be hard to achieve if the benefits of development are not widely shared.

Latin America has overcome difficult hurdles in the past decade. It has brought down inflation and begun to grow again. A hidden benefit of this effort is that it allows societies to think more about their long-term problems. Inequality has plagued the region for a long time and will take quite a while to quell. The first step is to increase understanding of its causes in order to be more successful in attempts to achieve equity.

PART ONE

MEASURING
THE PROBLEM

Chapter 1

MAGNITUDE OF INEQUALITIES

Latin America and the Caribbean have the greatest disparities in income distribution in the world. A quarter of all national income is received by a mere 5 percent of the population, and the top 10 percent receive 40 percent. Such proportions are comparable only to those found in some African countries, whose per capita income levels are half those of Latin America, and they are considerably higher than those of any other group of countries (Figure 1.1). In Southeast Asian countries, the wealthiest 5 percent receive 16 percent of all national income on average, while in the developed countries they receive 13 percent.[1]

The counterpart to the great concentration of income in the hands of the wealthy is found at the other end of the income scale in Latin America: the poorest 30 percent of the population receive only 7.5 percent of total income, less than anywhere else in the world, where it is over 10 percent. (Figure 1.2). This income concentration applies more to Latin America—which is the focus of this study due to the availability of information—than to the English-speaking Caribbean, where disparities are more moderate.

The indicator most commonly used to measure income inequality is the Gini index, which draws together information about the breakdown of income among all population groups (Box 1.1). The Gini average for all the countries in the world for which there is reliable information on income distribution is 0.4. A perfectly equal distribution would produce an index of zero, but in fact the best instances of distribution such as Spain, Finland and some other European countries show Gini indices of between 0.25 and 0.3 (Figure 1.3). At the opposite extreme, the indices of greatest income inequality are around 0.6, which are found almost solely in Latin America and the Caribbean. With the exception of Jamaica, whose inequality index of 0.38 is closer to European than to Latin American patterns, the other countries in the region for which there is reliable information for the 1990s show inequality levels higher than the world average, and 11 of them have indices higher than 0.5.[2]

---

[1] The source for these comparisons is the database in Deininger and Squire (1996), which has information on income distribution based on reliable household surveys in 108 countries. Southeast Asia includes only Hong Kong, Korea, Singapore and Taiwan.

[2] Henceforth, the IDB's own calculations based on the most recent household surveys are used, except for Colombia, Guatemala, Jamaica and the Dominican Republic, for which the most recent findings according Deininger and Squire (1996a) are used. Appendix 1.2 describes the characteristics of the surveys and the main socioeconomic indicators by income deciles and country.

Figure 1.1. Income Received by the Wealthiest 5 Percent of the Population

(*Percent of total income*)

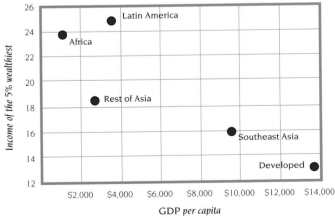

Source: IDB calculations based on Deininger and Squire (1996).

Figure 1.2. Income Received by the Poorest 30 Percent of the Population

(*Percent of total income*)

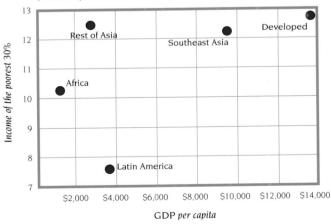

Source: IDB calculations based on Deininger and Squire (1996).

Box 1.1. Gini: A Simple Way to Measure Income Inequality

If incomes were distributed in a fully equitable manner, each person would receive the same share of income. The Gini index measures how far real distribution is from such a hypothetical reference point.

Real income distribution (or that of any other variable) can be represented as a cumulative curve showing what percentage of total income is received by each percentage of the population, lined up with its income level (which is called a Lorenz Curve). Consider points A and B in Figure 1. Point A indicates that the poorest 20 percent of the population receive 4 percent of income and that 90 percent receive 60 percent, which is actually more or less what happens in Latin American economies. Inasmuch as the diagonal represents the case of perfect distribution, the Gini coefficient is simply the area separating the Lorenz curve from the diagonal, divided by the area under the diagonal.

In theory, the Gini coefficient can vary between zero—perfect distribution—and one—complete concentration in a single person. In practice, Gini coefficients of per capita income vary between 0.25 and 0.60. Of the100 countries for which comparable information is available, only five have Gini coefficients outside of this range. Inequality indices in Latin America are on average 0.52, with a minimum of 0.43 for Uruguay and a maximum of 0.59 for Brazil.

There are other measurements of income inequality, such as the Theil index or the logarithmic income variance. Each inequality measure assigns a different weight to observations by income level, which can be interpreted as a way of aggregating individuals in order to obtain an overall measurement of social welfare. The empirical evidence shows that all the usual measurements of inequality produce highly correlated results, and hence for purposes of comparative analysis between countries, either one is adequate.

Instead of the Gini or one of the other measurements of concentration, some economists prefer to refer simply to the income gaps between the groups at either end, such as between the wealthiest 20 percent and the poorest 20 percent of the population (called the first and fifth quintiles, respectively), or between the wealthiest and poorest 10 percent (tenth and first deciles). This measurement is easy to understand, and it relates quite closely to the Gini coefficient (Figure 1). It is, however, a rather crude measurement, for it is based simply on comparing two points in the distribution curve, and that can be deceptive. For example, Ecuador and Panama have income gaps greater than Brazil's, but their Gini coefficients are better because the distribution among their middle groups is better.

Figure 1. Typical Lorenz Curve in Latin America
(*In percent*)

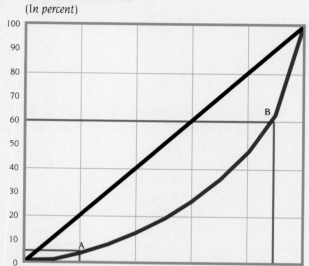

Figure 2. Gini Coefficients and Income Gaps

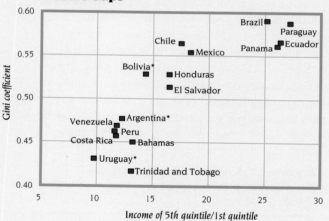

*Countries with urban data only.
Source: IDB calculations based on recent household surveys, and Deininger and Squire (1996a).*

Figure 1.3. Income Concentration Index

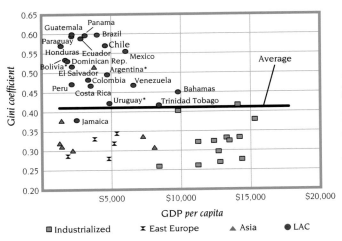

Countries with urban data only.
Source: IDB calculations based on recent household surveys, and Deininger and Squire (1996a).

Figure 1.4a. Observed and Expected Income Concentration by Level of Income

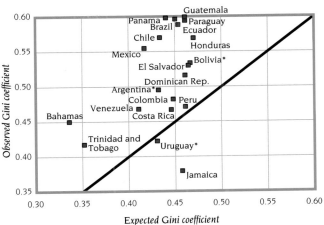

Countries with urban data only.
Source: World regressions based on IDB household survey data and Deininger and Squire (1996a).

It could be argued that comparing income inequality levels of countries that have very different levels of development is deceptive because economic development can go hand in hand with better distribution, whatever the causality between the two phenomena may be. In fact, all countries with high Gini coefficients belong to the medium- or low-income group (Figure 1.3). Nevertheless, admitting that there is a relationship between the level of development and income distribution, one finds that most Latin American countries are located above the level proper to that relationship, which is the same as saying that they have *excess* inequality, even after making allowance for the relationship between development and distribution.[3] The extra inequality in the region is 12 Gini percentage points, on average. The greatest excesses are found in Brazil, Chile, Guatemala, Ecuador, Mexico, Panama and Paraguay, while only Jamaica has a level of inequality significantly below the world pattern. Other countries in the English-Speaking Caribbean— the Bahamas and Trinidad and Tobago—also have income concentration indices that are modest compared to those of Spanish-speaking countries. Nevertheless, given their high income levels, they are also very unequal. (Figure 1.4a).

CONCENTRATION OF INCOME IS HIGH IN BOTH URBAN AND RURAL AREAS

Indices of income inequality in urban and rural zones resemble one another in almost all countries. Only in Paraguay is inequality substantially greater in the country-

Figure 1.4b. Urban and Rural Income Concentration

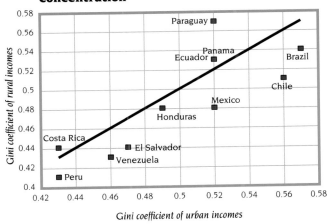

Source: IDB calculations based on recent household surveys.

side than in the cities (Figure 1.4b). In Brazil, Chile, Mexico and El Salvador, the differences go in the opposite direction, and are between three and five points. For all countries taken together, the urban and rural Ginis are practically identical, with an average value of 0.497.

---

[3] "Excess" or "extra" is defined here in relation to a worldwide pattern in which only income level is taken into account. As considered in Chapter 4, the stage of development is a determinant of inequality, particularly in the areas of capital accumulation, education, urbanization, demographic structure and the degree of formalization of employment.

Figure 1.5. Total and Urban Income Concentration

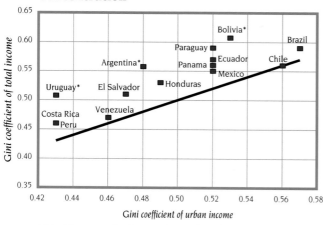

*Actual data cover urban incomes only. Gini for total incomes are estimates.
Source: IDB calculations based on recent household surveys.

Figure 1.6. Urban-Rural Income Gap

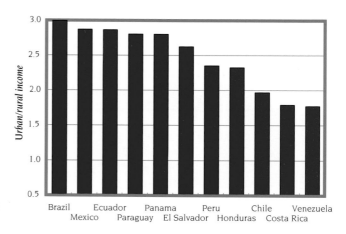

Source: IDB calculations based on recent household surveys.

Note that inequality of total income is greater than the average of the urban and rural inequalities taken separately, except in Chile, where the total and the urban Gini are the same (Figure 1.5). If the average income levels in the countryside and the city were similar, the inequality of total income would be located at some point between the separate concentrations of one region and the other. But urban incomes are substantially higher than rural ones, which means that, taken together, income inequality will be greater than in each region taken separately. The largest gaps are found in Brazil, where per capita income in urban areas is three times what it is in rural areas, and the smallest in Costa Rica and Venezuela, where urban incomes are 75 percent higher than rural ones (Figure 1.6). Due to these great differences in per capita income, total income inequality is greater than the separate concentration in the countryside and in the city. On average, the total Gini indices are 3.3 points higher than separate Ginis for rural and urban areas. It is important to keep this difference in mind, inasmuch as for three of the countries analyzed in this study—Argentina, Bolivia and Uruguay—information is not available on rural income distribution (and hence they do not appear in these comparisons). For example, the Ginis reported for countries that cover only urban areas (and only Greater Buenos Aires in the case of Argentina) tend to be underestimated. In Figure 1.5, we have assumed that the underestimate is by these 3.3 points. With this correction, Uruguay displays the same inequality index as Costa Rica, Argentina comes close to El Salvador, and Bolivia remains at inequality levels similar to those of Chile or Panama.

AS BAD AS BEFORE

Regardless of the measurement used, Latin America stands out among all regions for its high inequality. Income distribution has not improved during the 1990s, and according to the limited information available, it is as high today as it was two decades ago (Figure 1.7).

The period of rapid growth in the region, which began in the 1960s and lasted until the outbreak of the debt crisis in 1982, led to a notable improvement in income distribution. Between 1970 and 1982 the region's Gini coefficient[4] fell by 5 points (that is, by 10 percent), and the income ratio gap between the wealthiest 20 percent of the population and the poorest 20 percent fell from 23 to 18 during that same period. While low-income groups apparently improved their income share by around 10 percent, the highest groups stood still or fell, especially between 1980 and 1982 (Figure 1.8). The wealthiest 10 percent saw their share of income fall by 6 percent during this period and middle groups gained significantly. But these improvements in distribution were short-lived. During the 1980s, the decile with the highest incomes increased its share by over 10 percent at the cost of all other income deciles. The poorest 10 percent in Latin

---

[4] Approximations based on available information for the population of 13 countries that together make up 83 percent of the Latin American population (Londoño and Székely, 1997). Note that the Gini inequality index for the entire region is not the same as the average of Ginis by countries, since it is based on the incomes of all individuals combined. The Gini for the region is higher due to differences of average income between countries. Since these estimates are based on partial evidence of the evolution of distribution in each country, they should not be considered an exact description of the behavior of this variable over time.

Figure 1.7. Income Concentration in Latin America, 1970-95

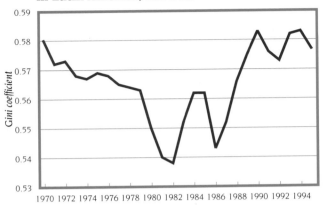

Source: Londoño and Székely (1997).

Figure 1.8. Participation of Each Income Group in Total Income, 1970-95

(*Percent of normalized income*)

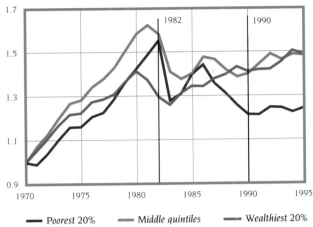

—— Poorest 20%   —— Middle quintiles   —— Wealthiest 20%

Source: Londoño and Székely (1997).

America suffered a 15 percent drop in their share of income. Thus the gaps widened again and the improvements in distribution from before the debt crisis were wiped out.

The economies of the region have undergone great changes in the 1990s. High inflation rates have been halted, deep economic reforms have been adopted to facilitate market operations, and productivity and economic growth have been restored. All these changes have brought about shifts of wealth and income. Concentration, however, has remained practically unchanged: the region's Gini has stood at around 0.58. What explains this apparent contradiction is that the changes have affected some groups differently from others. The poorest 10 percent in the region saw a 15 percent loss of their share in income between 1990 and 1995, and the next 10 percent a loss of 4 percent. The richest 10 percent also suffered a relative setback, while those who gained were the remaining groups in the middle. Hence, although the indicators of average concentration for the region have changed very little during the 1990s, distribution has by no means stood still.

Moreover, movement has not been homogeneous between countries. In Brazil, Chile and Mexico, income inequality worsened in the 1980s, but that was halted in the 1990s. In Colombia and Costa Rica, distribution patterns have remained quite stable, and indices of concentration in the 1990s have stood at levels similar to what they were a decade ago. In Honduras and Jamaica, income distribution worsened in the early 1990s, but in recent years it has been better than in the 1980s. In Venezuela, there have been periods of sharp decline, but they have been transitory.[5]

WHERE INEQUALITY IS FOUND

One of the most striking features of the poor income distribution in Latin America is the huge gap between the families in the highest income decile and everyone else. In relatively egalitarian societies such as Sweden or Canada, an individual who belongs to the wealthiest decile of the population earns on average 20 to 30 percent more than someone in the next decile. The succeeding differences in the next deciles are also lower, and hence there are no sharp gaps between social strata. In Latin America, the gaps within the middle-income groups are not so pronounced, but between the wealthiest decile and the next one there is an abyss: in the Dominican Republic or Chile, to cite the two most critical cases, the income of someone who belongs to the tenth decile is three times as great as in the previous decile and more than 30 times greater than that of the poorest decile (Figure 1.9a). These differences are possibly even greater, because income from capital, which is more important in the richest decile of the population, is most certainly underreported in the income surveys from which these calculations are taken (Box 1.2).

At the other end of the income scale there are also major gaps: because the incomes of the poorest 10 percent of the population are really quite low, the next 10 percent receive twice as much income in most countries, and in Ecuador and Panama close to triple the income of

---

[5] The countries mentioned are those for which there are at least five original observations since 1980. The interpolations and calculations used in the figures are by Londoño and Székely (1997).

Figure 1.9a. Income Gap

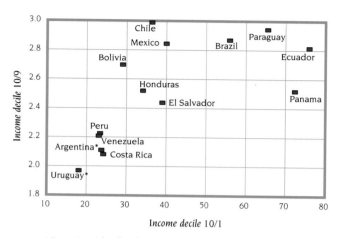

*Countries with urban data only.

Source: IDB calculations based on recent household surveys.

Figure 1.10. Income Concentration and Income Gap among the Rich

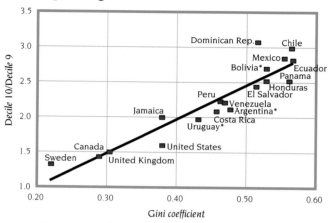

*Countries with urban data only.

Source: IDB calculations based on recent household surveys, and Deininger and Squire (1996a).

Figure 1.9b. Income Gap between Adjacent Deciles

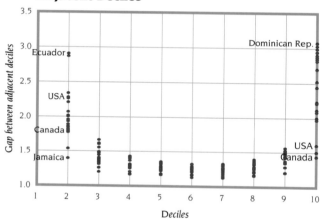

* Countries with urban data only.

Source: IDB calculations based on recent household surveys, and Deininger and Squire (1996a).

Figure 1.11. Total Income Concentration Excluding the Wealthiest 10 Percent

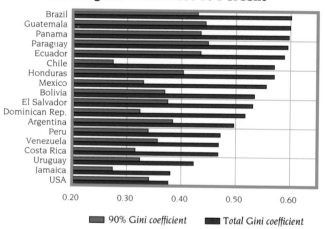

■ 90% Gini coefficient   ■ Total Gini coefficient

Source: IDB calculations based on recent household surveys.

the previous decile (Figure 1.9b). However, the existence of relatively significant gaps between the poorest groups is a phenomenon that is also seen in developed countries with better income distribution that have pockets of acute poverty, such as the United States or the United Kingdom.

Hence, the high income inequality is reflected in large income gaps between adjoining groups at both extremes of the income scale, but the gaps between the wealthy are sharper and more characteristic of countries with poor income distribution, such as those in Latin America. Indeed, the indices of overall income inequality in Latin American countries are closely associated with the size of the income gaps between the two richest deciles of the population (Figure 1.10). There is no equally

close connection with the gaps between the poorest deciles, or any other income gap.

Furthermore, the extra income inequality in Latin America is due to the gap between the highest incomes. If the Gini indices are recalculated without including the wealthiest decile, one finds that the income inequality of Latin American countries does not differ systematically from that of the United States (calculated in a similar manner). The Gini for 90 percent of the population would be on average only 0.36 instead of 0.52, and in six countries income inequality would be less than that of the United States (Figure 1.11). What makes the richest 10 percent of Latin America so different from the rest of the population? The answer offers the keys to factors explaining the extra inequality in the region.

Box 1.2. Household Surveys: A Basic Source of Information on Inequality

Information on income distribution comes mainly from the surveys made regularly by governments of representative samples of households on a national level. Besides information on the income of each household, such surveys provide information on education, age, occupation and other characteristics of each household member. They are therefore a rich source for studying the relationship between income distribution, work activity, participation in the education system, and the size and make-up of households. Hence, they are currently the most effective instrument for designing and evaluating all kinds of social programs. Even though this tool is now used around the world, surveys are still not carried out in some Latin American countries (Guatemala, Guyana and Haiti), while others perform surveys that leave out rural or nonmetropolitan areas (Argentina, Bolivia and Uruguay).

For the sake of studying income distribution, the most common shortcoming in some Latin American surveys is the lack of information on nonlabor sources of income (such as renting out of housing, noncash incomes, etc.) and on complementary variables that help establish the socioeconomic level of families (access to services, for example).

Because nonlabor incomes are often reported at less than their true value, especially among upper-income families, surveys tend to underestimate the level of real inequality in countries. If adjustments are made to correct this shortcoming, the results are subject to the arbitrary character of the method used. For Mexico in 1994, for example, Gini coefficients ranged from 0.477 to 0.60, depending on the adjustment method used.

The household surveys used in this study are of high quality and in keeping with international standards (Deininger and Squire, 1996a). Nevertheless, they do not all apply the same methodology for data gathering and sampling, and in a few cases with regard to the observation unit.[1] Since it is never possible to attain perfect comparability between surveys of different countries, differences in methodology do not necessarily invalidate the making of comparisons (Atkinson, 1995). In this study we have used reasonably comparable surveys, avoided any kind of subjective adjustment to the primary information, and applied identical methods of processing and statistical analysis to all surveys used. (See the Appendix to this chapter for the main features of the surveys used.)

In order to deal with the shortcomings in coverage and quality of the surveys and make them more relevant for policy design, the Inter-American Development Bank has implemented the Improvement of Surveys and Measurement of Living Standards (Mecovi) Program, in coordination with governments and other international agencies. The program provides financing and technical assistance for carrying out household surveys.[2]

---

[1] See Berry, et al (1983), Atkinson and Micklewright (1992), and Gottschalk and Smeeding (1997).

[2] The program has provided funding to carry out surveys in Argentina, El Salvador, Paraguay and Peru and will expand its operations to Bolivia and Nicaragua in the near future.

Who Are the Rich?

Among the many aspects that set the heads of households of the richest 10 percent of the population apart, four features in particular stand out: their level of education, the features of their work, where they live, and the number of children they have. These characteristics are valuable keys for determining the factors that cause and perpetuate poor income distribution.

Education is the main productive resource on which most people rely. This is even valid for the wealthiest 10 percent of the population. On average, in the 14 countries considered, the heads of household of the highest income decile have 11.3 years of education. Although this level amounts to slightly less than finishing secondary school (12 years in most countries), it is 2.7 years higher than the education level of the heads of household of the next decile and almost seven years higher than the heads of household of the poorest 30 percent of the population. The most pronounced education gaps between the two wealthiest deciles are found in Brazil, Mexico and

Honduras, where they are over three years, and only in Peru are they less than two years (Figure 1.12). Between the richest decile and the 30 percent at the bottom of the income scale, the average schooling gaps are over nine years in Mexico and between eight and nine years in Brazil, Panama and El Salvador, all countries with high income inequality. The lowest education gaps between rich and poor are found in Uruguay, Venezuela and Peru, countries whose income inequality is moderate when compared with patterns in the region. Thus, education is a factor differentiating the rich, not so much because their education level is so high, but rather because most others have not spent much time in school.

A second distinctive feature of the wealthy is the kind of work they do. A quarter of the heads of household of the highest income decile work directly as professionals, technical personnel or senior executives of companies. The portions range from 18 percent in Honduras and Paraguay to over 35 percent In Bolivia and Panama (Figure 1.13). In the next income decile, these proportions drop off noticeably in most countries, and between the

Figure 1.12. Years of Schooling in Rich and Poor Families

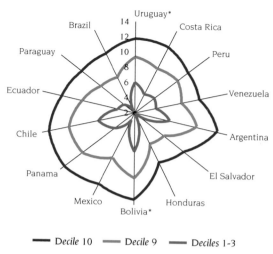

— Decile 10   — Decile 9   — Deciles 1-3

*Countries with urban data only.
Source: IDB calculations based on recent household surveys.

Figure 1.13. Percentage of Professionals and Executives in Rich and Poor Families

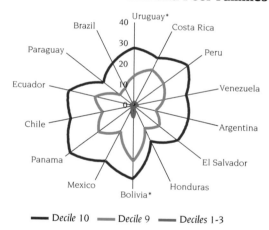

— Decile 10   — Decile 9   — Deciles 1-3

*Countries with urban data only.
Source: IDB calculations based on recent household surveys.

Figure 1.14. Percentage of Employers in Rich and Poor Families

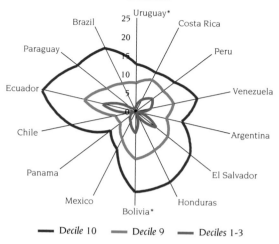

— Decile 10   — Decile 9   — Deciles 1-3

*Countries with urban data only.
Source: IDB calculations based on recent household surveys.

three lowest deciles only the tiniest number of heads of household reach leadership positions or have technical responsibilities. Most successful is Bolivia, where 6 percent of the poorest heads of households occupy such a position. Moreover, in most countries, between 10 percent and 20 percent of the population of the highest income decile are employers (Figure 1.14). Of the 14 countries for which such information is available, only in Panama is this proportion under 10 percent, while in Ecuador it represents around 25 percent of the wealthiest decile. In the next decile far fewer have the chance to employ other workers. Differences with the wealthiest

decile are especially marked in the countries where inequality is greatest, such as Brazil, Paraguay, Ecuador and Chile. The proportion of individuals who can employ others is considerably less in lower income groups, even though it is still somewhat significant in the lesser developed countries, such as El Salvador, Honduras, Bolivia and Ecuador.

A third feature differentiating the rich is where they live. In Latin America, poor households are found primarily in the countryside, while most of the wealthy live in cities. Among the countries in Figure 1.15, only in Brazil, Chile and Venezuela are over half of the households of the three lowest deciles in urban areas. By contrast, nine out of ten of the households of the two highest income declines are urban, except in Honduras, where the proportion falls below eight.

Number of children is another characteristic that varies between rich and poor households. In all the countries studied, the number of children in the highest income decile is lower than in any other decile. In Honduras, where the families of the wealthy are the largest relative to the wealthy in other countries, they do not even have on average two children under 18. In Argentina and Uruguay, only one out of two families of the highest decile has a minor child. The contrast with the poorest households is striking: the average number of children in the three lowest deciles is over two in all countries, reaches 3.5 in Mexico, Peru and Venezuela, and is four children per household in Paraguay (Figure 1.16). Hence, per capita income in each home is higher in the top decile not only because heads of household earn more, but because the number of persons among whom it must be distributed is smaller.

Figure 1.15. Percentage of Rural Families among Rich and Poor Families

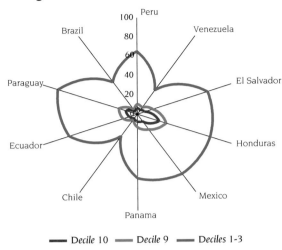

— Decile 10   — Decile 9   — Deciles 1-3

Source: IDB calculations based on recent household surveys.

Figure 1.16. Number of Children in Rich and Poor Families

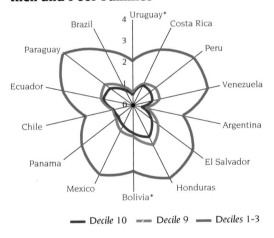

— Decile 10   -- Decile 9   — Deciles 1-3

Countries with urban data only.
Source: IDB calculations based on recent household surveys.

Figure 1.17. Income Concentration and Education Gap among the Rich

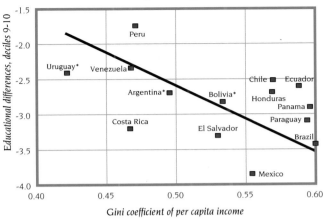

Countries with urban data only.
Source: IDB calculations based on recent household surveys.

one hand and the income inequality indices on the other. In Brazil, Chile, Ecuador, Honduras and Paraguay, where that gap is most pronounced, the greatest levels of income inequality are also found. The opposite is the case in countries with less inequality, such as Uruguay or Costa Rica. (Mexico and Panama, however, are cases apart in this relationship, as shown in Figure 1.18.) Likewise, the differences in the size of rich and poor households are greater in countries of high income inequality, such as Brazil, Ecuador or Paraguay, than in more equal countries like Costa Rica, Peru or Uruguay. (Panama once more appears as an isolated case, as shown in Figure 1.19.)

Hence, inequalities in income distribution in Latin American countries are related to the features that distinguish the two highest income groups from the rest. It is the gaps at the top of distribution, more than differences between groups in the middle or the poor, that make Latin America the most unequal region in the world.

The features that set the rich apart also say a great deal about the degree of income inequality in countries. The greater the gap between the tenth decile and the one following, the greater tends to be income inequality in general. Consider the relationship between the size of educational gaps and income inequality: heads of household in the richest decile in Brazil, the country with the greatest inequality, have 3.5 years more education than those of the next decile. In Uruguay, Peru and Venezuela, where concentration is less, these gaps are around two years (Figure 1.17). Now note the gap in the proportion of employers between the two wealthiest deciles on

Inequality in Per Capita Income and Labor Income

This study uses the household as the basic observation unit for analyzing income distribution, since it is the lowest observable unit of income distribution. Although household incomes derive from various sources, both work and nonwork, and although families differ in size and in the number of income earners, there is a close relationship between the inequality of the labor income of workers and household income inequality. For the average of 14 countries considered here, the Gini index of labor income inequality of workers is 0.51, similar to the

Figure 1.18. Income Concentration and Gap in the Proportion of Employers among the Rich

*Countries with urban data only.
Source: IDB calculations based on recent household surveys.

Figure 1.19. Income Concentration and Number of Children among the Rich

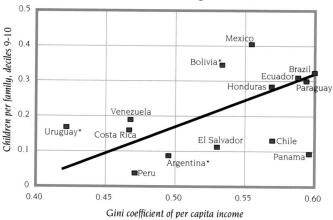

*Countries with urban data only.
Source: IDB calculations based on recent household surveys.

index of 0.52 that is the inequality of per capita household income. This similarity can also be seen in each country by itself, which indicates that it is not simply the result of aggregating individual cases that could be very dissimilar among themselves (Figure 1.20). The greatest differences between one coefficient and another are found in Bolivia and Panama, but even in these cases they only reach five points. Similar differences between household per capita income distribution and labor income per worker are also found in developed countries.

The connection between labor income inequality and how per capita income is distributed should not lead to the conclusion that the impact of income from capital (or from other sources) is secondary in income distribution. What it suggests is rather that such factors are not independent of one another. As will be seen in Chapters 2 and 4, the differences in income between some workers and others, or more precisely between workers who have greater or lesser education, can be explained by the relative demands for different types of work, which depend on the relative abundance of other factors and how they interact among themselves and with the labor factor.

WHY SHOULD WE CARE?

Social Justice

Income distribution should be a cause for concern for reasons of ethics and social justice. If income distribution reflected solely personal preferences about work, effort and savings, there would be no reason for it to constitute an ethical problem from the standpoint of distribu-

Figure 1.20. Concentration of Total and Labor Income

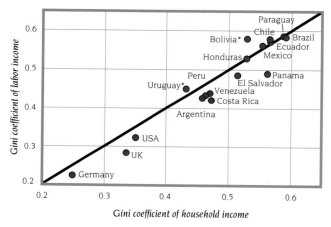

*Countries with urban data only.
Source: IDB calculations based on recent household surveys.

tive justice. Inequality and poverty become an ethical matter calling for outside intervention when it is acknowledged that the conditions generating them are not the choice of individuals but rather a result of circumstances beyond their control or a legacy of past problems.

Once it is acknowledged that effort and attitudes toward education, work, risk and savings are not independent of each individual's starting conditions, the way is opened for other concerns. The point is not simply to assure "equality of opportunity." If equality of opportunity is understood as equality of access (free basic education), it will not be enough to assure equality of capability of use (attendance at school), let alone equality of results (academic achievement). According to the social

Box 1.3. *Equality and Growth: Partners or Adversaries?*

Since Adam Smith, most economists have considered growth and equality to be largely incompatible. Only recently has a new school of theoreticians come to argue what seems plain to the eye: that high levels of economic development are found in relatively egalitarian societies where accumulating physical, human and social capital is attractive.

For classical economists, the capital accumulation needed for growth could only be obtained from the savings of capitalists, because workers would always consume their entire earnings. Equity and growth were incompatible. A similar conflict emerged within the pure neoclassical vision, but it was rooted in microeconomics: any redistribution would ultimately be at the expense of a productive factor, thereby lowering economic efficiency. Even a decade ago, these two visions had a great deal of influence on the position of economists on the issue of redistribution. Both implied that a shortage of productive resources would become sharper if a portion were set aside for redistribution purposes, thereby constituting an expenditure, not an investment. Because redistribution policies would have nothing to offer for economic growth or development according to these traditional approaches, income distribution was for a long time absent from the central agenda of economic theory and policy (Atkinson, 1997).

Over the past decade, the relationship between growth and equity has come back to the center of the academic debate, thanks to theories of endogenous growth and political economy. The central argument is that poor income distribution can weaken the pace of the accumulation of physical and human capital or affect productivity growth, which are the sources of economic growth.[1]

Education can be the channel through which poor income distribution lowers the possibilities of growth: families with limited resources are not in a position to put aside money for education, even though such an effort could be socially and economically profitable. Moreover, families with little education and few possibilities for future education for their children will prefer to have more children than those in the opposite situation, thereby reinforcing the vicious circle of inequality and poverty (see Banerjee and Newman, 1991; Galor and Zeira, 1993; Aghion and Bolton, 1997; Piketty, 1997; and Dahan and Tsiddon, 1998).

Restricted access to capital markets is another channel that perpetuates poor income distribution. Because access to credit requires being able to provide guarantees, those who initially have a higher level of wealth have more opportunity to invest in physical and human capital. Hence, in societies where wealth is very concentrated, many investments that could be profitable at the individual and social level cannot be made, thereby impeding growth (Aghion and Bolton, 1992; Galor and Zeira, 1993; and De Gregorio and Kim, 1994).

The connection between inequality and growth can also take place through various political and economic channels. The first is political participation, through which voters express their preferences for policies of economic redistribution. In a society where wealth and income are highly concentrated, most people will support redistribution policies financed with taxes on capital or similar measures that will discourage investment and productivity. The "median voter" is less inclined toward such policies to the extent that wealth is better distributed (Alesina and Rodrik, 1992 and 1994; Persson and Tabellini, 1992 and 1994; Alessina and Perotti, 1993; and Perotti, 1994). A second connection is that poor income distribution causes distributional and social tensions that lead to political instability and uncertainties that hinder investment. A third possibility is that the power groups that arise in unequal societies can erode genuinely distributive policies by seizing government institutions and other income-producing activities, perpetuating inequality and low growth (Benhabib and Rustichini, 1996; and Birdsall and Londoño, 1998).

Education, restricted access to capital markets, and political and economic mechanisms conditioning government policies are thus different channels by which income distribution affects growth.

---

[1] Alesina and Perotti (1994), Alesina and Rodrik (1994) and Solimano (1998) contain excellent reviews of this literature.

justice objectives pursued by society in each area, policy actions ought to be aimed at changing the distribution of capabilities of use (school subsidies, for example) or the distribution of results (leveling programs and other kinds of support).

Equality and Economic Development

After having been neglected for years in the academic debate among economists, the topic of income distribu-

tion has been regaining interest in recent years. The current debate centers precisely on determining whether, when governments try to improve distribution, they produce adverse consequences for the welfare of the population. Until recently, most theories on the subject presumed there was a conflict between equity and growth (Box 1.3). The usual arguments were either that greater concentration would allow for the generation of more savings, thereby facilitating investment and growth, or that concentration was the other side of the coin of effort and productivity. But empirical international evidence

Figure 1.21. Incidence of Poverty in Latin America if Income Distribution Were Different

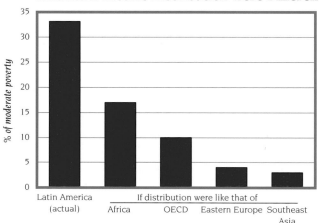

Source: Londoño and Székely (1997).

Figure 1.22. Income Concentration and Acceptance of Democracy

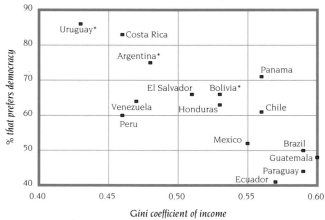

*Countries with urban data only.
Source: Latinobarómetro and IDB calculations based on recent household surveys.

does not offer much support to such theories. Comparative studies actually point in the opposite direction: countries with lower levels of income inequality tend to grow faster, even after isolating the influence that many other factors may have on growth (Box 1.4). According to this approach, we should care about inequality not only because it is an objective justifiable in itself for reasons of social justice, but because good income distribution is favorable to growth and common welfare.[6]

Poverty and Inequality

One serious implication of income inequality in Latin America is the extent of poverty in the region. The income level of more than 150 million Latin Americans—that is, around 33 percent of the population—is under $2 a day (corrected for differences of purchasing power of the currencies of the various countries). This is regarded as the minimum needed to cover basic consumption needs. If Latin America had the income distribution suited to its level of development by international standards, the incidence of poverty would be half of what it actually is. Other countries with similar levels of development have substantially reduced poverty. Per capita income levels of Eastern European countries are not appreciably different from those of Latin America, but poverty affects only 7 percent of their population. Although that may seem to be an extreme comparison, possibly affected by the socialist past of those countries, making comparisons with other regions of the world leads to a similar conclusion. For example, if income in Latin America were distributed as it is in the countries of Southeast Asia, poverty would

be a fifth of what it actually is. Even taking the distribution pattern of Africa, one finds that for Latin America's higher levels of development, it ought to have half as many poor people as it actually has (Figure 1.21).

If current income distribution of Latin American countries were to remain unchanged, the pace of poverty reduction would be slow, even with relatively high growth rates. With a 3 percent a year rise in per capita income, between 15 and 25 years would be required, depending on the country, to lower poverty rates to half of their current levels.[7]

Inequality and Democracy

Besides normative considerations of social justice, economic growth and poverty that explain why equality requires attention, international empirical evidence suggests that the issue of distribution is also important because inequality and democracy are clearly connected. Inequality can affect how democratic institutions function and can impede political decisionmaking processes.

---

[6] The reasons why more equal societies tend to grow more have only recently begun to be studied and understood thanks to developments in the theories of endogenous growth and of the political economy of growth (Box 1.3). The central idea is that poor income distribution may constrain the pace of the accumulation of physical or human capital or may lead to the adoption of policies and institutions that are harmful for productivity.

[7] See Londoño and Székely (1997), Lustig and Deutsch (1998) and Morley (1998) for alternative estimates of poverty levels by countries and the impact of growth on poverty.

Box 1.4. Inequality Hinders Growth: Summary of the Empirical Evidence

The relationship between income distribution and economic growth has been a recurring topic of discussion among economists. In theory, arguments can be found to justify both a direct and an inverse relationship between the two variables. What does the empirical evidence say?

The prevailing conclusion in recent empirical studies is that poor income distribution harms economic growth and that therefore, instead of the conflict between equality and development that used to be regarded as a serious constraint on distribution policies, the relationship is mutually reinforcing.

Studies by Clarke (1992), Alessina and Perotti (1993 and 1994), Persson and Tabellini (1994), Birdsall, Ross and Sabot (1995), Deininger and Squire (1996b) and Perotti (1996) conclude that poor income distribution reduces prospects for economic growth. This conclusion remains valid even after taking into account the influence on development of other factors, such as initial per capita income, education levels or other economic, political or demographic variables. Such empirical studies are no doubt open to question not only because of shortcomings in the quality of information, but also because of the possibility that the relationship between growth and equality over time by countries is different from what can be seen in these cross-sec-

tional comparisons between countries (Forbes, 1997). Nevertheless, the empirical studies that have focused on the channels connecting distribution with growth also support the conclusion that these variables tend to be mutually reinforcing rather than in conflict.

Econometric models that simply include income distribution as an extra variable explaining growth do not shed light on the channels that can determine this relationship. But several studies have tried to fill this vacuum. Perotti (1996) shows that joint decisions made by families regarding education and number of children may perpetuate a society's high inequality and low growth. Another possible channel is political instability: poor income distribution often goes hand in hand with political unrest that affects investment and growth (Alesina and Perotti, 1993 and 1994; Perotti, 1996). On a worldwide scale there is little evidence for the thesis of the "median voter," namely that poor distribution leads to higher tax levels that hinder growth.

Hence, even though the empirical evidence is not that of complete consensus, it does tend to favor those hypotheses according to which good income distribution tends to stimulate economic growth.

Recent public opinion surveys in Latin America indicate that income inequality can in fact change the way democratic institutions operate.[8] Income inequality can weaken acceptance of democratic institutions and principles. Where income inequality is less pronounced, as in Uruguay or Costa Rica, a high proportion of the population believes that "democracy is preferable to any other kind of government" (Figure 1.22). In the more unequal countries there is a greater tendency to accept authoritarian governments, and more people think that "it makes no difference whether a regime is democratic or nondemocratic." There also tends to be less trust in these countries in the institutions proper to a democracy, such as government, civil service, political parties, the legislature, large companies and business associations.

The lack of confidence in democracy and its institutions associated with poor income distribution in Latin America could have implications for national political systems. In fragmented societies where institutional confidence is low, the process of aggregating individual preferences is more complex and inexact, and conflicts over distributing public resources are more intense. Moreover, the social and economic integration of different groups is difficult and the state apparatus is more susceptible to the influence of interest groups, corruption and inefficiencies, all of which feed inequality.

---

[8] These surveys have been carried out annually in 17 countries since 1996 by Latinobarómetro, a private, nonpartisan and independent agency. Presented here are results for those countries that have comparable income distribution statistics.

Appendix 1.1. Main Features of Household Surveys Used in this Study

Country	Year	Name of the survey	Coverage	Reference month	Households	Individuals	Labor	Property rent	Capital rent	Transfers	Non-monetary	Imputed Rent
					Sample size				Income			
1 Argentina	80	Encuesta Permanente de Hogares	Greater Buenos Aires	October	3,400	11,905	X	X[a]	X[a]	X	na	na
	96	Encuesta Permanente de Hogares	Greater Buenos Aires	April and May	3,459	11,749	X	X[b]	X[b]	X[b]	na	na
2 Bolivia	86	Encuesta Permanente de Hogares	Urban	1986	2,788	12,226	X	X	na	na	na	na
	95	Encuesta Integrada de Hogares	Urban	June	5,455	25,314	X	X	X	X	na	na
3 Brazil	81	Pesquisa Nacional por Amostra de Domicilios	National	September	103,961	482,611	X	X	X	X	na	na
	95	Pesquisa Nacional por Amostra de Domicilios	National	September	85,270	334,263	X	X	X	X	na	na
4 Chile	94	Encuesta de Caracterización Socioeconómica Nacional	National	November and December	45,379	178,057	X	X	X	X	X	X
5 Costa Rica	81	Encuesta Nacional de Hogares - Empleo y Desempleo	National	July	6,604	22,170	X	na	na	na	na	na
	95	Encuesta de Hogares de Propósitos Múltiples	National	July	9,639	40,613	X	X[b]	X[b]	X[b]	na	na
6 Ecuador	95	Encuesta de Condiciones de Vida	Nacional	August to November	5,810	26,941	X	X	X	X	X	na
7 El Salvador	95	Encuesta de Hogares de Propósitos Múltiples	National	1995	8,482	40,004	X	X[b]	X[b]	X[b]	X	X
8 Honduras	89	Encuesta Permanente de Hogares de Propósitos Múltiples	National	September	8,727	46,672	X	na	na	na	na	na
	96	Encuesta Permanente de Hogares de Propósitos Múltiples	National	September	6,428	33,172	X	na	na	na	na	na
9 Mexico	84	Encuesta Nacional de Ingreso Gasto de los Hogares	National	Third quarter	4,735	23,985	X	X	X	X	X	X
	94	Encuesta Nacional de Ingreso Gasto de los Hogares	National	Third quarter	12,815	60,365	X	X	X	X	X	X
10 Panama	95	Encuesta Continua de Hogares	National	August	9,875	40,320	X	X[a]	X[a]	X	na	na
11 Paraguay	95	Encuesta de Hogares - Mano de Obra	National	August to November	4,667	21,910	X	X	X	X	na	na
12 Peru	85-86	Encuesta Nacional de Hogares sobre Medición de Niveles de Vida	National	July 1985 to July 1986	4,913	26,323	X	X[a]	X[a]	X	X	na
	96	Encuesta Nacional de Hogares sobre Niveles de Vida y Pobreza	National	Fourth quarter	16,744	88,863	X	X[a]	X[a]	X	X	na
13 Uruguay	81	Encuesta Nacional de Hogares	Urban	Second Semester 1995	9,506	32,610	X	X	X	X	X	X
	95	Encuesta Continua de Hogares	Urban	Second Semester	20,057	64,930	X	X	X	X	X	X
14 Venezuela	81	Encuesta de Hogares por Muestra	National	Second Semester	45,421	239,649	X	na	na	na	na	na
	95	Encuesta de Hogares por Muestreo	National	Second Semester	16,784	92,450	X	X[b]	X[b]	X[b]	na	na

[a] Cannot separate between property and capital rent.
[b] Cannot separate between property rent, capital rent, and transfers.

Appendix 1.2. Main Socioeconomic Indicators by Income Deciles
(Data from recent household surveys)

Appendix Table 1.2.1. Income Distribution (In percent)

A. Per capita total household income

| | Deciles | | | | | | | | | | Gini coefficient |
	1	2	3	4	5	6	7	8	9	10	
Argentina[1]	1.5	2.8	3.8	4.8	5.9	7.3	9.0	11.8	17.0	35.9	0.48
Bolivia[2]	1.5	2.6	3.4	4.2	5.2	6.3	7.9	10.5	15.6	42.1	0.53
Brazil	0.8	1.7	2.5	3.4	4.5	5.7	7.6	10.5	16.4	47.0	0.59
Chile	1.3	2.2	3.0	3.8	4.7	5.9	7.5	10.1	15.3	45.8	0.56
Costa Rica	1.4	2.9	4.0	5.2	6.3	7.7	9.6	12.2	16.4	34.2	0.46
Ecuador	0.6	1.7	2.8	3.9	5.2	6.5	8.3	10.9	15.6	44.0	0.57
El Salvador	1.0	2.4	3.4	4.5	5.7	7.1	8.9	11.4	16.2	39.4	0.51
Honduras[3]	na	na	na	na	na	na	na	na	na	na	na
Mexico	1.1	2.2	3.0	3.9	5.0	6.2	7.9	10.5	15.6	44.4	0.55
Panama	0.6	1.7	2.7	3.8	5.0	6.5	8.5	11.6	16.9	42.7	0.56
Paraguay	0.7	1.6	2.4	3.5	4.6	6.1	8.0	10.7	15.8	46.5	0.59
Peru	1.5	2.9	3.9	5.1	6.4	7.7	9.4	11.8	15.9	35.4	0.46
Uruguay[2]	1.8	3.2	4.3	5.4	6.6	8.0	9.7	12.2	16.4	32.3	0.43
Venezuela	1.6	2.9	3.9	4.9	6.1	7.5	9.3	11.8	16.2	35.8	0.47

B. Per capital household labor income

	1	2	3	4	5	6	7	8	9	10	
Argentina[1,4]	1.5	2.9	3.9	4.8	5.9	7.3	9.1	11.9	16.9	35.9	0.47
Bolivia[2]	1.4	2.6	3.4	4.3	5.3	6.4	8.0	10.6	15.6	42.4	0.52
Brazil	0.8	1.6	2.3	3.2	4.4	5.8	7.7	10.6	16.5	47.2	0.60
Chile	1.2	2.1	2.9	3.7	4.6	5.8	7.4	9.9	15.1	47.1	0.58
Costa Rica	1.4	2.9	4.1	5.2	6.4	7.8	9.6	12.2	16.5	33.9	0.45
Ecuador	0.6	1.7	2.8	3.9	5.1	6.5	8.3	10.9	15.6	44.8	0.57
El Salvador	1.1	2.3	3.3	4.4	5.6	7.1	8.9	11.6	16.4	39.2	0.51
Honduras[3]	1.2	2.3	3.2	4.1	5.3	6.7	8.6	11.4	16.3	40.9	0.53
Mexico	0.8	1.9	2.8	3.8	4.9	6.3	7.9	10.6	15.6	45.2	0.57
Panama	0.9	2.0	3.0	3.9	5.1	6.5	8.3	11.3	16.6	42.2	0.55
Paraguay	0.6	1.4	2.3	3.4	4.7	6.2	8.2	11.0	16.1	46.0	0.59
Peru	1.2	2.8	3.9	5.1	6.5	8.0	9.8	12.2	16.2	34.3	0.46
Uruguay[2]	1.3	2.7	3.8	5.0	6.2	7.8	9.6	12.3	16.9	34.4	0.47
Venezuela	1.5	2.9	3.9	5.0	6.2	7.5	9.4	11.9	16.2	35.5	0.47

C. Per capita household nonlabor income

	1	2	3	4	5	6	7	8	9	10	
Argentina[1,4]	na	na	na	na	na	na	na	na	na	na	na
Bolivia[2]	0.3	0.9	1.4	2.1	3.1	4.7	6.8	9.6	15.8	48.4	0.68
Brazil	0.5	1.4	1.9	2.6	3.4	4.7	6.3	9.3	14.9	55.0	0.66
Chile	0.2	0.4	0.7	1.5	2.7	4.1	6.3	9.6	17.3	57.1	0.72
Costa Rica	0.5	1.2	2.0	2.8	3.9	5.4	7.2	10.2	16.5	49.6	0.63
Ecuador	0.6	1.5	2.8	4.0	5.5	6.7	9.2	12.7	17.4	39.7	0.54
El Salvador	0.6	1.4	2.2	3.0	4.0	5.5	7.4	10.3	15.4	49.8	0.51
Honduras[3]	na	na	na	na	na	na	na	na	na	na	na
Mexico	0.5	1.2	1.8	2.8	3.8	5.0	6.8	9.8	16.4	51.7	0.64
Panama	0.5	1.1	1.5	2.1	2.9	4.0	5.7	8.7	15.4	57.9	0.69
Paraguay	0.3	0.8	1.3	2.1	3.0	4.3	6.2	9.4	14.8	56.9	0.70
Peru	0.3	0.8	1.3	2.0	2.9	4.2	6.5	9.9	16.8	55.3	0.69
Uruguay[2]	0.5	1.5	2.4	3.5	4.8	6.5	9.0	12.3	17.9	41.4	0.57
Venezuela	0.3	0.6	1.1	2.1	3.4	5.0	7.1	10.2	16.7	53.6	0.68

[1] The surveys for Argentina include only Greater Buenos Aires.
[2] The surveys for Bolivia and Uruguay include only urban areas.
[3] The surveys for Honduras include only labor incomes.
[4] Refers to main labor income only.
[5] No distinction is made between labor and non labor income.

| Appendix Table 1.2.II. Demographics | | | | | | | | | | |

A. Average size of household by income level

	Deciles										Total
	1	2	3	4	5	6	7	8	9	10	
Argentina[1]	6.27	5.25	5.44	4.42	4.80	3.96	3.79	3.61	3.37	3.06	4.40
Bolivia[2]	6.50	6.08	5.96	5.92	5.76	5.81	5.35	4.97	4.78	4.36	5.55
Brazil	6.49	5.93	5.49	5.10	4.66	4.79	4.37	4.25	4.01	3.59	4.87
Chile	5.63	5.25	5.24	4.92	4.88	4.76	4.46	4.27	4.08	3.87	4.74
Costa Rica	6.09	5.71	5.67	5.43	5.10	5.12	4.75	4.49	4.17	3.90	5.04
Ecuador	6.73	6.43	6.41	6.06	6.27	5.87	5.72	5.25	4.96	4.39	5.81
El Salvador	6.94	6.69	6.75	6.33	6.01	5.92	5.48	4.98	4.89	4.17	5.82
Honduras	7.22	7.53	7.09	6.87	6.77	6.39	6.48	5.93	5.65	4.86	6.49
Mexico	7.26	6.61	6.81	6.20	6.28	5.53	5.19	5.12	4.70	3.99	5.77
Nicaragua	8.37	7.59	7.69	7.49	7.33	7.06	6.53	6.80	5.98	5.17	7.00
Panama	6.32	6.17	6.06	5.56	5.26	5.29	4.92	4.62	4.22	3.57	5.20
Paraguay	7.26	7.32	6.53	6.14	6.42	5.81	5.73	5.27	4.87	4.37	5.97
Peru	7.71	7.38	6.61	6.39	6.36	6.03	5.82	5.76	5.34	4.68	6.21
Uruguay[2]	5.85	5.00	4.72	4.19	4.04	3.88	3.73	3.63	3.34	3.14	4.15
Venezuela	7.16	6.79	6.86	6.40	5.99	6.23	5.56	5.42	4.97	4.29	5.97

B. Number of children under 15 in household by income level

	1	2	3	4	5	6	7	8	9	10	Total
Argentina[1]	3.00	2.04	1.86	1.45	1.41	0.82	0.74	0.65	0.57	0.41	1.30
Bolivia[2]	3.40	2.99	2.77	2.46	2.40	2.26	1.93	1.73	1.47	1.31	2.27
Brazil	3.58	2.81	2.26	1.88	1.53	1.53	1.25	1.11	0.98	0.80	1.78
Chile	2.51	2.08	1.90	1.56	1.37	1.25	1.10	1.01	0.92	0.90	1.46
Costa Rica	3.30	2.76	2.65	2.30	1.98	1.76	1.55	1.27	1.14	1.03	1.97
Ecuador	3.42	3.06	3.08	2.69	2.58	2.25	2.07	1.76	1.49	1.37	2.38
El Salvador	3.70	3.50	3.22	2.90	2.49	2.34	1.92	1.53	1.43	1.06	2.41
Honduras	4.16	4.07	3.77	3.47	3.31	2.86	2.78	2.30	2.03	1.66	3.05
Mexico	3.99	3.20	3.32	2.60	2.39	2.04	1.72	1.54	1.30	1.06	2.32
Nicaragua	4.91	4.14	4.01	3.59	3.46	3.31	2.86	2.78	2.32	1.82	3.32
Panama	3.24	2.88	2.69	2.26	1.89	1.70	1.43	1.21	0.98	0.82	1.91
Paraguay	4.30	4.10	3.52	3.10	3.20	2.66	2.43	1.90	1.61	1.31	2.81
Peru	3.73	3.60	2.99	2.63	2.39	2.16	1.93	1.70	1.42	1.06	2.36
Uruguay[2]	2.78	1.89	1.59	1.14	0.92	0.84	0.76	0.70	0.56	0.49	1.17

C. Number of adults 65 or older in household by income level

	1	2	3	4	5	6	7	8	9	10	Total
Argentina[1]	0.41	0.40	0.49	0.48	0.42	0.44	0.41	0.38	0.35	0.33	0.41
Bolivia[2]	0.10	0.13	0.13	0.14	0.14	0.15	0.17	0.16	0.18	0.15	0.15
Brazil	0.06	0.12	0.21	0.22	0.26	0.23	0.22	0.21	0.20	0.21	0.19
Chile	0.15	0.16	0.26	0.28	0.28	0.32	0.34	0.27	0.27	0.26	0.26
Costa Rica	0.27	0.20	0.24	0.21	0.19	0.20	0.15	0.19	0.17	0.17	0.20
Ecuador	0.28	0.24	0.16	0.19	0.21	0.19	0.21	0.14	0.20	0.17	0.20
El Salvador	0.32	0.25	0.24	0.31	0.28	0.25	0.27	0.22	0.24	0.24	0.26
Honduras	0.22	0.23	0.22	0.23	0.17	0.17	0.20	0.18	0.22	0.14	0.20
Mexico	0.21	0.28	0.19	0.21	0.17	0.17	0.24	0.15	0.20	0.17	0.20
Nicaragua	0.16	0.20	0.23	0.22	0.23	0.17	0.24	0.20	0.17	0.13	0.19
Panama	0.24	0.26	0.21	0.19	0.25	0.26	0.21	0.25	0.28	0.21	0.23
Paraguay	0.17	0.14	0.20	0.22	0.23	0.19	0.21	0.27	0.20	0.23	0.21
Peru	0.79	0.77	0.58	0.58	0.66	0.53	0.52	0.49	0.45	0.51	0.59
Uruguay[2]	0.18	0.30	0.36	0.48	0.52	0.51	0.46	0.46	0.44	0.44	0.41
Venezuela	0.22	0.18	0.21	0.20	0.23	0.22	0.22	0.25	0.22	0.20	0.21

[1] The surveys for Argentina include only Greater Buenos Aires.
[2] The surveys for Bolivia and Uruguay include only urban areas.

Appendix Table 1.2.III. Education

A. Average years of education for 25 year olds by income level

| | Deciles | | | | | | | | | | Total |
	1	2	3	4	5	6	7	8	9	10	
Argentina[1]	7.04	7.48	7.74	7.71	8.52	8.82	8.99	9.91	11.13	13.57	9.44
Bolivia[2]	5.96	6.45	7.23	7.67	7.58	8.32	9.15	9.29	10.38	13.12	8.80
Brazil	1.98	2.49	2.97	3.41	3.66	4.40	4.99	5.98	7.43	10.53	5.22
Chile	6.24	6.88	7.09	7.40	7.69	8.16	8.47	9.80	10.88	12.83	8.79
Costa Rica	4.08	4.88	5.39	5.54	5.91	6.31	6.75	7.65	8.62	11.53	6.94
Ecuador	3.39	4.39	5.07	5.61	5.64	6.85	7.74	8.23	9.19	11.83	7.12
El Salvador	1.63	2.14	2.40	2.75	3.27	3.99	4.73	5.90	7.11	10.27	4.88
Honduras	2.07	2.33	2.47	3.06	3.59	3.90	4.70	5.76	6.86	9.58	4.74
Mexico	2.14	2.95	3.78	4.15	4.78	5.66	6.06	7.24	8.89	12.13	6.23
Nicaragua	2.17	2.05	2.65	3.33	4.11	4.55	4.94	5.46	6.46	8.49	4.74
Panama	4.31	5.36	6.30	7.07	7.53	8.16	8.78	9.90	10.88	13.57	8.68
Paraguay	3.37	3.67	3.88	4.59	4.81	5.46	5.96	6.62	7.88	10.72	6.06
Peru	3.87	4.17	4.95	5.69	6.60	7.05	7.66	8.28	9.04	10.80	7.20
Uruguay[2]	6.03	6.31	6.54	6.49	6.79	7.34	8.00	8.68	9.74	11.87	8.02
Venezuela	4.66	4.94	5.27	5.72	6.23	6.68	7.20	7.78	8.58	10.81	7.15

B. Primary Completion Rates for 20-25 year olds by income level
(In percent)

	1	2	3	4	5	6	7	8	9	10	Total
Argentina[1]	83	94	92	99	96	98	100	99	99	100	97
Bolivia[2]	84	89	90	87	94	94	93	94	95	94	92
Brazil	19	24	33	43	48	57	67	76	85	95	57
Chile	67	75	77	84	85	89	91	94	95	96	86
Costa Rica	64	69	78	77	81	84	92	95	95	99	86
Ecuador	76	85	81	85	83	89	92	93	94	98	88
El Salvador	17	17	22	25	34	37	52	63	75	85	47
Honduras	39	48	41	46	53	58	71	76	87	87	64
Mexico	52	66	65	70	84	87	91	93	95	92	83
Nicaragua	31	31	44	53	57	62	53	75	82	90	60
Panama	75	82	89	89	93	95	96	97	98	99	92
Paraguay	49	62	51	60	64	72	75	85	90	93	74
Peru	53	52	56	71	75	78	85	90	91	95	78
Uruguay[2]	88	94	92	95	97	98	99	98	99	99	96
Venezuela	76	79	79	79	89	91	91	94	96	97	88

C. Secondary completion rates for 20-25 year olds by income level
(In percent)

	1	2	3	4	5	6	7	8	9	10	Total
Argentina[1]	13	17	27	31	42	51	54	65	68	92	50
Bolivia[2]	51	48	55	52	59	60	60	64	65	83	61
Brazil	2	3	6	9	12	16	22	32	46	73	23
Chile	23	31	35	44	50	56	65	74	80	83	56
Costa Rica	10	10	11	14	13	18	29	42	44	70	30
Ecuador	14	15	18	29	26	33	40	46	49	73	36
El Salvador	8	6	10	9	14	15	27	35	47	69	27
Honduras	2	3	4	4	9	11	15	23	35	50	18
Mexico	4	9	12	16	18	26	32	39	53	70	32
Nicaragua	3	2	8	8	16	14	15	22	25	43	17
Panama	11	16	30	33	41	47	57	66	72	84	49
Paraguay	0	2	3	5	4	11	20	34	41	62	23
Peru	33	32	36	48	51	60	65	75	82	87	61
Uruguay[2]	16	21	24	35	35	43	46	51	63	72	42
Venezuela	15	17	26	24	31	32	44	48	53	74	40

[1] The surveys for Argentina include only Greater Buenos Aires.
[2] The surveys for Bolivia and Uruguay include only urban areas.

Appendix Table 1.2.IV. Labor

A. Female labor force participation rates (ages 25-45) by income level
(In percent)

| | Deciles | | | | | | | | | | Total |
	1	2	3	4	5	6	7	8	9	10	
Argentina[1]	41	47	45	48	46	62	64	69	74	88	60
Bolivia[2]	56	53	55	62	65	65	69	65	75	78	65
Brazil	48	50	53	54	58	61	63	67	70	78	61
Chile	20	25	28	37	43	49	53	63	70	76	47
Costa Rica	28	23	32	33	29	44	54	58	64	71	45
Ecuador	62	54	48	53	56	63	65	68	76	81	64
El Salvador	22	35	37	50	53	60	65	69	74	82	57
Honduras	27	39	31	39	42	48	54	58	69	77	50
Mexico	36	28	27	38	34	42	40	53	57	64	44
Nicaragua	27	36	46	52	57	51	55	66	65	72	55
Panama	28	30	32	32	39	47	59	68	77	84	52
Paraguay	69	75	70	63	66	67	68	75	79	83	72
Peru	65	68	65	64	63	68	68	69	73	74	68
Uruguay[2]	49	57	65	64	70	77	79	82	87	90	72
Venezuela	32	31	34	36	48	48	59	65	73	77	52

B. Percentage of men (ages 25-45), in informal sector by income level

	1	2	3	4	5	6	7	8	9	10	
Argentina[1]	68	50	42	40	47	45	39	43	41	34	44
Bolivia[2]	70	57	53	54	50	46	51	49	39	35	49
Brazil	39	33	29	26	22	21	20	20	19	20	22
Chile	37	32	29	30	29	28	28	29	28	30	30
Costa Rica	75	59	50	43	44	43	33	34	34	24	41
Ecuador	88	72	66	65	50	58	44	50	51	41	55
El Salvador	87	66	61	47	49	44	46	36	33	30	46
Honduras	90	89	81	74	60	57	55	51	41	34	59
Mexico	97	83	73	73	63	56	62	52	47	42	62
Nicaragua	93	82	84	82	76	81	76	70	71	64	76
Panama	84	67	51	42	42	32	30	28	27	19	38
Paraguay	82	83	83	71	68	56	59	45	47	46	57
Peru	71	67	68	68	62	62	50	52	47	35	56
Uruguay[2]	49	40	37	33	31	32	32	30	31	28	34
Venezuela	69	69	58	56	54	46	46	45	40	39	49

C. Percentage of women (ages 25-45), in informal sector by income level

	1	2	3	4	5	6	7	8	9	10	
Argentina[1]	77	72	68	63	48	42	54	37	27	31	47
Bolivia[2]	84	84	81	74	77	78	63	65	55	36	66
Brazil	43	30	25	27	26	21	20	21	20	20	22
Chile	47	47	52	42	47	41	36	30	32	39	39
Costa Rica	86	67	54	59	59	48	45	34	36	22	44
Ecuador	89	87	88	85	77	68	66	66	59	45	69
El Salvador	92	76	72	71	68	68	63	56	43	29	55
Honduras	93	89	88	81	72	67	64	50	50	30	60
Mexico	99	96	91	88	83	65	66	54	37	36	62
Nicaragua	99	90	87	93	90	92	89	82	86	78	87
Panama	87	80	67	58	45	34	29	20	18	10	32
Paraguay	97	97	92	90	91	73	75	64	59	56	70
Peru	70	74	78	79	75	73	69	65	62	46	68
Uruguay[2]	76	68	59	54	45	39	30	29	29	30	42
Venezuela	84	73	59	54	49	42	40	35	29	27	42

[1] The surveys for Argentina include only Greater Buenos Aires.
[2] The surveys for Bolivia and Uruguay include only urban areas.

REFERENCES

Aghion, P., and P. Bolton. 1992. Distribution and Growth in Models of Imperfect Capital Markets. *European Economic Review 36*.

_____. 1997. A Theory of Trickle-down Growth and Development. *Review of Economic Studies* 64(2) April: 151-72.

Alesina, A., and R. Perotti. 1993. The Political Economy of Growth: A Critical Survey of Recent Literature and Some Results. World Bank. Mimeo.

Alesina, A., and D. Rodrik. 1992. Income Distribution and Economic Growth: A Simple Theory and Empirical Evidence. In A. Cukierman, S. Hercovitz, and L. Leiderman, eds., *The Political Economy of Business Cycles and Growth*. Cambridge, MA: MIT Press.

_____. 1994. Distributive Politics and Economic Growth: A Critical Survey of the Recent Literature. *The World Bank Economic Review* 8(3).

Atkinson, A. B. 1997. Bringing Income Distribution in From the Cold. *The Economic Journal* (March): 297-321.

Atkinson, A. B., and J. Micklewright. 1992. *Economic Transformation in Eastern Europe and the Distribution of Income*. Cambridge: Cambridge University Press.

Banerjee, A., and A. Newman. 1991. Risk Bearing and the Theory of Income Distribution. *Review of Economic Studies* 58: 211-35.

Benabou, R. 1996. Inequality and Growth. Paper presented at Eleventh Annual Macroeconomics Conference, Cambridge, MA.

Benhabib, J., and A. Rustichini. 1996. Social Conflict, Growth and Income Distribution. *Journal of Economic Growth* 1(1): 125-42.

Birdsall, N., and J.L. Londoño.1997. Asset Inequality Does Matter: Lessons from Latin America. *American Economic Review* 87(2) May.

_____. 1998. No Tradeoff: Efficient Growth Via More Equal Human Capital Accumulation in Latin America. In *Beyond Tradeoffs: Market Reforms and Equitable Growth in Latin America*, Nancy Birdsall, Carol Graham and Richard Sabot, eds. Washington, D.C.: The Brookings Institution and the Inter-American Development Bank.

Birdsall, N., D. Ross, and R. Sabot. 1995. Inequality and Growth Reconsidered. *World Bank Economic Review* 9(3) September.

Clarke, G. 1992. *More Evidence on Income Distribution and Growth*. World Bank Working Paper 1064.

Dahan, M., and D. Tsiddon. 1998. Demographic Transition, Income Distribution and Economic Growth. *Journal of Economic Growth*. Forthcoming.

De Gregorio, J., and S. Kim. 1994. *Credit Markets with Differences in Abilities: Education, Distribution and Growth*. IMF Working Paper 94/97.

Deininger, K., and L. Squire. 1996a. New Ways of Looking at Old Issues: Inequality and Growth. World Bank. Unpublished.

_____. 1996b. A New Data Set Measuring Income Inequality. *World Bank Economic Review* 10(3), September: 565-91.

Forbes J., K. 1997. A Reassessment of the Effect of Inequality on Growth. Massachusetts Institute of Technology. October. Unpublished.

Galor, O., and J. Zeira. 1993. Income Distribution and Macroeconomics. *Review of Economic Studies* 60.

Gottschalk, P., and T. Smeeding. 1997. Cross-National Comparisons of Earnings and Income Inequality. *Journal of Economic Literature* 35 (June): 633-87.

Londoño, J. L., and M. Székely. 1997. *Persistent Poverty and Excess Inequality: Latin America 1970-1995*. Office of the Chief Economist Working Paper Series No. 357, Inter-American Development Bank.

Lustig, N. , and R. Deutch. 1998. The Inter-American Development Bank and Poverty Reduction: An Overview. Sustainable Development Department, Inter-American Development Bank. Mimeo.

Morley, Samuel. 1998. Poverty During Recovery and Reform in Latin America: 1985-1995. Inter-American Development Bank. Unpublished.

Perotti, R. 1993. Political Equilibrium, Income Distribution and Growth. *Review of Economic Studies* 60: 755-76.

_____. 1996. Growth, Income Distribution and Democracy. *Journal of Economic Growth* 1 (June): 149-87.

Persson, T., and G. Tabellini. 1991. Is *Inequality Harmful for Growth? Theory and Evidence*. NBER Working Paper No. 3599. National Bureau of Economic Research, Cambridge, MA.

_____. 1992. Growth, Distribution and Politics. *European Economic Review* 36.

_____. 1994. Is Inequality Harmful for Growth? *American Economic Review* 84(3).

Piketty, T. 1997. The Dynamics of the Wealth Distribution and the Interest Rate with Credit Rationing. *Review of Economic Studies* 64(2) April: 173-89.

Solimano, Andrés. 1998. The End of Hard Choices? Revisiting the Relationship Between Income Distribution and Growth. In Solimano, A., ed., *Social Inequality Values, Growth and the State*. University of Michigan Press. Forthcoming.

PART TWO

CAUSES

Part Two

INTRODUCTION

Income inequalities in Latin American countries are the greatest in the world, primarily because of the huge gaps between families belonging to the highest-income decile and everyone else. Four features set the wealthiest families apart: the higher education levels of their heads of households, the type of work they do, their urban location, and the smaller size of their households. Although household incomes come from various sources, overall income inequality as measured in household surveys is closely related to unequal income from work. Such are the facts, but what are their causes?

To answer that question, this section begins with more specific explanations associated with immediate observation of inequalities between individuals, and moves toward more general explanations that take into account the economic, social and institutional context in which individuals operate. Although only a limited number of variables can be observed and measured, their explanatory power is high. At the most immediate level, gaps in income can be explained primarily by differences in education. But these differences are the result of a decisionmaking process taking place in families, in which the economic, social and cultural conditions of parents play a role. In this process, families decide not only how much education to give their children, but whether or not the mother can be involved in economic activities outside the home and how many children it is desirable to have. Families that are poor because their parents have little education tend to be larger, offer fewer possibilities for women, and educate their children less. Thus, education and family are the channels through which income inequality is perpetuated. On a third level of analysis stands the context in which this process takes place. Parents make decisions on the basis of the relative rewards and opportunities they perceive for themselves and for their children. These rewards and opportunities depend on the abundance or scarcity of work and human capital in relation to other productive factors, particu-

larly capital and natural resources, and to other economic, social and institutional development conditions in their countries. The endowments and characteristics of productive resources and the state of development are therefore the two dimensions of the context in which income inequality unfolds and is perpetuated.

LABOR INCOME INEQUALITY AND EDUCATION

Given the many manifestations of income inequality, its causes can be explored on different levels. Differences in labor income constitute the most immediate level of observation. Because income inequality is greatest in Latin America, it is no coincidence that the region has the widest wage gaps in the world between more highly trained personnel who handle managerial and administrative tasks and unskilled workers who do manual production work.

The main explanation for such income differences is found in education and the power of experience to further widen the income gaps between those with a great deal of education and those with little. From the standpoint of income equality, education in Latin America is problematic in several ways. The average education of the workforce has advanced more slowly than it has elsewhere in the world, and by the early 1990s it had not even reached five years of schooling. Although initial access to school is comparable to or higher than it is elsewhere, the children of lower strata families withdraw quickly, while those who are better off remain in the education system, and growing numbers are even reaching the university level. Thus, a high proportion of the population has some primary education, and the proportion of those who attend the university is also high in terms of the development level of countries in the region, while the proportion at intermediate levels of education is low. Hence, the accumulation of human capital is not only weak, but its distribution is quite unequal (albeit increasingly less so for younger generations). This situation reflects problems of returns and of quality. The returns are low for the early years of schooling but high for university education, and are substantially less in the countryside than in the city. The quality is quite inferior for those who attend public school and have no access to higher quality private education. The result of this set of factors is highly stratified education that reproduces income inequality instead of helping to correct it.

Other factors help deepen differences of labor income between workers. Independent of education and experience, employers receive higher incomes than formal (subordinate) workers, and the latter earn substantially more than informal workers. Although Latin American women are reaching education levels similar to those of men, they do not receive equal pay, especially in informal sectors, where their numbers are increasing.

INEQUALITY AND THE FAMILY

Because decisions about education take place in the family, they are influenced by the same factors that affect other family decisions, such as the participation of women in the workforce and the number of children. Some of these factors are internal family matters. Aside from individual beliefs and values (which play a crucial role in all these decisions but are not observable), the most important internal factors are the educational level of the father and the mother, the time demands on the mother in the household (which depend primarily on the number of children), the presence of other adults in the home, and the availability of basic household services. Other factors are external, such as the pay that household members can earn given their education and experience, and their possibilities of being involved in formal and informal occupations.

As a result of this interaction, women in lower-strata families participate less in the workplace (and when they do so, usually in informal activities), and have more children and less education than women in the high-income strata. Inequalities are therefore reproduced in the next generation, although not in the same manner in all countries. Indeed, from the results of a model of estimated family behavior for 14 countries, it was found that two couples differing only in their educational level will make different decisions in countries that are currently more unequal than they will in more equal countries. Consequently, the family acts as a channel transmitting inequality between generations, and education is its basic mechanism. But the transmission of inequality operates with

varying strength from one country to another, depending on relative prices and other conditions of the economic and social context confronting individuals as they make key decisions. Higher pay for work and better facilities for performing household work induce women to participate more in the labor market and have fewer children. Better opportunities and more flexible employment conditions help bring women into formal rather than informal employment. High expected returns on the education of children, lower costs and better facilities for sending them to school encourage greater educational attainment, which translates into less inequality in future generations. All these price and cost signals coming from the context in which families operate are the result of aggregate economic and social conditions.

THE ROLE OF THE ECONOMIC AND SOCIAL CONTEXT

The last level of the causes of inequality is consequently of an aggregate character. What aspects of the economic and social environment tend to foster income inequality and facilitate its reproduction? The conclusion emerging from a comparative analysis for economies of all regions of the world is that inequality is connected both to a combination of aspects of the state of economic and social development, and to the more permanent conditions of countries associated with their natural resource endowment, geographical location, and other features of their productive resources (henceforth called "endowments").

Through a relationship of mutual causality and reinforcement, economic development is associated with falling levels of inequality. Development is multidimensional, and many of those dimensions affect inequality in the same direction, at least after certain minimal levels of development have been attained. Consider first the accumulation of physical capital, which is essential to the development process. At the early stages of accumulation, scarcity of capital leads to high returns, which are a cause of income inequality. But as capital becomes more abundant, its returns fall vis-à-vis other productive factors, especially labor. Since labor capacity is an asset that is better distributed than physical capital, income distribution tends to improve.

A similar mechanism is at work in education: low levels of schooling entail high returns for the few who are educated. As average educational levels rise, not only is the return for those who are educated reduced, but differences between the educational levels of some individuals and others tend to decline. Differences between individuals in the same generation tend to narrow first, although differences with past generations that received less education remain in place for several decades more. Thus, the micro-level analysis is confirmed in the aggregate: over time educational progress tends to help reduce inequality.

The same can be said of demographic patterns. Rapid population growth rates entail greater diversity in family size, which leads to worse distribution of per capita income. In part this is simply because in larger families the average income of individual members is less, but it also happens that in larger families women are less involved in formal employment and children receive less education. Hence, in countries with greater demographic growth, participation in the workforce is lower, as is educational achievement—even after isolating the effect of economic development on these variables.

The countryside offers fewer economic opportunities than the city: markets are not well integrated, costs of providing education are higher and access to it lower, employment possibilities are limited, and access to financing is restricted. This translates into lower income, less education and larger families in the countryside than in the city. Early in the urbanization process, income differences between city and countryside help increase income inequality of all individuals. But when most workers are based in cities, the rural-urban income gap will affect only a small fraction of the population, and its contribution to overall inequality will be reduced.

Similar reasoning can be applied to the formalization process. The existence of an informal sector makes it difficult to properly take advantage of the possibilities of specialization, greater access to capital and the economies of scale of higher volume production. Hence, the informal sector tends to generate lower incomes than those offered by the formal sector. Initially, as labor relations become more formal, the privileges of some wage workers are a source of inequality, but if the process takes hold and continues to advance, they become an equalizing factor.

Latin America is at a midpoint in this multidimensional development process, which partly explains the region's poor income distribution and suggests that pros-

pects are good if policies conducive to economic growth and the consolidation of changes are adopted to hasten the accumulation of physical capital and the expansion of education, improve women's chances to be part of the labor force, deal with the challenges of urbanization, and make productive activities more formal (see Part Three).

But that is not the whole story. The current development situation of Latin American economies only explains a third of the extra inequality as compared with developed countries (6 points of the 18 point differences between their respective Gini indices). The rest reflects factors of a more permanent nature, which constitute "endowments." Their influence on income distribution has occurred historically through varying institutional and political channels. Extensive agricultural lands, dependence on primary exports, and the geographical location of these countries are three interrelated variables that reflect characteristics of resource endowment. High economic volatility, which is also connected to these variables, is a manifestation of the influence of these endowments on economic institutions.

In keeping with other studies of geography and economic history, the statistical analysis on a world scale carried out for this section confirms the influence of tropical conditions on the structure of property and use of natural resources and unskilled labor. The colonial institutions of land ownership, forced labor and income distribution that prospered in tropical regions, influenced by those very geographical reasons, left their imprint on the distribution of land and other assets and continue to weigh on income distribution in Latin America.

But that imprint is not immune to change. Several countries, especially the English-speaking Caribbean countries, overcame slavery's legacy of inequality and today are among the countries with the least income inequality in the region. Furthermore, broad differences in distribution and tendencies toward change are found among countries with a Spanish or Portuguese heritage in tropical areas, thereby demonstrating that there is room for policies to have an effect. That is true both for policies favoring more equal distribution and for those that may reinforce the mechanisms that perpetuate inequality.

Chapter 2

LABOR INCOME INEQUALITY
AND EDUCATION

The world's largest per capita income inequalities are found in Latin America. The region's extreme income differences among workers lie at the heart of this inequality. Anywhere in the world, higher wages are paid to workers who are more skilled or occupy management and administrative positions than to workers having little education, who are normally placed in manual production jobs. Globalization and the introduction of new labor-saving technologies have widened these gaps in both industrial and developing countries. The gaps in Latin America, however, have widened even more rapidly.

Figure 2.1 is based on worldwide wage information by occupation, and uses the (relative) wage gap in industrial countries as a basis of comparison. The figure shows that Latin America's gaps are twice as wide as those of the industrial countries. In the Asian "four tigers," wage differentials between office workers and manual laborers are similar to those in industrial countries. Relative wage gaps are larger among other developing countries in Asia and Africa, but they are less pronounced than in Latin America. Further, while the wage differentials in these groups of countries have gradually been approaching those of industrial countries, this trend was interrupted in Latin America at the end of the 1980s, and has been on the rise during the 1990s.[1]

These earnings gaps between occupations illustrate why they serve as a conduit for the main factors in labor income differentiation. The most substantial differences arise from educational levels and from how the market remunerates different types of education. However, these are not the only factors in income differentiation. Persons with more experience earn more; men are paid more than women; and people with permanent jobs in formal sector enterprises earn more than those working for informal sector businesses or the self-employed. There are also differences between rural and urban areas and between economic sectors. In addition, some differentiation factors may be dependent on others. For example, while women earn less than men, the differences are less substantial in formal sector jobs, while they increase considerably among the self-employed.

This chapter analyzes the various dimensions of labor income inequality and discusses education's central (although not exclusive) role in explaining these differences.

**Figure 2.1. Relative Wages:
White Collar/Blue Collar, 1982-97**
(*Developed Countries*=1)

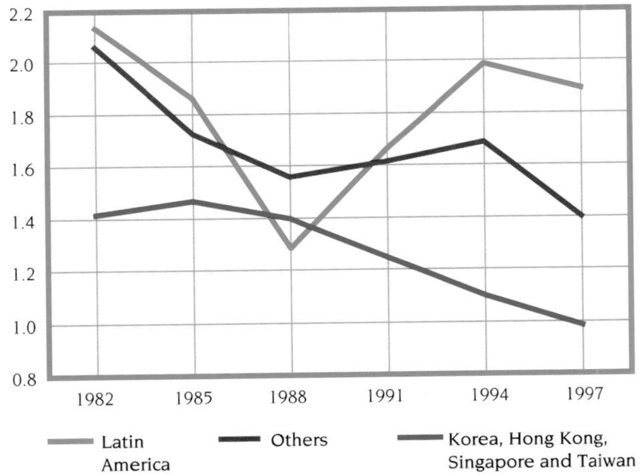

Legend: Latin America — Others — Korea, Hong Kong, Singapore and Taiwan

Source: Lora and Márquez (1998).

---

[1] See Lora and Márquez (1998) for a detailed description of these calculations, which compare earnings between workers having the same personal characteristics (education, experience, age and family status) and occupying similar jobs in different countries (department manager of a given size company, secretary, driver, construction worker, etc.). The calculation method ensures that the comparisons are not affected by changes in the composition of the labor supply or in employment, or by price phenomena at the macroeconomic level (inflation, exchange rate fluctuations, etc.).

Figure 2.2. Income Differentials by Education

(*Noneducated workers = 1*)

— No schooling   — 12 years
— 6 years   — 17 years

* *Countries with urban data only.*
Note: *Regressions of returns to education controlling for experience and experience squared.*
Source: *IDB calculations based on recent household surveys.*

Figure 2.3. Average Income of Earners by Age and Education Level, Brazil

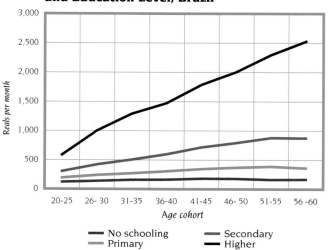

— No schooling   — Secondary
— Primary   — Higher

Source: *IDB calculations based on household surveys.*

Figure 2.4. Income Profiles by Education

(*Worker, 25 years of age, with no education =1*)

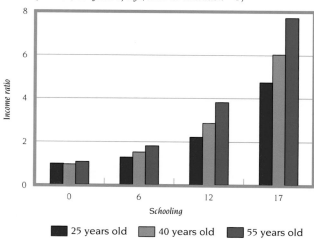

■ 25 years old   ■ 40 years old   ■ 55 years old

Note: *Estimates based on income regressions by education level, controlling for experience.*
Source: *IDB calculations based on recent household surveys.*

Figure 2.5. Income Gap by Gender

(*In percent*)

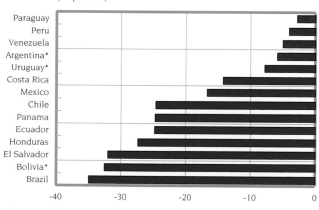

Percent difference between females and males

* *Countries with urban data only.*
Note: *Controlling for education, experience and experience squared.*
Source: *IDB calculations based on recent household surveys.*

DIMENSIONS OF LABOR INCOME INEQUALITY

Major Differences Attributed to Educational Level

A worker with six years of education (equivalent to completing primary school in most Latin American countries), employed for the first time, earns 50 percent more than a worker who has not attended school. The gap widens to 120 percent for a worker with 12 years of education (which normally corresponds to having completed secondary school), while it exceeds 200 percent for those with 17 years of education (university diploma).

These average gaps, calculated for 14 countries during the 1990s, differ widely from country to country (Figure 2.2). While in Brazil and Mexico workers with six years of education earn almost twice as much as those with no education, this gap is reduced to 40 percent in Peru, and to 35 percent in urban Argentina. With 12 years of education, the differences in income compared with workers having no education amount to 170 percent in the first two countries, while in Peru and Argentina the gap declines to about 80 percent. Further, for workers with 17 years of education, the gap is 280 percent in Brazil and 260 percent en Mexico, as compared with approximately 160 percent in Argentina and 145 percent in Peru.

It follows that income gaps attributable to educational level are significant, with substantial differences among countries. This implies that income inequality arises from education distribution patterns, as well as from the way the labor market compensates education in each country, and within each country, in light of other characteristics of the individuals, and their integration into the market in question.

Differences Increase with Age

Income gaps between educated and uneducated workers in first-time employment also tend to increase with age. The human capital developed with formal education can be enhanced with experience. This occurs at different rates in individuals with different levels of education. To understand this important point, consider the long-term earning patterns of two individuals—one is illiterate, and the other has completed a university education. At 25 years of age, the income difference between the two will be at a ratio of about four to one, according to the information on Brazil (Figure 2.3). As the workers accumulate years of experience, the skilled individual's income will increase steadily, while the illiterate worker's income will remain virtually unchanged. At 40 years of age, the income difference will be six to one, and at 55 years of age it will exceed

10 to one. Brazil has the largest income differences attributable to educational level and age. However, Latin America's average age profiles show that, at 25 years of age, income differences attributable to education are in the range of five to one, while at 55 years of age they are eight to one (for workers with 17 years of education compared with uneducated workers—see Figure 2.4).

Women Earn Less

Women earn significantly less per hour than men: the average gap for the 14 countries studied is 14 percent, although it exceeds 30 percent in Brazil, Bolivia and El Salvador, and is less than 10 percent (in increasing order) in Paraguay, Peru, Venezuela, Argentina and Uruguay (Figure 2.5).[2] These differences may be interpreted as the maximum possible effect of discrimination against women in each country, since the labor market does not provide equal pay for different types of employment. To the extent that more women tend to work in low-paying occupations, this is reflected in lower wages for women. Further, women earn less because they acquire less cumulative work experience than men, as a result of breaks in their work histories owing to the demands of motherhood and housework traditionally assigned to them.[3] While all this suggests that the effect of discrimination is modest, it can in fact be substantial in specific activities and certain types of work. Discrimination can also cause women to drop out of school or to abstain from participating in the workforce. These possible effects of discrimination are not reflected in the aforementioned income differentials.

Workers Earn Less in Rural Areas

The gap between rural and urban areas is a significant dimension of inequality in Latin America. Considerable disparities in average income levels in the two areas yield higher national income inequality figures than are found in rural or urban areas considered individually. Some per capita income differences can be attributed to the fact that families are larger in rural areas (see Chapter 3), and

---

[2] An earlier study found an average gap of approximately 25 percent, not reflecting differences in education and experience. See Psacharopoulos and Tzannatos (1992).

[3] It is difficult to account for women's workforce experience because the variable used as a proxy for experience is not the number of years effectively worked by each person, for which there is no information. Instead, it is an "apparent experience" variable that results when six years (of preschool) and the number of school years attained is subtracted from each person's age. This variable reasonably approximates men's workforce experience, but is much less accurate for women.

Figure 2.6. Labor Income Gap Between Rural and Urban Areas

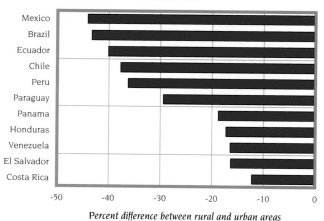

Percent difference between rural and urban areas

Note: Controlling for education, experience, experience squared and gender.
Source: IDB calculations based on recent household surveys.

Figure 2.7. Income by Occupation and Gender
(In percent, urban formal male worker = 1)

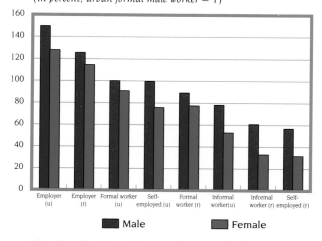

Note: Controlling for experience, experience squared and years of schooling. (u)=urban and (r)=rural.
Source: IDB calculations based on recent household surveys.

to the fact that rural workers are less educated. However, aside from these differences, workers having similar education, experience and gender characteristics earn an average of 28 percent less (per hour) than their counterparts in urban areas. The differences range from 12 percent in Costa Rica to 44 percent in Mexico (Figure 2.6).

Differences Attributable to Type of Employment

There are also significant differences in both urban and rural areas that can be attributed to type of employment. As can be seen in Figure 2.7, which uses a male wage earner employed by a formal sector enterprise with 10 or more workers[4] (controlling for differences related to education and experience), the following differentiating features are observed in hourly labor remuneration by type of job:

• Employers in both rural and urban areas are paid an average of 25 to 50 percent more;
• Self-employed workers' earnings do not differ systematically from those of their formal sector counterparts (though there may be differences in either direction, depending on the country);
• In the rural sector, subordinate workers in formal sector enterprises earn 10 percent less;
• In the urban sector, small enterprises (with less than 10 workers) associated with the informal sector pay their workers 20 percent less than formal enterprises;
• In the rural sector, informal workers, including both self-employed and employees in small enterprises,

earn approximately 40 percent less than urban formal sector workers.

Women earn less in all employment categories and in both urban and rural areas. The greatest differences are found in informal sector jobs (that is, the self-employed and persons working in small enterprises associated with informal sector activities), both in rural and urban areas. Women in informal sector jobs earn 25 percent less per hour than men having equal age and educational levels. Apparent discrimination against women is less pronounced in formal sector jobs. Women supervisors in urban sectors earn 20 percent less, while women in other formal sector jobs (rural employers or employees in rural or urban formal sector enterprises) are paid only 10 percent less than men. The wage differences for women in the formal sectors are apparently not significant, since, as we have observed, women have less work experience than men.

Income differences by type of job are not uniform between countries, or even between some formal sector occupations (Figures 2.8a-2.8d). Urban employers (both men and women) in Chile earn more than twice the wages of their counterparts in formal sector enterprises. This ratio is much higher than observed in most countries, with the exception of Brazil, where it is 1.8 times higher for supervisors. In Costa Rica and Peru, urban male employers earn only 1.2 times the pay of formal sector wage

---

[4] In some countries, a different number is used to define formal sector enterprises.

Figure 2.8a. Income of Formal Occupations
(*Urban formal male worker* = 1)

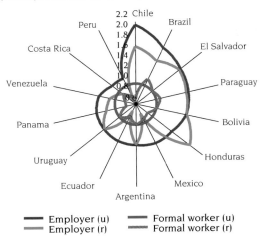

Employer (u) — **Formal worker (u)**
Employer (r) — **Formal worker (r)**

Note: Controlling for experience, experience squared and years of schooling.
Source: IDB calculations based on recent household surveys.

Figure 2.8b. Income of Formal Occupations, Women
(*Urban formal male worker* = 1)

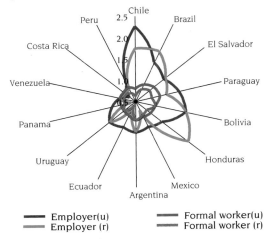

Employer(u) — **Formal worker(u)**
Employer (r) — **Formal worker (r)**

Note: Controlling for experience, experience squared and years of education level.
Source: IDB calculations based on recent household surveys.

Figure 2.8c. Income of Formal Occupations, Men
(*Urban formal male worker* = 1)

Self-employed (u) — **Self-employed (r)**
Informal worker (u) — **Informal worker (r)**

Note: Controlling for experience, experience squared and years of schooling.
Source: IDB calculations based on recent household surveys.

Figure 2.8d. Income of Informal Occupations, Women
(*Urban formal male worker* = 1)

Self-employed (u) — **Self-employed (r)**
Informal worker (u) — **Informal worker (r)**

Note: Controlling for experience, experience squared and years of schooling.
Source: IDB calculations based on recent household surveys.

earners, while rural employers earn less. Wages paid to male rural workers in the formal sector are much more similar to those of urban workers having similar characteristics, with differentials ranging from 14 percent (Brazil) to -30 percent (Chile).

Income differentials for women with formal sector jobs are similar to those of men in most countries. However, premiums for women employers (as compared with male formal sector employees in urban areas) are considerably lower than those paid to men (except in urban areas of Chile and Bolivia, and in rural areas of Honduras and Peru).

Where informal sector activities are concerned, only Chilean women in urban areas and self-employed Bolivian women receive pay comparable to male formal sector employees. Other women in the informal sector earn substantially less, and the gaps are generally more pronounced than for men. The greatest apparent discrimination against women in the informal sector is found in El Salvador, Honduras, Panama and Venezuela.

Figure 2.9. Labor Incomes by Sector
(*In percent, manufacturing = 1*)

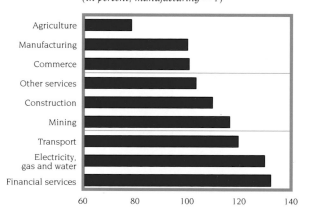

Note: *Controlling for experience, experience squared, education, gender, and type of employment.*
Source: *IDB calculations based on recent household surveys.*

Differences Due to Economic Sector

More formal sector workers are employed in industry than in agriculture, more women are employed in trade than in the transportation sector, and the financial sector has more stringent education requirements than any other sector. As a result, we might expect these conditions to be reflected in a typical worker's wages in each sector. However, even after taking into account all of the earnings differences attributable to education, experience, gender and type of occupation, workers in different sectors are not paid equally. The same individual employed as a formal sector worker in agriculture would be paid 20 percent less than in industry or trade, while in the transportation, public services and financial sectors, the individual could earn 20 percent or more than in industry (Figure 2.9).

However, it is difficult for any individual to be so versatile. Each sector might recognize and compensate some skills differently than others, and there is abundant proof that larger enterprises in all countries tend to pay their workers more in order to provide incentives, reduce supervision costs, and recognize the individual's investment in company-specific training, among other reasons.[5] As a result, sectors that require more specialized skills and in which larger enterprises operate tend to pay higher wages to workers having apparently similar years of education and experience and class characteristics, from the statistical standpoint. In any case, the differences by sector constitute an additional dimension of labor income inequalities.

The behavior of sectoral remuneration in Figure 2.9 is an average, from which some countries diverge appre-ciably. Although the agricultural sectors in all countries pay workers less than the industrial sectors, the difference is only slight in Panama, less than 10 percent in Honduras, and exceeds 40 percent in Peru and Mexico. At the other end of the scale, the financial and public service sectors (electricity, gas and water) compete as the highest paying sectors. Public services offer better jobs in Bolivia and Paraguay, with pay exceeding levels in the industrial sectors in these countries by 40 percent and 70 percent, respectively. By contrast, in Chile, Mexico and Venezuela, public service wages exceed industrial ones by more modest figures (between 3 and 10 percent). Brazil, Ecuador, Mexico and Uruguay offer much higher pay in the financial sector, with premiums of about 50 percent over industry.

Differences, Large and Small

We have described the income differences related to workers' different individual and labor characteristics; however, the relative importance of these factors should be considered along with a number of stylized figures for Latin America's average (Figure 2.10). From among all the angles of inequality considered, those associated with education are most significant. A 25-year old worker who has a university education earns four times more than a worker with only a primary education, and five times more than an illiterate worker. These gaps widen with experience—a delayed form of the influence of education on income. At 55, a worker who has a university education will earn 4.5 times more than a worker with a primary education, and eight times more than an illiterate worker of the same age. Owing to the effect of education through experience, there is also a generational dimension to inequality: older generations (of working age) earn more than younger ones, and these gaps widen in direct proportion with education at all levels.

Compared with inequalities associated with education and experience, those attributable to other factors are smaller, though not negligible. There is a gap of about 40 percent between supervisors and workers, and between the latter and their informal sector counterparts (employees and self-employed workers) the gaps are 20 percent for men and approximately 40 percent for women. Apparent discrimination against women seems to be concentrated in the informal sector, possibly owing in part to less cumulative experience, while reflecting the fact

---

[5] See Krueger and Summers (1988), Hamermesh (1998), and Raj Mehta (1998).

Figure 2.10. Labor Inequality

a. Between Workers with Different Schooling and Age
(*Noneducated 25-year old worker = 1*)

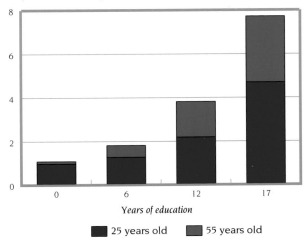

Years of education

■ 25 years old   ■ 55 years old

b. Between Workers with Different Types of Employment, by Gender
(*Noneducated 25-year old male worker = 1*)

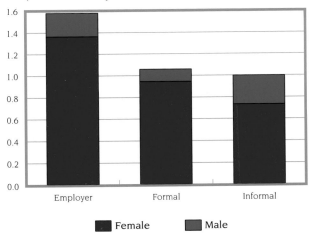

■ Female   ■ Male

c. Between Sectors
(*Manufacturing = 1*)

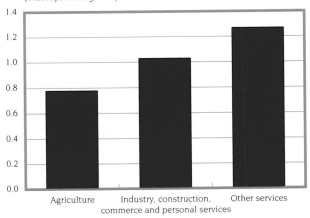

Source: IDB calculations based on recent household surveys.

that it is more difficult for women to access formal sector jobs because of the stringent requirements associated with these positions and the rigidities imposed by labor legislation (see Chapters 3 and 6).

Earnings for workers having similar characteristics and types of jobs, but in different economic sectors, differ by approximately 25 percent between agriculture and sectors such as industry, construction, trade and personal services. Between this group and the "modern" service sectors (transportation services, electricity, gas, water, and financial activities), there is an additional difference of about 25 percent.

How Much Do These Differences Explain?

All of these differentiation factors combined account for 55 percent of the labor income concentration in the typical Latin American country. The proportions are higher in Venezuela and Argentina, accounting for more than three-fourths of the concentration, while they explain just under half of the concentration in Brazil, Chile, Ecuador, Mexico and Paraguay (Figure 2.11). The unexplained share of income concentration is attributable to individual differences in talent, educational quality or other personal circumstances, or to differences in productivity conditions, and in how enterprises and businesses compensate their workers within each sector.[6]

Differences in the Characteristics of the Individual or the Job

Each individual's educational level, work experience and gender are associated with major labor income differences. These individual factors combined explain an average of 35 percent of the labor income concentration in the region, and approximately half of the concentration in Argentina, Costa Rica, El Salvador, Panama and Honduras (Figure 2.11). However, individuals are not the source of this inequality; it is instead the way in which the labor market compensates their characteristics and makes distinctions according to individual characteristics and labor market integration potential. Two individuals with different educational levels may earn much more unequal wages in a society in which education is a scarce commodity than in another society where the average educational level is high.

---

[6] However, income measurement errors and problems in defining observable characteristics also account for unexplained inequality.

Figure 2.11. Sources of Inequality
(Percent of the Gini coefficient of labor income)

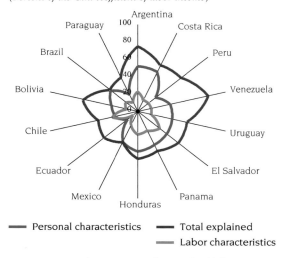

— Personal characteristics   — Total explained
— Labor characteristics

Note: *Regressions of income mixing all personal and labor characteristics.*
Source: *IDB calculations based on recent household surveys, and Barros, Duryea and Székely (1998).*

Figure 2.12. Inequality Associated with Personal Characteristics
(Percent of the Gini coefficient of labor income)

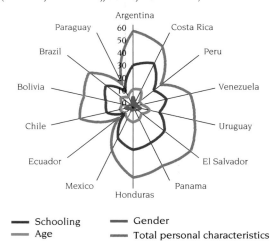

— Schooling   — Gender
— Age   — Total personal characteristics

Note: *Regressions of income mixing all personal and labor characteristics.*
Source: *IDB calculations based on recent household surveys, and Barros, Duryea and Székely (1998).*

Among individual characteristics, educational differences have the most significant effects on inequality, explaining an average of one-fourth of the labor income concentration and as much as one-third of the concentration in Argentina, Costa Rica, El Salvador, Panama and Honduras. Differences in experience, which constitute one conduit for amplifying educational differences, account for 10 percent of labor income concentration, while gender differences account for approximately 4 percent (Figure 2.12).[7]

On the other hand, the explanatory capacity of earnings differences by type of job, geographic area and economic sector averages 18 percent for the 14 countries studied, exceeds 10 percent in all cases, and is near 30 percent in El Salvador and Chile. This concentration is attributable to the fact that earnings differ among workers having similar personal circumstances. Although labor characteristics have less explanatory capacity than personal characteristics, this capacity is far from negligible. Differences in earnings associated with labor characteristics reflect a number of different segmentation factors that underlie inequality. In labor markets segmented by transportation problems or institutional or cultural rigidities, the same group of individuals will necessarily experience greater income inequalities than those in a homogeneous, integrated society with flexible labor markets. As we will observe in Chapter 6, ambitious labor protection and job security standards in the formal sector in Latin America have constituted an inequality fac-

tor, as they have limited worker mobility and reinforced income differences (as well as social security and stability differences) between those workers covered by legislation and those who are not.

The greatest inequalities associated with labor characteristics arise from the differences in earnings by type of job (supervisors, formal sector employees and informal sector workers). These differences account for an average of 13 percent of labor income inequality in Latin America. The highest levels of inequality by type of job are found in Chile, accounting for 27 percent of the concentration. Remuneration differences by economic sector explain an average of 5 percent of the concentration, with a maximum of 11 percent in El Salvador, while geographic differences account for about 3 percent. Greater segmentation between rural and urban areas is observed in Ecuador, El Salvador, Chile, Honduras, Panama and Peru, accounting for 5 to 6 percent of the concentration (Figure 2.13).

---

[7] The sum of these factors does not correspond to 35 percent of all factors mentioned in the preceding paragraph, as the latter figure reflects the influence of the interplay between the factors.

**Figure 2.13. Inequality Associated
with Employment Characteristics**
(*Percent of the Gini coefficient of labor income*)

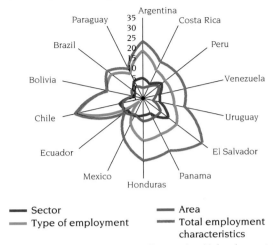

— Sector
— Type of employment
— Area
— Total employment
  characteristics

*Note: Regression of income mixing all personal and labor characteristics.
Source: IDB calculations based on recent household surveys,
and Barros, Duryea and Székely (1998).*

EDUCATIONAL INEQUALITIES

Since educational differences are the main factor in labor income inequality in Latin America, a more detailed analysis is warranted of the status of education in the region and its influence on wage inequality.

The population's average educational level is the most important indicator of the quantity of "human capital" a country's workers provide. However, this factor is only one dimension of the status of education, and does not suffice to explain the differences in worker earnings. We must also consider how this educational capital is distributed among the population. Societies having considerable disparities in educational levels might be expected to have a higher labor income concentration level than those in which education is more uniform. However, education dispersion is also insufficient to explain income differences. Its impact will depend on earnings gaps existing between the highly educated and the uneducated. Finally, among persons having the same number of years of education, there will also be earnings differences, resulting in part from differences in educational quality or characteristics.

The average educational level and distribution, earnings gaps by educational level, and quality differences are therefore the four dimensions that must be considered in analyzing the influence of education on labor income concentration. These dimensions are interrelated; for example, when a country's average educational level is very low, the distribution tends to be fairly equitable. The differences arise when some individuals begin to be more educated than others. Similarly, relative earnings of the highly educated will tend to be quite high initially, when these persons are in the minority, but will be lower in societies with higher and better distributed educational levels. Last, poor educational distribution will be reflected in differences in the number of years of education, as well as in lower earnings for persons with a lower quality education who are less likely to reach more advanced educational levels.

Educational Levels in Latin America

Educational levels have increased in Latin America. In the 1970s, the average Latin American over 25 years of age had 3.3 years of education. By the early 1990s, this average had increased to 4.8 years. During this period, the uneducated proportion of the population declined from 36 percent to approximately 23 percent, while the percentage of the population with some university education rose from 2 percent to more than 8 percent (Table 2.1).

However, educational progress in the region has lagged far behind other groups of countries. The Asian "miracle" countries, where the average educational level was 3.5 years during the 1970s (quite similar to Latin American countries), reached an average of more than six years of education in the early 1990s. While the average educational level in Latin America improved at a rate of only 0.9 percent per year, in East Asian countries it improved at a sustained rate of approximately 3 percent per year.

Comparison with the countries of East Asia highlights a major difference in the structure of education: in Latin America, a very small proportion of the population has a secondary education, while many people have had only some primary education. As surprising as this may seem, the educational differences between East Asia and Latin America cannot be attributed to the illiterate proportions of the population or to the university-educated component. On the contrary, in Latin America, a slightly higher proportion of the population has attended a university.

The disproportion between primary and secondary education groups is one feature that distinguishes Latin America not only from East Asia, but from any other region of the world. In fact, Latin America has the highest proportion of workers with some primary education, and after sub-Saharan Africa, it has the lowest proportion of workers with some secondary education.

As might be expected, however, this regional pattern includes tremendous differences between countries.

Figure 2.14. Average Years of Schooling

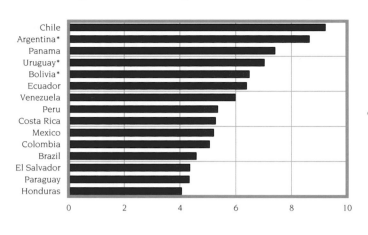

*Countries with urban data only.
Source: IDB calculations based on recent household surveys.

Figure 2.15. Population Distribution by Level of Education

(In percent)

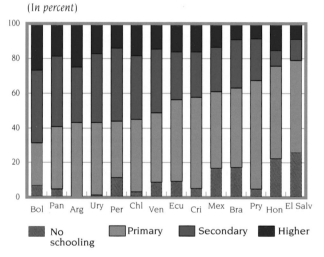

Note: Population 25 years of age or older.
Source: IDB calculations based on recent household surveys.

Figure 2.16. Mean Years of Schooling by Birth Cohort in Latin America

(Three-year moving average)

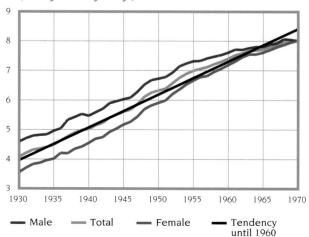

Source: Duryea and Székely (1998).

Figure 2.17a. Education by Cohort: Males Born in 1938-40 and 1968-1970

(Years of schooling)

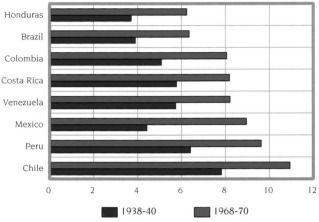

Source: IDB calculations based on recent household surveys.

Figure 2.17b. Education by Cohort: Females Born in 1938-40 and 1968-1970

(Years of schooling)

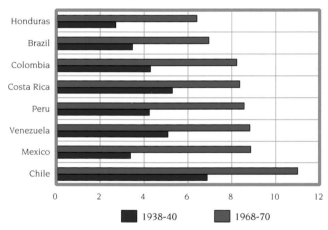

Source: IDB calculations based on recent household surveys.

Figure 2.18. Schooling Inequality and Level

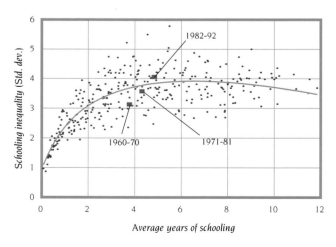

Note: Squares identified by years refer to Latin America.
Source: Calculations based on data from Barro and Lee (1996).

Table 2.1. Educational Levels in Latin America and East Asia, 1990

(*Percent of the population over 25 years of age at each level*)

	Latin America	East Asia
No education	23.6	20.1
Primary, complete or incomplete	50.8	43.8
Secondary, complete or incomplete	16.9	28.0
Higher, complete or incomplete	8.6	8.2

Source: Calculations based on data from Barro and Lee (1996).

At one extreme, approximately half of the population in Guatemala or Haiti has had no education, while the average adult has had less than three years of schooling. At the other extreme are relatively advanced countries such as Argentina and Barbados, where average education exceeds seven years, near the level of industrial countries (Figure 2.14).

The high relative share occupied by countries having some primary education, which is characteristic of Latin America as a whole, is seen in Brazil, Jamaica, Trinidad and Tobago and Costa Rica, where more than 60 percent of the population over 25 years of age has only had some primary education. The small proportion occupied by the group with some secondary education is particularly evident in Brazil and Guatemala, with only about 5 percent of the population in this group (Figure 2.15).

Since new educational efforts can only change the level of education in the younger groups, the time frame required to raise the average educational level of the entire adult population is quite lengthy. In addition, a comparison of average education rate increases in countries with different demographic structures and growth rates may be misleading. A more direct method for determining educational progress is to compare educational levels in different cohorts. Educational levels for both men and women in each generation have tended to exceed previous generations. However, the progress rate decelerated for generations born after the end of the 1950s and during the 1960s (Figure 2.16).

Comparison of educational levels up to 1995 for individuals born during the period 1968-70 (who were 25-27 years of age at the time) with those of persons born 30 years earlier shows that, on average, only about three years of progress was made in terms of years of education—approximately one year per decade. Women progressed more rapidly than men, although the levels are still modest (Figures 2.17a and b). In Chile, Peru and Mexico, for example, men gained more than three years while women gained more than four. However, men pro-

gressed by only about 2.5 years in Brazil, Costa Rica, Honduras and Venezuela, and women gained between three and 3.5 years in Brazil and Costa Rica. The more accelerated education rate increase for women means that they have now surpassed men in average years of education in almost all countries. Among the countries included in Figure 2.17, only in Peru do men still have a substantial advantage in educational level.

Distribution of Education

How does the distribution of education reflect the slow rise in Latin America's average educational levels and the fact that the educational structure is skewed toward a high proportion of individuals with some primary education and very few with secondary education?

Before answering this question, one should define the relationship between the average educational level and the distribution of education among the population. When educational levels are low, characteristic of societies that are less economically developed, there is a low degree of education dispersion, as very few people have had any education. There are few educational differences between generations and within each generation: all individuals tend to have similar educational levels. As the economy develops, educational progress is not uniform. Educational levels initially rise only in some limited groups. This causes educational differences to appear between the older and younger generations and within each generation, as the education system reaches only a fraction of the school-age population. As a result, during the initial stages of the development process, these two conduits lead to an increase in education dispersion.

Dispersion levels continue to rise, but the rate of increase decelerates as a higher proportion of the population achieves more advanced levels of education. The education dispersion between generations normally continues to rise in the long term, while the dispersion within generations begins to fall with broader basic education coverage. After a certain point, at which average educational levels are already very high, total dispersion (between and within generations) tends once again to decline, as there is a limit to the number of years individuals wish to remain in the education system. After the more educated groups reach this limit, higher average educational levels lead to smaller education gaps as compared with the subsequent groups. In the extreme case, we can consider a society in which everyone has a university education and there is no education dispersion.

Figure 2.18 shows this relationship between educational level and dispersion at the world scale. Each of the points represents the educational situation of a country during a given period.[8] When educational levels are extremely low, there is typically a difference of about one year between levels among various individuals. Dispersion levels increase rapidly at the beginning and then gradually approach a maximum of about four years. In Latin America during the 1960s, when the average educational level was about three years, dispersion was lower than might be expected in light of this international pattern. However, as average education increased, the region reached and then surpassed the normal education dispersion level. Beginning in the 1980s, education was more poorly distributed in Latin America than could be justified by the normal course of the process. The typical differences in educational levels between individuals in the same country now exceed four years for an average educational level of less than five years.

In most countries of the region, education is more poorly distributed than one might expect (Figure 2.19), with the exception of Guyana and a number of English-speaking Caribbean countries. This might be attributable to the pronounced influence of the British model on the school systems adopted by these countries, as the British system is more inclusive, and has fewer dropouts up to the secondary level. University access, on the other hand, tends to be more restrictive than the model adopted by Hispanic countries. In the English Caribbean, only 5.4 percent of the adult population has had no education, well below the 33 percent in Hispanic countries in the region. However, only 2.5 percent of the adult population has had some university education—half the level observed in Hispanic countries (Figure 2.15).

Education dispersion, on the other hand, has tended to increase in Latin America, depending on how the differences between and within generations interact. Average educational levels have increased in part because younger people are getting more education than their elders—which affects the dispersion between generations—but also because the dispersion within each generation is improving. These effects are more pronounced in some countries than in others, and Brazil and Venezuela illustrate the differences. In Brazil, the generation born in 1954-56 had an average educational level of five years, with a variance of approximately 30 percent. The 1939-41 generation reached the same level in Venezuela, but with a variance of approximately half, as this increase occurred through expanded primary education coverage rather than through a rise in more advanced education in some groups. In countries where educational levels have been sustained in a broader base (Chile, Costa Rica, Peru and Venezuela), education dispersion within each generation has been reduced vis-à-vis prior generations, beginning

Figure 2.19. Distribution of Education in Latin America

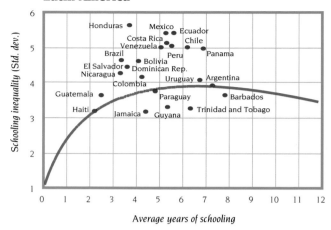

Source: Calculations based on data from Barro and Lee (1996).

with those born during the 1940s (Figure 2.20a). On the other hand, where the process of increased average education is farthest behind, or where coverage has been less extensive (Brazil, Colombia, Honduras and Mexico), dispersion did not begin to decline until the generations born during the 1960s (Figure 2.20b). Fortunately, education dispersion within the younger generations in all cases is lower than in the immediately preceding generations, suggesting that total education dispersion will tend to decline in the long term.

How can the excessive dispersion in the population's average years of education in most Latin American countries be explained? What tangible factor in the educational area underlies these apparently abstract indicators? Answering these questions starts with identifying certain features in Latin American school enrollment and dropout rates by social category and then comparing them with other regions of the world. This comparison can be made for 27 countries throughout the world, including seven in Latin America, using recent studies based on comparable household surveys to reconstruct the educational history of youth in the same cohort (15-19 years of age) by social category in all countries.[9] In each country, the "poor" category is defined as households in the lower 40 percent in terms of consumption and standard of living (not necessarily income) levels, and "wealthy" households are defined as those in the upper 20 percent.

---

[8] Three observations are included for each country, corresponding to averages for the periods 1960-70, 1971-81 and 1982-92.
[9] Filmer, Pritchett and Tan (1998). The majority of the surveys were conducted between 1991 and 1996.

Figure 2.20a/b. Variance of Male Schooling by Birth Cohort

Type A Countries

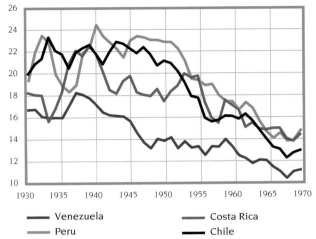

— Venezuela   — Costa Rica
— Peru   — Chile

Type B Countries

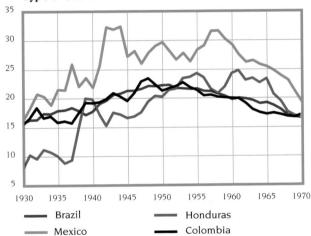

— Brazil   — Honduras
— Mexico   — Colombia

Note: *The y axis is the moving average of the variance of education.*
Source: *Duryea and Székely (1998).*

In Latin American countries, differences in educational achievement between the various social categories are less pronounced during the first few years of school, and increase appreciably thereafter. On average, 94 percent of the children in the poor categories of the four countries considered in South America (Bolivia, Brazil, Colombia and Peru), and 76 percent of the poor children in low-income countries in Central America and the Caribbean (Guatemala, Haiti and the Dominican Republic) enroll in and complete the first year of primary education. These percentages are lower than, but do not differ greatly from, those in the moderate categories (99 percent and 92 percent, respectively), and even in the upper categories (99 percent and 96 percent). However, as early as the fifth year of education, only about 63 per-

cent of the children in the poor category in South American countries, and approximately 32 percent in those of Central America and the Caribbean, remain in the system. During the ninth year of school, these figures decline to 15 percent and 6 percent, respectively. By contrast, in the upper category, 93 percent and 83 percent of children in the two groups of countries complete their fifth year of school, and 58 percent and 49 percent complete their ninth year (Figures 2.21a-2.21c).

It follows that the poor distribution of education in Latin America is not attributable to the lack of initial access to schools, but to increasing differences in school desertion among children from different categories as they advance through the system.

These patterns are far from universal (Figures 2.22a-2.22c). In some regions of the world, educational differences begin with first grade, reflecting access problems. For example, in West Africa and South Asia, less than half of the children in the poorer 40 percent of income levels complete first grade, which is accomplished by approximately four of every five children in the wealthier category.

Unlike Latin America, in other groups of countries with a high initial enrollment rate, a greater proportion of the children are kept in school, at least during the first five years, which reduces educational differences by income category (East Asia). In other regions with a high initial enrollment rate followed by a dropout problem, the latter is not concentrated so heavily among the poor—it also affects the middle and even upper classes (East Africa).

In summary, Latin America's poor educational distribution is not the result of problems of initial access for the poor to the education system. It results instead from high and more rapid dropout rates among the poor. Latin American school systems are quite stratified as a result, and do not constitute a mechanism for social mobility, or for reducing income differences, as is true in other areas of the world.[10]

RETURNS ON EDUCATION IN LATIN AMERICA

Educational progress in Latin America has been slow and education dispersion quite high, reflected in part by the normal relationship between the two variables, and strengthened by the stratification of educational achieve-

---

[10] Chapter 3 discusses the determinants of educational progress at the family level. Chapter 5 examines the implications of educational sector organization on the efficiency and quality of the services provided to different income groups and analyzes the distribution of the benefits of public expenditure on education.

Figure 2.21a. Percent of Population with First Grade Education, by Income Level

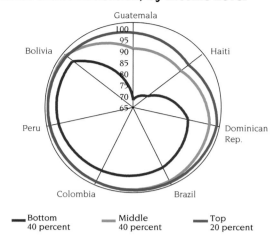

Bottom 40 percent Middle 40 percent Top 20 percent

Figure 2.22a. Percent of Population with First Grade Education, in Developing Regions, by Income Level

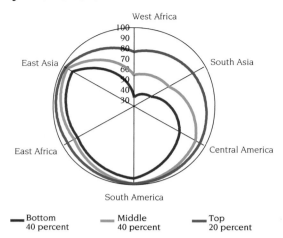

Bottom 40 percent Middle 40 percent Top 20 percent

Figure 2.21b. Percent of Population with Fifth Grade Education, by Income Level

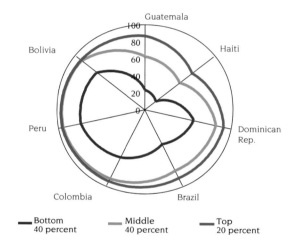

Bottom 40 percent Middle 40 percent Top 20 percent

Figure 2.22b. Percent of Population with Fifth Grade Education, in Developing Regions, by Income Level

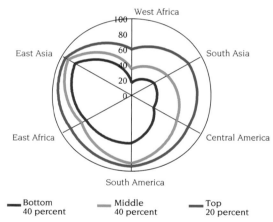

Bottom 40 percent Middle 40 percent Top 20 percent

Figure 2.21c. Percent of Population with Ninth Grade Education, by Income Level

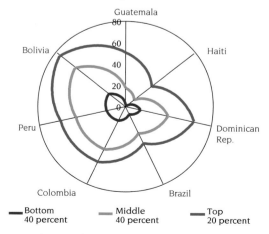

Bottom 40 percent Middle 40 percent Top 20 percent

Source: Filmer, Pritchett and Tan (1998).

Figure 2.22c. Percent of Population with Ninth Grade Education, in Developing Regions, by Income Level

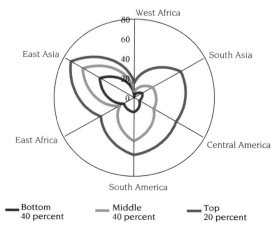

Bottom 40 percent Middle 40 percent Top 20 percent

Source: Filmer, Pritchett and Tan (1998).

ment. However, educational level and distribution are only two of the four dimensions that must be considered to understand the relationship between education and income distribution. Returns on education and educational quality must also be considered.

Individual returns on education are higher where the scarcity of this resource is most acute. An individual with an additional year of education in a country where educational levels are very low is likely to receive a much greater income increase than someone in a country where high educational levels are common. While in Africa income rises approximately 30 percent for each year of secondary or university education, in industrial countries, where average educational levels are high, one additional year of secondary or university education only represents an increase of approximately 12 percent in individual income. In between these two extremes, Latin America is closer to the industrial countries than it is to Africa (Figure 2.23).

These different returns can have an enormous impact on income gaps. With a 12 percent return on education, the income gap between an individual with a complete university education and an uneducated person is five to one. With an 18 percent return, it is 17 to 1, and with a 30 percent return, it is 86 to 1. The effects on income distribution also depend on the population distribution by educational level. If average education corresponds to the level reached by the majority of the population—however high the returns—there will be little difference in income distribution. However, when education is highly dispersed, as is true in Latin America, such high returns can have a considerable impact.

Low Returns on Little Education

Returns on education vary not only from country to country, but among educational levels. Returns on secondary education are typically lower than those at the university level, as observed in Figure 2.23. At the international level, there is also evidence that returns on primary education are significantly higher than at the subsequent levels, with rates exceeding 30 percent in many countries. While some earlier studies have estimated average rates of return of 26 percent on primary education in Latin America up to the end of the 1980s,[11] estimates based on household surveys for the 1990s show returns of only 10 percent on primary education, which do not differ greatly from returns on secondary education (11 percent), and are lower than those on university education (18 percent). The highest returns on primary education are found in Brazil (17 percent), Mexico and Peru (both 14 percent). While returns on secondary education do not exceed 16 percent

Figure 2.23. Returns to Education and Years of Schooling

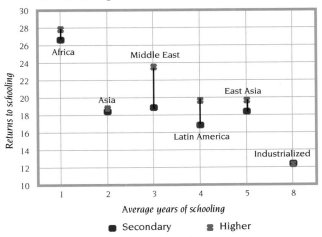

Source: Psacharopoulos (1994).

Figure 2.24. Returns to Education, by Level

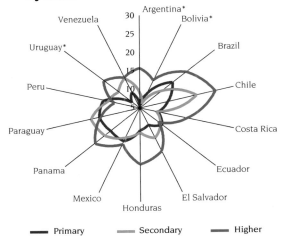

* Countries with urban data only.
Note: Regressions of returns to education by level controlling for experience and experience squared.
Source: IDB calculations based on recent household surveys.

in any of the countries, those on university education exceed 20 percent in Brazil, Chile, Costa Rica, El Salvador, Honduras and Panama, and never fall below 15 percent (Figure 2.24).

Low returns now offered by basic education in Latin America may reflect the influence of globalization, through a number of conduits. The incorporation of China and other less developed countries into world trade may have exerted adverse pressure on earnings for workers

---

[11] See Psacharopoulos and Ng (1994) and Psacharopoulos (1994).

Figure 2.25. Rates of Return to Primary Education in Urban and Rural Areas

(In percent)

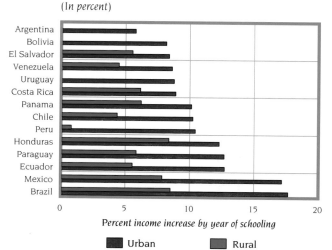

Percent income increase by year of schooling

■ Urban   ■ Rural

Note: Regression of return to education by level and areas controlling for experience and experience squared.
Source: IDB calculations based on recent household surveys.

Figure 2.26. Income Increase per Year of Experience, by Level

(In percent)

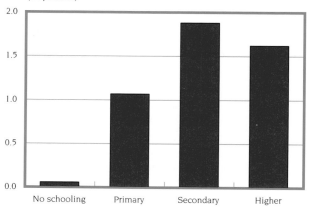

Note: Education level coefficients controlling for initial earnings and years of schooling.
Source: IDB calculations based on recent household surveys.

with only a basic education. Trade liberalization (by Latin American countries as well as those in other regions) may have raised the relative price of local natural resources, to the detriment of relative wages.[12] And, combined with macroeconomic policies, trade liberalization in Latin America seems to have fostered the adoption of technological change that has displaced labor demand to more skilled employment.[13] These demand factors have also interacted with a sharp expansion in the unskilled labor supply for demographic reasons, with no commensurate rise in educational levels.[14]

This profile of returns does not lend itself to imbalances any more than the typical profile of developing or industrial countries. The structure of returns in Latin America implies an income gap of eight to one between an individual with a complete university education and an uneducated worker; by contrast, the typical profile of industrial countries involves a gap of 11 to 1, while lower middle-income developing countries are found to have a gap of 33 to one.[15] However, the structure of returns on education in Latin America is conducive to the stratification of education, as it provides little incentive to advance in basic education unless there is the scope (and potential) to have access to a university education. The small proportion of the population that reaches secondary education in Latin America is consistent with this interpretation. However, the imbalancing effects are even greater. As we will note in the following chapter, inequalities arising from education are replicated and amplified within the family, as the number of children is largely dependent on the mother's income generation potential.

Women with low levels of education tend to have more children, who in turn will have little potential of receiving a good education.

Although returns on primary education are low, they are even lower in rural areas. While, on average, one additional year of primary education represents an 11 percent income increase for an urban worker, a rural worker's income only rises by 6 percent. The greatest differences in returns on education are found in Brazil, Mexico and Peru—possibly a reflection of quality differences between rural and urban areas, as well as a lack of adequate labor opportunities for more educated rural workers. These differences may be reinforced by the fact that the more motivated and capable workers might be more inclined to migrate to the cities (Figure 2.25).

A Note of Caution

Calculations of returns on education may be used misleadingly to support the argument that public education expenditure should focus on higher education, as it offers the highest returns. This assertion would be mistaken,

---

[12] See Rodrik (1997) and Wood (1997).
[13] See Robbins (1996) and Lora and Olivera (1998).
[14] See Duryea and Székely (1998).
[15] Rates of return for OECD countries used were 21 percent, 12 percent and 12 percent for the three respective levels; for developing countries with incomes of up to $2,450, they were 30 percent, 19 percent and 19 percent. Rounded averages reported by Psacharopoulos (1994).

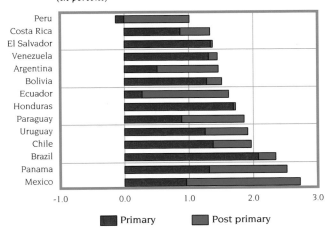

Figure 2.27. Income Increase per Year of Experience, by Country

(*In percent*)

Primary   Post primary

Note: *Level of education coefficient controlling for initial earnings and years of education by level.*
Source: *IDB calculations based on recent household surveys.*

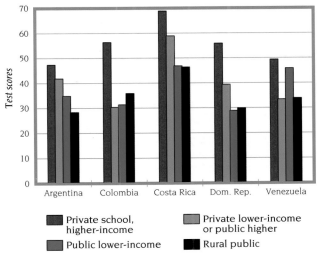

Figure 2.28. Performance in Mathematics and Science by Type of School, 1990s

Private school, higher-income

Private lower-income or public higher

Public lower-income

Rural public

Source: *Luna and Wolfe* (1993), *cited by Schiefelbein* (1995).

however, as public expenditure should aim at social returns, not private ones. Although basic education offers individuals low returns, it is socially desirable as it provides a basis for further benefits. Better basic education is necessary to improve the population's health conditions, reduce the birth rate, and raise the standard of living in urban areas, among many other factors.

The Multiplier Effect of Experience

Income differences resulting from education also tend to multiply with experience. Returns on experience vary at different levels of education. The rate at which income increases with years of experience is practically nil for uneducated workers, approximately 1 percent per year for workers with some primary education, and generally exceeds 1.5 percent per year for workers having a secondary or university education (Figures 2.26 and 2.27). Although as a rule the effect of experience on workers with primary education is greater than for those with no education (except in Peru), and is lower than for workers with some post-secondary education, there are considerable differences between countries. This may reflect the fact that the quality of education has not been constant over time, nor is it the same among countries. A deterioration in educational quality will be reflected in an apparent gain with experience, as older workers would tend to earn higher incomes because they have more experience, as well as because they are more educated. The opposite will occur if quality has improved.

QUALITY PROBLEMS

The number of years of education is only an approximate indicator of a person's educational level. An insufficient quality education yields a lower return and lower income during an individual's working life. If the education quality distribution is skewed against children from low-income sectors of the population, it will constitute an additional conduit for labor income concentration, and ultimately for the replication of inequality. All evidence for Latin America indicates that, in fact, the poor receive an inferior quality of education.

Judging from the comparison of international tests, academic performance among Latin American students is below the performance of industrial and East Asian countries.[16] Further, within each country, performance among public school students from low-income families or rural schools is far below achievement in middle- and upper-class schools, especially private secondary schools. Only students from elite private schools perform on par with international levels (Figure 2.28).

Private schools offer up to twice as many hours of instruction as public schools, and generally cover the full official curriculum, while, ironically, only about 50 per-

---

[16] Reading test performance by students from seven Latin American countries was below levels of industrial and East Asian countries. In a worldwide test of mathematics skills, in which only two Latin American countries participated, one occupied the penultimate position among 41 countries, and the other would not allow the results to be published. See Puryear (1997) and Preal, et al. (1998).

Figure 2.29. Use of Public Education by Income Decile

(*Percent of primary and secondary children*)

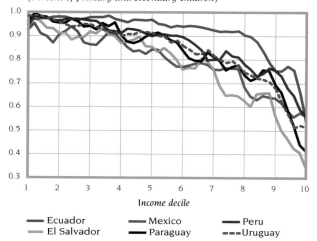

Income decile

— Ecuador   — Mexico   — Peru
— El Salvador   — Paraguay   ---Uruguay

Source: IDB calculations based on recent household surveys.

Figure 2.30. Educational Quality by Income Decile of Parents

(*In percent, decile 10 = 1*)

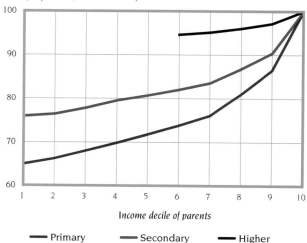

Income decile of parents

— Primary   — Secondary   — Higher

Note: Labor income regressions of dependents of the household as a function of experience, experience squared, education by level, education by level times education of the father, and father's and mother's education.
Source: IDB calculations based on recent household surveys.

vides over 90 percent of the primary and secondary education to the poorest 40 percent of the population and approximately 80 percent to the middle 40 percent. In the next highest income sectors, however, there is an exodus from the system, to the extent that only 25 to 40 percent of the children attend public schools among families in the highest income percentiles (Figure 2.29). Contrary to what is generally believed, private education is only a feasible option for the fraction of the population that can afford it. This is a clear element of distinction between the wealthiest 10 percent of the population and the rest, which possibly underlies the enormous income gaps pointed out in Chapter 1.

Poor educational quality severely affects the income generation potential of persons from the lower-income brackets. Higher-income families have greater purchasing power, allowing them to afford a better education for their children, and the parents are in a better position to make decisions regarding their children's education, and possibly to influence their achievement. Econometric analysis indicates that the rate of return for children per year of education is significantly dependent on the father's education or the father's permanent income.[19] This effect is independent of (and additional to) the possible direct impact of the father's income or the parents' education on the child's income for reasons other than years of education.[20]

Estimates show that individuals from the lower deciles receive a primary education whose quality (measured in terms of income generation capacity) is 35 percent lower than that of the next decile above.[21] Even between the ninth and tenth deciles, the average difference in primary education quality exceeds 10 percent. In secondary education, quality differences between the first four deciles and the last exceed 20 percent, and between the ninth and tenth deciles, they are still near 10 percent.

cent of the official curriculum is covered in official schools. Public schools also register high grade repetition rates, indicative of lower levels of academic achievement per year of study.[17] Inferior performance by public schools is not exclusively attributable to the students' socioeconomic situations. If the potential influence of students' observable characteristics is isolated, it confirms that scholastic achievement is lower in public schools.[18]

It is thus not surprising that high-income families turn away from public education. The public sector pro-

---

[17] Preal, et al. (1998).

[18] See Lockheed and Jiménez (1994), who conclude that, in addition to individual characteristics, performance in private secondary schools in Colombia is 13 percent better than in public schools, and 31 percent better in the Dominican Republic. See also Saavedra (1997) for Peru, and Savedoff (1998) for Chile and Venezuela.

[19] The father's permanent or expected income is the estimated function of income that reflects the father's education and experience. For purposes of these estimates, the "father" is defined as the male head of household at least 20 years older than the dependent in the same household.

[20] These results are based on the six cases in which the father's education is found to have a significant impact on the rates of return of the child's education, also including the father's and mother's education as separate explanatory variables. In the other countries, although this effect was significant when the latter variables were not included, it was no longer significant when they were introduced.

[21] The effect of the father's education on the return on the child's education and the parents' educational levels per income decile can be used to determine the expected quality of education the children will achieve for each income decile.

Not surprisingly, the quality differences are lower for secondary and university levels (Figure 2.30), since the system's selection process eliminates persons receiving the poorest quality education during the early years. However, smaller quality differences per income level in higher education (only about 3 percent between the last two deciles) suggest that access to quality universities can be influenced more by factors other than the income level of the family, such as individual aptitude.

Differences in the quality of secondary education available to the poor are quite significant. For individuals from a family in the most wealthy decile of Chile or Costa Rica, each additional year of education leads to an income increase that is 4 percentage points higher than for individuals from a family in the poorer decile. This is the magnitude of additional quality that wealthy individuals can buy owing to the segmentation of the education system. The differences are three points in Bolivia, Honduras, Panama and Uruguay. They are also appreciable between the last two deciles: in all of these countries, those from the wealthiest decile receive at least an additional 1 percent return per year of education over persons from the decile immediately below (Figure 2.31). These quality gaps are indicative of the degree of educational stratification in each country resulting from the interplay of the differences in quality of the education system with an individual's family history.

In conclusion, all available indicators point to the fact that there are major quality differences in the education received by the poor and the wealthy. These differences strengthen the influence of the distribution of education and the structure of returns on income concentration. As will be seen in Chapter 5, the source of these quality differences is not the level of expenditure, or even the fact that the wealthy have greater access to private education. The problem lies in the organization of the public education system, which is typically highly centralized, provides no incentives to adapt to the circumstances of students and their families or to improve quality, and does not involve families or even teachers in administrative or pedagogic decisions.

CONCLUSIONS

From the standpoint of income equality, education in Latin America involves four problem areas:
- *The level* of education has increased more slowly than in other regions in recent decades as a result of deficiencies in the scope of secondary education and early withdrawal from the school system by children from low-income families.

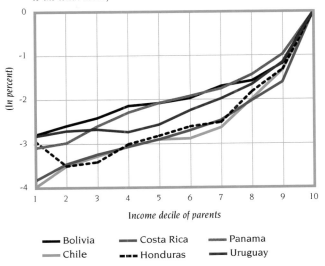

Figure 2.31. Cost of Lower Quality Education
(*Rates of return to education differentials with respect to the tenth decile*)

Income decile of parents

— Bolivia   — Costa Rica   — Panama
— Chile   ▬▬▬ Honduras   — Uruguay

Note: *Labor income regressions of the dependents of the household as function of the experience, experience squared, education by levels, education by levels times father's education, and father's and mother's education. Source: IDB calculations based on recent household surveys.*

- Education *dispersion* is high as, apart from younger generations having more education than earlier ones, within each generation there are major differences in educational achievement. However, these intragenerational differences are on the decline in all countries.
- *Returns* on education are low for the first years of school but high for university education, and are substantially lower in rural than in urban areas.
- Educational *quality* is much lower for students from low-income families, most of whom attend public school and do not have access to better quality higher education.

In summary, education is profoundly stratified in Latin America, an effect that is perpetuating, rather than correcting, income inequalities.

REFERENCES

Barro, R., and J. W. Lee. 1996. International Measures of Schooling Years and Schooling Quality. *American Economic Review Papers and Proceedings* 86(2) and accompanying database.

Barros, Ricardo Paes, Suzanne Duryea, and Miguel Székely. 1998. Explaining Inequality: An Investigation Using Microsimulation Techniques. Office of the Chief Economist, Inter-American Development bank. Unpublished.

Duryea, Suzanne, and Miguel Székely. 1998. Labor Markets in Latin America: A Supply-Side Story. Paper presented at the seminar "El empleo en América Latina: cuál es el problema y cómo enfrentarlo," Annual Meeting of the Inter-American Development Bank, Cartagena.

Filmer, Deon, Lant Pritchett, and Jee-Peng Tan. 1998. Educational Attainment Profiles of the Poor (and Rich): DHS Evidence from Around the Globe. Mimeo.

Hamermesh, Daniel S. 1998. *Changing Inequality in Markets for Workplace Amenities*. NBER Working Paper Series No. 6515, April.

Krueger, A. B., and L.H. Summers. 1988. Efficiency Wages and the Inter-Industry Wage Structure. *Econometrica* 56: 259-94.

Lockheed, Marlaine E., and Emmanuel Jiménez. 1994. *Public and Private Secondary Schools in Developing Countries*. World Bank HRO Working Paper No. 43.

Lora, Eduardo, and Gustavo Márquez. 1998. The Employment Problem in Latin America: Perceptions and Stylized Facts. Paper presented at the seminar "El empleo en América Latina: cuál es el problema y cómo enfrentarlo," Annual Meeting of the Inter-American Development Bank, Cartagena.

Luna, E., and R. Wolfe. 1993. A Feasibility Report on the Assessment of Mathematics and Science Education in Latin America. Technical Department, Latin America and the Caribbean Region, World Bank. Mimeo.

Preal, Diálogo Interamericano, and Cinde. 1998. El futuro está en juego. Report of the International Commission on Education, Equity and Economic Competitiveness. April.

Psacharopoulos, George. 1994. Returns to Investment in Education: A Global Update. *World Development* 22(9): 1325-43.

Psacharopoulos, G., and Y. C. Ng. 1994. Earnings and Education in Latin America: Assessing Priorities for Schooling Investments. *Education Economics* 2(2).

Psacharopoulos, G., and Z. Tzannatos. 1992. *Women's Employment and Pay in Latin America: Overview and Methodology*. Washington, D.C.: World Bank.

Puryear, Jeffrey M. 1997. *La Educación en América Latina: Problemas y Desafíos*. PREAL Working Paper Series No. 7. PREAL, Santiago.

Raj Mehta, Shailendra. 1998. The Law of One Price and a Theory of the Firm: A Ricardian Perspective on Interindustry Wages. *Rand Journal of Economics* 29(1) Spring: 137-56.

Robbins, Donald J. 1996. HOS Hits Facts: Facts Win. Evidence on Trade and Wages in the Developing World. Harvard Institute for International Development. Mimeo.

Rodrik, Dani. 1997. *Has Globalization Gone Too Far?* Washington, D.C.: Institute for International Economics.

Saavedra, Jaime. 1997. Private and Public Schools in Peru. GRADE. Mimeo.

Savedoff, W., ed. 1998. *Organization Matters: Agency Problems in Health and Education in Latin America*. Washington, D.C.: Inter-American Development Bank.

Schiefelbein, Ernesto. 1995. Programa de acción para la reforma educativa en América Latina y el Caribe. UNESCO-OREALC, Annual World Bank Conference for Latin American and Caribbean Development, Rio de Janeiro, June 12-13.

Wood, Adrian. 1997. Openness and Wage Inequality in Developing Countries: The Latin American Challenge to East Asian Conventional Wisdom. *The World Bank Economic Review* 11(1) January: 33-57.

Chapter 3

INEQUALITY
AND THE FAMILY

Inequality is not only a personal issue; it is a family issue as well. Just as each individual confronts different opportunities and makes decisions, families also face a variety of circumstances and respond to them. But family decisions are more complex because many are made jointly, whether they involve choices regarding work inside or outside the home, about raising children, or about whether and how much to educate children. Typically, parents save to benefit their children—either through financial instruments or more commonly by dedicating time and resources to their children that give them better education, skills or other assets that will enable them to fend for themselves when they are older. Hence, a fundamental intergenerational transfer of resources takes place within the family.

We have seen that household inequality is strongly related to wage inequality (Chapter 1) and that wage inequality is itself explained in large part by the unequal distribution of schooling (Chapter 2). This chapter asks questions about how these differences in schooling come about and shows how they are strongly influenced by decisions to enter the labor force and by fertility rates and family structure. We discuss how labor supply decisions are affected by available income earning opportunities in the market along with the alternative uses of time in the home.

There are some large variations between the average family at the top and bottom levels of income distribution in Latin America with respect to a few key characteristics.[1] The hourly wage of an individual in the top decile is, on average, almost nine times higher than for an individual in the bottom three deciles. Total household income (all earned and unearned income) of the average family in the top decile differs by a factor of little more than 12 from that of the average family in the bottom three deciles. And when we adjust for the size of households and measure the gap in per capita household income (i.e., income divided by the number of people in the household), the difference is even larger: the family in the top decile has per capita household income that is almost 20 times higher than the lower-income family.

Why are these gaps so large? How much of these gaps is related to characteristics of the family? And why do these differences vary so much across countries?

A large part of the differences have to do with the structure of the economy, culture, ethnicity and many other general social factors. But these differences are also related to the families' own resources—principally the education of the adults (Table 3.1). While the average family in the bottom three deciles has adults with five years of schooling, the adults in the top decile average family have completed about 12 years. The families also differ in terms of their likelihood of working outside the home. The men in each family have about the same probability of being in the paid workforce—approximately 83 percent for lower-income families and 86 percent for higher-income ones. But lower-income women are much less likely to be working outside the home. In fact, the woman in the average top decile family is almost twice as likely to be in the paid workforce as the woman from the lower three deciles—60 percent and 37 percent, respectively.

Table 3.1. Average Family Characteristics by Income

	Top 10%	Bottom 30%
Adult education-male (years)	12.1	5.0
Adult education-female (years)	11.6	4.7
Labor force participation-male (%)	85.8	82.5
Labor force participation-female (%)	60.9	36.7
Number of children	1.4	3.3
Expected educational attainment for children (years)	11.7	6.9

	Income ratio	
Household income	12.3	
Per capita household income	19.9	

Source: IDB calculations based on recent household surveys.

---

[1] This chapter relies heavily on household survey data. Box 1.2 and the Appendix in Chapter 1 provide details.

Another difference between families that affects their per capita income is the number of children they have. The average lower-income family has three or more children, while the average upper-income family has only one or two. Finally, the schooling of their children is likely to differ significantly. On their 21st birthdays, children of wealthier families will probably have finished 12 years of school, while children of the average lower-income family are likely to have finished only seven years.[2]

Thus, much of the inequality between lower- and upper-income families is related to differences in their own educational attainment, whether or not women work outside the home, and how many children they have. The differences in educational attainment of their children also have implications for future income inequality, just as the education of the adults was itself strongly affected by their parents' education. Nevertheless, family characteristics do not explain all of the differences. Families with similar characteristics in different countries generate different levels of inequality. This may be partly related to cultural or political factors, but it is also clearly related to such economic factors as prevailing wage rates and the level of informality. The economic context itself appears to alter family behavior in subtle ways that influence labor force participation decisions, the number of children, and children's educational attainment. This chapter will focus on the choices that families make with regard to these characteristics, and how these choices, in turn, affect income distribution. It will begin by looking at the direct impact of each of these factors on income distribution itself, and conclude with a discussion of the interrelationships of these factors and their combined direct and indirect effects on income inequality. This will make it possible to evaluate how much these factors combined contribute to income inequality, and how much remains unexplained in the income disparities experienced by people in different countries in the region.

LABOR FORCE PARTICIPATION

One household factor that contributes to income inequality is the variation in labor force participation by income level.[3] Individuals from lower-income households are much less likely to participate in the labor force than those in higher-income households. The only exceptions are Paraguay and Peru (Figure 3.1). The difference in participation averages is around 10 percent of the working age population in Ecuador, urban Uruguay, Brazil, urban Bolivia, and Mexico, and about 20 percent in the remaining countries.

Figure 3.1. Labor Force Participation by Country and Income
(*Ages* 15-65)

━━━ Top decile   ━━━ Bottom three deciles

* Countries with urban data only.
Source: IDB calculations based on recent household surveys.

Female Labor Force Participation Explains the Difference

Differences in participation rates between incomes groups are overwhelmingly explained by levels of female labor force participation, which remain substantially below male rates throughout the region by an average of 37 percent (Figure 3.2). The discrepancy is particularly large in Mexico, Costa Rica, Venezuela and Honduras. But even in countries with less of a difference, such as Paraguay, Peru and urban Bolivia, the gap remains significant. For most countries, this pattern differs markedly from the industrial countries, where the difference between male and female labor force participation is below 20 percent.

Male participation rates are relatively high in all income groups for all countries, averaging about 84 percent. The difference in the participation rates for men in the top decile and in the bottom three deciles is, on average, only 3 percent. However, for women, participation varies strongly with income. While on average more than 60 percent of women in the top decile are in the labor force, among the poorest three deciles this share is only 37 percent. In countries such as Paraguay and Peru, the difference in labor force participation rates apparently

---

[2] There is also evidence that the quality of schooling is likely to differ significantly by income, with wealthier families having access to better quality education for their children.

[3] A person is considered to be participating in the labor force if he or she is employed, self-employed, or seeking work. Therefore, unemployed workers who are looking for a job will be included. In most countries for which data is available, the unemployment rate is rather low—generally below 5 percent. The exception is Argentina, where unemployment has ranged above 10 percent.

Figure 3.2. Female and Male Participation Rates by Country

(*Ages* 15-65)

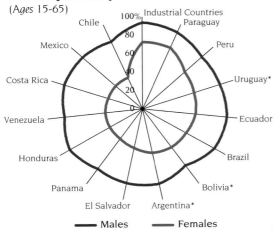

—— Males   —— Females

* *Countries with urban data only.*
Source: IDB *calculations based on recent household surveys.*
Industrial country data from Duryea and Székely (1998).

Figure 3.3. Female Participation Rates by Country and Income

(*Ages* 15-65)

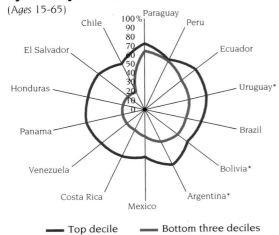

—— Top decile   —— Bottom three deciles

* *Countries with urban data only.*
Source: IDB *calculations based on recent household surveys.*

Figure 3.4. Female Labor Force Participation Rate in the 1980s and 1990s

(*In percent*)

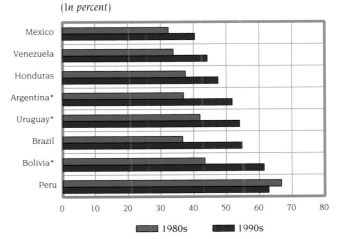

▨ 1980s   ■ 1990s

* *Countries with urban data only.*
Source: IDB *calculations based on recent household surveys.*

Figure 3.5. Female Participation in the Informal Sector by Country and Income

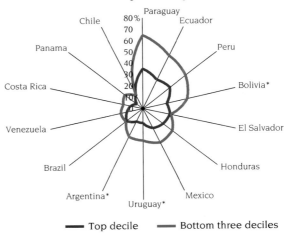

—— Top decile   —— Bottom three deciles

* *Countries with urban data only.*
Source: IDB *calculations based on recent household surveys.*

varies little at these extremes of the income distribution, but in countries like El Salvador and Panama, the difference is almost 40 percent. The urban samples—Uruguay, Argentina and Bolivia—are among those with the smallest differences; and the Central American countries are among those with the largest (Figure 3.3).

These participation rates are, nevertheless, higher than they were 10 or 20 years ago. Overall labor force participation increased between 1970 and 1995 because of a dramatic rise in female participation rates. In 1970, women represented only 23 percent of the total labor force, but in 1995 they accounted for more than 35 percent. Even over the single decade of the 1980s, rates rose consistently, except in Peru (Figure 3.4). In three of the eight countries in

Figure 3.4—the urban areas of Bolivia, Argentina and Uruguay—the participation of women from the top decile increased more than those from the bottom three deciles. In another four—Brazil, Venezuela, Mexico and Honduras—the relationship was reversed, with larger increases in participation for lower-income women.

Women Participate Disproportionately in the Informal Sector

When lower-income women do participate in the labor market, they do so mainly in the informal sector (Figure 3.5). Yet, women from the top 10 percent of the income distribution are much less likely to be working in the informal sector. The contrast is strongest in Paraguay, Ecuador, Peru and urban Bolivia, where lower-income women have high participation rates and are conspicuously concentrated in the informal sector. By contrast, women in these countries from the top decile, who have access to formal sector employment, are half as likely to work in the informal sector, even though they have comparable or greater participation in the labor force overall.

The decision to enter the labor force for both men and women is affected by their access to unearned sources of income, their age and physical health, cultural norms, and alternative uses of their time for leisure or work in the home. For adult men in Latin America, being in the workforce is almost automatic. Very few have the means to support themselves without working, and cultural norms encourage men to earn a living in the labor market. Male labor force participation has not changed dramatically over time, and is relatively unaffected by marriage, divorce or number of children.

For adult women in Latin America, the story is more complex and, indeed, changing. As discussed above, women's labor force participation rates vary considerably across countries, income levels and time. There is extensive literature on countries throughout the world that tries to understand these differences, and shows that a woman is more likely to participate in the labor force when she is unmarried, her spouse earns less, her family has more assets, her family has fewer children, she is more educated, or when she has higher income earning opportunities in the labor market.[4] These factors reflect the fact that traditionally women have been expected to assume the responsibilities of rearing children and doing household work.[5] Consequently, when choosing whether or not to enter the labor market, the alternative uses of their time in terms of these very important activities in the home frequently play a role.

Although such models clearly cannot explain any particular individual or family choice about working, they do help us understand social trends in female labor force participation. In general, when male earnings fall, female labor force participation rates are likely to rise, holding all other factors constant. Similarly, developments that raise the productivity of housework, such as access to running water and electricity, will be associated with rising female labor force participation. The number of women who are active in the labor force also increases when women have fewer children. When women are more educated, they can command higher earnings in the workplace, and this also encourages more of them to seek remunerated jobs. And when labor demand makes fewer distinctions between men and women in terms of pay by

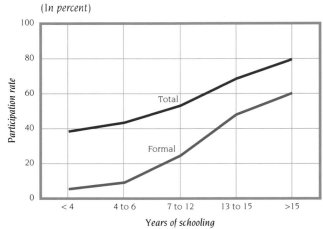

Figure 3.6. Female Labor Force Participation by Educational Level
(*In percent*)

Note: *Average of 14 Latin American countries.*
Source: *IDB calculations based on recent household surveys.*

reducing discrimination or occupational segregation, more women enter the labor market.

Hence, women's labor force participation in Latin America is likely to be higher whenever their spouses earnings decline, their education levels rise, and the number of children they have declines. These relationships are, in fact, very strongly supported by the available evidence. Policies that contribute to increasing women's labor market opportunities among lower-income groups can, in turn, contribute to reducing income inequality in the region.

First, women who are more educated are more likely to enter the labor market. (Figure 3.6). In fact, the differences are quite sharp. While only some 40 percent of women with four years or less of schooling participate in the labor market, over 78 percent of those with higher education do. The contrast is even sharper with respect to female participation in the formal sector, where a woman with a graduate degree is 11 times more likely to work than her counterpart with a year or two of schooling. This stands in contrast to the experience of men who, even with very little education, are still heavily represented in the formal sector (Figure 3.7).

---

[4] See Behrman and Wolfe (1984); Hill (1983); and Psacharopoulos and Tzannatos (1992).

[5] This is clearly an oversimplification of historical variations in women's social roles in Latin America, which varies through time, across countries and regions, and across income groups. A full account of these variations and their historical changes is beyond the scope of this study, which aims, instead, to focus on the aggregate changes in female labor force participation in recent years as a consequence of educational, demographic and labor market changes.

Figure 3.7. Share of Formal Sector Participation for Men and Women with Four to Six Years of Schooling

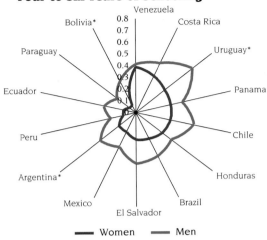

— Women   — Men

*Countries with urban data only.
Note: The share is calculated as the formal sector labor force participation rate divided by the total labor force participation rate for each sex.
Source: IDB calculations based on recent household surveys.

Figure 3.8. Female Labor Force Participation Rate by Number of Children
(In percent)

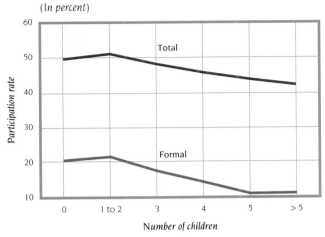

Note: Average of 14 Latin American countries.
Source: IDB calculations based on recent household surveys.

Figure 3.9. Female Labor Force Participation Gap and Education
(In percent)

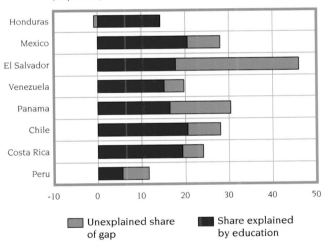

☐ Unexplained share of gap   ■ Share explained by education

Note: The gap is calculated as the difference between female labor force participation rates in the top 10 percent and bottom 30 percent of income distribution. Only countries with a gap of 10 percent or more are included.
Source: IDB simulations based on recent household surveys. See the Appendix for details.

Second, women who have fewer children are more likely to work in the labor market (Figure 3.8). Although this effect is not as dramatic, there is a clear declining relationship between the number of children and a woman's likelihood of participating in the labor force, and the effect is stronger in the formal sector. On average, women with five children participate about 7 percent less than do women with one or two children. In the formal sector, the difference in participation is 10 percent.

In simple tabulations, the relationship between female labor force participation and both education and number of children appears to be fairly strong. Even after controlling for other factors, such as the relative age of the children, the earning potential of the household head, and the presence of other adults and retired persons (over 65), women's education and number of children still have a significant impact on labor force participation decisions. Using an economic model to estimate the probabilities that a woman would be out of the labor force, working in the informal sector, or working in the formal sector, it was possible to show that women's education is by far the most relevant and important factor in explaining labor force participation decisions in almost all of the 14 countries analyzed (see Appendix). In eight countries, the gap in labor force participation between high- and low-income women exceeded 10 percent; and of these eight countries, the difference in educational levels of high- and low-income women explained between 40 and 100 percent of that gap (Figure 3.9).

By contrast, the number of children under six years of age is statistically significant but plays a relatively mi-

nor role in explaining the participation gap between high- and low-income women. After taking education and other factors into consideration, the number of children explains less than 2 percent of this labor force participation gap. The main explanation appears to be the strongly negative association between women's education and the number of children they have. More educated women tend to have fewer children. On average, each additional child under

Figure 3.10. Education and Women's Formal Sector Participation
(*In percent*)

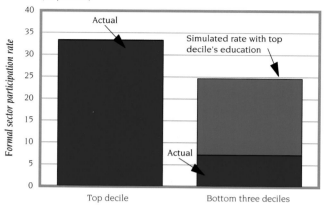

Note: *Average for 14 countries.*
Source: IDB *simulations based on recent household surveys.*

six reduces the participation rate by 4.1 percentage points, but the difference in the number of children between high- and low-income women is slightly less than two. By contrast, each additional year of schooling increases participation by 2.1 percent, and the difference in years of schooling between high- and low-income women typically exceeds six years. Consequently, women's education predominates in explaining differences in female labor force participation rates between income groups.

Education greatly affects participation, but it also affects the probability that a woman will work in the formal sector. For the region as a whole, the gap between formal sector participation is wide—33.5 percent and 7.5 percent for higher- and lower-income women, respectively. Using the same labor force participation model, it is possible to explain between 2 and 12 percent of this gap as a consequence of the different education levels of higher- and lower-income women (Figure 3.10). For men, after controlling for other factors, education has a much smaller impact on whether an individual is in the formal or informal sector. This compounded education effect—altering the likelihood that a woman will participate in the labor force and her probability of being in the informal sector—serves to exacerbate income inequality in the region.

The earning potential of the head of household also has an impact on participation, although the effect is much smaller than women's education. If the household head of the bottom three deciles were to have the same education as that of the top decile, women's participation in the formal sector would decrease by an average of 5 percentage points.

Hence, of the factors that we have considered, a woman's education is the most important for explaining

whether she is likely to be working at home, in the informal sector, or in the formal sector. Part of this effect is due to changes in preferences occasioned by schooling, and the accompanying exposure to alternative models of behavior and life choices. But education also plays a critical role in expanding a woman's income earning opportunities. Hence, the cost of staying out of the labor force in terms of what a woman could earn rises along with her educational attainment. It is not surprising, then, to find that in societies with rising educational levels for women, labor force participation rises. Under these conditions, the relative costs and benefits to the family of entering the labor market often shift in favor of working outside the home.

Why Do Fewer Women Work in the Formal Sector?

We have seen that women participate less in the labor force than men, and that there are several important factors that influence that decision. But the strong differences in the characteristics of jobs in the formal and informal sectors actually make this a three-way decision. Women decide whether or not to participate in the labor force not only by considering the relative benefits and costs of going to work, but by considering the relative benefits and costs of different kinds of jobs. In this context, why are women so much less likely to be in formal sector jobs? There are a variety of possible reasons, including those related to the ways formal sector firms contract and manage personnel and those related to women's own preferences for different kinds of work and working conditions.

If we consider the general characteristics of formal sector jobs and the pattern of female labor force participation, there are several related reasons that contribute to lower formal sector employment for women. First, formal sector firms tend to provide benefits, such as maternity leave, that are not generally provided in the informal sector. Hence, firms may be reluctant to hire younger women who have a significant probability of needing such leave and its attendant benefits (see Chapter 6).[6] Second, firms in the formal sector may be stricter about workers reliably showing up for work and putting in a regular number of hours each day. They are certainly more likely than informal firms to award upward career mobility to workers who have accumulated experience in their occu-

---

[6] Studies in the United States have demonstrated that even though women interrupt their careers to have children and care for them in their early years, they are, on average, more reliable than men in terms of lower rates of absenteeism. It is unclear how much firms have internalized these relative factors when make hiring decisions.

pation by maintaining a long-term and steady attachment to the firm, or at least to the occupation. By contrast, a large share of women in the informal sector are self-employed—almost 50 percent in both urban and rural areas. This provides greater flexibility in working hours and regularity. Furthermore, many jobs predominantly held by women in such sectors as retail trade and clothing frequently have flexible hours and locations, such as part-time shifts in a kiosk or piece work done at home.[7]

The relative inflexibility of formal sector jobs and their emphasis on steady career experience may make them problematic for many women in Latin America. To the extent that a woman is assuming traditional responsibilities in her home, going to work in the formal sector entails a significant commitment that places strict limits and penalties on dealing with unpredictable events at home. One way to deal with this is to rely on a network of support for fulfilling those traditional responsibilities; another way, for those who can earn enough money, is to contract domestic servants. Maternity leaves can also interrupt the accumulation of job experience, or may be interpreted by employers as indicating a less than complete commitment to a woman's job. Any of these factors can make it more difficult for women to enter and hold jobs in the formal sector than men.

Finally, Latin America, like many other societies, is characterized by significant occupational segregation. Women tend to be concentrated in the clerical, teaching, nursing, seamstressing and retail trades. Women work disproportionately in the service sectors, which have grown steadily as a share of total employment in recent decades. The service sectors are also characterized by jobs ranging from well-paid professional positions in formal sector activities to retail employment that may generate little income. The causes of this concentration of women in particular occupations are not well understood in Latin America, and probably result from the interaction of women's own preferences and their ascribed responsibilities in the home with specific choices by firms in hiring and managing personnel, and with the structure and technology of production.

Women's Earnings Vary More

Less educated women who enter the labor force tend to be concentrated in informal sector jobs that pay less than formal sector jobs for women with comparable levels of education. Because of the influence of educational attainment on both labor force participation and the probability of being in either the formal or informal sector, the variation in earnings for women is greater than for

men. These large disparities contribute to the overall inequality in income distribution.

As was discussed in Chapter 2, the difference between earnings in the formal and informal sectors for women is quite large, and the gap is larger for women than men. Using the relationships that were statistically analyzed in Chapter 2, it is possible to calculate the wage gaps between these sectors after accounting for other factors that affect income. For example, a 35-year old woman living in an urban area who has completed seven years of school would earn an average of 18.5 percent more in a formal sector job than a similar woman who was self-employed.[8] In 11 of the 14 countries for which data was available, the formal sector pays more to a woman with these characteristics (the exceptions are Argentina, Bolivia and Brazil). (For a summary of earning differentials, see Figure 2.7 in Chapter 2.) In all of the countries for which the gap was significant, the gap for women was much higher than for men. A man with the same personal characteristics living in an urban area and working in the formal sector would earn only 7 percent more than a similar man who was self-employed.

The gap between men and women in the formal sector is lower than in the informal sector. On average, women doing the same job as men earn 10 percent less than men in the formal sector, while the gap in the informal sector is about 25 percent. The smaller gender gap in the formal sector might indicate less gender discrimination, or it might mean that the occupations that women occupy in the formal sector pay closer to the average of their male counterparts. It is difficult to imagine that straightforward gender discrimination by employers could explain such a large gap within the informal sector, since this sector includes self-employment and other activities that are much more fluid. However, it may still be a contributing factor. Occupational segregation is very likely to play a role in the larger gender gap in the informal sector, since women's informal occupations (principally retail trade and domestic service) are significantly less well paid than the informal jobs available to men (including construction and small-scale manufacturing).

The larger gap for women between formal and informal sector activities, then, is likely to have at least two sources. One is that the traditional roles assigned to women in Latin American countries leads them to

---

[7] A fuller discussion of the impact of labor market patterns on labor force participation, earnings and inequality can be found in Chapter 6.

[8] To calculate these simulations, we first estimate earnings regressions, and use the coefficients to predict each person's income based on their personal characteristics. Secondly, we use the coefficients to evaluate the function at other mean levels, and recompute the predicted income.

seek out jobs that offer flexibility, while formal sector employers are seeking workers who can be predictable and continuously committed to their job. Poor and un-educated women may find it harder to commit to a strict schedule because they do not have the resources to generate the support network that would allow them to allocate their time more predictably. As the woman's educational level increases, so too does her salary, making such a network more affordable. Given the existing tendency in society to assign primary responsibility for household tasks to women, these factors are much less important for men, and hence the premium for men in the formal sector would be correspondingly lower. A second source for this earnings gap is, again, related to occupational segregation. The greater range in earnings for women compared to similar men is affected by the range of available jobs. This range of jobs may be larger for men, since highly educated women are concentrated in particular professional jobs in specific sectors, while poorly educated women are predominantly candidates for domestic service and retail trade occupations. Both of these reasons help explain why women with equal education and experience earn a premium in the formal sector compared to their potential income in the infor-mal sector, and why this premium is larger for women than for men of otherwise equal characteristics. This greater disparity, in turn, contributes to income inequal-ity overall.

Participation and Income Inequality

As discussed above, women are participating in the la-bor force in increasing numbers, and this trend is consis-tent for all ages and educational levels, and across most countries.[9] These trends are consistent with the observed role of women's educational attainment in influencing work choices. As women's educational attainment has risen, so too has their participation in the labor market. Using education and the other factors identified in our participation model allows us to compare how much women's labor force participation would be in the 1990s as a consequence of only the changes in education, in-come and family size.[10] When this predicted participa-tion rate is compared to the actual rate, it falls well short. These factors explain about 50 percent of the increase in participation rates.[11] Other factors, both economic and social, are also at work (Box 3.1).

Because women's labor force participation is di-rectly related to household income, the differences in participation rates exacerbate income inequality in the region. This direct effect is small but significant. Income

inequality is about 1.5 points higher on average (as mea-sured by the Gini index) than it would be if high- and low-income women had equivalent participation rates (Figure 3.11).[12] In seven countries—Argentina, Ecuador, Honduras, Panama, Paraguay, Uruguay and Venezuela—the direct effect is more than two points. It is interesting to note that in all of the Latin American countries, with the exception of Ecuador, the impact on inequality of dif-ferences in female labor force participation rates is smaller than it would be in the United States. Thus, the direct impact of women's labor force participation is significant but relatively modest in explaining income gaps. But la-bor force participation also influences other decisions that affect income inequality as well.

In sum, the patterns of women's labor force partici-pation have an impact on income inequality in the re-gion. Women participate in the labor force less than men, and when they participate, they are more likely to work in informal sector than in formal sector jobs. Female labor force participation is strongly influenced by women's edu-cational attainment and, to a lesser extent, by the num-ber of children they have. Since lower-income women tend to have less education and more children, they partici-pate less in the labor market than their higher-income counterparts. For those women with less education who enter the labor market, the available earnings opportuni-ties—primarily in the informal sector—also exacerbate income inequality. Women's labor force participation also affects future income inequality through its impact on children's educational attainment; as we will see below, the children of women who have entered the labor mar-ket are more likely to be enrolled in school and to com-plete more years of schooling.

---

[9] See Duryea and Székely (1998).

[10] The simulations that follow use econometric estimates performed in two stages. First, an earnings regression that uses education, experience and the geographic location of the household is estimated separately for men and women. The coefficients are used to predict the income that each individual would earn, given his or her labor market experience, education and location. In other words, this is an estimate of income generating capacity. The second stage consists of estimating a multinomial logit regression to predict the prob-ability that each person has for not participating in the labor market, partici-pating in the formal sector, or participating in the informal sector. This regres-sion uses the estimated income generating capacity of the individual in question as an independent variable. The simulations consist of using the coefficients from the regressions to evaluate the probabilities by using differ-ent mean values for each variable, depending on the experiment in question. The Appendix shows the coefficients of the multinomial regression and pro-vides a more detailed discussion.

[11] This simulation uses the coefficients from the multinomial logit regres-sions of the previous sections. The experiment consists of using the coeffi-cient estimates for the 1980s, but evaluating the probabilities at the variable means observed for the 1990s. This estimates the proportion of the change due to changes in the quantities of each of the variables in question.

[12] Calculated by comparing the Gini index for the average household income of each earner with the Gini for household income per adult. See Barros, Duryea and Székely (1998) for details.

Box 3.1. Female Labor Market Participation and Day Care Services in Brazil

Studies of female participation in the labor market agree that child care and labor force participation compete for a mothers' time. Lowering the cost of child care, either by increasing supply or subsidizing child care prices, is shown to increase the usage of "market care" (as opposed to care by the mother or a near relative) and, by lowering the reservation wage of women, also leads to greater female labor force participation. Individual characteristics of the mother, household composition, and supply-side characteristics of the child care market in which the household takes part all influence the type of child care used and labor force participation. In general, studies have found that married women's labor supply is more sensitive to child care costs than that of single women, given married women's access to their husband's income.

Research on the effects of child care on labor force participation and earnings for poor women in the favelas of Rio de Janeiro confirms these general findings. Study results indicate that expanding the supply of low-cost child care in the favelas would increase mothers' labor force participation and their use of publicly financed day care centers. When they work, women who avail themselves of external child care services are also likely to earn more.

Studies also indicate that women who pay more for child care in the private sector are compensated by greater returns in the labor market. The elasticity of earnings (corrected for selection into the labor force or child care market) with respect to the use of higher-cost market care ranges from 12 to 29 percent. Private care produces higher returns largely because it offers greater flexibility in operating hours. Limited hours of service in public centers reduces their utility and their net impact on the earnings of women who work longer hours or have long commutes to their places of employment. Greater access to high-quality child care services not only offers developmental benefits for the children receiving care, as has been documented by previous studies, but also expanded economic opportunities for their mothers.

Gelbach (1998) has found that free public schooling impacts positively on labor supply and negatively on the receipt of public assistance by single mothers. Specifically, he finds that for single mothers whose youngest child is five, access to free public schooling raises labor supply by 8 to 18 percent, boosts wage and salary income by 27 percent, and reduces receipt of public assistance by 18 percent.

Child care programs also have important indirect effects such as increased education for older siblings, since alternative child care options free them from these tasks and allow them to continue their schooling. Studies in Brazil, Mexico and Guatemala all indicate that older siblings, particularly females, tend to serve as "mother substitutes," allowing for higher female labor force participation rates, all other things being equal. Similarly, the presence of older siblings within the household reduces the likelihood of using market-based child care services outside the home.

Figure 3.11. Gini Coefficient Differences Due to Participation Rates

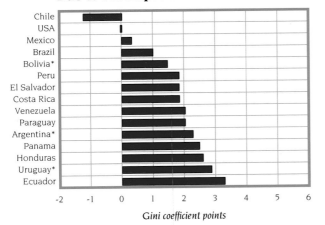

Gini coefficient points

* Countries with urban data only.
Source: Barros, Duryea and Székely (1998).

HOUSEHOLD SIZE AND INEQUALITY

The Poor Live in Large Households...

Low-income Latin Americans live in larger households than do upper-income people in the region. On average, Latin American families in the top 10 percent of the income distribution have four members, while those in the bottom 30 percent have 6.3 members. The number of Latin Americans who live alone is much higher among the top decile of the population than the bottom three deciles (Figure 3.12), particularly in the urban areas of Argentina and Uruguay, where the proportion is over 10 percent. Even there, however, the share of higher-income people living alone is less than half the rate of the United States, where 28 percent of the highest income group live by themselves. The people in the bottom three deciles, by contrast, rarely live alone in Latin America—fewer than 2 percent in all the countries for which household survey data was available. This contrasts with the United States, where almost 6 percent of the bottom three deciles live alone.

In Latin America, a similar pattern is apparent for three-person households which, throughout the region, encompass between a fifth and a quarter of the rich but

Figure 3.12. Share of Population by Household Size and Income

(*Number of people living in household*)

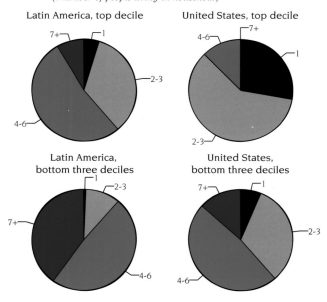

Source: IDB *calculations based on recent household surveys.*

Figure 3.13a. Adults per Household (Individuals 18 Years Old and Older)

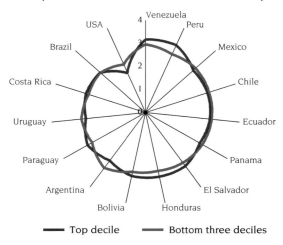

Source: IDB *calculations based on recent household surveys.*

Figure 3.13b. Children per Household (Individuals 17 Years Old and Younger)

Source: IDB *calculations based on recent household surveys.*

barely one-tenth of the poor. By contrast, in the United States, all income groups have a similar probability of living in three-person households. Nevertheless, the situation is sharply reversed for households with seven or more members. Barely one-tenth of the top decile live in such large families, while a little more than 40 percent of individuals in the bottom three deciles do, ranging from 22 percent in Chile to about 55 percent in Paraguay.

...Because They Have More Children

The larger households in the bottom three deciles are largely the consequence of more children, not more adults. In Latin America, the average household has slightly more than three individuals over 17 years old, and this is consistent across countries and varies little between the top and bottom of the income distribution (Figure 3.13a). By contrast, the number of children per household varies significantly across countries and income levels (Figure 3.13b). Even in countries that have low fertility rates, such as Argentina and Uruguay, there is a difference of about two children between the top 10 percent and the bottom 30 percent of the population. In higher fertility countries and regions such as Central America, the Andean region and Paraguay, the rich have between 1.5 and two children while the poor have between three and four children.

"Traditional" Families Still Predominate

Despite the differences in household size across income levels, household structures are strongly similar in all income groups. The traditional family remains the dominant form in Latin America. Most Latin American children live in nuclear or extended families; that is, in households with a parent, a spouse and their children (a nuclear family) or one which also includes other relatives (an extended family).[13] Between 70 and 90 percent of

---

[13] Note that we cannot determine if the spouse is the parent of all children present.

Figure 3.14a. Share of Children Living in Nuclear Households

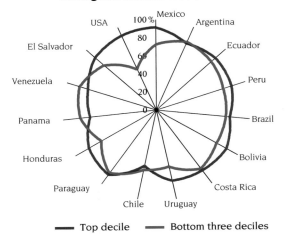

— Top decile — Bottom three deciles

Source: IDB calculations based on recent household surveys.

Figure 3.15. Gini Coefficient Differences Due to the Number of Children per Family

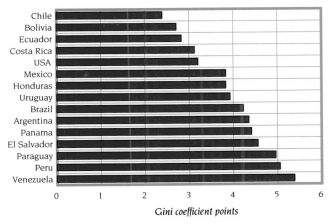

Gini coefficient points

Source: Barros, Duryea and Székely (1998).

Figure 3.14b. Share of Children Living in Single Parent Households

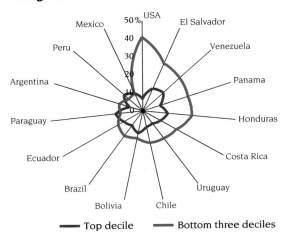

— Top decile — Bottom three deciles

Source: IDB calculations based on recent household surveys.

children in Latin America live in nuclear or extended families, ranging from as low as 66.3 percent in El Salvador to 83.4 percent in Mexico and 81.8 percent in Paraguay (Figure 3.14a). The number of children living in single-headed households (i.e., households with one adult and no spouse) is rather small. In the typical country, fewer than 20 percent of the children in the bottom three deciles live in single-headed households (Figure 3.14b). El Salvador, Venezuela, Panama and Honduras have the highest shares—close to 30 percent—while Mexico, Peru and Argentina are among the lowest, ranging close to 10 percent. This pattern varies considerably from the United States, where over 40 percent of the children in the bot-

tom three deciles live in single-parent households and where debates over poverty are concerned with changes in family structure. This kind of debate is less relevant to most Latin American countries, where the share of poor children living in single-parent households is considerably smaller.

There are several reasons why lower-income households may be larger. There are clearly different attitudes, norms and cultural standards regarding the appropriate age to marry, when and if to have children, divorce and separation, and when and how to combine families in a single household. In addition to cultural reasons and affective ties, economic factors also play a role. Poor families may live in larger households in order to pool economic resources, although the small income-related variation in the number of adults per household indicates that this is not a major factor. However, the number of children living in households headed by someone other than their parent is surprisingly large in some cases. In Venezuela, for example, almost 50 percent of children who are less than 2 years old live in such households, indicating that the choices people make about the structure of their households may be significant. Families may also live in larger households in order to improve income stability, avoid vulnerability and reduce the cost of transferring resources to other members of the family (Boxes 3.2 and 3.3).

Regardless of the reasons, the fact that lower-income individuals live in larger households with more children conspires to worsen per capita income distribution, as income must be shared between more household members. If poorer families had the same number of children as richer families, per capita income inequality, as measured by the Gini index, would be significantly

Box 3.2. Who Decides in This Family?

Much of the discussion in this chapter focuses on decisions made by families and households regarding the use of time and responsibilities for different tasks, as well as on such intimate family decisions as whether to limit their number of children. The chapter explores the factors associated with labor force participation, fertility and children's educational attainment, and it shows that there are reasonable explanations why families would modify their behavior in response to different economic contexts affecting their own resources and assets. But the chapter does not address how the decisions are made, nor who within the family is making these decisions. Economists have applied their analytical tools to understanding such family decisions in a language that is sometimes jarring, but within which some important insights can be found.

The economic literature models families and households in at least four different ways in order to address a variety of questions. All are simplifications, and each one has its particular insights. The four models can be characterized as monolithic, authoritarian, enlightened authoritarian and bargaining. Studies that characterize families as monolithic do not distinguish between the family members. These studies analyze such factors as how much labor families supply to the labor market and how they assign their incomes in order to maximize the utility of the whole group. For these studies, the differentiation within the family may be less important than the aggregate relationships. Studies that characterize families as authoritarian presume that the head of household makes the decisions, and optimizes her, or more frequently, his utility. The welfare of other family members does affect the head of household's own welfare and so the other family members will eat and be sheltered; however, the resulting welfare of each individual will not necessarily be maximized. An enlightened authoritarian family is similar to the authoritarian family in that a single individual, the head of household, is assumed to make all the decisions. However, in this model, the welfare functions of each member are specified, and the head of household seeks to maximize the

family's joint welfare. Finally, bargaining models treat the family as a grouping of individuals who bring different resources to the family and have differing demands. These models posit a variety of mechanisms through which all the family members come to joint decisions. In some cases the models treat the decision process as "trading," in which members offer certain resources or effort in return for benefits. In other cases, the decision process is modeled with game theory, in which each member pursues different strategies and the combined effects of these strategies have different "payoffs." These kinds of models tend to focus on the internal distribution of resources in the family, and can be quite helpful for studies that are trying to understand household formation.

Bargaining models have been used to understand such questions as why girls receive less education in certain countries, why families support the elderly, and why educational attainment is so highly correlated within couples. Behrman (1998) and Pitt and Rozensweig (1986) use such models to show that the allocation of resources within households appears to depend strongly on the expected future income of each member and its likely contribution to the household. Consequently, very low-income households tend to distribute more resources to their members who have higher earning capacities. Children who are likely to be more economically productive adults also receive greater shares of family resources, which further enhances their income-generating potential. When these children start using these capacities, they tend to transfer resources to the other members of the household. Thus, it appears that the outcomes of household decisions depend not only on cultural norms and affection but also significantly on the economic context within which the unit as a whole behaves as "consumer" and "investor," with strong consequences for family size, household structure, labor supply and income.

Sources: Sen (1984); Bourguignon and Chiappori (1992); Haddad and Kanbur (1992); Kapteyn and Kooreman (1992); and Katz (1997).

---

lower (Figure 3.15).[14] This effect would vary from just over two points in Chile (a 4 percent decline) to over 5 points in Venezuela and Panama, where the Gini indices are 0.47 and 0.56, respectively. Although family size contributes to inequality in all countries, and significantly in some, this factor cannot explain the difference between Latin America and other regions. For example, the potential impact of equalizing family size across income groups in the United States would have an effect comparable to what it would have on many Latin American countries.

In sum, the data indicates that poor families are larger, essentially because they have more children, but not necessarily because they have more adults. Family structure does not vary strongly by income, except with regard to size. The rich live more by themselves and in couples without children. But nuclear and extended fami-

lies are the most common structure for Latin American society for all income groups. The range in family size has a significant impact on the overall distribution of per capita income in society. But what determines family size?

Fertility and Family Size

Decisions by couples regarding having children are perhaps among the most intimate and important choices that they make. Many people do not even consider this to be a "choice" in the sense that they accept however

---

[14] The impact of the number of children on the Gini coefficient is computed by comparing the Gini index of total household per capita income with that of total household income per adult. See Barros, Duryea and Székely (1998) for details.

Box 3.3. *Where Do Elderly Latin Americans Live?*

One plausible explanation of why Latin Americans tend to live in extended households is that the household may act as a substitute for social security by grouping people from different generations and facilitating transfers from younger members to their elderly relatives. When adequate social security is not available or is deteriorating, the household can serve as a safety net for the elderly. Figure 1 shows the distribution of the population 65 years of age and older by household type for 15 Latin American countries and the United States. While in the United States most of these individuals live in single person households and as couples without children, a very large proportion of the Latin American elderly live in extended households, with very few living on their own.

Evidence from Mexico shows that when the oldest person in a household is over 50, households tend to increase their size and change composition toward extended units. In these units, significant transfers across generations take place, and the amount of the transfers increases as the oldest person in the unit grows older . The older the household head, the larger the number of individuals attracted to the unit. This suggests that the family is acting as a mechanism to provide security for the elderly. Strong family ties make it less necessary to rely on social security.

This pattern is also observed in other Latin American countries. According to Figure 1, Honduras, El Salvador, Mexico and Ecuador are the countries where the elderly seem to rely more on other family members, since a majority of them live in extended households and only around 42 percent live alone or in couples without children. Of those that live in extended households, about 40 percent are neither the household head nor the head's spouse.

Interestingly, Uruguay is where the largest proportion of elderly live on their own, perhaps owing to the fact that its social security system is the most advanced in the region. In Uruguay, 68 percent of the elderly live in single person units or as couples with no children, compared to the Latin American average of 48 percent (the proportion in the United States is 85 percent). Around 20 percent of the total reported income of individuals is from pensions and social security payments (the largest in the countries with available data). Looking at the types of income that people receive at different stages of their life, pensions are a key factor in the decisions made by the Uruguayan elderly. Figure 2 shows that after retirement age (60 years for women and 65 for men), the elderly on average obtain an income similar to the amount received by workers 25-30 years of age. This suggests that the average income of retirees does not decline after retirement because the value of pensions is high and more than compensates for the loss of labor income. This may make it less necessary to rely on the family for support and may be behind the large proportion of elderly living as couples without children or in single person households in this country.

Source: Székely (1998).

Figure 1. Where Do Latin Americans Live?
(*In percent*)

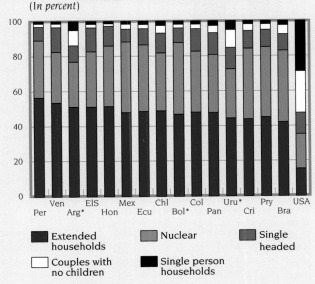

| Extended households | Nuclear | Single headed |
| Couples with no children | Single person households | |

* Countries with urban data only.
Source: IDB *calculations based on recent household surveys.*

Figure 2. Average Labor and Pension Incomes by Age in Uruguay, 1995

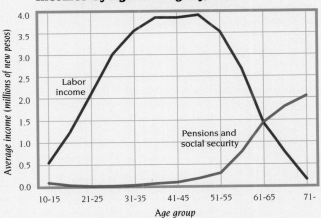

Source: IDB *calculations based on recent household surveys.*

Figure 3.16. Number of Children per Woman, by Education

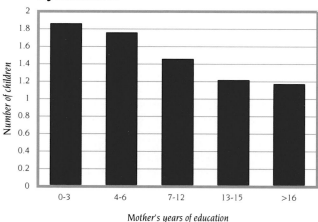

Note: Average for 14 Latin American countries.
Source: IDB *calculations based on recent household surveys.*

Figure 3.17. Number of Children in Urban and Rural Areas per Woman (30-40 Years Old) with 4-6 Years of Education

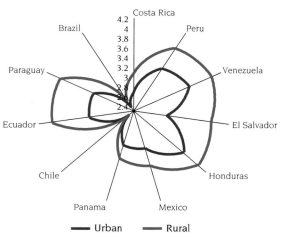

Source: IDB *calculations based on recent household surveys.*

many children they conceive. But many people also choose to influence when they will have their first child, the timing of births, and their total number of children. It is clear from available evidence that enough people make such decisions in response to changing social norms and economic factors that fertility rates are, in the aggregate, strongly influenced by a number of known factors, such as women's education, women's income-earning opportunities, and rural or urban location.

As discussed earlier, the number of children families have varies dramatically by income.[15] Rich households in Latin America have an average of two children less than poorer ones. The differences are widest in Paraguay and El Salvador, where the top 10 percent of households have fewer than two children on average, and the bottom three deciles have more than four. The difference appears to be smallest, although still significant, in Chile, where the top 10 percent of households have slightly more than 1.5 children on average, while the bottom three deciles have an average of around two children per household. This is puzzling in the sense that wealthier families have the resources to have and support more children, not less. Some of the clues to understanding the relationship between income and the number of children can be found by looking at relationships with other factors.

Educated People Have Fewer Children

As noted earlier, women who are more educated tend to have fewer children.[16] Not surprisingly, parent's schooling and fertility vary negatively, since education

is one of the main determinants of earnings. Figure 3.16 shows the relationship between the number of children and women's educational levels for 14 Latin American countries. The pattern is consistent throughout the region. Women with six years of schooling or less have 0.7 more children on average than those who finished more than 13 years of schooling.

Women's education can influence the number of children they have in at least two ways. First, education may change personal preferences and affect life choices by exposing women to more alternatives. Second, education increases a woman's earning power. This makes entering the workforce more attractive, and means that staying out of the labor force to have and care for children implies foregoing a higher income. Other things constant, men who are more educated or earn higher incomes are also likely to have somewhat fewer children on average, but this effect is smaller than for women.

---

[15] For the purposes of this study, the number of children per family or woman was estimated using the subsample of children living with mothers aged 30 to 35 years old. This subgroup was chosen because including younger women would bias the estimates downward (younger women have more childbearing years ahead of them and a higher probability that the observation does not accurately measure the total number of children that they will have). On the other hand, including older women would also bias the estimates downward because the household surveys only allow us to count the number of children living with the mother at the time of the survey. For the few household surveys that did not provide detailed information about relationships within the household, fertility rates were estimated by attributing all children in a particular household to women who are household heads or spouses of household heads (see Appendix). The estimates generated in this way are comparable to those measured by CELADE.

[16] Duryea and Lam (forthcoming) is a recent example of the analysis of these relations in a Latin American country.

Figure 3.18. Number of Children per Woman (30-40 Years Old), 1980s vs. 1990s

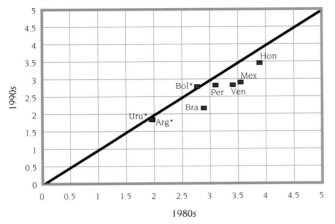

* Countries with urban data only.
Source: IDB calculations based on recent household surveys.

Economists say that for men the "income effect" (having more resources and therefore being able to care for more children) is larger relative to the "substitution effect" (entering the workforce and spending less time raising children) for men than for women.[17]

Rural Families Have More Children

Where people live also influences the number of children they have. Families in urban areas have consistently fewer children than their counterparts in rural areas. This is true in all the Latin American countries for which data was available, and is true throughout the world. Much of the difference can be explained by disparities in educational levels, which are lower in most rural areas. But if we consider women of a particular age and educational level, we still see that urban women have fewer children (Figure 3.17). This difference is greatest in Colombia, where rural women between 30 and 40 years of age who finished four to six years of schooling have three children, on average, compared with their urban counterparts who have slightly more than two children. After controlling for education in this way, however, the remaining unexplained differences are almost negligible in Chile and Brazil.

Rural areas differ from urban areas in a number of ways that explain part of the remaining gaps. First, children in rural areas typically can contribute earlier and more productively to their family than children in urban areas. This means that, in addition to cultural or social reasons, a rural family can consider children to be additional contributors to family income at an earlier age.

Second, rural areas have typically lacked social security arrangements that would secure pensions for the elderly. In this kind of situation, families may view having more children as a way of assuring support in old age. Third, as will be discussed below, the foregone earnings of women in rural areas are smaller than in urban areas, and this reduces any incentive to limit family size. Fourth, it has been suggested that high rates of mortality among children encourages families to have more children as a way of assuring that at least some of them reach maturity. Fortunately, as child mortality rates have declined in most of the region, this kind of explanation, if true, is likely to become less important with time.

Fertility Has Declined More Than Predicted

Fertility has declined steadily in Latin America for decades. Since the early 1980s, the decline has been particularly steep, especially in Brazil, Mexico and Venezuela (Figure 3.18). This decline has been accompanied by an increase in the average schooling of women in most countries. But education alone does not explain the pace of decline. Similarly, demographic models that predicted fertility rates on the basis of income have consistently underestimated the decline in births over the past decades, since fertility rates continued to fall even during the crisis years of the 1980s. With respect to income level, the pattern is less consistent across the region. The decline in fertility has been greater at the bottom than at the top of the income scale in Mexico, and in the urban areas of Argentina and Uruguay, while the opposite has been true for Brazil, Venezuela and Honduras (Figure 3.19).[18]

The Role of Women's Education

How much of the differences in fertility between high- and low-income women can be explained by the different rates of return they face in the labor market (i.e., the income-earning value of each school year attained) or by the resources they bring to the labor market in terms of their schooling level?

Using a model in which fertility and wages are simultaneously determined (see Appendix), it is possible

---

[17] See Becker (1964); Galor and Weill (1996); Becker, Murphy and Tamura 1990; and Dahan and Tsiddon (1998).

[18] The figures for the urban Bolivian sample indicate a rise in fertility rates. This is likely to be a consequence of rural-urban migration. The absence of information on migration and on rural areas makes it difficult to determine whether this increasing fertility rate is real or simply an artifact of the sample.

Figure 3.19. Change in the Number of Children per Household by Income, 1980s to mid-1990s

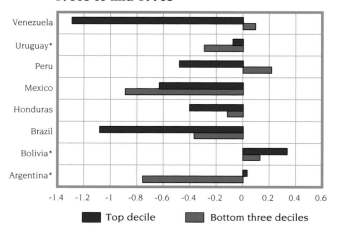

* Countries with urban data only.
Source: IDB calculations based on recent household surveys.

Figure 3.20. The Fertility Gap Due to Education and Returns

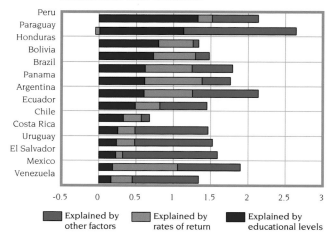

* Countries with urban data only.
Note: The fertility gap is calculated as the difference in the number of children per household in the top decile to the bottom three deciles.
Source: IDB simulations based on recent household surveys.

turn in all countries and the only remaining differences were educational levels—this would do relatively little to explain why high- and low-income families have different numbers of children (Figure 3.20). The returns to education can explain very little of the variation in El Salvador, urban Uruguay and Costa Rica. However, in Honduras, Peru, urban Bolivia, Chile and Paraguay the returns appear to account for around half of the predicted difference in the number of children in high- and low-income families. As noted above, these are underestimates of the true effect. If a higher rate were used, the explanatory power could be correspondingly larger. In such a case, the foregone earnings for women with more education would rise more than proportionally compared to women with less education, and the gap in the number of children per family would widen. Consequently, policies or economic trends that raise the returns to education may also exacerbate inequality through the effect on fertility decisions, but these effects will be relatively small.

Educational levels have an even larger effect on household fertility decisions throughout the region. After equalizing returns to education, if we also level education so that each woman has completed the same number of years of school, we can account for some 60 percent of the gap between high- and low-income women in terms of the number of children they have. (Figure 3.20). In Honduras, urban Bolivia, Chile, Panama, Peru and Brazil, the introduction of educational levels makes it possible to explain more than 80 percent of the differences between the rich and the poor. This shows that in most countries, the amount of education completed by high- and low-income parents is extremely important. However, variations in the relative prices they face in the labor market, which are shaped by the economic environment, also play some role in their decisions to have children.

EDUCATIONAL ATTAINMENT OF CHILDREN

While labor force participation and the number of children per household contribute to current income inequality, they also have implications for the education of today's

to estimate how much of the fertility difference between high- and low-income women can be attributed to either the schooling level or the rate of return.[19] By setting the rate of return to a year of schooling in each country to be equal, we can see how much of a difference this would make to the expected disparity in the number of children. By choosing a relatively low rate of return—6 percent—we also assure that the explanatory power is an underestimate of the true effect of prices on the number of children per family. The analysis shows, in fact, that if all households faced the same prices (returns to education)—that is, if each year of education generated the same re-

_____

[19] This exercise is similar to the simulations performed on the participation decision. It is based on two stage regressions. In the first stage, earnings equations are estimated based on experience, education and geographic location. The coefficients from the regression are used to predict each individual's income based on his or her personal characteristics. The predicted incomes are used in a second stage regression where the dependent variable is the number of children in the household, and the independent variables are the estimated income-earnings potential. See the Appendix for the regression results and a discussion of the methodology.

Figure 3.21. Education Gap by Age

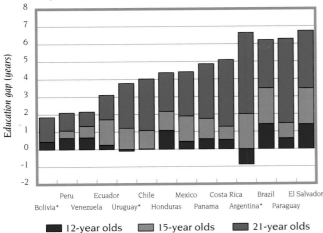

* Countries with urban data only.
Note: The education gap is calculated as the difference between the average years of schooling completed by children in the top decile and those in the bottom three deciles.
Source: IDB calculations based on recent household surveys.

Figure 3.22. Children's Education by Mother's Education (15-year olds)

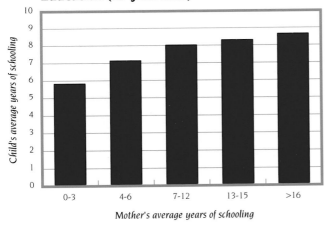

Note: Average of 14 countries.
Source: IDB calculations based on recent household surveys.

children, who will be making decisions about work and family in the future. Hence, the seeds of tomorrow's income inequality are being sown today, just as the seeds of yesterday affected income distribution today.

Despite public policies that talk of guaranteeing every child a full and free education, the schooling levels attained by children in Latin America are very different depending on the income of their parents. As discussed in Chapter 2, Latin America has relatively good primary school coverage for all income levels, when compared to other regions. However, there is some evidence that the

quality of this schooling may vary significantly by income. And the data clearly show that as children age, the gap in enrollment widens between children of high- and low-income families.

Regional averages for the 14 Latin American sample countries tell the story (Figure 3.21). For the 12-year old age group, the gap is not very evident: in many countries, the differences in attainment from one income group to another are less than half a year. Enrollment rates at this age remain relatively high in most of the region, with almost 90 percent of the bottom 30 percent of the income distribution attending school. However, the average difference of one-half a school year reflects higher rates of repetition among lower-income children. In countries such as Brazil, El Salvador and Honduras, the inefficiency of the schooling process is so bad that children from high-income households have finished a whole additional year of school compared to their lower-income 12-year old counterparts.

The picture worsens by age 15, when most children can be expected to be enrolled in high school. A 15-year old child should have completed between eight and nine years of schooling, a level attained by most children in the top decile. In most countries, lower-income children lag by about a year, but in Honduras, Mexico, Panama and Paraguay the gap is about two years, and in El Salvador and Brazil, almost four years. The larger gaps at this age are related as much to dropout rates as to repetition. By this age, many of the poorer children have already left school and effectively ended their education. Enrollment of 15-year olds in the poorest 30 percent of the population is barely 32 percent in Honduras, 42 percent in Paraguay and 50 percent in El Salvador and Ecuador. Brazil stands out for the impact of repetition, since this age group has attained barely 3.5 years of schooling, yet 68 percent are still enrolled.

By the time young people have reached 21, and most have effectively concluded their formal schooling, there is a wide gap in attainment between the top decile and the bottom 30 percent. In Peru and Venezuela, the difference is only about two years, but in Mexico, Panama, Chile and Costa Rica the gap ranges between four and five years, while in Brazil, Paraguay and El Salvador, the gap has widened to more than six years. At this age, fewer than 20 percent of the bottom three deciles are enrolled in school in all of the region's countries with the exception of Peru, Chile and Venezuela. By contrast, enrollment rates of the top 10 percent exceed 50 percent in Uruguay, Costa Rica, Argentina, El Salvador, Panama and Chile.

Although educational attainment of children varies strongly depending on household income, it is actually the education of parents that most strongly predicts

Figure 3.23. Children's Education by Age and Number of Children of the Mother

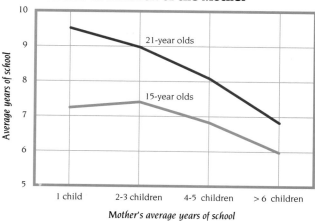

Note: *Average of 14 countries.*
Source: *IDB calculations based on recent household surveys.*

a child's final level of schooling.[20] Typically, there is a two to three year difference between the educational attainment of 15-year old children whose mothers have less than four years of education and those who have some secondary schooling (Figure 3.22). As in the case of women's labor force participation, education of parents has a variety of potential effects on children. First, education is very strongly related to an adult's long-term earning capacity. Therefore, education may indicate a parent's income—and consequently the resources available at the time the child was in school—better than the current level of income reported in the survey. Second, parents who are more educated may play a pedagogical role, reading to their children, discussing things, and paying more attention to performance on examinations and homework. Third, parents serve as a role model for their children. If children can see that their parents attended and valued schooling, and especially if educational attainment provided payoffs for the parents in the labor market, then these same children may see the advantages and look to follow that example.

By analyzing the performance of children whose mothers are in the labor force, we can infer that the role model or resources explanations are the more likely of these three explanations. Were this a pedagogical story, mothers who do not participate in the labor market would be expected to have more time to improve their children's schooling. However, children of working mothers actually attain higher educational levels than those of mothers who do not work. After controlling for numerous factors—including the number of children in the household, gender of the child, parents' education, household income, urban-rural location, age of the child, and the presence of elderly

members in the household—participation in the labor market by a child's mother increases that child's likelihood of being enrolled in school. In 13 of the 15 Latin American countries for which data was available, this positive effect of a mother's participation in the labor market on a child's educational enrollment is positive and statistically significant (the exceptions are Argentina and Peru; see Table 3.A1 in the Appendix). On average, if a mother participates in the labor market, the probability of her child being enrolled in school increases by around 5 percent.

The total number of children in the household is another factor that influences educational attainment. Fifteen-year-old children in households with six or more children have an average of two years less education than children in households with one or even three children (Figure 3.23 and Table 3A.1 in the Appendix). This is a reasonable relationship for a variety of reasons. One possibility is that older children may be drawn out of school to care for younger children.[21] Although this may happen among certain population subgroups, it cannot explain the difference in society as a whole because, as noted earlier, families in which both the mother and the father are working (that is, families with more resources and less time at home) have children who complete more schooling. Another explanation is that having more children makes it more difficult to finance the education of each one. The data strongly supports this explanation; in families with equivalent levels of income, structure and parental education, children in smaller families complete more years of school.[22] Numerous studies have demonstrated that couples try to limit the number of children they will have and simultaneously dedicate more resources to each child they do have. Parents with more education, income earning opportunities and incomes opt for fewer children and dedicate more resources to invest in the education of those offspring. This demonstrates the set of relationships between a mother's education, her income-earning opportunities, the number of children she may have, and her children's educational attainment (Figure 3.24).

These relationships are quite evident when urban and rural households are compared in terms of participation, fertility and educational attainment. Women living in

---

[20] See Behrman (1997) and Behrman and Knowles (1997). There is generally a stronger association between a mother's education and school attainment of children than for a father's education.

[21] See Chapter 5 for a lengthier discussion of the impact of children undertaking household activities on their educational attainment.

[22] This finding is consistent with a large economic literature that discusses a "quality and quantity" tradeoff in parental decisions about how many children to have and how much to invest in each one. See Becker (1991) and Cigno (1991).

Figure 3.24. Beneficial Effects of Educating Women

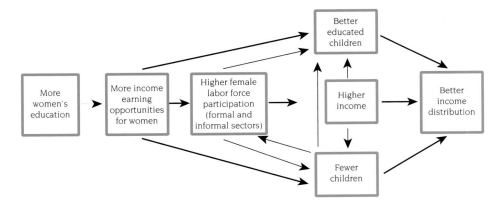

rural areas tend to complete fewer years of schooling, and the returns to that schooling are lower than in urban areas. Hence, women in rural areas are less likely to participate in the remunerated labor force, and when they do, they are more likely to work in lower paying informal sector activities. As discussed previously, there are numerous reasons why women in rural areas have more children, but poorer income earning opportunities for women play a part. Rural households have on average 0.6 more children than urban ones, and 15-year-old children in rural households have an average of 1.6 fewer years of education than their urban counterparts (Figure 3.25). This suggests a stronger tradeoff than in urban areas between the number of children in each family and the amount of time and resources dedicated to each one's schooling.

How much of the difference in educational attainment of high- and low-income children is due only to the fact that their parents have different educational levels? Using our model, we estimated that, on average, the variations in the parents' level of education explain about 30 percent of the predicted difference in their children's educational attainment (Figure 3.26). In El Salvador, Honduras, Panama and Mexico, the proportion of the expected difference reaches 50 percent. After accounting for the differences attributable to parental education, economy-wide factors also contribute to the gap in children's educational attainment. One important factor is how much the labor market values an additional year of schooling, i.e., the return to education. Equalizing returns to education between primary and higher education across coun-

Figure 3.25. Number of Children and Schooling in Rural and Urban Areas

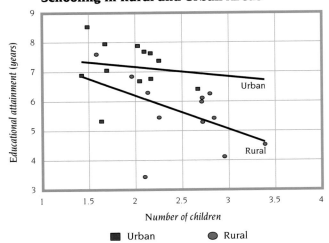

Note: Lines represent relationship between number of children and children's educational attainment after controlling for other factors. See econometric estimations in Appendix.
Source: IDB calculations based on recent household surveys.

Figure 3.26. Educational Attainment Gap Due to Parent's Education and Returns

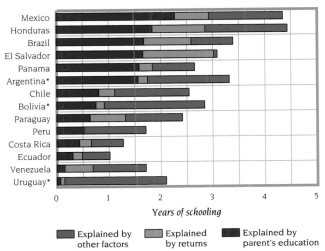

* Countries with urban data only.
Source: IDB simulations based on recent household surveys.
See details of the estimation in the Appendix.

Figure 3.27. Estimated Education Equilibrium for the Two Education Groups

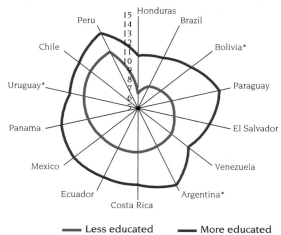

—— Less educated   —— More educated

Countries with urban data only.
Source: IDB *calculations based on recent household surveys.*

tries does indeed account for a significant amount of the educational attainment gap. On average, the combination of disparities in returns to education and parental education explains 55 percent of the expected difference in the educational attainment of high- and low-income children. However, in Mexico, Panama, Honduras, El Salvador and Brazil, these factors explain close to 80 percent of the predicted difference. These estimates represent the direct effect of parental education on children's educational attainment; the indirect effects upon other family characteristics will be addressed below.

INTERGENERATIONAL TRANSMISSION OF INEQUALITY

The education of children depends to a large extent on that of their parents. Just as the attainment of today's adults was affected by their parents' schooling levels, when today's children become parents, their children's education will also depend on theirs, and so on. Are different segments of society gradually moving towards the same levels of education, or will educational levels diverge into two classes—one highly educated and another relatively uneducated? Educational levels will converge whenever children of less educated parents have a continuing and high probability of finishing more school than their parents, and, conversely, when the children of more educated parents have some reasonably significant probability of finishing less schooling than their parents. Education levels will tend to diverge when the opposite situation holds.[23]

In order to find out if the educational levels of Latin American countries are converging or diverging, we estimated the current relationship between mothers' and childrens' educational attainment for two different groups of women—those who had completed more than nine years of school and those who had completed less.[24] The estimates took other family characteristics into account. The exercise demonstrates that if the current relationship between mothers' and children's education were to continue, all countries in Latin America would move toward a situation in which the less educated today would complete more than primary schooling in a "final" hypothetical equilibrium of the future (Figure 3.27). However, the less educated group would have educational attainment in excess of 10 years of schooling in only five of these countries—Peru, Chile, urban Uruguay, Panama and Mexico. In Honduras, Brazil, urban Bolivia and Paraguay, the less educated group would have 6.6, 7.6, 8.1, and 8.6 years of schooling, respectively. By contrast, the more educated groups are converging toward an average education of more than 13 years, i.e., effectively completing secondary school and with a significant number enrolling in college. The countries for which the more educated groups end up with the highest educational attainment are urban Argentina, Peru, Paraguay, Mexico, Ecuador and Costa Rica. In general, the hypothetical equilibrium level of education for the less educated group is closely related to the projected gap between the two groups. The relationship between these two outcomes is strongly negative: countries with low expected educational attainment for the lower income groups also tend to have a high projected level of educational inequality.

WEAVING THE STORIES TOGETHER

Thus far, we have shown that participation in the labor market, fertility and the educational attainment of children vary strongly by income. Furthermore, women's potential earning power, as influenced by their own educa-

---

[23] This assumes that the parent-child education relationship is smooth and with declining marginal educational "returns" to each additional year of parental education. If the relationship varies, with increasing and declining marginal returns at different levels, or if it is discontinuous, it is possible for a variety of equilibria to exist.

[24] The calculations were done for two separate samples. Using the estimated relationship, it was possible to calculate the final hypothetical equilibria in educational attainment for each of these groups in the future. The exercise is indicative of how educational attainment might move in the future if current relationships between mothers' and children's education remain the same. Also, the estimates of current relationships may understate the true relationships because they are calculated from cross-section, not panel, data.

tional attainment, plays an important role in all these outcomes. Up to this point we have looked only at the direct impact (shown in Figure 3.24 with thick arrows) of education on each of these family characteristics. But we know that these factors are interrelated in ways that introduce indirect effects (thin arrows). For example, as a woman's potential earnings rise, she is both more likely to enter the labor force and have fewer children. But having fewer children also increases her probability of entering the labor force. Hence, there are feedbacks in the complete model that address these indirect effects.

Despite the complexity of the interrelationships, the main relationships are both understandable and can be influenced by appropriate policies. Any policy or social trend that increases women's education will increase their potential earnings in the labor market and lead more women to seek paid work, since the advantages of being in the labor force will have increased relative to engaging primarily in work at home. Similarly, any policies that increase the productivity of household tasks—such as running water, electricity or community services—will also encourage families to allocate more work to the labor market. A more educated woman, with higher potential earnings, also has greater incentives to limit the number of children she has—partly in order to remain in her job longer, but also because it allows her family to focus more resources on fewer children. As a result, more educated women, and those who enter the labor force, have children with greater educational attainment. With greater earnings and fewer children per family among lower-income families, the overall distribution of income would tend to improve. And the higher educational attainment of children would, concomitantly, lead to lower income inequality in the future.

However, women's earning potential depends not only on their educational attainment but also on the returns to that education generated by the economy as a whole. Women's opportunities in the labor market will vary with the degree of occupational segregation, gender discrimination, and the formal versus informal jobs that are available. Rural opportunities, in particular, are significantly more limited than those in urban areas. Choices about fertility, labor market participation and schooling involve additional factors such as those related to the productivity of household work (e.g., availability of water, electricity and urban transport), the availability and total cost of child care, and the quality of education.[25] These elements vary across countries and across localities of the same country, and are difficult to measure directly. However, they enter into the explanation of why some countries are more unequal than others.

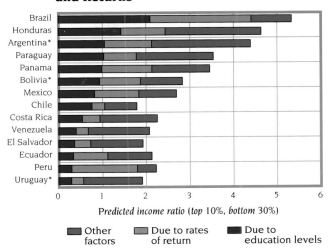

Figure 3.28. Income Gap Due to Education and Returns

Predicted income ratio (top 10%, bottom 30%)

□ Other factors   □ Due to rates of return   ■ Due to education levels

* Countries with urban data only.
Source: IDB simulations based on recent household surveys.
See the Appendix for details.

Following our earlier approach, in which we demonstrated how much of the income gap could be attributed to the direct effects of education and income opportunities upon family characteristics, we can now look at estimates of the total impact of these particular relationships.[26] Both personal characteristics and features of the economy influence the resulting levels of income inequality, so we estimate how the income gap between high- and low-income households is affected by the gap in educational levels between lower- and higher-income parents and by the fact that the returns to a year of primary education are much lower than the returns to a year of higher schooling (Figure 3.28).[27] On average, if the only difference between low- and high-income households were the amount of education the parents receive (in this case the return of each year is set equal across countries and educational levels), then 26 percent of the predicted

[25] Policies related to these factors are discussed in greater depth in Chapter 5.
[26] The method for the simulations is similar to the one already employed to estimate participation and the number of children in the household. The difference is that in this case, there are three kinds of decisions (rather than one) that are taken simultaneously. The simulation method is as follows: at a first stage earnings equations are estimated based on experience, education and geographic location. The coefficients from the regressions are used to predict each person's income earnings potential, based on personal characteristics. The estimated income feeds into three simultaneous equations that determine the number of children per household, the probability of participating formally and informally in the labor market, and children's educational attainment. By using the coefficients from the regressions and evaluating each equation at certain mean values, the estimated per capita income of the members of the household can be obtained. See the Appendix for more details.
[27] For the technical presentation of the economic model that was used, see the Appendix.

per capita income differentials could be explained. However, the wages paid for different types of education are not the same. When the wage variations are factored in, around 60 percent of the expected differences between the rich and poor can be explained using this model. In the case of Brazil, Peru, Mexico and urban Bolivia, the differences in relative wages and quantities of education for parents actually explain around 80 percent of the expected disparities in per capita income between the rich and the poor. Thus, the combined impact of direct and indirect effects on income inequality is significant in most countries. However, while personal differences matter, the model still only predicts a portion of the actual income gap. The magnitude of the income differential is also strongly determined by the economic environment in which people live.

TWO COUPLES TRAVELING THROUGH LATIN AMERICA

To understand better how the economic environment affects families' decisions and directly and indirectly affects income inequality in the region, we use our model to simulate the impact of different levels of educational attainment on labor force participation, fertility, children's educational attainment, and income inequality throughout the region. For the exercise, we can imagine two couples who always decide to live in urban areas, and who differ only in their educational attainment. The Altamira couple (Family A) is composed of two 35-year old adults each with about 11 years of schooling—the average educational attainment of Latin American adults from the top income decile. The Bajares couple (Family B) are also both 35 years old, but each has only about four years of schooling—the average for the bottom three income deciles. We will use these two fictional families to answer the following questions. How unequal would their incomes be if they lived in different countries of the region? How different would their choices be about labor market participation? How many children would they decide to have? And how much education would their children receive?

In this experiment, the people remain constant; only the environment changes. If the outcomes vary greatly from one country to another or they experience vastly different inequality, the blame cannot be placed on the educational gap, per se, which is going to remain the same. Rather, the inequality must be coming from the context, either directly through such factors as returns to education, indirectly through its influence upon the couples' decisions regarding labor force participation and how many children they have, or from other country-specific factors.

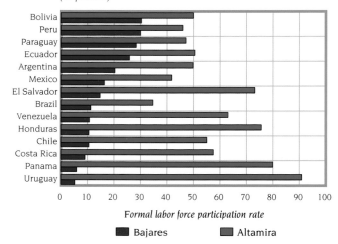

Figure 3.29a. The Altamira and Bajares Families: Women's Formal Labor Force Participation
(*In percent*)

Formal labor force participation rate

■ Bajares   ■ Altamira

Source: IDB simulations based on recent household surveys. See the Appendix for details.

Labor Force Participation

As noted earlier, men's labor force participation is generally high regardless of income level, so both Mr. Altamira and Mr. Bajares are more than 80 percent likely to be in the labor force. Interestingly, Ms. Altamira and Ms. Bajares are also equally likely to be in the labor force; the average difference by country is about 3 percent, with the largest projected gaps in urban Bolivia and Peru. Nevertheless, Ms. Altamira is much more likely to be working in the formal sector than Ms. Bajares (Figure 3.29a). In fact, for the region as a whole, Ms. Altamira is about 40 percent more likely to have a formal sector job than Ms. Bajares, with the largest predicted gaps in Panama and Uruguay, and the lowest in urban Bolivia and Peru. This demonstrates a key socioeconomic difference between different countries and their impact on family behavior. For example, with only four years of education in Uruguay, Ms. Bajares is at a substantial disadvantage relative to a population with a much higher average level of educational attainment. Her options are strongly restricted to informal activities, in contrast with Ms. Altamira. Also, the relatively small size of the formal sector in countries like Peru and Ecuador means that even Ms. Altamira has a somewhat low probability of getting one of these better kinds of jobs. The implications of being in different sectors are important because of the wide gap between formal and informal wages—more than 20 percent on average. The widely differing experiences simulated by the model are remarkable, given that the only difference between the two women is their education.

Figure 3.29b. The Altamira and Bajares Families: Number of Children

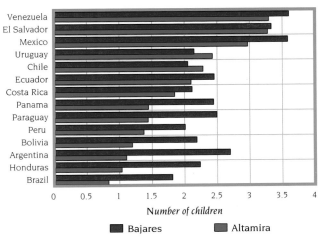

Source: IDB simulations based on recent household surveys. See the Appendix for details.

Figure 3.29c. The Altamira and Bajares Families: Children's Educational Attainment

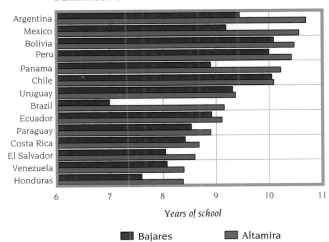

Source: IDB simulations based on recent household surveys. See the Appendix for details.

Number of Children

The number of children these couples are expected to have varies significantly depending on which country they are in (Figure 3.29b). Almost everywhere, the Bajares would be likely to have more children. In the countries with the largest expected families—Venezuela, El Salvador and Mexico—each couple would be expected to have three or four children, while in Brazil and Honduras, they would be expected to have one or two. However, the largest gaps between the two families can be found in the urban samples of Argentina and Bolivia (1.6 and 1.0, respectively), along with Honduras (1.2), Panama (1.0), Paraguay (1.1), and Brazil (1.0). These gaps in the number of children, which are purely a consequence of the expected effects of differing educational levels, contribute to income inequality across households.

Children's Attainment

The difference between the couples in terms of levels of education also generates very different patterns in their children's educational attainment (Figure 3.29c). On average, the children in a family like the Altamiras would complete 9.8 years of schooling, while the Bajares' children would complete only nine. The highest attainment for children of more educated parents would be found in urban Argentina, Mexico, Panama and Brazil; the lowest in Venezuela and Honduras. For the Bajares' children, educational attainment would be highest in the urban

samples of Bolivia and Argentina, Mexico and Peru, while it would be lowest in Honduras, El Salvador and Venezuela. The gap between the educational attainment of the Bajares' and Altamira's children would be lowest in Chile and urban Uruguay. This same gap would be greatest in Mexico, Panama, Argentina and Brazil—the same countries where the Altamira's children would have the highest expected attainment. The combined effects of parents' education, labor force participation and number of children upon educational attainment of children varies across countries, but in almost all cases it generates gaps that can be expected to perpetuate income inequality in the future.

The Income Gap: Direct and Indirect Effects of Education Gaps

The resulting income gaps between the two families, solely generated by their different educational levels, are generally large and vary significantly across countries. We can now distinguish two different steps in the chain of effects caused by differing educational levels. The first step, discussed in Chapter 2, is the impact of education on individual labor earnings and, consequently, upon the distribution of income across individuals. This is shown in Figure 3.30 as a labor earnings effect. If the Altamiras and Bajares went to Peru, both worked, and had no children, the income of the Altamiras would be 50 percent higher than that of the Bajares; with the same experience in Mexico, the gap would be over 150 percent.

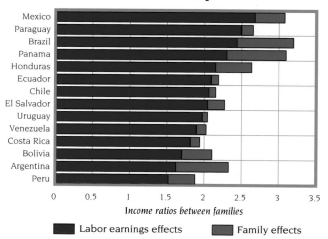

Figure 3.30. The Altamira and Bajares Families: The Income Gap

Income ratios between families

■ Labor earnings effects   ■ Family effects

Note: Income ratio is based on the expected per capita household income for each family.
Source: IDB simulations based on recent household surveys. See the Appendix for details.

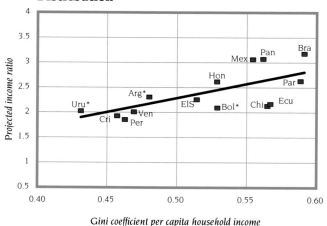

Figure 3.31. The Altamira and Bajares Families: Income Ratio and Income Distribution

Gini coefficient per capita household income

* Countries with urban data only.
Source: IDB simulations based on recent household surveys. See the Appendix for details.

The second step estimates the expected impact of education on income through family effects. That is, using the analysis developed in this chapter, we can calculate the effect on household income that would result from the differences in the expected decisions by the Altamiras and Bajares with respect to seeking jobs and having children. This family effect is also shown in Figure 3.30. It is much smaller than the direct impact of education upon income gaps that results from returns to education in the workforce. Nevertheless, it does exacerbate the expected income gap between the two families in all countries. In some cases, the family effect is rather small, such as in Ecuador, Chile, and Uruguay. In others, the effects are quite large, notably in Argentina, Brazil and Panama. In all cases, the combined results are quite remarkable considering that the Altamira and Bajares families differ only with respect to their education, and therefore can account for some of the income inequality in each country to differing degrees.

The income gaps between the Altamiras and the Bajares—which differ so markedly from country to country despite the fact that their personal education and age is the same—are strongly correlated with the actual levels of income inequality (Figure 3.31). These differences in per capita family income reflect the different wages families earn, their choices regarding participation in the labor market, and the number of children they decide to have. The simulation captures 25 percent of the variation in the Gini index. This is quite an achievement, considering that the results are abstracted from other factors that

affect income inequality in the various countries, including the distribution of earnings associated with individual educational attainment (see Chapter 2), rural and urban differences, and the distribution of assets. Hence, the travels of the Altamiras and the Bajares show us both the relevance and limitations of education and family effects on income inequality.

CONCLUSIONS

This chapter has examined the interrelated nature of critical choices that vary systematically with income distribution: labor force participation, fertility and educational attainment. It highlighted the critical role played by education for women, and along with it the opportunity cost for women of participating in the market. A high return for women in the labor force contributes to high participation, fewer children, and higher educational attainment by those children. That is the virtuous circle. However, this process depends not only on the educational attainment of the mother, but also on other factors that vary dramatically across the region. These variations were illustrated by simulating how the income gap between two hypothetical families would vary even though the characteristics of the family themselves remained constant. Different countries generate very different levels of inequality for these families. Hence, their education, age and location, as such, cannot fully explain the varying degrees of inequality across Latin America. Other factors in the structure of the economy are making wage gaps larger in some countries and smaller in others. Other factors are encouraging otherwise similar women to work at home, or seek out jobs in the informal or formal sectors. Even such personal choices as the number of children to have and how much resources to put into their education appear to be influenced, in the aggregate, by some important factors that go beyond individual characteristics and encompass factors in the broader market and society.

What broader factors could explain the differences that remain after accounting for the personal characteristics of the household? Part of the answer lies in the wages commanded by different levels of education, i.e., returns to schooling, which reflect the structure of supply and demand for people with different levels of education. High returns reflect, in part, a relative abundance of people with very low educational attainment, and a relative scarcity of highly educated individuals. However, these low levels of educational attainment are themselves partly a consequence of earlier educational outcomes that influenced fertility and educational attainment in previ-

ous generations. Part of the answer lies also in the demand for labor and the effectiveness of labor markets, which are themselves functions of technologies, productivity, organization of firms, and public economic policies. And the answer also has to do with the sensitivity of family decisions regarding labor force participation, fertility or educational attainment to relative "prices" such as wages for the skilled and unskilled, for formal and informal jobs, and for men and women.

Hence, by traveling this microeconomic road we have hit upon a macroeconomic and societal boundary. Forces larger than the characteristics of the families are driving a large part of income inequality; factors that lead otherwise similar people in different countries to make different choices. As this complex web of factors generates unequal incomes, it also feeds back into different choices regarding participation, fertility and attainment, so that over time households may become even more unequal in their family characteristics. The next chapter seeks to uncover what these larger economy-wide forces, including public policies, might be.

APPENDIX

Female Labor Market Participation Decisions

Female participation decisions have been studied extensively. A problem with econometric estimates is data availability; specifically, it is difficult to obtain a good measure of the opportunity cost that a woman faces when she decides to participate actively in the labor market or not. One way of tackling the issue is to produce a variable that approximates the income that a person would obtain in the labor market if he or she were to participate, and then use this to see if the decision to participate is statistically associated with this measure. This approach is followed here.

The exercise requires a two-stage process. In the first stage, we estimate wage regressions in the following form:

$$\ln(y_i) = c + \beta_1 e_i + \beta_2 \exp_i + \beta_3 \exp_i^2 + \beta_4 urb_i + u_i$$

where the dependent variable is the logarithm of the income of each earner, e represents the number of years of education of person i, exp denotes experience (measured as the age minus six, minus the years of education),[1] $\exp^2$ is its squared value, and urb is a dummy variable for urban areas. The regression is performed separately for men and women, correcting for sample selection bias.[2]

We use the estimated coefficients to predict the income (denoted y*) that each person would obtain if he or she participated in the labor market by using his or her education, experience and location. Then we use y* as an independent variable in a multinomial logit equation in the following form:

$$\ln(p_i) = c + \gamma_1 nkids_i + \gamma_2 y_f^* + \gamma_3 y_m^* + \gamma_4 urb_i + \gamma_5 age_i + u_i$$

where nkids is the number of children each female has, y_f^* is the predicted income of the female in question, y_m^* is the predicted income of the male spouse or male household head, and age is a dummy variable for age. The variable p_i is a variable that takes the value of 0 if woman i is not participating in the labor market, 1 if she participates in the informal sector, and 2 if she participates in the formal sector of the economy.

The coefficients from the multinomial logit estimation are presented in Table 3A.2.

With these two equations we performed several simulations. For example, given the coefficients and the mean value of the wage regression, one can estimate the income of a prototype person by simply multiplying the coefficients by the assumed education, experience and location. With this information we predict y_m^* and y_f^*, respectively, and if we had the number of children that each woman has, her age and her rural-urban location, we could multiply them by the coefficients of the multinomial logit regression to obtain the predicted probabilities of being types 0, 1 or 2.[3] With this method, one can vary the education of the woman, the education or income of the male head or male spouse, the number of children and the age to assess the impact on the probabilities of participating in the labor market.

Obviously, this kind of exercise is subject to econometric problems such as endogeneity. This is the case especially with variables such as the number of children in the household. Unfortunately, it is difficult to get around this problem with the information from household surveys because it is almost impossible to construct good instrumental variables. Several robustness tests were performed to the estimates presented in Table 3A.2 to check whether the conclusions changed when attempting to substitute the variable nkids with constructed instruments. The conclusions derived from the results did not vary from any of these estimates.

Fertility Decisions

One limitation of household survey data is that it typically does not contain retrospective fertility histories of household members. Typically, we are able to count the number of children living in a household and identify their mother, but we do not know if the woman has other children living elsewhere. Therefore, rather than strictly looking at fertility, the focus is on the number of children in the household, and whether this number is significantly correlated with other variables.

To perform the simulations on fertility discussed in the main text, we performed an exercise similar to the one described in the previous section. We also took a two-stage approach, where first we estimated earnings equations to predict y_m^* and y_f^* and then we used these predicted income-earning potentials in a regression where the dependent variable is the number of children in the household, and the independent variables are y_m^* and y_f^*

---

[1] To measure experience, the number of children each woman has is taken into consideration. The assumption is that a woman loses one year of labor market experience per child.

[2] For Argentina, Bolivia and Uruguay only urban data are available, so the dummy variable is not included.

[3] To assess the probabilities, we make the corresponding transformations to the coefficients so that they yield the predicted probabilities.

and the urban-rural location dummy.[4] With these two equations we can simulate the number of children that a prototype person would have, and test for the sensibility of that result to the education of the mother, the education and income of the male spouse or male household head, etc. by multiplying the regression coefficients by the mean values of the variables in question.

Binding the Stories Together

To put together the family's decisionmaking process regarding participation, fertility and children's education, a recursive model was estimated of earnings, participation, number of children and educational attainment of those children and estimated for 14 Latin American countries. Since all these are interrelated decisions, we estimate a simultaneous equation system following these steps:

First, we run an earnings regression of the following:

$$\ln(y_i) = c + \beta_1 e_i + \beta_2 \exp_i + \beta_3 \exp_i^2 + \beta_4 urb_i + u_i$$

with which we predict y_m^* and y_f^* as in the exercises previously described.

The predicted variables y_m^* and y_f^*, which represent the income generating potential of a person with a certain degree of education, experience and location, feed into the following regression:

$$nkids^* = c + \alpha_1 y_f^* + \alpha_3 y_m^* + \alpha_3 urb_i + \gamma_5 age_i + u_i$$

where the idea is that the coefficients of this regression can be used to predict the variable nkids for each household, based only on the opportunity cost (proxied by the earnings potential variables) and location. We denote nkids* the number of children in each household predicted by y_m^* and y_f^* and urb. From this perspective, the only reason why two couples in the urban sector would choose to have a different number of children is because they have different educational levels, and because the returns to their education (the opportunity cost) differ.

Thirdly, we reestimate the multinomial logit described at the beginning of this Appendix by running the following regression:

$$\ln(p_i) = c + \gamma_1 nkids_i^* + \gamma_2 y_f^* + \gamma_3 y_m^* + \gamma_4 urb_i + \gamma_5 age_i + u_i$$

where nkids has been substituted for nkids*. With the coefficients from this regression and the average values for y_m^*, y_f^*, nkids*, urb, and the age of each female, we can predict the probability of being out of the labor force, or participating in the informal or formal sector, which

we label p_1^* and p_2^* respectively.

Fourthly, we estimate earnings equations of the same form as in the first stage regression above, but we run them separately for men and for women in the formal and informal sectors, respectively. The coefficients allow us to predict the following income-earnings potentials

$y_m, f^* = $ income of males in the formal sector
$y_m, i^* = $ income of males in the informal sector
$y_f, f^* = $ income of females in the formal sector
$y_f, i^* = $ income of females in the informal sector

We estimate the income per capita of each family through the following formula:

$$ypc_i = \{y_m^* + [p_1 y_{f,1}^* + p_2 y_{f,2}^*]\}/(nkids^* + 2)$$

The formula says that the estimated income per capita (ypc*) of family i is calculated by adding up the predicted income of a male with a certain education, experience and geographic location, with the income of the female computed as the estimated probability (p_1^*) of being in the informal sector times the informal sector predicted income (the income is also predicted based on education, experience and rural-urban location), plus the estimated probability of being in the formal sector (p_2^*) times the formal sector predicted income. All this is divided by the number of children expected of a couple with a certain education, experience and rural-urban location, plus two adults to account for total family size.

Finally, we estimated the educational attainment of each family with the following regression:

$$educkids_i^* = c + \eta_1 y_m^* + \eta_2 [p_1^* y_{f,1}^* + p_2^* y_{f,2}^*]\} \eta_3 nkids^* + \eta_4 sex_i + u_i$$

where educkidsi* represents the predicted educational attainment of the child, and sex is a dummy variable for the gender of the child.

Therefore, the system of equations uses the number of years of education, experience and geographic location as exogenous variables, and with this information it predicts the income earning potential in the formal and informal sectors, the probability for females of being out of the labor force or in the formal or informal sectors, the number of children that a couple with the above characteristics would have, and their attainment. The main advantage is that, as explained in the text, the methodology allows simulations of several scenarios by making an explicit distinction between the effects of the number of years of schooling (the quantity effect), and the returns to education (the price effect).

---

4 This second-stage regression was only estimated for the sample of 35-40 year old females.

Table 3A.1. Dependent Variable:
Probability of 15–18 Year Olds Being Enrolled in School

Independent Variable	Argentina	Bolivia	Brazil	Chile	Costa Rica	Ecuador	El Salvador	Honduras	Mexico	Panama	Paraguay	Peru	Uruguay	Venezuela
Age	-0.0891**	-0.0292**	-0.0811**	-0.0382**	-0.0911**	-0.0643**	-0.0963**	-0.1466**	-0.1446**	-0.0571**	-0.1070**	-0.0691**	-0.0818**	-0.0937**
Gender	-0.0186	0.0026	-0.0329**	-0.0224**	-0.0693**	-0.0110	-0.0024	-0.1104**	0.0705**	-0.0350**	0.0463*	0.0087	-0.0912**	-0.0955**
Father's education	0.0131**	0.0071**	0.0119**	0.0043**	0.0174**	0.0225**	0.0126**	0.0217**	0.0201**	0.0052**	0.0171**	0.0102**	0.0144**	0.0086**
Mother's education	0.0242**	0.0051**	0.0210**	0.0177**	0.0326**	0.0335**	0.0271**	0.0287**	0.0303**	0.0140**	0.0269**	0.0071**	0.0214**	0.0253**
Log of household pc income	0.0841**	-0.0056	0.0299**	0.0092*	-0.0033	0.0013	0.0118	0.0277*	-0.0036	0.0314**	0.0119	-0.0166**	0.0538**	-0.0213**
Urban-rural			0.0970**	0.0730**	0.1618**	0.1943**	0.2472**	0.1881**	0.1263**	0.1394**	0.2141**	0.1438**		0.1196**
No. of other children in household	-0.0482**	-0.0050**	-0.0079**	-0.0209**	-0.0347**	-0.0279**	-0.0045	-0.0096*	-0.0363**	-0.0187**	-0.0173**	-0.0185**	-0.0279**	-0.0146**
Mother participates	-0.0579	0.0258**	0.0432**	0.0050	0.0561**	0.0416*	0.0593**	0.0605**	0.0442**	0.0208	0.1302**	-0.0105	0.0334**	0.0054
No. elderly members of household	-0.0481	0.0478**	0.0259**	0.0437**	0.0740**	0.1074**	0.0593**	0.0546**	0.0643**	-0.0218	0.0779**	-0.0019	0.0618**	0.0782**

*Statistically significant at the 95 percent level.
**Statistically significant at the 99 percent level.

Table 3A.2. Coefficients from Multinomial Logit Regression
Dependent Variable, Female Labor Market Participation (Baseline, p = 0)

p = 1	Argentina	Bolivia	Brazil	Chile	Costa Rica	Ecuador	El Salvador	Honduras	Mexico	Panama	Paraguay	Peru	Uruguay	Venezuela
Number of children	-0.11	-0.00	-0.03	-0.14	-0.05	-0.06	-0.04	-0.06	-0.01	-0.04	0.01	-0.09	-0.06	-0.07
Women, income	-1.28	-2.23	-0.10	-0.61	0.19	-0.75	-0.39	0.12	-0.11	-0.44	-0.37	-2.46	-0.72	-0.59
Men, income	-0.45	-0.24	-0.19	-0.14	-0.19	-0.13	-0.21	-0.34	-0.36	-0.39	-0.01	-0.21	-0.06	-0.14
Urban-rural			0.57	1.07	0.16	0.28	0.97	0.46	0.10	0.27	-0.74	0.04		0.57
Age 20-25	0.19	0.63	0.17	0.25	0.15	0.28	0.38	0.47	0.52	0.30	0.22	0.19	0.18	0.29
Age 25-30	0.53	0.74	0.24	0.49	0.05	0.27	0.75	0.45	0.43	0.77	0.55	0.29	0.30	0.52
Age 30-35	0.47	0.92	0.19	0.62	0.24	0.33	0.43	0.46	0.26	0.61	0.46	0.41	0.38	0.42
Age 35-40	0.25	0.78	0.14	0.36	-0.13	0.28	0.37	0.16	0.26	0.43	0.41	-0.02	0.22	0.13
Age 40-45	0.00	0.38	-0.01	0.11	-0.52	-0.34	0.08	-0.03	-0.05	0.31	0.32	-0.24	-0.04	-0.39
Age 45-50	-0.64	-0.39	-0.37	-0.35	-0.99	-0.43	-0.28	-0.07	-0.38	-0.47	0.21	-0.58	-0.78	-0.66
Constant	3.49	5.69	-1.65	2.94	-1.39	7.34	0.38	-0.24	0.09	-0.38	3.60	5.92	7.68	2.91
p = 2														
Number of children	-0.19	0.02	-0.17	-0.17	-0.11	-0.03	-0.05	-0.06	-0.18	-0.11	-0.03	0.05	-0.17	-0.04
Women, income	2.37	3.07	1.05	2.07	2.04	1.94	2.21	2.54	1.92	2.54	1.97	2.76	1.59	2.11
Men, income	-0.45	-0.23	-0.26	-0.13	-0.24	-0.12	-0.27	-0.43	-0.38	-0.33	-0.07	-0.20	-0.06	-0.15
Urban-rural			1.27	0.19	0.28	-1.33	0.32	0.38	-0.29	0.21	-0.68	-2.23		-0.05
Age 20-25	-0.12	0.08	-0.13	-0.13	-0.28	0.05	0.13	-0.25	0.20	0.09	-0.28	-0.12	-0.01	0.22
Age 25-30	-0.11	-0.17	-0.27	-0.23	-0.34	0.18	0.29	-0.09	-0.09	0.53	-0.26	-0.22	0.00	0.42
Age 30-35	-0.26	-0.41	-0.51	-0.37	-0.61	0.10	-0.60	-0.76	-0.40	0.00	-0.18	-0.26	-0.12	0.24
Age 35-40	-0.79	-0.87	-0.98	-0.95	-0.84	-0.65	-0.80	-0.67	-0.84	-0.22	-1.07	-0.49	-0.64	0.05
Age 40-45	-0.91	-1.62	-1.47	-1.21	-1.66	-0.51	-1.31	-1.41	-0.99	-1.05	-0.90	-1.07	-0.99	-0.58
Age 45-50	-1.72	-2.36	-1.98	-1.89	-2.71	-1.18	-2.23	-1.60	-2.33	-2.95	-0.58	-1.74	-1.92	-1.52
Constant	-5.36	-8.89	-3.84	-15.03	-13.20	-16.21	-7.26	-7.51	-5.31	-4.96	-18.02	-4.75	-16.56	-13.80

REFERENCES

Barros, R., S. Duryea, and M. Székely. 1998. What Is Behind the Latin American Income Inequality? Office of the Chief Economist, Inter American Development Bank. Mimeo.

Becker, Gary S. 1964. *Human Capital*. 1st edition. New York: Colombia University Press for the National Bureau of Economic Research.

_____.1991. *The Economics of the Family*. Cambridge: Harvard University Press, Second Edition.

Becker, G., K.M. Murphy, and R. Tamura. 1990. Human Capital, Fertility and Economic Growth. *Journal of Political Economy* 98(5) October.

Behrman, J. R. 1998. Intrahousehold Allocation of Nutrients in Rural India: Are Boys Favored? Do Parents Exhibit Inequality Aversion? *Oxford Economic Papers* 40.

_____. 1997. Women's Schooling and Child Education: A Survey. University of Pennsylvania, Philadelphia. Mimeo.

Behrman, J.R., and J. Knowles. 1997. How Strong is Child Schooling Associated with Household Income? University of Pennsylvania, Philadelphia. Mimeo.

Behrman, J.R., and B.L. Wolfe. 1984. Labor Force Participation and Earnings Determinants for Women in the Special Conditions of Developing Countries. *Journal of Development Economics* 15: 259-88.

Birdsall, N., and R. Sabot, eds. 1991. Unfair Advantage: Labor Market Discrimination in Developing Countries. World Bank.

Bourguignon, F., and Chiappori P. 1992. Collective Models of Household Behavior. *European Economic Review* 36.

Cigno, Alessandro. 1991. *Economics of the Family*. Oxford: Clarendon Press.

Connelly, Rachel, Deborah S. DeGraff, and Deborah Levison. 1996. Women's Employment and Child Care in Brazil. *Economic Development and Cultural Change* 44(3-4): 619-56

Dahan, M., and Tsiddon. 1998. Demographic Transition, Income Distribution and Economic Growth. *Journal of Economic Growth* (March).

Deutsch, R. 1998. Does Child Care Pay? Labor Force Participation and Earnings Effects of Access to Child Care in the Favelas of Rio de Janeiro. Poverty and Inequality Advisory Unit, Inter-American Development Bank, Washington, D.C. Mimeo.

Duryea, S., and Lam. Effects of Schooling on Fertility, Labor Supply, and Investment in Children, with Evidence from Brazil. *Journal of Human Resources*. Forthcoming.

Duryea, S., and M. Székely. 1998. *Labor Markets in Latin America: A Supply-Side Story*. Working Paper No. 374, Office of the Chief Economist, Inter American Development Bank, Washington, D.C.

Engle, Patrice L. 1991. Maternal Work and Child Care Strategies in Peri-Urban Guatemala: Nutritional Effects. *Child Development* 62: 954-65

Galor, O., and Weil. 1996. The Gender Gap, Fertility and Growth. *American Economic Review* 86.

Gonzales de la Rocha, M. 1998. *The Resources of Poverty*. Blackwell Publishers.

Haddad, Lawrence, and Ravi Kanbur. 1992. Intrahousehold Inequality and the Theory of Targeting. *European Economic Review* 36.

Hill, M.A. 1983. Female Labor Force Participation in Developing and Developed Countries—Consideration of the Informal Sector. *Review of Economics and Statistics* 63(3):459-68.

Kapteyn, Arie, and Peter Kooreman. 1992. Household Labor Supply: What Kind of Data Can Tell us How Many Decision Makers There Are? *European Economic Review* 36.

Katz, Elizabeth. 1997. The Intra-Household Economics of Voice and Exit: Evaluating the Feminist-Institutional Content of Family Resource Allocation Models. Columbia University. Mimeo.

Pitt, Mark, and Rosenzweig Mark R. 1986. Agricultural Prices, Food Consumption, and the Health and Productivity of Indonesian Farmers. In *Agricultural Household Models*, I. Singh, L. Squire, and J. Strauss. Baltimore: The Johns Hopkins University Press.

Psacharopoulos, G., and Z. Tzannatos. 1992. Women's Employment and Pay in Latin America: Overview and Methodology. World Bank.

Sen, A.. 1984. Economics and the Family. In *Resources, Values and Development*, A. Sen, ed. Oxford: B.Blackwell..

Singh I., L. Squire and J. Strauss. 1986. In *Agricultural Household Models: Extensions and Applications*. Baltimore: The Johns Hopkins University Press.

Sorrentino, C. 1990. The Changing Family in an International Perspective. *Monthly Labor Review*: 41-58.

Székely, M. 1998 *The Economics of Poverty, Inequality and Wealth Accumulation in Mexico*. London: Macmillan, and New York: St. Martin's Press.

Wong, R., and R. Levine. 1992. The Effect of Household Structure on Women's Economic Activity and Fertility: Evidence from Recent Mothers in Urban Mexico. *Economic Development and Cultural Change* 41(1): 89-102.

Chapter 4

THE ROLE OF
THE ECONOMIC ENVIRONMENT

The preceding chapters have explored the determinants of income inequality at the level of the individuals and families who live, work and raise their children within a national economy. We have seen that certain key characteristics of the individuals in the family, most notably the education of the household's adult members, are important determinants of the household's decisions about labor force participation, fertility and the education of the children. The household's decisions interact with the economic environment that surrounds them—wages and employment opportunities—to determine household income and the earning capacity of the next generation. The message has been that a substantial part of income inequality in the region is attributable to differences across households in educational attainment and in other characteristics that determine household earning capacity. Thus, an important part of the Latin American income inequality story is that education and other determinants of earning capacity are unequally distributed across the population.

This is an important part of the story, the policy implications of which are very different from those that would have followed, for example, from a finding that the large differences in household earnings were inexplicable and unrelated to education or other individual characteristics. But we have also learned that this is not the whole story. This is so for two reasons. First, we have so far shed only limited light on why the distribution of education and other determinants of earning capacity are so skewed in Latin

America, and why they are so much more skewed in some countries of the region than in others.

And further, we have uncovered evidence that a given difference in educational attainment or some other determinant of earning capacity generates much more inequality in some countries of the region than it does in others. It seems that in some countries there is something about the economic environment that translates a given difference in educational attainment into a larger difference in earning capacity, thus generating more unequal distribution of income, which is then amplified and transmitted to the next generation through the family decisions described in the previous chapter.

To understand this part of the story, we turn our attention away from detailed investigations of individual household behavior within a country, where households face a relatively common economic environment, and toward comparisons across countries, where we find some key differences in the underlying economic environment. We can then try to learn how these differences affect distribution of income.

To motivate the discussion that follows, let us return for a moment to the Altamira and Bajares families introduced in Chapter 3. The families were identical in all respects except in the education of the family's adults. The more educated Altamira family had higher income than the Bajares family in all countries of the region, but that gap in income was much larger in some countries than in others; something about the economic environ-

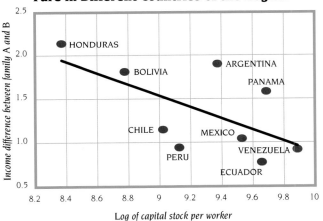

Figure 4.1. How the Altamiras and Bajares Fare in Different Countries of the Region

Log of capital stock per worker

Income difference between family A and B

Source: *IDB calculations based on recent household surveys, and Technical Appendix.*

ment was acting to magnify inequality in some countries. Figure 4.1 suggests that this aspect of the economic environment is not random or inexplicable, but is instead related to key characteristics of the economy in which the families are embedded. The figure suggests that in those countries of the region where workers have more capital to work with, the gap between the incomes of the Altamiras and the Bajares tends to be substantially smaller than in countries where less capital has been accumulated. This experiment seems to suggest that economic development promotes a more egalitarian distribution of income.

This chapter examines the international experience to explore in more detail the idea that certain aspects of the economic environment tend to promote income inequality. The stage of economic development is indeed importantly related to the distribution of income, and this factor helps explain why the distribution of income is so much more unequal in Latin America than it is in the industrial countries. We are also able to shed some light on the mechanisms through which the stage of development affects the distribution of income.

But we also find that the stage of development is only part of the story. After accounting for its stage of development, Latin America remains by international standards a region of very high income inequality. We thus turn to some other dimensions of the economic environment that may help to explain this excess inequality. While this investigation is exploratory, and hampered in some key respects by data limitations, the evidence suggests that the region's endowments of land and natural resources, including factors related to climate and geography, appear to have played an important role. We also find, not completely unrelated to this, that Latin America's volatile macroeconomic environment accounts for a significant share of the region's excess inequality. We say "not unrelated" because we also uncover evidence that this volatility results in part from the large external shocks that affect the region, which are themselves related to the region's rich endowment of natural resources.

The story is thus a complex one, in which circumstances associated with Latin America's stage of economic development interact with longer-lasting characteristics of the region, including its geography and climate, and its endowments of land and natural resources, to determine the income inequality observed today. But while we will have relatively little to say about policy until subsequent chapters, the explanations for income inequality provided here are not deterministic ones that leave no scope for remediation by good policies, or aggravation by bad policies. Indeed, one important motivation for laying out as fully as we can the underlying determi-

nants of income inequality is to lay the foundation for a more complete and productive strategy for policies to address the inequalities that may be generated by the region's history and economic circumstances.

INEQUALITY AND STAGES OF DEVELOPMENT

Perhaps the oldest and most prominent empirical speculation about the distribution of income focused on the development process as a key driver. The idea was that very primitive economies, in which virtually all of the population engages in very simple and labor-intensive activities, were likely to be very equal. During the process of development workers are pulled from the traditional sector into a gradually expanding "modern" sector with higher productivity and wages. This opens up an important wage gap between workers in the traditional and the modern sectors, and inequality thus emerges and increases in the early stages of development. By the end of the process every worker would be in the modern sector, earning roughly similar wages, and thus inequality would decline once again in the later stages of development. This story suggests a hump-shaped relationship between the level of development and income inequality, in which inequality first rises then declines as development proceeds, a relationship that came to be known as the Kuznets curve, after the economist who elaborated the idea in a famous 1955 paper.

Figure 4.2 illustrates the relationship between the stage of development, as measured by purchasing-parity adjusted income per capita, and income inequality. It also shows the predicted value implied by the statistical relationship that relates income inequality to per capita income and the squared value of per capita income.[1] Though some recent studies have had difficulty identifying a Kuznets curve relationship between income and inequality, in our data set there is in fact evidence of such a hump-shaped relationship between per capita income and inequality.

However, the upward-sloping part of the relationship between income and inequality appears to be relevant only for a few countries with very low income levels. The dominant feature of the relationship between development and inequality is a fairly strong tendency for inequality to decline as income rises. In particular,

---

[1] We used the log of per capita income rather than the level, so that equal changes in the variable would correspond to percentage rather than absolute changes in per capita income. We also conducted the same analysis using (the log of) per capita income and its inverse, as suggested by Anand and Kanbur (1993), with essentially identical results to those reported above. See the Technical Appendix for the regression results that are summarized in the figure.

Figure 4.2. Development and Income Distribution

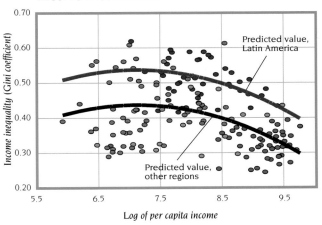

Note: In this and all subsequent figures, Latin American observations are graphed in red, the industrial economies are shown in blue, emerging East Asian economies are shown in green, and other countries are shown in grey. For the purposes of this report, emerging East Asia comprises Hong Kong, Indonesia, Korea, Malaysia, Singapore, Taiwan and Thailand.
Source: See Technical Appendix.

Figure 4.3. Development and Income Distribution, 1982-92

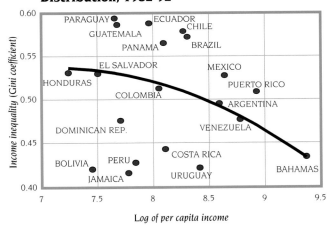

Source: See Technical Appendix.

Figure 4.4. Income Inequality and Capital Intensity

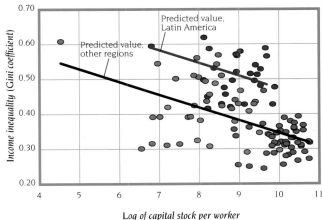

Source: See Technical Appendix.

America than in the rest of the world, we also included a dummy variable for Latin America in the statistical relationship. The results suggest that the stage of development cannot explain all of Latin America's inequality; at any given level of development, Latin America exhibits roughly 10 percentage points more inequality than does the rest of the world.

Economic development is associated with changes in the distribution of income because it involves economic and social transitions that affect the position of different economic and social groups. Here we discuss five of these transitions: the accumulation of physical capital, which affects the returns to labor; the educational transition, which affects the returns to skilled workers; the demographic transition, which carries with it profound implications for family size, labor force participation and educational attainment; urbanization; and formalization of the workforce.

Capital Accumulation Is Associated with Less Income Inequality

Development is, in essence, the accumulation of capital, both physical and human. It is natural therefore to begin with the role of capital accumulation. As Figure 4.4 illustrates, there is in fact a strong negative correlation between inequality and capital accumulation.

It is easy to understand how an increase in the stock of capital with which labor can work might affect the distribution of income. Basic economic theory suggests that, as capital is accumulated and becomes less scarce, the return that it earns should fall, while the return that is earned by other factors of production, such as skilled and

few of Latin America's economies have income levels low enough to put them in the range where increased income would be associated with an increase in inequality, though several of them are near the peak of the estimated curve.

This predicted relationship between per capita income and inequality suggests that development is a powerful force; as a country moves from the level of development that puts it at the peak of the hump to the per capita income that characterizes the industrial economies, the Gini coefficient is predicted to fall by over 10 percentage points.

To allow for the possibility that the relationship between development and inequality is different in Latin

Figure 4.5. Nonlabor Income Share Falls as Capital Intensity Rises

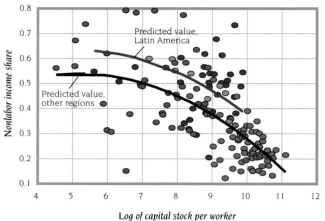

Source: See Technical Appendix.

Figure 4.6. Returns to Education Decline as Education Rises

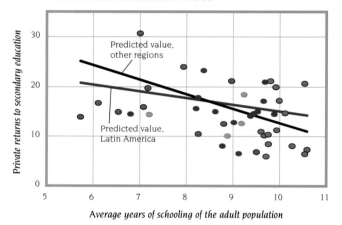

Note: Two observations with very high returns to education (Botswana and Zimbabwe) have been deleted from this chart to enhance readability. Source: See Technical Appendix.

unskilled workers, would rise. Since the returns to capital accrue disproportionately to a small and wealthy subset of the population, this change in factor returns would be expected to improve the distribution of income.

Internationally comparable data on wages and the return to capital are hard to find, but most countries report rough estimates of the share of income that accrues to workers in the form of labor compensation, and that which is earned by entrepreneurs and businesses. Using this information, we see that there is a strong association between capital intensity and factor payments.

Where capital is more abundant, labor compensation tends to comprise a larger share of the national income and nonlabor income's share declines. This implies

that the return to capital declines sharply as capital becomes more abundant, since, despite the rise in the amount of capital that is employed in the economy, capital income (the product of the return to capital and the stock of capital) declines as a share of total income. The counterpart of this decline is a rise in the share of income paid to skilled and unskilled labor. Since labor power and skills are much more equally distributed among the population than is ownership of claims on the economy's capital stock, this tends to be equalizing.

As seen in Chapter 3, these direct effects of capital accumulation on factor returns are only the beginning of the story, for the increase in wages and the expanded opportunities for market work associated with capital deepening also trigger important changes in labor force participation, fertility and education, with powerful implications for the distribution of income.

Educational Progress Affects Returns to Education, Reducing Inequality

Development involves not only the accumulation of investments in buildings and equipment, but also in the education of the workforce. High returns to and an unequal distribution of educational attainment are important sources of income inequality. How does the human capital accumulation that accompanies economic development affect these determinants of income inequality?

Just as with physical capital, the private returns to education would be expected to decline as the population becomes more educated. And as seen in Figure 4.6, the returns to secondary education do in fact tend to decrease in countries where the population is more educated.[2]

How important is this effect? On average in Latin America, the population between the ages of 25 and 65 possesses roughly 4.8 years of education, while in the industrial economies the same population possesses about 8.4 years. Figure 4.6 suggests that this difference in average educational attainment is associated with an increase in the private returns to education in Latin America of roughly 7 percentage points, an increase in wage differentials that would have a major impact on the distribution of income. This suggests that increasing educational attainment in the region could be highly equalizing for income distribution, even if the educational

---

[2] The returns to secondary education shown in Figure 4.6 and the remainder of this chapter are from Psacharopoulos (1994), and may differ in some instances from the computations presented in previous chapters.

progress were not accompanied by reductions in the inequality of educational attainment.

There is also an important interaction between human and physical capital accumulation, since the data suggest that, holding constant the population's average educational attainment, a larger supply of physical capital is associated with higher returns to education. This is consistent with the idea that capital-intensive industries also require skilled labor and implies that a country or region is likely to experience particularly high returns to education if its investment in people lags behind its investment in capital.

We have seen that development affects the distribution of income through its effects on factor returns. Development tends to be equalizing because it reduces the returns to human and physical capital, ownership of which tends to be concentrated in the hands of a relatively small, wealthy segment of the population. But this is not the end of the story, for educational progress is also associated with systematic changes in educational inequality. This relationship was discussed in Chapter 2, where it was explained that educational inequality tends to rise with educational progress at first, but eventually declines as progress continues. Educational inequality is thus, in part, a transitory byproduct of educational progress, a point that is highly relevant for Latin America since, while measures of aggregate inequality of educational attainment have been rising, the inequality of educational attainment within cohorts has already started to fall.

The impact of educational progress on inequality is thus something of an open question; while we expect such progress to drive down the premium that skilled workers earn and thus make the distribution of income more equal, it may at the same time be associated with an increase in educational inequality, which tends to increase income inequality. The international experience, summarized in Figure 4.7, suggests that, on balance, educational progress is in fact equalizing.

There is a strong negative relationship between educational attainment and income inequality, even after one controls for per capita income.[3] Other things being equal, educational progress is equalizing; we shall provide some estimates of the significance of this factor below.

The Demographic Transition

The previous chapter highlighted the strong links between female labor force participation, fertility and educational attainment, showing that in families at the lower end of

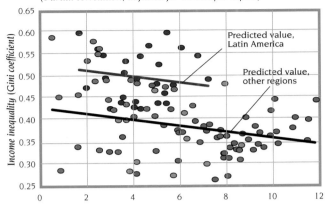

Figure 4.7. Inequality and Educational Attainment
(*Partial correlation, adjusted for income per capita*)

Average years of schooling of the adult

Source: See Technical Appendix.

the income distribution, labor force participation was generally low and families tended to be large, undermining the family's capacity to invest in their children's education. The opposite tended to be true of high-income families, where labor force participation is higher and families have fewer children who are provided with more education.

A central element of this story is the role of fertility decisions and family size as key influences over income inequality in both the current and subsequent generations. This is of great relevance to Latin America because, along with much of the rest of the world, the region has been undergoing a wrenching demographic transition from the high birth and death rates common only a few generations ago to a world with much lower rates of fertility and death, longer life spans, and correspondingly older populations. This transition is due in substantial part to important advances in medical technology and public health practices, and their gradual diffusion in recent decades through the developing world. These innovations reduced death rates, and particularly infant mortality, resulting in a substantial increase in population growth and a decrease in the average age of the population. Over time, fertility rates have declined, and in most of the developing world populations are now beginning to grow more slowly and to become older.

While the demographic transition through which most of the developing world is now passing is related to

---

[3] It is useful to control for per capita income to avoid confusing the effects of educational progress with other elements of the development process with which educational progress is likely to be correlated. If one does not control for per capita income, the correlation between education and the distribution of income is substantially stronger than that shown in Figure 4.7.

Figure 4.8. Development and Female Labor Force Participation

(*In percent*)

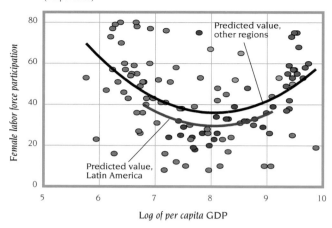

Source: See Technical Appendix.

Figure 4.9. Female Labor Force Participation and Population Growth

(*In percent*)

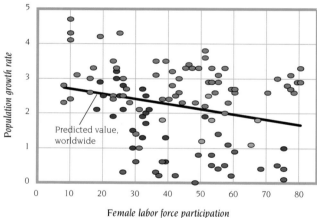

Source: See Technical Appendix.

Figure 4.10. Demography and Income Distribution

(*Partial correlation, adjusted for income per capita*)

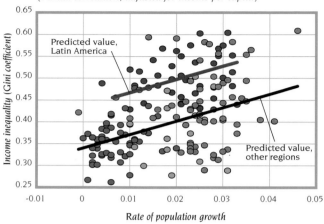

Source: See Technical Appendix.

medical advances of the past half century, it is also strongly related to economic development, since that process affects family decisions about fertility, labor force participation and education. Through these decisions, the demographic transition is having an important impact on the distribution of income.

As development proceeds and employment opportunities expand, it becomes increasingly advantageous for women to enter the labor market. At the same time, the process of urbanization that is typical of development, and the extension of water supplies, electrical power and communication networks, reduce the time and effort required to manage a household, making it easier for secondary earners to enter the labor force.

Figure 4.8 suggests that female participation in the labor force tends to follow a U-shaped pattern. It tends to be relatively high at very low levels of development, perhaps reflecting the fact that very low-income economies are predominantly rural, where female participation tends to be high, and that at very low income levels many women simply cannot afford to forgo work. Starting at low levels of income, female participation tends to decline as per capita income rises until, at moderate income levels, participation begins to rise along with income, reflecting the enhanced incentives and possibilities for workforce participation that we have discussed. The figure also shows that female labor force participation tends to be lower in Latin America than in other countries with similar income levels.

As Chapter 3 emphasized, the decision to participate in the workforce and the decision on how many children to raise are closely related. Families in which both parents are in the workforce tend to choose to have fewer children than families where the potential secondary earner stays out of the labor force and in the home. Thus, as economic development proceeds and female labor force participation rises, fertility rates and the rate of population growth tend to decline.

Development is thus an important driver of the demographic transition through its impact on the incentives and the possibilities for labor force participation that face families. What does this have to do with the distribution of income? Quite a lot, it seems. Figure 4.10 shows that there is a strong positive correlation between population growth and income inequality, even after controlling for the level of development. The association is very strong. Holding constant the level of development, Figure 4.10 suggests that a 2 percentage point decline in the rate of population growth would be associated with a reduction in the Gini coefficient of income inequality of more than 7 percentage points, more than a third of the actual difference in income inequality between Latin America and the industrial countries. And the link between demographic factors and income inequality is also evident within Latin America, as seen in Figure 4.11.

What explains this important link between demography and distribution? A number of explanations have been put forward. Some focus on implications for the age structure of the population growth. For example, it has been well documented that earnings differentials between skilled and unskilled workers tends to rise significantly as workers progress in their careers, and then decline significantly after workers retire.[4] Thus, in a population with many more experienced workers, earnings differentials created by differing educational attainments will be larger, and income inequality higher, than in a population where most of the workforce is young. This cannot, however, explain why countries with rapid population growth and younger populations tend to have higher, not lower, income inequality than countries with older populations.[5]

An alternative explanation arises from the interaction between the wages of unskilled workers, family decisions and inequality that we have been emphasizing in this report. In the previous chapter we saw that when the returns to employment are low, participation in the workforce is lower, families are larger, and education of children is more limited. In this view, high fertility rates and the associated rapid population growth reflect a situation in which the returns to market work are low compared with the benefits of staying home and having a larger family.

It is thus not surprising to see that educational attainment tends to be low in countries where population growth rates are high. Figure 4.12 illustrates the strong negative correlation between the average educational attainment of the adult population and the rate of population growth.

This correlation should of course not be read as a structural relationship in which the causality runs only from demography to educational attainment. It is likely that the reverse causality is important as well. Other things being equal, higher educational attainment is likely to be associated with lower rates of fertility and population growth. Indeed, this mutual relationship between fertility and the education decisions was a key point of the argument in Chapter 3. The very strong empirical relationship between fertility and education provides support for this story, which in turn helps us understand the strong empirical link between demography and the distribution of income.

Figure 4.11. Demography and Income Distribution

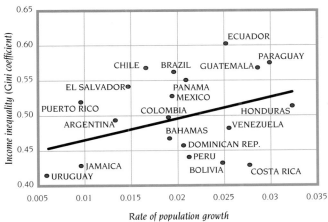

Source: See Technical Appendix.

Figure 4.12. Demography and Educational Attainment

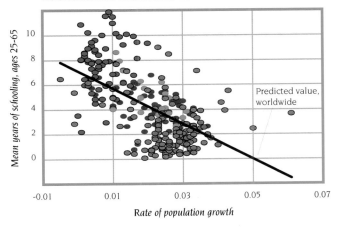

Source: See Technical Appendix.

But there is more. To the extent that high fertility and rapid population growth reflect an economic environment that offers low returns to market work, the effects are likely to be particularly strong in poor families, whose unskilled parents face the lowest rewards for entering the labor force. Rapid population growth should thus be associated not only with low levels of educational attainment on average, but also with a more unequal distribution of educational attainment across the population. And we do in fact see this.

---

[4] See Atkinson (1982, p.100) for evidence on industrial economies, and Duryea and Székely (1998) and Chapter 2 of this report for evidence on Latin America.
[5] On the other hand, if there are many retired workers, income inequality will tend to decline. There is some evidence that large retirement-age populations are associated with lower inequality; in a multivariate statistical framework, high rates of population growth—and therefore younger populations— are associated with higher inequality, while at the same time the share of the population over 65 is associated with significantly lower income inequality.

Figure 4.13. Demography and Educational Inequality
(*Partial correlation, controls for mean schooling*)

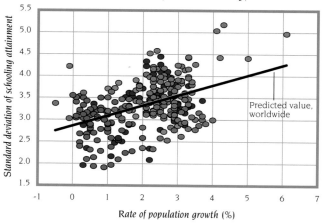

Source: *See Technical Appendix.*

Figure 4.14. Urbanization and Inequality
(*Partial correlation, controls for per capita income*)

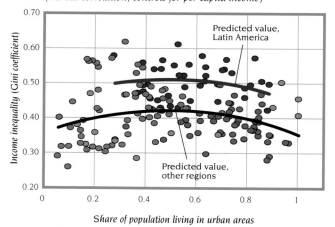

Source: *See Technical Appendix.*

After accounting for the relationship between average educational attainment and educational inequality discussed in Chapter 2, we see that there is a strong positive correlation between population growth and educational inequality, as measured by the standard deviation of educational attainment. This suggests that the underlying factors leading families to choose higher fertility rates are adversely affecting not only the country's rate of investment in human capital, but also the distribution of those investments across the population, with adverse consequences for the distribution of income.

In summary, we have identified a number of channels through which demographic factors affect the distribution of income. The story about households that was laid out in Chapter 3 finds support in international comparisons; in general, high fertility rates, low female labor force participation and low educational attainment tend to go together, and these are associated with higher income inequality.

This is relevant for Latin America because different countries of the region are at very different stages of the demographic transition, ranging from relatively young countries like Nicaragua, Haiti and Guatemala, where the average age of the population is just over 20, to countries like Argentina, Jamaica and Uruguay, where the average age of the population is over 30, matching or exceeding that of the industrial economies. These differences in demographic structure help explain differences in the degree of inequality that characterize countries of the region, and they also help explain why Latin America is so much more unequal than the industrial economies.

The link between demography and distribution is also important and interesting because as birthrates and

family sizes decline, most countries of the region are in the midst of a major demographic transition. Looking ahead, this demographic transition should be good news for income distribution in the region.

Urbanization

Development is also associated with urbanization, and like much of the developing world Latin America is experiencing a gradual urbanization of the population. The share of the population living in urban areas has risen from about 50 percent in the 1960s to 53 percent in the 1970s, 58 percent in the 1980s and well over 60 percent in the 1990s. This transition affects income distribution because the economic environment in rural areas differs dramatically from that of the cities. As we saw in Chapter 2, a key feature of the economic landscape in Latin America is a very large gap between the income of families in urban and rural areas. Holding constant other determinants of wages such as education and experience, workers in rural areas earn roughly 20 percent less than workers in urban areas. But the earnings gap is in fact substantially larger than this, because everything is not equal in the countryside and the city; in fact, educational attainment is dramatically lower in rural areas, a reflection of low wages, lower returns to educational investment and large family sizes. Finally, because rural families tend to be larger, reflecting both larger numbers of children and greater tendencies for extended families to live together, differences in the per capita incomes of urban and rural households is increased even further.

What does this earnings gap mean for the distribution of income? In the very early stages of the transition

Figure 4.15. Informality and Inequality
(Partial correlation, controls for per capita income)

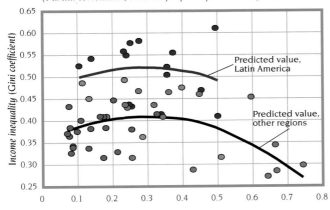

Source: *See Technical Appendix.*

to an urban society, when nearly everyone lives in low-wage rural areas, income inequality would be expected to be relatively low. But as people begin to move to the higher-wage urban areas, the substantial gap between urban and rural earnings will contribute to gradually increasing inequality. Near the end of the process, when most workers have made the transition to the urban sector, the urban-rural earnings gap will affect only a small fraction of the population, and its contribution to the country's income inequality will thus be small.

We thus expect to see a hump-shaped relationship between urbanization and inequality, and this is in fact what emerges from the data. Even after controlling for per capita income, urbanization has an important effect on the distribution of income. Urbanization is predicted to have the most unfavorable consequences for income distribution at an urbanization rate of about 50 percent of the population, roughly where Latin America has been for the past several decades. The international experience suggests, however, that as the process of urbanization continues, it should begin to exert an equalizing rather than an unequalizing impact on the region.

Formalization

The final manifestation of Latin America's stage of development is its large informal sector. The incorporation of increasing shares of the workforce into formal employment relationships is one hallmark of the development process, and internationally the size of the informal sector tends to decline with per capita income. As development proceeds in the region, it is natural to expect that the incidence of informality will tend to decline as well.

What will this transition mean for income inequality?

As we saw in earlier chapters, informal sector employment generally pays less than employment in formal sectors. This is not true for all workers and for all types of informal employment, but it is true for most, and is especially true for women. Also, freed from the constraints imposed by minimum wages and collective bargaining, informal sector earnings are substantially more unequal than are earnings in the formal sector.

As with urbanization, we might therefore expect an inverted U-shaped relationship between informality and inequality. Because of differences between the average incomes of workers in the informal and formal sectors, inequality might increase in the early stages of formalization. However, as the process of formalization proceeds and the informal sector gradually shrinks in size, inequality will eventually begin to decline as an increasing share of the labor force becomes incorporated into the formal sector, where wage differentials are more limited than in the informal sector.

Figure 4.15 suggests that the process of formalization involves an increase in inequality until the rate of informality declines to about 25 to 30 percent of total employment, after which further declines in the size of the informal sector are associated with declines in inequality. This is an important point for Latin America, where the rate of informality ranges from about 11 percent of the workforce to nearly 60 percent, and the median rate for the region is 27 percent. This means that roughly half the countries of the region are now in the category where international experience suggests that further formalization of the workforce will tend to reduce inequality. Most other countries of the region have rates of informality ranging between 30 to 50 percent, where formalization is predicted to have only small adverse effects on the distribution of income, and only a few countries are still in the range where formalization of the workforce is predicted to have adverse consequences.

While we have suggested that formalization of the workforce is a normal part of the development process, this does not mean it is an automatic outcome of the process. We find, for example, that in Latin America informality is associated with shallow financial markets, which is consistent with the idea that many entrepreneurs are forced to continue in a state of informal, small-scale development because they cannot obtain the credit that might finance an expansion and formalization of their business activities.

This highlights the fact that, while formalization normally accompanies development, the process could be short-circuited if the domestic financial system is not

Figure 4.16. Financial Depth and Informality, 1982-92

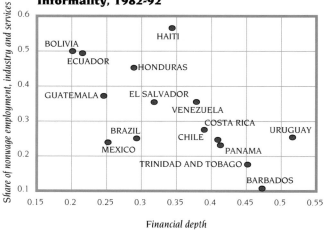

Source: See Technical Appendix.

Figure 4.17. Land Intensity and Income Inequality

(*Partial correlation, adjusted for per capita income*)

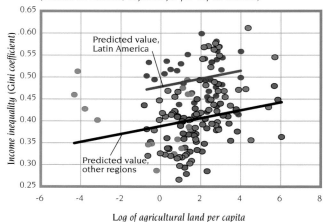

Source: See Technical Appendix.

up to the task of supporting the transition. By the same token, policy measures that promote the development of a robust financial system with the capacity to serve small enterprises can promote formalization.

Summing Up: Stages of Development and Inequality

Economic development is associated with declining income inequality, at least over the range that is relevant for most countries of Latin America today. As Latin America develops, the distribution of income will be favorably influenced by the transitions associated with development, including capital deepening, educational progress, the demographic transition, urbanization and formalization of the labor force. This is no cause for complacency, however. Development is a slow process and any improvements in income distribution may be a long time in coming. The mechanisms discussed in this chapter may provide potential levers for policy to secure lasting improvements in income distribution.

In short, looking to the future, the message is an optimistic one. Latin America is undergoing several transitions that in some cases have been unequalizing, but which can in the near future be expected to exert a more equalizing influence on income distribution. However, while the eventual payoff of these transitions is likely to be significant, it will not bring Latin America's inequality to East Asian levels. Put differently, there is something about the Latin American economic environment that is generating persistently higher inequality, even after correcting for the impact of the region's stage of development.

THE STRUCTURAL BACKDROP FOR INCOME INEQUALITY

We now explore two longer-term or "structural" factors. The first is Latin America's geographical heritage, which has endowed it with specific types of land, natural resources, and climatic conditions that form the backdrop for the region's economic development. The second factor, fundamentally related to these endowments, is the region's exposure to large economic shocks, which has been associated with a history of macroeconomic volatility. This has colored prospects for development in the region, and affected, most importantly, the poorer members of these societies.

Geography and Natural Resources

Latin America is distinctive for many reasons. One of them is the region's rich endowment of natural resources, which has played a crucial role in its history, and which distinguishes it from most of the economies of South and East Asia that are generally less richly endowed in land and mineral wealth. What do these endowments mean for the distribution of income?

Figures 4.17 through 4.20 illustrate the relationship between income inequality and various measures of resource intensity and climatic conditions. They show, respectively, the quantity of agricultural land per capita, primary commodity exports as a share of GDP, and latitude, or distance from the equator, first comparing Latin America to other regions and then within Latin America itself. Each of the figures shows the correlation between

Figure 4.18. Primary Commodity Exports and Income Inequality

(*Partial correlation, adjusted for per capita income*)

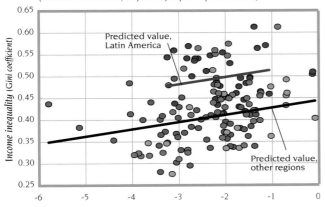

Log of primary commodity exports as share of total exports

Source: See Technical Appendix.

Figure 4.19. Latitude and Income Inequality

(*Partial correlation, adjusted for per capita income*)

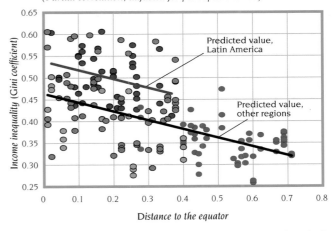

Distance to the equator

Note: The "latitude" variable is the absolute value of the actual latitude of the center of the country divided by 90. It thus lies between zero and one, being equal to zero at the equator and one at the North and South Poles.
Source: See Technical Appendix.

Figure 4.20. Latitude and Income Inequality in Latin America

(*Partial correlation, adjusted for per capita income*)

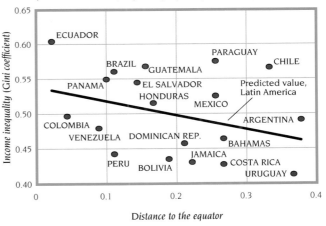

Distance to the equator

Note: The "latitude" variable is the absolute value of the actual latitude of the center of the country divided by 90. It thus lies between zero and one, being equal to zero at the equator and one at the North and South Poles.
Source: See Technical Appendix.

income inequality, as measured by the Gini coefficient, and the explanatory variable after accounting for the empirical relationship between income inequality and the stage of development discussed above.

The correlations are striking. Countries with large amounts of agricultural land per capita are substantially more unequal that countries with relatively little land per capita. Countries that rely upon large exports of primary commodities are also substantially more unequal than countries with lower primary commodity exports.

Particularly striking is the correlation between latitude and inequality. Countries near the equator have systematically higher income inequality, even after accounting for the fact that countries in the tropics tend to be far less developed than are countries in more temperate regions. This is true at the global level, and also within Latin America.

This correlation between latitude and inequality is, in fact, the strongest and most robust of all those prepared for this report, as seen in Table 4.1, which measures the power of various potential explanations for income distribution. The number in the table is the fraction of the variance in the Gini coefficient explained by the simple statistical framework that includes the indicated explanatory variable.

As the table indicates, the correlation between latitude and income inequality is higher than any other explanatory variable. While comparison of the numbers in the table is complicated by the fact that the different variables have different missing observations, and therefore the subsample of the data being explained by each variable differs somewhat, the importance of latitude as an explanation of inequality is also supported by the robust-

ness of the variable to the inclusion of alternative explanatory variables. In all of the many specifications explored here, the variable measuring distance to the equator is highly significant in statistical and, as we shall see below, economic terms. The measures of land intensity and reliance upon primary commodity exports also proved fairly robust predictors of inequality, though the correlation between these variables is less dramatic.

It is impossible to ignore this strong relationship between geography and inequality. But the relationship is an unsettling one because it is not immediately clear

Table 4.1. Explanatory Power of Various Potential Determinants of Income Inequality

Latitude (Distance to the equator)	.532
Land intensity (Log of agricultural land per capita)	.207
Primary commodity exports as a share of GDP	.144
Stage of development (Per capita income and its square)	.442
Capital intensity (Log of capital stock per worker)	.280
Average schooling attainment	.396
Standard deviation of schooling attainment	.202
Rate of population growth	.430
Urbanization (Urban population times one minus the urban population)	.275
Informality (Share of nonwage employment in industry and services)	.261
Real GDP volatility (Standard deviation of the real GDP growth rate)	.198
Terms of trade volatility (Standard deviation of percent changes in terms of trade)	.198
Financial depth (Ratio of the broad money supply to GDP)	.272
Inequality of land ownership (Gini coefficient)	.197

Note: The numbers in the table give the R-squared of a linear regression of the Gini coefficient on the explanatory variable. The regression also included a dummy variable to distinguish between measures of income inequality that come from surveys of household expenditure, rather than surveys of income, since there is a tendency for expenditures to be less unequal than income. A dummy variable was also included for communist countries, since they experienced much less inequality than noncommunist countries. Because of missing data for the different explanatory variables, different regressions included different subsamples of the data set.

what the correlation means. What are the mechanisms that make for this strong association between income inequality and tropical land and climates? There are a number of explanations, all of which may contain at least a grain of truth.

Tropical Conditions Reduce Labor Productivity and Wages

One explanation for this association emphasizes the difficulties that tropical conditions create for workers, and the impact of tropical conditions on the productivity of labor. While progress has been made in ameliorating some of these conditions, life in tropical areas remains complicated by disease and by problems associated with climate, pests and soil and water quality. All hamper the productivity of labor, and particularly undermine agricultural efficiency. This is amplified by the fact that many of the most important innovations in agricultural technology have been associated with agricultural products and production techniques that are well suited to temperate rather than tropical regions.

Recent studies have begun to quantify the enormous toll that these conditions impose on progress for economic growth.[6] This interruption of development prospects itself contributes to inequality, since economic development tends to be good for distribution, except at quite low income levels. But there is also good reason to expect that tropical conditions exert an independent effect on income

inequality. At least in the earlier stages of development, when industrialization is drawing labor out of the rural workforce, wages and working conditions in the modern sector will be linked, at least loosely, to conditions in the rural areas.

If an independent worker without a lot of capital can make a good living in farming—as was the case in the United States during much of its industrialization—a fairly high floor will be placed on wages that workers will accept in the industrial sector. Under these conditions, industrialization can take place with relatively high wages and low income inequality. If, on the other hand, workers in rural areas face the life of low productivity and difficult living conditions that are to be found in many tropical regions, industrialization may take place in a "buyer's market" for labor, with low wages and high inequality. Moreover, the resultant income inequality is likely to be amplified and perpetuated by the impact of these difficult labor market conditions in rural and modern sectors alike on family decisions about fertility, labor force participation and education.

Tropical Crops Are Associated with Unequal Distribution of Land and Income

These labor market conditions may be reinforced by mechanisms that are emphasized in a second, complementary explanation for the association between tropical environments and inequality.[7] This explanation emphasizes the nature of the technologies appropriate for tropical crops, as compared with crops grown in temperate climates. Many of the most important tropical crops, including cotton, sugar and tobacco, are efficiently produced on large-scale plantations. This is much less true of most temperate crops such as wheat, maize or barley, for which, until the relatively recent introduction of agricultural mechanization, relatively small-scale production was reasonably efficient.

It has been argued that the returns to scale associated with many tropical crops facilitated an extreme concentration of land ownership. This idea is certainly borne

---

[6] See Sachs and Warner (1995) and Gallup and Sachs (undated).
[7] See Engerman and Sokoloff (1998) for a persuasive presentation of this view.

Figure 4.21. Latitude and Inequality of Land Ownership

(Partial correlation, adjusted for per capita income)

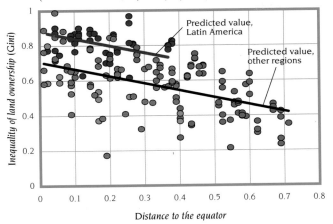

Source: See Technical Appendix.

out by the data, which show that the ownership of land is much more concentrated in tropical than in temperate areas.

In fact, the correlation between latitude and the concentration of land ownership is even more impressive than the correlation between latitude and the distribution of income, suggesting that promotion of highly concentrated land ownership is an important mechanism through which climate and geography have influenced income distribution.

The concentration of land ownership facilitated by the increasing returns to scale in the production of tropical crops reduces competition among employers and may provide them with substantial market power over their employees, thus compounding the difficulties faced by workers in tropical areas. The most extreme manifestation of this market power was slavery, a phenomenon that developed almost exclusively in tropical and subtropical climates, these being parts of the New World where agricultural technology presumably made it most profitable. One view is that inequality in many parts of Latin America is in substantial part the legacy of tropical labor markets, including slavery.

The concentration of land ownership that typifies countries in tropical regions was facilitated in Latin America by the land, immigration and labor policies of governments from early colonial times. But the interesting historical question is whether these policies were accidents of history, or whether they were themselves the result of the natural resource endowments, climate and other geographical conditions of the Latin American colonies. It has been argued that such policies, as well as many of the institutional features that have long been invoked

as explanations for Latin America's highly skewed income distribution, have their roots in the factor endowments that awaited the Spanish and Portuguese colonizers of the region.[8]

An important exception to the general rule that countries in tropical regions have more concentrated land ownership is provided by the economies of emerging East Asia, which lie close to the equator but nevertheless have very low concentrations of land ownership. This may be one of those rare exceptions that actually proves the rule, for the crop upon which these societies were generally built was rice, which does not exhibit the economies of scale in production associated with other tropical crops such as sugar, cotton or tobacco. While other factors may certainly be at play, it seems plausible that East Asia's relatively more egalitarian distribution of income has much to do with the economic, social and institutional structures left behind by a rice culture.

But this example also highlights data limitations. While they have substantial predictive power, variables such as distance to the equator are clearly no more than crude proxies for important structural differences closely associated with, but not identical to, the indicator. The same is true of, for example, aggregate measures of land intensity if, as we have argued, there are important differences between different types of land.

Natural Resources—A "Capital Sink"?

There are other explanations for the link between natural resource endowments and inequality. It has been argued, for example, that mineral resources and certain types of land require considerable physical capital and very little labor. In developing countries, where capital is scarce and labor abundant, this may increase the relative price of capital and reduce the market size to support a growing manufacturing and modern services sector. This leaves workers in a difficult situation, lowering real wages and worsening the distribution of income. And, to the extent that growth is generally facilitated by the development of manufacturing and nonresource-based industries, natural resources may even undermine prospects for long-run development, with deleterious implications for the distribution of income.[9]

A final reason for the association between abundant natural resources and inequality lies in the implica-

---

[8] See Engerman and Sokoloff (1998).

[9] See Sachs and Warner (1995) for evidence that natural resources are associated with slower growth. A number of theoretical ideas have been floated to explain how large natural resource endowments may undermine growth prospects. These typically involve externalities, increasing returns to scale, or important learning-by-doing dynamics in industries that tend to be crowded out by the presence of natural resource wealth. See Matsuyama (1992).

Figure 4.22. Natural Resources Are Associated with Large External Shocks

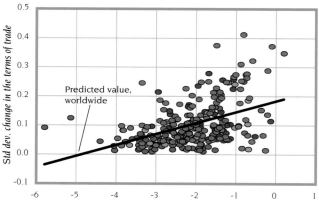

Log of primary commodity exports as share of GDP

Source: See Technical Appendix.

Figure 4.23. Macroeconomic Volatility and Inequality

(*Partial correlation, adjusted for per capita income*)

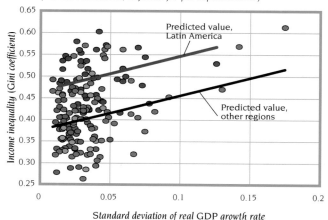

Standard deviation of real GDP growth rate

Source: See Technical Appendix.

Figure 4.24. Volatility and Income Distribution

(*Impact of GDP volatility by quintile*)

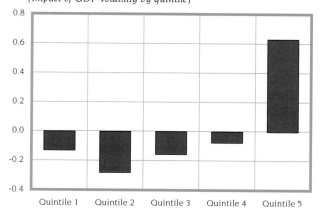

Source: See Technical Appendix.

tions of such abundance for macroeconomic volatility. Large external shocks to which Latin America is exposed have much to do with the region's rich endowments of natural resources and consequent reliance upon volatile primary commodity exports. Macroeconomic volatility worsens income inequality in a number of ways. As Figure 4.22 shows, volatility in the terms of trade is closely associated with reliance upon primary commodity exports.

Macroeconomic Volatility Worsens Income Distribution

The volatile macroeconomic environment with which Latin American families and businesses have had to cope has taken an enormous toll on the region, reducing the rate of long-term growth by as much as one percentage point per year, worsening the distribution of income, and lowering educational attainment.[10]

Figure 4.23 presents the correlation between macroeconomic volatility, as measured by the standard deviation of the real GDP growth rate, and inequality, after accounting for the influence of the stage of development (as measured by per capita income and squared per capita income) and geography (as measured by distance to the equator). The positive relationship between volatility and the distribution of income is significant in both statistical and economic terms. The statistical relationship suggests that a three percentage point reduction in the volatility of real GDP growth would reduce the Gini coefficient of income inequality by roughly 2 percentage points. To the extent that the reduction in volatility also produces more rapid economic growth, the beneficial effects on income distribution would cumulate over time.

Who gets hurt by a volatile macroeconomic environment? The statistical relationship between macroeconomic volatility and the income shares that accrue to different quintiles of the population—accounting for the estimated impact of the stage of development and geographical factors as before—shows that all except the richest 20 percent of the population are adversely affected by macroeconomic volatility. The hardest hit are the second and third quintiles from the bottom.

What are the mechanisms that underlie this relationship between economic instability and inequality? During the past few decades, a substantial body of economic research has documented the adverse impact of inflation and macroeconomic shocks and crises on the poor.[11] But there is more at work than the simple fact

---

[10] Inter-American Development Bank (1995).
[11] See Lustig (1995) and Morley (1995).

Box 4.1. The Scars of Volatility: Mexico 1994-96

Macroeconomic shocks do not affect all groups the same way, nor do their effects recede entirely with economic recovery. Many heads of households are forced to retire early from their formal jobs, passing into the informal sector or into inactivity, perhaps permanently. To make up for the reduction in family income, many young persons drop out of school, sometimes never to return. Once the crisis is over, employment is higher than before but at the cost of higher rates of informal sector employment and fewer young persons in the education system.

These are the preliminary conclusions of a study that has tracked the effects of the Mexican crisis that broke out at the end of 1994 (Márquez, 1998). Although this episode is still not over, some effects have been so profound that they will likely be felt for some time.

In the year after the crisis, the economy contracted 6.2 percent. Although this drop corrected itself almost completely in the following year, many other changes did not recede quite as quickly. The unemployment rate, which had risen 3.5 percent in 1995, fell by only one point in 1996. But this was not due to a lack in the creation of jobs, which increased 3 percent in 1996 (after a decrease from 0.2 percent in 1995), but rather to the expansion of the labor market in both 1995 and 1996.

Moreover, although employment recovered, the share of formal jobs in private sector companies decreased, while the share of informal sector jobs increased. In 1996, 55.1 percent of job growth was generated by small businesses and other informal activities (self-employment or family helpers). Two years earlier the rate was 53.7 percent. In this period, the number of informal sector jobs rose by more than 900,000, while the number of formal jobs in the private sector fell by 200,000. Had it not been for the government, which created a similar number of jobs, expansion of the informal sector would have been even greater.

The 1995 crisis forced more than 5 percent of young persons between the ages of 12 and 25 to enter the labor market: 1 percent found formal employment, 2 percent were employed in small businesses or in informal jobs, and 1.7 percent joined the unemployment lines. The 1996 recovery reinforced this trend even more: 1.9 percent more were employed in formal business, and 3.2 percent in informal activities. The recovery also allowed a large number of young persons who in the previous year had informal jobs or who were unemployed to pass into the formal sector. Thus, in the two years that followed the crisis, 9 percent of all young persons joined the job market and more than one-half of them found employment in the formal sector.

By contrast, adult workers ended up swelling the size of the informal sector, and, above all, the ranks of the unemployed. Between 1994 and 1996, 2 percent of all Mexicans between the ages of 25 and 55 lost their formal jobs. During the recession year, the economic downturn produced a rise in unemployment, further aggravated by workers who left the informal sector. In the following year, workers who left formal jobs were for the most part directly involved in the informal sector.

Workers 55 and older also left their formal jobs, and a large number withdrew entirely from work activity. In 1995, 1.4 percent of all workers 55 and older left their formal jobs, one-half of them for the informal sector and one-half for inactivity, where they were joined by many others discouraged by their work in informal occupations. This situation did not correct itself in 1996: 0.6 percent of all older workers went from the formal sector to retirement and 5.6 percent more abandoned informal jobs to become inactive.

Figure 1. Labor Market Recomposition, Mexico, 1994-96

(*Percent of the corresponding age group*)

Young persons, ages 12 to 25
(*40% of the working age population*)

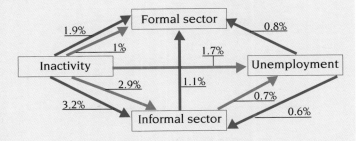

Adults, ages 25 to 55
(*48% of the working age population*)

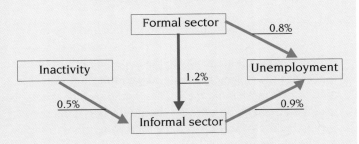

Persons 55 and older
(*12% of the working age population*)

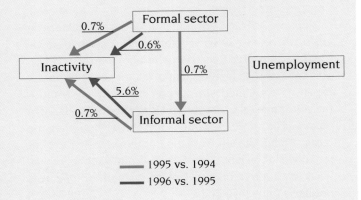

── 1995 vs. 1994
── 1996 vs. 1995

Source: Márquez (1998). *Note*: Only net flows greater than 0.5 percent of the corresponding age group are shown.

The end effect of the crisis was a great loss of human capital. Young persons abandoned their studies, companies lost the accumulative experience of thousands of middle-age and older workers, and older workers abandoned all productive activity. Thus, although economic activity recovered from the beginning of 1996, society lost resources, and for many families, prospects for improvement faded.

Figure 4.25. Macroeconomic Volatility and Educational Attainment

(*Partial correlation, adjusted for per capita income*)

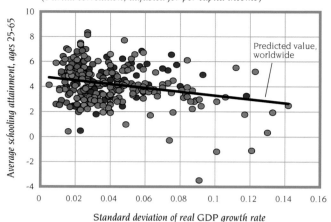

Source: See Technical Appendix.

that the poor are more exposed to the ups and downs of a shock-prone economy. Macroeconomic volatility contributes to higher inequality in the long run because the poor lack the means available to wealthier individuals and families to handle the shocks, and they may therefore be forced by an adverse shock into decisions that have adverse consequences for their long-run earning potential or that of their children.

When industrial economies fall into recession, their students tend to remain in school longer, since it makes sense to wait out the bad labor market until conditions improve. In developing economies, many students lack this option. As Box 4.1 documents for the recent Mexican crisis, when the economy suffers a major adverse shock, the young are often forced into the labor market, presumably because their families cannot afford the out-of-pocket expenses associated with school, or more likely because the young person's contribution is needed for the family's income. The Mexican example also shows that, when the crisis abated, the students did not return to school, but remained in the labor force. Once a child's schooling has been interrupted for any significant length of time, it is not likely to be resumed.

Recent research has shown that this link between volatility and educational attainment is a general pattern; in countries with greater volatility, educational attainment tends to be significantly lower.[12] This is, of course, bad for income inequality because where education is more scarce, the wage premium earned by well-educated workers tends to be higher. But there is more, for it is not only the country's average level of educational attainment that is affected by volatility. Because the poor are particularly exposed to adverse macroeconomic shocks, it is plau-

sible that children from poor families will be the ones forced out of school in the event of a crisis.

We thus expect macroeconomic volatility to increase educational inequality at the same time it reduces average attainment. After accounting for the normal relationship between educational inequality and the average level of schooling attainment discussed in some detail above, countries with more severe macroeconomic volatility also tend to have more inequality in educational attainment. Macroeconomic volatility is thus doubly unequalizing, both reducing the average level and raising the inequality of educational attainment.

A volatile macroeconomic environment also undermines investment, which translates over time into a lower capital stock.[13] This tends to increase income inequality because a scarcity of capital means that the returns to capital are high, and because the reduction of investment slows all of the transitions associated with development.

THREE INTERACTIONS

We thus see that two longstanding features of the Latin American economic terrain—endowment of land, natural resources and climate, and macroeconomic volatility—have contributed in important ways to the problem of inequality in the region. Shortly we will make some very rough estimates of the quantitative importance of these factors, and of the factors associated with the region's stage of development. But before doing so, we note that the story is in fact somewhat more complex than the one that we have presented so far, because it involves not only these two sets of factors, but also interactions between them.

Wages for Unskilled Work and Inequality— A Virtuous Circle

The family is the decisionmaking nexus through which inequality generated by the economic environment may be amplified and transmitted to the next generation. In particular, anything that reduces the wages of low-skilled workers or impedes the ability of secondary wage earners to enter the labor market will not only result in high

---

[12] See Flung, Spilimbergo and Wachtenheim (1998).

[13] There is a very large theoretical and empirical literature on the relationship between macroeconomic volatility and investment, including Inter-American Development Bank (1995). Servén (1998) handles the econometric issues with particular care, and provides a brief overview of the issues and the literature. Leamer, et al. (1998) present a trade-theoretic argument about why natural resource-intensive economies may be particularly risky for capital.

inequality for the current generation, but will also reduce low-income families' capacity to educate their children. At the level of the family, one generation's educational gap is transmitted to the next generation. At the economy-wide level, the resulting scarcity of skilled workers contributes to the premium that well-educated workers receive, and amplifies existing inequalities. This compounds the unequalizing impact of anything that reduces the incomes that can be earned by unskilled labor, and may perpetuate inequality for generations, even after the initial cause of the low wages is removed. This will be the case if a country's geography and natural resource endowments lead to low wages for unskilled labor. The natural resource endowments may thus impede the demographic transition described above.

High costs or barriers to the labor force participation of adults in poor families can also perpetuate inequality. If a community lacks running water, electricity or other utilities that ease the task of maintaining a household, and thus facilitate labor force participation by secondary earners, the family is more likely to be trapped in a high-fertility, low-education equilibrium for this and the next generation. The same will be true if women face discrimination in the labor market, or if excessively restrictive regulation of labor contracts makes it difficult for secondary earners to participate in the formal labor market on terms consistent with their responsibilities at home.

We have presented this interaction in somewhat negative terms. But it also offers important opportunities for policy, for the family's amplification and intergenerational transmission of inequality means that policy changes that increase the earnings of unskilled workers and that facilitate labor market participation may have substantial and long-lasting effects on inequality. Such policies could trigger a virtuous cycle of lower fertility, increased participation, and more complete education of the family's children.

A Volatility Trap

We have seen that macroeconomic volatility adversely affects the distribution of income. This volatility is in large part the consequence of the region's exposure to large external shocks—itself a consequence of the region's rich endowment of natural resources—combined with inadequate policy responses, which have tended to amplify rather than absorb external shocks.

Why is it that policy has so frequently been destabilizing in Latin America? One explanation is inequality itself, which generates deep political and social cleav-

ages that make it much more difficult to mount a prompt and effective response to the shock. Recent research by Rodrik (1998b) lends support to the idea that divided societies, where income inequality or ethnic fragmentation are pronounced, are much less likely to respond adequately to an external shock and, consequently, more likely to suffer an output collapse should one occur.

This leads to the possibility of a volatility-inequality trap in which the region's exposure to external shocks creates a volatile environment that, due to social fissures associated with the income inequality, tends to be amplified by inadequate policy responses. This amplified macroeconomic volatility then worsens the distributional problem both directly and indirectly by undermining development prospects. The political economy of inequality thus interacts with external volatility, and carries with it the danger of a self-reinforcing cycle of volatility and inequality.

The outcome is not, however, inevitable, for recent research has also established that strong institutions can help overcome both the social conflicts generated by the need to adjust to large shocks and the difficulties created by inequality. Rodrik (1998b) provides evidence that countries with strong institutions of conflict management, as indicated by measures of the quality of governmental institutions, rule of law and democratic rights, as well as effective social safety nets, were less likely to suffer output collapses in the aftermath of a large external shock. Similarly, recent research on the role of budgetary institutions has documented the fact that stronger institutions can promote more adequate fiscal policymaking.[14] The challenge for policymakers in the region is to find institutions up to the task of promoting effective adjustment to shocks in order to ensure that Latin America will not become locked in a volatility-inequality trap.

Globalization and Distribution

The world has been undergoing an important process of globalization for at least the past 20 years. This new international environment has brought developing economies into far closer economic contact with industrial economies, and has also exposed middle-income developing economies like most of Latin America to formidable competition from much lower-income economies like China and India, which with roughly a third of the

---

[14] See von Hagen and Harden (1994) for evidence on Europe, Poterba (1996) on the United States, and Fukasaku and Hausmann (1998) on Latin America.

Box 4.2. *Democracy and Distribution*

Latin America is living through a process of political as well as economic development. In recent decades, democracy has spread throughout the continent, and it continues to sink deeper roots as political decentralization brings the region's governments closer to their constituents. What might this democratic transition mean for income distribution in the region?

Economic and social policy choices are heavily influenced by the economic, social and political institutions that exist to express societal preferences and to mediate social conflicts. There is a large body of evidence that these institutions—which include an array of arrangements such as the nature of the electoral system, the degree of respect for property rights and the rule of law, and the legal institutions surrounding the monetary and fiscal policy decisionmaking process—influence economic policy choices and prospects for economic development.

There is also a growing body of evidence that political institutions affect the distribution of income as well as its average rate of growth. For example, Li, Squire and Zou (1998) present evidence that countries that enjoy more extensive civil liberties tend to have less inequality than do countries with fewer liberties. This association between democracy and equality seems particularly strong in Latin America, where the correlation between a widely-used index of civil liberties and the Gini coefficient of income distribution is about 0.46, which is in fact higher than the correlation with per capita income and many other explanatory variables. Similarly, Rodrik (1998c) shows that in countries where democratic institutions are stronger, wages tend to be higher than in weaker democracies, after controlling for other determinants of real wage levels, including labor productivity. Though Rodrik does not make an explicit link between the level of real wages and the distribution of income, it is likely that the higher real wages would be associated with more equal distribution of income.

What are the mechanisms through which political institutions might affect the distribution of income? While firm evidence is lacking, it seems plausible that effective democracies—where the principle of "one man, one vote" is generally respected and politicians are held accountable to their constituents—tend to do a better job of delivering essential social services such as health and education to low-income neighborhoods than do political systems that lack this accountability, if only because the distribution of voting power is more equally distributed than the distribution of economic power. Democratic governments

may also tilt the market scales in favor of workers; Rodrik interprets his finding that wages tend to be higher in democratic countries as evidence that democratic governments act in ways that enhance the bargaining power of workers.

There may also be indirect effects of governance structures on economic growth. Firm adherence to the rule of law, a credible policymaking framework, and the existence of civil liberties may reassure investors that their investments will not be subject to arbitrary confiscation or unpredictable and unreasonable taxation, thus promoting investment and the pace of development. Barro (1996) argues that the rule of law and free markets are positively correlated with economic growth and that, holding constant these and a number of other factors, political freedom is associated with more rapid growth up to a certain point, after which it may have negative effects. Along similar lines, the World Bank (1997) presents evidence that credible policymaking institutions are strongly associated with higher investment and more rapid economic growth. And, as we have argued, there are good reasons to believe that this more rapid growth will, over time, tend to promote more equitable distribution of income.

Democracy may also promote equality by reducing macroeconomic volatility and the likelihood of disruptive economic crises. While we often lament the delays that can be generated by the process of democratic decisionmaking, the process provides a means to resolve social conflicts that has far more legitimacy than nondemocratic alternatives. Because they provide a means of resolving the social conflicts often associated with economic crises, democratic political institutions may also facilitate more effective adjustment to external economic shocks. Rodrik (1998b) presents evidence that countries with latent social conflicts such as ethnic or linguistic differences or racial tensions have a more difficult time adjusting to economic shocks. Conversely, strong institutions of conflict management—including adherence to the rule of law, democratic rights, and robust social safety nets—tend to promote more effective management of economic shocks, thus reducing the likelihood that a shock will lead to a major collapse. This may explain why democracies tend to produce less macroeconomic volatility than do countries where democratic rights are weaker (Rodrik, 1997). Given the high cost of economic crisis for the poor, the less volatile economic environment that democracies deliver should translate into a more equitable and secure place to live.

world's population have recently burst onto the economic scene. It has opened up new possibilities for businesses to locate their production in the most cost-effective locations, and has vastly increased the size of the markets where talented and skilled individuals can earn their living. And financial market globalization is taking place every bit as rapidly as are markets for goods and services.

Will this new economic environment facilitate or impede an equalizing development process in Latin America?

International Trade and Distribution in Latin America

The outstanding feature of most developing countries is their scarcity of capital and abundance of labor. The basic theory of international trade suggests that its expansion will increase the income earned by a country's most abundant factor of production. Thus, the prediction is that when industrial countries increase their trade with developing economies, the returns to capital rise in the industrial economy and wages fall, while in the developing economies wages rise and the returns to capital fall. This would, of course, be equalizing in the developing economies, and unequalizing in the industrial economies.

This prediction has received a lot of attention in the industrial economies, because the years of globalization have seen strongly declining demand for unskilled workers. This has resulted in a massive decline in the real wages of unskilled workers in the United States and a large increase in unemployment in much of Europe. However, a large body of research has come to a rough consensus that, while increased trade with developing economies has probably contributed to the decline in demand for labor, other trends, such as technological advances like computers, have probably played a somewhat more important role.[15] This is partly because there has been little evidence of the relative price shifts that this theory relies upon to generate large wage effects, and partly because industrial country trade with developing countries—though much larger than it was two decades ago—remains relatively small, on the order of 5 percent of GDP, making it seem implausible to many economists that the effects on labor markets could have been so large.

To the extent that this mechanism is important, it is good news for Latin America and other developing economies, which should expect to see wage increases as a result of greater integration with the industrial economies. But things are not so simple, for several reasons.

First, and most ominous, while Latin America is labor intensive relative to the industrial economies, labor is scarce and quite expensive by the standards of countries like China and India, both of which are rapidly inserting their very large economies into the world trading system. This raises the theoretical possibility that the need to compete with China will drive Latin American wages down toward Chinese levels rather than up toward industrial-country levels.

This is a daunting possibility, but seems theoretical for the moment. The world is more complicated than the simplest trade theory. There are more than two factors of production (labor and capital) in the world. There is labor with different degrees and kinds of skill, a large variety of natural resource endowments, and many different kinds of goods that are traded. A more sophisticated approach that takes these considerations into account suggests that wages and other factor prices will

tend to be driven together only for those countries that produce and trade similar combinations of goods.[16] And, at the moment, most countries of the region do not in fact compete with the labor-intensive economies of Asia, mainly because Latin America's rich endowment of land and natural resources provides it with a comparative advantage in the production and export of resource-intensive goods, rather than the raw labor-intensive goods that China and India generally export.

So, for the moment, most Latin American workers would appear to be somewhat insulated from direct competition with the very low-wage economies of China and India. Having said that, it is also true that several countries of the region have established important *maquila* sectors, which produce labor-intensive exports such as textiles for export to industrial country markets. For these countries, the prospect of increased competition from low-wage Asian countries may be more real and imminent.

Globalization and Wages—the Educational Imperative

Given the likely inability of resource-based industries to indefinitely provide a basis for economic development sufficient to absorb Latin America's growing labor force, countries of the region will eventually be faced with the need to develop new industries based on different comparative advantages. Here there are two possiblities. One is that the new industries will be based on comparative advantage derived from abundant supplies of unskilled labor, which will place countries in direct competition with the low-wage Asian economies. The other is that the new industries will be based on comparative advantage derived from the skills and education of the workforce, an outcome that offers the possibility of escaping the downward pressure on wages that would be implied by direct competition with low-wage Asian economies.[17] This highlights an important interaction between globalization and

---

[15] For overviews of the debate, see Sachs (1998), Freeman (1995), Ricardson (1995) and Wood (1997). The latter argues that the impact of trade on unskilled workers' wages in industrial economies has been much larger than the conventional wisdom would suggest.

[16] Technically, factor prices will tend to be equalized among countries that lie within the same "cone of diversification." This is an important point, because it means that the impact of trade on factor prices in a country will depend not on how abundantly endowed the country is by comparison with world patterns, but rather how abundantly endowed the country is in comparison with other countries that produce similar goods, that is, that are in the same "cone of diversification." To take a hypothetical example, Brazil may be labor intensive by global standards, but if it mainly produces tradable products that are produced by even more labor-abundant economies such as China or India, Brazil is in fact capital intensive by the relevant comparison, and trade liberalization would tend to raise the return to Brazilian capital, not labor. Davis (1996) explains this important point clearly, and highlights the challenge that it presents for empirical research in this area.

[17] Leamer, et al. (1998) provide a more complete explanation of this point.

the educational transition, and suggests that promoting education is particularly urgent in the new international economic environment.

Implications of Globalization for a Resource-Rich Region

Globalization also interacts importantly with Latin America's abundant endowment of land and natural resources. Globalization can be expected to raise the returns that can be earned by these natural resources, and to expand possibilities for the international capital flows required to develop them more aggressively. While the case for exploiting the region's abundant supply of natural resource is strong, the danger is that the increased reliance upon natural resource-based industries that has followed trade liberalization in some countries of the region may expose them to the difficulties discussed above in yet more exaggerated forms.

"Footloose Capital"—A Threat to Workers?

Another factor that the simplest theory of international trade overlooks is the operation of labor markets and its implication for income inequality. Whereas the theory assumes that labor markets are perfectly competitive, many labor markets in the world are characterized by a bargaining process that can have an important impact on wages and the distribution of income. Because globalization has increased the ability of capital to move from one country to the next in search of efficiencies and lower wages, while labor mobility has remained largely unchanged, it has been argued that capital's bargaining power has increased to the detriment of labor. Grant us wage concessions, workers are told, or we will pack up our capital and take it elsewhere. Note that the simple threat to leave may have significant effects on wages, even if there are no trade or capital flows actually triggered by the globalization. Rodrik (1998a) presents evidence that in countries that are more open to international trade, as measured by the value of international trade as a share of GDP, wages tend to be significantly lower than in more closed economies, after controlling for productivity and other determinants of wages. He also argues that increased mobility of capital makes it more difficult to tax profits, with the result that an increasing share of the tax burden falls upon workers.

Openness, Investment and Development

More fundamentally, it needs to be borne in mind that openness to international trade will affect income distribution through a number of channels. Most importantly, there is now a rough consensus that open trade regimes are conducive to growth, which contains important equal-

izing forces that may eventually outweigh the direct, unequalizing effects of international trade, if any. While the impact of openness on growth may be felt in a number of ways, an important one is its effect on increased international investment.

To test this impact, we investigated the statistical relationship between openness, as measured by an index of trade policy orientation compiled by Jeffrey Sachs and Andrew Warner, and capital intensity, as measured by the log of the capital stock per worker. The analysis was confined to developing countries, since virtually every industrial country was already categorized as "open." We controlled for a number of other potential determinants of capital intensity, including the capital intensity in the previous decade (to account for gradual adjustment of the capital stock), the land intensity of the economy in question, its latitude, and the average inflation tax. A strong positive relationship between openness and capital intensity was found. The results suggested that in the medium run[18] a switch from a closed to an open trade orientation was associated with an increase in the capital stock of about 22 percent, with much larger results over the long run. As we have argued in some detail above, such an increase in the capital stock would be good news for the distribution of income, as the greater abundance of physical capital raises wages and reduces the returns to capital.

These results are far from definitive. But they do serve to highlight the fact that openness and globalization are multifaceted phenomena whose impact on income distribution requires an assessment in a number of areas.

LESSONS FROM INTERNATIONAL COMPARISONS: A BOTTOM LINE

While we have emphasized the limitations imposed by the data available to investigate the various influences on income inequality—some variables are measured poorly and others are only rough proxies—the data do roughly correspond to most of the influences on distribution that we can identify. It is natural to ask whether the stories that we have been telling explain a significant portion of Latin America's inequality, and if so, which of the stories are most important?

Our approach was to gather empirical measures summarizing the various factors discussed in general

---

[18] Over a time horizon of about a decade, which was the periodicity of our panel data.

Table 4.2. Why Is Latin American Inequality So High?
(Estimated impact on the Gini coefficient)

Dimensions of economic development included in the analysis	Comparison group			
	Industrial economies		Emerging East Asia	
	Dimension of development	Latitude, land and volatility	Dimension of development	Latitude, land and volatility
1. Per capita income and demography	6.00	11.08	1.30	4.91
2. Capital intensity	0.73	15.07	0.21	4.60
3. Education	3.60	11.68	0.97	6.22
4. Urbanization	1.96	14.84	3.23	4.10
5. Demography	2.80	11.78	0.30	5.02
6. Schooling, demography and urbanization	4.56	12.20	3.84	4.59

Source: Study calculations as described in the text. Demography refers to the rate of population growth. Capital intensity refers to the log of the capital stock per worker. Education refers to the mean educational attainment of the population aged 25-65, and the standard deviation of educational attainment across that population. Urbanization refers to the share of the population living in urban areas and that variable squared. The measures of endowments used in all cases were the log of agricultural land per capita, distance of the country to the equator, and the standard deviation of real GDP growth. The data set included three subperiods: 1960-1970, 1971-1981 and 1982-1992. See Technical Appendix.

terms above, and to use them in a multivariate statistical analysis to determine the strength of their association with the Gini coefficient of income inequality. The resulting relationship was then used to examine how much of the difference between Latin America's inequality and that of some benchmark can be explained by differences between the various measures of transition in Latin America and the benchmark. We considered two different benchmarks—the industrial economies and emerging East Asia—since comparisons against these rather different regions highlight different aspects of the Latin American experience.

Missing data for many countries made it impractical to simply introduce measures summarizing all five of the development-related transitions in a single statistical relationship. For this reason, the discussion that follows describes a number of different exercises, in which we took different combinations of the variables representing the five dimensions of the development process. Each exercise included all three variables selected to estimate the importance of a country's natural endowments, including the log of agricultural land per capita to summarize the economy's natural resource intensity; latitude, to summarize the influence of climate and geography; and the volatility of real GDP growth, to summarize the volatility of the macroeconomic environment.

Table 4.2 summarizes the results. The first column lists the dimensions of economic development included in each of the several statistical exercises. For example, the first exercise captures in a broad way all of the transitions related to the economic development process and the demographic transition by including in the statistical

analysis linear and quadratic terms in per capita income and the rate of population growth. The next number gives the estimated impact of these variables on Latin America's income distribution, using the industrial countries as the counterfactual. More precisely, this means that if per capita income and the population growth rate were equal to the average for the industrial economies, rather than those that were actually observed in Latin America, the Gini coefficient would be about 6 percentage points lower than it actually was. In the next column, we calculate the counterfactual for differences in latitude and land intensity. The first row shows that if the region had the latitude and land intensity of the industrial economies, the Gini coefficient would be about 11 points lower than it actually was.

In this sense, Latin America's stage of economic development, as characterized by per capita income and demography, explains about six percentage points of the difference between the region's Gini coefficient and that of the industrial countries. Since the actual difference is about 18 percentage points, we can say that the region's stage of development explains about a third of the difference between Latin American and industrial country inequality. By the same logic, the longer-term factors that we have identified—latitude, land intensity and volatility—are estimated to account for 11 percentage points, or nearly two-thirds, of the difference. Taken together, the two stories explain nearly all of the difference between Latin American and industrial country Gini coefficients.

The more important of the two factors associated with Latin America's stage of development is per capita income, which accounts for nearly 5 of the 6 percentage point difference in the Gini coefficient explained by the stage of development, while demographic factors account for about 1.2 percentage points of the difference. Of the "structural" factors, by far the most important quantitatively is latitude, which is estimated to account for over 9 percentage points of the difference between industrial country and Latin American inequality. Volatility explains roughly 2 percentage points, and land intensity explains quite little.[19]

---

[19] The reason for this is that the industrial countries include several countries, such as Canada, New Zealand, and the United States, with huge endowments of agricultural land per capita. If the counterfactual were, for example, Europe, the results would of course be different.

Why Is Inequality Higher Than in Emerging East Asia?

Comparisons with the industrial economies shed interesting light on Latin America. But it is also revealing to compare the Latin American experience with that of emerging East Asia, a region at roughly the same stage of development but with substantially lower inequality. The last columns of Table 4.2 provide counterfactuals that ask how Latin America's income inequality would change if it resembled emerging East Asia in the dimensions that we have been discussing?

There we see that factors associated with the stage of development have little to do with Latin America's higher inequality; differences in per capita income and the rate of population growth explain only 1.3 percentage points of the 11 percentage point difference between the two region's average Gini coefficients. This is not surprising, since emerging East Asia's incomes are not much higher than the average for Latin America. Our indicators of the region's "endowments"—latitude, land intensity and volatility—account for about 5 percentage points of the difference. Taken together, these variables account for just over half the difference between income inequality in the Latin American and East Asian economies.

There are at least two reasons why more than half the difference between East Asian and Latin American income inequality remains unexplained. The first is that the analysis so far has summarized all of the processes associated with development with per capita income. This misses the important role played by differences in the nature of urbanization.

A second reason is that for East Asia, "latitude" is a particularly poor proxy for differences in agricultural technologies that have influenced the evolution of income inequality. While these countries are located relatively close to the equator, the rice culture that shaped their economic and social development was not conducive to the same kinds of large-scale plantation production structures seen for many other tropical crops. In addition to these factors, there may of course be other factors that we have not included from the analysis.

Table 4.2 investigates the separate influence of measures summarizing the five dimensions of the development process. For explaining the difference between Latin America and the industrial economies, schooling, urbanization and demography appear to be the quantitatively most important elements of the development process. When these variables are included in a single statistical exercise, the estimated impact of the transitions is roughly equal to the estimate that emerges using per capita income as a proxy for all of the transitions.

The degree of urbanization emerges as an important difference between Latin America and East Asia, a difference not captured by differences in per capita income. The difference emerges not because the average degree of urbanization is very different in the two regions; at just over 50 percent of the population, they are similar. It emerges instead because the East Asian average results from the combination of two almost completely urbanized populations (Hong Kong and Singapore, where the rates of urbanization are 93 and 100 percent, respectively) and two very rural populations (Indonesia and Thailand, where the rates of urbanization are only 28 and 18 percent of the population, respectively.) Only two countries, Korea and Malaysia, have the moderate rates of urbanization found to be associated with the most inequality. In Latin America, on the other hand, very high and very low rates of urbanization are rare, and most countries of the region have rates of urbanization associated with high inequality. When schooling, demography and urbanization are considered together, the analysis explains roughly 8.5 percentage points, or about 75 percent, of the difference in income inequality between Latin America and East Asia.

CONCLUSIONS

This chapter has attempted to identify a number of economic factors associated with income inequality in order to gain some understanding of the manner in which they may be contributing to the problem. The discussion has had relatively little to say about the role of policy, but that does not mean that policy does not matter. Policies can either ameliorate or aggravate the inequality that may be generated by some aspect of a country's economic circumstances. For example, in countries where unskilled workers earn very low wages, there will be a tendency for lower female labor force participation, which is associated with larger families and lower educational attainment of the next generation, with the result that educational and income inequality is transmitted from one generation to the next. But policy can weaken this intergenerational transmission of inequality in a number of ways, such as by lowering barriers to female labor force participation, lowering the costs of access to education, improving the quality of educational services available to low-income families, and strengthening social safety nets so that poor children are not forced to withdraw from school during bad economic times. The purpose of the chapter was to improve understanding of the determinants of income inequality, with the aim of promoting more comprehensive and productive policy responses.

TECHNICAL APPENDIX

Data Definitions and Sources

The data set that was used for Chapter 4 was generated from annual data from a variety of sources. Because measurements of income inequality and some of the other data are made at infrequent and irregular intervals, we aggregated the time series into three 11-year time intervals: 1960-1970, 1971-1981, and 1972-1982 inclusive, and used the average of the available annual data for each time period. The variables that we discuss in the chapter are shown in Table 4A.1.

Stage of Development and Income Distribution

Figure 4.2 illustrates the link between the stage of economic development, as measured by per capita income, and inequality, as measured by the Gini coefficient. In addition to the individual data points, we also show predicted values for Latin America and other regions. These predicted values are based upon the regression summarized in column (1) of Table 4A.2. In that regression, we regressed the Gini coefficient on a dummy variable that indicates whether the measurement was based upon a survey of household expenditure, rather than income, a dummy variable for Latin America and the Caribbean, per capita income, and squared per capita income.

Two relevant points emerge from this analysis. First, there is statistical support for a curvilinear relationship between development and distribution, which is reflected in the statistically significant coefficient on squared per capita income. (We conducted the same analysis using per capita income and its inverse, as suggested by Anand and Kanbur [1993] and obtained results that were similar in statistical terms and visually almost indistinguishable from the curve shown in Figure 4.2.) Second, after controlling for per capita income, there is a statistically significant estimate of the coefficient on the Latin American dummy, which indicates that at any given stage of development, countries in Latin America tend to have a Gini coefficient that is about 10.2 percentage points higher than do countries in other regions of the world. The "pre-

Table 4A.1. Variable Definitions and Sources

Gini	Gini coefficient of income inequality. Source: Deininger and Squire (1996) database.
Expsurvey	Dummy variable = 1 if the measurement of income inequality is based upon a survey of household expenditure and = 0 if the measurement is based upon a survey of household income. Source: Deininger and Squire (1996).
Comm	Dummy variable = 1 if the country was communist and = 0 if the country was noncommunist. Source: Deininger and Squire(1996).
Latam	Dummy variable = 1 if the country was in Latin America and the Caribbean.
Lppp	Log of per capita income in constant, purchasing parity adjusted dollars. Source: *World Penn Tables* (1995).
LKapw	Log of capital stock per worker in constant U.S. dollars. Source: World Bank, *World Tables*, 1995.
MeanSchool	Average years of schooling of the population aged 25-65. Source: Barro and Lee (1994).
StdSchool	Standard deviation of years of schooling of the population aged 25-65. Computed using Barro-Lee data.
Urban	Share of the population living in urban areas. Source: World Bank, *World Tables*, 1995.
Popgrow	Rate of growth of the population. Computed using data from IMF *International Financial Statistics*.
Meanage	Average age of the population. Computed using data from the World Bank, *World Tables*, 1995.
Latitude	Distance of the country from the equator. Computed as the absolute value of the latitude divided by 90.
LLand	Log of arable land per capita. Source: World Bank, *World Tables*, 1995.
RGDPStd	Standard deviation of real GDP growth. Computed using annual data from IMF *International Financial Statistics* and the IDB *Economic and Social Database*, 1995.
FDep	Ratio of the broad money supply (M2) to GDP. Source: IMF *International Financial Statistics*.
CivLib	Index of civil liberties, ranging from 1 to 7, with higher numbers representing stronger civil liberties. Source: Barro and Lee (1994).

dicted values" that are shown in the various figures of Chapter 4 are derived in the same manner. Because of space considerations, we do not present all of the underlying regressions here.

Counterfactual Exercise

Here we explain in more detail the counterfactual exercises that are summarized in Table 4.2. The six rows of that table are based upon the six regressions that are summarized in columns (2)-(7) of Table 4A.2. Each of these regressions includes as explanatory variables Latitude, LLand, and RGDPStd, and also one or more dimensions of the stage of adjustment. In all cases, the coefficients on Latitude, LLand, and RGDPStd are statistically significant at conventional confidence levels.

In column (2) we see the results of using per capita income and the population growth rate as measures of the stage of development and the country's position in the demographic transition. The link between per capita

Table 4A.2. Summary of Econometric Results

	(1)	(2)	(3)	(4)	(5)	(6)	(7)
Expsurvey	-3.04 (-2.26)	-6.33 (-5.44)	-7.34 (-5.08)	-7.04 (-5.77)	-6.65 (-6.30)	-6.64 (-5.65)	-8.04 (-7.09)
Comm			-10.38 (-1.72)	-11.52 (-4.90)	-13.80 (-6.22)	-11.47 (-4.41)	-13.14 (-5.65)
Latam	10.20 (7.46)						
Lppp	28.64 (2.61)	41.03 (4.62)					
Lppp²	-2.02 (-2.97)	-2.59 (-4.66)					
LKapw			11.48 (2.09)				
LKapw²			-.716 (-2.20)				
MeanSchool				-.906 (-3.34)			-.449 (-1.48)
StdSchool				1.85 (2.20)			.002 (0.003)
Urban					.812 (0.35)		
Urban(1-Urban)					48.09 (6.21)		45.22 (5.24)
Popgrow		86.34 (1.21)				75.19 (0.91)	70.40 (0.94)
Meanage						-.231 (-1.42)	
Latitude		-24.72 (-7.21)	-30.74 (-7.70)	-25.50 (-7.80)	-31.69 (-11.58)	-25.77 (-6.68)	-26.10 (-7.91)
LLand		1.31 (4.33)	1.19 (3.22)	1.68 (5.19)	.973 (3.46)	1.28 (3.83)	1.05 (3.05)
RGDPStd		54.09 (2.67)	90.01 (3.00)	62.71 (2.43)	66.25 (3.44)	63.62 (2.91)	73.94 (3.14)
Nobs	173	172	112	159	175	158	157
RBarSq	.459	.630	.625	.602	.650	.585	.668

Note: Dependent variable is the Gini coefficient (in percent). In the first regression the communist economies are excluded. All regressions include a constant, which is not reported. The t-statistics are in parentheses.

Table 4A.3. Further Econometric Results

	(1)	(2)	(3)	(4)	(5)	(6)
Expsurvey	-4.36 (-3.83)	-3.31 (-2.65)	-4.79 (-3.59)	-3.58 (-1.86)	-1.10 (-0.68)	-3.39 (-1.71)
Latam	5.32 (4.19)	3.46 (2.27)	7.33 (4.27)		15.30 (7.09)	4.15 (1.71)
Latitude	-22.03 (-6.54)	-23.75 (-5.96)	-26.17 (-5.78)			-24.70 (-4.02)
LLand	1.152 (4.036)	2.06 (4.86)	1.503 (4.23)			1.258 (2.48)
RGDPStd	55.98 (2.84)	36.87 (1.65)	54.38 (2.20)			85.86 (1.77)
LKapw²			-.716 (-2.20)			
Lppp	31.10 (3.32)	36.09 (3.02)	46.71 (4.21)			28.71 (1.71)
Lppp²	-1.99 (-3.41)	-2.23 (-2.94)	-2.89 (-4.23)			-1.81 (-1.72)
FDep		-2.06 (-0.52)				
LndGini			-15.49 (-3.37)	18.98 (3.51)	-5.81 (-1.03)	
CivLib						-0.60 (-0.079)
Nobs	168	123	103	104	104	72
RBarSq	.529	.584	.735	.116	.406	.529

Note: Dependent variable is the Gini coefficient (in percent). Communist economies are excluded. from the regression. All regressions include a constant, which is not reported. The t-statistics are in parentheses.

income and the Gini remains strong, though the statistical evidence for an independent link between demographic factors and income distribution is not strong, after one also controls for the "environmental" factors, latitude, land intensity and macroeconomic volatility. In order to obtain the counterfactual estimates reported in the first row of Table 4.2, we used these coefficient estimates to compute how much the Gini would change if the explanatory variables were changed by enough to bring the value for Latin America to the average value for the industrial countries (or emerging East Asian in the second set of counterfactuals.)

The remaining counterfactuals, summarized in rows 2-6 of Table 4.2, were computed in the same manner, using the regression results summarized in columns 3-7 of Table 4A.2, respectively.

Other Results

In this chapter we emphasize a number of variables that have not been emphasized in recent work, and we do not emphasize a few that have figured prominently. Table 4A.3 presents additional statistical evidence on three variables that were emphasized in a recent study (Li, Squire and Zou, 1998) that exploits essentially the same data on income inequality used here. That study emphasized the role of financial depth, an index of civil liberties, and inequality in land ownership as predictors of inequality in the distribution of income.

Column (1) of Table 4A.3 is a base regression, which includes none of these variables but does include indicators of geography and climate (latitude), resource intensity (lland), macroeconomic volatility (RGDPStd), and the stage of development.

If we add an indicator of financial depth to this regression, the estimated coefficient is negative, as in Li, Squire and Zou (1998), but it is not statistically significant. Meanwhile, the coefficient estimates for the rest of the variables remain similar to those of the base regression, and they remain statistically significant.

While Li, Squire and Zou (1998) found that higher concentration of land ownership should be associated with higher income inequality, our results suggest the opposite result. This is of course highly counterintuitive. Something of an explanation can be found in the regressions summarized in columns (4) and (5), which focus solely on the correlation between the land Gini and the income Gini. If there is no dummy variable for Latin America in the equation, there emerges a strong positive correlation between the two. But if a dummy variable for Latin America is included in the regression, the estimated (conditional) correlation becomes negative. This suggests that the main reason for the positive correlation between the land Gini and the income Gini results from the fact that Latin America has a very high land Gini and a very high income Gini—but after accounting for Latin American regional differences with a dummy variable, the positive correlation vanishes. Given this sensitivity to simple changes in the specification, we thought it most prudent not to emphasize the role of the land Gini.

In column (6) of Table 4A.3 we add an index of civil liberties to the regression. We find that this index has limited explanatory power, once one controls for the variables emphasized in this chapter. As we note in Box 4.2, this is not true if we restrict the sample to Latin America; in this restricted sample, civil liberties are associated with less inequality, a correlation that is statistically quite significant.

There are differences between these results and the previous published work, in terms of periodicity of the data (annual vs. 11-year periods) and econometric technique. However, these do not seem to be the reason for the difference in results, as we can very roughly replicate the previous results with our data set. What seems to be generating the difference in results is our inclusion of alternative explanatory variables.

REFERENCES

Anand, Sudhir, and S.M.R. Kanbur. 1993. The Kuznets Process and the Inequality-Development Relationship. *Journal of Development Economics* 40: 25-52.

Atkinson, A.B. 1982. *The Economics of Inequality*. Oxford: Clarendon Press.

Barro, Robert. 1996. Democracy and Growth. *Journal of Economic Growth* 1(1) March: 1-27.

Barro, Robert, and Jon-Wha Lee. 1994. Data Set for a Panel of 138 Countries. Unpublished.

Behrman, Jere R., Nancy Birdsall, and Miguel Székely. 1998. Schooling Gaps, Family Background, and Macro Conditions in Latin America. Inter-American Development Bank. Forthcoming.

Birdsall, Nancy, Carol Graham, and Richard H. Sabot. 1998. *Beyond Tradeoffs: Market Reforms and Equitable Growth in Latin America*. Washington, D.C.: Inter-American Development Bank and The Brookings Institution.

Davis, Donald R. 1996. *Trade Liberalization and Income Distribution*. NBER Working Paper No. 5693.

Deininger, Klaus, and Lyn Squire. 1996. A New Data Set Measuring Income Inequality. *World Bank Economic Review* 10(3) September: 565-91.

Duryea, Suzanne, and Miguel Székely. 1998. *Labor Markets in Latin America: A Supply-Side Story*. Working Paper No. 374, Office of the Chief Economist. Inter-American Development Bank, Washington, D.C.

Edwards, Sebastian. 1993. Openness, Trade Liberalization and Growth in Developing Economies. *Journal of Economic Literature* (September): 1358-93.

Engerman, Stanley L., and Kenneth L. Sokoloff. 1998. Factor Endowments, Institutions, and Differential Paths of Growth among New World Economies: A View from Economic Historians of the United States. In Stephen Haber, ed., *How Latin America Fell Behind: Essays on the Economic Histories of Brazil and Mexico, 1800-1914*. Stanford, CA: Stanford University Press.

Flug, Karnit, Antonio Spilimbergo, and Erik Wachtenheim. 1998. Investment in Education: Do Economic Volatility and Credit Constraints Matter? *Journal of Development Economics*. Forthcoming.

Frank, Robert, and Philip Cook. 1995. *The Winner Take All Society*. New York: Simon and Schuster.

Freeman, Richard B. 1995. Are Your Wages Set in Beijing? *Journal of Economic Perspectives* 9(3) Summer: 15-32.

Fukasaku, Kiichiro, and Ricardo Hausmann. 1998. *Democracy, Decentralization and Deficits in Latin America*. Washington, D.C.: Inter-American Development Bank and OECD.

Gallup, John, and Jeffrey Sachs. Undated. Geography and Economic Development. Harvard University. Mimeo.

Inter-American Development Bank. 1995. *Economic and Social Progress in Latin America. 1995 Report*. Washington, D.C.: IDB.

Kuznets, S. 1995. Economic Growth and Income Inequality. *American Economic Review* 45.

Leamer, Edward E., Hugo Maul, Sergio Rodríguez, and Peter K. Schott. 1998. Natural Resources as a Source of Latin American Income Inequality. University of California, Los Angeles. Mimeo.

Li, Hongyi, Lyn Squire, and Heng-fu Zou. 1998. Explaining International and Intertemporal Variations in Income Inequality. *Economic Journal* 108: 26-43.

Lustig, Nora. 1995. *Coping with Austerity: Poverty and Inequality in Latin America*. Washington, D.C.: The Brookings Institution.

Márquez, Gustavo. 1998. *The Impact of Volatility on the Labor Market: Mexico 1994-96*. OCE Working Paper, Inter-American Development Bank. Unpublished.

Matsuyama, Kiminori. 1992. Agricultural Productivity, Comparative Advantage, and Economic Growth. *Journal of Economic Theory* 58.

Morley, Samuel A. 1995. Structural Adjustment and the Determinants of Poverty in Latin America. In Nora Lustig, ed., *Coping with Austerity: Poverty and Inequality in Latin America*. Washington, D.C.: The Brookings Institution.

Poterba, James. 1996. Budget Institutions and Fiscal Policy in U.S. States. *American Economic Review* 86(2).

Psacharopoulos, George. 1994. Returns to Investment in Education: A Global Update. World Development 22(9): 1325-44.

Richardson, J David. 1995. Income Inequality and Trade: How to Think. What to Conclude. *Journal of Economic Perspectives* 9(3) Summer: 33-55.

Rodrik, Dani. 1997. Democracy and Economic Performance. Harvard University. Mimeo.

————. 1998a. Capital Mobility and Labor. Harvard University. Mimeo.

————. 1998b. Where Did All the Growth Go? *External Shocks, Social Conflict, and Growth Collapses*. NBER Working Paper No. 6350.

————. 1998c. Democracies and Economic Performance. Harvard University. Mimeo.

Sachs, Jeffrey. 1998. International Economics: Unlocking the Mysteries of Globalization. *Foreign Policy* (Spring): 97-111.

Sachs, Jeffrey D., and Andrew M. Warner. 1995. Economic Reform and the Process of Global Integration. *Brookings Papers on Economic Activity* 1(August): 1-118.

Servén, Luis. 1998. Economic Uncertainty and Private Investment: an Empirical Investigation. World Bank. Mimeo.

Sheahan, John, and Enrique V. Iglesias. 1998. Kinds and Causes of Inequality in Latin America. In N. Birdsall, C. Graham and R. Sabot, eds., *Beyond Tradeoffs: Market Reforms and Equitable Growth in Latin America*. Washington, D.C.: Inter-American Development Bank and The Brookings Institution.

Spilimbergo, Antonio, Juan Luis Londoño, and Miguel S. Székely. 1997. *Income Distribution, Factor Endowments, and Trade Openness*. Inter-American Development Bank, Office of the Chief Economist Working Paper No. 356.

von Hagen, Jürgen, and Ian Harden. 1994. Budget Processes and Commitment to Fiscal Discipline. *European Economic Review* 39.

Wood, Adrian. 1997. Openness and Wage Inequality in Developing Countries: The Latin American Challenge to East Asian Conventional Wisdom. *The World Bank Economic Review* II (I) January: 33-57.

World Bank. 1997. *World Development Report*. Washington, D.C.: World Bank.

PART THREE

POLICIES

INTRODUCTION

Latin America's severe income inequality is connected to its level of development and to the characteristics of its natural resource endowment. That would seem to provide a twofold reason for doing nothing: the first implies waiting and the second resignation. Nothing could be further from the spirit of this study, whose intention and content have to do with the policies that should be adopted to attain development with equity.

More developed societies tend to be more equal, and that equality is aided by various aspects of development. Higher and better distributed levels of education are tantamount to greater equality of opportunity. High levels of capital accumulation mean competition and productive uses for labor capacity. Moderate rates of population growth represent better opportunities for the employment of women and education for children, and hence broader and more solid income generation for present and future generations. High rates of urbanization entail economies of scale, specialization in both countryside and city, and better average living conditions. High levels of formal employment bring about greater labor productivity and broader mechanisms for worker protection.

But these dimensions of development do not necessarily advance at an even pace, nor are they the spontaneous result of economic growth. There are great differences in each of these dimensions between countries with the same level of per capita income and even among those that share a common history and similar resource endowments. Some of these dimensions have their own specific dynamic only partly connected to other aspects of development or economic growth.

DEMOGRAPHIC OPPORTUNITY

One such dimension is the demographic transition, which involves an increase and subsequent slowing of the population growth rate. For reasons only partly related to the previous development of countries, mortality rates have fallen before fertility rates, giving rise to a transitory pe-

riod of rapid population growth. In the early phases, this process has led to an increase of lower age groups, entailing a greater burden of dependent children on the working-age population. At the intermediate phase of this process, these majority groups that reach productive ages find themselves in a favorable and unique situation. They have fewer children than their parents had, and at the same time, because they come from the generation of large families, they are less burdened by the dependency of older people, much less so than their children will be. This intermediate stage thus constitutes a period of transitory opportunity that may or may not be exploited.

Figure III.1: The Demographic Window of Opportunity in Latin America

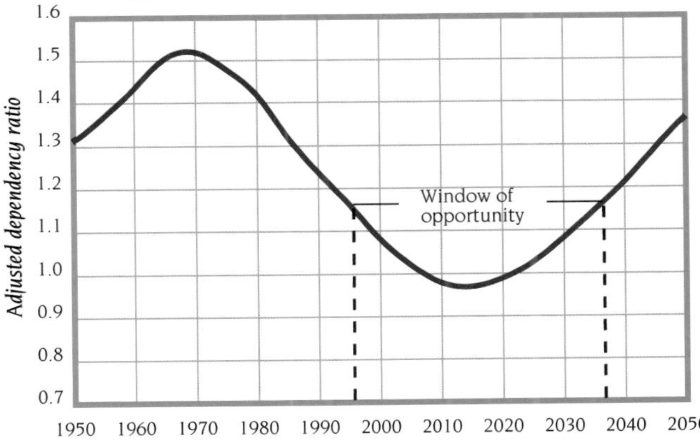

Source: Duryea and Székely (1998).

Latin America as a whole stands at this period of demographic opportunity. For the regional average, the combined rates of dependence that the working-age population will have to support will fall for approximately two decades before rising steadily until after the middle of the next century (Figure III.1). But not all countries have this much time. In the more demographically mature countries such as Trinidad and Tobago, Cuba, the Baha-

Figure III.2: Expected Changes in the Dependency Ratio

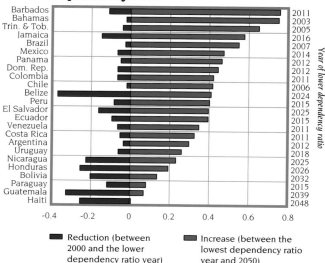

Year of lower dependency ratio

	Year
Barbados	2011
Bahamas	2003
Trin. & Tob.	2005
Jamaica	2016
Brazil	2007
Mexico	2014
Panama	2012
Dom. Rep.	2012
Colombia	2011
Chile	2006
Belize	2024
Peru	2015
El Salvador	2025
Ecuador	2015
Venezuela	2011
Costa Rica	2011
Argentina	2012
Uruguay	2018
Nicaragua	2025
Honduras	2026
Bolivia	2032
Paraguay	2015
Guatemala	2039
Haiti	2048

-0.4   -0.2   0   0.2   0.4   0.6   0.8

■ Reduction (between 2000 and the lower dependency ratio year)

■ Increase (between the lowest dependency ratio year and 2050)

Source: IDB *calculation based on* UN *Population Statistics* (1996).

mas or Uruguay, the rates of dependency will fall very little and in a much more fleeting way than in countries with a younger population, such as Honduras, Bolivia, Guatemala, Paraguay or Haiti (Figure III.2).

This period of demographic opportunity opens up a set of possibilities for improving income distribution. If policies exploit the opportunity, more work, greater savings, and more education can be generated, and therefore the mechanisms that perpetuate current inequality can be attenuated.

MORE WORK

During the demographic opportunity period, sources of family income generation can be multiplied, since more members of the household will be at working age. Moreover, since fewer children will have to be taken care of, there will be fewer demands for domestic work than in earlier generations. That will open up possibilities for greater participation of women in the labor force, a process already under way throughout the region. Because women are joining the work force, the economically active population will grow even faster than the working-age population or the total population. Hence, there will be an opportunity, if adequate employment is generated, for the average income of the entire population to rise rapidly, and for inequalities between families to decline. If the opportunity is not exploited, however, the growing labor supply will bring about more informal employment and unemployment, and the gaps in pay will widen be-

tween skilled and unskilled workers, formal and informal workers, and men and women. Economic and social policies can make the difference.

Trade Policy

To take advantage of growing labor resources, trade policy must make it easy to use them. During the days of import substitution, trade policies encouraged the use of capital in industrial activities and allowed the cost of protecting the incipient manufacturing sectors to be passed on to consumers. Workers had to endure a higher cost of living and less demand for employment than they would have had under other circumstances. Despite the profound trade reforms of the past decade, such conditions have not disappeared entirely. With a few exceptions, tariff structures offer more protection to consumer goods than to intermediate goods or capital.[1] To take advantage of the demographic opportunity, trade policy must advocate a flat and moderate tariff structure that protects all sectors alike, does not discriminate against labor, and does not squander the tax revenue potential of imports of intermediate goods and capital, which constitute the bulk of imports in almost all countries.

Labor Legislation

Traditional mechanisms for protecting labor in Latin America were designed to provide stability to formal employment and strengthen workers vis-à-vis large companies, rather than to encourage involvement of women in economic activities or stabilize income from labor and offer social protection to all workers. But with the demographic shift, legislation that leads companies to discriminate against women and against more disadvantaged workers should be avoided. Examples are restrictions on temporary and part-time hiring and imposing maternity costs on companies. These efforts at protection have aggravated rather than corrected labor inequality, and they should be replaced by collective protection mechanisms against unemployment, illness and old age. The high minimum wages in effect in some countries also cause discrimination against women and against workers with less education, and constitute inefficient mechanisms for redistributing income. (Labor policies for generating greater income and distributing it better are discussed in Chapter 6).

---

[1] See Part Two of both the 1996 and 1997 Reports on *Economic and Social Progress in Latin America* by the Inter-American Development Bank.

Infrastructure of Household Services

In order for women to be incorporated into high productivity economic activities, they must be freed up from household tasks. The lack or unreliability of water, electricity or sewage services limits women's participation and lowers their productive potential. Such deficiencies also keep children from remaining in the school system and hinder school performance. Hence, improving utilities can impact equity and the productive capacity of families in several ways. It is often argued that reorganizing public utility companies is essential for assuring the efficiency of productive sectors and international competitiveness. Equity is no less important a reason (see Chapter 5).

Health and Child Care

The incorporation of women into formal employment, where they can be better paid and enjoy greater stability, is also limited by lack of help with child care. As various experiences show, child care services can facilitate not only the involvement of women in the work force, but subsequent improvement in school performance of children as well. Preventive health services with special emphasis on illnesses that affect younger children are also an effective instrument for child welfare that promotes women's participation as paid workers (see Chapter 5).

MORE SAVINGS

Because families have fewer children to raise and educate during the period of demographic opportunity, family expenses are lower than for previous generations. This presents an opportunity for saving. But saving is also a necessity: today's parents cannot expect that their small number of children will support them when they are old. In the aggregate, this means that the period of demographic opportunity ought to increase the savings rate for a time. Whether such savings are generated and really provide support for the old age of current generations will depend essentially on pension and financial policies.

Pension Policy

Traditional pension systems in Latin America are distribution mechanisms through which workers of today's generations cover the expenses of workers from previous generations who are now retired, with the implicit commitment that when today's workers reach retirement the workers of the future will pay for them. But this mechanism does not impose the same costs on all generations. Due to the demographic moment when the pay-as-you-go systems were introduced, and their initial low coverage, they now offer benefits that will not be sustainable in the future with such low annual contributions. Today's generations are not contributing at the level of the benefits to which they are becoming entitled. Hence, with the current distribution system, the present generation of workers will become a heavy burden for future generations. The countries that are enjoying the demographic opportunity ought to take advantage of it to pay for their pensions by generating the savings that will make it possible to cover such expenses in the future. Otherwise, their pensions will require heavier burdens, and future generations will be less free to consume. Countries that did not avail themselves of this opportunity are today supporting pension burdens that require them to maintain contribution rates of over 20 percent and that restrict the possibility of saving and investing.

Despite their redistributional potential, simple pay-as-you-go systems have not operated as effective mechanisms for distributing income toward the poor. Low initial obligations have allowed the better-off groups of workers to obtain generous benefits, restraining room for broadening coverage of the system. The new pension systems will be able to make minimum protection universal with funds from the general budget and the generation of individual savings based on a capitalization system managed by the private sector and strictly monitored by the state, as now exists in several countries in the region. (See the discussion of social security policies in Chapter 6).

Financial Policy

Good use of the savings potential during the period of demographic opportunity requires efficient and secure mechanisms for channeling these resources toward productive investments. Savings will thus finance the capital accumulation that will be the basis for the yields that older people will enjoy in the future. Financial policy must offer the legal and regulatory framework to attain that objective. It also ought to assure protection of savings against the volatility typical of Latin America.[2]

---

[2] See a more complete description of this policy agenda in Hausmann and Stein (1995), and Gavin, Hausmann, Perotti and Talvi (1996).

But financial policies should also help savings serve to finance small producers and self-employed workers who today do not have access to credit resources. The imperfections of credit markets are a factor aggravating income inequalities because they limit the productive potential of those without capital. Lack of access results primarily from the absence of institutions to assure individual willingness to honor obligations and to reduce the perception of credit risk for lenders. The most common mechanism for resolving the problem is collateral, but its use is limited to the financing of assets with a secondary market. Alternative strategies include creating rewards for good reputation (and costs for poor reputation) in meeting obligations through the use of credit information services; raising the cost of nonfulfillment by making it a criminal offense and punishing it effectively; and creating group credit systems that use social control to reduce monitoring and transaction costs. All these options require policy actions to help establish and operate institutions under legal protection (see Chapter 7).

MORE EDUCATION

The period of demographic opportunity will allow families to devote greater effort and more economic resources to educating their children. In the aggregate, the increase in the proportion of workers per school-age person makes it possible to extend school coverage without having to raise the tax burden per worker. In order to take advantage of this opportunity, there must be, on the supply side, better organization of education systems, enabling them to respond to the needs of families, and on the demand side, support mechanisms to help pay the costs incurred by low-income families in sending their children to school.

Organization of the Education System

Public education systems in Latin America are centrally organized around a Ministry of Education that handles financing, resource allocation, staff hiring and administrative oversight. Such monopolistic organization leads to weak users because families and students have no way to affect decisions; it leads to strong teacher organizations because it creates incentives for them to become centrally organized to deal with the government; and ultimately it leads to weak command structures in government because decisions on education (and labor union pressures) operate on time horizons that are much longer than the lifetime of any individual administration. Hence,

in many countries public spending on education is high but poorly allocated. Resource allocation is biased toward paying employees and is shaped by payment commitments, not by the level and quality of education results. The escape route for higher income families is private education, where competition and standards of quality are in effect. The upshot is that education is heavily stratified, thereby aggravating differences of income rather than eliminating them.

The alternative to this centralized organization system involves strengthening the user, giving the provider independence, and redefining the government's role. As users of the system, parents can be stronger if they have more information on quality and performance of schools (for example, through national standardized tests), if they can participate in decisions over the leadership and direction of schools, and if they have the possibility of choosing between alternative schools. In their role as providers, schools can be more independent if they have the basic operational decisions about staff hiring and resource allocation, and if they have to be responsible to parents and communities for the services they provide. The government can play a more decisive role if it devotes itself not to bureaucratic control but to generating information, setting quality standards, and assuring that schools receive funds from public financing based on the quantity and quality of the education they can provide, rather than on expenses (see Chapter 5).

Lowering the Private Costs of Education

The high dropout rate in Latin America cannot be attributed solely to the problems of supply that have to do with the organization of education systems. Demand for education is limited by low returns and by high (real and opportunity) costs that families must incur to send their children to school. Better educational organization would help improve returns. Suitable labor policies and a growth-oriented macro context would also be helpful. Even with promising returns, however, keeping students in the education system may be limited by high private costs that low-income families cannot meet. Possible solutions include direct subsidies as well as providing school supplies, meals, transportation or health services for students. Experiences in the region are rich and provide many lessons on the possibilities and limitations of such policies (see Chapter 5).

In short, the different dimensions of development associated with inequality are not independent of economic and social policies. Past policies help explain why Latin American economies have educational levels below world patterns, and are more informal, more urbanized and unquestionably more unequal than other economies with the same income level. Policies adopted during this moment of demographic opportunity can help not only to lower this extra inequality but also to hasten economic and social development. Equity and development are not at odds.

DEALING WITH NATURAL ENDOWMENTS

The extra inequality in Latin America is also rooted in the characteristics of its natural resource endowment. Tropical countries have disadvantages in their struggle against poverty and inequality for reasons associated with disease control, the productivity of land, and people's capacity for physical exertion. Where there are no seasons, there is no natural control over the continual reproduction of disease-bearing agents, and hence they are difficult to eradicate. Even with the best combination of inputs, lands in tropical zones are less productive than in temperate zones, and properly exploiting them requires technologies that have greater economies of scale and that need more capital. Moreover, the physical effort that an individual can make when at the mercy of the tropics is substantially less than in a country with moderate seasons.

Inequality is affected not only by geographical location, however, but also by the characteristics of resources. Countries that have abundant agricultural or extractive mining resources tend to generate greater inequality and a lower level of development. One reason is that these activities absorb the scarce capital available and require very little employment, thereby slowing the development of other sectors due to the lack of both capital and markets. Another reason is that such abundance encourages opportunism rather than cooperation. Finally, dependence on natural resources leads to volatility, thereby discouraging investments that are slow to mature, especially in education.

No country is utterly at the mercy of geography, however. Some tropical countries, such as those in Southeast Asia, have reached levels of development and distribution comparable to or better than those of European countries. Some natural resource-dependent economies such as Australia or New Zealand are among the most highly developed and their income distribution is among the best in the world.

Several policies are decisive for overcoming the constraints of geography. In the area of health, the key is coverage of preventive health care services in order to keep the influence of tropical diseases under control. For

its part, rural education can facilitate the spread of preventive health care practices, and also help raise productivity in the countryside and stimulate migration to the cities. Provision of basic services is another piece of the struggle against geography. Access to potable water, still quite limited in rural areas of many countries in the region, is essential for improving health conditions and chances for ending poverty. To mitigate the rigors of warm climates on labor productivity and on people's welfare, nothing is more necessary than electricity.

Natural resource extraction has been a source of inequality in Latin America that has drawn productive resources away from other activities that have the potential for generating more employment and well-being. This does not mean that policies must be artificially limited in terms of developing natural resource-based activities. For reasons of efficiency, however, it is not justifiable to grant tax exemptions and special investment conditions to these sectors, especially when they are nonrenewable resources whose social opportunity cost is much greater than the costs incurred by producers. Tax incentives are often granted with the justification that such activities require large amounts of capital to remain unmoved for very long periods, but that is one of the very reasons why they tend to promote inequality. Because revenues from natural resources are potentially very unstable, tax systems must not transfer instability to the government by artificially lowering the risk perceived by investors. Government must also develop mechanisms for stabilizing tax revenues from primary sectors in order to avoid spreading volatility to the entire economy.

FISCAL SUPPORT FOR REDISTRIBUTIONAL POLICIES

Income distribution in Latin American countries will depend heavily on government in the next century. The distributional impact of fiscal policies is usually measured by the magnitude of the resources redistributed through the tax system and by social expenditures. In Latin America, as elsewhere in the world, the ultimate result of these operations tends to be redistributional, since taxes come from higher income groups in a greater proportion than the benefits that they receive through schools, hospitals or other social services. But this distributive impact of fiscal policy is not necessarily the most important, and can be a deceptive guide for policy.

Indeed, in Latin America tax systems traditionally have been quite progressive, but at the cost of sacrificing great revenue collection potential that could be directed to financing expenditures with great redistribution potential. Moreover, the highly progressive structure of taxes in theory and their concentration in some activities and sectors has limited public control over fiscal policy, leaving it more exposed to powerful interest groups. The vexing tax systems typical of Latin America have been difficult to administer and easy to evade. Simplifying income taxes and gradually adopting broadly-based taxes such as the value-added tax are ameliorating these problems in many countries in the region (see Chapter 8).

More important than how progressive the tax system or social spending may be is how efficiently taxes are collected, how low-income groups are provided adequate education, health care and household infrastructure services, how effective and well-focused safety nets are created, and how economic policies are adopted to promote a pattern of redistributive growth without sacrificing productivity.

Chapter 5

SOCIAL POLICIES
TO REDUCE INCOME DISPARITIES

WHICH SOCIAL POLICIES MAKE A DIFFERENCE?

As explained in previous chapters, factors such as women's participation in the labor force, fertility rates, and education all are important determinants of income inequality in Latin America and the Caribbean. In countries where women work more, and particularly where they have access to formal sector jobs, family incomes are higher. When women are more educated and participate more in the labor force, families have fewer children, and their children tend to be better educated. Countries that have done a better job of increasing the level and quality of education have also been able to reduce disparities in education. In countries with higher participation by women in the labor force, and with reduced fertility and better education, income is more equitably distributed (Figure 5.1).

A variety of policies can act on these primary factors to improve the ability of women to seek and gain employment in good jobs. Some are related to labor market policies and will be discussed in Chapter 6. But others fall clearly within the purview of social policy, such as promoting appropriate day-care and preschool services that make it easier for women to get jobs, while at the same time improving their children's ability to learn, develop and complete school. Ensuring that women get an education also increases the probability that they will enter the labor force and that their children will have improved schooling levels. Even infrastructure investments for utilities like water and electricity can increase women's participation in the workforce, or their productivity when working at home, by reducing the burden and time dedicated to domestic chores. Reproductive health services, which include

voluntary family planning, improve women's health and ability to work while giving families the option to delay their first child and ultimately focus their care, resources and attention on fewer children.

Promoting better educational outcomes requires policies that act on a variety of fronts. The public sector is primarily responsible for the supply of education services in most countries. These education systems generally are failing to provide the amount and quality of education needed to keep pace with international trends, and to significantly reduce income inequalities. Reforming education systems to improve children's progress through schooling is an important part of the solution. However, public policy can only be effective if it takes into consideration the factors that affect family decisions regarding their children's schooling. These determinants of the demand for education are another significant subject for social policies aimed at reducing inequality.

Social policies cover a wide range of goals and programs directed toward reducing income disparities. But

Figure 5.1. Reinforcing Positive Links: How Social Policies Affect Income Distribution

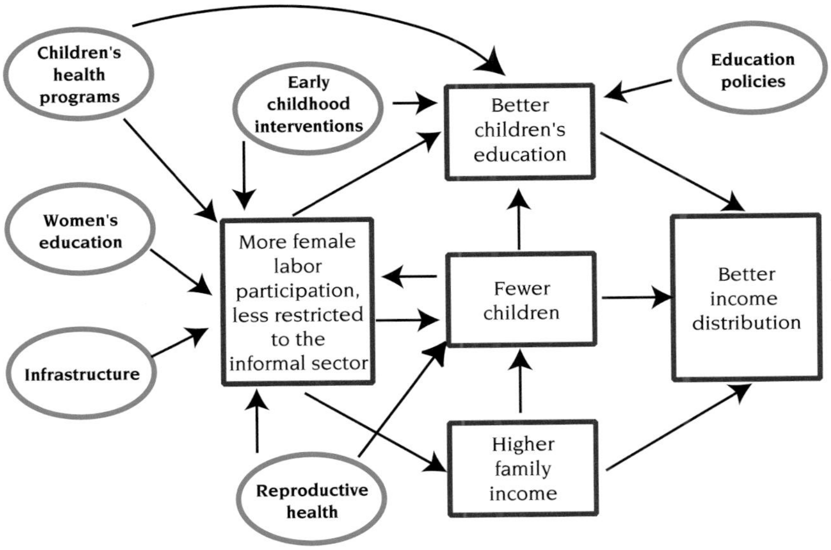

Box 5.1. *Economic Shocks, Inequality and Poverty: The Need for Safety Nets*

Empirical evidence suggests that macroeconomic shocks can seriously exacerbate inequality and poverty. Latin America has experienced two major crises in the last 15 years. In the 1980s, Mexico's debt crisis spread throughout Latin America by way of trade shocks and weak public finances. In 1995, Mexico's liquidity crisis spread only to Argentina.

How did poverty and income distribution change when countries endured stagnant or negative growth? Poverty and inequality increased during the 1980s in Brazil, Guatemala, Mexico, Panama and Venezuela, as well as in urban areas of Argentina, Bolivia, Chile, Honduras and Peru. Similarly, urban poverty and inequality in Argentina rose sharply during the 1995 crisis. Although the poorest quintile of the population was not always hurt disproportionately, its average income fell. Income downturns can have a more devastating impact on those living close to subsistence. Furthermore, in country after country hit by the 1980s crisis, the income share of the top 10 percent increased, sometimes substantially.

Although social indicators such as infant mortality rates and average years of schooling continued to improve in Latin America during the 1980s, they did so at a slower pace than in previous years. Some of the more detailed indicators of health and education worsened. For example, in Mexico, infant and pre-school mortality caused by nutritional deficiency rose in the 1980s, reversing the trend of the previous decade. In Chile, the data on low birthweight infants and undernourished children followed the trends in economic conditions, after a systematic improvement in both indicators in the 1970s. In Venezuela, the literacy rate for ages 15-19 fell in the 1980s. In Mexico, the proportion of children entering first grade shrank, as did that of students moving to high school after completing junior high. These trends also imply that investment in human capital probably became more skewed, making the observed increase in inequality more entrenched.

The fact that adverse shocks have more devastating effects on the poor, and that the rich tend to have access to income-protecting mechanisms (including capital flight), is not circumscribed to macroeconomic slumps. Natural disasters or sudden changes in the terms of trade can have similar effects. For example, in Ecuador it is estimated that more than 50 percent of the population in areas affected by El Niño is poor. The sharp fall in coffee prices following the dismantling of the International Coffee Agreement led to a sharp rise in poverty in coffee-producing states in Mexico in the early 1990s.

In the 1980s, Latin American governments responded to the social costs of the economic crises in many ways. Measures included food assistance programs, unemployment insurance, social funds, extension of health care coverage to the unemployed, scholarships and training, and retraining and workfare programs. However, with the partial exception of Chile, the overall response was too little, too late. What are the lessons?

First, tackling social issues means putting them at the top of the agenda. Too often during the Latin American crises, policymakers' energy was devoted only to restoring macroeconomic stability and implementing structural reform. Argentina waited until 1997 to introduce an emergency employment program, despite the sharp rise in unemployment earlier in the decade and the fact that the existing severance payment and small-scale unemployment insurance schemes provided no safety nets for the unemployed poor. Second, the design of the response is crucial. Even in the case of the Social Emergency Funds designed to cushion the social costs of economic adjustment, success was at best mixed because beneficiaries were not necessarily those most affected by the crises. In Mexico and elsewhere, general subsidies were cut without the introduction of effectively targeted alternatives. Of greatest importance is the need to maintain support for core education and health services to avoid irreversible losses in human investment; yet this was done poorly in Latin America in the 1980s, as evidenced by the slower progress in health and education indicators mentioned above. Third, evidence suggests that programs put in place and operating before crises hit (albeit on a smaller scale) are better equipped to protect the target population than ad hoc emergency measures.

At present, most Latin American countries still do not have adequate mechanisms to mitigate the impact of adverse shocks on the poor and to temper the unequalizing character of economic crises. While there is a widespread perception that social funds were put in place for precisely that purpose, most were more effective at building small-scale social infrastructure than at creating employment opportunities for those hurt by the emergency. In fact, most countries in the region lack unemployment insurance or other types of consumption-smoothing safety nets to protect the poor from output, employment and price risks associated with systemic adverse shocks.

Because the institutional mechanisms to protect the poor from the brunt of the shocks are not in place beforehand, responses often have to rely on improvised programs designed for purposes and beneficiaries other than those affected by the crisis. Emergency responses to emergency situations do not have the time for adequate technical analyses, either to clarify the socioeconomic profile of groups most vulnerable to the adverse shocks or to evaluate the cost-effectiveness of different social protection options.

There are, however, some examples of safety nets that work well. In the 1980s, Chile implemented a large-scale public works program that provided employment for a large portion of the work force. It targeted the most needy by paying below market wage rates. Furthermore, it is possible to adapt social funds to function as safety nets when the need arises. Because many governments lack the resources to put social safety nets in place, the alternative of setting up social funds proved useful both to mobilize external resources and to respond rapidly to pressing needs. Whatever their form, implementing efficient and cost-effective safety nets to cope with emergencies can be of great value in the quest for greater social equity in the region.

social policies also aim to reduce poverty, assure social cohesion, and share costs of public goods. Although all social programs influence income inequality, this chapter will focus on those policies that can most directly influence the distribution of income in the short and medium term. In the short term, policies that assure that women can participate effectively in the labor market can have a strong impact, while in the medium term, increasing children's educational attainment is the key to reducing inequality. The chapter begins by discussing the rationale of public programs that improve women's options for entering the labor force and raising their earnings. It then examines those policies and programs that hold promise for increasing educational attainment.

The common element of the policies discussed here is their intention to equalize access to services, resources and opportunities that affect family decisions regarding labor participation, fertility and education. These are permanent contributing factors toward the region's high levels of inequality. However, macroeconomic shocks, sudden changes in the terms of trade and natural disasters can have devastating effects on inequality and poverty, independent of longer-term social policy. Such transitory events require policies that address emergencies or establish safety nets (Box 5.1).

EARNING OPPORTUNITIES FOR WOMEN

As we have seen in earlier chapters, whether or not women participate in the labor force makes a significant difference in the distribution of family income. When women have the option to enter the labor force, they can better contribute to increasing household income. Regardless of whether women actually get jobs, the option itself has beneficial effects on the intrahousehold distribution of consumption, reduces women's vulnerability to violence, and improves investments in children. While women's labor force participation is strongly influenced by their education, the most immediate influences include child care, health and family planning, and infrastructure.

Child Care Improves Women's Earnings and Children's Cognitive Development[1]

In Latin America, women generally assume more responsibilities for the care of children than men. As a result, any social trends or public policies that affect the opportunities and costs for child care and schooling have an important impact on the capacity of women to enter the labor force and earn income. Numerous studies have shown that child care and labor force participation are competing uses of the time of mothers.[2] Women with small children, particularly younger than three years old, are much less likely to work than those without young children. The cost of child care also affects the kinds of care and the decision to work, and the implicit costs that families face depend on the availability of alternative care options, including the presence of relatives or friends willing to provide low-cost care. Lowering child care costs, either through increased supply or subsidies, increases the options to use "market care" as an alternative to care by the mother or a relative. For those who choose to purchase child care services and enter the labor force, lower costs reduce what a woman needs to earn before the associated expenditure on child care services is covered. Other factors also affect women's participation in the labor force, including the woman's education and the presence of other income earners in the household. But the cost, quality and kinds of child care available in the market clearly have an overriding impact.

A recent study in Rio de Janeiro confirms these general findings.[3] It indicates that if the supply of low-cost child care for children under six years old in the favelas of Rio de Janeiro were increased, more mothers would join the labor force and use publicly-financed day care centers. Women fortunate enough to obtain free child care from municipalities increased their earnings by as much as 20 percent. For those who paid private providers to care for their children, earnings were between 12 and 29 percent higher, even after controlling for selection effects and the features of the child care market. In the case of private providers, the higher returns may reflect the advantage of greater flexibility in operating hours, since public centers had limited hours.[4]

Lowering the costs and increasing the availability of child care can have a large impact on family income, particularly among poorer families, by making it possible for women to bring in additional incomes. Furthermore, giving women the option to enter the labor force and maintain a capacity to earn incomes independently of spouses has benefits in terms of the intrahousehold distribution of resources and reduction of domestic violence.

---

[1] This section is based on Deutsch (1998a).

[2] Starting with Heckman (1974).

[3] Deutsch (1998b).

[4] Recent findings from the United States provide further corroboration for the strong labor supply effects of access to child care. Free public schooling has a significant positive effect on labor supply and a significant negative effect on receipt of public assistance by single mothers. Specifically, for single mothers whose youngest child is five, access to free public schooling raises labor supply by 8 to 18 percent, raises wage and salary income by 27 percent, and reduces receipt of public assistance by 18 percent. See Gelbach (1998).

Access to child care services may also have an impact on the schooling of some older siblings, particularly girls, to the extent that they are involved in caring for younger siblings while their mothers work.[5]

However, labor market benefits for mothers or benefits for older siblings generally are not explicit objectives of most early childhood interventions. These programs usually focus on improving the children's health, nutrition and development, with a resulting improvement in future opportunities for learning and earning.

Recent studies confirm that early childhood intervention programs can be very beneficial to children. A study of U.S. programs documented improvements in emotional or cognitive development; parent-child relationships; educational processes and outcomes; and health-related indicators such as child abuse, maternal reproductive health, and maternal substance abuse.[6] Preliminary findings from a control group evaluation of an early childhood intervention program in Bolivia are also positive. Upon enrollment, some 40 percent of the children in the PIDI program in urban Bolivia showed stunted psycho-social development. After the children spent one year in the program, this percentage declined to 20 percent, and after two years, it was only 5 percent. The child mortality rates of PIDI participants was less than 1 percent, in contrast to the 20 percent rate among the target population.[7]

Children also appear to benefit from well designed child care programs over the long run through better performance in school, and ultimately in higher earnings as adults.[8] Early childhood intervention programs in the United States also appear to reduce negative social behavior. Program participants exhibit lower rates of juvenile delinquency, significantly less antisocial behavior, and have significantly fewer lifetime arrests.

The many benefits described above appear to justify a significant role for government in ensuring that quality early childhood programs be available to families. However, there is no prescribed or predefined role for how the state should be involved. The appropriate kinds of child care—whether in public programs or in the home with a parent or relative—depend on many factors that differ from one family, woman and child to the next. Furthermore, each program has its own set of costs and benefits, and relatively little is known about the optimal design and mix of such programs. Nonetheless, a few basic precepts can be drawn from experiences in the region that can help contribute to cost-effective programs.

• *Be Flexible and Promote Choice*. Governments should not presume to impose a one-size-fits-all approach to child care. By encouraging and supporting a variety of programs, public policy can empower individuals, fami-

lies, communities and local governments to demand the kind of care that best fits their circumstances. Given the panoply of possible interventions available,[9] and the wide array of family structures, tastes, cultures and concerns—all within national settings with extreme variations in incomes by region and in the implementation capacity of local governments—it is impossible to provide a single national solution.

• *Leverage Public Resources*. Households have already developed numerous strategies to care for the children of working mothers, with or without government support. The challenge for public policy is to work with these existing options to guarantee the desired quality in terms of the custodial, emotional, cognitive and nutritional support provided to the children. The best option is probably not to build new government daycare centers. Instead, it will be possible to reach more people, and leverage greater benefits, by supporting informal initiatives that are already underway, and by working both to improve their quality and to provide financial support to the poorest families so as to guarantee access.

Another way to leverage scarce public resources is to build partnerships with community groups, nongovernmental organizations, religious organizations, existing social service agencies and the private sector. Governments should avoid "bureaucratic creep," which would add large numbers of employees to the public payroll and more public facilities to maintain, if more flexible and effective alternatives are available through partnerships. Recent programs in Bolivia and Ecuador exemplify this approach to program design by fostering increased involvement of nongovernmental actors in financing and providing child care services.

• *Target Well*. Targeting public funds to expand child care options is important if governments are going to increase the options for a significant number of households without creating fiscal problems. Targeting poses a chal-

---

[5] Connelly, et al. (1996), Deutsch, (1998b), Engle (1991), Wong and Levine (1992).

[6] Karoly, et al. (1998).

[7] Tan and van der Gaag (1998).

[8] Karoly, et al. (1998) and University of Wisconsin-Madison, Institute for Research on Poverty (1997). When adults who as children had attended the Perry preschool program reached age 27, their earnings were 60 percent higher than their peers.

[9] As stated by Karoly, et al. (1998): "The term early childhood intervention is a broad concept. It covers programs concerned with low-birthweight babies and those concerned with toddlers in low-income families; interventions targeting children as well as those targeting their mothers; services offered in homes and those offered in centers; programs aimed at improving educational achievement and those aimed at improving health; and services as diverse as parent skills training, child health screening, child-abuse recognition, and social-services referral."

lenge because middle-class families who already have the resources to care for their children will be tempted to seek and demand access to subsidized services, particularly if programs are of high quality. Even low-income families may change their behavior in counterproductive ways to gain access to public programs. It would hardly help to reduce income inequality and poverty if subsidized child care for families below a particular income level led women to leave the labor force in order to gain or maintain access to the program. Effective targeting requires designs that can clearly identify the target group—through selection or self-selection—and criteria that do not encourage counterproductive behavior. One fairly common design for meeting these criteria is to target subsidies or child care programs geographically in low-income neighborhoods.[10] Some programs try to be cost-effective and target by giving advice, training and supervision to women who are already providing daycare for neighbors in poorer neighborhoods.[11]

While this discussion of early childhood interventions particularly applies to children under the age of six who attend child care centers, much of it applies equally to preschool programs in this age group and to the early years of primary schooling. Many countries in the region are already expanding preschool systems, although such programs are not necessarily cost-effective, may substitute for private expenditures by wealthier households, and could create serious fiscal burdens for the future. But policies to promote the provision of good custodial care for young children, if done wisely, can give women and their families options that in many cases are critical to household well-being and to reducing income disparities. In primary school, as well, the relatively short school day makes it difficult for women to participate more fully in the labor market. Several countries are increasing the school year to cover the same number of days as in more developed economies. Similarly, the number of school hours per day is being increased in such countries as Panama and Uruguay by reducing the number of schools with several shifts.

Reproductive and Children's Health

While social policy, broadly speaking, needs to address the entire range of health services, the kinds of health investments that reduce inequality are quite specific and frequently inexpensive. The hospitals and curative services that consume the lion's share of national health expenditures (at least 4 percent of regional GDP) have a limited impact on income distribution. Rather, the services that affect women's labor force participation rates,

increase children's educational attainment, and reduce fertility are mainly those related to reproductive and child health care. Yet, the region traditionally spends very little on these services; in Brazil, for example, spending on mother and child health programs represents only about 1 percent of total health expenditures.

Government actions that address income inequality are mainly in the area that is traditionally known as maternal and child health, more recently expanded to reproductive and child health. Reproductive and child health policies, programs and practices can improve household welfare in two ways. First, they break the intergenerational transmission of poverty because children who are born healthy, at full term, well nourished, and protected from communicable diseases are more likely to flourish and take advantage of educational and other opportunities. Second, these services influence a woman's ability to enter and remain in the labor force and to participate in relatively high-earning sectors of the economy, since they promote better health and the ability to affect the timing and number of children.

Giving poorer households the same access to reproductive health services as wealthier ones is an essential part of reducing social inequality, since this opens options to the poor that would otherwise be out of reach. As shown in Chapters 2 and 3, families at opposite ends of the income distribution tend to differ in both the number of children and the extent to which women are involved in income-generating activities. Reducing the disparities in access to reproductive health services would allow those lower-income families who would like to increase women's remunerated work or focus their resources on fewer children to better act on what they determine is best for them.

The role of reproductive health services in reducing death, morbidity and illness among women cannot be ignored. In countries like Bolivia, Peru and Honduras, maternal mortality rates are frighteningly high—at 390, 265 and 221 maternal deaths per 100,000 live births, respectively. Reproduction-related ailments are responsible for 14 percent of the total burden of disease (death and disability) in Latin America. These causes are thus the single largest contributors to the burden of disease in the region, and hit the poorest and most vulnerable populations particularly hard. Reproductive health services include a wide range of essential preventive and curative services, such as prevention and treatment of sexually transmitted diseases and other infections of the repro-

---

[10] For discussions of targeting see Van de Walle and Nead (1995).

[11] Such programs include *Mãe Crecheira* in Brazil and *Madres Comunitarias* in Colombia.

ductive tract, cervical cancer screening, routine prenatal and postnatal care, management of high-risk deliveries, and contraceptive services and counseling for men and women. Taken together, these services address most of the basic health needs of women in their reproductive years, which are also potentially the years of greatest contribution to family income. For women, better health care can mean fewer days of work lost to illness and higher productivity on the job. For them and their families, this can mean more income and a reduction in income disparities.

Reproductive health services can also play a role in reducing income disparities by allowing couples to choose whether to delay having children, extend the period between pregnancies, and eventually have smaller families. Each of these—particularly delaying the first birth—allows women greater opportunities to continue in school or enter the labor force. Availability of means to control fertility helps women to reduce the number and frequency of interruptions in their jobs due to pregnancy and childbearing, and to gain access to better jobs that require more continuity of commitment and investments in training. Control over fertility can also make an important contribution to gender equity if the prevention of unwanted or mistimed pregnancies improves employers' perceptions about the reliability of female workers.

There is, in fact, evidence of considerable unmet demand for contraceptive services, particularly among poor and marginalized populations. In household surveys, one-quarter to one-third of currently married women in Guatemala, El Salvador and Mexico state that they do not want to have another birth within two years (or ever), and yet are not using a contraceptive method. This figure rises to 40 percent among women with no more than primary schooling, and yet is very low (less than 10 percent) among women who have completed secondary school— evidence of their greater ability to access family planning services. Although it is difficult to accurately determine the demand for contraceptive services in such surveys, there is corroborating evidence from other sources. The extraordinarily high rates of illegal and unsafe abortions— the primary cause of high maternal mortality rates in many countries in the region—are a strong signal to policy-makers that the lack of access to high quality family planning services is exacting a terrible toll. In short, the provision of reproductive health services is a vital instrument in a broader policy framework to reduce social gaps.

Publicly-funded reproductive health programs are undergoing important changes in many countries. In years past, public health sector resources for maternal and child health services were directed primarily toward fostering healthy children through prenatal, delivery and postnatal care programs, as well as preventive and curative services for infants and young children. Some governments also sponsored or accepted external funding for family planning services, generally delivered alongside but separate from maternal and child health services. Family planning services often were justified as a means to slow population growth and thereby improve social welfare, rather than as a means to improve the welfare of households and individuals.

Today, reproductive health is viewed as a service that women need, rather than as a mechanism that utilizes the woman as an instrument to reduce population growth or improve the welfare of children. Women's demands, preferences and needs are increasingly being taken into account in the design of programs throughout the region. One of the most important lessons is to recognize that women are fully capable of determining their own destinies. This requires that public programs be sensitive to cultural and social norms and respect human rights. The current generation of reproductive health program benefits from decades of theory, research, and trial and error. Outlined below are some of the important lessons that have emerged about how such programs can be designed to make the greatest contribution to women's welfare.

• *Policy.* Government decisions about family planning and other reproductive health services go far beyond the health sector. They touch on core social, cultural and religious values, often stirring strong emotions. While in some countries the controversies surrounding family planning have been major obstacles, in others, these sensitive issues have been skillfully managed. Increasingly, greater public dialogue and the participation of civil society is essential for widespread understanding of public family planning investments.

As governments develop or refine reproductive health and family planning policies, investments in these health services will be more cost-effective if paired with significant investments in education, particularly for girls. While making high-quality services available is one part of the equation, ensuring that women at all levels in society have educational opportunities remains an essential ingredient in any social sector strategy.

• *Integrating Services with Other Programs.* Family planning services are most effective when delivered within the larger package of reproductive health services. Programs designed to help couples achieve better individual and family health are more likely to engender the confidence required for successful delivery of family planning services than stand-alone, target-oriented approaches. One way to stimulate higher quality, integrated service delivery is to monitor the results of reproductive health interventions, focusing on the outcomes—that is, a couple's ability to have the number of children desired and a decline in morbidity associated with births—rather than on the number of couples using contraception or other standard family planning targets.

• *Taking Advantage of the Private Sector.* The private sector has been shown in household surveys to be the provider of choice for most couples throughout the world and is an important partner for government. The private sector affords greater confidentiality and is perceived by most couples to deliver services of higher quality than the public sector. Currently in the region, more than 60 percent of family planning services are delivered through private providers, with shares ranging from 23 percent in El Salvador and 36 percent in Mexico to 70 percent in Brazil and 72 percent in Colombia. The public sector can foster greater (and higher quality) participation of the private sector by financing services delivered by the private sector, subsidizing preservice or in-service training in reproductive health, and supporting social marketing campaigns to educate people about the availability of particular services or products.[12]

• *Voluntary and Appropriate Care.* Medical and counseling services must be adjusted to accommodate a broad range of ages, socioeconomic conditions, and ethnic and cultural groups. Programs adapted to the needs of adolescent girls are particularly important. In many countries, while overall fertility rates are declining, the rate of pregnancy is increasing (or slowing at a lower rate) among very young women. Opportunities for adolescents are negatively affected by pregnancy, and the welfare of their children is at risk. In addition, because pregnancy is just one of the outcomes of troubled behavior by adolescent girls, it is a strong signal that more attention is needed for this generation of mothers.

• *Financing.* Despite the high externalities associated with family planning, program designers should strongly consider incorporating user fees or other cost recovery mechanisms to partially offset the costs of service delivery. Given the pattern of demand for family planning services—with better-off families generally having greater demand for contraception—a fully subsidized program can be regressive. In addition, user fees can help guarantee that the services are used on a voluntary basis—the touchstone of quality and important as well for reasons related both to culture and human rights. It is important to note, however, that in virtually no country in the world are family planning services financially self-sustaining. Even in the for-profit private sector, family planning services are cross-subsidized by payments for other obstetrical and gynecological care, and are offered primarily because they attract patients, not because they are inherently profitable.

Finally, given that health insurance is currently part of health reform efforts in many countries, the benefits packages should include family planning services, along with the larger set of reproductive health services, to ensure equitable access.

Better Children's Health Helps Women Work and Improves Educational Attainment

Financing or providing infant and child health services represents a clear opportunity to improve individual and family welfare over the long term and to reduce social inequalities. In general, effective targeting of the poor can be achieved simply by investing in services that prevent or treat the types of diseases that disproportionately affect them. Children born to families on the margins of society are vulnerable to debilitating diseases and high risk of death due to preventable causes. Measles, cholera, tuberculosis and other infectious ailments are the cause of 85 percent of deaths among children under five in the region as a whole, and a significantly larger share of deaths among poor families. Care for sick children requires large amounts of parents' (and typically mothers') time, competing for time in school, the workplace or other domestic production, such as home-based agriculture.

As with family planning services, policymakers and child health program designers can benefit from decades of experience in Latin America and throughout the world. The single greatest determinant of children's health is the education of their mothers. While public investment in health care for children is important and necessary, the critical role of girls' education must be recognized by policymakers in all sectors. Given the importance of nutrition for growth, a strong immune system, and quick recovery from common childhood diseases, greater attention should also be paid by policymakers and program managers to integrating nutrition education and services within the health sector. This includes promotion of breastfeeding, school feeding programs within poor communities, nutrition education, promotion of home gardening to increase dietary variety, and distribution of micronutrients.

Program designers should keep in mind the time constraints within the household. Some widely promoted

---

[12] For example, the International Planned Parenthood Federation, which has affiliates throughout Latin America and the Caribbean, has had productive partnerships with many governments, often providing family planning and other reproductive health services using grants or contractual arrangements.

treatments place additional burdens on mothers who have many other critical daily obligations inside and outside the home. For example, the regimen of oral rehydration solution for treatment of diarrhea is extremely effective, but only when an adult (generally the mother) devotes many hours each day to mixing the solution and feeding it to the sick child. While all care requires time—and mothers are almost always strongly committed to ensuring that their child gets the best care they can give—the work of mothers as adjuncts to the health care system should be recognized by professionals, and every effort should be made to ensure that they are not excessively burdened.

Similarly, program managers can facilitate the use of child health services simply by making clinic hours and locations compatible with the other demands on parents' time. When health facilities are open early or late in the day or located near markets where farmers come to sell their produce, they make taking care of children more compatible with earning income for the family.

Infrastructure Services Make Household Time More Productive

Traditionally, women in the region have been responsible for most domestic tasks.[13] But the relatively poor performance of utilities such as water, electricity and telecommunications has meant that an inordinate amount of women's time, effort and strength has been expended on getting water and cooking fuel, cleaning and washing. Public policy that improves the efficient expansion of utilities, particularly into poor urban and rural areas, can therefore have a significant impact on expanding women's opportunities in ways that reduce income disparities.

Ironically, one of the greatest impediments to effective provision of infrastructure services has been an almost single-minded focus on keeping prices and tariffs low. Although such a policy would appear to favor the poor, in practice it has meant that wealthy and middle-class families with connections to water, electricity and telephone systems have received subsidized services, while lower-income households in rural and marginal urban areas have had to do without. In fact, by restructuring the provision of public utilities to operate on a commercial basis, as much as possible with private sector participation, equity can be improved as a direct consequence of improving efficiency.

Telecommunications, for example, are undergoing a veritable revolution with the privatization of telephone companies in several countries. The number and loca-

tions of telephone lines are expanding rapidly because these new frameworks give utility companies the incentives and capacity to respond to demand and compete for expanding their client base. In several cases, the increased investment, efficiency and scale of operation has reduced average costs and resulted in lower rates.[14] The electricity sector is also changing as public monopolies begin to accept private partners, establish concessions, or privatize their operations. Clearly there are regulatory challenges posed by the involvement of the private sector, but overall there have been substantial social benefits from the resulting reduction in communications and electricity costs, and from a more rapid expansion of these networks to marginal urban and rural areas.

Among utility services, water probably consumes the most time and money for poor households. Families without access often pay 10 times more per liter than richer families connected to the urban water system. For example, in Tegucigalpa, families without potable water paid 27 lempiras per cubic meter of water and used 3.7 m^3 per month, whereas those fortunate enough to be among the 46 percent of households connected to the water system paid only 2 lempiras per cubic meter and consumed an estimated 33 m^3 per month.[15] When public water systems are poorly managed, families have to purchase water from tank trucks, haul it from distant unsafe surface water sources, or build leaky pipes to extract water from trunk lines and aqueducts. For those who are connected to public water systems, pressure often fails and rationing is common. Unless water companies are financially autonomous and can charge sufficient prices, the investments required for expansion will continue to be constrained by the degree to which government and external funding agencies are willing to pitch in. It has been demonstrated that the best way to ensure quality water services is to make water companies financially autonomous, allow them to charge adequately, and create a proper regulatory framework. When prices are adequate, even poor communities can get service, often at lower prices.[16]

Other initiatives worth mentioning include creating consumer cooperatives, particularly in rural areas, that allow individuals to collectively resolve their water needs. Governments are also making large investments in water infrastructure through Social Investment Funds and mu-

---

[13] Detailed time studies have been done in Africa and Asia, but were unavailable for Latin America. See Fafchamps and Quisumbing (1998).

[14] Levy and Spiller (1996).

[15] Walker, et al. (1997).

[16] See Walker, et al. (1997) for a discussion of how the current institutional framework can be characterized as a "low-level equilibrium" with proposals for improving water service to the poor.

nicipal development programs.[17] These generally operate by establishing criteria to select projects proposed by communities and municipalities and then financing investments that meet certain conditions. The Social Investment Funds have generally been effective in reaching communities historically neglected by government agencies. But the funds have had difficulties assuring that these new water investments are maintained and operated, often for precisely the same reasons that the traditional institutional frameworks have failed. In short, effective reform of utilities, particularly water, is another ingredient for increasing household productivity and freeing women to focus on other tasks related to remunerated work, education or child rearing.

IMPROVING EDUCATION

Education is the single area where public policy should be able to have a large impact on reducing inequality. Generally, improvements in education have their largest influence on income inequality in the medium and long term: young adults with more education tend to experience shorter unemployment spells and earn more, marry later and have fewer children, and invest more in their own children's education and health. But education also has shorter-term effects on income inequality, since having children in good custodial care makes it possible for women to reenter the labor force sooner and in better jobs, and nontraditional training improves the earnings opportunities for lower-income groups (see Chapters 2 and 3).

Despite the importance of education, Latin America has raised its schooling levels much more slowly than other regions. And while it is true that the educational disparities within younger cohorts are declining in most countries, the overall dispersion continues to rise in many places because of the slow pace of past improvements. Furthermore, the returns to primary schooling are extremely low, due in part to the poor quality of education, particularly for children from less advantaged households. A large effort is required in two principal areas to accelerate the pace and quality of education: first, by improving the supply of quality education through institutional reforms, and second, by increasing the demand for education through improved quality and reduced costs.

Reforming the Organization of Education to Increase Coverage and Quality

One notable feature of education in Latin America, noted in Chapter 2, is that coverage is almost universal in the early grades, but falls off rapidly toward the secondary level. Latin America has underemphasized secondary schooling relative to other levels. While similar shares of the population over 25 years old have attained primary education in both East Asia and Latin America, East Asia has a 50 percent higher share of secondary level graduates. Only 25 percent of Latin Americans have some secondary schooling, compared to 36 percent in East Asia. These poor outcomes reflect problems with both the supply and demand for education. Because the supply of education is of poor quality and at relatively high cost, students end up repeating grades excessively. At the same time, those who complete school have learned less than students at comparable ages in other countries. On the demand side, high private costs of attending school coupled with low private returns encourage many children to leave school early.

The region is not behind for lack of resources. Public spending on primary and tertiary education is comparable to its expected level, based on a regression for 61 countries that controls for the level of national income. Thus, in Figures 5.2a and 5.2c, which refer to these two types of expenditures, Latin American countries are scattered above and below the international norm. Only spending on secondary education, which appears in Figure 5.2b, is significantly below its expected level (by almost 1 percent of GDP for the region as a whole).

There are numerous explanations for this lagging performance, but a leading factor is the institutional organization of the public education sector. Public education systems are structured in ways that generally insulate teachers, administrators and managers from being accountable to the government and families they serve. Rather than seeking to improve pedagogical techniques, gather information about student performance, or reward excellent teachers, the systems traditionally have sought to impose uniformity and reward mediocrity.[18] As a consequence, while teacher organizations are strong, the ability of governments, families and even administrators to modify the system is quite limited.

A consequence of these institutional imbalances is that expenditures are biased toward salaries, which account for more than 90 percent of the total educational budget in 15 of the 21 countries for which data was available. In some countries these expenditures are a consequence of high wages, while in others they are an indica-

---

[17] For an overview of Social Investment Funds, see Inter-American Development Bank (1998).

[18] For a broader discussion of the organization of the education sector and its impact on outcomes, see IDB (1996) and Savedoff (1998). On education sector reforms in Latin America, see Alvarez and Ruiz-Casares (1997), Partnership for Educational Revitalization in the Americas (PREAL, 1998), and Economic Commission for Latin America and the Caribbean (1997).

Figure 5.2. Education Spending and GDP

a. Primary level

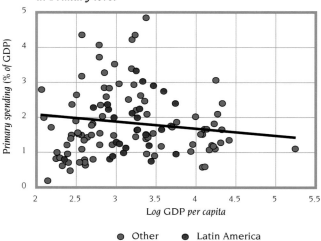

b. Secondary level

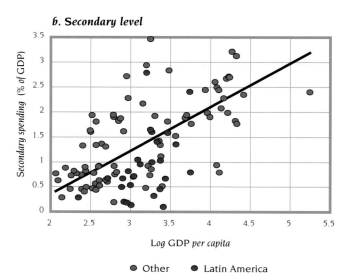

c. Higher education

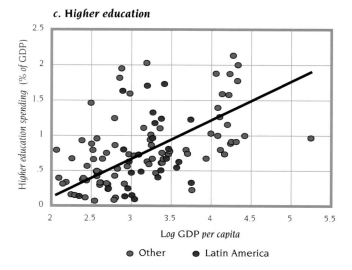

Source: IDB calculations based on expenditure data by UNESCO (1997).

tion of excess employment. Furthermore, in seeking to limit managerial abuses, governments and teachers' unions have created rigid labor regimes that make it difficult, if not impossible, to discipline poor workers and reward good ones. School principals are so limited in their decisionmaking powers that they are little more than passive channels for administrative tasks. In order to reverse this situation, countries in the region are already taking important initiatives to empower consumers, give teachers and school directors more autonomy, and redefine the role of the state.

• *Empowering Consumers.* Teachers and principals can be given even greater control over their working conditions and professional work if they are made accountable to groups with an interest in ensuring that the system educates children well. This requires making more information regarding student performance available to parents, the community, educators and the government. Measures related to internal efficiency, such as reducing repetition rates, indicate when schools are doing well. Student examinations are a critical tool for developing education policy, identifying schools with special problems, and helping citizens evaluate the use of their tax dollars. At least six countries have introduced or reintroduced national student examinations since 1991 in an effort to measure the performance of the education system and guide education policy. And each year more countries are participating in the TIMMS Project, which seeks to compare student performance across countries.

Consumers are also empowered when they have opportunities to voice their satisfactions and dissatisfactions with the school system. Many countries are increasing community and family participation in schools in ways that go beyond the traditional parent association. In El Salvador, Nicaragua, Brazil and Bolivia, local school boards are being created with parental involvement and given significant responsibilities that range from choosing school principals (Brazil) and managing funds (Bolivia and Nicaragua) to evaluating and paying teachers (El Salvador).

Finally, consumers have an even greater lever to hold schools accountable when they are given choice. Chile is the one education system in Latin America where families can officially choose their children's school, with the government paying a fixed sum per student to the school regardless of whether it is run by a municipality or a nonprofit or for-profit institution. The rapid expansion of nonmunicipal schools over the last decade—they now account for over 35 percent of student enrollment—is an indication of dissatisfaction with the municipal schools. At the same time, the capitated payment scheme helps Chile ensure the most progressive educational spending in the region (see Chapter 8).[19] Although Chile is the only country to promote choice systemically, many parents in other countries also choose to opt out of public school systems. This is mainly an option for wealthier families, but a substantial share of lower-income families make whatever sacrifices they have to in order to get their children the best education possible.[20]

• *Autonomy for Providers.* Because education systems are extremely large, efforts to impose similar models, allocate resources and manage personnel across an entire national educational system have generally failed. Once consumers are empowered and accountability mechanisms are in place, most decisions can be delegated to schools or school districts. The critical role of personnel management, which requires evaluating teachers for a variety of nonquantifiable activities, is better left to school principals and local boards, which can gather and evaluate relevant information. Schools with control over their own budgets can do a better job of allocating resources between salaries and textbooks, administrative and teaching personnel, and maintenance and investment. Many countries are experimenting with greater autonomy for schools in day-to-day decisions and in control of funds, but more ambitious efforts are needed.[21]

• *Redefining the Government's Role.* When the government delegates more decisions and power to schools, it can concentrate on functions needed at the national level or in the public sphere. The most critical task for the government is to finance education efficiently. This means allocating resources based on desired outcomes—for example, financing students rather than funding installed capacity of schools, or recovering some costs of public universities through tuition while providing scholarships for lower-income students. Funding alone is not enough. The money allocated to education must be spent in ways that holds the education system accountable for improving its performance. The government can also play an important role by generating and disseminating information related to student performance (e.g., national examinations) and pedagogy and curriculum (e.g., research and dissemination). Finally, government can play a productive role by setting standards to aid consumers and local boards in holding their schools accountable.

Throughout the region, major efforts are required to initiate, maintain and expand on these institutional reforms, either at the primary or secondary levels. By increasing involvement of parents and local communities, addressing constraints in personnel management, improving financing allocation mechanisms, and expanding the delegation of functions, countries in the region can accelerate educational progress and create conditions for substantially reducing income inequality in the future.

Private Costs and Benefits Affect the Demand for Schooling[22]

Increasing the quality and supply of educational services is critical to improving education, but these investments alone are not sufficient. Families and their children make decisions every day regarding school attendance and the amount of effort they put into schooling. These decisions comprise the "demand" for education, which is affected not only by the quality of schooling being offered but also by the costs and benefits of attendance. As discussed earlier, women's educational attainment has a marked effect on the decision as to whether children remain in school. Mothers who are active in the labor market also have children who perform better in the school system.

When children do not complete schooling, it suggests there are problems of information and uncertainty, unobserved complementary factors, private costs, and constraints.[23] Regardless of the exact source of the problem, it is apparent that better educated parents have better educated children (see Chapter 2). Hence, there is either an informational advantage or a change in preferences that leads parents with more education to put a greater emphasis on their children's schooling.

A frequently mentioned factor in school attendance is private costs. Although public primary and secondary education is officially free of charge in the region, parents or other family members must make financial outlays when sending children to school. Direct costs include uniforms, books, school supplies and transportation. The time devoted by parents to the school and to help their children can also be considered a private cost of schooling. Schools may also request fees, tuition, levies to parent-teacher associations, and cash or in-kind donations. All of these tend to increase both in absolute terms and relative to family income as children go from primary to secondary school. These expenses can be difficult for poor parents, especially at the secondary level, where tuition, uniforms, textbooks and transportation are often more expensive.

Few countries in the region have detailed studies of the private costs of education, but the available evi-

[19] See Aedo (1998).

[20] See Navarro and de la Cruz (1998) for Venezuela, Flores (1997) for the Dominican Republic, and Saavedra-Chanduvi (1996) for Peru.

[21] See Mello (1993).

[22] See Schiefelbein (1996).

[23] Birdsall (1982) and Jiménez (1987) contain comprehensive lists of studies of the determinants of enrollment or educational attainment in developing countries, with estimates of the responsiveness of demand for education. Schiefelbein (1996) provides a recent overview of determinants of education demand with policy implications.

dence is quite striking. An assessment in Colombia in 1992 showed that the household income share allocated to education is not only significant but also larger for lower income groups. Households in the top quintile with children attending public schools spent 1 percent of average income on primary education, while those in the bottom quintile spent 4.4 percent. Moreover, these disparities increased at higher levels of education. Families in the top quintiles with children attending secondary school spent 1.7 percent of their income on education compared to 10.9 percent for the bottom quintile, while at the tertiary level the shares were 3.5 percent and 19.4 percent, respectively.[24] In Ecuador, households below the poverty line spent over 3 percent of their total income for each child enrolled in public primary education, while nonpoor families allocated only 2.3 percent. At the secondary level, the expenditures rose to 3.8 percent for the nonpoor and 4.9 percent for the poor.[25]

In some countries, public schools charge small fees, even at the primary level. Usually they are masked as contributions, although they may not really be voluntary. Such is the case in certain schools in Bolivia, Colombia, Costa Rica, the Dominican Republic, Venezuela and Ecuador. Although these fees are often extremely modest, they may create obstacles for the poorest families.

Inefficiency at the central level also imposes additional costs on families. In Venezuela, there have been cases where poor parents interested in keeping children in school have hired and paid for a substitute teacher's salary when the regular one is on maternity leave.

Although private costs clearly affect schooling decisions, the effect is not necessarily large. Demand for education appears to be relatively inelastic. Studies in Colombia, Peru and El Salvador showed that an increase in most components of private costs would result in a less than proportionate decrease in the demand for education.[26] Similar results are found in several rigorous studies in the United States, where estimated price elasticities are reported to be as low as -0.15. However, the range is large, and some studies demonstrated much higher elasticities, making this an issue that requires empirical verification in each particular context.[27] Nevertheless, in most studies on Latin America, the effect of parental education, particularly mother's education, is shown to have a much stronger impact on educational attainment than factors like costs.

In addition to direct out-of-pocket expenses, the decision to enroll children in school is affected by the alternative uses of their time. This so-called "opportunity cost" of a child's time is the value of earnings or household work that the family has to forego if the child attends school, and includes time spent in the classroom,

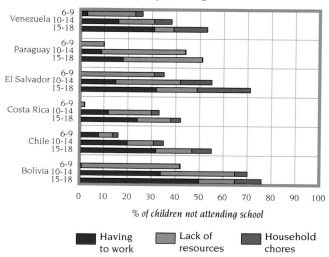

Figure 5.3. Reasons for Not Attending School, by Age Group

% of children not attending school

Having to work   Lack of resources   Household chores

Source: IDB calculations based on recent household surveys.

in traveling to and from school, and in doing homework. Opportunity costs of schooling are particularly important in developing countries, where both remunerated and household work can represent significant contributions to family income and well-being.

Few studies have estimated the opportunity cost of children's time and its impact on the full costs faced by households in Latin America. But results from other developing countries are illustrative. In Tanzania, it is estimated that the opportunity cost of children's time is between two and three times the value of direct expenditures on primary education, and between 50 and 80 percent of the direct costs at the secondary level. Similarly, recent evidence from Indonesia suggests that the opportunity cost of attending lower secondary school can be as high as twice the direct costs of schooling for low-income households. This ratio is even more impressive considering the relatively high levels of direct costs of education in Indonesia, which are estimated at 17 percent of household income.[28]

The available evidence from Latin America is consistent with these findings. In Peru, children in rural areas between the ages of 10 and 18 worked 37.2 hours per week if they were not in school, but only 20.3 if they at-

[24] Molina, et al. (1993).
[25] Research Triangle Institute (1995).
[26] See Jiménez (1987, pp. 80-81) for studies on Colombia and El Salvador and Gertler and Glewwe (1989) for Peru.
[27] Perkins (1984) summarizes the results of 10 studies.
[28] Mason and Khandker (1996).

tended school.[29] In rural Peru, 51 percent of children contribute to the family by working on the family farm, and working significantly reduced the probability that a child would enroll in school and increased the probability that he or she would drop out before completion.[30] The same conclusion can be drawn from the school attendance pattern of rural students in Honduras. They drop out after five or six months of classes to work the harvest, returning the following year to repeat the same grade.[31]

As with direct costs, opportunity costs rise with age and education level. As children get older, they are more employable outside the home and their potential wages rise. In fact, more than 30 percent of children between 15 and 18 years old not attending school report having to work as the reason for leaving school in Venezuela, El Salvador, Chile and urban Bolivia (Figure 5.3). As children get older, they also become more capable at contributing to the household through home production or household chores. By helping with domestic tasks, such as taking care of younger siblings or cultivating family plots, older children who don't go to school can release their mother's or father's time for other productive activities. Gender differences are particularly apparent here. In some countries, like Bolivia, El Salvador and Venezuela, there are important differences in the alternative occupation of boys and girls. While boys tend to work outside the house, girls tend to help with household chores. In Venezuela and El Salvador, the share of girls reporting household chores as the reason for not attending school exceeds the share of those who are working. By contrast, girls in Costa Rica, Chile and urban Bolivia not attending school are more likely to be working outside than inside the home (Figure 5.4). Despite the obvious impact of leaving school to attend to household chores, overall, the children of women who work outside the home have higher educational attainment (see Chapter 3). There are two explanations for this apparent contradiction. First, the children of mothers who work and take responsibility for household tasks may have still completed more years of school than children in similar situations whose mothers are not in the labor force. Second, the overall relationship estimated for the entire population may not hold for some specific subgroups, such as the extremely poor. In either case, further information about these children and their families is needed to identify which factor predominates and to promote policies to encourage children—and especially girls—to remain in school.

In some cases, children may leave school even when it would be worthwhile to stay because the direct and indirect costs are too high relative to the family's income. In such cases, access to credit might make the difference between continuing in school or not. There is suggestive

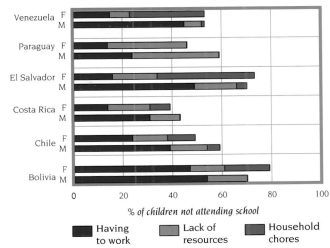

Figure 5.4. Reasons for Not Attending School, 15-18 Year Olds, by Gender

% of children not attending school

Having to work   Lack of resources   Household chores

Source: IDB calculations based on recent household surveys.

evidence that access to credit can make a difference, particularly for secondary school.[32] But except in the case of higher education, it is difficult to evaluate the importance and significance of this potential constraint.

Educational attainment for girls in the region is generally as good or better than for boys. However, in certain countries, including Guatemala, Bolivia and Peru, girls are more likely to drop out of school and to do so earlier than boys. This is particularly true in rural areas and among indigenous populations. Many of the factors that influence the demand for education—cultural attitudes, alternative uses of time for household and family chores, and costs—play a role in these gender inequities that must be addressed by public policy. Given the strong impact of women's education on all of the factors that contribute to inequality—women's income-earning opportunities, fertility choices, and educational attainment of their children—assuring more education for girls in these countries is critical.

Increase Demand for Education by Reducing Costs and Improving Quality

Almost every country in the region has made attempts during the last decade to increase attendance and reten-

---

[29] Gertler and Glewwe (1989) estimated the amount of hours worked both in housework and outside the house.
[30] Ilon and Moock (1991).
[31] World Bank (1995).
[32] Flug, Spilimbergo, and Wachtenheim (1998).

tion. The range of programs is large. Most interventions aim to reduce the private costs of education, either by giving pure cash subsidies or by providing in-kind transfers such as textbooks, uniforms and transportation. Some programs have been designed to increase the benefits of education by improving school quality or by providing nutritional supplements that have been shown to positively affect performance in school. A relatively recent trend has been the use of marketing campaigns to inform families of the advantages of sending children to school.

One of the most frequently-used policies by Latin American governments to reduce the private costs of education has been to provide free textbooks. But these programs historically have been inefficient because of the way they are implemented. First, by giving national contracts to one or a few publishers, the government creates a protected sector with little interest in the kinds of research, design and innovation necessary to make textbooks useful, current and captivating. Second, students who receive textbooks for free have a reduced incentive to care for the books, which then deteriorate rapidly. Third, education ministries have been ineffective at delivering textbooks at the right place and the right time. In Brazil, the delay in textbook delivery was resolved one year by simply mailing the books to the schools through the postal service—itself not always known for speedy delivery.

Other private costs have been addressed as well. Some countries have attempted to provide uniforms, although one study suggests that these programs did not yield the expected returns. Promoting less strict rules regarding uniforms might be a more effective way of reducing this particular direct cost of schooling.[33] Transportation subsidies for students in the form of reduced prices on urban buses have been used for many years in many countries, including Venezuela. Finally, some countries have provided students with a backpack or other school supplies. In 1992, Honduras started a project called *Bolsón Escolar*, targeted to low-income students attending first and second grade in public schools. Venezuela also has put in place programs called *Bulto Escolar* and *Uniformes Escolares* that provide school supplies and uniforms to all primary students in public schools. However, in neither case has there been an evaluation of the effectiveness of these programs.

School nutrition programs have been widely used in the region.[34] These programs are attractive because they not only alleviate nutritional deficiencies that affect children's health and constrain their learning, but because they encourage students to attend school so they can have access to the lunch or snack. Although recent evaluations of school feeding programs in the Dominican Republic

and Honduras showed encouraging results in terms of dropout rates and enrollment,[35] the impact of such programs on school attendance, retention and repetition is not clear in the empirical literature.[36]

The most direct mechanism to reduce both direct and indirect costs of education is through cash transfers, scholarships and vouchers. In spite of some initial resistance, these programs are becoming more common. Mexico, Honduras, Brazil and Argentina have recently implemented some kind of cash transfer to increase the demand for education at the primary and secondary level.

Voucher programs, though still seldom used in Latin America, can reduce the burden of education costs on low-income families. Students, or the schools they attend, receive a certain monetary value financed from public funds that can only be used to pay for school-related costs. There are many possible variations in the design of such programs, which differ by the particular beneficiaries, school providers, items covered, and distribution mechanisms. If the low quality of public education is considered a deterrent to student enrollment, or if the supply of public schools is insufficient, making such subsidies available to poor families to help them pay private tuition can provide the incentive to parents to keep their children in school. This was the objective of Colombian voucher programs for secondary schools.[37] The Dominican Republic provides funding for private schools to operate in areas not reached by the public system. And in Venezuela, schools operated by nonprofit religious groups receive funding to expand education services to disadvantaged areas.[38] The most successful and systematic use of such a mechanism is in Chile, where schools receive funds based on their average enrollment during the month. Since nongovernmental and even for-profit institutions are eligible, this financing mechanism creates incentives to seek out students and keep them in school.

The federal government in Mexico recently launched an ambitious education, health and nutrition program that gives a cash transfer and school supplies to qualifying students as long as they maintain a minimum of 85 percent school attendance. This program attempts to cover the opportunity costs of children's time by increasing the amount provided as the grade level rises, and addresses households' different schooling decisions for

---

[33] Bellew and King (1991).

[34] Bolivia, Brazil, Chile, the Dominican Republic, El Salvador, Guatemala, Honduras and Venezuela have had some sort of school feeding program since 1989.

[35] Miller Del Rosso and Marek (1996).

[36] USAID (1986).

[37] Calderon (1996).

[38] Navarro and de la Cruz (1998).

boys and girls by giving a higher transfer for females than for males. An evaluation of this program has only just been initiated.

In 1995, Brasilia's state government also initiated a project, *Bolsa-Escola*, that provides a cash transfer in the amount of a minimum salary to low-income families whose children between 7 and 14 years old are enrolled in public schools. In order to receive the scholarship, families must have all their children in the age group in school and every child must maintain an attendance record above 90 percent. A sister program known as *Poupança-Escola* seeks to reduce repetition and dropout rates, both severe problems in Brazil, through a savings incentive. The government establishes a bank account for each child enrolled in the program and deposits 100 *reais* every year only if the child passes the grade. Before children graduate from high school, families are allowed to withdraw from the account only half of the accumulated balance, and only when children reach certain grades (after the fourth and eighth grade). So far the results of both programs are promising. Although studies have not evaluated these programs rigorously to adjust for the effects of self-selection, the differences in outcomes are still quite dramatic. Dropout rates among beneficiaries have dropped to 0.4 percent compared to 7.4 percent for all basic education students in the Federal District. Repetition rates have also decreased, from 18.1 percent for all primary students to 8 percent for those participating in the program.[39]

The *Programa de Asignación Familiar* (PRAF), launched in Honduras in 1994, provides a monthly bonus to mothers living in extreme poverty for each child enrolled in public schools from first to third grade. To qualify, families must be below a certain income level and have three or more unsatisfied basic needs, and the children must regularly attend school without repeating. Preliminary evaluations show some encouraging results in terms of enrollment, repetition and dropout rates, all of which are better than rates in nonparticipating schools.

A recent trend in the region is the use of education and information campaigns to raise parent's awareness about the benefits of educating their children. Communication strategies to increase the demand for education have been implemented in Argentina, Bolivia, Brazil, Chile, Guatemala, Paraguay and Uruguay. To date, little is known about the effectiveness of these programs.

In sum, increasing educational attainment in the region to break the pattern that perpetuates high levels of inequality requires encouraging and expanding the demand for education. One of the key factors for increasing demand is to improve the quality and performance of the main provider of schooling: the public education system. As quality rises, students will progress more efficiently through the school system, which reduces private costs. To complement this effort on the supply side, countries can consider the effectiveness of interventions to increase the demand for schooling, particularly among the poor. These include cash transfers, school feeding programs, targeted provisioning of materials, scholarships and vouchers.

OTHER SOCIAL PROGRAMS TO IMPROVE INCOME INEQUALITY

There are numerous other social programs that can be designed to improve income inequality. Among them are programs that focus on women's labor force participation, fertility and educational attainment.

Labor Force Training to Expand Opportunities

Formal education has a clear impact on income inequality through its long-term effects on earning capacity, reducing family size, and improving the attainment levels of children. However, for those who have left school, training programs can still make a difference for family income and welfare. One category of training is aimed at providing skills required by the modernization of economic sectors. In order to be effective, this kind of training must target those who already have sufficient schooling, that is, technical training that is complementary to basic skills, usually at the secondary schooling level. This kind of training is not likely to have a large impact on income inequality, but a second category of training that targets those who did not complete school can potentially have more of an impact by reaching those who lack basic reading, writing and reasoning skills required by most jobs. Training programs that give women access to jobs outside of those traditionally reserved for women, and particularly in the formal sector, can make the biggest difference in reducing income disparities.

Improving the Link between Market and Nonmarket Activities

In most societies, the division between unremunerated and remunerated work in the market creates inequities within households, between men and women, and be-

---

[39] Buarque (1998).

tween income groups (see Chapters 2 and 3). Public policies that focus on benefits for remunerated workers necessarily exclude those who are producing unpaid services at home or work in the informal sector. These policies can also have a counterproductive impact on those they are meant to serve, i.e., the less advantaged and more vulnerable workers, among whom women are prominent.

Other Public Policy Opportunities

There are many areas of public policy that involve low-cost solutions that address these imbalances and income inequalities. An important one is to enforce financial responsibility by men. Families are the product of a generally unequal partnership between men and women. When a couple splits, men generally have better alternatives for income generation than women. Also, women in the region tend to retain responsibilities for any children. By enforcing financial responsibility by men, some of these inequalities can be reduced. There are many sensitive issues that arise with this kind of program, since many men may also be extremely poor. Designing such policies requires seeking ways to increase enforcement without being counterproductive, particularly regarding spousal abuse. Innovative programs to combat domestic violence are important in their own right, but it has also been shown that among women who were working in Nicaragua and Chile, those who had been abused earned less than those who had not.[40] Some programs are as simple as establishing confidential counseling services for women to gain access to judicial systems that are frequently difficult to approach. Others could address legal inequities in the treatment of women and men with regard to separation and divorce. Still other policies could address this imbalance by sharing the costs of maternity

leave or encouraging the movement from nonmarket to market activities, as discussed in Chapter 6.

Access to the court system, promoting social capital, better transportation, improved housing conditions, and safety nets to respond to natural disasters and emergencies are other examples of public policies that can play a role in increasing women's opportunities, reducing fertility, and raising educational attainment, all directed toward reducing income inequality.

CONCLUSIONS

For public policy to reduce inequality, it must establish and improve programs that expand women's opportunities and increase education. Effective child care, family planning and preventive health services, along with improvements in the provision and quality of utilities, can all help the capacity of women to choose whether or not to enter the labor force and raise their family's incomes. Institutional reforms in education that improve the quality of schooling, along with programs targeted to increase the demand for education among particular disadvantaged groups, could go a long way toward redressing income inequality in the medium and long term. Smart policies need to take advantage of the interconnections of social programs—such as school nutrition programs that both improve children's health and encourage them to attend school, or longer school hours that both improve student learning and free women to attend to other activities. Such programs lay the foundation for expanding the options and opportunities for families and their children. But these policies alone are not sufficient; to ensure that they bear fruit, it is also necessary to address shortcomings in the labor market and in access to nonlabor assets in the economy.

---

[40] Morrison and Orlando (1998).

REFERENCES

Aedo, C. 1998. *Diferencias entre escuelas y rendimiento estudiantil en Chile.* In W. Savedoff, ed., *La organización marca la diferencia: educación y salud en América Latina.* Washington, DC: Inter-American Development Bank.

Alvarez H. B., and M. Ruiz-Casares, eds. 1997. *Paths of Change: Education Reforms Under Way in Latin America and the Caribbean.* USAID, Advancing Basic Education and Literacy Project, Educational Policy in Latin America and the Caribbean, Technical Paper 1, Washington, D. C.

Bellew, R., and E. King. 1991. *Promoting Girls' and Women's Education. Lessons from the Past.* Policy Research Working Paper 715. Policy and Human Resources Department, World Bank, Washington, D.C.

Birdsall, N. 1982. *Child Schooling and the Measurement of Living Standards.* Living Standards Measurement Study Working Paper No. 14. World Bank, Washington, D.C.

Brown, L. R., and L. Haddad. No date. *Time Allocation Patterns and Time Burdens: A Gender Analysis of Seven Countries.* International Food Policy Research Institute (IFPRI), Washington, D.C.

Buarque, Cristovam. 1998. *Lugar de Criança e na Escola. Com qualidade!* Gabinete do Governador, Secretaria de Comunicação, Secretaria de Educação. Brasília: Governo do Distrito Federal.

Calderon, A. 1996. *Voucher Program for Secondary Schools: The Colombian Experience.* HCDWP66, World Bank, Washington, D.C. May.

Connelly, et al. 1996. Women's Employment and Child Care in Brazil. *Economic Development and Cultural Change:* 619-56

Deutsch, R. 1998a. How Early Childhood Interventions Can Reduce Inequality: An Overview of Recent Findings. SDS/POV Policy and Strategy Research Study, Inter-American Development Bank, Washington, D.C.

_____. 1998b. Does Child Care Pay? Labor Force Participation and Earnings Effects of Access to Child Care in the Favelas of Rio de Janeiro. SDS/POV, Inter-American Development Bank. Mimeo.

Economic Commission for Latin America and the Caribbean. 1997. *La Brecha de la Equidad: América Latina, El Caribe y La Cumbre Social.* Santiago: ECLAC.

Engle, Patrice L. 1991. Maternal Work and Child Care Strategies in Peri-Urban Guatemala: Nutritional Effects. *Child Development* 62: 954-65

Fafchamps, M., and A. R. Quisumbing. 1998. Social Roles, Human Capital, and the Intrahousehold Division of Labor: Evidence from Pakistan. Stanford and IFPRI. Mimeo.

Flores, R. 1997. *La escuela basica de la zona marginal de Santo Domingo.* Latin America Research Centers Network Working Paper R-304. Inter-American Development Bank, Washington, D.C.

Flug, K., A. Spilimbergo, and E. Wachtenheim. 1998. Investment in Education: Do Economic Volatility and Credit Constraints Matter? *Journal of Development Economics* 55: 465-81.

Gelbach, Jonah. 1998. How Large an Effect Do Child Care Costs Have on Single Mothers' Labor Supply? Evidence Using Access to Free Public Schooling. MIT. Mimeo.

Gertler, P., and P. Glewwe. 1989. *The Willingness to Pay for Education in Developing Countries. Evidence from Rural Peru.* Living Standards Measurement Study Working Paper No. 54. World Bank, Washington, D.C.

Heckman, James J. 1974. Effects of Child-Care Programs on Women's Work Effort. *Journal of Political Economy* 82, supplement (March-April): 136-63.

Ilon, Lynn, and Moock, Peter. 1991. School Attributes, Household Characteristics, and Demand for Schooling: a Case Study of Rural Peru. *International Review of Education* 37(4): 429-51.

Inter-American Development Bank. 1996. Making Social Services Work. In *Economic and Social Progress in Latin America.* Washington, D.C.: IDB.

_____. 1998. The Use of Social Investment Funds as an Instrument for Combating Poverty: A Bank Strategy. SDS/POV, Inter-American Development Bank. March. Mimeo.

Jiménez, E. 1987. *Pricing Policy in the Social Sectors.* Baltimore: Johns Hopkins University Press.

Karoly, Lynn, et al. 1998. *Investing in Our Children: What We Know and Don't Know About the Costs and Benefits of Early Childhood Interventions.* Santa Monica: Rand.

Levy, B., and P.T. Spiller. 1996. *Regulations, Institutions, and Commitment: Comparative Studies of Telecommunications.* Political Economy of Institutions and Decisions Series. Cambridge, New York and Melbourne: Cambridge University Press.

Mason, A., and S. Khandker. 1996. *Measuring the Opportunity Costs of Children's Time in a Developing Country: Implications for Education Sector Analysis and Interventions.* Human Capital Development Working Paper No. 72. World Bank, Washington, D.C.

Mello, G. 1993. *Autonomia da Escola: Possibilidades, Limites e Condições.* Brasilia: Cadernos de Educação Básica.

Miller Del Rosso, J., and T. Marek. 1996. Class Action: Improving School Performance in the Developing World through Better Health and Nutrition. *Directions in Development.* World Bank, Washington, D.C.

Molina, C., et al. 1993. El gasto público en educación y distribución de subsidios en Colombia. FEDESARROLLO.

Morrison, A., and M. B. Orlando. 1998. The Economic Impact of Domestic Violence in Chile and Nicaragua: Labor Force Participation, Earnings, Service Utilization and Children's Educational Performance. SDS/WID, Inter-American Development Bank, Washington, D.C. Mimeo.

Navarro, J.C., and R. de la Cruz. 1998. Escuelas federales, estatales y sin fines de lucro en Venezuela. In W. Savedoff, ed., *La Organización Marca La Diferencia: Educación y Salud en América Latina.* Washington, D.C.: Inter-American Development Bank.

Perkins, G. 1984. Public Education: Comment. *American Economic Review* 74(4).

Partnership for Educational Revitalization in the Americas (PREAL). 1998. The Future at Stake: Report of the Task Force on Education, Equity, and Economic Competitiveness in Latin America and the Caribbean. Inter-American Dialogue (IAD), Washington, D.C., and the Corporation for Development Research (CINDE), Santiago.

Research Triangle Institute. 1995. Ecuador: la crisis educativa. USAID, Washington, DC.

Saavedra-Chanduvi, Jaime. 1996. Educación Pública y Educación Privada en el Perú: Su impacto relativo sobre los ingresos. Evidencia basada en encuestas de hogares. In Richard Webb and Gilberto Moncada, eds: Cómo estamos? Análisis de la Encuesta Nacional de Niveles de Vida. Lima: Instituto Cuánto.

Savedoff, W., ed. 1998. Organization Matters: Agency Problems in Health and Education in Latin America. Washington, D.C.: Inter-American Development Bank.

Savedoff, W. and P. Spiller, eds. Spilled Water: Institutional Commitment in the Provision of Water Services. Inter-American Development Bank. Forthcoming.

Schiefelbein, E. 1996. School-Related Economic Incentives in Latin America: Reducing Drop-Out and Repetition and Combating Child Labour. Child Right Series No.12, UNICEF.

Tan, Jee-Peng, and Jacques van der Gaag. 1998. The Benefits of Early Child Development Programs: An Economic Analysis. Washington, D.C.: World Bank.

UNESCO. 1997. Statistical Yearbook. New York: UNESCO Publishing and Bernan Press.

University of Wisconsin-Madison, Institute for Research on Poverty. 1997. Investing in Young Children. Special issue of FOCUS 19(1) Summer/Fall.

USAID. 1986. School Feeding Programs in Developing Countries: An Analysis of Actual and Potential Impact. AID Evaluation Special Study No. 30.

Van de Walle, D., and K. Nead. 1995. Public Spending and the Poor. Baltimore and London: Johns Hopkins University Press/World Bank.

Walker, I., et al. 1997. Regulation, Organization and Incentives: The Political Economy of Potable Water Services in Honduras. Latin America Research Centers Network Working Paper R-314. Inter-American Development Bank, Washington, D.C.

Wong, Rebecca, and Ruth Levine. 1992. The Effect of Household Structure on Women's Economic Activity and Fertility: Evidence from Recent Mothers in Urban Mexico. Economic Development and Cultural Change 41(1): 89-102.

World Bank. 1995. Honduras: Basic Education Project. Staff Appraisal Report. World Bank, Washington, D.C.

Chapter 6

LABOR POLICIES TO IMPROVE
INCOME DISTRIBUTION

Labor policies in Latin America have been greatly influenced by redistributive objectives. Workers have benefited from protection in their relationships with enterprises, and attempts have been made to stabilize their income during both their working and retirement years. These policies as applied have attempted to increase labor's income participation vis-à-vis profits, rather than to distribute income among workers. However, to the extent that these policies have been designed to oversee a labor relationship established in a contract between formal enterprises and permanent workers, they have left out many workers, particularly those with less income generation capacity, thus accentuating differences among workers.

The conflict between protecting employment and income distribution cannot be resolved without considering workers' demands for economic stability and security. The solution could reduce the discriminatory aspects of the present social security and protection systems, extending basic benefits to all workers, and reducing restrictions on job creation in the formal sector. The changes required by labor and social security laws and regulations cannot be made at the expense of workers, and certainly not to their detriment. In many countries, owing to the great deficiencies and low coverage levels in existing social security and protection systems, major workers' groups should step in as the main advocates of reform.

Latin American labor protection laws and regulations have traditionally involved placing restrictions on probationary periods and temporary and fixed-term contracts, and imposing penalties on labor contract terminations. For the workers that they cover, these laws and regulations have increased job stability and protection against loss of income associated with unemployment. In most countries, however, the law provides low and poorly distributed levels of coverage, favoring workers who are more educated, more experienced, and higher-paid. Protection in many countries has aggravated wage differentials between workers covered by the laws and those who are not. In the end, such laws have protected only a few workers and have widened the differences in incomes, benefits and job stability.

Nor has social security protection covered everyone equally. In practice, in order to participate in the system workers must be associated with a formal sector enterprise, and even in these enterprises many workers are also excluded. The workers who remain outside of the system have the lowest income-generating potential, in part because enterprises can easily replace them, and in part because the workers themselves prefer to waive coverage in exchange for higher pay. On the other hand, social security systems have also failed to generate the progressive redistribution among participants that they were theoretically designed to create because of evasion by higher-income workers, special schemes for certain privileged groups of workers, or simply because, in many cases, such systems have operated in deficit, using general tax funds.

The establishment of minimum wages has not been particularly effective in improving the income of the poorest groups, in part because it is not a targeted redistribution mechanism. The minimum wage applies equally to a poor head of household and to a recent university graduate from a high-income family. While reasonable minimum wage levels have been established in many countries and have not interrupted normal operation of the labor market, in other countries they have been ineffective in redistributing income because they have been set too high. In such cases, the minimum wage in fact helps protect higher-income workers rather than poor ones.

The central policy conclusion of this chapter is that the objective of income distribution is only compatible with the aim of protecting workers if it corrects discrimination in laws and regulations against formal contracting for less privileged workers. Action is therefore suggested in four areas: contracting conditions, unemployment protection, pension systems, and minimum wage regulations. During the past decade, a number of countries have made progress in these areas.

Where *contracting conditions* are concerned, greater flexibility should be introduced into the contracts permitted by law. As has occurred in a number of countries, restrictions applied to part-time and temporary contracts should be removed, and benefits associated with permanent contracts should be extended to part-time and temporary workers. This would give workers and enterprises greater scope to choose the type of contract that best meets their needs, without losing social security benefits. Work days should be more flexible to allow for greater margin for negotiation between workers and enterprises. Biases in labor legislation against employment for women should be eliminated by having the social security system collectively cover maternity costs rather than charging them to enterprises.

In the area of *unemployment protection*, penalties for arbitrary dismissal should be distinguished from income protection in connection with unemployment. The legislation should aim to prevent arbitrary dismissal—that is, dismissals that the enterprise cannot attribute to economic reasons or to the worker's lack of effort or integrity—and to penalize enterprises that unjustly dismiss their workers. Unemployment protection mechanisms should be carefully designed to stabilize income for workers who lose their jobs or who wish to change jobs, while protecting against abuse of the system. Many countries have established individual savings accounts to be used for periods of unemployment, potentially supplemented with low-interest loans or transfers from a mutual interest fund established with workers' contributions. The new protection systems should be designed to cover the maximum possible number of workers from potential loss of income, without impeding employment mobility. Additionally, since it will be difficult for unemployment savings schemes to protect lower-income workers vulnerable to unstable employment, collectively-financed social safety nets must be established to support them.

In the area of *pensions*, the simple pay-as-you-go system still predominant in Latin America should be replaced with a two-pillar system that establishes basic universal protection while narrowing the relationship between individual benefits and contributions for workers. The basic protection pillar should offer a minimum pension to workers who have no other old-age resources, and should be covered with general budget funds. The contribution pillar might consist of a savings system under which individual accounts are administered with the assistance of the private sector under strict government supervision. Such systems already exist in eight countries in the region.

Last, in connection with the *minimum wage*, a level should be set to protect the incomes of the poorest individuals, with a reduced minimum for young workers to ensure that there is no negative stimulus to employment.

JOB PROTECTION REGULATIONS

Labor legislation in most Latin American countries aims to defend workers in their relations with enterprises by specifying conditions for contracting and dismissal and establishing standards on extending the work day and compensation for overtime. To guarantee stable employment, labor legislation emphasizes standard labor contracts and places severe restrictions on contracts for temporary and part-time contracts. This section will show that while the labor situation is better for groups of workers covered by such legislation, income distribution does not improve. The existence of an informal sector, where income levels are different than those in the formal sector, and where stability is less favorable, cannot be exclusively attributed to labor protection regulations. The segmentation between formal and informal sector workers can be largely explained by the preference among many individuals (women in particular) for more flexible work that enables them to make better use of certain skills; different incentives and remuneration mechanisms depending on the activity; and credit market imperfections.[1] But labor regulations exacerbate rather than alleviate the segmentation and inequalities between formal and informal sector occupations.

Regulations to Provide Job Stability

Given the high degree of economic volatility in Latin America, it comes as no surprise that most countries in the region have established protection systems to soften the impact of economic crises on workers. While this objective may be pursued either by ensuring income or job stability, most Latin American countries have traditionally elected the second option. Promoting stable labor relations is the backbone of labor codes throughout the region. To that end, legislation focuses on standard labor contracts, in which a permanent relationship is established between the enterprise and the worker, and severe restrictions placed on their termination.

To protect employment, labor regulations include provisions pertaining to:[2]

- *Length of the Probationary Period*. During this period, the labor contract between the enterprise and the worker may be unilaterally terminated. In Latin America, the typical probationary period is three months.

---

[1] See Chapters 2, 3 and 7.

[2] For a detailed description of the legislation by country, see IDB (1996), Part Two, Chapter 6.

- *Type of Contract and Length of the Work Day.* Typical Latin American legislation limits the work day and rates for overtime hours, night and holiday work, and imposes severe restrictions on temporary contracts. In some countries, such contracts are prohibited from carrying out "typical and ongoing operations of the enterprise," or are greatly restricted in terms of the duration or number of renewals permitted.

- *Advance Notice for Dismissing a Worker.* This period normally depends on the worker's length of service. The average period is one month, although, for example, regulations in Guatemala, Peru and Uruguay do not provide for any advance notice.

- *Severance Pay.* Labor legislation typically requires enterprises to pay dismissed workers severance pay equivalent to one month's wages per year of service. These amounts may be higher in some cases, when seniority exceeds 10 to 15 years. In some countries, workers also receive a separation payment that is determined by seniority, although this payment must be made on termination of the labor contract, even when the worker has not been dismissed.

- *Just Cause for Dismissal.* Legislation in most countries determines the causes that justify dismissal. Argentina and Chile, for example, stipulate lower levels of compensation for dismissal arising from economic difficulties experienced by the enterprise. However, in many other countries, such economic difficulties are not considered just cause for dismissal.

- *Rehiring of Workers.* The law stipulates in some cases that enterprises are required to rehire workers who have been dismissed for unjustified causes.

These regulations are much more restrictive in Latin America than in most industrial countries (Figure 6.1). This figure assigns higher values to more restrictive regulations (on an ordinal scale of all countries considered), implying that workers enjoy greater protection from the risk of dismissal. The regulations themselves provide high levels of job protection, even in comparison with Southern European countries, traditionally considered to provide high levels of protection. Within the region, some of the Caribbean countries provide lower levels of protection similar to those in industrial countries with more flexible legislation, such as the United States, the United Kingdom and the Netherlands.

Only a few countries have undertaken labor regulation reform during the 1990s. In 1991, Argentina established a ceiling on involuntary dismissal indemnities, and incorporated cases of economic need as justified cause for dismissal. New formulas were also established for contracting youth and other groups severely affected by

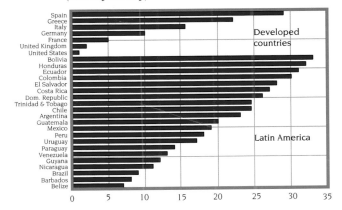

Figure 6.1. Labor Code Rigidity Index
(*Country ranking*)

Source: Márquez and Pagés (1998).

unemployment. In Panama, a 1995 reform changed the computation scale for severance pay, reducing the forced severance pay for some groups of workers and creating new fixed-term and temporary contracting procedures. In Colombia (1990), Peru (1991), and Venezuela (1997), legislation on severance pay was changed, and a requirement was established for enterprises to make periodic deposits of a proportion of each worker's wages into individual accounts with specialized financial institutions. These funds yield market interest rates and are available to workers in the event of forced dismissal or voluntary termination of the labor relationship. The allowed duration for temporary contracts was also changed (Colombia) and new contracting procedures were created for specific activities and groups (Peru). In Ecuador, new temporary contracting options (virtually nonexistent prior to the reform) were created, although dismissal regulations were not changed.

However, a number of other attempted reforms have been unsuccessful. In 1993, there were discussions in Chile of a draft law on unemployment insurance, but the Congress did not approve it. In 1997, the Argentine government decided not to support a proposed reform that would have converted dismissal indemnities into an individual savings system. Reforms of current worker protection systems normally run into problems, particularly because of insufficient knowledge of alternatives, but also because reform involves redistributing rights and income from those who benefit from the existing system to those marginalized by its coverage.

Regulations Increase Stability for Some....

Typical job protection standards in Latin America might appear to increase worker turnover and decrease workers' average length of service in an enterprise. Although this theory is plausible, there is no evidence that it is true.

International data show that, in general, a worker's length of service in a job is directly related to his or her level of education and the size of the enterprise. These patterns tend to occur in Latin America, although in Peru and Bolivia turnover for more educated workers is as high if not higher than for less educated workers, and in Brazil worker seniority in large enterprises is low and no greater than the levels found in small enterprises (Figure 6.2)

Moreover, international comparisons of length of service also yield surprising results, attributable to labor protection regulations. Although volatility is higher in Latin America than in industrial countries, workers in the region who have permanent affiliations with enterprises,[3] as well as workers having similar age and education characteristics and employed in similar sized enterprises, achieve greater seniority in Latin America than in the United States, where job protection does not exist.

Labor protection laws therefore do achieve the objective of increasing employment stability for workers covered by the law. However, coverage of the laws is often incomplete and poorly distributed: workers with low education levels, who are younger or less experienced and have lower incomes and heavier family burdens, are very unlikely to have access to job protection.

...But Increase Levels of Informal Activity and Wage Gaps

Job protection regulations have come under frequent criticism for having a paradoxically negative impact on employment. In industrial countries, broad literature exists regarding the impact of wage-earning employment regulation on employment and unemployment, with inconclusive results. While some studies have found more severe job protection regulations to be associated with a higher unemployment rate or a lower employment rate, others show no significant relationship between protection and unemployment in the labor market. Insufficient evidence for developing countries still prevents precise conclusions from being drawn in this connection. One recent study that examined the subject found no clear correlation between protection and employment or unemployment.[4] While there may be a negative correlation between levels of protection and employment rates in

Figure 6.2. Employees with Ten or More Years of Service
(*In percent*)

a. Size of firms

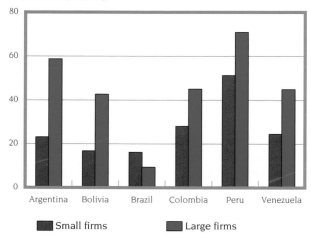

b. Level of education

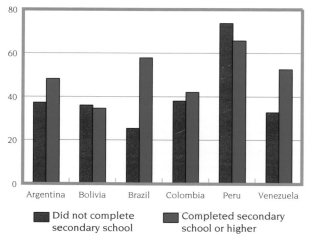

Source: *Márquez and Pagés* (1998).

some countries, this seems to be attributable to the fact that both issues are related to level of development and not to the existence of true causality between them. The conclusions are quite similar when analyzing events in the long term in countries that have undergone changes in labor protection standards. Chile is a good example, as its protection regulations have been changed since the 1960s on a number of occasions in either direction. Employment and unemployment levels there have under-

---

[3] In countries of the region, this is tantamount to being affiliated with social security, making it possible to identify them.
[4] See Márquez and Pagés (1998).

gone pronounced changes, but they do not seem to have been influenced significantly by changes in labor protection regulations.[5]

However, while labor protection standards might not have a significant effect on total employment or on unemployment rates, they appear to affect the composition of employment in ways that are unfavorable to equity. In countries where labor protection is more severe, the proportion of self-employed workers is significantly higher than might be explained by the level of development or per capita income. In countries such as Venezuela, Nicaragua, Bolivia, Colombia and Honduras, which have more severe labor protection laws, the percentage of workers employed in independent activities might be 5 to 10 points lower than its present level had there been more flexible labor legislation (Appendix 6.1 and Figure 6.3). Labor protection standards also seem to affect youth employment. Data from Chile, for example, shows that periods of greater employment protection have been accompanied by a significantly reduced level of youth employment, offset by an increase in employment for more experienced workers with more job seniority (Appendix 6.2).

Labor legislation also affects the composition of employment, as it makes it less attractive to contract wage earners, especially women. Contrary to the objective of the legislation, the proportion of wage earners in Latin America holding permanent contracts is very low. In Chile (1996) and Venezuela (1995), only 38 percent of wage earners were employed using this option. In Mexico (1994), this percentage was even lower, accounting for only 19 percent of wage earners. The differences between men and women are considerable. In Chile, Venezuela and Mexico, 55, 56 and 27 percent, respectively, of male wage earners held permanent contracts; for women, the figures were 25, 26 and 12 percent.

A more detailed study of the determinant factors that affect the probability of being employed under a permanent contract in the three countries mentioned above indicates that, regardless of the size of the enterprise in which the worker is employed, persons who are more educated, in the 35-55 year age bracket, live in urban areas, and have fewer children are more likely to be covered by labor legislation (Appendix 6.3A). Being a woman reduces this probability in Chile, regardless of marital status, and in Venezuela and Mexico, this applies to married women. This might reflect a bias against contracting women with family obligations; alternatively, women who have such obligations might prefer more flexible employment arrangements. In any event, legislation does not help solve the problem, as it leads to more rigid hours and working conditions than would be acceptable to enterprises and potential workers.

Figure 6.3. Labor Rigidity and Self-Employment

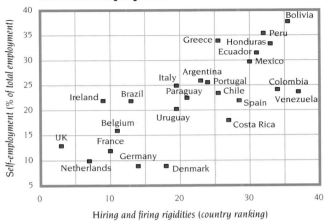

Source: Márquez and Pagés (1998).

The foregoing discussion highlights considerable inequalities in labor legislation coverage. Regardless of whether they work in large or small enterprises, the weaker and less educated workers are the ones excluded from the benefits of permanent contracts. It is not surprising, then, that different levels of coverage are reflected in income differences. In Chile (1996), a worker employed under a permanent contract was paid approximately 13 percent more than a worker not covered by the law, although both had the same age, education and gender characteristics, were employed in the informal sector and in enterprises of the same size, and performed the same activity (Appendix 6.3B). In Mexico (1994), this differential was 26 percent, and in Venezuela (1995), 17 percent. Accordingly, the benefits guaranteed by law lead to income differences that magnify existing gaps between workers employed in large and small enterprises. These differentials are normally greater for women and youth than for men and older workers.

As labor regulations provide particularly negative stimulus for female employment, income differences between men working in the formal sector and women in the informal sector are greater in countries having more rigid labor relations (Figure 6.4). These differences are less pronounced in Brazil, where the labor market is relatively flexible, than in Honduras or Venezuela, where labor legislation is more rigid. Although this is only one of the possible income differentials, it was found that the magnitude of many other differentials (for example, between men in the formal and informal sector, or between

---

[5] See Pagés and Montenegro (1998).

Figure 6.4. Labor Protection and Compensation of Women in the Informal Sector

(*Relative to the salary of men in the formal sector*)

Hiring and firing rigidities (country ranking)

Source: *IDB calculations based on recent household surveys.*

urban and rural areas) tends to be greater in countries that have more rigid legislation.[6] Therefore, while rigid labor relations are not the only explanation for the existence of considerable wage differences between workers having similar personal characteristics, it does help enhance these differences.

WHAT COULD JOB PROTECTION REGULATIONS ACCOMPLISH?

The analysis above has shown that labor protection systems generate inequalities between workers in three dimensions: income levels, opportunities for protection under the laws and regulations, and job stability. This is indicative of the need to undertake reforms in current protection schemes, extend the benefits of protection to more workers, reduce biases in the present system against less advantaged groups, and reduce income inequalities among workers.

Undertaking labor protection system reforms is a complex task that requires its share of political initiative and consensus among representatives of workers, enterprises and the government. As this consensus can be achieved more easily in some areas than in others, reforms are more likely to succeed when they are comprehensive in scope and combined with other institutional changes that can benefit all groups of workers. The solution to the problems found in labor schemes is not to dismantle the protection that some groups of workers now enjoy, but to replace this protection with more comprehensive schemes that meet the basic needs for protection and stability of larger groups. The solution, then, is

to find a balance between protection, equity and competitiveness in the changing world in which workers and enterprises now must operate. Some countries have already undertaken reforms with these aims. The four areas for reform presented in this chapter reflect this experience to some extent. They are summarized as follows:

- Reform in contractual relations to facilitate part-time contracts and alternative solutions, without associating them with a loss of basic benefits.
- Review of legislation governing maternity to avoid biases against contracting for women.
- In the area of unemployment protection, separation between the system of penalties for arbitrary dismissal and the unemployment income protection system. Penalties should be applied to employers for arbitrary dismissal and collected by the Ministry of Labor. In the area of worker income protection, severance pay mechanisms should be replaced with individual savings-based systems, and supplemented with transfer or credit schemes for unemployed workers.
- Improvement of social safety net systems in order to protect the poorer workers who do not participate in contribution-based systems.

Reform in Contractual Procedures

Current contractual procedures severely restrict part-time and temporary contracts. This bias is the result of the economic situation at the time when many of the Latin American codes were drafted. At that time, men were much more predominantly responsible for supporting the family, a role that they assumed at an early age. However, in recent decades, women's participation in the labor market has increased substantially. Between 1970 and 1994, the proportion of women in the total work force in Latin America rose from 23 to 35 percent. In addition, as a result of higher education levels, men and women now enter the labor market later. These two factors imply that more workers would now prefer jobs that offer flexible schedules to enable them to combine productive activities with family or educational ones. Labor laws and regulations need to be adapted to these changes to reduce segmentation and provide more equal opportunities, benefits and income in the labor market.

---

[6] Appendix 6.4 shows that all correlations between income differentials and legislation rigidities have the same sign. The same 15 differentials were analyzed in Chapter 2 (see Figure 2.7). Wage-earning men in the urban formal sector were used as a basis for comparison in all cases.

In many areas, the establishment of new contractual procedures is associated with a relative loss of workers' rights and benefits. This can occur if basic benefits enjoyed by permanent workers are not extended to new contracts, and if the latter bear the full brunt of job and wage instability. This has in fact occurred in a number of countries where labor legislation has become flexible "at the margin," excluding temporary workers and those employed in sectors considered apart from coverage, such as free trade or *maquila* areas. This could be resolved by finding the best possible balance between the benefits and contributions associated with new contractual procedures and those applicable to permanent contracts. In addition, to the extent that the employment protection system is reformed based on severance pay, it will not be necessary to use temporary contracts as a mechanism to achieve more flexible conditions for hiring and dismissal.

Revision of Labor Legislation Applicable to Women

Chapters 2 and 3 of this report show that there are major wage differences between men and women. A factor that clearly helps to explain these differences is the real or perceived costs of contracting a woman as opposed to a man. Laws and regulations governing paid maternity leave, child care facilities in enterprises and other benefits may have an adverse effect if they encourage enterprises to hire men. Such regulations require careful review so that the costs of protecting women, which are now borne by enterprises, can be socialized. Depending on the type of cost involved, this might be achieved through the social security system, or in connection with health and education programs covered by general budgets.

New Unemployment Protection Mechanisms

The previous section showed how the protection system, which is based on guaranteeing employment stability, generates biases in contracting and dismissing certain groups of workers and contributes to wage inequalities. However, the system exists in response to the need to protect workers from the risks of losing their jobs, a need inherent in any economic activity. New unemployment protection systems should avoid the biases and coverage gaps that are found in the present system, while preserving the objective of protecting workers.

First, the distinction should be made between penalizing for unjustified dismissal and protecting workers who lose or decide to change their jobs. The current system uses worker indemnification as an instrument to achieve these objectives, resulting in a less transparent system, and confusing the issues of protection and penalties. In the future, the economic requirements of an enterprise should be considered a justified cause for dismissal, while arbitrary dismissal should constitute grounds for an enterprise to be levied a penalty, payable to the Ministry of Labor, rather than to the worker, as is now true in many countries. The amount of the penalty should be determined by the authorities of each country, taking into account that an excessively high penalty may increase incentives to initiate legal proceedings regardless of the reason for dismissal.

Where income protection for the unemployed is concerned, it might be argued that the best defense against the economic risk of unemployment is voluntary personal saving and a sufficiently flexible labor market that enables workers to find new jobs with relative speed. However, for a number of reasons, a system based on these principles would be insufficient. First, workers may not save enough money to cover a period of unemployment, attributable to inadequate assessment of their unemployment risks, or their perception that the government would help them should they become unemployed. Second, although a flexible and efficient labor market is synonymous with finding a job easily, there are times when labor market fluidity is disrupted. During economic recessions, dismissals exceed new hires. Also, some workers may require time to readapt their skills, should their specific skills fall into disuse.

Unemployment insurance is the main protection mechanism used in industrial countries. The principal advantage of unemployment insurance, as compared with voluntary or mandatory saving mechanisms, is that, like fire insurance, it diversifies risk and does not require each individual to save enough money to cover himself fully against this contingency. However, such programs do entail problems, hence the principle known as "moral hazard," whereby individuals behave more recklessly precisely because they are insured. In the case of fire insurance, for example, an individual may be more careless with his property, and in an extreme case, may burn it down in order to collect insurance benefits. In the case of unemployment insurance, the problem is to make the distinction between the possibility of unemployment and potential voluntary inactivity. In addition, as insurance transfer payments are associated with being unemployed, insurance may reduce a worker's incentive to find a job, or encourage him to find one and not declare it.

In practice, most unemployment subsidy schemes pose restrictions aimed at reducing moral hazard and abuse. In many countries, job search activities must be documented, waiting periods are required, and the amount and duration of transfers are limited. However, the more conditions and complexities are built into the system, the higher its administrative costs. In addition, the existence of a large informal sector in many countries makes it impossible to determine whether or not a worker finds a job. Accordingly, in countries where there is no institutional capacity to administer relatively complex programs, or where there is a large informal sector, unemployment insurance is not a viable alternative to current programs that focus on job stability.

Perhaps a more appropriate system in moderately developed countries would be a mandatory savings-based scheme, such as separation funds in Colombia, Ecuador and Peru, where enterprises deposit a percentage of wages into individual accounts in the worker's name. These accounts are managed commercially by private administrators, who invest the funds and guarantee a market return. The government supervises the administrators and guarantees a minimum return should market returns fall short of a preestablished limit. Experience has shown that it is important to define a ceiling beyond which workers would be permitted to withdraw funds, in order to avoid oversaving.

Such schemes provide the major advantage of being relatively simple to manage, as they do not involve the moral hazard problems inherent with insurance. Another important advantage is that the benefits are portable, and therefore workers can easily change jobs as they wish without fear of losing seniority rights under the traditional protection schemes. The major disadvantage is that workers may not deposit sufficient funds in their accounts to cover a period of unemployment. One way to solve this problem is to introduce provisions to give workers who have deposited a certain level of funds into their accounts the option to receive additional amounts in the form of loans or transfers. This would ensure that workers receive the amount deemed appropriate to cover a period of unemployment. To ensure the solvency and equity of the system, these provisions should be financed entirely with contributions from workers deposited periodically in a mutual interest fund.

Of course, there will be difficulties involved in converting from the present scheme to a new protection scheme. Workers who are older and more experienced—who in fact are the ones who benefit from the current system—will press against the implementation of such reforms. If overall system reforms do not prove to be politically viable, a transitional system would be the next best alternative. New contracts would be included in a savings-credit or savings-transfer scheme, while entitlements acquired by workers employed prior to the reform could be kept in their current form, or exchanged for deposits in individual accounts.

Coverage under current employment protection schemes is quite low. Any new protection scheme should aim to expand coverage to workers not participating in the existing systems. As we have observed, workers who are less educated, women, those living outside of major cities, and those with greater family burdens tend to be marginalized by the employment protection system, even if they work in large enterprises. These coverage gaps may be corrected at least partially with an individual savings program managed by private financial concerns aiming to extend their customer portfolio. However, incorporating workers at higher risk of unemployment into the system may increase the costs of savings-credit or savings-transfer systems and therefore raise the contributions that each participant must make to the mutual interest fund. This dilemma could be solved by requiring higher-risk individuals to pay larger contributions, or by partially subsidizing higher-risk workers through the government budget.

New unemployed workers' protection systems will be increasingly effective if supplemented with policies to assist workers in reentering the labor market. For example, job exchanges and other job search assistance mechanisms are effective when coordinated with unemployment benefits. In addition, adequately targeted training programs supplemented with apprenticeships have been effective in increasing employability among young workers in Chile, Argentina and Mexico (see Box 6.1).

Improving Social Safety Net Systems

It is not feasible to try to extend unemployment protection systems to workers in the informal sector or to the poorest workers. Lack of employment records makes it difficult to determine how long an informal sector worker has been unemployed. Thus, the participation of these workers should be limited to individual savings accounts without access to credit or transfer systems in the event of unemployment. Participation should also be voluntary, owing to the lack of records.

It is quite probable that the poorest workers will not participate in the contribution-based programs described above, even if their contributions are partially subsidized. Poor workers do not have the economic means to forgo present consumption for the sake of stabilizing future consumption. A reasonable alternative would be to extend social safety net systems so that they respond—in the form of income transfer programs, food or work—

Box 6.1. *Training and Employability Programs*

Traditionally, training in Latin America has been dependent on centralized government agencies financed through payroll taxes. It is difficult for such programs to meet the present needs of employment and qualified labor because they were designed to support the early stages of import substitution in a context of slow technological change.

As a result of their monopolistic and government nature, these training programs often operate at high cost, with little administrative and occupational flexibility. And their connection to demand for skills in the productive sectors prevents them from keeping up with changing technological requirements of enterprises.

Some countries in the region have already taken steps to remedy this situation. Youth programs provide a much-used model for such intervention. Chile was a pioneer in these efforts in 1994, followed soon thereafter by Argentina and by pilot programs now being developed in six other countries.

Under these programs, the Ministry of Labor allocates funds to train unemployed youth, in connection with competitive bidding procedures involving various training providers, which constitutes a departure from the monopolistic nature of supply. To participate in the competitive process, training providers must hold contracts with enterprises that assure that a certain number of trainees will be hired, thus ensuring that these services are linked to demand.

Another successful activity has been a comprehensive training and modernization program (CIMO—*Capacitación Integral y Modernización*) implemented by Mexico's Secretariat of Labor. This program targets workers employed in small and me-dium-scale enterprises. The Secretariat creates local units to promote and organize training demand, and define training programs. Competitive bidding procedures are used to contract independent suppliers to provide the training courses. The costs of the program are partially subsidized for a limited period of time. This methodology has proven useful where local production lines provide a natural forum for the organization of training activities.

Though these systems have been successful to the extent that they have adapted workers' skills to enterprise demand, they cannot contribute substantially to job creation, let alone to the reduction of income inequality. First, no training system can create jobs when this is prevented by adverse growth trends or regulatory rigidities. An effective training system can only improve worker employability by providing workers with varied and timely skills necessary to enter the labor market. Second, training programs have often been presented as part of a social safety net system, based on the assumption that a better-trained worker will be more likely to obtain employment and support his or her family. The alternative would be direct transfers to households, which may be more decisive in the critical situations of the poorest sectors of the population. Experts are divided as to which option is preferable, and under what circumstances, and there are a limited number of studies on existing programs (Ravallion, 1998). In summary, while government intervention is justified to provide training to help protect workers and address changing demands for skills, it is not viable for purposes of generating jobs or as an income transfer mechanism.

---

to the needs of the poorest workers who lose their jobs and are temporarily without another source of income (see Box 5.1 in the preceding chapter). To prevent these initiatives from reducing incentives to contribute to the above-mentioned protection systems, assistance must target the poorest individuals, and must be carefully designed to prevent people from becoming dependent on protection systems.

SOCIAL SECURITY SYSTEMS

Labor protection mechanisms in Latin America focus on the typical relationship between the enterprise and the worker, as do the region's traditional social security systems. Workers join the system through enterprises that make contributions, part of which are deducted by arrangement from the worker's wages. The social security system is typically administered by a government agency, which is responsible for providing health services and payment of old-age pensions and disability or death indemnities. While this social security system is inherently redistributive, the redistributive aims are often a double-edged sword that can favor those in a privileged position to begin with. Such is the case with the traditional pay-as-you-go system, the model still in effect in most countries. In many cases, the individuals most vulnerable to instability and uncertainty have been excluded, as have workers who are less educated, women, and rural workers. In addition, the principles of redistribution among members of the system have often become distorted.

Whom Does Social Security Protect?

Social security protection does not provide equal coverage for all, due in part to the fact that to be affiliated with the system, a worker must be associated with a formal sector enterprise. However, this is not the full explanation, as many workers in these enterprises are also ex-

Figure 6.5. Whom Does the Social Security System Protect?

(*In percent*)

a. Less equitable systems: Brazil (1995), Peru (1985) and Venezuela (1995)

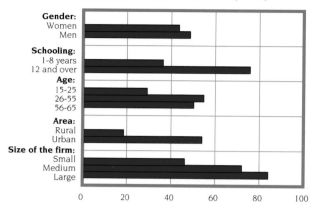

b. More equitable systems: Argentina (1996), Chile (1994) and Costa Rica (1995)

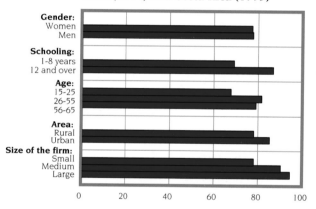

Source: Márquez and Pagés (1998).

cluded. Workers who remain outside the system are those with the lowest income-generating potential, since they are easier for enterprises to replace and they prefer to waive protection in exchange for higher pay.

These are the conclusions of a comparative analysis of social security system coverage in six Latin American countries. Persons under 25 and older than 55 receive less protection than persons in the more productive moderate age categories. Women have less access than men, and rural workers have less access than those who live in the cities. A worker with five or six years of education, that is, a typical worker according to Latin American standards, is as likely to be affiliated with social security as not, while a university graduate can almost take affiliation for granted. However, these inequities in protection are not inevitable. They are much lower in Argentina, Chile and Costa Rica than in Brazil, Peru and Venezuela (Figure 6.5).

A detailed econometric analysis shows that these inequalities are even observed within medium- and large-scale enterprises.[7] Data for Argentina and Venezuela show that the probability of being affiliated with social security, regardless of the size of the enterprise and economic sector, is significantly greater for a person with 15 years of education than for someone with only five, and is much greater for an employee who earns the equivalent of four or five times the wages of a rank-and-file worker.

We might expect some enterprises to evade the rules and deceive workers. It is also possible, however, that these low-income workers themselves prefer to waive social security voluntarily in exchange for higher pay, which may make the difference between covering or not covering their basic needs. (This explanation is also corroborated with data indicating that most social security contributions paid by enterprises correspond to affiliated workers, and hence the actual cost to the enterprise is virtually unchanged.[8]) And in a number of countries that have introduced more flexible contracting conditions, affiliation is not a legal requirement, as workers with temporary or part-time arrangements do not receive the same social security benefits as those who have permanent contracts.[9]

Systems Are Designed for Redistributive Purposes...

Pay-as-you-go pension schemes are inherently redistributive, since contributions from active workers are earmarked to pay the pensions of persons who are already retired. Under this "inter-generational arrangement," some current income of present generations is transferred to cover the pensions of earlier generations; in exchange, it is expected that pensions for the present generations will be covered in the future by new generations. Theoretically, this system of redistribution between generations could work indefinitely, with provisions to adjust the combination of benefits and contributions to growth trends in terms of the number of pensioners, on the one hand, and the active population of workers, on the other. In practice, however, this balance is difficult to maintain. Initially, the relationship between contributors and retirees tends to be quite favorable, and leaves scope to pro-

---

[7] Calculated based on results from Márquez and Pagés (1998).

[8] Based on the case of Chile and analyzed by Gruber (1997).

[9] In the United States as well, unskilled workers have less social security coverage and receive fewer benefits than skilled workers employed by the same enterprises. Further, protection inequalities have worsened since the early 1980s. See Hamermesh (1998).

vide the first generations with substantial pensions, which are subsequently difficult to sustain. Under present demographic conditions, paying out large pensions is a great temptation for most Latin American countries, but one that would result in a severe burden for future generations. In fact, the number of working-age persons per individual over 60 years of age exceeds nine in most countries (Figure 6.6). Only Argentina, Barbados and Uruguay now have six or less persons of working age for each person older than 60. However, in three decades, the demographic situation in most countries will be similar to the present situation in these three countries. And in five decades, there will be an average of only four working-age persons for each person over 60. Further, in more demographically mature countries, there will be only about three economically active persons for each retirement age person. This will involve a proportionally greater burden that will increase as coverage, which is still very limited in many countries, is expanded.

In addition to this redistribution among generations, pension systems also redistribute benefits among individuals in the same generation, since some beneficiaries receive more substantial pension benefits than others in absolute terms as well as in relation to the contributions that they have made during their economically active lives. In principle, substantial progressive and equity elements are incorporated into defined-benefit pension systems, the traditional characteristic of all systems in Latin America until the recent reforms that incorporated individually funded mechanisms into systems in Argentina, Bolivia, Chile, Colombia, El Salvador, Mexico, Peru and Uruguay.

Defined benefit systems include the following main progressive factors:

- Establishment of minimum pensions for persons with lower incomes, and whose contributions are therefore lower;
- More career interruptions with periods of unemployment and informal activity for the poor;
- Shorter working lives and longer retirement periods for women.

...But Implemented Inequitably

However, a number of factors lead to perverse redistribution—that is, from the poor to the rich—in the same generation:

- Higher pension levels for the rich, since retirement benefits are determined by wage level;

Figure 6.6. Working Age Population per Person Older than 60

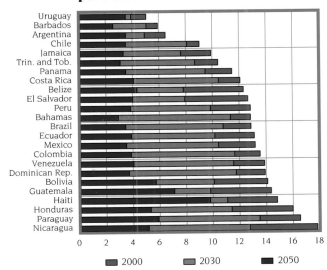

Source: IDB calculations based on UN Population Statistics (1996).

- Longer life expectancies for wealthier persons;
- Shorter careers for the wealthy, as they spend more time in the education system;
- Exclusion from the system of those who do not have permanent contracts, typically the poorest members of society.

While it is impossible to determine a priori whether the progressive factors are dominant, some studies based on individual characteristics and behavior patterns among persons with different income levels suggest that progressive factors may be important in an "ideal" system with total coverage and totally faithful contributions.[10] In addition, regulations on contributions and pension computation may theoretically aim to reinforce redistributive objectives. For example, contribution rates may be higher for higher incomes. In Brazil, wage-earners contribute 8, 9 or 10 percent, depending on the wage level (in addition to the 20 percent paid by the enterprises); in Colombia, persons earning more than four times the minimum wage are required to make a mutual interest contribution of 1 percent of wages; and in Ecuador and Uruguay, employees in some sectors make higher contributions. Redistribution objectives may also be supported by establishing a ceiling on pension value, as is true in Brazil, Costa Rica, Guatemala, Peru and Uruguay (Table 6.1).

However, the actual situation in any pension system may change the distributive results to the point that

---

[10] See Falkingham and Johnson (1993).

Table 6.1. Redistributive Features of Pay-As-You-Go Social Security Systems in 1996

	Special systems	Different contribution rates by income level or sector	Ceiling wage for contributions (as proportion of income per capita)	Minimum pension (as proportion of per capita income)	Relevant wage for the benefits calculation
Argentina	Military	No	na [1]	na [1]	10 years
Bahamas		1.7% if weekly insurance wage is under B$60, 3.4% for others	1.17	0.16	
Barbados		No	2.7	0.34	Best 3 years of the last 15
Belize		Between B$0.12 and $B1.30 according to four wage classes ($B40 - $B110)		12.5	Best 3 years of the last 15
Bolivia	Bank employees, military personnel, drivers, miners, railroad employees, petroleum workers	No			12 months
Brazil	Public employees and military, aircraft crew, journalists, veterans and teachers	8%, 9% and 10%	8.54 times minimum wage	100% minimum wage	3 years
Colombia	Public petroleum enterprise employees, teachers and military	1% extra for employees with more than 4 minimum wages		100% minimum wage	10 years
Costa Rica		Between 4.5% and 7% for independent workers		0.61	48 months of the last 5 years
Dominican Republic	Public employees	No		0.49	2 years
Ecuador	Congressmen	6% in industry, 8% by bank employees and teachers, 6% in agriculture		0.74	5 years
El Salvador	Public employees	No	21.7	0.82	10 years
Guatemala	Some public employees	No	9.4	0.39	5 years
Guyana		No		50% of the minimum wage	5 years
Haiti	Public employees	Between 2% and 6% according to wage level (200-1,000 gourdes)			10 years
Honduras	Public employees, doctors, teachers and the military	No	0.92		
Jamaica	Armed forces	No			
Mexico	Petroleum employees, public employees and military	No	25 times the federal minimum wage	100% federal minimum wage	
Nicaragua	Teachers	No		66% of the minimum wage	Last 5, 4 or 3 years
Panama	Rural employees	No		0.86	7 years
Paraguay	Public, railroad, bank employees	No			3 years
Peru		No		Between 0.24 and 0.48	12 months
Trin. and Tob.		No	0.47	0.062	
Uruguay	Bank employees, notaries, university graduates, armed forces, police	15% in industry and commerce and public employees, 16% rural employees		100% minimum wage	10 years
Venezuela	Public employees and armed forces	No			5 years during the last 10 years

[1] 60 AMPOs. AMPO is determined dividing the total employee contribution to the system by the total number of contributors.

Source: *Social Security Programs Throughout the World,* 1997, U.S. Social Security Administration, Office of Research, Evaluation and Statistics.

they become regressive. An important factor in regressiveness is attributable to the fact that pensions in many countries are calculated based on declared wages from the past few years, rather than from an individual's entire working life. In many countries, only the highest pay in the past four to five years is considered; in some countries, the reference period is as long as 10 years. This tends to benefit the higher income groups, which may substantially underreport their wages during most of their careers and make substantial contributions only at the end. To avoid these tactics, some countries impose maximum declarable wage limits, which is not a proper solution to the problem as it reduces the contribution base and redistribution potential of the overall system. It is also a common practice for social security contributions to be exempt from other taxes, which implies more favorable treatment for higher-income individuals, who should pay higher direct taxes.

Progressive potential in pension systems is also changed by the creation of special schemes for certain groups of workers. This has been a common practice in Latin America, primarily benefiting government employees, teachers and military personnel, who enjoy special conditions such as early retirement or higher replacement rates, which often correspond only to their lobbying and organizing capacity. In some countries, certain associations for professionals such as bank staff, physicians, notaries and university professors have created pension funds that receive budgetary support through taxes, surcharges and other specifically-earmarked funds.

These are extreme cases of the use of budgetary funds for clearly regressive purposes; however, they are not the only ones. Many pay-as-you-go pension systems are operating in deficit and are financed with general budget resources (Figure 6.7), which implies that persons who are excluded from the system make indirect contributions.

Reforms in the Proper Direction

More and more Latin American countries have reformed their pay-as-you-go pension systems, replacing them partially with individually funded systems. Since Chile established a private pension system in 1981, seven more countries have moved in this direction: Peru (1993), Colombia (1993), Argentina (1994), Uruguay (1996), Bolivia (1997), El Salvador (1997), and Mexico (1997). In principle, funded systems do not involve any income redistribution mechanism, as pensions inherently depend exclusively on individual contributions (and market yields). However, all countries have introduced mutual interest and redistribution components into their new systems.

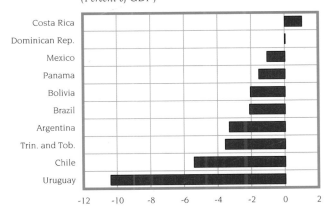

Figure 6.7. Operational Balance of Public Social Security Systems, 1995
(*Percent of* GDP)

Source: International Monetary Fund, Government Financial Statistics (1997).

In Chile, although the defined benefits scheme has only remained in effect for those who were already retired and those who decided to remain in the system at the beginning, the government guarantees everyone a minimum pension under the new system after 10 years of contributions. In Mexico, where the old system will also be eliminated, there is a government-sponsored minimum guaranteed pension. The final consolidation of the new systems in these two countries will for all intents and purposes eliminate the regressive mechanisms of pension benefits in the prior system.

The situation is more complex in other countries where many components of the earlier systems are still in place. In Colombia, workers may select between the old and new system, but in either case are guaranteed a minimum pension. In addition, under the pay-as-you-go system, retirement conditions are quite favorable to women, individuals over 40 years of age at the time of the reform, and those who have less potential to accumulate contributions during their overall working life. Regardless of which system they select, higher-income employees must also contribute 1 percent of their wages to the pay-as-you-go system. This approach has preserved a number of mutual interest components, which may be progressive. However, it has also retained more regressive factors such as very generous retirement conditions for civil servants and options for private fund participants to claim pensions from the pay-as-you-go system in the event that the yields in private funds are unsatisfactory. In addition, as all of these guarantees will lead to financial imbalance in the pay-as-you-go system, eventual dependence on tax revenue will accentuate its regressive features.

The two systems are complementary in Argentina and Uruguay: the basic component, to which all workers contribute, provides basic pensions up to a maximum amount, which has a progressive feature. The individual funding component, which is mandatory in Uruguay and optional in Argentina, theoretically has no significant distributive impact. While this component should have resulted in an enhanced distributive effect for the entire pension system in the two countries, it is not clear that it is in fact progressive. In Uruguay, the schemes were maintained for special groups (military personnel, police and other groups of employees affiliated with parastatal social security funds). In Argentina, an additional benefit was established for remaining in the old pay-as-you-go system, in the form of ample guarantees on returns for the state bank pension fund, and guaranteed retirement benefits from the old system up to an amount specified in the national budget for persons choosing the funded system.

In summary, Latin American pension systems have not served as progressive income redistribution mechanisms. Countries that have introduced purer forms of individually funded systems, such as Chile or Mexico, will in the long term eliminate the most significant regressive components, which will disappear with the pay-as-you-go system (although there will be a considerable temporary operating deficit to be covered with tax revenue). Progress will be less evident in countries that have opted for a combination of the pay-as-you-go and funded systems, maintaining acquired privileges for various groups and offering government guarantees, with unclear progressive features. However, a pure individually funded scheme is inherently neutral in distributive terms, and hence in and of itself would be an incomplete solution to social security problems and should be supplemented with a purely redistributive component.

WHAT THE PENSION SYSTEM CAN DO

A social security system with two or more pillars may achieve objectives in terms of redistribution, savings and insurance that traditional pay-as-you-go systems in Latin America cannot:

• The payment of minimum pensions to persons not earning subsistence incomes—a basic component financed with general budget resources—may address the objective of reducing poverty and providing the elderly with insurance.

• A mandatory, individually funded component based on defined contributions should address the old-age saving function for persons with regular labor income. This component should be operated under competitive conditions by the private sector, although it should be publicly regulated to avoid systemic risks and protect participants' rights.

• The two components could optionally be supplemented with voluntary long-term savings plans offered by financial institutions or other private organizations to those who wish to have additional old-age coverage.

One of the main problems with the design of any social security system in Latin America is the incorporation of informal sector workers. As it is impossible to monitor, participation of these workers must be voluntary, although they would seem to have little incentive to participate because their incomes are lower and more unstable than formal sector workers, and because the opportunity cost of saving is high due to limited access to credit for informal activities.[11] An incentive that might favor poorer informal sector workers would be a periodic direct subsidy in a fixed per capita amount, strictly targeted and subject to continued participation in the system. Another option is to provide seed capital for membership in the form of paper with a future maturity (possibly related to the worker's age). A variation of this option is to allow workers to share in ownership of public enterprises that have been "capitalized" or privatized.

It is a good time for Latin American countries to make the necessary reforms in their social security systems. The state of demographic transition in most countries in the region indicates that the proportion of the population of productive age will peak in the next few decades. The number of children each active worker must support has declined, and the proportion of persons of retirement age has still not increased. As a result, present workers are able to generate savings to cover their future retirement without having to transfer the burden to future generations. Pension system reform can therefore not only improve income distribution among present generations, but also between present and future generations.

---

[11] See Chapter 7.

WHAT THE MINIMUM WAGE ACCOMPLISHES

The minimum wage in Latin America has traditionally been considered a redistributive instrument and an income protection mechanism for the poorest workers. However, as with other labor protection instruments, when goals are excessively ambitious they become irrelevant, if not counterproductive, in terms of helping the poor.

What Is Needed for the Minimum Wage to Protect the Poor?

There is intense debate both in industrial and developing countries as to whether minimum wages constitute an effective mechanism for distributing income and protecting the income of the poorest workers (see Box 6.2). Evidence for Latin America suggests that changes in the minimum wage have a discernable effect on income distribution, although the magnitude is low (see Box 6.3).

For the minimum wage to raise real incomes for the poorest workers, it must meet three difficult conditions. First, it should not adversely affect aggregate employment demand. Income of the poor cannot be protected if income increases for some workers result in a significant rise in unemployment. Second, levels of compliance with regulations must be high. Ambitious wage increase regulations are of little help if they cannot be enforced owing to informal labor contracting practices or to the government's insufficient means to prevent evasion, especially by organized enterprises operating in the formal sector. However, these two conditions are not sufficient. After all, if the minimum wage were established at an extremely low level, it would not reduce employment or generate evasion problems—nor would it improve anyone's income. The third condition, therefore, is that the minimum wage be situated at a level that covers a substantial group of low-income workers.

These three conditions can easily conflict with one another, depending greatly on the minimum wage level. It is widely agreed that, at relatively low levels, the minimum wage does not appreciably change aggregate employment demand, while at high levels its effects can be quite negative. A number of different studies on developing countries have found that low minimum wage levels affect the composition more than the level of employment: although youth employment tends to be reduced, this effect is typically offset with higher adult employment levels.[12] However, when the minimum wage is set at a high level, job destruction effects predominate, as demonstrated by Puerto Rico's experience when it adopted the U.S. minimum wage during the 1970s. Experience in Puerto Rico and other developing countries indicates that, at high levels, a 10 percent increase in the minimum wage (exceeding inflation) can reduce employment in proportions that vary widely from country to country, but that in some cases can be as high as 12 percent.[13]

If a high minimum wage level leads to reduced employment demand, it will also affect compliance with regulatory requirements because displaced workers and the affected enterprises will benefit from collusion to evade the regulations. Noncompliance will be higher the greater the divergence between the minimum wage and the market level for wages, and will also depend on the government's institutional capacity for oversight and enforcement.

It follows that the selected minimum wage level is the principal determining factor in its efficiency and its potential impact on income distribution. Excessively high minimum wages can have job destroying effects and prove to be ineffective in raising income levels of the poor.

Is the Minimum Wage in Some Countries Too High?

Answering this question for Latin America requires comparing the minimum wage in each country with the average wage level, which reflects general worker productivity conditions. In 1995 and 1996, minimum wage levels in most Latin American countries represented less than half the average minimum wage level (Figure 6.8). In Bolivia, Brazil and Argentina, the minimum wage was less than 30 percent of the average wage, and in Chile, Mexico and Peru, it was between 30 and 40 percent. These proportions are low in comparison with industrial countries. However, in a number of Latin American countries, the minimum wage exceeded the average by 50 percent, and in the extreme case of Venezuela in 1995, it represented approximately 90 percent of the average wage, well above the level in any industrial country.

High minimum wage levels will only affect remuneration of high-income workers. In fact, in Honduras, Paraguay, El Salvador and Venezuela, those who earn

---

[12] See Brown, Gilroy, and Kohen (1982), Hamermesh (1982), Wellington (1991), Card (1992), and Card and Krueger (1994) for the effects of the minimum wage in the United States; Schaafsma and Welsh (1983) for Canada; Bazen and Martin (1991) for France; and Dolado, et al. (1996) for France, the Netherlands, England and Spain.

[13] On the subject of Puerto Rico, see studies by Santiago (1989) and Castillo-Freeman and Freeman (1990). For Mexico and Colombia, see Bell (1997).

BOX 6.2. *Minimum Wages and Income Inequality: The Discussion*

There is intense debate both in industrial and developing countries as to whether minimum wages constitute an effective mechanism for distributing income and protecting the income of the poorest workers. Evidence for Latin America suggests that changes in the minimum wage have a discernable effect on income distribution, although the magnitude is low (see Box 6.3). Overall evidence on the impact of minimum wages on income distribution points to some positive but small declines in inequality and somewhat larger positive effects on poverty. In the United States, for example, the discussion evolves around whether the sharp decline in the real value of minimum wages during the 1980s can explain the increase in wage and income inequality experienced during that period. The evidence is far from conclusive. Dinardo, Fortin and Lemieux (1996) find that the decline in the real value of the minimum wage explains about one-third of the change in wage inequality, but Horrigan and Mincy (1993) find modest effects on earnings inequality and virtually no effects on family income inequality. Regarding minimum wages and income distribution in developing countries, World Bank (1995) states that while minimum wages might help protect the incomes of the poorest workers in industrial countries, they clearly do not do so in developing countries. The claim is that the workers affected by minimum wage provisions are really the most needy. Moreover, by reducing formal sector employment, minimum wages exert downward pressure on the wages of informal poor workers. However, there is little evidence that minimum wages might yield declines in wage inequality in developing countries. Bell (1996) documents that in Colombia, minimum wage increases were accompanied by a decline in inequality even when the economy was going through recession. On the empirical side, Lustig and McLeod (1997) find that in a sample of about 30 developing countries, an increase in statutory minimum wages is associated with a decrease in the level of poverty. They describe various channels for which this effect may arise. Besides the direct impact of minimum wages, they cite mechanisms that link higher minimum wages with higher wages for informal workers. Demand-link models, for instance, state that an upward push in formal sector wages might increase the demand for informal sector products, leading to an increase in informal sector demand and wages. Finally, Ramos and Almeida Reis (1995) undertake an exercise of simulation to assess the impact of minimum wage policy in Brazil very similar to the one performed by Horrigan and Mincy for the United States. As did Horrigan and Mincy, they find that minimum wages have positive but small effects on income inequality.

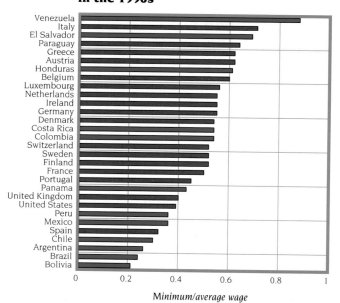

Figure 6.8. Minimum Wage in OECD Countries and in Latin America in the 1990s

Minimum/average wage

Source: OECD: *European Industrial Relations and OIT Yearbook.* Latin America: *Ministries of Labor.*

minimum wage are moderate-income workers in the third labor income quintile.[14] Even in Mexico, Panama and Costa Rica, where the minimum wage represents a smaller proportion of average wages, it applies to workers in the second quintile, and not the poorest. The minimum wage level should be relatively low, less than 40 percent of the average wage, so that, at least in principle, it favorably affects remuneration among the lowest-income workers.

Effectiveness of High Minimum Wages Is Limited

Where minimum wages are higher with relation to average wages, noncompliance with the regulatory system is greatest: in Paraguay and El Salvador, approximately half of workers earn wages under 80 percent of the minimum, which is true for 30 to 40 of every 100 workers in Honduras and Venezuela. By contrast, noncompliance levels fall below 10 percent in countries where the minimum wage is below 30 percent of the average wage (Figure 6.9). Judging from the ratio of relative minimum wage level compliance, a 10 percent minimum wage reduction can in-

---

[14] All calculations in the rest of this section reflect minimum wage data for 1994, 1995 or 1996, depending on the country.

Box 6.3. *Minimum Wages in Latin America: Trends and Effects on Inequality*

The purchasing power of the minimum wage in most Latin American countries is now much lower than it was during the early 1980s. The debt crisis and subsequent adjustment processes led to decreases in minimum wages, which were only partially corrected during the 1990s. Only Colombia, Costa Rica and Panama succeeded in maintaining relatively stable minimum wages in real terms (see Figure 1).

An econometric analysis indicates that reductions in minimum wage purchasing power have been inversely associated with increases in income concentration (and vice versa) in all 11 countries considered (after isolating the influence of a number of other variables that may even have affected distribution—see Appendix 6.5). However, the effects have been surprisingly modest. For every 10 percent minimum wage reduction, the income concentration index has increased by just under 0.2 points (equivalent to approximately 0.4 percent of the initial inequality level).

Other studies, both of Latin America and at the international level, have found that while minimum wage increases may effectively reduce poverty in the short term, they cannot be used indiscriminately for that purpose, as they can generate unemployment and reduce growth, adversely affecting the poor in the long term (Morley, 1992 and 1997; de Janvry and Sadoulet, 1995; Lustig and McLeod, 1997).

In Latin America, minimum wages have distributive effects through a number of different channels that normally have little to do with the nature of this instrument. In many countries, they serve as a basis to define the amounts of pensions

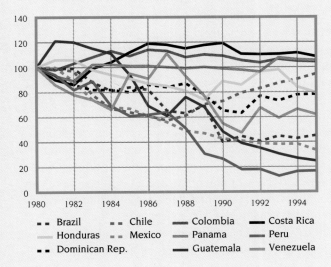

Figure 1. Minimum Wage Index

and other transfers, to adjust civil servants' wages, or to establish rates for public services. And in inflationary situations, minimum wage adjustments may influence other wages and prices. All of these factors are indicative that minimum wages constitute an untargeted income distribution instrument.

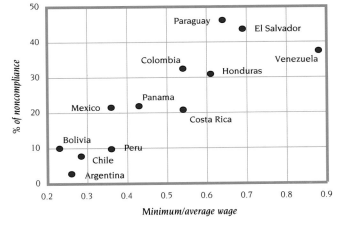

Figure 6.9. Noncompliance and the Minimum Wage Level

Source: *IDB calculations based on most recent household surveys.*

crease compliance by approximately eight points. Although this figure is merely indicative, it suggests that evasion is quite sensitive to incentives. It is mutually beneficial for enterprises and workers at risk or in unemployment situations to agree to remunerations below the minimum wage.

It is commonly believed that noncompliance with wage standards is limited to small-scale enterprises and informal concerns, reflecting a highly simplified theoretical conception according to which a minimum wage requirement above the equilibrium labor market wage leads to the appearance of an informal sector that evades the regulations.[15] Reality is quite different, as much minimum wage evasion occurs in large enterprises.[16] As indi-

---

[15] This theory was proposed by Welch (1976) to explain why the minimum wage did not seem to generate unemployment in the United States to the extent that might be expected based on the single market model.

[16] As also observed by Ashenfelter and Smith (1979) in the United States, demonstrating the limitation of the simple segmentation approach.

cated above, labor regulations are just one of the factors that influence the existence and scope of the informal sector. Typically, 40 percent of workers paid less than 80 percent of the minimum wage work in enterprises with 10 or more employees. In El Salvador and Venezuela, six of every 10 workers paid less than 80 percent of the minimum wage are employed by large enterprises.[17] In Brazil, Panama and Paraguay, young workers can legally be paid below minimum wage (in the former two countries, they must be apprentices). However, in many cases, observed noncompliance is tantamount to evasion of the law. Governments lack the resources to supervise compliance and impose fines on violators. Insufficient supervision tends to occur in very large and unrepresentative enterprises. While unions can perform supervisory functions, the levels of unionization are insufficient in most countries to make an impact. In addition, unions are concentrated in high-wage enterprises, where few workers are directly affected by minimum wage regulations.

To summarize, the higher the minimum wage levels with relation to the average wage earned by all workers, the greater the noncompliance. Young workers, who are less educated, along with those employed in small enterprises, are the most likely to remain below this level. However, compliance is far from perfect in large-scale enterprises. Noncompliance with wage regulations softens the impact on employment, but also reduces the possibility for the minimum wage to operate as an income protection mechanism for poorer workers.

Minimum Wage Earners Are Often Not the Poor

Aside from problems of compliance and potential job destruction effects, the minimum wage is a fairly tenuous instrument for protecting the incomes of poor families. Even when the minimum wage is very low, workers who earn it are not exclusively (and often not even in the majority) from poorer families. In the best of cases, when the minimum wage is fairly low, such as in Argentina, only 30 percent of the wage earners paid near the minimum wage level (0.8 to 1.2 times this amount) are members of families in the poorest quintile of the population. Just above 20 percent belong to the second poorest quintile, and the rest are members of middle- and upper-class families (Figure 6.10). More than half of those who earn the minimum wage are not heads of household, but rather young people who may or may not come from families whose fathers are low earners. In countries with high minimum wage levels, such as Venezuela, more minimum wage earners are adult heads of household, although most are in the middle and upper categories. Youth who

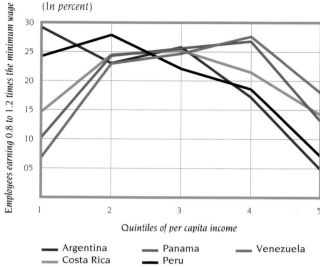

Figure 6.10. Minimum Wage Incidence according to Per Capita Household Income
(*In percent*)

Employees earning 0.8 to 1.2 times the minimum wage

Quintiles of per capita income

— Argentina   — Panama   — Venezuela
— Costa Rica   — Peru

Source: IDB *calculations based on recent household surveys.*

earn minimum wages are predominantly highly educated and come from wealthy households. In other words, a high minimum wage is targeted more at the wealthy than a low minimum wage is at the poor.

In these conditions, an increase in the minimum wage affects income distribution modestly, even with the assumption that it is totally effective and does not adversely affect employment. With these assumptions, a 10 percent minimum wage increase in Argentina would reduce the Gini wage income concentration coefficient by 0.04 percentage points, and the Gini household income concentration coefficient by 0.0035 percentage points, quite a modest change. Similarly, in Costa Rica, the Gini wage coefficient would be reduced by .035, and in other countries the reduction would be somewhat lower.[18] These calculations only reflect the direct effect of a minimum wage on wages of workers at this income level, but do not include any indirect effect that they may have as a reference price for other incomes (for example, informal sector wages or social security transfers). However, although indirect effects are not considered, these changes are similar in magnitude to those obtained from the time series analysis (results are summarized in Box 6.3).

---

[17] We used 80 percent of the minimum as a cutoff line, as the wages actually received by workers can be affected by social security contributions and other deductions paid by workers.
[18] These results are based on Pagés (1998).

What the Minimum Wage Can Do

As we have observed, the minimum wage is a very limited income redistribution instrument. Part of the problem is that a single minimum wage does not reflect differences in household structures. Of course, minimum wages that vary with the number of dependents or other household characteristics would be both unmanageable and counterproductive, as they would cause enterprises to discriminate against those in greatest need. A better solution is to establish a lower minimum wage for youth, as is done in European countries (and in Paraguay, among countries in the region). This would make it possible to address the main problem of the targeting of the minimum wage based on its effects on the income of youth in middle- and high-income families. This approach could also reduce youth unemployment, as enterprises would prefer, given a minimum wage, to employ more experienced workers and to hire youth on a selective basis. Young people, in turn, would find it more advantageous to keep looking for formal sector employment, given its relative advantages over other activities.

The minimum wage is limited in its ability to protect the income of the poor, as well as in income redistribution, because of evasion problems, potential adverse effects on employment and insufficient targeting. These problems are less severe, although they are not eliminated, when the minimum wage is set at moderate levels and when a lower minimum wage for youth is established.

OTHER INCOME PROTECTION MECHANISMS FOR THE POOR

Are there other, less limited options? Wage supplements for low-income workers provide an alternative, although they do entail some problems. With this technique, low-income workers receive a wage supplement if their income is below a certain level. In Colombia, this system is financed with a payroll tax levied on all workers, which is also used to finance health, education and recreation programs administered by private "equalization funds." In the United States, the earned income tax credit is a similar instrument, with the advantage that it serves as a negative tax for low-income workers, and is administered by the tax collection office. Under these schemes, the tax credit or supplement that workers receive can be adjusted to reflect the number of dependents or the income level without affecting the cost of a worker to the enterprise. However, these programs have serious disadvantages in that they encourage workers to report lower wages in order to receive higher subsidies. Accordingly, they require

greater administration and supervision than minimum wages. Apart from their high administrative costs, these systems can generate poverty traps, which occur when an increase in gross income is not reflected by a net gain because part of the subsidy is forgone. In this case, workers may become dependent on social welfare systems.

A similar option is to subsidize enterprises that contract workers whose wages are below a certain income level. The subsidy might operate as a payroll tax exemption, with the advantage that it stimulates, rather than discourages, demand for this type of worker. A further advantage is that, unlike the minimum wage, if the aim is to focus incentives on workers who have more dependents, enterprises would prefer them to other workers. In principle, employment subsidies should be granted only under new worker contracts to prevent transfers costly to enterprises in connection with existing jobs. Experience in industrial countries has shown that enterprises often simply replace existing workers with new ones, with few gains in terms of employment. Another problem is that this is a temporary system that lasts as long as the subsidy policies remain in effect. Last, poverty traps can also appear in this connection, as subsidies reduce the incentive for enterprises and workers to raise productivity and wages above the minimum level eligible for the subsidy.

There are other problems as well with subsidizing workers or companies in order to increase employment and incomes of the poorest workers. The limitation of any of these schemes is that fraud and evasion can only be kept under control with adequate information systems and supervision, which normally do not exist in the poorer countries. And in these countries, these types of programs are often not feasible because of the large proportion of unskilled, low-income workers.

Appendix 6.1. Econometric Results: Effect of the Labor Code on Employment

Dependent variable:	Employment rate (Share of working age population)		Self-employment rate (Share of employment)	
Labor rigidity index	-0.77 (-3.4)	-0.39 (-0.9)	0.63 (3.2)	0.38 (2.4)
GDP per capita		0.0002 (0.3)		-0.0005 (-2.5)
Dummy for Latin America		-6.11 (-0.5)		
No. of observations	34	27	24	23
Adjusted R^2	0.243	0.152	0.531	0.659

Note: T-statistics in parentheses.
Source: Márquez and Pagés (1998).

Appendix 6.2. Econometric Results: Effect of the Labor Code on Dependent Employment by Age Group, Chile, 1960-96

Dependent variable:	Total employment (% growth)	Employment population aged		
		15-25 (% growth)	26-50 (% growth)	51-60 (% growth)
Labor rigidity index (log)	-0.002 (-1.44)	-0.009 (-3.08)	0.0007 (0.18)	0.004 (0.99)
Salary (change in log, lagged)	-0.023 (-1.43)	-0.015 (-1.21)	-0.018 (-1.067)	-0.014 (-0.75)
GDP growth	0.241 (8.22)	0.28 (7.142)	0.22 (4.61)	0.12 (2.13)
Adjusted R^2	0.53	0.63	0.35	0.21
Durbin-Watson	2.75	2.34	2.47	2.31

Source: Pagés and Montenegro (1998), based on household surveys from Santiago University.
Note: In addition to the reported variables, a constant, a lag of the dependent variable and its interaction with the protection index are included in the regressions. T-statistics in parentheses.

Appendix 6.3A. Probability of Obtaining a Permanent Contract

Estimation method: PROBIT
Dependent variable:
Dummy =1, if obtain a permanent contract
= 0, if not

Women

	Chile	Mexico	Venezuela
Marital status (dummy = 1 if married)	-0.34 (-4.94)		-0.02 (-3.41)
Number of children	-0.2 (-8.95)	-0.005 (-1.18)	-0.006 (-3.41)

Men

	Chile	Mexico	Venezuela
Marital status (dummy = 1 if married)	0.08 (14.60)		0.57 (6.84)
Number of children	-0.015 (-8.82)	0.13 (4.87)	-0.07 (-4.64)

Note: In addition to the above variables. five dummies of age, years of education, size of the firm, zone, occupation and sector of activity are included. T-statistics in parentheses.

Dependent workers aged 15-65

	Chile	Mexico	Venezuela
Age 25-35 (dummy = 1 if in this age)	0.06 (11.84)	0.09 (7.51)	0.049 (7.48)
Age 35-45 (dummy = 1 if in this age)	0.09 (16.64)	0.21 (14.91)	0.056 (7.54)
Age 45-55 (dummy = 1 if in this age)	0.11 (19.05)	0.19 (10.62)	0.067 (7.49)
Age 55-65 (dummy = 1 if in this age)	0.1 (13.54)	0.17 (6.38)	0.066 (4.91)
Years of education	0.14 (23.32)	0.025 (19.25)	0.0042 (4.76)
Marital status (dummy = 1 if married)	0.036 (8.15)		0.019 (3.22)
Zone (dummy = 1 if urban)	0.02 (3.85)	0.11 (10.06)	0.89 (10.82)
Gender (dummy = 1 if man)	0.014 (3.18)	0.013 (1.29)	-0.007 (-1.12)
Type of employment (dummy = 1 if formal)	0.04 (8.43)	0.54 (58.9)	0.111 (16.73))
Number of children	-0.015 (-11.52)	0.008 (3.44)	-0.006 (-5.19)

Note: In addition to the above variables, a constant and controls for occupation and sector of activity are included. T-statistics in parentheses.
Source: IDB calculations based on recent household surveys.

Appendix 6.3B. Wage Differentials Associated with Type of Contract			

Dependent variable: Hourly wage (log)
Sample: Dependent workers aged 15-65

Women

	Chile	Mexico	Venezuela
Type of contract (dummy = 1 if has permanent contract)	0.06 (4.4)	0.33 (11.55)	0.19 (8.06)

Men

	Chile	Mexico	Venezuela
Type of contract (dummy = 1 if has permanent contract)	0.176 (19.67)	0.23 (12.3)	0.17 (11.1)

Total sample

	Chile	Mexico	Venezuela
Type of contract (dummy = 1 if has permanent contract)	0.13 (18.4)	0.27 (16.8)	0.171 (13.2)
Marital status (dummy =1 if married)	0.1 (15.9)		0.08 (7.87)
Zone (dummy = 1 if urban)	0.27 (29.3)	0.27 (18.1)	0.15 (10.42)
Type of employment (dummy = 1 if formal)	0.2 (24.9)	0.17 (11.3)	0.41 (35.01)
Gender (dummy = 1 if man)	0.21 (31.3)	0.24 (16.8)	0.16 (15.5)

Note: In addition to the above variables, a constant and controls for years of education, years of education squared, experience, experience squared, occupation and sector of activity are included. T-statistics in parentheses.
Source: IDB calculations based on recent household surveys.

Appendix 6.4. Relationships between Labor Protection Indices by Country and Earnings Differentials, Estimated by Type of Employment

(For Urban Male Wage Earners)		
	Men	**Women**
Employer, urban	-0.3765	-0.283
Employer, rural	-0.3508	-0.4215
Formal worker, urban	na	-0.1346
Self-employed, urban	-0.2845	-0.2167
Formal worker, rural	-0.6931	-0.2036
Informal worker, urban	-0.2217	-0.3983
Self-employed, rural	-0.1841	-0.2706
Informal worker, rural	-0.6717	-0.692

Source: IDB calculations based on household surveys, and Labor Rigidity Indices from Figure 6.1.
Note: Correlations are calculated for 14 countries for urban earnings and 11 countries for rural earnings. Earning differentials are estimated for each country controlling for education, experience and experience squared (see Chapter 2, where these results are reported).

Appendix 6.5. Econometric Results: Effect of the Minimum Wage on Income Distribution, 1981-95

Dependent variable:	Gini coefficient of per capita income (Three-year average for 11 countries)			
Minimum wage index	-0.02 (-2.40)	-0.02 (-2.68)	-0.02 (-2.25)	-0.02 (-2.27)
Share of manufacturing and commerce in GDP		0.51 (2.29)		
GDP growth			2.7 (0.25)	
GDP volatility				-2.75 (-0.11)
Adjusted R^2	0.13	0.22	0.11	0.12
Durbin-Watson	2.38	2.61	2.38	2.47
No. of observations	37	37	37	37

Note: T-statistics in parentheses.
Source: Income distribution according to Deininger and Squire (1996); minimum wage from ECLAC; and macro variables from IDB's Economic and Social Database.

REFERENCES

Ashenfelter, Orley, and Robert Smith. 1979. Compliance With the Minimum Law. *Journal of Political Economy* 87: 333-50.

Bazen, S., and J. P. Martin. 1991. L'impact du salaire minimum sur les salaires et l'emploi des jeunes et des adultes en France (Impact of the Minimum Wage on Wages and Employment of Youth and Adults in France). *Revue Economique de l'OCDE* 16 (Spring).

Bazen, S., G. Benhayoun, and N. Skourias. 1995. The Impact of Minimum Wages in France: A Regional Approach. IERSO, Université de Bordeaux IV.

Bell, Linda A. 1997. The Impact of Minimum Wages in Mexico and Colombia. *Journal of Labor Economics* 15(3). University of Chicago.

Brown, C., C. Gilroy, and A. Kohen. 1982. The Effect of the Minimum Wage on Employment and Unemployment. *Journal of Economic Literature* 20(2) June: 487-528.

Card, D. 1992. Using Regional Variations in Wages to Measure the Effects of the Federal Minimum Wage. *Industrial and Labor Relations Review* 46(1) October: 22-37.

Card, D., and A. Krueger. 1994. Minimum Wages and Employment: A Case Study of the Fast Food Industry in New Jersey and Pennsylvania. *American Economic Review* 84(4): 772-93.

Castillo-Freeman, Alida, and Richard Freeman. 1990. Minimum Wages in Puerto Rico: Textbook Case of a Wage Floor? Industrial Relations Research Association Proceedings: 243-53.

Deininger, Klaus, and Lynn Squire. 1996. Measuring Income Inequality: A New Data Base. *The World Bank Economic Review* 10(3) September.

de Janvry, Alain, and Elizabeth Saldoulet. 1995. Poverty Alleviation, Income Redistribution, and Growth during Adjustment. In *Coping With Austerity*, Nora Lustig, ed. Washington, D.C.: Brookings Institution Press.

DiNardo, John, N.M. Fortin, and T. Lemieux. 1996. Labor Market Institutions and the Distribution of Wages, 1973-1992: A Semiparametric Approach. *Econometrica* 64(5) September: 1001-44.

Dolado, Juan, et al. 1996. The Economic Impact of Minimum Wages in Europe. *Economic Policy* 23.

Falkingham, Jane, and Paul Johnson. 1993. *Life-Cycle Distributional Consequences of Pay-as-you-Go and Funded Pension Systems*. Policy Research Working Paper 1200, World Bank, Policy Research Department, Washington, D.C.

Gruber, J. 1997. The Incidence of Payroll Taxation: Evidence from Chile. *Journal of Labor Economics* 15(3) July: 72-101.

Hamermesh, Daniel. 1982. Minimum Wages and the Demand for Labor. *Economic Inquiry* 20: 365-79.

————. 1998. Changing Inequality in Markets for Workplace Amenities. April. Mimeo.

Horrigan, Michael W., and Ronald B. Mincy. 1993. The Minimum Wage and Earnings and Income Inequality. In *Uneven Tides: Rising Inequality in America*, Sheldon Danzinger and Peter Gottschalk, eds. New York: Russell Sage Foundation.

Inter-American Development Bank. 1996. *Economic and Social Progress Report in Latin America*. Washington, D.C.: IDB.

Lustig, Nora C., and Darryl McLeod. 1997. Minimum Wages and Poverty in Developing Countries: Some Empirical Evidence. In *Labor Markets in Latin America: Combining Social Protection with Market Flexibility*, Sebastian Edwards. Washington, D.C.: Brookings Institution Press.

Márquez, Gustavo, and Carmen Pagés. 1998. Ties That Bind: Protecting Employment and Labor Trends in Latin America. Prepared for the seminar "¿Cuál es el problema de empleo de América Latina y cómo enfrentarlo?" at the Annual Meeting of the Board of Governors, Inter-American Development Bank, Cartagena, Colombia.

Morley, Samuel A. 1992. Structural Adjustment and the Determinants of Poverty in Latin America. Department of Economics and Business Administration, Vanderbilt University, Nashville, Tenn.

————. 1997. Estrategia para reducir la pobreza. (Strategy for Reducing Poverty). Washington, D.C., Inter-American Development Bank.

Pagés, Carmen. 1998. Minimum Wages and Inequality in Latin America. Inter-American Development Bank. Mimeo.

Pagés, Carmen, and Claudio Montenegro. 1998. Job Security, Tenure and Employment Dynamics: Theory and Evidence from Chile. Mimeo. June.

Ramos, Lauro, and José Guilherme Almeida Reis. 1995. Salário mínimo, distribuição de renda e pobreza no Brasil. (Minimum Wage, Income Distribution and Poverty in Brazil). *Pesquisa e Planejamento Econômico* 25(1) April.

Ravallion, Martin. 1998. *Appraising Workfare Programs*. IDB-SDS-POP Working Paper. Inter-American Development Bank.

Santiago, Carlos. 1989. The Dynamics of Minimum Wage Policy in Economic Development: A Multiple Time-Series Approach. *Economic Development and Cultural Change* 38: 1-30.

Schaafsma, Joseph, and William Walsh. 1983. Employment and Labour Supply Effects of the Minimum Wage: Some Pooled Time-Series Estimates from Canadian Provincial Data. *Canadian Journal of Economics* 16: 86-97.

Welch, Finis. 1976. Minimum Wage Legislation in the United States. In *Evaluating the Labor Effects of Social Programs*, Orley Ashenfelter and James Blum, eds., Princeton University, Industrial Relations Section.

Wellington, Alison. 1991. Effects of the Minimum Wage on the Employment Status of Youths: an Update. *Journal of Human Resources* 26: 27-46.

World Bank. 1995. Workers in an Integrating World. *World Development Report*. Oxford: Oxford University Press for the World Bank.

Chapter 7

FINANCIAL MARKET POLICIES
TO REDUCE INCOME INEQUALITY

Previous chapters of this report have emphasized the role of factor prices, and particularly the wages of unskilled workers, as a key determinant of income inequality. Through their impact on family decisions about fertility, labor force participation and education, low wages promote and perpetuate high levels of income inequality. The returns to labor are also importantly affected by the amount of capital with which workers can operate. As economies develop and capital becomes less scarce, the return to labor tends to rise and the return to capital tends to fall, and these changes in factor returns are reflected in lower income inequality.

Here is where financial markets come in. Financial markets provide the institutional framework within which savings are mobilized and intermediated to generate the productive investments required to raise workers' productivity and wages. If financial markets are not functioning effectively, domestic investment will not match its potential, and the scarcity of capital will adversely affect not only prospects for economic growth, but also the distribution of income.

But there is more to the story because the scarcity of credit that comes with inadequately functioning financial systems is likely to be particularly severe for small businesses and potential entrepreneurs, whose financial needs may be more expensive to service (as a proportion of the typical loan size) than larger businesses, and whose creditworthiness is more difficult to assess. The severe shortage of credit will restrict the capacity of small businesses and microentrepreneurs to obtain access to the working and physical capital required to raise their productivity and expand their businesses, thus leaving those working in the sector with severely reduced earnings capacity.

Finally, inefficient financial systems offer particularly poor terms to small savers who, if located in underserved rural markets, may even be locked out of the opportunity to place their savings in a financial institution. They may therefore be faced with the need to invest in very low-earning or risky assets, such as currency or durable goods. This reduced access of low-income families to deposit and other nonlending services of the financial system may also worsen the distribution of income.

Reforms to improve the functioning of the domestic financial system and ensure that it adequately supports productive investments by entrepreneurs and small businesses thus have the potential to improve income distribution, while at the same time promoting economic growth and efficiency. This chapter details the linkages between the operation of financial markets and the distribution of income. It also discusses concrete reforms that could improve the functioning of financial markets, particularly their capacity to support the small enterprise sector in which so many of the region's low-income wage earners are employed.

FINANCIAL MARKETS AND INEQUALITY: WHAT ARE THE LINKAGES?

Shallow Financial Markets Are Associated with More Inequality...

It is not easy to measure the quality or efficiency of a domestic financial system, especially in terms of such dimensions as its ability to reach small entrepreneurs and businesses. Despite this difficulty, there is evidence that financial systems matter. A recent study by Li, Squire and Zou (1998) finds that deep financial markets, as measured by the ratio of the broad money supply to GDP, are strongly associated with lower income inequality.[1] The study argues that this measure of financial depth has one of the largest quantitative impacts on the Gini coefficient among all the variables that were considered. In the results reported in Chapter 4, which controlled for a different and

---

[1] The study employs the Deininger and Squire (1996) set of Gini coefficients for 49 developed and developing countries from 1947-94. It uses five-year averages of these and all explanatory variable data.

somewhat broader set of explanatory variables, the relationship between income inequality and financial depth was somewhat weaker. But while weaker, the correlation between financial depth and income inequality was still negative, providing some corroboration for the earlier finding that deep financial markets are associated with less inequality.[2]

...And Latin America Has Shallow Financial Systems

In the 1960s, financial depth—measured either by the ratio of the broad money supply to GDP or financial system credit to the private sector as a percent of GDP—was only about 25 percent higher in the emerging East Asian countries than it was in Latin America. But the region's macroeconomic and financial instability, financial repression and relatively slow growth during much of the following decades slowed its financial development. East Asian financial depth steadily pulled away, and it now stands at two to three times the Latin American average. Latin America also has shallow financial systems compared to the industrial economies. To the extent that shallow and inefficient financial markets contribute to inequality, then, there is good reason to believe that Latin America's financial systems contribute to a meaningful and growing share of the difference between the region's high income inequality and the lower degree of inequality observed in other regions such as emerging East Asia and the industrial economies.

Why Do Financial Markets Matter? A Macroeconomic Channel

Financial markets pervade the economic system and affect income inequality in a number of ways. Deep financial markets facilitate the accumulation of capital, raising labor productivity and wages while driving down the returns to capital.[3] As seen in Chapter 4, this tends to improve the distribution of income, because so much capital income accrues to a relatively small group of higher-income individuals, and because the accelerated rate of economic development promotes all of the development-related transitions that tend to be equalizing.[4] The initial impact on wages is amplified over time, because the higher wages that come with increased capital accumulation eventually influence family decisions about labor force participation, fertility and education in ways that reinforce the initial beneficial impact of higher wages on income distribution.

Access to Credit is Unequal

If financial markets are weak, credit is not only limited in general but is particularly inaccessible to low-income individuals and small businesses. This reinforces the adverse distributional consequences of weak financial systems, because it limits the ability of small-scale and low-income producers to obtain the credit they need to produce more efficiently and expand their businesses. Scarcity of credit may also discourage potential entrepreneurs from entering the labor force. This is likely to be particularly important for secondary earners in a household. If a woman has access to credit, she can obtain the materials required to start a small business to supplement the family's income. This in turn enables women to work part-time and at irregular hours, thus posing less conflict with family responsibilities than would working in the formal sector. However, without access to the requisite credit, a woman may be restricted to such a small scale of operation, or to the use of such labor-intensive and inefficient methods, that she is forced either to work at a very low level of productivity and income, or to abandon the venture and stay home. Inadequate access to credit may thus be one explanation for the finding of Chapter 2 that women who work in the informal sector earn particularly low wages.

There is plenty of evidence that the banking system provides limited credit to small enterprises. Table 7.1 reviews a number of studies that indicate that few of these firms, generally less than five percent, have ever received credit from the banking system.[5]

Even the lending institutions that lead the way in making microloans in Latin America have small loan portfolios compared with the formal financial system (Table 7.2). And even when semiformal sources (nongovernmental organizations and credit unions) are included, total credit going to microenterprises is less than 1 percent of the $425 billion that commercial banks provided to the Latin American private sector in 1995, and probably about

---

[2] One reason why we found a weaker correlation between financial depth and income inequality may be that we controlled for several variables, such as capital intensity or the level of development, that may be mechanisms through which financial depth is affecting income inequality.

[3] King and Levine (1993) is among the most influential studies on the relationship between the depth of the domestic financial system and economic growth. Their results suggested that a 10 percentage point rise in the ratio of private banking system credit to GDP is associated with an increase in the annual GDP growth rate of about one-third of a percentage point. Ghani (1992) finds an even larger growth effect, approximately half a point. Westley (1994) discusses several channels through which increased intermediation may result in productivity and growth rate gains.

[4] See Wolff (1991).

[5] IDB (1995) estimates, based on existing survey and other evidence, that less than 5 percent of Latin American microentrepreneurs have access to credit from the banking system, which is corroborated by Table 7.1.

Table 7.1. Where Are the Banks?
(Share of Micro or Small Enterprises with Credit from Banking Institutions)

Country	Share	Reference	Survey	Source
Mexico	4.5% received credit after start-up 1.9% received business start-up credit	Microenterprises[1]	February-May, 1994	INEGI (1994, pp. 31-36)
Guyana	1.9% received credit for current operations 3.4% received business start-up credit	Microenterprises[2]	November 1995	Bresnyan (1996, Tables C-10, C-11a)
Dominican Republic	4.2% received credit for current operations	Micro and small enterprises[3]	1993-1995 (four surveys)	Pons and Ortiz (1995, Table 4.13)

[1] Nonmanufacturing firms with up to five employees, manufacturing firms with up to 15 employees.
[2] Firms with less than 10 employees.
[3] Firms with up to 50 workers.

Table 7.2. Leading Banking Institutions That Make Microloans in Latin America
(Real Loan Rates and Volume)

Country	Lender	Microenterprise credit: Real loan rate (%)	Volume of microenterprise loans outstanding (US$ millions)	Number of microenterprise loans outstanding (thousands)	Microenterprise credit: Average loan size (US$)
Bolivia	Banco Sol	42	30.2	57.7	523
Bolivia	Caja Los Andes	34	8.6	17.9	480
Chile	Banco de Desarrollo	44	17.6	17.5	1,006
Colombia[1]	Corposol/Finansol	52	11.7	32	366
Ecuador	Banco del Pacífico	27	4	4	1,000
El Salvador	Banco Agrícola	na	14.8	9.3	1,591
Guatemala	Banco Empresarial	21	2	0.84	2,381
Guyana	Bank of Nova Scotia	18	1.2	9	133
Panama	Multicredit Bank	31	8.6	1.45	5,931
Paraguay	Financiera Familiar	83	4.5	4.66	966
Peru	Banco Wiese	26	19	4.76	3,992
Mean		38	11.1	14.5	762
Total			122.2	159.11	

[1] Data for 1993 from Christen, Rhyne, and Vogel (1995); all other data are from 1995-96, as reported by Baydas, Graham and Valenzuela (1997).

1 percent of banking system credit going to businesses in the region.[6]

In contrast, it has been estimated that microenterprises account for approximately 20 percent of Latin American GDP.[7] Although the concept of microenterprise used in these estimates may not be entirely comparable,

it would appear that, relative to their output, these firms receive a disproportionately small share of credit from formal and even semi-formal sources.

Unsatisfied Demand for Credit from Small Borrowers

Does this minimal use of credit mean that small borrowers need less credit, or that they face highly restricted access to it? It is difficult to measure access to credit directly because limited use of it could in principle reflect either minimal demand or a restricted supply. However, there is evidence that small borrowers face more restricted access to credit than do larger borrowers. A number of studies have presented evidence that small borrowers show clear signs that their activities are restricted by the inability to obtain credit, and that larger borrowers are less affected by such credit constraints. (Box 7.1 surveys some of these studies.)

Another piece of evidence that smaller enterprises have many high-return projects waiting in the wings, frustrated by lack of finance, is the very high loan rates routinely paid by these firms when formal credit is made available to them (see Table 7.2). Moreover, when good microlending programs are started up, they often attract huge demand despite charging high real loan rates. Banco Sol in Bolivia is only 10 years old (five years as an NGO followed by five years as a bank) and already has one-third of the total clients served by the entire Bolivian banking system. And, as the numerous impact studies surveyed by Sebstad and Chen (1996) make clear, owners of smaller firms, including those below the poverty line, do derive substantial income gains from access to credit, with the gains typically increasing over time as additional larger loans are extended to them.

These studies also report substantial employment creation by microloan programs. There is good reason to believe that this job creation expands opportunities primarily for low-income workers, since microenterprise employees and self-employed microentrepreneurs (30

---

[6] The figure of $425 billion is obtained from IMF (1997, line 22d). It represents total private credit extended by commercial banks in the 26 borrowing member countries of the Inter-American Development Bank at the end of 1995. This $425 billion omits other banking institutions' credit to the private sector and thus is an underestimate of total banking system credit. However, consumer lending (credit cards, residential mortgages, etc.) is perhaps 25 to 30 percent of total banking system private credit, the bulk of it going to traditional business lending in such sectors as industry and commerce. Hence, any overestimation is probably slight (the two omissions tending to cancel each other out). Total microenterprise credit from the banking system, NGOs and credit unions can be estimated between $2.3 billion and $4 billion (calculations based on Baydas, Graham and Valenzuela, 1997; Acción International, 1997, and WOCCU, 1996).

[7] From Westley (1997).

Box 7.1. Credit Constraints

National surveys of microenterprises and small businesses often ask about the major business problems they face, including lack of finance. Although these self-reporting data are properly deemed less reliable than market data, they are useful to detect credit constraints in market data. It is often difficult to determine statistically whether businesses that receive no formal credit simply are not demanding it or are judged not to be good credit risks, or whether they are really being rationed by the financial intermediaries. Because of this difficulty, evidence of credit constraints based on analyses of market data is limited.

Among the few studies to distinguish credit constraints from observed market behavior using reasonably recent Latin American data are Mushinski (1995) and Barham, Boucher and Carter (1996). Based on data from three regions in Guatemala, these studies find that smaller firms desiring bank credit received it much less often than larger firms. However, credit unions in these three areas provided loans to a substantial percentage of these smaller, bank-rationed firms. This suggests that these companies were creditworthy enterprises. Jaramillo, Schiantarelli and Weiss (1996) estimate the Euler (accumulation) equation for capital stock allowing for adjustment costs in a panel data set covering 420 Ecuadorean manufacturing firms over 1983-88. They find that smaller firms faced significant credit constraints both before and after interest rate ceilings were removed in Ecuador, while larger firms never did. Since smaller firms are defined as those with a capital stock of up to $600,000 in 1975 prices, this study shows that even fairly sizable firms with substantial collateralizable assets can face credit constraints.

Asking firms directly if they want to obtain credit but cannot get it can also show whether microenterprises and small businesses face a credit constraint. Nonetheless, these data must be interpreted with care, because they are not based on actual behavior, the price of credit is rarely made explicit (though may be understood to be "market rates"), and not all firms desiring credit would be deemed good credit risks by financial intermediaries.

Pons and Ortiz (1994) provide perhaps the most straightforward estimate of this type. Based on a national survey, they find that 42 percent of the smaller enterprises in the Dominican Republic would like to have credit and do not, and another 16 percent are not sure. (The remaining 42 percent did not want credit for a variety of reasons, including the fact that some already had it.) The impact of credit market restrictions extends even beyond this sizable group, however, as there are an unknown number of households that would like to begin their own businesses but do not for lack of credit to finance their start-up or subsequent operations.

Several other national surveys ask about major business problems, including credit constraints. In Guyana, Bresnyan (1996) finds that 62 percent of microenterprises face a severe or very severe "lack of cash in running their business," as opposed to a constraint that is "not severe." In the same survey, 39 percent cited the lack of finance as affecting the ability of the firm to grow. Magill and Swanson (1991) find that lack of sustained access to finance is by far the biggest problem that microenterprises face in Ecuador, placing ahead even of lacking markets. EIM/International's (1996) survey of Trinidad and Tobago and ESA Consultores (1996) survey in Honduras both find that market opportunities are the biggest problem microenterprises face, followed in each case by lack of finance.

---

and 40 percent, respectively) together make up about 70 percent of Latin America's low-income earners.[8,9] To the extent that microcredit programs create jobs for such earners, these programs are likely to contribute to strongly lessening income inequality. In addition to all of these credit effects, the provision of deposit services, particularly in rural areas where liquid savings facilities are often unavailable, can also increase the income levels of low-income households, which are disproportionately located in rural areas.[10]

How the Absence of Deposit and Other Nonlending Financial Services Hurts the Poor

Even very poor households in rural areas save, if only to carry over income from one harvest to the next. In the absence of a financial institution offering deposit accounts, however, savings must be done in nonmonetary form (building materials; livestock, crops and other capital and inventory; jewelry and other valuables, etc.) or by

holding cash.[11] These forms of savings have serious disadvantages, including erosion of value with the passage of time (due to wear and tear or to inflation), possibility of theft, high transaction costs that typically accompany the conversion of illiquid assets into cash (with a likelihood of additional losses if a sale must be made quickly because of an emergency), and problems of indivisibility (one cannot slaughter half a cow, sell half a ring, etc.).[12]

With their savings in commodities, rural households that suddenly find themselves in need of cash may be

---

[8] Within the context of these household surveys, microenterprises are defined as firms with five or fewer employees.

[9] "Low-income" wage earners are defined as workers in the bottom 30 percent of the wage distribution. The statistics discussed here are based on a simple average of results from household surveys for 14 countries.

[10] The discussion of Small Cap Rural Banks below outlines some of the mechanisms through which this might occur.

[11] See Gadway and O'Donnell (1995).

[12] In periods of rapidly rising prices, commodities may, of course, serve as an inflation hedge, much as a reasonably priced deposit account does. The other disadvantages of holding savings in nonmonetary form, however, still apply.

forced to choose between borrowing from informal markets at high interest rates or paying the high transaction costs (and facing any indivisibility problems) associated with converting illiquid physical assets into cash. Access to a liquid savings account would allow rural families to meet their routine and emergency liquidity needs more easily and cheaply, and thus avoid erosion of their income and wealth. A deposit facility might also help poor farmers increase their incomes by giving them a readily available cushion of financial support in case their crops fail. This might allow them, for example, to shift out of a lower risk, diversified cropping pattern, and specialize to a greater extent in higher valued crops, with the knowledge that they have saved resources readily available to meet their families' most urgent needs in case things go badly. Finally, with more liquid savings services available in the rural areas, the supply of funds used for informal lending may expand, driving down the informal lending rate and widening the use of such credit. This may particularly benefit smaller farms and enterprises and lower-income households, which, lacking access to formal loans, may disproportionately use informal credit.

What Obstacles Impede the Credit Relationship?

Before discussing potential policies to promote a more adequate functioning of the credit market, we need to understand why credit markets are so complicated, and why smaller and lower-income borrowers face particular obstacles in obtaining credit. After all, the financial landscape is littered with failed institutions whose mission it was to provide credit to various underserved groups, but which were in the end incapable of solving the underlying problems.

A fundamental problem lies in the first step in a credit relationship: the creditor must give a borrower money based on a promise of repayment. Although the lending institution will do its best to ensure that it is lending to borrowers who are going to be able and willing to repay the loan, there are no assurances that the borrower will not renege on his promise. The credit relationship thus depends upon ways of ensuring both *ability* and *willingness* to repay loans. This is a complicated matter under any circumstances, but even more so in emerging markets like Latin America, and the problems are particularly severe for small borrowers.

To ensure *ability* to repay, lenders may rely upon a careful review of a borrower's balance sheet, business plans and track record, and after a loan is granted may monitor the use to which the funds are put. All of this is, of course, expensive—especially so if accounting standards and disclosure practices are not high. What is more, these costs are likely to be particularly high as a share of the typical loan size for small borrowers, which means that simple economics often dictate that small borrowers have to pay higher interest rates for credit, a point whose policy implications are discussed below.

Ensuring *willingness* to repay is equally important, and in many ways more complicated. There are four main mechanisms to ensure that borrowers with the financial capacity to repay a loan will also have the incentive to do so: punishment, collateral, reputation and relationships.

Punishment relies upon the capacity to impose, through the legal system or in some other way, a penalty on debtors who do not repay. Delinquent debtors may be thrown in jail or suffer other punishment. While this punishment provides no relief to the lender who has suffered from the default, it does provide incentives for borrowers to repay if they possibly can. While effective in many circumstances, enforcement mechanisms that rely upon punishment cannot solve all problems. Even where judicial systems operate well, enforcement of a claim through the judiciary can be a drawn-out, complicated and expensive process. If it were too often necessary to rely upon this expensive process, many credit contracts would be too expensive to support. This is all the more true of small loans that are required by microenterprises and small businesses, for which the legal costs of enforcing repayment through judicial proceedings would be prohibitive. If they are going to be able to serve smaller borrowers, therefore, financial systems need to seek more efficient ways to ensure willingness to pay.[13]

Collateral is one of the most important of these mechanisms. In a collateralized loan, the borrower pledges to the lender that, in the event of a default, he will turn over some item of value—the "collateral"—thus protecting the lender at least partly from the cost of the default. When collateral works well, it can provide important protection to the lender and thus greatly improve access and reduce the cost of credit to the borrower. However, collateral in general works less well for small borrowers than it does for large enterprises and wealthy individuals.

---

[13] This is not to say that punishment strategies are irrelevant. An interesting example is the role of post-dated checks in the Paraguayan financial system. It used to be difficult in that system to enforce repayment of a claim through the legal system. But another way was found to use the legal system to enforce debt claims. Since it was illegal to write post-dated checks, a lender would require a borrower to write a post-dated check in the amount that would come due when the loan matured. If the lender repaid the loan in full and on time, the post-dated check would be returned to the borrower. If the borrower defaulted, the lender could present the post-dated check, exposing the borrower to a serious risk of jail. This mechanism apparently worked well until the law was changed, decriminalizing the writing of post-dated checks.

Collateral works best when it is the object that is to be purchased with the proceeds of the loan, and when that object has substantial value to someone other than the borrower. Mortgages work well because in the event of a default, the buildings and property that are seized by the lender can be sold to some other user at a reasonable price. It works less well when the object being financed is something like a specialized industrial machine or tool, which may be of little value to any other business and thus provides little security to the lender. And collateral is much less useful to support loans needed to finance the accumulation of intangible assets or working capital, which may be particularly important for small businesses or microenterprises in many services or retail trades. In principle, such a loan could be collateralized with property other than the object whose purchase is being financed by the loan. A business owner, for example, could in principle secure a loan to finance working capital for his business by offering his home as collateral. However, many legal systems limit lenders' ability to enforce such pledges, and even when such pledges are permitted, they provide a solution only for borrowers wealthy enough to own collateralizable assets. Having said all of this, collateral is an essential instrument of a well-functioning financial system, and the section that follows proposes reforms to improve the operation of collateral in the region.

Reputation is another mechanism commonly used to ensure willingness to repay loan obligations. Borrowers may have an incentive to repay if they perceive that default would limit their access to future additional credit. An advantage of reputation is that, in principle, anybody can develop a good one, regardless of income level. And indeed, a technique of many successful microenterprise lending programs is to grant progressively larger loans to an individual or group, with a default resulting in loss of access to future loans. There are two main problems here. The first is information. In a world with many lenders, a borrower might hope to default on a loan from one lender but then obtain credit from another lender, who he hopes does not know about the previous default. The solution to this problem is credit bureaus or other information-sharing institutions. A second problem is that a solution based on the borrower's reputation may make it difficult for new borrowers, who face a "catch-22": no credit history means no reputation, but no reputation means no credit and therefore no possibility to develop a credit history. Successful attempts to bring credit to microenterprises are often based on developing ways to permit borrowers to develop a credit history with a microlending institution.

Finally, *relationships* are another important mechanism to ensure willingness to pay. If a lender has an ongoing relationship with the borrower in some other area, it may be possible to use that relationship to enforce repayment. Or the lender may be able to take advantage of relationships that the borrower has with others, as in the case of group lending. In group lending, the loan is to a group of borrowers, and a default by one results in loss of access to further credit for the entire group. If the other members of the group know one another and interact in a number of different capacities, they may be better able than the lender to persuade a potentially recalcitrant borrower to honor his repayment obligations. Group lending is another of the techniques commonly used by successful microlenders.

Credit Can Reach the Poor

Having discussed in such detail the many obstacles to the credit relationship, and how they particularly complicate the situation of small borrowers, it is worthwhile to remember that credit can, despite these obstacles, reach the poor. In Bolivia, a large percentage of the clientele of several microenterprise finance institutions (MFIs) are poor borrowers:[14] Banco Sol (36 percent), Caja los Andes (26 percent), FIE (20 percent), Prodem (81 percent), and Sartawi (76 percent). The first three institutions serve urban areas, and Banco Sol and Caja los Andes are regulated financial institutions, while Prodem is an NGO (in 1996 when the data were collected). The last two MFIs are NGOs that serve rural areas. The extremely high percentages of poor among the borrowers of these latter two MFIs partly reflect Bolivia's high rural poverty rates, together with the MFIs' mission to bring credit to poor microentrepreneurs. Together, these five institutions have 167,000 microenterprise clients,[15] of whom 67,000 are poor, suggesting that credit can reach poor microentrepreneurs in substantial numbers. In fact, many more poor have been reached than are even indicated by this last number, considering the employment effects noted earlier. In addition, even considering only firm owners, the five poverty percentages given above understate the share of poor microentrepreneurs who were assisted by the five MFIs. While many MFI clients start off poor, after several loans some of their incomes will have increased beyond the poverty line. Even better than just serving poor customers, the institutions seem to be helping to lift their borrowers out of poverty.

---

[14] Gulli (1998, p. 12).
[15] Ibid. (p. 13).

FINANCIAL MARKET POLICIES TO REDUCE INEQUALITY

What can be done to make financial systems more efficient, and in particular to promote expanded access to credit by smaller enterprises? Most countries in Latin America have already taken important steps in this direction by stabilizing their economies, eliminating interest rate ceilings, dismantling subsidized and targeted credit programs and other forms of state-imposed credit allocation, and lowering reserve requirements to prudential levels. These changes have greatly expanded the capacity of the private financial system to serve domestic borrowers, and have been particularly conducive to the delivery of financial services to smaller firms. The liberalization of lending interest rates makes it possible for financial institutions to charge the high interest rates such lending often requires. By fostering greater competition and efficiency in serving traditional large-firm customers, liberalized lending interest rates encourage intermediaries to look for new and unexploited market segments, such as smaller firms.

For countries that have yet to eliminate interest rate ceilings or create more competitive financial markets, these are certainly important steps to take toward providing smaller firms with increased financial services, and thereby attempting to reduce income inequality. However, little formal or even semiformal credit has become available to microenterprises, and many smaller firms face significant credit constraints. Reforms to promote broader availability of credit might include appropriate regulation and supervision of banking institutions that lend to microenterprises, improving the legal and institutional framework for secured transactions, reducing informality, establishing or strengthening credit bureaus, improving the legal framework for leasing and factoring, facilitating the development of small capitalization rural banks, modernizing and supervising credit unions, "downscaling" commercial banks to serve microenterprises, and "upgrading" NGOs into full-fledged financial institutions.

Appropriate Regulation and Supervision of Banking Institutions that Lend to Microenterprises

Most countries in Latin America have prudential banking regulations and supervisory practices that—because they are typically designed with traditional commercial bank lending technologies and large loan sizes in mind—may unintentionally and unnecessarily impede lending to microenterprises. Box 7.2 describes the salient features of the microlending technology that has been used suc-

cessfully by a large number of financial institutions around the world and in the region to make small loans (e.g., $100 to $1,000) while at the same time achieving commercial bank-level delinquency rates (2 to 3 percent) and containing administrative costs. This technology is fundamentally designed to ensure willingness to repay, in addition to verifying borrowers' ability to repay.

This lending technology differs in important ways from that which is appropriate for lending to larger customers. Applying supervisory norms appropriate for larger loans to microenterprise lending may unnecessarily drive up the cost of microloans and reduce supply.[16] Areas where adaptations of the regulatory framework might improve microlending are cited below.

Operational restrictions. As noted in Jansson and Wenner (1997), most Latin American countries place minimum and sometimes maximum limits on the number of hours per day and days per week that branches of regulated financial institutions can operate, usually mandating at least five days per week and five to eight hours per day. This often poses a particular problem for microlenders, who may wish to open branches in marginal urban or rural areas where demand is not sufficient to justify such lengthy hours. Banco Sol in Bolivia, for example, has complained of having wanted to open branches in some areas for only two days per week.

Documentation requirements. Bank superintendencies throughout Latin America typically require that regulated banking institutions gather extensive documented information in the course of granting each loan in order to help the lender and regulator assess loan risk. Among the standard requirements for business loans are the borrower's past three to five years of balance sheets and income statements, documents establishing the value of physical assets owned, and information on existing liens. Some countries require notarization of these formal documents, with notary costs ranging as high as $40 per loan,[17] clearly a burdensome requirement for a $500 credit. As explained in Box 7.2, individual microenterprise loans are normally extended on the basis of a current cash flow analysis of the combined household and business, and, perhaps even more importantly, on the basis of a character assessment of the borrower. Group loans are extended on the basis of group guarantees and screening. Unless reporting requirements are adjusted to fit the nature of the methodology being used to make microloans, the already-high administrative costs of making these loans will be further increased.

---

[16] See Jansson and Wenner (1997) and Rock and Otero (1997).

[17] Jansson and Wenner (1997, p. 35).

Box 7.2. The Microlending Technology

In group lending, credits are granted to small, self-formed groups. These groups serve three purposes. First, they screen out bad credit risks, since the whole group is held responsible if anyone in the group defaults, and hence they reduce the costs of gathering information on creditworthiness. Second, they exert social pressure in the event a borrower fails to repay. Third, they offer the potential to further reduce administrative costs by allowing the bank to make and service a single group loan in place of several individual loans.

Individual lending is grounded in a detailed investigation and assessment of the borrower's character and willingness to repay. Initial loan screening often includes visits to the business site and home, and talks with neighbors and business associates. An analysis is also performed of the cash flow (ability to repay) of both the business and the household. Loans are generally extended based on these assessments, rather than being secured with physical collateral, of which the microentrepreneur typically has little, and which would in any case entail prohibitive costs to seize and sell. Thus, in contrast to traditional bank lending, group and particularly individual microlending is said to be information-intensive instead of intensive in the use of physical collateral.

The remaining elements of the microlending technology apply to both individual and group lending.

- Repayment is further encouraged by a progressive lending scheme in which borrowers are first given very small loans and short loan terms. If successfully repaid, the loan amount and term are progressively increased in subsequent rounds of borrowing. In addition to rewarding repayment, this also serves to establish a credit history for borrowers who typically have none to begin with, allowing the lender to decide whether to make larger, riskier loans based on this history.

- Frequent repayment schedules are employed to facilitate monitoring of borrowers.

- Incentive pay is used to help solve the principal-agent problem, with a loan officer's remuneration determined to a significant degree by loan volume and portfolio delinquency rate.

- Staff are drawn from the local service area, so they have better access to information about potential borrowers.

- To help keep delinquency rates low in larger microlending programs, specialized software is used that tracks individual loans and provides daily delinquency reports to loan officers. Delinquencies are followed up the next day or soon thereafter.

- In order to reduce the borrower's transaction costs and the intermediary's loan default losses, loan officers spend much of their time in the field, screening new clients and checking on old ones, particularly those who are delinquent. The lender's administrative costs are held down by using inexpensive transportation (e.g., motorcycles), directly entering field-collected data into portable computers (in lending programs of larger size), and maintaining relatively modest branch offices, in keeping with the fact that the program serves a clientele of more limited means.

- In order to increase the value to borrowers of the lending institution's credit services, and thus encourage loyalty and repayment, the loan approval and disbursement period is normally very rapid (often a matter of a few days).

- Microloan interest rates are set considerably above average commercial bank lending rates in order to cover the higher administrative cost margins of making much smaller loans. These cost margins are typically 15 to 30 percentage points or more, depending on average loan size, total program volume (due to economies of scale), and other factors.

Capital requirements. For example, Argentina has risk-weighted capital adequacy standards in which the required capital increases with the interest rate that the lender charges. Indeed, for loans that charge a very high interest rate, the required capital is 69 percent of the loan amount (six times the basic 11.5 percent requirement). This makes sense for normal lending because high-lending interest rates are generally associated with a high risk of default. However, with microloans, high loan rates are the result of high administrative costs, not necessarily of high default risk, and unless this is reflected in capital requirements, the costs of making microloans will be unnecessarily increased. A way needs to be found to distinguish between high administrative costs and high default risk when basing capital requirements on lending interest rates.

Emphasis on collateral. As noted in Box 7.2, traditional bank lending is collateral-intensive while microlending is information-intensive. Yet both systems are capable of producing high rates of repayment. Accordingly, the common practice of requiring 100 percent specific loan provisions for any noncollateralized loans whose repayment is overdue by even a single day, or general provisioning of 20 percent for all noncollateralized loans (late or not) vs. 1 to 3 percent for collateralized loans, may exaggerate the difference in the risk of loss between collateralized lending and microlending, and thus unnecessarily raise the cost of making microloans.

Improving the Legal and Institutional Framework for Secured Transactions

In much of Latin America, poorly formulated laws and inadequate or nonexistent legal registries impede using either movable goods or real property as collateral to secure loans. While this problem affects firms of all sizes, its greatest impact is on small firms. This problem has three major components—in the creation of security interests, in the perfection of those interests, and in enforcement.[18]

The *creation* of security interests means making a legal agreement to assign some object as collateral for a loan. However, the laws of many Latin American countries impose important restrictions on the kinds of goods that may be used as collateral. Many countries do not allow for a "continuing security interest," so that if the pledged asset is sold, the creditors often cannot automatically attach the proceeds (as creditors can, for example, in the United States and Canada). Another useful device frequently not available in the region is the "floating security interest." In Uruguay, for example, if a bank lends $50,000 against 100 head of cattle, it must identify a particular 100 head by tattoo or other means, which makes loan monitoring very expensive. By contrast, in the United States and Canada, a loan can be based on a floating security interest in "$50,000 in cattle," which provides much better security to the lender.

The *perfection* of security interests means ensuring that there are no prior superior claims on an asset that a borrower has pledged as collateral. To do this, lenders must be able to search for such claims in a legal registry. In Latin America, this is often unnecessarily difficult. In Uruguay, for example, the lender must know the date of the prior pledge; one cannot search by the name of the borrower or by using a description of the pledged asset. This process is even more cumbersome in Bolivia, where claims are filed chronologically and one must look through the entire registry for prior pledges. Further complications arise when, as occurs often in Latin America, one needs official permission to search a registry. This permission may be difficult to obtain, perhaps involving uncertain access, bribes or delays. Much can be done to create accurate registries that are accessible to the public and inexpensive to search. Strengthening or privatizing public registries is one possibility, as is introducing competition among public registries or permitting private registries to compete with public ones.

Finally, collateral is of little value if the pledge cannot be *enforced* in the event of a default. But enforcement is often slow and costly in the region, where a lengthy legal process involving the courts is typically required, rather than a rapid administrative procedure outside the court system. With their attendant risks and costs, such delays undermine the usefulness of all collateral, and particularly the use of movable property as collateral. During the lengthy period of time it takes the lender to repossess and sell the pledged equipment or inventory, the collateral may be sold or moved out of the economy, machines left to rust, grain to rot, or cattle to die or be slaughtered. The resulting decline in the usefulness of movable collateral is particularly problematic for smaller and less wealthy borrowers, since while wealthier businessmen and larger businesses are likely to have real property assets, small firms may have only their inventory, or perhaps some equipment, to pledge as security for a loan. This means that improving the legal and institutional framework surrounding collateral is of particular importance to small borrowers.[19] Recognizing the potential importance of these reforms, several countries in Latin America have recently examined the issue of overhauling their secured transactions laws, including Argentina, Bolivia, El Salvador, Honduras, Mexico, Peru and Uruguay.

Reducing Informality[20]

Banking institutions typically lend only to officially sanctioned businesses, not to unregistered enterprises.[21] These unregistered firms tend to be very small and owned by low-income individuals. One way to improve their access to credit is to encourage formalization by reducing the barriers to formality. (The other strategy, discussed later, is to strengthen the unregulated financial institutions, such as NGOs and in many cases credit unions, that willingly lend to firms in the informal sector.) Formalization would increase access to bank credit and also permit firms to register their business property, which can then potentially be used as loan collateral.

Costs of formality. The costs of simply registering a business can be very substantial. In an actual experiment to set up a small garment factory in Lima, de Soto (1989) found that it took 10 months, involved 11 separate and time-consuming procedures with various ministries and other state institutions, and cost $1,232 in fees, bribes and lost profits, all of which equaled nearly three years of

---

[18] See Fleisig, Aguilar and de la Peña (1994) and Fleisig (1995a; 1995b).

[19] Microenterprise loans, on the other hand, are less affected by collateral problems, because in contrast to small firm loans, they are normally based on a character assessment or on group guarantees rather than collateral. Nonetheless, microenterprise credit could become more available if improvements in collateral systems were to give their suppliers access to credit, and make it easier for suppliers to offer credit to microentrepreneurs.

[20] "Informality" is used in this chapter in the classic sense of denoting a firm that is unregistered (and out of compliance with tax, labor and other codes), rather than a firm with few employees. The latter (ILO) definition is used in other chapters of this volume.

[21] See de Soto (1989), Loayza (1996), McPherson and Liedholm (1996), and Orlando (1998). As an example of the high cost of borrowing, de Soto notes that in Lima in 1985 the nominal borrowing rate for informal firms was 22 percent per month, versus 4.9 percent for formal firms of comparable size.

Table 7.3. Gini Regressions for 14 Latin American Countries, Using Loayza's Informality Measure

Variable	Regression 1	Regression 2	Regression 3
INFORMAL	0.45 (2.00)	0.41 (1.63)	0.50 (1.73)
Constant	30.15 (2.73)	37.9 (1.68)	28.6 (1.06)
EXPSURVEY	-6.66 (3.97)	-7.06 (1.66)	-7.41 (1.69)
MEANAGE		-0.22 (.40)	-0.28 (.47)
MEANSCHOOL			1.18 (.68)
R^2	0.32	0.36	0.44

Note: The countries covered by the regression are Argentina, Bolivia, Brazil, Chile, Colombia, Costa Rica, Ecuador, Guatemala, Honduras, Mexico, Panama, Peru, Uruguay and Venezuela. The table reports regression coefficient estimates, with t-statistics in parentheses. Explanatory variables: INFORMAL - Loayza's informality measure; EXPSURVEY - dummy variable equals 1 if the Gini coefficient is based on a household expenditure survey, equals zero if based on a household income survey; MEANAGE - mean age of the population; MEANSCHOOL - mean number of years of schooling completed for the population aged 25-64.

wages at the minimum salary level. Tokman (1992) also finds high access costs to legality in other Latin American countries. The time to register a small firm in his group of Latin American countries was 10 months on average, ranging from about one month in Bolivia, Brazil and Chile to two years in Guatemala. By contrast, Chickering and Salahdine (1991) report that a similar procedure takes about three or four hours in Florida or New York. Clearly, streamlining registration procedures could go a long way toward encouraging formalization of enterprises in Latin America.

Formal enterprises also face ongoing costs in the form of income, payroll and other taxes; minimum wages and mandated fringe benefits; constraints on and additional costs of dismissal; and compliance with government-imposed procedural and paperwork requirements. On this last point, de Soto (1989) surveyed 37 formal firms operating in sectors with high levels of informality and found that 40 percent of the working time of administrative personnel was spent complying with the government's bureaucratic procedures, a cost that seems clearly exorbitant. The question of whether state-imposed taxes and regulations make labor costs too high and dismissal restrictions too strict is treated in Chapter 6 of this volume. It is argued there that most countries in Latin America would be well advised to reduce many of these barriers to formality as a way to increase formalization rates and extend labor code protections and benefits—as well as

the other advantages of formality, including better access to capital—to a larger percentage of earners.

Land titling. Greater integration in the formal economy could also be achieved through programs to regularize the land titles of small farmers and urban squatters. Among the many benefits of such a reform would be to provide beneficiaries with a potentially acceptable form of collateral and thus greater access to credit.

Does informality contribute to inequality? To answer this question, we employed estimates of the size of the informal sector in 14 Latin American economies to explain the average value of the Gini coefficient of income inequality over 1982-92. Although the data sample is limited, and it is generally difficult to explain inequality in the Latin American cross-section alone, we do find that greater informality is significantly associated with greater inequality, as the preceding discussion has suggested (Table 7.3). This result is consistent with Chapter 2 of this report, which showed that earnings tend to be somewhat lower and are much more concentrated within the informal sector than in the formal sector. This holds out the hope that policies to reduce barriers to informality may improve the distribution of income.

Credit Bureaus

As we noted above, knowing a borrower's reputation is one way to help ensure repayment of a loan, since even the smallest borrowers can, in principle, develop a reputation. However, this requires some arrangement to facilitate the gathering and sharing of information about borrowers' credit histories. This is the purpose of credit bureaus, which typically gather together the credit histories of all banking system borrowers, or all such borrowers with loans above a certain size. Improving the functioning of credit bureaus, and encouraging them to cover the population of small borrowers, thus has the potential to improve small borrowers' access to credit. Ways to achieve this include establishing public credit reporting systems or, where they already exist, extending their coverage to smaller banking system loans, and ensuring widespread access to this information by the lenders and, for reasons of accuracy and transparency, by the borrowers themselves.

Candidates for these reforms include a number of countries in Latin America that currently do not have a credit bureau, including Costa Rica, Honduras, Panama, Guyana and Belize. Several other countries have credit bureaus with substantial loan size cutoffs (of approximately $20,000 or more), which do not track many loans to smaller firms. These include Brazil, Colombia, Paraguay and Uruguay. At the other end of the spectrum, a number of countries have very extensive loan reporting systems. For example, the credit bureaus in Bolivia, Chile, Ecuador and Venezuela cover all loan sizes, while the Argentine system tracks loans down to $50. A recent example of reform is Peru, where until 1996 the superintendency's database included only loans of $5,000 or more. Today, all loans there are tracked.

Leasing and Factoring

Leasing and factoring offer ways for firms that currently have little or no physical collateral to obtain loans, and thus may be of special interest to smaller firms. Unfortunately, a variety of legal, regulatory and tax obstacles may impede more widespread use of these instruments to obtain durable equipment financing (in the case of leasing) or loans based on accounts receivable (in the case of factoring).

In *leasing*, the lending institution buys and retains ownership of a piece of equipment that the firm would like to use. The enterprise uses the equipment and pays a monthly rent (which represents interest on the credit outstanding plus amortization). This arrangement offers the advantage over a collateralized loan in that the lender, as the owner of the equipment, does not have to be concerned about creating or perfecting a security interest—it can be sure that no one else has a legal claim on it. In addition, if the firm defaults on its lease and the lending institution takes possession of the equipment, it can sell it immediately in the second-hand market (since it is the owner), avoiding the lengthy proceedings required to obtain a court order to sell the pledged asset. However, the lender often must still go through a long legal process to take possession of the equipment, since it resides on the firm's property. Thus, with leasing one escapes some but not all of the problems associated with secured transactions. To facilitate leasing, the legal system should permit parties to contract for rapid and low-cost repossession of leased equipment in cases of default.

Unnecessary tax and regulatory barriers to the widespread use of leasing should also be avoided. For example, since banks were allowed to enter the leasing business in Chile in the 1980s (as partial or sole owners of leasing companies), leasing has become one of the major ways that credit has been made available to smaller enterprises. As another example, if bank loan interest payments are tax deductible but lease payments are not, leasing will not flourish. In Argentina, until recently, there was a double taxation problem. The leasing company paid the 21 percent value-added tax when it bought the equip-

ment, and then the lessee paid it again when it leased the equipment. Only recently has legislation repealed the former levy, eliminating this problem.

A pioneer in the microcredit field, Bangladesh's Grameen Bank, has also recently been demonstrating the feasibility of microleasing. The Grameen program began with leasing power looms to poverty-level weavers in the Dhaka Zone in 1992 and has since expanded to cover a wide variety of products (including sugarcane grinders, power tillers, battery chargers, ballpoint pen production machines, baby taxis, and mini transport) and to all 14 zones covered by the bank's operations. As of October 1996, the Grameen Bank had booked $1.5 million in leases, with an average lease size of $760 and a default rate of 1.5 percent. Nearly 20 percent of the lessees had moved into ownership of the equipment financed. The leasing program is open to second-time borrowers from the bank's microloan program, with leasing terms of up to three years and rental payments collected on a weekly basis.[22]

In *factoring*, the firm obtains a loan by making use of a somewhat nontraditional form of movable property collateral, its accounts receivable. This form of finance may be of particular interest to smaller firms, since they are often labor-intensive and may not have significant amounts of real property or even equipment that could be used to secure a loan. If, however, the smaller firm has substantial accounts receivable, particularly from large, bankable firms (for example, because they supply parts, other inputs, or services to these large firms), the smaller firm may be able to secure low-cost financing. This is because the interest rate charged on its receivables financing is primarily a function of the credit rating of the large firm, rather than of its own credit rating.

Since factoring is merely a special case of using movable property collateral to secure a loan, the obstacles to wider availability of such credit include all of the barriers to the use of movable capital discussed above. Hence, to expand the use of factoring—and thus the opportunities for smaller firms to obtain credit—the law must allow security interests to be created using invoices as collateral, there must be a way to verify that no one else has a prior claim on these invoices, and there needs to be a low-cost means for lenders to enforce their security interests in case of default.

---

[22] For more on microleasing and the Grameen Bank's program, see Gallardo (1997).

Small Cap Rural Banks

Financial services are generally much less available in rural than in urban areas of Latin America. This, together with the fact that rural areas typically have much greater concentrations of low-income households, means that improving the delivery of financial services to smaller farms and other rural enterprises may be a useful strategy for creating more equal income distribution. One interesting approach is to permit the creation of small capitalization rural banks, as has been done in Indonesia and the Philippines. In the case of the Philippines, Agabin and Daly (1996) note that there are some 745 small "cap banks" serving 75 percent of the country's secondary and tertiary cities and towns and supplying small loans to a large share of the Philippine countryside. The minimum capitalization required for bank start-up is between $77,000 and $770,000 (depending on location), which is significantly less than what is required to open a large urban bank.

The idea behind small cap rural banks is that in the countryside there are local entrepreneurs who understand the local culture and agriculture, and know many of the potential borrowers as well. Some of these entrepreneurs would make excellent bankers, but many do not have access to the several million dollars of capital normally required to start up a bank. This requirement was typically written with larger, urban commercial banks in mind, and may not be appropriate for rural areas. The minimum capitalization requirement exists for two reasons. First, it helps ensure that the intermediary will have a healthy start-up of operations, without difficulties in obtaining an appropriate location, purchasing equipment, meeting initial payrolls, making initial loans out of capital, and so forth. Second, it helps to avoid moral hazard problems by placing a significant amount of the owner's capital at risk so that he or she does not make excessively risky loans and is not so tempted by the lure of fraudulent schemes, loan kickbacks, etc. These purposes might require smaller capitalization levels in less prosperous rural areas, or might be more efficiently served through a special regulatory regime such as higher capital-loan ratios. Policymakers may want to consider making such adaptations to the prudential regulatory framework to facilitate the creation of small cap rural banks.

Though this chapter has thus far focused primarily on credit solutions for the income distribution problem in Latin America, providing deposit services can also help to increase the incomes of poor households and thus potentially lessen inequality, particularly if these services are provided in rural areas with large poor populations.

Modernizing and Supervising Credit Unions

Credit unions provide credit and deposit services in rural areas that are often too isolated or sparsely populated to support a bank branch. They have also traditionally played and continue to play the role of a "poor man's bank" in both urban and rural areas of Latin America, serving lower- and some middle-income households and smaller firms that banks have served less well. Credit unions are also the dominant supplier of microenterprise credit in Latin America, though total supply is still quite limited. Modernization and supervision of credit unions offer the possibility of increasing the quantity and quality of credit and deposit services delivered to lower-income households, thus lessening income inequality.

Credit unions throughout the region were established from the 1950s through the 1970s with a strong social welfare purpose in mind. Many were organized by Catholic priests and U.S. Peace Corps volunteers. They typically lacked professional management, were weak at loan recovery and at earning and retaining profits for future expansion, and usually kept loan rates low in order to benefit borrowing members. Low lending rates meant that deposit rates were also normally kept low, but with substantial grant and soft loan funds available from external donors, many credit unions grew rapidly despite the lack of deposit mobilization, loan recoveries and retained earnings. With the drying up of much of these donor funds in the 1980s and 1990s, the credit union movements in many Latin American countries became moribund.

Rehabilitation (or modernization) programs and prudential regulation and supervision have shown great potential for improving the performance of the region's credit unions, including their sustainability and outreach. Rehabilitation programs that began in the mid to late 1980s in Guatemala and the Dominican Republic have produced excellent results, while those in Honduras and Bolivia have also made substantial strides. (Box 7.3 presents highlights of the Guatemala case.)

Modernization programs must of course be tailored to the particular weaknesses and needs of the credit unions being rehabilitated. Among the major weaknesses in credit union policies and practices commonly addressed in these programs are low wage levels, poor labor quality, low deposit rates and weak deposit mobilization, low loan rates and little capitalization of profits, opaque financial information and undisciplined financial practices, and inadequate risk management. Obviously, such major failings seriously jeopardize the performance and sustainability of credit unions and their ability to reach large numbers of households with quality financial

Box 7.3. Credit Union Rehabilitation in Guatemala

When the technical assistance team from the World Council of Credit Unions arrived in Guatemala, it found that credit unions there suffered from all of the problems described in this section and more: uncompetitive salary levels, low deposit and loan rates, little institutional capital, erratic provisioning, poor quality of financial information, and weak risk management practices. Working with a group of 20 of the largest and most promising credit unions, the team helped overhaul key prices, policies and practices, and improve or establish auditing and control, strategic planning, marketing, information and other systems. The effort was highly successful by nearly any measure.

From program initiation in 1985 until its end in 1993, the delinquency rate on the consolidated portfolio of the 20 credit unions fell from 30 percent to 7.9 percent. Provisioning of loans overdue more than one year increased from 36 percent to 100 percent. Institutional capital rose from 4.5 percent of assets to 10.7 percent, while total assets in real terms increased at an average compounded rate of 17 percent per year. The total number of credit union members nearly doubled. With the modernization program having created a base of financially solid, well-managed credit unions, growth then further accelerated. In the next four years (1994-97), real assets nearly tripled and the number of members nearly doubled. At the same time, financial solidity was maintained, with the delinquency rate on the consolidated portfolio falling slightly to 7.5 percent and the consolidated capital/assets ratio increasing somewhat to 11.6 percent.

services. In addition to addressing these principal problems, modernization programs often improve other important areas of credit union operations and management, including strategic business planning, internal auditing and controls, general personnel and incentive policies, marketing, and information systems.

Supervision. Bringing credit unions under the financial supervisory umbrella helps impose much of the financial discipline they have traditionally lacked, and which they need in order to provide more and better financial services. But superintendencies in only five Latin American countries currently supervise credit unions (Bolivia, Colombia, Ecuador, Mexico and Paraguay), and all of these programs were begun too recently to assess their impact on credit union performance. A number of important differences between supervising credit unions and banks stem from differences in the credit unions' ownership structure (cooperative instead of stock company) and resulting governance issues; the fact that credit unions make a large number of small, often uncollateralized loans (so that reporting requirements and the methods used to assess portfolio quality must be adjusted); and the probable need for tougher provisioning and capital adequacy standards due to the greater volatility of credit union earnings, which in turn is the result of a frequent lack of geographical diversification of the loan portfolio, the effect of credit union governance problems and a tendency (partly born of cooperative philosophy) to slip into lax loan collection procedures.[23] Like supervision of intermediaries that specialize in microlending, then, supervision of credit unions requires a number of special considerations in order to be carried out effectively. When done well, however, credit union supervision, like rehabilitation, has the potential to contribute to economic development and reduce income inequality.

Downscaling and Upgrading

Downscaling refers to efforts by commercial banks and other similar banking institutions, such as financing companies, to offer loans to microenterprises, while upgrading refers to the process of turning NGO microlenders into regulated financial intermediaries. Downscaling is important; all but three of the financial institutions listed in Table 7.2 are intermediaries that have downscaled, the exceptions being Banco Sol and Caja los Andes in Bolivia and Corposol/Finansol in Colombia, which are upgrades. For several reasons, banks are attractive platforms from which to begin offering services to a large number of microfinance clients:[24]

- They are regulated institutions, fulfilling the conditions of ownership, financial disclosure and capital adequacy that help ensure prudent management.
- They have the infrastructure, including branch networks, from which to reach out to a substantial number of microfinance clients.
- They have well-established internal controls and administrative and accounting systems to keep track of a large number of transactions.
- Their ownership structures, made up of private capital, encourage sound governance, cost-effectiveness and profitability, all of which lead to sustainability.
- They offer deposit services as well as loans.

Downscaling operations typically focus on transferring the lending technology (see Box 7.2) to the commercial bank and fitting it into the framework of the en-

---

[23] See Poyo (1998).
[24] This discussion is taken from Baydas, Graham, and Valenzuela (1997).

tire institution in as cost-effective a manner as possible. The impact of downscaling programs on income inequality may not be very great, at least at first, as banks may not reach down to the poorest microentrepreneurs.[25] They may choose instead to serve the larger and wealthier microentrepreneurs, finding this to be more profitable if there is little competition as yet in this market segment. Over time, of course, additional competition may appear, and some banks may find it profitable to lend to lower-income firm owners.[26]

By contrast, upgrading operations typically start with a financial NGO that is committed to reaching low-income microentrepreneurs.[27] The difficulty here is that most such NGOs do not possess the skills or mindset that would enable them to become regulated financial institutions. Those that do must learn many of the same financial disciplines described earlier for credit unions: keeping loan rates up (despite the high costs this imposes on the group they are trying to assist); containing costs and earning and capitalizing profits (to help ensure sustainability and underwrite future growth); and provisioning adequately, controlling risks and submitting themselves to the prudential regulatory norms imposed on deposit-taking institutions. They must also become proficient at looking after the vastly more complex liabilities side of their operations: liquidity management, asset/liability matching, selection and pricing of appropriate deposit instruments, and so forth. Offsetting these costs is the leverage provided by deposit-taking, which allows the former NGO to greatly expand its credit outreach, as well as to provide valuable savings services to its target population. Training programs designed to assist in the process of upgrading may thus be a cost-effective way of expanding access to credit to small, low-income borrowers.

A combination of downscaling and upgrading occurs when commercial banks or other banking institutions decide to work in tandem with financial NGOs to serve microenterprises more effectively. This can be done by combining the financial expertise and better access to funds and supervision of commercial banks with the financial NGOs' knowledge of and closeness to microenterprise clients.

---

[25] Judging from their average loan sizes in excess of $2,000, this would appear to be true of several downscales listed in Table 7.2.

[26] Even wealthier microentrepreneurs, however, may hire low-income workers, which would have important beneficial impacts on income distribution.

[27] Evidence of this commitment is seen in the low average loan sizes of the three upgrades in Table 7.2.

REFERENCES

Acción International. 1997. *1996 Annual Report*. Somerville, Mass.: Acción International.

Agabin, Meliza, and Jorge Daly. 1996. An Alternative Approach to Rural Financial Intermediation: the Philippine Experience. Chemonics International, Inc., Washington, D.C.

Bank of Japan. 1996. *Economic Statistics Monthly* 8(1) January. Tokyo.

Barham, Bradford, Stephen Boucher, and Michael Carter. 1996. Credit Constraints, Credit Unions, and Small-Scale Producers in Guatemala. *World Development* 24(5): 793-806.

Baydas, Mayada, Douglas Graham, and Liza Valenzuela. 1997. *Commercial Banks in Microfinance: New Actors in the Microfinance World*. Microenterprises Best Practices Working Paper, USAID and Development Alternatives, Inc., Washington, D.C.

Bresnyan, Jr., Edward. 1996. The Microenterprise Sector in Guyana. Regional Operations Department 3, Inter-American Development Bank, Washington, D.C.

Chickering, A., and M. Salahdine. 1991. Introduction and the Informal Sector Search for Self- Governance. In A. Chickering and M. Salahdine, eds, *The Silent Revolution*. San Francisco: International Center for Economic Growth.

Christen, Robert. 1997. Issues in the Regulation and Supervision of Microfinance. In R. Rock and M. Otero. *From Margin to Mainstream: The Regulation and Supervision of Microfinance*. Acción International Monograph Series No. 11. Somerville, Mass.

Christen, Robert, Elisabeth Rhyne, and Robert Vogel. 1995. *Maximizing the Outreach of Microenterprise Finance: The Emerging Lessons of Successful Programs*. Washington, D.C and Cambridge, Mass: Harvard Institute for International Development and USAID.

Deininger, Klaus, and Lyn Squire. 1996. Measuring Income Inequality: A New Data Base. *The World Bank Economic Review* 10(3) September.

de Soto, Hernando. 1989. *The Other Path: The Invisible Revolution in the Third World*. New York: Harper & Row.

Deutsche Bundesbank. 1995. Monthly Report 47(3) March. Frankfurt.

EIM/International. 1996. Characteristics and Constraints of Small Businesses in Trinidad and Tobago: Final Report National Baseline Survey. A Sample Survey among 2,104 Businesses. Small Business Development Company and EU, Port of Spain/Zoetermeer.

ESA Consultores. 1996. Estudio de la Pequeña y Micro Empresa en Honduras. USAID, Tegucigalpa.

Fleisig, Heywood. 1995a. The Power of Collateral. Private Sector Department Note No. 43. World Bank, Washington, D.C.

_____. 1995b. The Right to Borrow. Private Sector Department Note No. 44. World Bank, Washington, D.C.

Fleisig, Heywood, Juan Carlos Aguilar, and Nuria de la Peña. 1994. How Legal Restrictions on Collateral Limit Access to Credit in Bolivia. World Bank Report 13873-BO, Office of the Chief Economist, Latin America and the Caribbean Region, Washington, D.C.

Gadway, John, and Michael O'Donnell. 1995. Rural Finance and Small Farmer Liquidity. Inter-American Development Bank, Washington, D.C. Unpublished.

Gallardo, Joselito. 1997. *Leasing to Support Micro and Small Enterprises*. Policy Research Working Paper No. 1857. World Bank, Washington, D.C.

Ghani, Ejaz. 1992. *How Financial Markets Affect Long-Run Growth: A Cross-Country Study*. PRE Working Paper No. 843. World Bank, Washington, D.C.

Gulli, Hege. 1998. Microfinance and Poverty: Questioning Common Beliefs. Microenterprise Unit, Inter-American Development Bank, Washington, D.C.

INEGI. 1994. Encuesta Nacional de Micronegocios. Aguascalientes, Mexico.

Inter-American Development Bank. 1995. The IDB and Microenterprise: Promoting Growth with Equity. Microenterprise Unit, Inter-American Development Bank, Washington, D.C.

International Monetary Fund (IMF). 1997. *International Financial Statistics* 50(8) August.

Jansson, Tor, and Mark Wenner. 1997. Financial Regulation and its Significance for Microfinance in Latin America and the Caribbean. Microenterprise Unit, Inter-American Development Bank, Washington, D.C.

Jaramillo, Fidel, Fabio Schiantarelli, and Andrew Weiss. 1996. Capital Market Imperfections Before and After Financial Liberalization: An Euler Equation Approach to Panel Data for Ecuadorian Firms. *Journal of Development Economics* 51: 367-86.

King, Robert, and Ross Levine. 1993. Finance and Growth: Schumpeter Might Be Right. *The Quarterly Journal of Economics* 108(3): 717-37.

Li, Hongyi, Lyn Squire, and Heng fu Zou. 1998. Explaining International and Intertemporal Variations in Income Inequality. *The Economic Journal* 108: 26-43.

Loayza, Norman. 1996. The Economics of the Informal Sector: A Simple Model and Some Empirical Evidence from Latin America. World Bank, Washington, D.C. Unpublished.

Magill, John, and Donald Swanson. 1991. Ecuador Micro-Enterprise Sector Assessment: Summary Report. GEMINI Technical Report No. 8, USAID, Washington, D.C.

McPherson, Michael, and Carl Liedholm. 1996. Determinants of Small and Micro Enterprise Registration: Results from Surveys in Niger and Swaziland. *World Development* 24(3): 481-87.

Mushinski, David. 1995. Credit Unions and Business Enterprise Access to Credit in Guatemala. The College of William and Mary, Williamsburg, VA. Unpublished.

Orlando, María Beatriz. 1998. How Informal Are Microenterprises? The Role of Human and Physical Capital on Institutional Participation in Urban Mexico. Department of Economics, Tulane University, New Orleans. Unpublished.

Pons, Frank Moya, and Marina Ortiz. 1994. Indicadores de las microempresas en la República Dominicana 1993-1994. Fondomicro, Santo Domingo.

_____. 1995. Indicadores de las microempresas en la República Dominicana 1994-1995. Fondomicro, Santo Domingo.

Poyo, Jeffrey. 1998. A Conceptual Framework for the Regulation and Supervision of Credit Unions: How Does It Differ from Stockholder-Owned Banking Institutions? Paper presented at the conference "Building Modern and Effective Credit Unions in Latin America and the Caribbean, Inter-American Development Bank, Washington, D.C.

Psacharopoulos, George. 1993. Poverty and Income Distribution in Latin America: The Story of the 1980s. Latin America and the Caribbean Technical Department, World Bank, Washington, D.C.

Rock, Rachel, and María Otero. 1997. *From Margin to Mainstream: The Regulation and Supervision of Microfinance*. Acción International Monograph Series No. 11, Somerville, Mass.

Sebstad, Jennifer, and Gregory Chen. 1996. *Overview of Studies on the Impact of Microenterprise Credit*. AIMS Project Working Paper, USAID Office of Microenterprise Development, Washington, D.C.

Tokman, V. 1992. The Informal Sector in Latin America: From Underground to Legal. In V. Tokman, ed., *Beyond Regulation: The Informal Economy in Latin America*. Boulder: Lynne Rienner.

Westley, Glenn. 1994. *Financial Liberalization: Does It Work? The Case of Latin America*. DES Working Paper No. 194, Inter-American Development Bank, Washington, D.C.

_____. 1997. *Credit Union Policies and Performance in Latin America*. OCE Working Paper No. 355, Inter-American Development Bank, Washington, D.C.

Wolff, Edward. 1991. The Distribution of Household Wealth: Methodological Issues, Time Trends, and Cross-Sectional Comparisons. In Lars Osberg, ed., *Economic Inequality and Poverty: International Perspectives*. Armonk, NY: M.E. Sharpe Publishers.

World Council of Credit Unions (WOCCU). 1995. 1994 *Statistical Report*. Madison, WI: WOCCU.

_____. 1996. 1995 *Statistical Report*. Madison, WI: WOCCU.

Chapter 8

THE DISTRIBUTIONAL AIMS
OF FISCAL POLICY

Income distribution in the Latin American countries in the next century will depend heavily on government action. Governments will not be able to change the historical or geographical conditions that have influenced the region's high levels of inequality. Nor will they be able to suddenly alter the resource endowments that contribute to the inequalities of reward between productive factors and between skilled and unskilled labor. But with the appropriate policies, government can help modify the channels through which inequality is perpetuated. Government can help improve women's opportunities to participate in the work force, assure that children attend and remain in the educational system, lower the barriers to formal work, create conditions to make informal work productive, and improve the economic situation of the poor during unemployment and old age. In terms of macroeconomic policy, government has the power to mitigate the effects of external shocks and volatility on the economy by developing adequate fiscal or monetary policies.

In some instances, the actions that must be taken to attain these objectives do not entail major fiscal effort, but in others they do. As we have argued in the introduction to these policy chapters, for distributional reasons, spending aimed at basic needs that the market cannot supply and that the poor cannot pay for individually must be covered with public funds, including basic education and health care, and minimum pensions for the poor. Day care and various child health and education programs that support participation of women in the work force must also be financed with public funds. Moreover, although there must be private participation in providing infrastructure, investments in the delivery of water, sewerage and electricity to low-income households will continue to demand public funds.

By international standards, Latin American governments are small, and they only partially cover some of these areas of redistributive spending. That should not lead to the conclusion, however, that poor income distribution is a consequence of the small size of Latin American governments. There is no convincing international evidence that shows that larger governments lead to better income distribution. Moreover, in Latin America, even though governments are small, the expenditures that could have redistributive potential, such as those on education, health and social security, are not small. The main difficulty of governments in the realm of social spending is efficiency, not volume.

Moreover, one reason Latin American governments are small is that the design of tax policies has become so burdened with supposedly distributive considerations, and the upshot has been the sacrifice of vast amounts of tax resources that could be utilized on expenditures with greater potential for redistribution. The distributive impact of public spending has been measured by how the benefits are distributed. Under this traditional criterion, public social spending is moderately redistributive. But this is not the criterion by which the distributive impact ought to be judged. That impact depends on the *efficiency* with which resources are used and on their being *targeted* to basic social spending needs in those areas that will make it possible to remove the mechanisms that perpetuate inequality.

Expanding the size of government ought to be a way to accomplish basic social objectives, and that can only be justified if spending is done in an efficient and targeted way. Expanding government in a way that disregards these principles will quite surely be regressive, if only because the resources will be used to pay the salaries of public officials who typically have higher educational levels and greater opportunities for earning income than most people.

SIZE OF GOVERNMENT AND INCOME DISTRIBUTION

Improving income distribution is one of the functions that societies have entrusted to government around the world. In Latin American countries, a broad majority believes that the state ought to play a redistributive role. Public opinion surveys show, for example, that at least four of five Latin Americans think that the government has a responsibility to "reduce the differences between the rich and the poor," and an even higher percentage thinks that the government ought to accept responsibility for "providing health care to the sick" as well as "a decent living standard of living" for old people and the unemployed (Figure 8.1).

Government Spending Is Small in Latin America...

While in developed countries central government spending typically represents 40 percent of GDP, in Latin America that rate is around 20 percent. There is no simple criterion for pinpointing the size of spending, but international comparisons indicate that it tends to rise in proportion to the level of development (see Appendix Table 8.1a, regression 1). If this is accepted as a guideline, it can be said that the size of the Latin American state, measured by public spending as a percentage of GDP, is on average 9 points below the international norm for the level of development of its countries (regression 2). Although international patterns for the size of the state, like many other variables, are generally established in relation to the development level of countries, that does not seem to be its most important determinant. The proportion of the population over 65 and the degree of ethnic and linguistic fragmentation are two much more crucial factors (regressions 3 and 4). The first variable reflects claims for social safeguards, the cost of which tends to be quite high: for every percentage point rise in the aging population, public spending also rises by 1 percent. Although this relationship is affected by developed countries (where the ratio is even greater), it is not limited to such countries (regression 5). Ethnic and linguistic fragmentation, moreover, reflects the willingness of the society to show solidarity with group demands as expressed in public spending. The various groups making up a fragmented society may fear that their taxes are benefiting those with whom they do not identify, and such lower willingness to pay taxes limits the size of government. Taking into account these two variables, which together explain around half of the differences in size of governments around the world, Latin American governments are significantly smaller than would be suited to their demographic, social and political conditions (Appendix Table 8.1a, regressions 6 and 7). On average the variation from the worldwide pattern is around 8 percent of GDP.

Figure 8.1. Demand for Redistributive Public Policies
(*Percent of people in favor*)

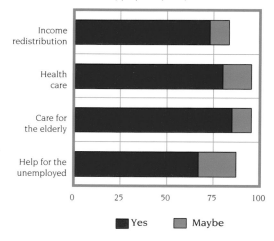

Source: *Latinobarómetro* (1997).

...But Bigger Isn't Always Better

Developed countries, where government spending represents around 40 percent of GDP, have the best income distribution in the world. By contrast, Latin America, where income distribution is worst, is also the region where governments are smaller (Figure 8.2). These relationships could lead to the conclusion that the small size of Latin American government *causes* poor income distribution. That is not necessarily the case, for two reasons. The first is that there is no guarantee that better income distribution will result from larger government. The analysis of the determinants of income distribution on a world scale for Chapter 4 did not reveal that the size of government is not a major factor in explaining differences in income distribution between countries worldwide or in Latin America. Within the region, the economies with larger governments are not necessarily the most equitable. The most notable case is Brazil, where the size of the government resembles that of a developed country, yet the country's inequality is one of the worst in the region and the world. Likewise, some countries with levels of inequality that are moderate for the area, such as Argentina or Peru, have modest sized governments. It is true that Uruguay and Costa Rica, the countries with the best income distribution in the region, have rather extensive governments, and that in Guatemala, where income is very unequal, the size of the government is insufficient for performing the necessary redistributive tasks. However, no clear pattern for the entire region can be concluded from these cases.

Figure 8.2. Income Concentration and Government Size by Region

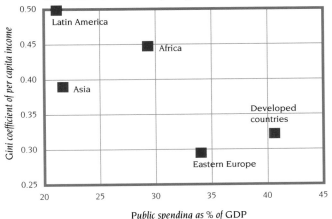

Source: Deininger and Squire (1996) and International Monetary Fund, Government Financial Statistics (1997).

Figure 8.3. Public Spending by Region
(*Percent of GDP*)

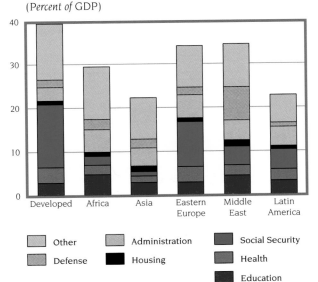

Source: International Monetary Fund, Government Financial Statistics (1997).

Latin American Social Spending

The second reason why it is difficult to argue that the small size of government causes poor income distribution is that public spending aimed at redistributive operations is not small in Latin America, contrary to widespread belief in the region. Redistributive expenditures, such as those on education, health and social security, represent on average over 10 percent of GDP in the typical Latin American country, practically the same as in countries in the Middle East and considerably above countries in Asia or Africa (Figure 8.3). Social spending is low in Latin America only in comparison to European patterns (both the developed countries and those in transition), and that is due to the huge weight of social security transfers in those countries. But if the close connection existing between such social spending and the percentage of the population over 65 (or the development level) is kept in mind, Latin America is not below the world standard in the area of social security expenditures, nor in social spending as a whole (Appendix Table 8.1b, regressions 8 to 11). In Uruguay, Costa Rica, Panama and Nicaragua, social spending is substantially greater than one might expect for the development levels of these countries, and on average throughout Latin America it is slightly above the world pattern (Figure 8.4). This does not suggest that one should ignore the fact that in some countries, such as Mexico, Colombia, Guatemala and the Dominican Republic, there are indeed glaring inadequacies in government social spending. The small size of government in Latin America is due above all to the modest size of economic expenditures such as investments in infrastructure and subsidies to productive sectors (grouped under the category of "other" in Figure 8.3). However, there are no grounds for claiming that the lack of a redistributive impact of governments in the region is because such expenditures are small.

INTERFERENCE OF DISTRIBUTIVE AIMS IN TAX POLICY

Paradoxical as it may seem, the small size of the typical Latin American government is largely due to the design of tax policy that has been unduly contaminated by supposedly redistributive considerations. Income taxes become progressive through rates that rise with taxes and various exemptions and deductions. In order to prevent consumption taxes from disproportionately burdening the poor, in many countries the main items of popular consumption are exempted. As a result of such distributive concerns, the application of taxes in Latin America has tended to be progressive, thereby sacrificing large amounts of revenue, which paradoxically has operated to the benefit of higher-income groups and has severely limited the possibility of carrying out redistribution through spending.

Figure 8.4. Observed vs. Expected Social Spending by Worldwide Standards
(*Percent of* GDP)

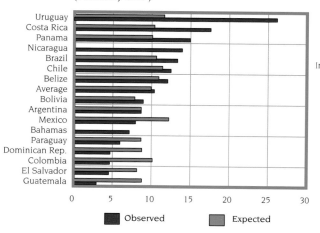

Note: *Social spending regression (as % of* GDP) *as a function of per capita income.*
Source: *Social spending,* IMF, *Government Financial Statistics* (1997); *per capita income, World Bank* (1993a).

Figure 8.5. Tax Sources
(*Percent of* GDP)

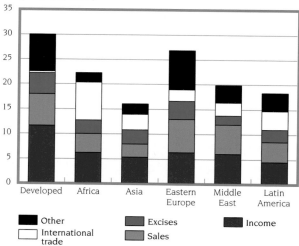

Source: *International Monetary Fund, Government Financial Statistics* (1997).

Figure 8.6. Latin America's Observed and Expected Tax Revenue by Global Standards
(*Percent of* GDP)

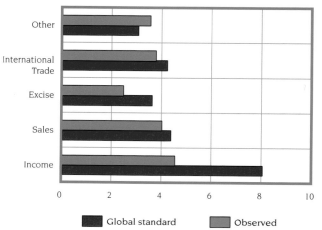

Note: *Income tax regressions (as % of* GDP) *as a function of per capita income.*
Source: *Income tax, International Monetary Fund, Government Financial Statistics* (1997); *per capita income, World Bank* (1993a).

Figure 8.7. Maximum Marginal Income Tax Rates
(*In percent*)

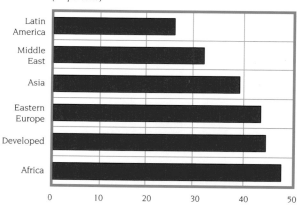

Source: *Price Waterhouse, Individual Taxes: A Worldwide Summary* (1997), *and The Heritage Foundation.*

Latin America Collects Little in Taxes, Especially More Progressive Taxes

The counterpart to the small size of the public sector in Latin America is low tax collection. For the development level of the countries, average tax burdens ought to be 24 percent of GDP, not 18 percent as they are currently (Appendix Table 8.1b, regressions 12 and 13). The primary deficiency in tax collection is for taxes on income and property, which on average amount to only 4.5 percent of GDP; in keeping with the development level of the countries, those taxes ought to generate 8 percent (Appendix Table 8.1c, Figures 8.5 and 8.6 and regressions 14 and 15). Revenue from specific taxes imposed on such products as gasoline and alcoholic beverages is also significantly less than might be expected. On average, these taxes produce 2.5 percent of GDP, a point less than the world norm (Appendix Table 8.1c, regression 16). Even with the spread of the value added tax (VAT) as a tool for taxing consumption in Latin America, revenue from taxes of this type is slightly (though not significantly) less than what might be expected (Appendix Table 8.1c, regression 17).

Income Tax: Victim of Redistributive Intentions

Income tax rates in Latin America are currently the lowest in the world, but this was not so a decade ago. Until then, maximum tax rates on individuals were 40 percent or more in practically all countries in the region, and in 10 countries they were at least 50 percent. These levels have been cut to an average that stands currently at around 25 percent and is less than that of any other region. In developed countries, maximum tax rates are on average over 40 percent, and in Asian countries they are slightly below that figure. In Latin America, only Barbados, Belize, Chile (and Honduras until 1997) have maximum tax rates on individuals of 40 percent or over (Figures 8.7 and 8.8). The trend in business taxes has been similar. Maximum marginal rates of over 40 percent, which were common a decade ago, have practically disappeared. The average of maximum tax rates on businesses in Latin America is currently around 27 percent, substantially lower than averages of all the other groups of countries, with the exception of Eastern Europe (Figures 8.9 and 8.10).

Although taxes were cut to make the tax system more effective, that goal is far from achieved. Current productivity levels of the income tax, which is defined as the ratio of tax rates and revenue collected as a percentage of GDP, are around 15 percent in Latin America. This is tantamount to saying that (maximum) tax rates of 25 to

Figure 8.8. Maximum Individual Tax Rates, 1997 vs. 1986

(*In percent*)

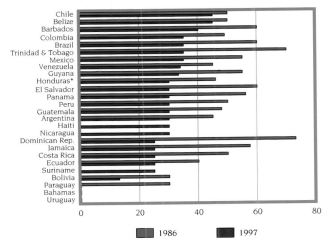

* *Refers to 1998 instead of 1997.*
Source: *Price Waterhouse, Individual Taxes: A Worldwide Summary (1997).*

30 percent generate revenues of 3.7 to 4.5 percent of GDP. Although this is higher productivity than a decade ago, it is still low and it is lower than international norms for the development levels of the countries of the region (Appendix Table 8.1c, regression 18).

Low collection rates for income and other taxes in Latin America reflect the limited institutional capacity of public administration to enforce the law. Although it is difficult to demonstrate empirically, countries that have tried to improve their administrative capacity have shown this to be true. For example, Peru's program to modernize its tax administration system was decisive in boosting collections from 5 percent of GDP at the beginning of the decade to 14 percent today. However, it is important to remember that the troublesome tax systems typical to Latin America demand an administrative prowess that is difficult to come by in the region.

Paradoxically, the blame for the complicated design and ineffectiveness of tax systems may lie in an excess of redistributive considerations. Even after all the tax reforms of the past decade, where other criteria have been given preference, the countries with greatest income inequality have maintained the highest income tax rates (Figure 8.11). Redistributive aims are explicit in the tax codes. In the case of the personal income tax, the following characteristics are aimed at redistribution (Table 8.1):

- Minimum incomes below which no tax is collected;

- Tax rates rising by income level;

Figure 8.9. Corporate Tax Rates
(In percent)

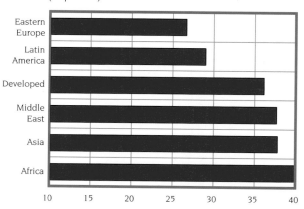

Source: Price Waterhouse, Corporate Taxes: A Worldwide Summary (1997), and The Heritage Foundation.

Figure 8.11. Income Concentration and Maximum Income Tax Rates

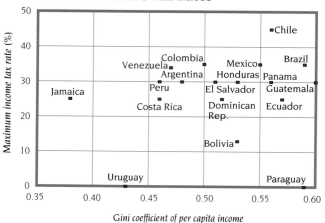

Source: Price Waterhouse, Corporate Taxes: A Worldwide Summary (1997), IDB calculations based on recent household surveys, and Deininger and Squire (1996).

Figure 8.10. Maximum Corporate Tax, 1997 vs. 1986
(In percent)

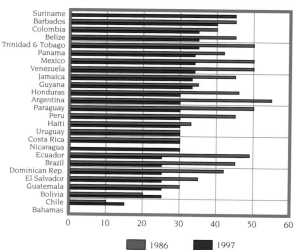

1986   1997

Source: Price Waterhouse, Corporate Taxes: A Worldwide Summary (1997).

Figure 8.12. Income Tax Incidence

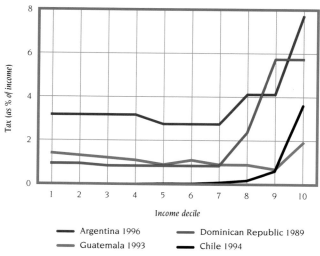

Argentina 1996   Dominican Republic 1989
Guatemala 1993   Chile 1994

Source: Argentina: Centro de Estudios Bonaerense (1997); Chile: Engel, Geltovic and Raddatz (1997); Guatemala: Bahl, Martínez-Vásquez and Wallace (1996); Dominican Republic: Santana and Rathe (1992).

• Marginal maximum tax rates applied only to high-income levels;

• Various deductions for the number of dependent children and for basic expenditures on education, health and housing;

• Lower rates on income from labor or other types of income.

As a result of these distributive considerations, income taxes fall quite disproportionately on high-income

groups. The two highest income deciles pay taxes that as a proportion of their incomes are several times higher than those of all previous deciles, which are usually exempt. (Nevertheless, in Figure 8.12, where the impact of the tax on income is shown, the lowest deciles in some countries are seen to be taxed because in these cases it has been assumed that a portion of business taxes has been transferred to prices of consumption goods.)

Even at the highest decile, in no case is the tax burden over 8 percent of income, although the theoreti-

Table 8.1. Redistributive Features of the Personal Income Tax

	Minimum income taxable (times per capita income)	Increasing marginal tax rate? (%)	Maximum rate applicable from (times per capita income)	Differential treatment according to income source?	Other deductions (dependents, education, health, housing)?
Argentina	1.6	6-33	19.4	No	Yes
Bahamas*					
Barbados	0.31	25-40	1.76	No	Yes
Bolivia		13		No	No
Brazil	3.46	15-25	6.91	No	Yes
Chile	0.15	5-45	1.91	No	No
Colombia	1.45	0-35	23.53	No	Yes
Costa Rica	1.28	10-25	11.96	Yes	Yes
Ecuador	9.13	10-25	45.65	No	No
El Salvador	2.0	10-30	18.18	No	Yes
Guatemala	11.83	15-30	32.75	No	Yes
Guyana		33.33		Yes	No
Honduras	5.9	10-30	118.7	No	Yes
Jamaica	1.38	0-25		No	No
Mexico	0.11	3-35	7.17	No	Yes
Nicaragua	9.33	7-30	42.0	Yes	No
Panama	1.14	4-30	15.15	No	Yes
Paraguay*					
Peru		15-30	24.17	No	Yes
Trinidad & Tobago	1.94	28-35		No	
Uruguay*					
Venezuela		6-34	6.82	Yes	Yes

* Countries with no personal income tax.
Source: IDB calculations based on Price Waterhouse, *Individual Taxes: A Worldwide Summary* (1997).

cal tax rates are far higher. That means that even in the upper deciles, the productivity of the income tax is quite modest. Low efficiency is largely a result of evasion due to deficiencies in tax administration and in the design of the systems themselves. In effect, the low effectiveness of taxes is largely the result of manipulation of supposedly redistributive purposes, which in practice have served to lower the tax burdens of upper-income groups.

For example, the minimum levels of taxable income, which in principle are aimed at excluding the poorest, tend to be set at high levels due to pressures from the middle and upper classes. In Brazil, the minimum taxable income is over three times per capita income; in Honduras it is approximately six times; and in Ecuador, Nicaragua and Guatemala it is close to 10 times per capita income (Table 8.1). Likewise, although maximum income tax rates in Latin America are currently the lowest in the world, in many cases they apply only to extremely high incomes. For example, Ecuador has a maximum tax rate of only 25 percent, which begins to apply only to incomes equivalent to 45 times per capita income. Guatemala and

Peru have maximum rates of 30 percent that apply to incomes starting at 32 and 24 times per capita income, respectively. Before its 1998 tax reform, Honduras was simply beyond comparison: the maximum rates only applied to incomes representing over 100 times the average income. As can be seen in Figure 8.13 (which excludes this extreme case) the effectiveness of income tax is severely limited by these excessive attempts at progressiveness.

Thus it is clear that the attempt to make the income tax progressive has meant a very serious sacrifice in collection. To the extent that public expenditures are much more redistributive than any tax could be, the ultimate impact on income distribution may have been the very opposite of what was intended. Flaws in revenue collection have also led governments to be increasingly dependent on indirect taxes, especially the VAT.

Figure 8.13. Income Tax Effectiveness and Maximum Income Tax Rate

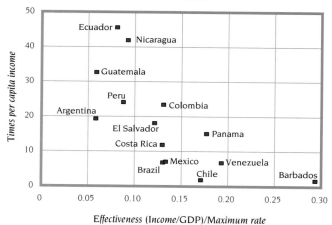

Source: Calculations based on Price Waterhouse, Corporate Taxes: A Worldwide Summary (1997) and International Monetary Fund, Government Financial Statistics (1997).

The VAT: The Dilemma between Effectiveness and Progressiveness

Until a decade ago, many countries tried to compensate for poor income tax revenue collection with high taxes on foreign trade, but since 1985, out of a concern for efficiency, average duties have been reduced from 42 percent to around 14 percent. The proportion of taxes on foreign trade within tax collection as a whole fell on average from 30 percent in the early 1980s to 16.6 percent in 1995.

In the absence of this resource, the value-added tax has become a central part of tax systems in Latin America. Twenty-one countries in the region now have the VAT, and two more are in the process of implementing it. The spread of the VAT reflects not only the aim to increase tax revenues, but also to improve neutrality and avoid the distortions of other forms of levies (such as taxes on foreign trade or sales). As it exists in most countries, the VAT is a consumption tax. The fiscal burden results from the difference between the taxes collected on sales, minus those paid in purchases. Thus the tax paid at successive states of production and distribution is a partial payment on the total tax that ultimately falls on the sale price to the consumer.[1]

In principle, a single-rate VAT for all consumption goods is a regressive tax because higher-income groups presumably have higher rates of saving. This characteristic may be reinforced by the practical impossibility of observing and taxing the consumption of some goods that are not traded on the market and that weigh significantly in the consumption of the upper classes (for example, the use of owner-occupied dwellings).

In Argentina (after the 1996 reform) or in Chile, where the VAT has flat rates and few exceptions, it is indeed true that its application is regressive. In Argentina, the weight of the tax drops from 9 percent of the income of the first four deciles to around 7 percent of the ninth and less than 4 percent of the richest decile. In Chile, the three lowest income deciles bear a weight that as a percentage of their income is four points higher than on the two highest deciles (Figure 8.14). The regressivity of the VAT can be avoided only at the cost of making it substantially less effective. In Guatemala and Colombia (or as was the practice in Argentina before the reform), the VAT excludes some of the main articles in the basic consumption basket. In the Colombian case, the theoretical VAT rates would entail a slightly "regressive" structure, where the lowest deciles would pay 2 percentage points more of their income than the highest groups (Figure 8.15). This regressive impact is eliminated through exemptions, but the overall productivity of the tax falls to less than half.

The Cost of Progressive Rates with Low Revenue Collection

Due to excessive distributional considerations in the design of the income tax, and to the difficulties of administration and control that severely limit the effectiveness of this tax, the only way to substantially raise the total tax load is through a broadly based VAT with few exceptions. This leads to the regressive impact that can be seen in the Chilean and Argentine systems. Hence, countries face the alternative of having either a tax system that is pitifully small but progressive like Guatemala's, or a system that is more effective in its revenue collection capability but regressive (Figure 8.16).

In the past, that choice could be avoided through taxes on foreign trade. Such was the case, for example, of the Dominican Republic, where in 1989 such taxes contributed around a half of tax revenue and entailed a tax load of close to 7 percent of the income of all groups of families. But this option entails high efficiency and productivity costs, which has prompted almost all countries to abandon it.

What position then should be taken toward the choice between either greater tax effectiveness or having an entire tax system that is more progressive? Can sacri-

---

[1] A more detailed description of the VAT structures is found in IDB (1996), Part Two, Chapter 3.

Figure 8.14. VAT Incidence

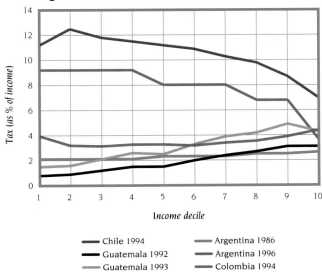

Source: *Argentina: Centro de Estudios Bonaerense, (1997); Chile: Engel, Galetovic and Raddatz (1997); Colombia: Steiner and Soto (1998); Guatemala: Bahl, Martínez-Vásquez and Wallace (1996).*

Figure 8.16. Tax System Incidence

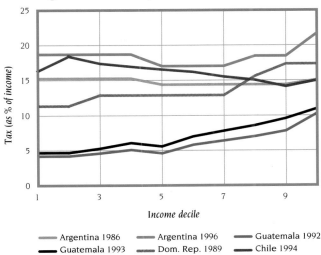

Source: *Argentina: Centro de Estudios Bonaerense (1997); Chile: Engel, Galetovic and Raddatz (1997); Dominican Republic: Santana and Rathe (1992); Guatemala: Bahl, Martínez-Vásquez and Wallace (1996).*

Figure 8.15: Theoretical and Effective Incidence of the VAT: Colombia, 1994

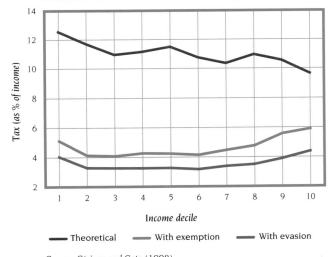

Source: *Steiner and Soto (1998).*

ficing a major proportion of revenue be justified to prevent tax burdens from affecting low-income groups disproportionately? The answer to these questions depends on the potential distributional impact of additional tax resources. Analyses of the distributional impact of taxes often ignore this important consideration, implicitly assuming that the use made of tax resources benefits each

individual in accordance with his or her share in the total revenue of the society. Such is rarely the case. Wherever the use of fiscal resources provides benefits that are better distributed than the tax burden, the final distribution that emerges after taxes and government spending will be better than it was at the outset (Box 8.1).

Obviously it does not suffice that a tax and expenditure system be redistributive for it to be socially acceptable or desirable, especially if it produces losses of efficiency that harm the general welfare. However, the redistributive potential of a tax and expenditure system tends to be greater when tax distortions are minimized and spending efficiency is maximized. Instead of a conflict between redistribution and efficiency, in practice there is complementarity.

The more significant social expenditures, such as basic education or health care, benefit poor individuals more than the wealthy. These expenditures are progressive in absolute terms (that is, per capita, and hence they are more progressive with regard to income), since poor individuals receive more basic education services or more public health care than the rich. Therefore, even if they are financed with a tax that is regressive (relative to income), the redistributive impact can be significant. For example, for each 1 percent of GDP collected via the Chilean VAT, which is regressive (relative to income), there can be a redistributive impact (measured solely by the amount of spending) equal to a 0.4 point drop in the Gini index, simply assuming that spending is distributed in

Box 8.1. *The Distributive Impact of Taxes and Government Spending*

In popular terminology, a tax is considered "regressive" if it falls disproportionately on low-income groups. This means that the distribution curve of taxes is located above the original income distribution curve (Figure 1). Usually, only a tax that falls more heavily on wealthier groups—meaning that taxes are more unequal than incomes—is regarded as progressive.

With regard to spending, the terms "progressive" and "regressive" refer, respectively, to situations in which the per capita benefits are greater or less for poor than for wealthy individuals (Figure 2).

This colloquial use of the terms is imprecise, because the basis of comparison is not the same in each case: whereas distribution of taxes is compared to the income distribution curve, the distribution of benefits from spending is compared to the diagonal line, that is, the one of equal distribution.

This lack of precision explains an apparent contradiction: a "regressive" (with regard to income distribution) tax that is used to finance "regressive" (per capita) government spending, can nevertheless *improve* income distribution. Suppose that a tax takes 15 percent of the income of the poorer half of the population and only 10 percent of the richer half, whose income is four times greater than that of the poor; suppose, moreover, that the government uses these funds to provide education subsidies in proportions of 5 and 6, respectively, to the poor and the rich. Such a fiscal policy *improves* income distribution, as can be seen in the following calculations:

	Initial Income	Minus Taxes	Plus Subsidies	Final Income
Poor	20	15%=3	5	22
Rich	80	10%=8	6	78
Total	100	11	11	100

The explanation of this paradox lies simply in the fact that the distribution of spending is less unequal than income distribution. That is all that is required for the combination of taxes and expenditures (of the same amount) to improve income distribution; or to use the usual terms, what suffices for the tax to be more "progressive" than the spending, both being measured in relation to initial income, or both in absolute terms individually.

In the strictest form, the change in the Gini, ΔG, equals the difference between the inequality ratio of expenditures by income level Gg (quasi-Gini of expenditures), minus the inequality ratio of taxes by income levels Gt (quasi-Gini of taxes), multiplied by the amount of the operation as a proportion of the sum of incomes of all individuals, v:

$$G_1 - G_0 = \Delta G = (Gg - Gt)\, v$$

If the tax falls on all incomes at rate v, and therefore the distribution of the tax is the same original tax distribution, G_0, and if the distribution of spending is completely equal (and therefore Gg is zero), the initial Gini will fall exactly by the tax rate, v.[1]

Therefore, an expenditure whose impact is "equal" (the same amount per person) and is financed with a tax that falls "equally" (that is applied to all incomes equally) has a powerful redistributive effect.

Conventional analyses of impact assume that the benefit that individuals derive from government spending corresponds to the sum of spending that they receive through education, health care and other social spending. This is a useful approximation, but it is deceptive, because the benefit derived from very modest spending, such as vaccinations, may be much greater than that of a very large expenditure, such as a sports stadium, that reaches the same group of poor individuals. Moreover, many benefits of government spending may take much longer to emerge, even if they are quite large, such as greater income-generating potential resulting from education. Finally, many expenditures can have indirect effects on distribution that are difficult to trace and quantify. This can happen, for example, because government spending, taxes, or mechanisms used to finance the deficit cause real interest rates to rise, raise the relative salaries of more highly qualified workers, generate rents for higher-income groups, or cause inflation.

---

[1] This equation is exact only when income and spending are the same. See Kakwani (1977) and Vélez (1996), Chapter 3.

Figure 1. Progressive and Regressive Taxes

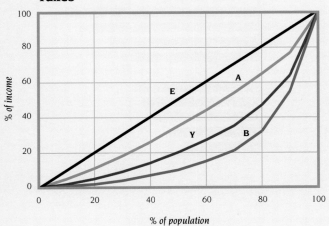

E: Equidistribution diagonal
A: Regressive tax distribution (in relative terms)
Y: Income distribution
B: Progressive tax distribution (in relative terms)

Figure 2. Progressive and Regressive Public Spending

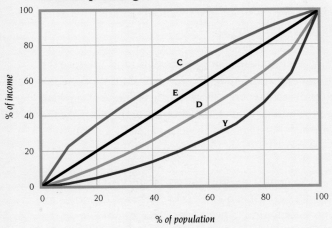

C: Progressive Spending Distribution (in per capita terms)
E: Equidistribution diagonal
D: Regressive spending (in per capita terms)
Y: Income distribution

equal amounts throughout the population. Obviously, if expenditures are distributed in a more targeted way toward the poor, as in fact happens in Chile, the effect on income inequality would be even greater.

Figure 8.17 presents the hypothetical impact that income and VAT taxes of different countries have on the Gini indices, given the way they are applied and assuming in all cases that benefits are distributed equally (in absolute terms) among all individuals and are the same as the amounts of expenditures. Income taxes produce a greater distributive impact: in Chile, each 1 percent of GDP in revenues can lower the income Gini more than 0.8 percentage points; in the Dominican Republic it is lowered by 0.7 points, and in Argentina by 0.6. The distributive potential of the VAT is lower in all cases, but it is positive in any case: the effect is between 0.4 and 0.6 points in Guatemala, Colombia and the Dominican Republic, and between 0.3 and 0.4 in Chile and Argentina.

Nevertheless, the impact on income distribution depends not only on how progressive the tax is but also on the amount collected. Argentina substantially increased the VAT's distribution potential with the 1996 reform, because whereas in the previous situation it was more progressive (the quasi-Gini[2] of revenue collected was 0.53), collection was very low. With actual sums collected in mind, the redistributive potential of the VAT (always under the assumption that spending is distributed equally) went from a 1.2 drop of the Gini prior to the reform to almost 2 points subsequently (Figure 8.18). The Argentine tax reform also affected the income tax, which became slightly more progressive (from 0.56 to 0.63). But the greatest distributive effect (which went from 2.2 to 3.2 points of a potential reduction of the Gini) was due to a 25-percent increase in revenue collection. Chile is an equally illustrative case: the strongly progressive impact on income has a very limited potential impact on income distribution because it would potentially lower the Gini by 1.2 points, while the VAT, as regressive as it might be in the usual meaning given to this term, has a much greater distribution effect, lowering the Gini by around 3.5 points.

In short, within the ranges between which the distributive impact of taxes move, the redistributive potential of the tax system depends not only on how progressive it is, but also on the revenue raised by taxes. The margin for improving the progressivity ratio of the entire tax system is quite limited, since efforts at progressivity on any particular base entail major sacrifices of revenues

---

[2] It is called "quasi-Gini" because it is the Gini of the tax paid, but calculated on the basis of the ordering of family incomes.

collected, which must be compensated with other taxes. Hence, the progressivity of all systems tends to be similar. In the five countries appearing in Figure 8.19, the lowest quasi-Gini of the distribution of tax burdens is that of Chile (0.44) and the highest that of Guatemala (0.58). Within these cases, we have included the Philippines as an example of a country from another region with an index of distribution of tax loads that falls right in the middle of the narrow margin in which those of Latin American countries move. However, in that country the tax system generates a potential reduction of the Gini by over 13 points, merely from better collection. Between the cases studied in the region, the Argentine tax system generates a potential reduction of some 10 points, and that of Guatemala only 5 points.

Under such conditions, the aim of tax policy should not be to make collection as progressive as possible in order to enhance its redistributive effect. It is much more feasible and effective to moderate the degree of theoretical progressivity insofar as doing so makes it possible to raise revenue collection, thereby raising the fiscal resources available for financing expenditures that can modify income distribution. That requires simplifying income tax systems, reducing exemptions and differential treatments by types of income that facilitate evasion, and lowering the levels of personal income at which the tax begins to be collected and to which maximum tax rates apply. In the area of the business tax, the adjustment that many systems in the region most need is to eliminate differences in the fiscal treatment between some sectors and others. Finally, the region has progressed a great deal in implementing the VAT, but in many countries the effectiveness of this tax is severely limited by exemptions that seek to avoid regressivity. In lower-income countries, incorporating some basic consumer goods, such as unprocessed foods, will continue to be limited by the few possibilities for administration and supervision, and in such cases it would be a mistake to seek to make the VAT universal. But there is no justification for leaving outside the tax base other items of mass consumption, such as processed foods, beverages or clothing, which are primarily consumed by middle- and upper-income groups anyway.

SOCIAL SPENDING: MODERATELY PROGRESSIVE, PLAINLY INEFFICIENT

Distribution of social spending is much more progressive than is generally believed. As a general rule, social expenditures taken together are distributed in an approximately equal way among the various income groups. This relatively flat distribution pattern of the benefits of so-

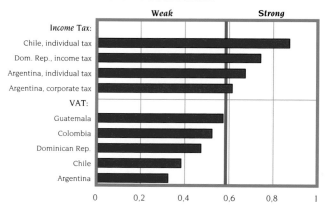

Figure 8.17. Hypothetical Impact of 1 percent of GDP Tax Revenue on the Gini coefficient

Reduction in Gini coefficient points (Quasi-Gini coefficient of the tax)

Source: See Figures 8.12 and 8.14.

cial spending is not necessarily true of each of its components, however. Typically, while basic spending on education and health benefits the poor disproportionately, advanced education and subsidies on prices and fees reach upper-income groups to a greater extent.

The redistributive impact of social spending does not depend solely on the volume of spending received by each income group. It is far more important that such spending be efficient and focused on those services that can have an influence on the factors that perpetuate inequality. This means that governments must improve the efficiency of the systems that provide education, health care and social security, more effectively reorienting them toward attaining results. Too often governments make the mistake of thinking that to reach "a higher level of health" or "a better education" they need only build more hospitals and schools.

Figure 8.20 presents the distribution of total social spending by income quintiles. Of the seven countries for which information is available, Chile stands out as the one where the lowest income groups receive a greater proportion of spending than the percentage of the total population that they represent: the poorest quintile of households receives over 35 percent of total social spending, while the richest quintile receives under 10 percent. Distribution is moderately progressive in Colombia, where the poorest quintile of the population receives almost 25 percent of social spending, while the wealthiest quintile receives less than 15 percent. In most of the other countries, spending seems to be distributed among the various population groups in a proportion more or less equal

Figure 8.18. Redistributive Potential of the VAT and Income Tax

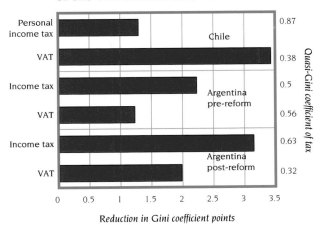

Source: See Figures 8.12 and 8.14. The redistributive potential is defined as the quasi-Gini coefficient of the tax times its revenue as a percentage of GDP.

Figure 8.19. Redistributive Potential of Tax Systems

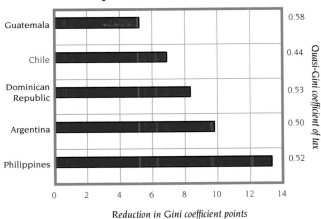

Source: See Figures 8.12 and 8.14. For the Philippines, see Devarajan and Hossain (1995).The redistributive potential is defined as the quasi-Gini coefficient of taxes times their revenues as a percentage of GDP.

Figure 8.20. Distribution of Social Spending by Quintiles

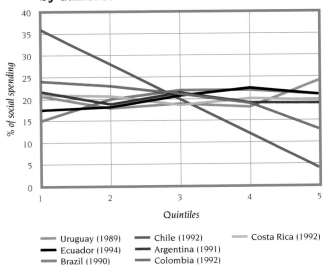

Source: World Bank (1993, 1995, 1996, 1997a and 1997b), Vélez (1996) and FIEL (1995).

Figure 8.21. Progressiveness of Public Spending

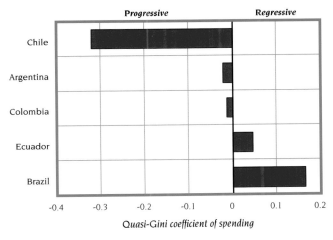

Source: Calculations based on World Bank (1993, 1995, 1996 and 1997a). Public spending progressiveness is defined as the Gini coefficient of the benefits of social spending by income levels.

to the percentage of the population that they represent, with the exception of Brazil, where distribution is somewhat regressive: the poorest quintile receives only 15 percent while the wealthiest quintile receives around 22 percent. Another way of demonstrating these results is to calculate the inequality ratio of social spending by the income levels of the beneficiaries (or quasi-Gini of social spending). When each group of households receives a proportional share of spending, this indicator equals zero, and when spending is progressive the index is negative.[3] Figure 8.21 confirms that social spending in Chile is re-

markably progressive, while in other countries it is neutral or slightly regressive.

When these spending structures are combined with tax systems whose weight is roughly proportional to income, they actually produce a net redistributive effect

---

[3] According to Box 1.1 in Chapter 1, the Gini index equals the proportion of the zone located *beneath* the 45-degree line and the distribution curve. With regard to social spending, the area located beneath the curve is regressive (with a positive Gini index) and a distribution curve located above the 45-degree line is progressive (with a negative Gini index).

Figure 8.22. Redistributive Impact of Taxes and Public Spending

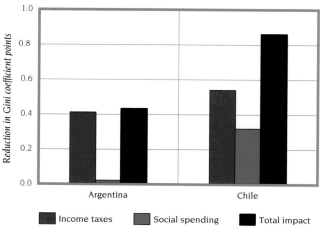

Source: See Figures 8.21 and 8.18.

Figure 8.23. Distribution of Educational Spending
(*Percent of total*)

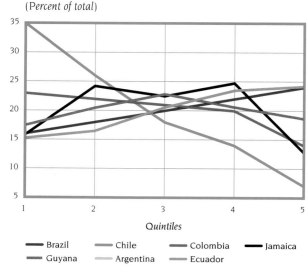

Source: World Bank (1993, 1995, 1996, 1997a) and FIEL (1995).

favoring lower-income groups. Taking a typical country as an example, the quintile of households with the lowest incomes may receive only 5 percent of national income and pay approximately 5 percent of taxes, but they receive a volume of public spending in services equaling 20 percent of total social spending. Hence, the difference between the quasi-Gini of social spending and the quasi-Gini of the taxes that finance it represents the potential impact of an increase in social spending above the Gini index that measures income inequality (Box 8.1). In the two Latin American countries for which complete information is available, if an additional 1 percent of GDP were to be collected in accordance with current tax distribution, and it were spent in accordance with current social spending, the Gini index would fall between 0.4 and 0.8 points. In fact, the net redistributive impact of taxes and spending in Chile is much greater than in Argentina, even though Argentina's tax burden is relatively regressive because its social spending is progressive (Figure 8.22). Analytical studies carried out by the ILO and ECLAC corroborate these conclusions in the sense that the fiscal policy of the region has a redistributive effect that favors lower-income groups.[4]

Unfortunately, the redistributive impact of fiscal policies is small in relation to the high levels of income inequality found in the region. Even in the case of Chile, although social spending seems to be progressive and reaches a relatively high level (more than five times that of Argentina), the redistributive impact of this policy only enables it to counteract the Gini coefficient of income distribution by 3.4 points. In Argentina, the impact is extremely moderate according to estimates: just 0.5 points.

Even if it were possible to efficiently spend a greater volume of resources, Chile would have to raise taxes and the spending level by over 8 percent of GDP—while maintaining current distribution structures—to overcome the difference of around 10 points found in income inequality in comparison with other regions of the world. In other words, the net impact of redistributive policies based on taxes and spending can be positive, but its potential effects are limited.

The empirical results on how social spending is applied are not enough to quantify its impact on inequality. The redistributive impact of social spending depends both on how it falls and on its efficiency. Two countries that present the same distribution of spending can register different redistributive impacts; indeed, the greater redistributive impact will be registered in the country whose social spending is more effective. A more efficient health care system can provide low-income groups essential preventive medical services for their current income levels, thereby lowering the number of days lost because of illness or having to deal with sick children. A more efficient education system can provide lower-income groups with training and knowledge that will affect their income-earning capabilities in the future. In fact, even in a country where social spending is essentially progressive, the impact can be regressive if the quality of public services is poor, especially services provided to

---

[4] See Lecaillon, et al. (1984). ECLAC has done several studies on the distribution of social spending. See ECLAC (1997a and 1997b) and Jiménez and Ruedi (1998).

Table 8.2. Spending on Education: Impact and Results

	Argentina	Brazil	Chile	Colombia	Ecuador
Income Inequality (Gini)	**0.46**	**0.57**	**0.55**	**0.56**	**0.54**
Impact of spending	0.01	0.08	-0.27	-0.08	0.10
Spending (% of income of households)	1.75	3.75	3.54	1.99	2.44
Net impact	0.008	0.018	0.029	0.013	0.011
Spending per student (in 1990 dollars)					
Primary	421	526	619	297	186
Secondary	562	621	557	495	341
Higher	796	5,258	1,795	1,782	589
Schooling (average years)					
At age 24	10.5	6.8	11	8.1	8.9
Of the population between 25-65	9.9	5.6	9.2	6.6	7.5

Source: World Bank (1993, 1995, 1996, 1997a) and FIEL (1995).

lower-income groups. The primary means by which the government deals with inequality need not be in determining who spending reaches but in how efficient that spending is. This issue is analyzed in greater detail by considering three major categories of public spending: education, health, and subsidies for public utilities.

Spending on Education Is Generally Progressive

Total spending is made up of a number of items, each of which presents a different distribution structure. One of the main components of social spending is education, and as can be seen in Table 8.2, the structure in this instance is similar to that of total spending, as might be expected. However, this component presents some more striking tendencies. In Ecuador and Brazil, the structure is more clearly regressive, while in Colombia, spending on education seems to go in a slightly progressive direction (Figure 8.23). At a greater degree of detail, it can be seen that spending on basic education[5] is clearly progressive in all countries, although to different extents. In Chile, the poorest quintile of households still receives around 35 percent of public spending on primary education, but Colombia spends around 40 percent on this group and Argentina also devotes approximately 35 percent to them (Figure 8.24).[6] Total spending on education is less progressive in most countries, particularly because of the proportion of spending on higher education, which is largely regressive. Spending on higher education clearly benefits the wealthy disproportionately, but this benefit continues to be less than that represented by their share in national income (Figure 8.25). The fact that net spending on education is progressive reflects the predominance of spending on the primary level within total spending on education.

Figure 8.24. Distribution of Spending on Elementary Education
(In percent)

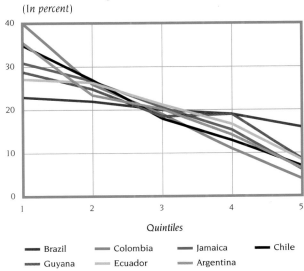

Source: World Bank (1993, 1995, 1996, 1997a) and FIEL (1995).

[5] Basic education includes levels of primary education, generally first to sixth grade, although sometimes up to the ninth grade is included.

[6] The progressivity indicators used here are spending per quintile of households, not individuals. It could be argued that such indicators exaggerate the degree of progressivity insofar as the poorest quintile of households generally makes up over 20 percent of the population, since on average poorer families are larger. Although that could have some effect on the results, the net result is relatively small, given the demographic profile in Latin America. In most countries the ratio between the size of the poorest families and that of the wealthiest is less than 1.2. In comparison with other regions in the developing world, particularly Africa, most children in Latin America tend to be enrolled in the first grade of school. This relatively complete coverage at the primary level means that the bias between rural and urban zones, which is so pronounced in Africa, is much less relevant for explaining the impact of spending on education in Latin America.

Figure 8.25. Distribution of Spending on Higher Education

(In percent)

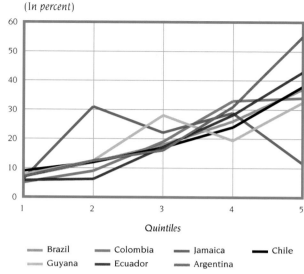

Source: World Bank (1993, 1995, 1996, 1997a) and FIEL (1995).

Figure 8.26. Spending and Fourth Grade Attainment

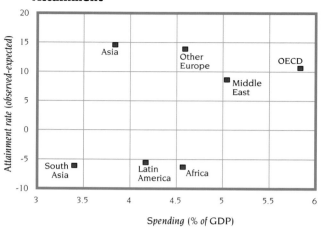

Note: The expected attainment rate is estimated as a function of per capita GDP and public spending on education as a percentage of GDP.
Source: Calculation of 95 countries based on UNESCO (1997) data.

Subsidies to higher education benefit well-off families disproportionately. Children from such families are more likely to finish secondary studies, they have a higher level of training and a greater tendency to finish advanced study, and they have access to savings or credit, and hence are better prepared to handle the opportunity costs represented by attending the university. One way to make spending on education more progressive would be to encourage the creation of private universities, charge enrollment fees at government universities to cover at least some of the costs, and offer scholarships to students on the basis of their economic situation. All these policies, in combination, would make it possible to increase the supply of university education, mobilize further financial resources, and reorient public spending toward the students who most need it. As things are now, the better-off families, who can handle paying all or some of the costs of a university education, end up absorbing public resources that otherwise could be used to grant a scholarship to a student without resources. Moreover, such sums represent a particularly high proportion of spending on education in countries like Venezuela, Costa Rica and Brazil.[7]

As is the case with total data on social spending, the redistributive impact of spending on education, even though it might be quite progressive, remains relatively limited. Chile and Argentina represent the extreme cases in this regard. In Argentina, spending on education is distributed approximately in a proportional per capita manner, that is, the poorest quintile of households receives around 20 percent of funds devoted to this item. This level of spending represents approximately 1.7 percent of household income, and hence counteracts by less than a point the country's 0.46 income distribution inequality. In Chile, spending is much more progressive: the poorest quintile receives approximately 35 percent of spending on education. Moreover, Chile devotes almost twice as much funding to this item. Even so, the net result is a reduction of less than three percentage points of the 0.55 inequality in income distribution (Table 8.2).

Progressivity Is Not as Important as a Good Education

The most important effect of spending on education is not measured by the amount of money that each income group receives but by the level and quality of education. Spending on education may be quite heavy, but if teachers do not show up for class or schools do not operate reliably, it will not provide the benefits that it should, and of course it will not have any impact on trends in income inequality.

Judging by the information available, there is only a limited correlation between the results of education and how progressive spending is on this item. Countries as

---

[7] Birdsall and James (1993) offer a perspective on the issue of spending on university education.

different as Brazil, Ecuador and Argentina have in common the fact that spending on education is slightly regressive, but the average levels of school achievement fall along a range of values extending from 5.6 years to around 10. Disparities of this nature indicate that the different education systems provide a very different service to their respective populations, regardless of how spending is apportioned. Moreover, education systems in Latin America are generally mediocre. Compared internationally, the rate of completion of fourth grade in Latin America ought to be 83 percent, with the level of national income and the percentage of GDP spent on education taken into account. But in a sample of 19 countries, the average is only 72 percent—a divergence from other regions in the world with similar spending levels, such as Asia and Eastern Europe (Figure 8.26). Spending on education will only be effective in reducing inequality if it translates more effectively into higher levels of learning and school achievement. That statement is valid regardless of how progressive spending might be in this area.

Spending on Health Is Also Progressive

Another major component of social spending is health care services. Public spending on this category in Latin America is 4 percent of GDP on average, ranging from 1.8 percent in Haiti and 2.5 percent in Honduras to over 5 percent in Argentina and Costa Rica. Except for Guyana, the distribution of public spending on health is generally progressive. Chile consistently devotes a larger amount of resources to poor households, while in Jamaica, Honduras and Ecuador, distribution seems to favor the second and third quintiles (Figure 8.27). The progressive nature of Chile's health care system may be attributable to the fact that it explicitly offers the wealthy the chance to opt for private sector services, thereby enabling public resources to be devoted to the less favored strata. At the other extreme of the spectrum are Ecuador and Brazil. The weakness of the redistributive impact in Ecuador is a result of the small amount and low quality of private sector services; hence, the wealthy insist that they be provided good services and have privileged access to the public sector. In Brazil, the private sector is huge, but the mechanism for reimbursement of expenses—which provides coverage to rich and poor alike—is based on services provided and hence disproportionately favors the wealthy, who call on the system more often and use the more expensive services.

Spending on health is excessively concentrated on hospital and curative services, which, important as they are, constitute a glaring example of ineffective use of public funds.[8] Too much of public spending on health in Latin America goes to treatment services, and relatively less to more cost-effective prevention programs. Building hospitals and clinics and hiring the staff needed for their operation—physicians, nurses and administrators—is relatively attractive for politicians and voters, while services that can really have an impact on inequality but are less visible or less prestigious are continually deprived of needed funding. Programs such as public hygiene campaigns, infant development programs, prenatal testing, infant care or family planning are relatively cheap and have a much greater impact on health conditions, especially among the poor, who tend to know less about how to care for their health and have fewer resources for doing so.

Inefficiency in allocating and using resources also has an important effect on public health. A regression for 19 countries in Latin America, controlling for the level of national income, showed that the statistical relationship between spending on health and infant mortality rates is insignificant. The results indicate that increasing by 1 percent the proportion of GDP spent on health lowers infant mortality by less than 0.1 deaths per 1,000 live births. In a region where infant mortality rates remain on average at over 45 per 1,000 live births, government resources for this purpose are going to have to be used much more effectively if the health of the population is to be improved. Many studies on different public health systems show how the inefficiency and misallocation of resources prevent those systems from improving health conditions.

Where there *is* funding for health care services such as prevention and treatment, the resources are generally used inefficiently. The number of physicians per persons treated tends to be quite high, and administrative expenses are often excessive. Services and staff are concentrated in the major urban centers. In many countries, the physicians on the public payroll do not fulfill the number of consultation hours specified in their contract, and instead they refer patients to their private offices. Maintenance of equipment and installations is often deficient, and it is not at all unusual that essential materials and medications are lacking when and where they are most needed.[9]

As happens in education, wealthier families who are able to pay for medical insurance tend to use the costly services of public hospitals as a backup. If they were to pay for private medical insurance, public funds would be

---

[8] See World Bank (1993a) and Fundación Mexicana para la Salud (1997).
[9] For a more detailed analysis of inefficiency in health systems, see IDB (1996).

Figure 8.27. Distribution of Spending on Health

(*In percent*)

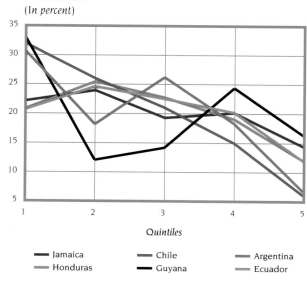

Quintiles

— Jamaica   — Chile   — Argentina

— Honduras   — Guyana   — Ecuador

Source: World Bank (1993, 1995, 1996, 1997a) and FIEL (1995).

Figure 8.28. Distribution of Subsidies of Utility Prices and Rates

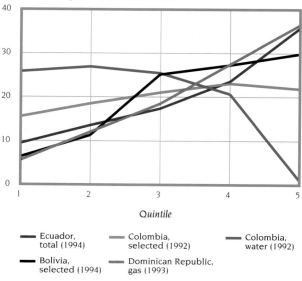

Quintile

— Ecuador, total (1994)   — Colombia, selected (1992)   — Colombia, water (1992)

— Bolivia, selected (1994)   — Dominican Republic, gas (1993)

Source: World Bank (1993, 1995, 1996) and FIEL (1995).

available to subsidize or pay for insurance policies of lower-income groups. The contrast noted between the reforms of the health care system in Brazil and Chile in the 1980s is a clear example of the different approaches. Under the 1988 Brazilian Constitution, the state must provide obligatory and free health care service that is unlimited in nature and universal in coverage. The starting point was the assumption that it would be possible simply to extend social security services to those who were not covered. However, under the new "Unified Health System," the wealthy continued to receive services that were paid at the expense of the public treasury and to which they continued to have privileged access. Consequently, between 1987 and 1996, health care spending in Brazil became even more regressive. Despite the policy of free and universal medical care, the poor ended up paying disproportionately larger sums in order to have access to the services they needed, whether in medicines, private consultations or transportation.[10] This is merely a dramatic example of something that is common to many health systems where middle-class groups have greater access to public health services, and use them more, because they have more weight in political matters.[11]

By contrast, the reform of the health care system in Chile in the 1980s—which sought to raise efficiency rather than promote equality—has often been criticized as regressive. The reform enabled citizens to opt out of being covered by the public health system (FONASA) and apply the withholdings of the payroll tax to financing the premiums offered by private sector insurance plans

(ISAPREs). At the same time, however, the government extended coverage of FONASA to make it universal. The net impact of these changes has been the creation of one of the most progressive social spending structures in Latin America and possibly the world. Services provided by the Chilean public health system are actually more progressive than those of the United Kingdom or Hungary, "because of the fact that public spending on health coexists with private spending and that the beneficiaries of the former are disproportionately poor households."[12] More recent studies have confirmed the progressive nature of spending on health in Chile, calculating that "leakage" to wealthy households is less than 2.5 percent of the total public subsidy to the health sector.[13]

Subsidizing Public Utility Charges: Not the Best Use of Public Resources

Subsidies of public utility charges and other costs are not a topic generally included in discussions on social spending, but in fact they represent a major loss of budget resources, often justified on grounds of redistribution. Paradoxically, charging "social" fees for public utili-

---

[10] Medici (1998).

[11] See other examples and an analysis of the political economy of these regressive results in Birdsall and Hecht (1995).

[12] Milanovic (1995).

[13] Bitrán (1998).

ties and other goods is the only area of economic policy that turns out to be regressive from any standpoint. Except in rare circumstances, the upper and middle classes in Latin America consume more of these goods and services than the poor, and therefore benefit disproportionately from public subsidies. For example, in Bolivia in 1994, the wealthiest quintile of households reaped 30 percent of electricity subsidies while the poorest quintile received less than 10 percent (Figure 8.28). In Ecuador, the combination of subsidies on prices and rates provides the richest quintile of households with over 35 percent of total subsidies, while the poorest quintile receives only 10 percent. Such subsidies represent a significant percentage of national income in most countries, amounting to 1 percent of GDP on average for the region. These resource transfers do not heighten disparities in consumption simply because they are distributed less unequally than income. However, action by government in this area can become more progressive by covering the cost of sale to the public. Such a policy would free up resources for direct income transfers or subsidizing the prices that the poor sectors pay. For example, Colombia applies moderately effective methods for targeting water bill subsidies. In Chile, all public utilities are billed at their normal sale price, but a household survey and a study of ability to pay is used to subsidize the water and electricity bill of lower-income households.[14]

Summary: Social Spending

Social spending is not as regressive in Latin America as might often be expected. Especially in the areas of health and education, public spending seems to be on the whole proportional to the number of people making up a specific income group. Combined with tax systems that are proportional to income, public policies in general do redistribute toward the poor. Expenditures on health and education may be two of the more progressive components of total public spending because they are so visible and because they can be more easily connected with the number of people who receive a service (students, patients). By contrast, subsidies for utilities and even other components of public spending, such as defense or subsidies for industrial and farm prices, are less visible and more regressive in their impact. But spending on education and health systems, even though generally equitable, tends to be inefficient. Schooling levels and results in the area of health could be much better, given income and spending levels in the region. The upshot is that children do not attend school for as many years as they should nor receive the preventive health care ser-

vices that they need, thereby affecting other factors that maintain the high levels of inequality existing in Latin America.

PUBLIC SECTOR EMPLOYMENT: A POTENTIALLY REGRESSIVE ASPECT OF PUBLIC SPENDING

Although the combined impact of taxes and public spending may be progressive, government actions—such as excessive public sector employment—may bring about other distributive effects that go in the opposite direction. In some countries, public sector employment can be a very important channel through which fiscal policy indirectly influences income distribution. In the past, when many countries in the region experienced high fiscal deficits, inflation was another significant channel of indirect redistribution that operated against lower-income groups.[15]

Some take the view that government has the social obligation to provide large-scale employment opportunities, which should have a healthy redistributive effect. Or, put differently, they believe that the cutbacks in public employment effected in many countries since the 1980s have contributed to their income distribution problems. Examining the nature of most public sector employment shows these theories to be wrong.

Public sector employment represents a significant proportion of total employment. In Bolivia, Panama and Uruguay, at least one of every five employed persons is a public sector employee. In countries where the share in public employment is lower, at least 7 percent of those employed work for the public sector (Figure 8.29).

Public sector activities employ workers with high educational levels. A public sector worker typically has completed high school, while those who work in the rest of the economy have an average of six or seven years of schooling. The differences in educational levels between public and private sector workers are over five years in Ecuador, Paraguay, Mexico, El Salvador and Honduras (Figure 8.30).

Because public sector employees have more education than other workers, they belong on average to higher-income strata. This means that the way in which spending on government employees is distributed among the population is more unequal than income distribu-

---

[14] Vélez (1996) provides an analysis of the case of Colombia; Morandé and Doña (1997) study targeted subsidies to water rates in Chile.
[15] See estimates of the impact of the inflation tax for Argentina in Chisari and Romero (1997) and for Mexico in Gil Díaz (1987) and Reyes (1988).

Figure 8.29. Share of Public Employment in Total Employment

(Percent of total employment)

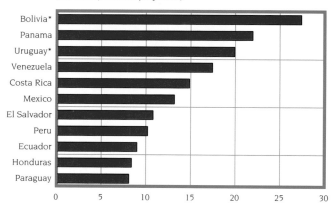

* Countries with urban data only.
Source: IDB calculations based on recent household surveys.

Figure 8.30. Education of Private and Public Employees

(Years of schooling)

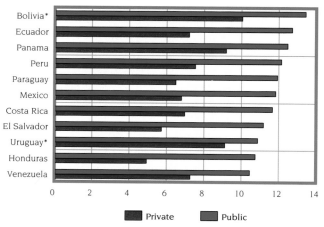

* Countries with urban data only.
Source: IDB calculations based on recent household surveys.

Figure 8.31. Distribution of Public Salaries by Income Deciles

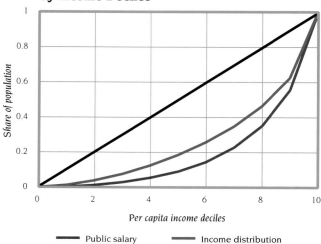

Source: IDB calculations based on recent household surveys.

tion, as represented in the Lorenz curves in Figure 8.31 for simple averages of the 11 countries considered. More precisely, the quasi-Gini index of distribution of spending on employment among the population is on average 0.61, substantially higher than the Gini of per capita income distribution, which on average for these same countries is 0.51. It should be noted that this does not imply that distribution of government salaries between public employees is more unequal than total income distribution. Indeed, there is much greater equality between incomes of public employees than between incomes of private workers. This simply means that public sector salaries go disproportionately to individuals who belong to the upper-income strata.

The regressive distribution of spending on public sector employees is perhaps clearer if it is compared with that of income from private labor. Only in Uruguay is public sector spending on pay and salaries distributed among the entire population in a way that is more equitable than private labor incomes (Figure 8.32). In other countries, the quasi-Gini of the distribution of public sector employee spending among the entire population is greater than that of incomes from private labor. The differences are over 15 points in Costa Rica, El Salvador, Honduras, Mexico and Peru. Not surprisingly, in several countries there are also major differences between educational levels of workers in both sectors, as was noted earlier. With differences of distribution of this magnitude, public spending can increase overall income inequality quite considerably. Indeed, with a 15 point difference in Gini coefficients, if spending on public sector salaries represents 15 percent of total family incomes, the Gini would drop by 2.2 percentage points, a figure sufficient to cancel out the combined distributive effect of taxes and social spending.

The overall regressive effect of public spending on salaries is nevertheless even greater than these calculations suggest. The reason is that given the importance of the public sector and demand for workers with high educational levels, public employment must have a notable effect on relative wages. At schooling levels of up to nine years, public sector employment represents relatively modest proportions of total spending. But typically, two of every 10 workers who have 11 years of schooling work in the public sector, and of those who have studied in the university, four of every 10 are public employees. In Bo-

Figure 8.32. Distribution of Public Salaries and Private Labor Income

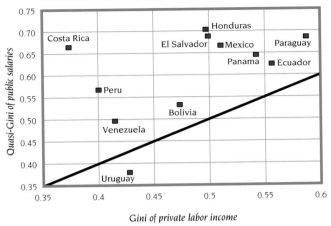

Source: IDB calculations based on recent household surveys.

Figure 8.33. Public Employment by Years of Schooling
(*Percent of public employees/total*)

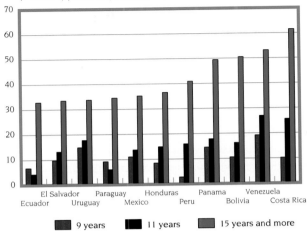

Source: IDB calculations based on recent household surveys.

livia, Venezuela and Costa Rica, over half of the workers with 15 or more years of education are public sector employees (Figure 8.33).

Pressure on pay for more highly trained workers does not necessarily depend on public sector salaries being higher than those in the private sector for workers with the same level of education and experience. (On this point the evidence obtained from household surveys does not display any clear pattern except for the highest income decile, where private sector work offers greater income opportunities than the public sector.) The government need only reduce the (relative) supply of highly trained workers available to the private sector and the result will be a rise in their relative salaries.

As is the case with other aspects of government action previously examined, the real effects of the regressive nature of spending on public sector employment may be less important for overall income distribution than the efficiency with which such spending is made. One way to attract productive, highly trained staff to the public sector is to offer salaries that are competitive with those of the private sector. If the public sector attracts such professionals and employs them efficiently, it may have a very effective way of providing high-quality public services. However, if pay in the public sector is not higher than that offered by the market, or if the people hired are used unproductively, such spending will have a negative impact on lower-income groups, who are more dependent on public services. An extreme case is the Dominican Republic: the Dominican Social Security Institute (IDSS) employs over 15 administrators per 1,000 members, while in prepaid private medical insurance plans this propor-

tion is one for each 1,000 members. Something similar happens with physicians, who are the most highly trained employees and who cost the most money: the IDSS has 4.8 physicians per 1,000 members, while in private companies the ratio is one physician per 1,000 members.[16] In short, properly rewarding the delivery of good service can largely serve greater equity in public sector services, but generously rewarding poor service is a highly regressive practice.

In itself, creating public service employment does not fulfill any redistributive purpose. The creation of public sector employment as an objective in itself, far from providing social protection, contributes indirectly to making fiscal policies regressive in Latin America. It not only redistributes incomes to upper-income strata, but it also raises the relative pay of more highly educated workers, accentuating the differences between rich and poor. If such employees are used efficiently, it can be a progressive channel for government activity, but otherwise, it will be highly regressive.

CONCLUSIONS

The fiscal policies applied in Latin America on the whole seem to be progressive. The countries of the region tax different income groups in proportion to their income level and devote a large amount of funding to social ser-

---

[16] See Santana (1998).

vices, normally in proportion to the percentage that their population represents. Hence, the net effect is that public spending on the poor is much higher as a proportion of household income than spending on rich sectors. Of the various components of social spending, spending on university education and subsidies in the prices of public utilities are the only ones that are clearly regressive. Moreover, Chile is the only country among those for which information is available that unquestionably devotes more resources per household to poor than to wealthy sectors.

But how progressively fiscal resources are collected and distributed is just one aspect of the distributive effect of fiscal policy, and perhaps not the most important one. More important is the effectiveness with which taxes are collected, lower-income groups are provided with adequate services, higher-income group resources are mobilized, well-focused safety nets are created, and economic policies stimulating redistributive growth without sacrificing productivity are adopted. A tax policy that is effective in collecting fiscal revenues, even when it is neutral or slightly regressive in terms of income, can be the most suitable way to mobilize the resources needed to correct income inequality through social spending and specific programs. Social service systems, even if they devote the same amount of resources per household, will only have a significant impact on poverty and inequality if they are effective in providing the health and education services that they are supposed to supply. Similarly, setting a price at below cost for electricity and drinking water represents a considerable waste of resources and is an inefficient approach to providing such services to lower-income groups. The most important conclusion is that to the extent that the services offered by the public sector are more efficient, they will be more useful than policies seeking to be directly redistributive in order to reduce inequities.

Appendix Table 8.1a. Econometric Results: Government Size

Dependent variable:	Size of the government (% of GDP)						
Regression number	1	2	3	4	5	6	7
Constant	-21.97 (-1.81)	-15.96 (-1.37)	32.20 (2.13)	22.39 (7.25)	19.74 (8.74)	28.58 (7.80)	32.74 (8.37)
Per capita income (log)	6.20 (4.27)	5.69 (4.12)	-2.16 (-1.03)				
Dummy for Latin America		-9.20 (-2.86)				-8.00 (-2.79)	-7.41 (-2.68)
Population older than 65 (%)			1.94 (4.89)	1.34 (5.36)	0.96 (2.87)	0.99 (3.72)	-0.09 (-0.18)
Population older than 65 (%) in developed countries					0.57 2.16		0.91 (2.42)
Index of ethno-linguistic fragmentation				-0.08 (-2.03)		-0.13 (-3.06)	-0.13 (-3.22)
Number of observations	61	61	61	59	68	59	59
Adjusted R^2	0.22	0.31	0.44	0.45	0.44	0.51	0.55

Appendix Table 8.1b. Econometric Results: Social Expenditure

Dependent variable:	Social Security expenditure		Social expenditure	
Regression number	8	9	10	11
Constant	-3.37 (-.79)	-34.61 (-5.36)	1.54 (0.88)	-33.91 (-4.27)
Population older than 65 (%)	1.29 (10.50)		1.38 (7.79)	
Per capita income (log)		5.02 (6.65)		5.63 6.06
Dummy for Latin America	1.22 (0.92)	-0.96 (-0.54)	1.61 (0.83)	-1.12 (-0.51)
Number of observations	55	54	55	54
Adjusted R^2	0.69	0.46	0.54	0.41

Appendix Table 8.1c. Econometric Results: Tax Revenues

Dependent variable:	Total tax revenues		Income tax revenues		Excise tax revenues	Sale tax revenues	Compliance of income tax revenue
Regression number	12	13	14	15	16	17	18
Constant	-22.25 (-2.67)	-14.10 (-1.12)	-10.69 (2.79)	-7.07 (-1.25)	0.02 (0.01)	-5.27 (-1.87)	-0.32 (-2.99)
Per capita income (log)	5.58 (5.66)	4.44 (2.71)	2.23 (4.91)	1.72 2.33	0.41 (2.10)	1.17 (3.49)	0.06 (4.84)
Dummy for Latin America	-6.38 (-2.72)	-5.31 (-2.00)	-3.44 (-3.24)	-2.97 (-2.48)	-1.15 (-2.61)	-0.35 (-0.46)	-0.03 (-1.35)
Dummy for developed countries		3.41 (0.87)		1.55 (0.87)			
Number of observations	69	69	67	67	61	61	47
Adjusted R^2	0.38	0.38	0.35	0.35	0.14	0.15	0.35

REFERENCES

Bahl, Roy, Jorge Martínez-Vásquez, and Sally Wallace. 1996. *The Gua-temalan Tax Reform*. Boulder: Westview Press.

Birdsall, N., and R. Hecht. 1995. Swimming Against the Tide: Strategies for Improving Equity in Health. In *Marketising Education and Health in Developing Countries: Miracle or Mirage?*, ed. Christopher Colclough. Oxford: Oxford University Press.

Birdsall, N., and E. James. 1993. Efficiency and Equity in Social Spending: How and Why Governments Misbehave. In *Including the Poor*, eds. Michael Lipton and Jacques van der Gaag. New York: Oxford University.

Bitrán, R. 1998. *Equity in the Financing of Social Security for Health in Chile* Partnerships for Health Reform (PHR). Bethesda, MD: Abt Associates, Inc.

Centro de Estudios Bonaerense. 1997. *Informe de Coyuntura* 7(65/66) May. La Plata, Argentina.

Chisari, Omar O., and Carlos A. Romero. 1997. *Promotion of Equity and Poverty Alleviation in Argentina. An Appraisal of the Consequences of the Recent Economic Reform and CGE Evaluation of Alternative Policies*. Buenos Aires. Unpublished.

Deininger, Klaus, and Lyn Squire. 1996. A New Data Set Measuring Income Inequality. *World Bank Economic Review* 10(3) September: 565-91.

Devarajan, Shanta, and Shaikh I. Hossain. 1995. *The Combined Incidence of Taxes and Public Expenditures in the Philippines*. World Bank. Policy Research Working Paper No. 1543.

Economic Commission for Latin America and the Caribbean (ECLAC). 1997a. *El gasto social en América Latina: Un examen cuantitativo y cualitativo*. Santiago: ECLAC.

⸺. 1997b. *La brecha de la equidad*. Santiago: ECLAC.

Engel, Eduardo, Alexander Galetovic, and Claudio Raddatz. 1997. Taxes and Income Redistribution in Chile: Some Unpleasant Redistributive Rithmetics. National Bureau of Economic Research and Centro de Estudios Públicos. Paper presented at the 10th annual Inter-American Economic Seminar, Santiago.

FIEL. 1995. *El sistema de seguridad social, una propuesta de reforma*. Buenos Aires: FIEL.

Fundación Mexicana para la Salud. 1997. *Observatorio de la salud: necesidades, servicios, políticas*. Mexico City: Fundación Mexicana para la Salud.

Gil Díaz, Francisco. 1987. Some Lessons from Mexico's Tax Reform. In *The Theory of Taxation for Developing Countries*, eds. David Newbery and Nicholas Stern. World Bank Research Publication.

Inter-American Development Bank. 1996. *Economic and Social Progress Report*. Washington, D.C.: IDB.

Jiménez, L., Luis Felipe Ruedi, and Nora Ruedi A. 1998. *Stylized Facts of Income Distribution in Five Countries of Latin America and General Guidelines for a Redistributive Policy*. Santiago: Economic Commission for Latin America and the Caribbean.

Kakwani, Nanak. 1977. Measurement of Tax Progressivity: An International Comparison. *Economic Journal* 87(345): 71-80.

Latinobarómetro. 1997. Cruces Totales Latinobarómetro 1996. Santiago. Mimeo.

Lecaillon, Jacques, Felix Pauqertin, Christian Morrison, and Dimitri Germidis. 1984. Income Distribution and Economic Development. An Analytical Survey. International Labor Organization, Geneva.

Medici, A. 1998. O SUS e a Política "Hood Robin" de Saúde. Inter-American Development Bank. Unpublished.

Milanovic, B. 1995. The Distributional Impact of Cash and In-Kind Transfers in Eastern Europe and Russia. In *Public Spending and the Poor: Theory and Evidence*, eds. D. van de Walle and K. Nead. Washington, D.C.: World Bank.

Morandé, Felipe, and Juan E. Doña. 1997. *Los servicios de agua potable en Chile: Condicionantes, institucionalidad y aspectos de economía política*. IDB-OCE Working Paper Series no. R-308. September.

Reyes Heroles, Jesús. 1988. Las políticas financieras y la distribución del ingreso en México. *El Trimestre Económico* 55(3) July-September: 649-702.

Santana, Isidoro. 1998. Seguridad social y planes privados prepagos en la República Dominicana. In *La organización marca la diferencia: Educación y salud en América Latina*, ed. William Savedoff. Washington, D.C.: Inter-American Development Bank.

Santana, Isidoro and Magdalena Rathe. 1992. *El Impacto Distributivo de la Gestión Fiscal en la República Dominicana*. Santo Domingo: Ediciones de la Fundación Siglo 21.

Steiner, Roberto, and Caroline Soto. 1998. IVA, productividad, evasión y progresividad. Fedesarrollo, Bogota. Mimeo.

UNESCO. 1997. *Statistical Yearbook*. New York: UNESCO Publishing and Bernan Press.

Vélez, Carlos Eduardo. 1996. *Gasto Social y Desigualdad: Logros y Extravíos*. Bogotá: Departamento Nacional de Planeación and Tercer Mundo.

World Bank. 1993a. *World Development Report*. Washington, D.C.: World Bank.

⸺. 1993b. *Uruguay Poverty Assessment: Public Social Expenditures and Their Impact on the Income Distribution*. Washington, D.C.: World Bank.

⸺. 1995. *Brazil: A Poverty Assessment*. Washington, D.C.: World Bank.

⸺. 1996. *Ecuador Poverty Report*. Washington, D.C.: World Bank.

⸺. 1996. *Poverty, Equity and Income: Selected Policies for Expanding Earning Opportunities for the Poor*. Washington, D.C.: World Bank.

⸺. 1997a. *Chile: Poverty and Income Distribution in a High-Growth Economy, 1987-1995*. Washington, D.C.: World Bank.

⸺. 1997b. *Costa Rica: Identifying the Social Needs of the Poor. An Update*. Washington, D.C.: World Bank.

PART FOUR

STATISTICAL APPENDIX

Part 4

STATISTICAL APPENDIX

Prices, Money and Credit and International Reserves

Statistical Profiles, by Country

TABLE A-1. TOTAL POPULATION

Country	1988	1989	1990	1991	1992	1993	1994	1995	1996	1997p	1970 1980	1980 1990	1990 1997
					Thousands						In Percent		
Argentina	31,636	32,081	32,527	32,974	33,421	33,869	34,318	34,768	35,220	35,672	1.6	1.5	1.3
Bahamas	247	251	256	260	264	268	272	276	280	284	2.4	2.0	1.5
Barbados	255	256	257	258	259	260	261	262	263	264	0.4	0.3	0.4
Belize	179	184	189	194	199	204	209	215	221	227	1.8	2.5	2.6
Bolivia	6,283	6,425	6,573	6,729	6,894	7,064	7,238	7,414	7,592	7,773	2.4	2.1	2.4
Brazil	143,078	145,593	148,030	150,375	152,641	154,849	157,022	159,182	161,314	163,404	2.4	2.0	1.5
Chile	12,667	12,883	13,100	13,320	13,545	13,771	13,994	14,210	14,419	14,622	1.6	1.6	1.6
Colombia	31,307	31,953	32,596	33,239	33,887	34,534	35,178	35,814	36,442	37,065	2.2	2.1	1.9
Costa Rica	2,876	2,956	3,035	3,113	3,191	3,269	3,347	3,424	3,500	3,575	2.8	2.9	2.4
Dominican Republic	6,815	6,964	7,110	7,255	7,399	7,542	7,684	7,823	7,961	8,097	2.6	2.3	1.9
Ecuador	9,794	10,029	10,264	10,502	10,741	10,981	11,221	11,460	11,698	11,937	2.9	2.6	2.2
El Salvador	4,858	4,938	5,031	5,139	5,262	5,395	5,530	5,662	5,792	5,924	2.5	1.1	2.3
Guatemala	8,325	8,532	8,749	8,978	9,215	9,462	9,715	9,976	10,244	10,519	2.7	2.5	2.7
Guyana	792	794	796	802	809	817	825	835	844	854	0.8	0.5	0.9
Haiti	6,227	6,355	6,486	6,619	6,754	6,893	7,035	7,180	7,329	7,482	1.7	1.9	2.1
Honduras	4,592	4,734	4,879	5,028	5,180	5,336	5,494	5,654	5,816	5,981	3.2	3.2	3.0
Jamaica	2,344	2,355	2,366	2,382	2,398	2,414	2,431	2,447	2,465	2,483	1.3	1.1	0.7
Mexico	80,117	81,666	83,226	84,803	86,391	87,983	89,571	91,145	92,712	94,275	3.0	2.1	1.8
Nicaragua	3,411	3,484	3,568	3,667	3,776	3,891	4,008	4,124	4,236	4,349	3.1	2.5	2.8
Panama	2,305	2,351	2,398	2,444	2,491	2,538	2,585	2,631	2,677	2,722	2.6	2.1	1.8
Paraguay	3,969	4,095	4,219	4,340	4,460	4,580	4,703	4,828	4,958	5,089	2.8	3.1	2.8
Peru	20,751	21,163	21,569	21,966	22,354	22,740	23,130	23,532	23,947	24,371	2.8	2.2	1.8
Suriname	391	395	400	404	409	414	418	423	428	433	-0.2	1.0	1.1
Trinidad and Tobago	1,205	1,220	1,236	1,250	1,264	1,278	1,292	1,306	1,320	1,335	1.1	1.3	1.1
Uruguay	3,060	3,077	3,094	3,112	3,131	3,149	3,168	3,186	3,204	3,221	0.4	0.6	0.6
Venezuela	18,542	19,025	19,502	19,972	20,441	20,910	21,377	21,844	22,311	22,777	3.5	2.6	2.3
Latin America	**406,028**	**413,758**	**421,454**	**429,123**	**436,776**	**444,412**	**452,027**	**459,622**	**467,191**	**474,736**	**2.5**	**2.1**	**1.7**

Source: IDB estimates based on data from the Latin America Demographic Center and the United Nations Population Division.

TABLE A-2. URBAN AND RURAL POPULATION

	1980			1990			1997p			Average Annual Growth Rates: Urban			Average Annual Growth Rates: Rural
	Urban	Rural	% Urban	Urban	Rural	% Urban	Urban	Rural	% Urban	1970 1980	1980 1990	1990 1997	1990 1997
Country	Thousands									In Percent			
Argentina	23,401	4,693	83.3	27,887	4,640	85.7	30,970	4,702	86.8	2.2	1.8	1.5	0.2
Bahamas	123	87	58.6	161	95	63.1	193	90	68.1	2.1	3.0	2.6	-0.5
Barbados	100	149	40.1	114	143	44.4	124	141	46.8	1.1	1.3	1.2	-0.3
Belize	75	71	51.7	90	99	47.7	108	118	47.8	...	1.8	2.5	2.7
Bolivia	2,365	2,990	44.2	3,435	3,137	52.3	4,701	3,072	60.5	3.2	3.8	4.5	-0.2
Brazil	80,334	41,338	66.0	112,643	35,387	76.1	135,272	28,132	82.8	4.2	3.5	2.7	-3.1
Chile	9,054	2,093	81.2	11,314	1,786	86.4	12,900	1,723	88.2	2.3	2.2	1.9	-0.6
Colombia	17,200	9,325	64.8	23,079	9,517	70.8	27,717	9,349	74.8	3.5	3.0	2.7	-0.2
Costa Rica	985	1,299	43.1	1,420	1,615	46.8	1,780	1,795	49.8	3.7	3.7	3.3	1.6
Dominican Republic	2,877	2,820	50.5	4,329	2,781	60.9	5,429	2,668	67.1	5.0	4.2	3.3	-0.6
Ecuador	3,739	4,223	47.0	5,775	4,490	56.3	7,452	4,485	62.4	4.7	4.2	3.8	0.0
El Salvador	1,880	2,667	41.3	2,332	2,699	46.4	2,941	2,983	49.6	3.0	2.2	3.3	1.4
Guatemala	2,587	4,233	37.9	3,628	5,121	41.5	4,729	5,790	45.0	3.4	3.4	3.8	1.8
Guyana	232	527	30.5	261	535	32.8	316	538	37.0	1.1	1.1	2.6	0.0
Haiti	1,272	4,081	23.8	1,840	4,646	28.4	2,422	5,060	32.4	3.7	3.7	4.0	1.2
Honduras	1,281	2,287	35.9	2,132	2,747	43.7	2,953	3,028	49.4	5.5	5.2	4.8	1.4
Jamaica	1,017	1,116	47.7	1,319	1,047	55.7	1,610	873	64.8	2.8	2.6	2.9	-2.5
Mexico	42,783	24,787	63.3	58,971	24,255	70.9	71,008	23,267	75.3	4.2	3.3	2.7	-0.6
Nicaragua	1,480	1,310	53.1	2,313	1,255	64.8	3,273	1,076	75.3	4.4	4.5	5.0	-2.0
Panama	970	980	49.7	1,281	1,116	53.4	1,518	1,205	55.8	3.2	3.0	2.5	1.1
Paraguay	1,312	1,802	42.1	2,030	2,189	48.1	2,685	2,404	52.8	4.1	4.5	4.1	1.4
Peru	11,153	6,171	64.4	15,132	6,437	70.2	17,385	6,986	71.3	4.0	3.1	2.1	1.0
Suriname	158	197	44.5	173	227	43.1	201	232	46.4	...	0.8	2.1	0.4
Trinidad and Tobago	616	466	56.9	839	397	67.9	883	452	66.2	5.1	3.3	0.8	1.7
Uruguay	2,442	472	83.8	2,644	450	85.4	2,795	426	86.8	0.6	0.8	0.8	-0.7
Venezuela	12,510	2,581	82.9	17,859	1,643	91.6	21,588	1,189	94.8	4.9	3.7	2.8	-4.5
Latin America	**221,946**	**122,763**	**64.4**	**303,001**	**118,453**	**71.9**	**362,953**	**111,783**	**77.7**	**3.8**	**3.2**	**2.7**	**-0.8**

Source: IDB estimates based on data from the Latin America Demographic Center and the United Nations Population Division.

TABLE B-1. GROSS DOMESTIC PRODUCT

Country	1988	1989	1990	1991	1992	1993	1994	1995	1996	1997p	1970 1980	1980 1990	1990 1997
					Millions of 1990 U.S. Dollars						In Percent		
Argentina	166,852	155,364	153,216	169,073	186,470	198,057	214,798	205,008	214,308	232,310	2.6	-0.9	5.2
Bahamas	3,085	3,147	3,134	3,050	2,989	3,039	3,067	3,076	3,205	3,317	...	2.8	0.7
Barbados	1,710	1,796	1,711	1,660	1,578	1,601	1,673	1,711	1,801	1,874	2.8	1.5	0.5
Belize	320	362	402	413	445	464	474	498	505	513	...	...	4.4
Bolivia	5,086	5,279	5,524	5,815	5,910	6,163	6,450	6,752	7,029	7,323	4.4	0.0	4.2
Brazil	440,504	454,445	435,458	436,929	433,332	451,480	478,537	498,810	513,775	529,195	8.7	2.3	1.9
Chile	28,948	32,004	33,188	35,833	40,232	43,043	45,500	50,336	54,044	57,861	2.5	3.4	7.7
Colombia	45,234	46,743	48,547	49,337	51,284	54,272	57,624	61,052	62,328	64,412	5.6	3.8	4.1
Costa Rica	5,349	5,635	5,838	5,959	6,406	6,805	7,106	7,258	7,219	7,441	5.6	2.2	3.5
Dominican Rep.	6,061	6,340	5,985	6,018	6,513	6,705	7,009	7,350	7,897	8,556	7.3	2.3	3.8
Ecuador	12,657	12,573	12,975	13,694	14,228	14,613	15,323	15,714	16,032	16,621	9.4	2.0	3.6
El Salvador	6,187	5,101	5,348	5,539	5,957	6,396	6,783	7,217	7,365	7,663	...	-1.5	5.2
Guatemala	7,354	7,644	7,881	8,170	8,565	8,902	9,261	9,719	10,005	10,411	5.7	1.1	3.9
Guyana	406	382	369	400	432	488	529	556	597	634	1.6	-3.1	6.5
Haiti	2,147	2,115	2,051	1,989	1,695	1,650	1,475	1,541	1,582	1,600	4.4	-0.3	-3.4
Honduras	2,960	3,088	3,091	3,191	3,371	3,581	3,531	3,683	3,820	4,006	5.3	2.3	3.3
Jamaica	3,660	3,914	4,125	4,157	4,228	4,288	4,343	4,376	4,313	4,253	0.1	1.5	1.0
Mexico	245,921	254,196	265,948	275,636	283,519	285,284	298,530	279,204	294,191	315,563	6.6	2.3	2.7
Nicaragua	1,780	1,768	1,766	1,764	1,775	1,758	1,836	1,923	2,023	2,137	0.0	-1.1	2.4
Panama	4,879	4,942	5,313	5,791	6,249	6,569	6,758	6,899	7,066	7,357	6.7	3.7	5.1
Paraguay	5,765	6,093	6,271	6,414	6,528	6,792	6,983	7,307	7,387	7,576	8.4	3.7	2.8
Peru	44,618	38,792	36,869	37,953	37,636	39,852	45,403	49,048	50,127	53,836	4.0	-0.6	4.2
Suriname	313	328	329	338	302	264	258	275	294	308	3.7	-1.2	-0.8
Trinidad & Tobago	4,979	4,932	4,987	5,150	5,077	5,003	5,221	5,355	5,545	5,730	5.1	-2.1	1.9
Uruguay	8,177	8,282	8,355	8,624	9,303	9,582	10,190	10,011	10,539	11,072	3.2	1.0	3.7
Venezuela	60,392	55,262	59,411	65,385	70,208	69,817	68,095	70,639	70,374	74,423	4.0	0.7	3.8
Latin America	**1,115,343**	**1,120,527**	**1,118,092**	**1,158,280**	**1,194,232**	**1,236,465**	**1,306,758**	**1,315,319**	**1,363,371**	**1,435,992**	**6.0**	**1.6**	**3.1**

TABLE B-2. GROSS DOMESTIC PRODUCT PER CAPITA

Country	1988	1989	1990	1991	1992	1993	1994	1995	1996	1997p	1970 1980	1980 1990	1990 1997
					1990 Dollars						In Percent		
Argentina	5,274	4,843	4,710	5,128	5,579	5,848	6,259	5,896	6,085	6,512	1.0	-2.4	4.3
Bahamas	12,492	12,515	12,243	11,735	11,328	11,349	11,280	11,145	11,452	11,694	...	0.7	-1.0
Barbados	6,696	7,010	6,656	6,435	6,092	6,158	6,410	6,532	6,847	7,092	2.4	1.2	0.2
Belize	1,786	1,968	2,128	2,130	2,235	2,271	2,261	2,318	2,289	2,261	...	...	2.0
Bolivia	809	822	840	864	857	872	891	911	926	942	2.0	-2.0	2.0
Brazil	3,079	3,121	2,942	2,906	2,839	2,916	3,048	3,134	3,185	3,239	6.1	0.3	0.5
Chile	2,285	2,484	2,534	2,690	2,970	3,126	3,251	3,542	3,748	3,957	0.8	1.7	6.9
Colombia	1,445	1,463	1,489	1,484	1,513	1,572	1,638	1,705	1,710	1,738	3.3	1.7	2.5
Costa Rica	1,860	1,906	1,924	1,914	2,007	2,081	2,123	2,120	2,063	2,081	2.7	-0.7	1.3
Dominican Rep.	889	910	842	829	880	889	912	940	992	1,057	4.6	0.1	2.2
Ecuador	1,292	1,254	1,264	1,304	1,325	1,331	1,366	1,371	1,370	1,392	6.3	-0.6	1.5
El Salvador	1,274	1,033	1,063	1,078	1,132	1,186	1,227	1,275	1,271	1,293	...	-2.5	3.3
Guatemala	883	896	901	910	929	941	953	974	977	990	2.9	-1.4	1.4
Guyana	513	481	464	499	534	597	641	666	707	743	0.8	-3.5	6.4
Haiti	345	333	316	300	251	239	210	215	216	214	2.6	-2.1	-6.1
Honduras	644	652	633	635	651	671	643	652	657	670	2.0	-0.9	0.4
Jamaica	1,562	1,662	1,744	1,745	1,763	1,776	1,787	1,788	1,750	1,713	-1.2	0.4	0.4
Mexico	3,070	3,113	3,195	3,250	3,282	3,242	3,333	3,063	3,173	3,347	3.5	0.1	1.0
Nicaragua	522	508	495	481	470	452	458	466	478	491	-2.9	-3.5	-0.5
Panama	2,117	2,102	2,216	2,369	2,508	2,588	2,615	2,622	2,640	2,702	5.4	0.6	0.0
Paraguay	1,452	1,488	1,487	1,478	1,464	1,483	1,485	1,513	1,490	1,489	1.2	-2.8	2.7
Peru	2,150	1,833	1,709	1,728	1,684	1,752	1,963	2,084	2,093	2,209	3.9	-2.2	-2.2
Suriname	802	830	823	836	738	639	616	650	687	712	3.9	-3.4	0.9
Trinidad & Tobago	4,132	4,041	4,035	4,121	4,018	3,916	4,042	4,101	4,199	4,292	2.8	0.3	3.6
Uruguay	2,672	2,692	2,700	2,771	2,972	3,043	3,217	3,142	3,290	3,437	0.5	-1.9	1.7
Venezuela	3,257	2,905	3,046	3,274	3,435	3,339	3,185	3,234	3,154	3,267	0.5	-1.9	1.7
Latin America	**2,747**	**2,708**	**2,653**	**2,699**	**2,734**	**2,782**	**2,891**	**2,862**	**2,918**	**3,025**	**3.3**	**-0.4**	**1.6**

TABLE B-3. TOTAL CONSUMPTION

Country	1988	1989	1990	1991	1992	1993	1994	1995	1996	1997p	1970 1980	1980 1990	1990 1997
					Millions of 1990 U.S. Dollars							In Percent	
Argentina	131,060	124,304	123,815	138,839	154,472	162,374	172,378	164,155	172,351	183,318	2.5	-0.2	5.0
Bahamas	...	...	...	...	...	...	...	...	...	...	...	...	...
Barbados	1,380	1,432	1,393	1,411	1,350	1,343	1,370	1,413	...	...	0.3	2.5	...
Belize	258	279	292	318	325	333	346	375	362	370	...	...	3.6
Bolivia	4,670	4,797	4,941	5,095	5,252	5,439	5,650	5,849	5,974	6,168	5.3	0.6	3.2
Brazil[1]	332,003	345,086	341,380	346,248	344,468	362,190	387,294	418,297	432,751	447,735	8.3	2.8	3.3
Chile	21,093	22,679	23,134	25,165	27,987	29,453	31,598	33,451	36,019	38,284	1.6	2.2	6.8
Colombia	35,138	36,600	37,722	38,483	39,418	41,051	43,476	46,227	47,897	49,386	5.6	3.6	3.8
Costa Rica	4,210	4,436	4,626	4,706	4,968	5,281	5,559	5,720	5,840	5,851	4.9	1.8	3.5
Dominican Rep.	5,973	5,878	4,882	5,601	6,287	6,186	6,411	7,331	7,864	9,156	7.4	1.1	5.7
Ecuador	9,120	8,991	9,824	9,277	9,835	10,413	10,659	10,720	11,652	11,270	8.1	3.0	2.9
El Salvador	5,660	4,578	5,258	5,416	5,819	6,264	6,730	7,341	7,466	7,581	...	-0.4	6.5
Guatemala	6,678	6,875	7,053	7,364	7,990	8,294	8,733	9,149	9,234	9,647	5.3	1.2	4.3
Guyana	368	299	282	285	261	327	372	387	421	...	0.1	-4.5	...
Haiti	2,054	2,039	1,998	2,060	1,808	1,910	1,672	1,921	1,938	1,956	4.8	0.1	-0.5
Honduras	2,405	2,534	2,475	2,528	2,627	2,669	2,642	2,860	2,879	3,001	5.5	2.7	2.1
Jamaica	2,924	3,129	3,149	3,150	2,957	3,042	3,091	2,773	3,170	...	4.7	2.1	...
Mexico	180,569	193,993	207,513	219,295	226,964	228,940	238,892	221,815	222,754	234,407	6.4	2.7	2.4
Nicaragua	1,992	1,760	1,715	1,880	1,845	1,730	1,747	1,768	1,714	1,859	2.4	-1.3	0.7
Panama	3,912	4,436	4,168	4,678	4,829	4,908	4,857	4,805	5,418	5,497	3.1	2.1	2.7
Paraguay	4,465	4,537	5,051	5,255	5,648	5,902	6,728	6,927	7,116	7,285	6.8	4.9	6.1
Peru	35,865	30,049	29,045	30,260	30,348	31,457	34,543	37,092	38,391	40,406	3.0	0.0	3.8
Suriname	244	225	256	277	235	191	155	188	232	255	4.9	-1.0	1.6
Trinidad & Tobago	3,820	3,652	3,437	3,892	3,680	3,817	3,426	3,574	3,734	3,992	5.7	-2.3	1.1
Uruguay	7,034	7,005	6,940	7,239	7,994	8,462	9,003	8,875	9,352	9,816	2.2	1.3	4.3
Venezuela	44,482	42,230	43,986	48,186	52,377	51,749	49,622	49,929	47,856	50,414	12.5	0.1	2.2
Latin America[2]	847,376	861,823	874,333	916,908	949,745	983,727	1,036,957	1,052,944	1,082,386	1,127,655	6.0	1.9	3.4

[1] Includes changes in inventories from 1987. [2] Latin American aggregate excludes Barbados (1996-97), Guyana (1997), and Jamaica (1997).

TABLE B-4. GROSS DOMESTIC INVESTMENT

Country	1988	1989	1990	1991	1992	1993	1994	1995	1996	1997p	1970 1980	1980 1990	1990 1997
					Millions of 1990 U.S. Dollars							In Percent	
Argentina	32,253	25,286	21,446	28,210	37,666	43,695	53,205	44,555	48,253	61,330	4.1	-6.3	11.7
Bahamas	...	...	...	...	...	...	...	...	...	...	...	...	...
Barbados	289	340	322	287	140	206	212	227	...	...	4.2	0.6	...
Belize	86	113	115	124	127	147	113	113	109	114	...	...	0.2
Bolivia	693	588	692	895	943	942	842	946	1,143	1,415	1.6	-4.4	11.6
Brazil[1]	96,581	97,731	87,092	85,510	78,129	83,718	94,261	106,914	108,812	118,090	9.5	-1.1	2.4
Chile	6,535	8,268	8,719	8,782	10,689	12,955	13,035	17,536	18,843	21,251	3.3	3.8	12.5
Colombia	9,831	9,121	9,004	8,229	11,631	16,064	20,320	22,322	22,011	22,895	7.0	2.0	12.2
Costa Rica	1,384	1,524	1,595	1,382	1,908	2,157	2,035	1,896	1,579	2,100	9.7	1.3	4.1
Dominican Rep.	1,614	1,790	1,505	1,353	1,681	1,806	1,919	2,484	2,735	3,290	11.6	1.5	7.9
Ecuador	2,872	3,088	2,265	3,568	3,227	2,888	3,164	3,563	2,586	3,696	10.7	-5.1	2.3
El Salvador	702	886	741	870	1,116	1,226	1,401	1,614	1,282	1,355	...	-3.2	5.5
Guatemala	1,102	1,123	1,072	1,257	1,622	1,611	1,610	1,643	1,441	1,471	5.0	-2.9	3.4
Guyana	74	125	156	131	129	136	145	159	159	...	0.6	0.4	...
Haiti	242	247	250	230	60	55	24	45	45	44	14.8	-1.9	-19.4
Honduras	722	686	710	845	935	1,206	1,308	1,165	1,229	1,254	5.8	-0.6	7.8
Jamaica	943	1,121	1,150	1,219	1,158	1,146	1,162	1,599	1,111	...	-8.6	3.2	...
Mexico	55,060	56,466	61,545	65,921	77,925	74,858	83,621	49,336	68,789	83,587	9.1	-0.1	5.0
Nicaragua	464	390	340	368	382	375	510	601	719	806	0.3	-2.8	9.5
Panama	431	302	894	1,091	1,523	1,827	2,062	2,231	1,673	1,861	5.0	-1.4	25.5
Paraguay	1,185	1,308	1,434	1,538	1,439	1,473	1,539	1,653	1,652	1,699	16.1	2.8	3.3
Peru	9,561	7,552	7,790	8,004	8,235	9,246	12,167	14,571	13,731	15,538	7.8	-2.0	9.4
Suriname	54	70	70	75	70	67	90	74	86	73	5.2	-2.3	0.4
Trinidad & Tobago	600	710	689	717	539	555	803	691	771	693	17.5	-9.1	-0.3
Uruguay	1,025	1,003	916	1,140	1,343	1,553	1,594	1,557	1,695	1,833	8.2	-6.5	7.8
Venezuela	15,540	6,867	6,071	11,716	16,465	13,226	8,814	12,936	11,412	13,047	4.7	-8.9	8.4
Latin America[2]	239,841	226,706	216,584	233,464	259,082	273,137	305,957	290,432	311,863	357,442	7.6	-1.7	5.9

[1] Excludes Changes in Inventories from 1987. [2] Latin American aggregate excludes Barbados (1996-97), Guyana (1997), and Jamaica (1997).

TABLE B-5. EXPORTS OF GOODS AND SERVICES[1]

Country	1988	1989	1990	1991	1992	1993	1994	1995	1996	1997p	1970 1980	1980 1990	1990 1997
					Millions of 1990 U.S. Dollars							In Percent	
Argentina	11,787	12,668	14,800	14,045	14,340	14,682	17,018	20,885	22,201	23,910	5.0	4.1	8.3
Bahamas	...	...	...	...	...	...	...	...	...	...	...	...	...
Barbados	891	984	873	837	779	803	878	891	...	...	8.3	0.4	...
Belize	202	230	245	246	293	295	301	290	293	323	...	...	4.4
Bolivia	706	879	977	1,048	1,060	1,116	1,284	1,401	1,496	1,488	1.5	2.0	6.8
Brazil	35,214	37,004	35,170	35,039	41,446	46,893	46,893	44,845	45,760	49,421	10.3	8.4	3.7
Chile	6,638	7,708	8,372	9,413	10,724	11,103	12,394	13,755	15,135	16,640	9.5	6.8	10.1
Colombia	6,808	7,381	8,679	9,717	10,260	10,898	10,903	11,797	12,292	13,533	5.2	5.1	7.9
Costa Rica	1,567	1,815	1,963	2,138	2,398	2,668	2,878	3,090	3,370	3,508	6.6	5.4	8.6
Dominican Rep.	1,584	1,675	1,832	1,578	1,733	1,862	2,084	4,558	4,922	5,562	8.8	0.1	16.2
Ecuador	3,013	2,962	3,263	3,605	3,951	4,117	4,474	4,696	4,866	5,040	13.2	4.5	6.9
El Salvador	909	786	973	968	1,031	1,342	1,455	1,658	1,768	2,213	...	-4.8	13.8
Guatemala	1,299	1,471	1,568	1,491	1,615	1,771	1,830	2,060	2,242	2,508	5.7	-1.4	6.9
Guyana	249	250	251	292	404	418	447	456	493	...	-2.3	-3.8	...
Haiti	320	314	318	284	148	202	131	198	211	228	7.6	-0.7	-3.9
Honduras	978	1,027	1,033	1,012	1,092	1,080	971	1,103	1,192	1,203	4.3	0.3	2.0
Jamaica	1,946	1,952	2,217	2,352	2,470	2,575	2,660	2,851	2,994	...	-0.1	3.9	...
Mexico	46,045	47,090	48,805	51,043	51,902	53,842	63,235	84,095	99,828	117,099	7.8	7.2	12.1
Nicaragua	251	332	392	333	400	415	455	527	726	755	1.4	-4.7	10.8
Panama	3,379	3,791	4,438	6,185	5,663	5,075	4,901	5,380	5,416	6,163	9.9	6.2	6.3
Paraguay	1,448	1,571	1,880	2,018	1,936	2,702	2,877	3,362	2,972	2,948	10.5	5.5	8.2
Peru	4,080	4,844	4,120	4,594	4,631	4,796	5,693	6,130	6,824	7,725	3.3	-2.6	6.0
Suriname	92	124	93	67	146	76	78	108	107	126	4.5	-7.4	0.2
Trinidad & Tobago	2,037	1,969	2,289	2,486	2,474	2,522	2,682	2,957	3,117	3,257	1.9	1.9	6.5
Uruguay	1,736	1,916	2,159	2,215	2,433	2,499	3,019	2,992	3,293	3,726	7.0	4.6	8.7
Venezuela	15,560	16,423	18,806	19,608	19,208	21,517	23,252	24,224	26,247	28,862	-3.5	1.7	7.3
Latin America[2]	**148,737**	**157,166**	**165,513**	**172,616**	**182,537**	**195,269**	**212,794**	**244,309**	**267,765**	**296,238**	**4.6**	**4.9**	**8.2**

[1] Non-Factor Services. [2] Latin American aggregate excludes Barbados (1996-97), Guyana (1997), and Jamaica (1997).

TABLE B-6. IMPORTS OF GOODS AND SERVICES[1]

Country	1988	1989	1990	1991	1992	1993	1994	1995	1996	1997p	1970 1980	1980 1990	1990 1997
					Millions of 1990 U.S. Dollars							In Percent	
Argentina	8,248	6,894	6,846	12,020	20,009	22,694	27,802	24,587	28,497	36,248	9.0	-3.8	23.1
Bahamas	...	...	...	...	...	...	...	...	...	...	...	...	...
Barbados	849	961	878	876	692	751	788	820	...	...	4.4	1.6	...
Belize	225	259	248	276	301	311	286	279	259	295	...	...	1.6
Bolivia	982	985	1,086	1,223	1,344	1,335	1,326	1,444	1,584	1,747	3.0	0.6	7.4
Brazil	23,294	25,377	28,184	29,868	30,710	41,322	49,912	71,246	73,548	86,051	9.2	-0.1	16.5
Chile	5,319	6,651	7,037	7,526	9,168	10,468	11,527	14,406	15,953	18,314	4.6	3.2	13.5
Colombia	6,544	6,359	6,858	7,093	10,025	13,741	17,074	19,294	19,872	21,403	7.4	2.1	16.4
Costa Rica	1,812	2,141	2,346	2,267	2,868	3,302	3,367	3,448	3,570	4,018	7.6	3.1	8.2
Dominican Rep.	3,109	3,003	2,233	2,514	3,188	3,149	3,406	7,023	7,624	9,453	10.1	-1.9	15.4
Ecuador	2,348	2,469	2,377	2,757	2,785	2,806	2,973	3,266	3,073	3,384	9.8	-1.1	4.0
El Salvador	1,083	1,148	1,624	1,715	2,009	2,437	2,803	3,396	3,152	3,486	...	-1.6	14.9
Guatemala	1,724	1,825	1,812	1,943	2,662	2,774	2,912	3,133	2,912	3,214	4.5	-3.0	7.3
Guyana	285	292	320	308	363	393	436	446	477	...	-2.8	-3.6	...
Haiti	469	486	515	584	322	516	352	624	611	628	14.5	-0.2	3.3
Honduras	1,146	1,160	1,127	1,194	1,284	1,374	1,389	1,445	1,480	1,452	5.1	-0.5	2.9
Jamaica	2,152	2,287	2,390	2,565	2,357	2,475	2,570	2,847	2,961	...	-1.0	5.9	...
Mexico	35,753	43,353	51,915	60,624	73,272	72,357	87,218	76,043	97,179	119,530	12.0	4.4	13.5
Nicaragua	927	714	682	817	852	763	876	972	1,136	1,284	7.2	1.2	7.6
Panama	2,843	3,588	4,187	6,163	5,765	5,242	5,062	5,517	5,441	6,164	5.7	2.8	7.0
Paraguay	1,334	1,323	2,093	2,397	2,495	3,284	4,161	4,635	4,353	4,356	11.2	8.1	16.1
Peru	4,888	3,652	4,086	4,906	5,577	5,647	6,999	8,745	8,819	9,834	4.3	-1.4	13.2
Suriname	76	91	90	80	150	70	66	95	131	146	6.6	-7.6	6.0
Trinidad & Tobago	1,477	1,399	1,427	1,946	1,616	1,891	1,690	1,868	2,077	2,212	13.1	-2.9	5.9
Uruguay	1,618	1,641	1,659	1,970	2,468	2,932	3,427	3,413	3,801	4,304	6.7	-0.2	12.8
Venezuela	15,190	10,259	9,451	14,125	17,841	16,675	13,594	16,449	15,141	17,899	9.2	-7.1	7.2
Latin America[2]	**123,696**	**128,316**	**141,472**	**167,757**	**200,121**	**218,708**	**252,017**	**275,442**	**303,651**	**355,422**	**8.9**	**0.6**	**13.6**

[1] Non-Factor Services. [2] Latin American aggregate excludes Barbados (1996-97), Guyana (1997), and Jamaica (1997).

TABLE B-7. VALUE ADDED BY AGRICULTURE, FORESTRY AND FISHING

Country	1988	1989	1990	1991	1992	1993	1994	1995	1996	1997p	Average Annual Growth Rates 1970 1980	1980 1990	1990 1997
					Millions of 1990 U.S. Dollars						In Percent		
Argentina	12,559	11,481	12,446	12,976	12,852	13,249	13,730	14,050	14,275	14,346	2.4	0.7	2.8
Bahamas	...	...	...	...	...	...	...	...	...	...	...	...	...
Barbados	81	74	79	77	69	66	66	66	77	79	-0.6	-1.8	0.9
Belize	61	65	74	76	87	87	89	95	103	115	...	...	7.3
Bolivia	823	811	848	932	892	929	779	790	824	863	5.7	1.7	0.8
Brazil	29,821	30,671	29,530	30,346	31,976	31,583	33,942	35,941	37,063	...	5.4	3.1	...
Chile	2,509	2,666	2,909	2,979	3,344	3,441	3,701	3,957	4,109	4,101	2.3	5.8	5.5
Colombia	7,141	7,448	7,882	8,210	8,059	8,320	8,398	8,838	8,856	8,873	4.3	2.9	2.2
Costa Rica	837	899	922	979	1,019	1,043	1,074	1,117	1,113	1,105	2.7	2.8	2.6
Dominican Rep.	934	955	873	910	965	972	954	1,012	1,108	1,146	3.1	0.8	2.3
Ecuador	1,598	1,641	1,740	1,844	1,907	1,875	1,948	2,010	2,081	2,146	3.5	4.3	3.4
El Salvador	863	859	915	912	985	960	937	980	999	995	...	-1.8	1.9
Guatemala	1,901	1,959	2,040	2,103	2,166	2,211	2,268	2,347	2,407	2,474	4.8	1.3	3.0
Guyana	148	140	124	139	164	172	188	202	214	218	0.1	-3.3	5.7
Haiti	716	708	682	681	674	657	645	580	579	564	1.4	-0.7	-2.8
Honduras	555	610	617	655	678	674	680	739	758	782	2.3	2.6	3.1
Jamaica	263	239	267	266	301	331	356	363	375	338	0.7	0.3	4.4
Mexico	20,162	19,708	20,871	21,072	20,863	21,158	21,352	21,564	21,814	22,120	3.4	1.6	1.5
Nicaragua	502	548	548	525	537	536	601	635	682	743	-0.9	-2.5	3.9
Panama	470	498	504	510	533	534	548	572	576	570	0.8	2.4	1.7
Paraguay	1,582	1,706	1,742	1,726	1,726	1,825	1,810	1,961	1,986	2,068	6.3	4.5	2.4
Peru	3,008	2,865	2,681	2,733	2,566	2,832	3,265	3,426	3,623	3,754	0.4	1.4	3.4
Suriname	34	33	33	39	39	38	35	34	33	32	3.5	0.6	-0.6
Trinidad & Tobago	101	107	125	129	127	138	139	135	140	139	-0.6	-1.3	3.3
Uruguay	913	946	947	969	1,084	1,045	1,140	1,176	1,275	1,261	1.4	1.7	3.7
Venezuela	3,427	3,251	3,201	3,276	3,344	3,445	3,407	3,389	3,454	3,548	3.3	2.0	1.1
Latin America	**91,010**	**90,888**	**92,598**	**95,064**	**96,955**	**98,120**	**102,053**	**105,979**	**108,522**	**...**	**3.8**	**2.1**	**...**

TABLE B-8. VALUE ADDED BY INDUSTRY

Country	1988	1989	1990	1991	1992	1993	1994	1995	1996	1997p	Average Annual Growth Rates 1970 1980	1980 1990	1990 1997
					Millions of 1990 U.S. Dollars						In Percent		
Argentina	63,394	57,131	55,194	61,195	68,028	72,552	78,312	73,674	77,540	...	2.1	-2.3	...
Bahamas	...	...	...	...	...	...	...	...	...	...	...	...	...
Barbados	259	275	270	207	232	231	243	260	266	276	2.5	1.2	0.0
Belize	70	81	90	94	102	111	106	109	107	109	...	...	3.7
Bolivia	1,523	1,645	1,761	1,835	1,868	1,970	2,062	2,206	2,280	2,359	3.4	-1.3	4.6
Brazil	149,583	153,903	141,087	138,293	132,850	141,715	151,659	154,412	158,303	...	9.1	1.1	...
Chile	12,403	13,446	13,639	14,771	15,914	16,936	17,803	19,313	20,735	22,074	1.8	3.5	6.4
Colombia	16,749	17,502	17,831	17,925	18,290	19,023	19,925	21,077	21,205	21,714	5.0	5.1	2.7
Costa Rica	1,399	1,465	1,500	1,518	1,653	1,775	1,851	1,890	1,816	1,917	8.3	1.8	3.4
Dominican Rep.	2,001	2,122	1,989	1,922	2,180	2,230	2,420	2,476	2,657	2,952	10.4	2.6	4.2
Ecuador	5,342	5,025	4,935	5,171	5,383	5,669	6,077	6,237	6,293	6,527	13.7	0.9	3.3
El Salvador	1,363	1,400	1,430	1,488	1,625	1,618	1,747	1,864	1,896	2,043	...	-2.7	4.8
Guatemala	1,485	1,537	1,560	1,599	1,714	1,770	1,823	1,911	1,965	2,072	7.0	0.4	3.8
Guyana	94	81	81	92	95	114	123	125	140	156	-0.4	-5.8	8.6
Haiti	511	509	472	417	286	283	195	226	242	251	7.1	-1.6	-8.5
Honduras	685	731	725	731	812	890	832	882	919	952	5.6	2.6	3.4
Jamaica	1,447	1,666	1,781	1,748	1,756	1,745	1,745	1,746	1,733	...	-1.9	1.8	...
Mexico	67,556	71,467	75,578	78,196	80,559	80,653	84,379	78,350	86,475	94,432	7.2	2.3	3.5
Nicaragua	397	386	377	392	381	383	394	418	442	465	0.9	-0.6	2.4
Panama	735	706	778	897	988	1,137	1,185	1,201	1,241	1,288	5.3	0.1	7.8
Paraguay	1,485	1,562	1,605	1,643	1,684	1,743	1,819	1,908	1,913	1,943	10.6	3.5	2.8
Peru	17,189	14,673	14,068	14,762	14,627	15,679	18,623	20,062	20,185	22,306	4.0	-1.0	5.4
Suriname	84	83	82	80	81	68	63	80	90	93	4.4	-3.1	1.3
Trinidad & Tobago	2,237	2,215	2,251	2,331	2,276	2,145	2,312	2,388	2,452	2,535	4.7	-3.2	1.7
Uruguay	2,758	2,743	2,678	2,714	2,830	2,703	2,784	2,677	2,787	2,938	3.9	-1.2	0.9
Venezuela	29,343	26,863	29,832	33,112	34,996	36,017	35,877	37,837	39,063	41,934	3.4	1.7	5.7
Latin America	**380,093**	**379,215**	**371,594**	**383,133**	**391,210**	**409,159**	**434,357**	**433,328**	**452,746**	**...**	**5.8**	**0.8**	**...**

TABLE B-9. INDUSTRY: VALUE ADDED BY MINING AND QUARRYING

Country	1988	1989	1990	1991	1992	1993	1994	1995	1996	1997p	1970 1980	1980 1990	1990 1997
					Millions of 1990 U.S. Dollars							In Percent	
Argentina	4,295	4,261	4,383	4,508	5,009	5,511	5,998	6,397	6,883	...	3.4	0.6	...
Bahamas	...	...	...	...	...	...	...	...	...	...	...	...	...
Barbados	1	1	10	1	1	1	1	1	1	1	11.4	30.1	2.2
Belize	1	2	2	3	3	3	3	3	3	3	...	...	7.4
Bolivia	459	526	566	579	586	621	642	689	682	680	-0.4	-0.6	3.3
Brazil	6,035	6,274	6,446	6,506	6,557	6,593	6,903	7,117	7,810	...	7.7	7.4	...
Chile	4,693	5,059	5,106	5,738	5,656	5,646	6,149	6,722	7,594	8,206	2.8	3.9	6.2
Colombia	3,824	4,269	4,522	4,493	4,319	4,248	4,317	5,084	5,475	5,656	-1.8	17.8	3.6
Costa Rica[1]	...	...	...	...	...	...	...	...	...	...	...	...	...
Dominican Rep.	256	254	224	211	174	111	210	229	235	242	18.0	-1.6	-0.6
Ecuador	2,153	1,944	1,926	2,089	2,210	2,452	2,713	2,816	2,763	2,891	10.4	2.4	5.1
El Salvador	20	20	20	22	23	26	29	30	32	33	...	2.3	6.3
Guatemala	20	21	20	21	28	31	32	37	45	58	23.9	-0.2	13.6
Guyana	38	28	33	40	35	52	56	50	57	66	-4.3	-6.3	11.3
Haiti	3	3	3	3	2	2	2	3	3	4	-2.0	-21.2	2.9
Honduras	45	51	47	49	54	56	54	63	67	71	3.8	-0.6	4.2
Jamaica	230	312	383	404	394	396	423	394	424	...	3.7	1.3	...
Mexico	6,094	6,054	6,223	6,272	6,384	6,441	6,604	6,428	6,963	7,263	8.6	4.3	2.3
Nicaragua	9	12	9	9	11	11	10	13	17	21	-13.9	-8.1	7.2
Panama	4	3	4	6	9	10	11	10	10	11	4.1	-4.5	20.8
Paraguay	20	22	22	23	25	24	26	26	27	27	26.7	6.7	2.9
Peru	1,026	976	891	911	887	959	1,001	1,024	1,050	1,111	6.5	-3.5	1.6
Suriname	9	10	10	10	10	11	14	14	15	18	-2.5	-0.4	7.3
Trinidad & Tobago	1,067	1,054	1,060	1,027	976	889	942	945	928	891	3.1	-3.2	-2.1
Uruguay	18	19	15	18	20	22	24	29	31	32	...	...	7.1
Venezuela	11,836	11,804	13,830	14,995	15,268	16,650	17,598	18,657	20,177	21,966	0.6	2.5	8.1
Latin America	**42,157**	**42,979**	**45,755**	**47,938**	**48,641**	**50,767**	**53,761**	**56,781**	**61,293**	**...**	**3.4**	**3.5**	**...**

[1] Included in Manufacturing.

TABLE B-10. INDUSTRY: VALUE ADDED BY MANUFACTURING

Country	1988	1989	1990	1991	1992	1993	1994	1995	1996	1997p	1970 1980	1980 1990	1990 1997
					Millions of 1990 U.S. Dollars							In Percent	
Argentina	45,444	41,994	41,046	45,095	49,716	52,269	55,509	51,642	54,328	59,869	1.6	-2.1	4.5
Bahamas	...	...	...	...	...	...	...	...	...	...	...	...	...
Barbados	115	121	118	113	102	99	106	114	114	117	5.0	-0.5	-0.4
Belize	43	48	53	53	57	60	63	65	65	67	...	...	4.3
Bolivia	828	869	937	982	983	1,023	1,078	1,152	1,197	1,248	6.8	-0.9	4.6
Brazil	103,652	106,637	96,549	94,268	90,413	97,596	105,416	107,103	107,981	...	9.1	0.8	...
Chile	5,377	5,966	6,025	6,346	7,071	7,584	7,893	8,488	8,784	9,174	1.2	2.9	5.5
Colombia	8,798	9,292	9,685	9,764	10,202	10,370	10,532	10,638	10,351	10,610	6.0	2.8	1.7
Costa Rica[1]	1,066	1,103	1,131	1,155	1,274	1,356	1,403	1,454	1,394	1,457	7.9	2.1	3.5
Dominican Rep.	1,016	1,063	1,018	1,044	1,172	1,195	1,229	1,221	1,267	1,366	9.0	2.4	3.2
Ecuador	2,624	2,494	2,511	2,591	2,684	2,751	2,872	2,935	3,033	3,129	9.8	0.7	2.9
El Salvador	1,078	1,107	1,161	1,230	1,351	1,331	1,429	1,527	1,551	1,677	...	-2.9	5.3
Guatemala	1,134	1,161	1,186	1,214	1,254	1,290	1,329	1,372	1,398	1,433	6.0	0.4	2.7
Guyana[2]	42	39	34	37	44	46	49	55	59	64	4.8	-6.8	6.5
Haiti	354	347	323	265	208	207	138	151	156	157	7.1	-1.8	-9.4
Honduras	430	446	449	457	485	515	506	534	558	593	6.4	2.3	3.6
Jamaica	720	774	804	744	756	741	744	735	713	684	-1.5	1.7	-1.5
Mexico	48,652	52,149	55,312	57,532	58,837	58,393	60,769	57,837	64,115	70,399	7.1	2.3	3.8
Nicaragua	308	302	298	317	300	300	303	312	319	329	3.0	-1.3	1.1
Panama	436	441	502	555	606	644	671	673	678	700	3.9	1.2	5.9
Paraguay	998	1,057	1,084	1,096	1,100	1,122	1,139	1,173	1,147	1,159	8.3	3.1	1.2
Peru	12,515	10,554	9,942	10,556	10,306	10,801	12,503	13,070	13,423	14,295	3.5	-1.2	3.9
Suriname	39	39	40	38	34	29	29	29	31	31	3.5	-3.8	-2.9
Trinidad & Tobago	620	652	670	726	744	722	769	798	845	905	2.0	-1.0	4.2
Uruguay	2,232	2,228	2,195	2,184	2,217	2,018	2,100	2,040	2,122	2,246	3.1	-0.8	0.1
Venezuela	13,041	11,499	12,193	13,382	13,723	13,580	13,249	14,300	13,921	14,485	5.6	3.2	2.9
Latin America	**251,563**	**252,384**	**245,265**	**251,744**	**255,640**	**266,041**	**281,827**	**279,416**	**289,549**	**...**	**5.8**	**0.6**	**...**

[1] Includes Mining and Quarrying. [2] Includes Electricity, Gas and Water.

TABLE B-11. INDUSTRY: VALUE ADDED BY CONSTRUCTION

Country	1988	1989	1990	1991	1992	1993	1994	1995	1996	1997p	1970 1980	1980 1990	1990 1997
					Millions of 1990 U.S. Dollars							In Percent	
Argentina	10,763	8,123	6,812	8,540	9,986	11,109	12,793	11,399	11,524	13,921	3.3	-6.0	7.0
Bahamas	...	...	...	...	...	...	...	...	...	...	...	...	...
Barbados	99	107	96	89	82	84	86	93	97	101	-0.9	1.2	-0.7
Belize	19	24	27	29	32	37	30	29	27	26	...	...	0.5
Bolivia	156	165	170	180	200	211	214	227	250	269	3.5	-6.0	6.3
Brazil	30,564	31,508	28,436	27,450	25,649	26,914	28,488	28,528	30,089	...	9.0	-0.2	...
Chile	1,430	1,589	1,748	1,721	1,956	2,416	2,390	2,627	2,865	3,060	-0.3	5.9	8.5
Colombia	3,009	2,764	2,403	2,408	2,583	3,053	3,641	3,831	3,812	3,828	4.6	3.2	4.2
Costa Rica	171	192	188	173	178	207	220	202	182	212	9.4	-1.7	1.3
Dominican Rep.	637	721	671	588	731	805	858	907	1,025	1,201	11.1	5.3	6.6
Ecuador	588	611	520	515	513	491	517	510	523	533	5.3	-2.3	-1.7
El Salvador	206	213	186	205	218	226	252	267	274	290	...	-3.1	3.9
Guatemala	158	170	157	159	200	193	193	210	212	223	11.9	-3.0	3.5
Guyana	15	14	15	15	15	16	19	21	24	27	1.0	-1.1	8.1
Haiti	132	136	124	128	59	57	43	56	66	73	13.4	0.6	-7.5
Honduras	137	157	141	138	184	223	183	184	177	164	3.6	1.9	0.5
Jamaica	405	477	485	488	490	488	457	490	463	489	-6.9	1.9	0.3
Mexico	9,545	9,748	10,426	10,678	11,511	11,833	12,830	9,820	10,940	12,055	6.6	0.4	2.7
Nicaragua	63	53	50	46	50	51	60	70	82	89	-1.5	7.9	6.6
Panama	83	50	58	135	185	260	266	277	265	278	6.8	-11.1	24.1
Paraguay	337	345	342	352	370	380	394	409	422	434	19.0	2.8	2.9
Peru	3,428	2,924	3,017	3,069	3,202	3,662	4,838	5,672	5,411	6,564	5.1	0.5	10.6
Suriname	27	24	21	20	24	17	11	25	30	29	8.3	-5.1	2.6
Trinidad & Tobago	490	449	459	513	487	466	529	571	601	657	12.4	-6.2	4.9
Uruguay	322	329	281	310	358	432	438	368	384	395	8.6	-5.9	2.3
Venezuela	3,410	2,489	2,682	3,512	4,728	4,469	3,693	3,509	3,577	4,028	9.4	-5.3	6.2
Latin America	**66,191**	**63,385**	**59,515**	**61,462**	**63,992**	**68,100**	**73,443**	**70,304**	**73,320**	**...**	**6.6**	**-1.2**	**...**

TABLE B-12. INDUSTRY: VALUE ADDED BY ELECTRICITY, GAS AND WATER

Country	1988	1989	1990	1991	1992	1993	1994	1995	1996	1997p	1970 1980	1980 1990	1990 1997
					Millions of 1990 U.S. Dollars							In Percent	
Argentina	2,891	2,752	2,953	3,051	3,317	3,664	4,011	4,235	4,804	...	7.1	3.1	...
Bahamas	...	...	...	...	...	...	...	...	...	...	...	...	...
Barbados	44	45	46	5	47	47	49	52	53	56	7.2	4.8	2.7
Belize	7	7	8	9	10	11	11	12	12	13	...	...	7.7
Bolivia	79	84	89	95	100	115	128	139	151	163	5.1	4.8	8.6
Brazil	9,332	9,483	9,656	10,069	10,232	10,612	10,852	11,664	12,423	...	11.5	6.4	...
Chile	903	833	760	965	1,231	1,291	1,371	1,475	1,493	1,635	5.0	2.0	8.8
Colombia	1,118	1,177	1,222	1,259	1,186	1,352	1,436	1,524	1,566	1,621	8.7	4.8	4.1
Costa Rica	162	170	181	189	201	212	228	234	240	248	10.1	6.0	4.8
Dominican Rep.	92	84	76	80	103	119	123	118	130	144	8.4	0.2	6.9
Ecuador	-23	-24	-23	-24	-24	-25	-25	-24	-25	-26	9.3	9.6	0.9
El Salvador	59	59	62	31	32	35	37	39	40	42	...	1.6	-4.1
Guatemala	172	186	197	205	232	255	269	292	310	357	9.3	4.5	8.5
Guyana[1]	...	...	...	...	...	...	...	...	...	...	...	...	...
Haiti	22	23	22	20	16	17	12	15	17	17	12.6	4.8	-3.8
Honduras	73	77	87	88	88	95	88	101	117	125	12.0	9.5	6.3
Jamaica	92	102	109	111	116	121	122	127	133	...	4.1	5.1	...
Mexico	3,265	3,515	3,617	3,714	3,826	3,986	4,176	4,266	4,457	4,715	9.4	6.0	3.7
Nicaragua	17	18	20	20	20	21	21	23	24	25	2.4	2.2	4.2
Panama	212	213	214	202	189	223	237	241	289	298	9.5	6.1	4.3
Paraguay	130	138	157	171	190	217	261	300	318	323	18.8	8.8	11.2
Peru	220	217	218	227	232	257	280	297	301	335	9.3	3.7	5.6
Suriname	10	10	11	12	12	11	10	12	14	15	10.2	3.3	4.7
Trinidad & Tobago	60	60	62	65	69	68	72	75	77	81	6.6	6.6	3.9
Uruguay	186	167	187	203	234	231	223	239	250	265	4.2	4.0	5.9
Venezuela	1,057	1,070	1,126	1,223	1,278	1,318	1,337	1,371	1,388	1,455	8.6	5.3	3.9
Latin America	**20,182**	**20,468**	**21,058**	**21,989**	**22,937**	**24,251**	**25,327**	**26,828**	**28,584**	**...**	**9.3**	**5.3**	**...**

[1] Included in Manufacturing.

TABLE B-13. VALUE ADDED BY SERVICES

Country	1988	1989	1990	1991	1992	1993	1994	1995	1996	1997p	1970 1980	1980 1990	1990 1997
					Millions of 1990 U.S. Dollars						In Percent		
Argentina	90,899	86,753	85,576	94,902	105,590	112,256	122,757	117,284	122,493	...	3.0	-0.1	...
Bahamas	...	...	...	...	...	...	...	...	...	...	...	...	...
Barbados	967	1,003	910	961	886	900	931	950	992	1,029	3.3	1.2	0.3
Belize	139	160	175	179	193	201	208	215	216	222	...	...	4.2
Bolivia	2,313	2,387	2,457	2,558	2,649	2,748	2,860	2,960	3,091	3,231	4.9	0.5	3.9
Brazil	187,196	194,119	193,949	202,143	200,753	214,207	225,488	233,511	241,295	...	8.2	3.2	...
Chile	12,621	13,974	14,563	15,729	17,955	19,135	20,055	22,125	23,632	25,364	3.2	2.3	7.7
Colombia	21,344	21,792	22,834	23,202	24,935	26,929	29,301	31,137	32,267	33,824	6.5	3.2	5.6
Costa Rica	3,113	3,271	3,416	3,462	3,735	3,987	4,180	4,251	4,290	4,419	5.4	2.1	3.8
Dominican Rep.	3,127	3,263	3,122	3,186	3,369	3,503	3,634	3,863	4,132	4,458	7.5	2.6	4.0
Ecuador	5,716	5,906	6,300	6,679	6,937	7,068	7,299	7,467	7,658	7,948	8.4	2.2	3.8
El Salvador	3,961	2,843	3,004	3,139	3,347	3,818	4,099	4,374	4,470	4,625	...	-0.7	6.3
Guatemala	3,968	4,148	4,282	4,468	4,685	4,920	5,170	5,461	5,634	5,865	5.6	1.3	4.4
Guyana	120	118	121	121	123	127	136	144	154	163	3.2	-0.4	4.1
Haiti	919	898	897	891	735	711	635	735	762	786	5.7	0.9	-1.7
Honduras	1,389	1,428	1,408	1,418	1,491	1,626	1,606	1,668	1,724	1,816	9.2	2.0	3.1
Jamaica	1,951	2,009	2,077	2,143	2,171	2,212	2,242	2,266	2,205	...	1.9	1.4	...
Mexico	158,203	163,022	169,498	176,368	182,097	183,473	192,799	179,289	185,902	199,011	6.8	2.4	2.5
Nicaragua	881	834	841	847	857	839	841	871	899	929	0.2	-0.2	1.4
Panama	3,674	3,738	4,031	4,384	4,728	4,898	5,025	5,126	5,249	5,499	8.1	4.7	4.9
Paraguay	2,697	2,825	2,924	3,046	3,119	3,225	3,354	3,437	3,488	3,565	8.5	3.4	3.0
Peru	24,420	21,255	20,120	20,459	20,444	21,341	23,515	25,560	26,319	27,777	4.4	-0.5	3.4
Suriname	169	186	184	188	177	151	137	145	151	162	5.0	-0.6	-1.7
Trinidad & Tobago	2,641	2,610	2,611	2,690	2,674	2,721	2,771	2,833	2,952	3,056	5.8	-1.0	2.0
Uruguay	4,506	4,594	4,730	4,940	5,390	5,834	6,266	6,158	6,477	6,873	3.1	2.3	5.2
Venezuela	27,622	25,148	26,378	28,997	31,868	30,355	28,811	29,414	27,857	28,940	4.6	-0.4	1.8
Latin America	**564,558**	**568,283**	**576,410**	**607,099**	**630,908**	**657,187**	**694,122**	**691,245**	**714,309**	**...**	**6.0**	**1.9**	**...**

TABLE B-14. SERVICES: VALUE ADDED BY WHOLESALE AND RETAIL TRADE

Country	1988	1989	1990	1991	1992	1993	1994	1995	1996	1997p	1970 1980	1980 1990	1990 1997
					Millions of 1990 U.S. Dollars						In Percent		
Argentina	25,898	24,066	23,897	27,564	31,536	32,852	35,641	32,815	...	...	3.3	-1.5	...
Bahamas	...	...	...	...	...	...	...	...	...	...	...	...	...
Barbados	301	308	293	275	253	259	272	281	299	313	2.1	1.8	0.2
Belize	46	56	63	62	66	69	72	74	73	79	...	...	4.3
Bolivia	600	636	671	714	728	750	777	798	831	868	6.2	2.1	4.0
Brazil	41,592	42,715	39,738	39,405	38,459	41,167	43,588	46,826	49,201	...	9.2	1.0	...
Chile	4,105	4,754	4,974	5,452	6,409	6,875	7,227	8,250	9,023	9,762	3.2	3.1	9.4
Colombia	6,557	6,677	6,865	6,895	7,071	7,717	8,186	8,611	8,585	8,920	5.7	2.4	3.7
Costa Rica	1,062	1,119	1,173	1,175	1,322	1,421	1,492	1,517	1,526	1,586	5.3	1.3	4.5
Dominican Rep.	1,029	1,046	904	946	1,027	1,090	1,151	1,280	1,405	1,568	6.7	0.0	5.2
Ecuador	2,592	2,647	2,747	2,855	2,942	2,992	3,100	3,168	3,306	3,415	8.4	1.7	3.2
El Salvador	763	789	814	865	1,158	1,032	1,127	1,248	1,265	1,320	...	-3.2	6.6
Guatemala	1,805	1,868	1,898	1,977	2,066	2,150	2,272	2,410	2,475	2,568	5.2	-0.1	4.1
Guyana	22	21	22	23	24	25	27	28	30	31	2.2	-3.1	5.2
Haiti	357	357	354	343	206	176	132	164	165	166	5.7	-0.2	-9.1
Honduras	335	320	318	325	334	361	361	382	399	413	5.1	-0.9	3.2
Jamaica	802	829	868	887	934	971	988	1,027	1,041	...	-2.3	2.0	...
Mexico	60,903	63,198	65,773	68,612	71,072	70,120	74,873	63,228	65,817	72,333	5.6	1.9	1.7
Nicaragua	420	408	409	429	435	425	432	454	477	501	-0.4	-0.6	2.6
Panama	632	667	810	934	1,054	1,110	1,163	1,150	1,136	1,233	5.3	1.2	8.0
Paraguay¹	1,462	1,530	1,585	1,655	1,664	1,728	1,802	1,830	1,812	1,840	8.5	3.5	2.3
Peru	8,421	7,078	6,877	7,107	6,853	7,147	8,390	9,248	9,600	10,320	6.1	-0.9	4.8
Suriname	50	65	61	60	64	40	35	39	40	47	3.9	-5.2	-4.0
Trinidad & Tobago	877	826	716	745	739	763	805	828	903	1,011	4.6	-2.7	2.6
Uruguay	1,062	1,052	1,054	1,142	1,297	1,513	1,664	1,510	1,595	1,725	4.2	0.2	6.4
Venezuela	11,954	10,070	10,450	11,289	12,420	11,919	10,967	10,978	9,943	10,358	2.9	-0.7	0.4
Latin America	**173,646**	**173,102**	**173,331**	**181,735**	**190,133**	**194,673**	**206,544**	**198,143**	**...**	**...**	**5.6**	**0.8**	**...**

¹ Includes Financial Services except property rents.

TABLE B-15. SERVICES: VALUE ADDED BY TRANSPORT AND COMMUNICATION

											Average Annual Growth Rates		
											1970	1980	1990
	1988	1989	1990	1991	1992	1993	1994	1995	1996	1997p	1980	1990	1997
Country					Millions of 1990 U.S. Dollars							In Percent	
Argentina	8,387	8,296	8,033	8,866	10,003	10,551	11,569	11,598	...	...	2.0	0.9	...
Bahamas	...	...	...	...	...	...	...	...			...	...	...
Barbados	114	122	122	119	115	116	120	123	128	132	2.2	3.3	1.0
Belize	26	33	37	40	48	51	51	54	56	57	...	...	7.1
Bolivia	453	488	515	548	574	599	635	672	731	781	8.6	3.6	6.0
Brazil	17,945	19,398	19,687	21,549	22,383	23,888	25,522	27,748	33,577	...	11.4	6.1	...
Chile	1,841	2,104	2,269	2,460	2,887	3,054	3,219	3,691	4,080	4,605	4.0	4.9	10.3
Colombia	4,131	4,264	4,423	4,575	4,819	5,028	5,320	5,639	5,892	6,146	7.8	2.8	4.7
Costa Rica	253	277	296	304	347	384	414	439	450	468	10.9	4.7	6.8
Dominican Rep.	466	497	465	497	572	608	639	704	780	874	9.5	3.0	7.3
Ecuador	993	1,072	1,120	1,187	1,255	1,312	1,366	1,408	1,451	1,497	11.0	4.7	4.3
El Salvador	365	369	393	411	450	480	508	536	542	562	...	-0.3	5.4
Guatemala	536	591	628	665	715	749	780	840	870	924	8.1	2.8	5.7
Guyana	26	24	25	25	26	27	30	32	36	39	2.8	-0.1	6.0
Haiti	43	45	45	42	37	33	19	21	21	21	4.2	-1.1	-8.9
Honduras	157	167	173	178	186	192	187	201	210	218	4.8	4.9	3.4
Jamaica	332	345	357	372	392	423	444	489	533	...	2.2	3.7	...
Mexico	21,764	22,666	24,173	25,585	27,532	28,445	30,922	29,398	31,962	34,998	10.9	2.7	5.6
Nicaragua	70	68	68	71	73	70	69	73	76	80	1.2	-1.3	2.1
Panama	846	823	847	868	900	871	910	995	1,022	1,066	19.8	10.3	3.3
Paraguay	223	233	242	254	260	269	280	290	297	305	9.0	4.3	3.4
Peru	2,236	2,027	1,917	1,956	1,997	2,108	2,257	2,454	2,626	...	6.2	0.2	...
Suriname	21	20	19	21	20	24	23	22	25	27	4.3	-0.9	3.9
Trinidad & Tobago	391	401	402	414	408	409	402	414	421	530	6.2	3.7	3.6
Uruguay	499	541	544	595	668	745	863	918	968	1,013	3.2	2.0	8.2
Venezuela	2,910	2,727	2,716	2,845	3,001	3,028	2,925	3,021	3,056	3,256	7.4	-0.6	2.2
Latin America	**65,027**	**67,597**	**69,515**	**74,449**	**79,667**	**83,463**	**89,474**	**91,777**	...	...	**8.2**	**3.2**	...

TABLE B-16. SERVICES: VALUE ADDED BY FINANCIAL SERVICES

											Average Annual Growth Rates		
											1970	1980	1990
	1988	1989	1990	1991	1992	1993	1994	1995	1996	1997p	1980	1990	1997
Country					Millions of 1990 U.S. Dollars							In Percent	
Argentina	23,324	21,469	21,014	24,763	28,276	30,873	34,821	32,930	...	...	4.1	-0.9	...
Bahamas	...	...	...	...	...	...	...	...	...	...	...	...	...
Barbados[1]	...	...	...	...	...	...	...	...	...	...	...	...	...
Belize	14	15	16	17	17	18	19	20	21	21	...	3.1	4.1
Bolivia	477	463	471	481	499	522	549	563	586	603	6.3	-2.0	3.6
Brazil[2]	25,985	26,341	25,520	23,469	22,385	21,903	21,285	19,706	17,954	...	7.5[a]	2.5	...
Chile	3,117	3,428	3,467	3,951	4,277	4,529	4,860	5,257	5,566	5,909	4.1	0.7	7.9
Colombia	4,770	4,792	5,320	5,432	6,239	7,299	8,639	9,207	9,644	10,008	6.1	3.4	9.4
Costa Rica	633	676	719	729	788	863	912	906	917	947	4.5	4.3	4.0
Dominican Rep.	596	649	672	677	681	680	685	694	706	726	6.9	5.3	1.1
Ecuador[3]	1,002	1,042	1,270	1,449	1,537	1,567	1,627	1,674	1,673	1,791	7.7	0.1	5.0
El Salvador[4]	1,836	704	730	751	796	1,151	1,258	1,320	1,356	1,398	...	...	9.7
Guatemala	664	690	722	754	787	826	868	928	969	1,024	3.9	2.4	5.1
Guyana	37	38	39	39	40	41	44	47	51	54	3.6	1.7	4.7
Haiti	118	118	124	126	120	112	100	104	106	107	7.5	1.8	-2.1
Honduras	361	384	398	424	452	489	516	548	577	622	22.4	4.5	6.6
Jamaica	277	293	308	349	309	276	273	209	91	...	...	...	...
Mexico	30,241	31,134	32,209	33,245	34,345	35,589	37,065	37,876	38,849	41,025	6.6	4.0	3.5
Nicaragua	101	100	98	98	98	98	98	102	105	110	0.6	-1.0	1.6
Panama	975	1,020	1,169	1,360	1,559	1,690	1,679	1,674	1,758	1,819	5.6	2.0	6.5
Paraguay[5]	339	348	356	368	394	404	418	431	444	446	6.9	1.1	3.3
Peru[1]	...	...	...	...	...	...	...	...	...	...	...	...	...
Suriname	41	43	43	45	49	46	40	46	46	47	8.0	2.5	1.1
Trinidad & Tobago	372	358	401	432	453	464	476	489	494	505	8.2	-8.3	3.4
Uruguay	1,440	1,476	1,540	1,606	1,777	1,928	2,091	2,048	2,189	2,361	2.4	1.7	6.3
Venezuela	6,150	5,537	5,930	7,014	7,552	7,368	6,744	6,883	6,341	6,814	3.0	0.5	2.0
Latin America	**102,872**	**101,117**	**102,536**	**107,580**	**113,430**	**118,735**	**125,070**	**123,664**	...	...	**7.6**	**1.9**	...

[1] Included in Other Services. [2] Includes Government until 1979. [3] Includes Value-Added Tax from 1990. [4] Included in Other Services before 1988. [5] Property Rents only. [a] 1970-1979.

TABLE B-17. SERVICES: VALUE ADDED BY GOVERNMENT

Country	1988	1989	1990	1991	1992	1993	1994	1995	1996	1997p	1970 1980	1980 1990	1990 1997
					Millions of 1990 U.S. Dollars						In Percent		
Argentina[1]	...	...	...	...	...	...	...	...	...	...	...	...	...
Bahamas	...	...	...	...	...	...	...	...	...	...	...	...	...
Barbados	266	269	273	267	254	254	254	257	259	260	1.6	1.5	-0.4
Belize	32	33	35	36	38	38	40	40	39	37	...		1.4
Bolivia	554	562	555	560	583	600	616	632	639	664	6.7	-0.9	2.1
Brazil[2]	65,875	67,041	68,174	69,271	70,351	71,391	72,405	75,446	76,472	...	...	1.8	...
Chile[1]	...	...	...	...	...	...	...	...	...	...	...	...	...
Colombia	3,607	3,749	3,856	3,844	4,325	4,334	4,453	4,800	5,395	5,605	7.0	5.1	5.2
Costa Rica	840	857	870	879	887	905	928	947	952	957	6.1	1.2	1.4
Dominican Rep.	472	485	498	492	502	518	537	539	570	588	7.7	4.0	2.4
Ecuador	596	597	611	617	615	601	594	595	589	590	8.5	2.2	-0.2
El Salvador	393	389	395	397	383	385	395	412	413	418	...	3.1	0.9
Guatemala	508	532	552	578	610	668	705	719	736	748	6.4	4.4	4.4
Guyana	28	28	28	27	26	26	27	27	28	28	...	-0.8	0.3
Haiti	293	257	247	244	249	274	288	286	289	289	11.3	1.3	1.5
Honduras	228	235	201	193	201	230	192	185	190	197	19.8	1.3	-2.2
Jamaica	365	358	349	346	347	345	340	340	339	...	8.0	-1.0	...
Mexico[1]	...	...	...	...	...	...	...	...	...	...	...	...	...
Nicaragua	196	164	170	149	149	146	138	135	130	124	4.6	3.2	-3.5
Panama	837	808	766	782	739	744	768	794	808	837	5.6	2.8	0.4
Paraguay	178	202	207	214	230	240	256	274	301	316	5.2	5.2	5.8
Peru	2,935	2,518	2,213	2,061	2,087	2,149	2,214	2,268	2,222	...	8.3	0.1	...
Suriname	55	55	56	58	41	38	36	35	37	38	7.4	7.5	-4.5
Trinidad & Tobago	510	509	532	522	506	507	487	492	492	492	5.0	1.6	-0.4
Uruguay[1]	...	...	...	...	...	...	...	...	...	...	...	...	...
Venezuela	3,267	3,401	3,660	3,944	3,987	3,878	3,892	3,920	3,770	3,644	6.8	2.2	0.9
Latin America	**82,034**	**83,048**	**84,248**	**85,481**	**87,109**	**88,273**	**89,563**	**93,143**	**94,670**	**...**	**7.2**	**1.8**	**...**

[1] Included in Other Services. [2] Included in Financial Services before 1980.

TABLE B-18. SERVICES: VALUE ADDED BY OTHER SERVICES

Country	1988	1989	1990	1991	1992	1993	1994	1995	1996	1997p	1970 1980	1980 1990	1990 1997
					Millions of 1990 U.S. Dollars						In Percent		
Argentina[1]	33,289	32,922	32,631	33,709	35,775	37,979	40,725	39,942	...	...	2.4	0.5	...
Bahamas	...	...	...	...	...	...	...	...	...	...	...	...	...
Barbados[2]	285	304	223	300	264	270	286	290	307	325	7.6	-0.8	0.8
Belize	22	23	23	24	24	25	26	26	27	28	...	...	2.8
Bolivia	228	239	245	254	266	277	284	294	304	314	-3.6	0.2	3.5
Brazil	35,800	38,624	40,831	48,449	47,175	55,858	62,688	63,785	64,091	...	...	...	...
Chile[1]	3,558	3,689	3,854	3,866	4,381	4,677	4,749	4,927	4,963	5,087	2.1	0.8	4.1
Colombia	2,279	2,310	2,370	2,456	2,481	2,551	2,704	2,881	2,751	3,146	6.4	2.4	3.9
Costa Rica	325	342	358	374	390	413	434	441	445	461	3.2	2.2	3.8
Dominican Rep.	565	586	584	574	588	607	623	647	672	702	8.0	3.5	2.3
Ecuador	534	550	553	570	588	597	612	623	638	655	7.1	3.7	2.2
El Salvador[3]	604	593	673	715	559	771	811	858	894	927	...	-6.4	5.8
Guatemala	456	467	483	494	509	527	545	564	583	602	6.5	1.2	3.2
Guyana	7	7	7	7	8	8	9	9	10	11	-10.5	-0.2	5.2
Haiti	108	119	127	135	123	116	95	160	180	202	-2.9	4.7	6.8
Honduras	308	321	318	298	318	353	350	352	349	367	7.4	2.2	1.7
Jamaica	174	184	196	190	190	196	197	202	201	...	11.1	-7.6	...
Mexico[1]	45,294	46,023	47,344	48,926	49,148	49,320	49,939	48,786	49,274	50,655	7.1	1.9	1.2
Nicaragua	94	94	96	100	102	100	103	107	110	114	-1.4	-1.4	2.5
Panama	384	419	440	440	477	484	505	513	525	544	18.9	0.3	3.3
Paraguay	496	513	534	555	569	583	598	613	634	658	10.8	3.2	3.2
Peru[2]	10,828	9,633	9,113	9,335	9,507	9,938	10,655	11,591	11,871	...	2.4	-0.5	...
Suriname	4	4	4	3	3	3	3	3	3	3	1.3	-0.7	-1.5
Trinidad & Tobago	492	517	560	578	567	577	600	610	641	518	4.7	3.3	0.0
Uruguay[1]	1,505	1,525	1,592	1,597	1,648	1,648	1,647	1,682	1,725	1,773	2.7	4.6	1.9
Venezuela	3,341	3,414	3,623	3,905	4,908	4,162	4,283	4,613	4,747	4,869	8.7	-2.5	4.5
Latin America	**140,979**	**143,420**	**146,781**	**157,855**	**160,569**	**172,042**	**183,471**	**184,517**	**...**	**...**	**7.1**	**4.0**	**...**

[1] Includes Government. [2] Includes Financial Services. [3] Includes Financial Services before 1988 and Value-Added Tax from 1993.

NATIONAL ACCOUNTS
METHODOLOGICAL NOTE

In order to permit comparisons of gross domestic product and its major aggregates among countries and calculate values for Latin America, Statistics and Quantitative Analysis computes a consistent set of National Accounts estimates in constant 1990 dollars.

The estimates presented in this section of the Statistical Appendix cover 10 sectors of origin for value added, their aggregates for the sectors of Industry and Services, and four main components of expenditure on gross domestic product.

The preparation of the estimates is done as follows:

1. Rebasing each country's national accounts in constant local currency to a common base year; and

2. Conversion of the estimates obtained in step one into U.S. dollars.

The first step is necessitated by the fact that countries use different base years for the calculation of constant price series in their own national accounts.[1]

While the rebasing is only partial and therefore imperfect, it nonetheless allows for more meaningful comparisons of national accounts aggregates across countries by using the relative price systems of a common base year.[2]

1. The rebasing was done in a series of steps:

1.1. On the origin side, each of the 10 sectors was rebased (rescaled) to 1990 using the implicit price deflator calculated for the sector:

$$S_t^{90} = S_t^b \times PS_{90}$$

Where S_t^{90} = constant value added of sector S in prices of 1990

S_t^b = constant value added of sector S in prices of national base year b

PS_{90} = value of the implicit price deflator of sector S in 1990

Gross domestic product was obtained as the sum of the ten[3] sectors.[4]

1.2. On the expenditure side, the same exercise (i.e., taking the main components, rebasing them, and summing them) could generate a series for gross domestic product that is different from that calculated on the sector side.

Therefore, to ensure consistency between the two measures, the rebasing procedure on the expenditure side is carried out for each component except for consumption, which is treated as a residual category. The adjustment is made on the expenditure side because in most countries of the region, gross domestic product is first calculated on the origin side. Private consumption, or total consumption when the former is not available, is taken as the residual category because, in most Latin American countries, it is derived as a residual in the elaboration of the National Accounts by the local authorities.[5]

2. The conversion of the rebased expenditure and sector of origin estimates from local currency into U.S. dollars was also done in a series of steps:

2.1. Exports and imports of goods and non-factor services were each converted into 1990 dollars[6] such that their values in 1990 coincided with the "equivalent" concepts in the Balance of Payments.

2.2. The remaining elements (gross domestic product, investment and each of the sectors of origin)[7] were converted by using the conversion factor calculated for 1990 according to the following method:

The conversion factor cf_t^j is estimated as a function of the ratio of the implicit price deflator of GDP for country "j" over the implicit price deflator of the United States. The use of alternative price indicators does not significantly change the results. However, for Trinidad and Tobago the consumer price index is preferred.

$$cf_t^j = a^j \times (IPD_t^j)^{b^j} \times (IPD_t^{US})^{c^j} \qquad (1)$$

Where cf_t^j = conversion factor for year t for country j

IPD_t^j = implicit price deflator for year t for country j

j = country for which estimate is being carried out

US = United States

t = year

The estimation of the parameters a^j, b^j and c^j were carried out through a least squares regression for annual data for the period 1960-95. The exchange rate observed is the principal rate published in *International Financial Statistics* by the International Monetary Fund. The use of alternative exchange rates in the case of multiple exchange rate systems or parallel rates does not significantly modify the estimate of the coefficients over this period of time. The regression was performed for each country where exchange rates varied sufficiently to allow reasonable estimates. There were 17 such cases. Of the remaining countries, several had only recently experienced exchange rate variations (e.g., Guatemala and the Dominican Republic), while others have not modified their exchange rates (Bahamas, Panama). In these cases GDP-weighted averages of three years around 1990 were used to estimate the conversion factor in 1990:

$$cf_t^j = \left(\sum_{k=1989}^{1991} GDP_k^j \times EX_k^j \right) \qquad (2)$$

Where EX^j = market exchange rate of country j

GDP^j = nominal gross domestic product of country j

If the assumption is that in the long run the exchange rate moves in line with the relative prices of the country vis-à-vis the United States, the coefficients b^j and c^j should be equal to 1 and -1, respectively.

The classification by economic activity corresponds to the major divisions of the International Standard Industrial Classification of all Economic Activities (ISIC), Series M, No. 4, Rev. 2, United Nations (1968), as published in A System of National Accounts, Studies in Methods, Series F, No. 2, Rev. 3, United Nations, New York, 1968.

Each activity has been briefly identified in each table. The complete description under each heading for those which are incomplete is as follows:

Agriculture, Forestry and Fishing: Agriculture, Hunting, Forestry and Fishing.

Wholesale and Retail Trade: Wholesale and Retail Trade, Restaurants and Hotels.

Transport and Communications: Transport, Storage and Communications.

Financial Services: Financing, Insurance, Real Estate, and Services to Enterprises including adjustments for banking services, and in those cases where series are presented at market prices, payments of import duties less subsidies on imports.

Other Services: Community, Social and Personal Services.

The aggregation of activities into major sectors is as follows:

Industry: Includes Mining and Quarrying, Manufacturing, Electricity, Gas and Water, and Construction.

Services: Includes Wholesale and Retail Trade, Transport and Communications, Financial, Government and Other Services.

Growth Rate Calculations:

Growth rates for any period (e.g., 1970-80) are based on a geometric average formula between 1970 and 1980. The growth rate for the Latin American region is calculated over the set of countries for which data are available both for the beginning and the end of the period.

Source:

The original National Account data used for this presentation come from official sources in the member countries. For each country, the source is identified under the heading "Total GDP" in the list of sources accompanying the Statistical Profile for each country chapter.

[1] Argentina, 1986; Barbados, 1974; Bolivia, 1990; Brazil, 1980; Chile, 1986; Colombia, 1975; Costa Rica, 1966; Dominican Republic, 1970; Ecuador, 1975; El Salvador, 1990; Guatemala, 1958; Guyana, 1988; Haiti, 1976; Honduras, 1978; Jamaica, 1986; Mexico, 1993; Nicaragua, 1980; Panama, 1982; Paraguay, 1982; Peru, 1979; Suriname, 1980; Trinidad and Tobago, 1985; Uruguay, 1983; and Venezuela, 1984.

[2] The determination of a common base year across a group of countries is not without its problems given the different economic situations affecting individual countries and the difficulty of evaluating the degree of "normality" of a system of relative prices.

[3] For those countries that measure value added by sector at factor cost or basic prices rather than market prices (see the note to Table B-3), an adjustment has been made for net indirect taxes (the difference between the two).

[4] As Gross Domestic Product is calculated as the sum of the rebased sectors, the growth rate for it may differ in some years from that calculated using a country's constant price series on its original base year. However, the observed differences between the two series over the period 1960 to 1995 were, on average, less than 1 percent.

[5] Since consumption is a residual item, its annual growth rate in 1990 prices may be different from the growth rate obtained from the original series for a few countries in some years, but the trend remains the same.

[6] Converting local currencies into dollars remains a difficult operation due to the large and sometimes erratic movements in relative prices and exchange rates in the countries of the region, not to mention the difficulty of arriving at a correct statistical estimation of these movements. If available, conversion factors based on the Purchasing Power Parity methodology of the International Comparison Project would have been preferred. This option will be pursued in the future. For the time being, it was decided to temporarily adopt a method of smoothing out the market-based exchange rate. This last method is based on the idea that an underlying real long-run exchange rate, or fundamental equilibrium exchange rate, exists. However, it is realized that this method is imperfect because the market exchange rate bears little reference to the relative prices of non-tradable goods and services.

The intensity of the bias depends on the importance of the non-tradable sector in the country, and on the situation of the relative prices between tradable and non-tradable goods. In extreme low-income countries where the agriculture and services sectors are important, the bias may be higher and the estimate of per capita GDP will probably be underestimated. Smoothing out the exchange rate helps to avoid sharp swings due to variable supply and demand conditions for foreign currency.

[7] Consumption is directly available as a residual component in dollars. The implicit conversion factor for consumption changes slightly over time, and is somewhat different from the conversion factor (calculated in step two). For this reason, the growth rate of consumption in 1990 dollars may differ slightly from the growth rate in local currency. In general, the difference is small, and the trend is the same.

TABLE C-1. CURRENT REVENUES

(As a Percent of GDP)

Country	1988	1989	1990	1991	1992	1993	1994	1995	1996	1997p
Argentina	13.1	14.0	13.4	15.4	17.7	17.5	16.8	17.1	15.6	...
Bahamas	16.8	15.2	15.9	15.9	17.0	16.5	18.0	18.5	18.5	18.6
Barbados	28.9	29.2	27.3	30.4	31.4	31.5	30.0	31.0	29.7	32.7
Belize[1]	25.5	26.1	26.1	24.8	25.2	23.8	24.4	22.1	23.4	22.8
Bolivia[2]	12.3	6.4	7.8	7.8	9.6	10.2	11.8	...	...	...
Brazil	21.4	21.5	22.9	20.9	23.5	25.5	...	...	...	...
Chile	31.4	29.6	25.7	27.1	26.3	25.8	25.5	26.2	25.5	25.6
Colombia	10.1	10.1	10.1	12.0	12.2	13.3	13.2	13.0	13.6	14.1
Costa Rica	15.5	15.3	14.5	14.8	15.5	15.7	15.1	16.3	16.8	17.0
Dominican Rep.	14.9	15.7	12.5	13.6	15.3	15.9	15.1	15.0	14.1	15.9
Ecuador	15.1	16.6	18.3	15.5	15.9	16.0	15.7	17.4	16.8	17.2
El Salvador	11.4	9.4	9.5	10.3	11.0	11.1	11.8	13.0	13.4	12.0
Guatemala	10.1	9.5	8.1	9.1	10.6	9.1	7.6	8.6	9.2	9.5
Guyana	41.6	31.1	34.1	31.4	38.6	37.8	31.6	33.5	34.8	31.9
Haiti	...	...	7.3	7.6	5.5	5.5	3.2	8.0	9.2	11.4
Honduras	15.6	14.8	16.5	17.7	17.3	16.9	16.0	18.2	16.7	16.0
Jamaica	28.5	29.9	27.6	28.8	28.7	31.4	32.0	34.5	33.0	32.0
Mexico	15.7	16.4	15.9	18.7	18.7	15.4	15.0	15.2	15.4	15.5
Nicaragua	20.3	23.0	14.6	19.3	20.4	19.5	20.1	22.5	22.6	25.3
Panama	12.4	11.6	24.3	18.5	19.0	18.3	17.7	18.6	18.7	18.3
Paraguay	8.0	11.4	12.4	11.8	13.3	12.2	14.5	15.3	14.7	13.1
Peru	8.2	6.5	8.8	9.1	11.0	11.1	13.0	13.6	14.2	14.0
Suriname	29.3	31.2	31.5	27.2	22.8	12.6	19.0	34.7	34.4	30.8
Trinidad & Tobago	28.6	26.3	25.7	29.9	26.3	27.4	25.6	26.8	28.1	25.4
Uruguay	16.8	15.6	17.8	18.3	18.9	18.5	18.7	18.7	19.2	...
Venezuela	18.2	19.7	22.4	22.8	17.2	16.5	17.1	12.5	15.0	19.7

[1] Fiscal year (April - March) used.
[2] Due to changes in methodology and coverage, data from 1989 are not comparable with those of earlier years.

TABLE C-2. TOTAL EXPENDITURES

(As a Percent of GDP)

Country	1988	1989	1990	1991	1992	1993	1994	1995	1996	1997p
Argentina	17.5	16.8	15.6	17.5	18.8	17.9	17.0	18.0	17.5	...
Bahamas	20.1	19.3	18.3	20.2	19.2	17.2	18.7	19.8	19.0	20.7
Barbados	31.2	31.4	34.8	32.3	33.9	31.6	32.0	30.2	33.3	34.5
Belize[1]	18.8	27.7	27.1	29.7	30.0	31.9	32.8	26.8	27.5	27.0
Bolivia[2]	17.6	12.3	15.5	14.3	16.5	17.8	19.6	...	...	...
Brazil	37.9	41.7	37.5	26.3	30.9	39.6	...	...	...	...
Chile	28.1	24.9	24.5	25.1	23.6	23.8	23.6	22.7	23.1	23.4
Colombia	11.8	11.8	11.2	12.8	14.5	14.3	14.9	15.2	17.3	18.2
Costa Rica	18.0	19.4	19.0	17.9	17.5	17.6	22.0	20.8	22.1	21.0
Dominican Rep.	15.5	15.3	12.5	10.8	12.5	16.3	16.3	14.5	14.7	15.4
Ecuador	17.1	16.2	14.8	14.1	16.2	15.6	15.8	19.0	19.3	18.5
El Salvador	16.3	14.9	13.4	15.5	16.2	14.6	14.2	14.4	15.5	13.3
Guatemala	12.9	13.2	10.2	9.1	10.7	10.5	9.1	9.4	9.4	10.7
Guyana	74.9	48.0	69.8	60.3	59.6	48.5	40.5	40.1	39.8	41.4
Haiti	...	...	9.1	8.3	8.6	9.6	7.4	14.7	11.9	14.0
Honduras	22.4	21.3	23.0	21.9	24.8	27.4	23.0	22.6	19.6	19.0
Jamaica	34.9	32.2	26.8	27.8	26.7	29.2	30.1	33.8	42.0	38.8
Mexico	24.8	21.1	18.6	15.7	14.6	15.0	15.5	15.9	15.9	16.7
Nicaragua	45.9	29.9	34.8	27.0	28.1	27.4	30.3	33.8	32.9	32.2
Panama	17.4	18.3	18.0	18.7	22.9	18.2	18.4	17.3	17.2	19.4
Paraguay	6.6	7.6	7.2	7.4	13.7	13.0	13.8	16.0	15.7	13.2
Peru	12.0	12.8	12.3	10.7	12.7	13.0	14.8	16.8	15.9	14.9
Suriname	51.5	48.6	41.7	46.5	40.0	42.5	29.0	44.4	52.6	45.5
Trinidad & Tobago	34.3	30.7	27.4	30.2	29.2	27.7	25.8	26.8	27.6	26.9
Uruguay	18.7	19.0	17.8	17.9	18.6	19.6	20.7	20.9	21.1	...
Venezuela	24.3	20.8	24.5	24.2	21.0	19.0	24.0	20.3	19.1	21.5

[1] Fiscal year (April - March) used.
[2] Due to changes in methodology and coverage, data from 1989 are not comparable with those of earlier years.

TABLE C-3. CURRENT SAVINGS

(As a Percent of GDP)

Country	1988	1989	1990	1991	1992	1993	1994	1995	1996	1997p
Argentina	-2.3	-0.2	-0.8	-0.8	-0.3	0.6	0.7	0.2	-0.8	...
Bahamas	-0.2	-0.6	0.2	-1.1	0.6	1.5	1.9	1.7	1.1	0.8
Barbados	4.5	4.5	-0.6	3.0	0.6	3.1	2.3	3.3	0.9	4.9
Belize[1]	7.3	8.6	9.3	7.3	5.7	2.9	2.6	-0.6	2.2	2.6
Bolivia[2]	-2.1	-0.6	0.4	2.0	0.1	-0.9	-2.0	...	...	...
Brazil	-13.3	-21.7	-23.4	-5.2	-8.3	-13.3	...	...	...	...
Chile	10.4	8.9	6.4	6.5	7.1	6.4	6.6	7.6	7.1	6.8
Colombia	1.1	0.7	1.1	2.7	2.0	1.7	0.9	0.1	-1.1	-1.1
Costa Rica	-0.1	-1.1	-2.3	-1.6	-0.2	0.0	-4.6	-2.6	-3.4	-1.7
Dominican Rep.	7.0	9.0	6.0	8.2	9.4	7.7	7.4	7.1	5.9	4.7
Ecuador	0.1	2.7	6.3	3.2	2.5	3.2	3.3	2.4	2.1	2.5
El Salvador	-1.4	-2.6	-1.9	-1.8	-0.6	-0.2	0.3	1.9	1.1	1.0
Guatemala	-0.2	-0.6	-0.3	1.5	2.9	1.7	0.8	1.9	2.5	2.7
Guyana	-10.3	-4.9	-14.6	-17.4	-11.5	1.9	5.4	6.4	10.8	4.0
Haiti	...	...	-1.5	-0.6	-2.9	-3.7	-3.9	-5.7	-2.3	-0.9
Honduras	-1.9	-2.7	-0.7	1.5	0.0	-1.5	-0.6	2.5	1.3	-0.1
Jamaica	2.3	4.1	4.9	6.1	7.3	6.7	6.0	7.4	-1.6	-0.7
Mexico	-7.3	-2.9	-0.2	5.0	6.3	2.3	1.6	1.1	1.5	0.4
Nicaragua	-19.5	-3.6	-18.6	-4.2	-1.8	-1.1	-1.2	0.2	0.2	2.5
Panama	-4.5	-5.8	6.7	2.6	-2.2	2.1	1.6	3.3	4.1	1.9
Paraguay	2.6	4.7	6.2	6.1	2.1	1.1	3.2	3.3	2.0	2.2
Peru	-2.5	-4.2	-2.2	-0.1	1.0	1.1	1.9	0.4	1.5	2.3
Suriname	-19.7	-13.5	-6.3	-17.8	-14.8	-26.4	-6.7	-3.8	-11.2	-7.2
Trinidad & Tobago	-2.3	-2.0	-0.1	3.1	-1.2	1.4	1.4	2.0	2.2	1.4
Uruguay	0.1	-1.1	1.9	2.1	2.0	1.1	0.6	0.2	-0.1	...
Venezuela	1.4	2.7	3.7	5.9	1.6	2.6	2.6	-2.5	0.3	2.9

[1] Fiscal year (April - March) used.
[2] Due to changes in methodology and coverage, data from 1989 are not comparable with those of earlier years.

TABLE C-4. OVERALL SURPLUS OR DEFICIT

(As a Percent of GDP)

Country	1988	1989	1990	1991	1992	1993	1994	1995	1996	1997p
Argentina	-3.8	-2.6	-1.7	-1.2	-0.1	0.3	0.1	-0.4	-1.7	...
Bahamas	-3.4	-4.1	-2.4	-4.3	-2.2	-0.7	-0.7	-1.1	-0.5	-2.1
Barbados	-2.3	-2.2	-7.5	-1.9	-2.5	0.0	-1.9	0.9	-3.6	-1.8
Belize[1]	7.1	-0.8	0.7	-3.2	-3.4	-6.7	-7.4	-3.5	-2.0	-1.6
Bolivia[2]	-4.5	-1.8	-1.4	0.8	-1.0	-4.2	-3.8	...	...	...
Brazil	-16.3	-17.5	-5.8	-0.4	-3.8	-9.3	...	...	...	...
Chile	3.6	5.0	1.4	2.2	2.8	2.0	2.0	3.5	2.5	2.2
Colombia	-1.4	-1.7	-0.1	-0.8	-2.2	-0.9	0.8	-2.2	-3.8	-4.2
Costa Rica	-2.5	-4.1	-4.4	-3.1	-1.9	-1.9	-6.9	-4.5	-5.3	-4.0
Dominican Rep.	0.0	0.7	0.5	3.6	3.8	0.5	-0.1	1.2	0.1	1.0
Ecuador	-2.0	0.4	3.5	1.4	-0.3	0.4	-0.1	-1.6	-2.5	-1.3
El Salvador	-3.0	-3.7	-1.5	-3.2	-3.3	-1.3	-0.7	-0.4	-1.9	-1.1
Guatemala	-1.7	-2.9	-1.8	0.0	0.5	-1.3	-1.4	-0.7	-0.1	-1.1
Guyana	-31.6	-7.0	-21.7	-24.3	-17.4	-6.9	-1.5	-3.3	-1.9	-4.6
Haiti	...	...	-1.3	-0.5	-2.8	-3.8	-4.1	-8.3	-2.7	-0.7
Honduras	-4.1	-6.0	-4.1	-3.2	-5.4	-7.8	-6.4	-4.0	-2.2	-2.3
Jamaica	-1.5	-0.2	3.0	4.4	4.2	3.5	3.6	1.9	-8.1	-6.1
Mexico	-9.1	-4.7	-2.6	2.9	4.1	0.3	-0.5	-0.7	-0.4	-1.2
Nicaragua	-25.1	-3.5	-18.7	4.1	-3.3	0.0	-5.1	-5.1	-4.0	-2.8
Panama	-4.9	-6.6	6.4	-0.1	-3.7	0.1	0.0	1.4	1.7	-0.3
Paraguay	1.4	3.8	5.2	4.5	-0.2	-0.8	1.0	-0.3	-0.8	0.2
Peru	-3.9	-6.3	-3.5	-1.5	-1.5	-1.6	2.9	-1.6	2.2	0.1
Suriname	-21.3	-14.0	-6.3	-17.4	-8.7	-9.4	4.1	4.6	0.5	-4.0
Trinidad & Tobago	-5.7	-4.2	-1.2	-0.2	-2.8	-0.2	0.0	0.2	0.5	0.7
Uruguay	-2.0	-3.4	-0.1	0.4	0.3	-1.1	-2.1	-2.2	-2.0	...
Venezuela	-6.1	-1.1	-2.1	-1.4	-3.8	-2.5	-6.8	-4.6	0.2	2.0

[1] Fiscal year (April - March) used.
[2] Due to changes in methodology and coverage, data from 1989 are not comparable with those of earlier years.

TABLE C-5. DOMESTIC BORROWING

(As a Percent of GDP)

Country	1988	1989	1990	1991	1992	1993	1994	1995	1996	1997p
Argentina	0.2	1.5	-0.7	0.3	-0.8	...	...	...	...	...
Bahamas	3.8	4.3	3.9	4.0	...	...	...	...	...	...
Barbados	...	...	...	...	...	...	...	...	...	...
Belize[1]	...	...	...	...	...	4.0	4.5	3.2	-0.8	1.3
Bolivia	...	1.1	1.8	-0.6	1.1	2.1	2.3	...	...	...
Brazil	...	...	...	...	...	...	...	...	...	...
Chile	-5.8	-5.8	-1.3	-0.9	-0.4	-0.2	-0.2	-0.4	-1.1	-0.5
Colombia	0.2	1.0	0.3	0.7	1.9	1.0	...	...	...	...
Costa Rica	2.3	3.7	3.5	4.2	2.5	2.8	7.0	5.5	6.6	5.1
Dominican Rep.	-0.3	0.9	-0.1	-3.9	-1.9	-0.3	0.3	-0.1	0.9	0.2
Ecuador	1.5	0.8	-0.1	...	...	...	...	...	...	...
El Salvador	2.3	3.0	-0.1	1.5	0.7	-0.3	-1.2	-0.8	-0.3	-0.5
Guatemala	1.5	2.4	1.5	0.9	0.1	1.3	-0.4	0.3	-0.2	0.0
Guyana	33.4	24.7	4.7	0.6	2.6	-11.2	-2.2	8.3	-3.3	-7.8
Haiti	...	...	1.1	0.4	2.5	3.2	3.6	-0.2	2.4	-0.3
Honduras	3.4	4.6	-0.9	-1.2	-0.4	1.5	2.5	0.1	1.0	-0.4
Jamaica	-0.6	-2.8	-5.1	-8.2	-3.4	-4.3	...	...	...	...
Mexico	...	...	...	...	...	...	...	...	...	...
Nicaragua	24.7	-0.1	10.7	-4.6	-6.1	0.0	-1.2	2.8	-0.4	2.1
Panama	0.4	0.2	0.0	0.0	0.0	...	...	...	...	...
Paraguay	-1.2	-3.7	-4.5	-5.8	0.0	0.3	-1.1	-0.4	0.4	...
Peru	0.5	3.4	1.7	-0.5	0.6	0.1	-4.1	-0.5	-3.0	0.1
Suriname	20.9	16.7	2.2	18.9	8.7	8.5	-2.2	-5.8	1.9	3.7
Trinidad & Tobago	5.8	5.0	3.3	1.9	3.6	-1.9	-1.1	2.4	-0.5	1.5
Uruguay	1.9	3.3	0.1	-0.3	-0.3	0.7	1.6	...	...	...
Venezuela	...	...	...	...	...	...	...	...	...	...

[1] Fiscal year (April - March) used.

TABLE C-6. FOREIGN BORROWING

(As a Percent of GDP)

Country	1988	1989	1990	1991	1992	1993	1994	1995	1996	1997p
Argentina	1.2	1.0	1.4	-0.2	-0.1	...	...	...	...	...
Bahamas	0.2	1.0	0.8	0.8	...	...	...	...	...	...
Barbados	...	...	...	...	...	...	...	...	...	...
Belize[1]	...	...	...	...	...	2.7	3.0	0.3	-1.5	-1.2
Bolivia	...	0.7	-0.2	0.0	0.9	2.7	2.0	...	...	...
Brazil	...	...	...	...	...	...	...	...	...	...
Chile	2.0	0.4	0.4	0.6	0.2	-1.3	0.0	-2.0	-1.0	-0.5
Colombia	1.2	0.7	0.3	-0.3	-0.7	-0.6	...	...	...	...
Costa Rica	0.2	1.2	0.9	1.7	1.5	-0.9	-0.1	-1.0	-1.4	-1.1
Dominican Rep.	0.3	-0.1	-0.1	-0.8	-1.4	-1.6	-1.3	-1.1	-1.0	-1.1
Ecuador	-0.7	-1.8	-1.9	...	...	...	...	...	...	...
El Salvador	0.7	0.7	1.3	1.6	2.6	1.7	1.9	1.2	2.1	1.6
Guatemala	0.7	0.4	0.4	0.2	-0.1	0.0	1.4	0.4	0.3	1.1
Guyana	-5.9	2.8	17.4	16.3	7.7	2.0	0.4	1.4	6.5	7.0
Haiti	...	...	0.2	0.1	0.3	0.6	0.5	8.4	0.3	1.0
Honduras	3.7	1.9	7.1	1.4	5.3	6.8	3.9	3.9	1.2	1.5
Jamaica	3.5	1.6	1.2	3.0	-0.7	0.8	...	...	...	...
Mexico	...	...	...	...	...	...	...	...	...	...
Nicaragua	0.4	3.6	8.0	0.5	9.4	0.0	6.3	2.4	4.4	0.7
Panama	0.0	0.0	0.0	2.7	1.4	...	...	...	...	...
Paraguay	-0.2	-0.1	-0.7	1.3	0.2	0.5	0.2	0.7	0.4	...
Peru	3.4	2.9	1.8	2.0	0.9	1.5	1.2	2.2	0.7	-0.2
Suriname	0.8	0.4	0.1	0.5	0.0	0.9	-2.0	1.1	-2.3	0.7
Trinidad & Tobago	-0.1	-0.8	-2.0	-1.7	-0.8	2.1	1.1	-2.6	0.0	-2.2
Uruguay	0.1	0.1	0.0	-0.1	-0.1	0.4	0.5	...	...	...
Venezuela	...	...	...	...	...	...	...	...	...	...

[1] Fiscal year (April - March) used.

TABLE C-7. TAX REVENUES

(As a Percent of Current Revenue)

Country	1988	1989	1990	1991	1992	1993	1994	1995	1996	1997p
Argentina	92.1	93.2	92.1	92.3	95.0	94.0	94.0	93.3	97.1	...
Bahamas	88.7	88.0	88.0	86.5	90.0	89.6	90.4	90.5	89.8	89.8
Barbados	85.6	92.1	92.9	93.2	91.9	90.3	90.0	90.9	90.6	93.5
Belize[1]	89.4	84.7	84.3	86.1	85.2	87.7	89.6	88.0	88.9	89.6
Bolivia[2]	...	93.3	93.9	94.7	96.7	96.7	95.4	...	...	...
Brazil	73.3	73.2	83.6	75.9	70.0	72.4	...	...	...	...
Chile	57.7	58.6	63.2	64.8	67.4	68.9	69.6	67.2	72.3	69.4
Colombia	92.6	91.5	90.1	87.9	90.4	87.4	87.8	85.8	84.4	86.2
Costa Rica	93.0	94.4	96.3	97.0	97.2	98.1	97.6	98.2	98.2	99.2
Dominican Rep.	78.3	78.7	83.6	86.9	90.3	92.9	93.4	93.3	93.9	93.5
Ecuador	51.2	50.6	43.0	49.2	46.1	47.9	50.3	45.8	43.6	54.7
El Salvador	89.9	92.4	93.2	92.4	88.0	93.2	92.1	92.4	83.5	90.0
Guatemala	87.0	83.2	84.4	81.0	78.4	87.4	88.9	91.7	95.0	96.2
Guyana	92.1	89.4	94.3	94.1	96.0	95.2	94.6	94.2	93.1	93.1
Haiti	...	...	100.0	100.0	100.0	100.0	100.0	77.4	84.2	77.5
Honduras	82.2	84.8	89.8	87.4	92.6	92.4	93.0	89.5	88.0	86.9
Jamaica	88.9	89.4	87.1	85.0	87.0	89.9	89.8	88.7	90.0	88.8
Mexico	72.2	67.5	67.2	58.4	60.1	72.7	75.0	60.7	57.5	61.8
Nicaragua	92.2	94.2	89.8	92.0	94.6	95.4	95.2	95.8	95.8	95.0
Panama	73.5	72.4	48.2	67.8	65.4	65.0	66.8	67.3	63.7	65.3
Paraguay	86.7	76.6	72.3	73.4	65.2	69.9	67.5	73.3	71.2	70.5
Peru	92.7	95.5	95.7	94.0	88.0	85.8	85.6	85.2	84.3	85.5
Suriname	66.1	62.9	64.8	74.4	72.4	67.7	80.0	87.1	90.4	87.1
Trinidad & Tobago	80.9	82.7	86.7	84.6	86.8	84.8	83.6	85.1	84.5	83.6
Uruguay	90.7	92.0	90.5	87.7	88.3	87.2	84.6	84.1	83.2	...
Venezuela	79.9	74.9	76.9	77.5	76.3	78.4	79.3	98.8	90.2	87.5

[1] Fiscal year (April - March) used.
[2] Due to changes in methodology and coverage, data from 1989 are not comparable with those of earlier years.

TABLE C-8. DIRECT TAXES

(As a Percent of Current Revenue)

Country	1988	1989	1990	1991	1992	1993	1994	1995	1996	1997p
Argentina	...	...	...	...	...	...	...	...	...	...
Bahamas	3.3	3.3	3.9	4.1	3.2	3.7	3.1	3.0	4.6	3.4
Barbados	34.0	38.6	40.6	43.3	43.8	40.3	36.3	39.2	40.0	36.3
Belize[1]	21.5	19.7	20.4	22.1	25.9	24.6	27.2	23.3	20.3	19.4
Bolivia	...	...	...	...	...	...	...	...	...	...
Brazil	49.6	53.1	57.3	52.4	50.6	51.7	...	...	...	...
Chile	19.0	16.7	17.4	19.3	17.7	18.2	18.8	19.6	21.2	20.0
Colombia	34.5	35.4	34.9	41.6	43.9	35.3	37.4	35.5	...	...
Costa Rica	17.4	17.4	18.3	16.7	16.7	20.3	22.2	22.3	21.7	22.1
Dominican Rep.	17.9	19.9	21.9	18.6	16.5	16.6	16.3	17.9	18.8	18.3
Ecuador	9.2	11.1	7.3	9.6	9.3	8.7	10.1	11.6	11.2	12.8
El Salvador	26.5	28.5	26.7	27.9	25.3	24.2	25.2	25.9	23.1	25.4
Guatemala	21.7	20.2	19.7	25.3	18.5	20.9	15.9	19.0	22.9	21.8
Guyana	36.6	34.2	33.8	30.2	33.6	33.6	35.9	38.6	38.3	37.5
Haiti	...	...	15.4	16.4	19.0	15.9	18.1	11.3	17.1	14.6
Honduras	24.5	24.9	21.6	22.2	27.3	28.3	24.7	28.5	25.4	24.1
Jamaica	38.5	38.4	41.5	36.4	36.4	34.6	37.3	34.2	36.0	34.9
Mexico	30.4	29.4	28.7	24.9	28.2	35.0	33.6	26.3	24.8	26.5
Nicaragua	18.6	23.5	24.9	17.6	16.6	13.2	10.8	12.4	13.5	14.0
Panama	38.5	31.5	21.1	31.3	29.9	29.1	29.5	30.5	28.3	29.0
Paraguay	19.9	13.5	11.3	11.9	12.6	12.0	13.8	14.9	15.1	14.2
Peru	27.4	23.6	14.3	14.2	16.5	18.7	18.3	19.4	23.4	23.4
Suriname	34.7	35.1	37.4	42.1	38.5	38.2	46.8	47.9	48.2	50.2
Trinidad & Tobago	55.8	54.7	48.6	52.0	47.8	43.5	46.4	51.9	53.7	48.0
Uruguay	19.8	15.2	14.0	11.8	14.7	16.2	15.6	16.4	...	...
Venezuela	57.8	62.5	67.6	65.5	56.5	53.9	43.1	58.0	55.8	54.5

[1] Fiscal year (April - March) used.

TABLE C-9. INDIRECT TAXES

(As a Percent of Current Revenue)

Country	1988	1989	1990	1991	1992	1993	1994	1995	1996	1997p
Argentina	...	...	...	...	...	...	...	...	...	...
Bahamas	85.4	84.6	84.1	82.4	86.8	85.9	87.2	87.5	85.2	86.5
Barbados	51.7	53.5	52.4	49.9	48.1	49.9	53.6	51.6	50.6	57.2
Belize[1]	67.9	65.0	64.0	64.0	59.3	63.2	62.4	64.7	68.6	70.1
Bolivia	...	...	...	...	...	...	...	...	...	...
Brazil	23.7	20.1	26.3	23.5	19.4	20.7	...	...	...	...
Chile	38.7	41.8	45.8	45.5	49.7	50.7	50.7	47.6	51.0	49.4
Colombia	58.1	56.0	55.2	46.4	46.4	51.6	50.5	50.3	...	...
Costa Rica	75.6	77.0	78.1	80.2	80.5	77.8	75.4	75.9	76.4	77.1
Dominican Rep.	60.4	58.7	61.6	68.3	73.8	76.2	77.1	74.9	74.7	74.8
Ecuador	42.0	39.5	35.8	39.5	36.8	39.2	40.1	34.2	32.5	41.9
El Salvador	64.5	63.9	69.7	64.3	62.6	67.1	65.4	66.5	60.4	64.6
Guatemala	65.3	63.0	64.7	55.7	59.9	66.5	73.0	72.7	72.1	74.4
Guyana	55.5	55.2	60.6	63.9	62.3	61.6	58.7	55.6	54.8	55.7
Haiti	...	...	84.6	83.6	81.0	84.1	81.9	58.8	49.4	63.6
Honduras	57.7	59.9	68.2	65.1	65.4	64.2	68.3	61.0	62.6	62.8
Jamaica	50.4	51.0	45.6	48.6	50.6	55.2	52.5	54.5	54.1	53.9
Mexico	41.8	38.1	38.5	33.4	31.9	37.7	41.4	34.4	32.7	35.2
Nicaragua	73.6	70.5	64.7	74.4	77.9	82.2	84.4	83.4	82.3	81.1
Panama	35.0	40.9	27.1	36.5	35.6	35.9	37.3	36.8	35.5	36.3
Paraguay	64.2	58.4	54.8	55.0	47.6	56.3	52.6	57.1	55.1	56.4
Peru	65.3	71.9	81.4	79.9	71.5	67.0	67.2	65.8	60.9	62.1
Suriname	31.4	27.7	27.4	32.3	33.9	29.5	33.2	39.1	42.1	36.9
Trinidad & Tobago	25.1	28.0	38.0	32.5	39.0	41.3	37.2	33.1	30.8	35.6
Uruguay	70.9	76.9	76.5	75.8	73.6	71.0	68.9	67.8	...	...
Venezuela	22.1	12.3	9.3	12.0	19.9	24.5	36.2	40.8	34.5	33.0

[1] Fiscal year (April - March) used.

TABLE C-10. NON-TAX REVENUES

(As a Percent of Current Revenue)

Country	1988	1989	1990	1991	1992	1993	1994	1995	1996	1997p
Argentina	7.9	6.8	7.9	7.7	5.0	6.0	6.0	6.7	2.9	...
Bahamas	11.3	12.0	12.0	13.5	10.0	10.4	9.6	9.5	10.2	10.2
Barbados	14.4	7.9	7.1	6.8	8.1	9.7	10.0	9.1	9.4	6.5
Belize[1]	10.6	15.3	15.7	13.9	14.8	12.3	10.4	12.0	11.1	10.4
Bolivia	...	2.4	2.4	2.2	1.9	2.1	1.9	...	...	...
Brazil	26.7	26.8	16.4	24.1	30.0	27.6	...	...	...	...
Chile	42.3	41.4	36.8	35.2	32.6	31.1	30.4	32.8	27.7	30.6
Colombia	7.4	8.5	9.9	12.1	9.6	12.6	12.2	14.2	15.6	13.8
Costa Rica	7.0	5.6	3.7	3.0	2.8	1.9	2.4	1.8	1.8	0.8
Dominican Rep.	21.7	21.3	16.4	13.1	9.7	7.1	6.6	6.7	6.1	6.5
Ecuador	48.8	49.4	57.0	50.8	53.9	52.1	49.7	54.2	56.4	45.3
El Salvador	10.1	7.6	6.8	6.9	10.2	4.3	6.1	7.6	16.5	10.0
Guatemala	13.0	16.8	15.6	19.0	21.6	12.6	11.1	8.3	5.0	3.8
Guyana	7.9	10.6	5.7	5.9	4.0	4.8	5.4	5.8	6.9	6.9
Haiti	...	...	...	...	...	...	...	22.6	15.8	22.5
Honduras	17.8	15.2	10.2	12.6	7.4	7.6	3.9	7.7	8.0	13.1
Jamaica	11.1	10.6	12.9	15.0	13.0	10.1	10.2	11.3	10.0	11.2
Mexico	27.8	32.5	32.8	41.6	39.9	27.3	25.0	39.3	42.5	38.2
Nicaragua	7.8	5.8	10.2	8.0	5.4	4.6	4.8	4.2	4.2	5.0
Panama	26.5	27.6	51.8	32.2	34.6	35.0	33.2	32.7	36.3	34.7
Paraguay	13.3	23.4	27.7	26.6	34.8	30.1	32.5	26.7	28.8	29.5
Peru	7.3	4.5	4.3	6.0	12.0	14.2	14.4	14.8	15.7	14.5
Suriname	33.9	37.1	35.2	25.6	27.6	32.3	20.0	12.9	9.6	12.9
Trinidad & Tobago	19.1	17.3	13.3	15.4	13.2	15.2	16.4	14.9	15.5	16.4
Uruguay	9.3	8.0	9.5	12.3	11.7	12.8	15.4	15.9	16.8	...
Venezuela	20.1	25.1	23.1	22.5	23.7	21.6	20.7	1.2	9.8	12.5

[1] Fiscal year (April - March) used.

TABLE C-11. CURRENT EXPENDITURES

(As a Percent of Total Expenditures)

Country	1988	1989	1990	1991	1992	1993	1994	1995	1996	1997p
Argentina	87.9	84.2	90.7	92.6	95.7	94.6	95.0	94.0	93.5	...
Bahamas	84.2	82.0	85.9	84.1	85.0	87.5	85.8	84.7	91.5	85.6
Barbados	78.4	78.7	80.2	85.0	90.9	89.7	86.4	91.6	86.5	80.6
Belize[1]	97.2	62.8	61.9	58.7	65.1	65.4	66.7	84.6	77.2	74.9
Bolivia[2]	82.0	83.6	82.9	83.8	83.3	82.5	80.6	...	...	...
Brazil	91.6	103.6	123.5	99.3	103.1	98.0	...	...	...	...
Chile	74.6	83.2	78.7	82.2	81.3	81.2	79.9	81.4	79.7	80.1
Colombia	77.1	79.3	80.5	72.7	71.0	80.7	83.1	84.4	84.7	83.3
Costa Rica	86.6	84.5	88.7	92.0	90.0	88.8	89.5	90.8	91.2	88.9
Dominican Rep.	51.5	43.8	52.2	50.6	47.8	50.1	47.2	54.7	56.2	72.7
Ecuador	88.2	86.0	81.1	86.8	83.2	82.4	78.1	78.9	76.1	79.1
El Salvador	78.8	80.3	85.0	78.1	71.6	77.2	82.7	77.5	79.7	82.7
Guatemala	80.7	76.2	83.0	83.0	72.8	70.9	74.9	71.6	71.8	63.7
Guyana	69.4	74.8	69.7	80.9	84.0	74.1	64.7	67.4	60.1	67.5
Haiti	67.7	69.6	97.0	98.0	98.0	96.6	95.4	93.3	96.6	87.8
Honduras	78.0	81.9	74.6	74.3	69.6	67.1	71.8	69.2	78.6	84.7
Jamaica	74.9	80.0	84.5	81.7	80.1	84.6	86.6	80.1	82.3	84.3
Mexico	92.7	91.4	86.7	86.9	84.8	86.7	86.5	88.4	87.7	90.7
Nicaragua	86.7	88.9	95.5	87.0	78.7	75.2	70.3	66.0	67.9	70.5
Panama	97.2	95.2	97.6	84.6	92.7	88.7	87.5	88.7	85.4	84.3
Paraguay	80.7	88.1	85.0	77.9	82.5	84.6	82.0	75.6	80.4	83.4
Peru	88.5	83.5	89.5	86.4	79.2	76.8	75.3	78.3	79.6	78.7
Suriname	95.1	92.2	90.6	96.7	94.2	91.6	88.5	86.7	86.7	83.5
Trinidad & Tobago	89.9	92.2	94.2	88.7	94.4	94.2	93.6	92.6	93.8	89.3
Uruguay	88.9	87.9	89.1	90.6	90.9	88.7	87.0	88.7	91.3	...
Venezuela	68.9	81.5	76.4	69.7	74.3	73.1	60.8	73.6	77.0	78.1

[1] Fiscal year (April - March) used.
[2] Due to changes in methodology and coverage, data from 1989 are not comparable with those of earlier years.

TABLE C-12. PURCHASE OF GOODS AND SERVICES

(As a Percent of Total Expenditures)

Country	1988	1989	1990	1991	1992	1993	1994	1995	1996	1997p
Argentina	22.4	21.2	21.5	20.0	18.9	17.1	17.2	17.3	17.2	...
Bahamas	68.4	67.4	69.6	67.3	67.3	67.4	66.5	65.0	67.6	63.9
Barbados	45.2	46.9	45.6	49.1	52.0	50.0	49.1	50.0	47.0	43.6
Belize[1]	78.7	51.6	52.4	49.0	55.6	53.2	53.5	58.2	60.9	58.7
Bolivia[2]	46.8	54.8	52.6	54.6	52.0	49.6	47.4	...	...	...
Brazil	15.4	15.5	14.7	18.3	12.2	11.8	...	...	...	...
Chile	27.6	28.8	28.4	30.2	31.5	32.4	32.9	32.7	33.9	33.4
Colombia	23.2	24.4	27.1	22.3	21.8	24.9	25.8	24.8	21.9	21.3
Costa Rica	35.6	34.0	35.3	34.9	33.1	34.8	29.8	30.9	29.9	30.6
Dominican Rep.	24.8	23.9	27.4	25.1	26.4	24.6	25.8	29.6	28.2	34.3
Ecuador	39.0	37.8	42.6	47.2	43.8	45.5	45.3	39.0	40.0	42.3
El Salvador	59.3	60.5	61.1	49.1	45.4	45.9	47.0	48.9	47.1	51.1
Guatemala	51.0	47.0	56.0	47.8	47.9	46.3	48.0	41.3	39.6	38.3
Guyana	34.9	35.4	19.6	20.8	24.1	25.3	30.7	30.4	32.8	34.8
Haiti	...	...	84.5	89.2	81.9	78.0	83.3	74.4	80.8	72.0
Honduras	56.0	60.7	53.6	47.9	43.1	37.3	40.6	40.3	44.0	47.1
Jamaica	35.6	37.2	40.4	39.6	34.3	50.0	48.9	47.7	47.3	55.1
Mexico	13.5	16.6	17.0	22.1	17.2	18.6	19.1	16.3	15.9	12.7
Nicaragua	66.2	76.5	81.2	58.3	50.4	46.9	37.7	36.5	40.7	35.0
Panama	71.0	66.6	63.3	53.4	55.0	50.7	46.6	47.9	48.2	43.7
Paraguay	45.0	50.0	52.1	53.7	49.8	56.6	53.8	52.3	55.9	...
Peru	39.1	38.4	35.5	34.8	38.5	36.6	36.3	36.7	40.4	40.1
Suriname	67.9	63.5	60.5	58.1	62.9	65.5	57.5	68.0	68.0	67.0
Trinidad & Tobago	47.0	43.6	43.6	42.1	45.1	45.6	44.0	44.6	43.5	37.5
Uruguay	71.6	69.5	69.6	72.4	73.8	74.1	74.1	74.9	79.2	...
Venezuela	23.0	24.5	20.3	22.1	26.4	24.6	21.4	21.6	16.1	20.8

[1] Fiscal year (April - March) used.
[2] Due to changes in methodology and coverage, data from 1989 are not comparable with those of earlier years.

TABLE C-13. INTEREST PAYMENTS

(As a Percent of Total Expenditures)

Country	1988	1989	1990	1991	1992	1993	1994	1995	1996	1997p
Argentina	4.9	5.1	4.1	8.2	8.6	5.5	6.6	8.1	8.9	...
Bahamas	10.6	9.3	10.8	11.7	11.0	13.4	11.6	11.8	12.3	11.5
Barbados	11.3	10.4	12.1	13.8	17.2	13.7	13.9	15.4	15.6	13.2
Belize[1]	11.3	6.7	5.0	4.2	4.4	6.2	6.5	7.6	7.5	7.5
Bolivia[2]	...	7.2	8.3	10.0	9.7	11.4	12.5	...	...	...
Brazil	45.9	58.0	72.5	31.2	45.2	48.8	...	...	...	...
Chile	7.9	11.4	8.2	7.3	6.0	5.2	4.1	3.2	2.4	1.9
Colombia	11.5	11.5	11.9	10.9	8.4	9.3	9.1	9.3	12.2	12.6
Costa Rica	15.2	15.2	17.6	23.2	20.8	17.7	18.6	26.9	27.5	24.4
Dominican Rep.	9.1	4.5	3.3	6.5	4.2	7.8	5.4	6.4	3.8	3.3
Ecuador	26.2	30.2	22.5	23.0	22.8	23.3	21.7	18.2	21.2	25.2
El Salvador	6.1	6.8	9.1	16.5	13.3	13.7	11.2	9.5	10.0	9.9
Guatemala	11.4	10.4	11.1	17.5	9.2	8.6	9.7	10.8	11.9	6.9
Guyana	27.2	23.3	38.3	43.7	41.5	35.2	27.3	24.4	19.2	23.0
Haiti	...	...	8.3	6.6	7.3	9.9	9.5	5.8	5.8	6.8
Honduras	13.5	14.3	11.4	14.2	18.6	17.2	21.7	20.6	23.9	23.4
Jamaica	26.1	30.6	33.1	31.8	33.7	32.9	37.7	32.4	35.0	29.2
Mexico	57.4	49.5	41.9	28.4	21.7	15.0	12.2	24.0	23.3	21.0
Nicaragua	0.2	0.0	0.0	4.2	10.2	14.0	17.1	14.1	10.6	16.5
Panama	13.2	15.6	17.2	13.1	17.4	15.0	18.2	9.8	9.3	14.6
Paraguay	10.8	11.7	10.3	0.0	6.7	6.0	4.8	4.5	3.2	...
Peru	28.2	23.4	27.6	25.1	16.4	17.5	14.0	18.0	13.8	10.8
Suriname	9.2	10.5	10.9	10.0	10.1	9.3	7.0	2.1	2.0	1.4
Trinidad & Tobago	11.3	16.0	16.7	15.9	18.3	21.3	20.8	18.6	16.9	16.5
Uruguay	8.7	10.3	10.4	9.5	7.7	7.2	6.1	7.1	...	...
Venezuela	11.0	16.6	16.0	14.3	16.6	15.9	16.7	23.4	21.9	10.6

[1] Fiscal year (April - March) used.

[2] Due to changes in methodology and coverage, data from 1989 are not comparable with those of earlier years.

TABLE C-14. CURRENT TRANSFERS AND SUBSIDIES

(As a Percent of Total Expenditures)

Country	1988	1989	1990	1991	1992	1993	1994	1995	1996	1997p
Argentina	60.7	58.0	64.4	63.7	68.2	72.1	37.6	37.2	37.6	...
Bahamas	5.2	5.2	5.6	5.1	6.7	6.8	7.7	7.9	11.6	10.2
Barbados	21.9	21.4	22.5	22.1	21.7	26.0	23.4	26.2	24.0	23.8
Belize[1]	7.2	4.5	4.5	5.5	5.0	6.0	6.7	6.4	8.8	8.8
Bolivia[2]	16.3	11.4	13.5	9.7	8.0	7.2	10.9	...	...	...
Brazil	30.3	30.1	36.3	49.8	45.7	37.5	...	...	...	...
Chile	39.1	43.0	42.2	44.7	43.9	43.6	43.0	45.6	43.4	44.9
Colombia	42.0	43.2	41.0	39.4	38.8	46.5	48.1	50.2	50.4	49.4
Costa Rica	35.8	35.2	35.9	33.9	36.1	36.3	41.0	32.9	33.8	34.0
Dominican Rep.	15.3	12.2	17.1	14.7	11.5	11.0	8.7	12.7	17.6	24.0
Ecuador	21.5	17.3	14.7	14.3	12.1	12.0	8.2	6.3	7.1	11.3
El Salvador	13.3	13.0	14.8	12.5	12.9	17.6	22.8	19.1	22.6	21.7
Guatemala	18.3	18.8	15.8	17.8	15.7	16.0	17.2	19.4	20.3	18.6
Guyana	7.3	16.1	11.8	16.4	18.4	13.6	6.7	12.3	7.7	9.3
Haiti	...	...	1.3	1.0	0.6	1.9	0.0	8.4	7.2	4.5
Honduras	8.5	6.8	9.6	12.2	7.8	12.6	9.5	8.3	10.7	14.2
Jamaica	13.2	12.3	11.0	10.3	12.1	1.6	...	...	...	...
Mexico	21.5	23.4	25.1	31.9	43.8	49.9	53.7	47.1	47.4	57.0
Nicaragua	20.3	12.4	14.4	24.5	18.1	14.3	15.6	15.4	16.7	18.9
Panama	13.0	13.0	17.1	18.1	20.2	23.1	22.6	30.5	27.2	23.3
Paraguay	16.9	19.4	21.0	22.7	24.3	21.3	18.7	18.1	20.6	...
Peru	21.1	21.7	26.5	26.5	24.3	22.6	25.0	23.7	25.4	27.8
Suriname	18.0	18.2	19.2	28.6	21.1	16.8	24.0	16.5	16.7	15.1
Trinidad & Tobago	31.6	32.6	33.9	30.8	30.9	27.3	28.8	29.4	33.5	35.3
Uruguay	6.0	5.6	9.0	8.7	9.4	7.4	6.9	6.7	6.5	...
Venezuela	34.9	40.4	40.1	33.3	31.3	32.6	22.6	28.6	39.0	46.8

[1] Fiscal year (April - March) used.

[2] Due to changes in methodology and coverage, data from 1989 are not comparable with those of earlier years.

TABLE C-15. CAPITAL EXPENDITURES[1]

(As a Percent of Total Expenditures)

Country	1988	1989	1990	1991	1992	1993	1994	1995	1996	1997p
Argentina	12.1	15.8	9.3	7.4	4.3	5.4	5.0	6.0	6.5	...
Bahamas	15.8	18.0	14.1	15.9	15.0	12.5	14.2	15.3	8.5	14.4
Barbados	21.6	21.3	19.8	15.0	9.1	10.3	13.6	8.4	13.5	19.4
Belize[2]	2.8	37.2	38.1	41.3	34.9	34.6	33.3	15.4	22.8	25.1
Bolivia[3]	18.0	16.4	17.1	16.2	16.7	17.5	19.4	...	...	...
Brazil	8.4	-3.6	-23.5	0.7	-3.1	2.0	...	...	...	...
Chile	25.4	16.8	21.3	17.8	18.7	18.8	20.1	18.6	20.3	19.9
Colombia	22.9	20.7	19.5	27.3	29.0	19.3	16.9	15.6	15.3	16.7
Costa Rica	13.4	15.5	11.3	8.0	10.0	11.2	10.5	9.2	8.8	11.1
Dominican Rep.	48.5	56.2	47.8	49.4	52.2	49.9	52.8	45.3	43.8	27.3
Ecuador	11.8	14.0	18.9	13.2	16.8	17.6	21.9	21.1	23.9	20.9
El Salvador	21.2	19.7	15.0	21.9	28.4	22.8	19.0	22.5	20.3	17.3
Guatemala	19.3	23.8	17.0	17.0	27.2	29.1	25.1	28.4	28.2	36.3
Guyana	30.6	25.2	30.3	19.1	16.0	25.9	35.3	32.6	39.9	32.5
Haiti	32.3	30.4	3.0	2.0	2.0	3.4	4.6	6.7	3.4	12.2
Honduras	22.0	18.1	25.4	25.7	30.4	32.9	28.2	30.8	21.4	15.3
Jamaica	25.1	20.0	15.5	18.3	19.9	15.4	13.4	19.9	17.7	15.7
Mexico	7.3	8.6	13.3	13.1	15.2	13.3	13.5	11.6	12.3	9.3
Nicaragua	13.3	11.1	4.5	13.0	21.3	24.8	29.7	34.0	32.1	29.5
Panama	2.8	4.8	2.4	15.4	7.3	11.3	12.5	11.3	14.6	15.7
Paraguay	19.3	11.9	15.0	22.1	17.5	15.4	18.0	24.4	19.6	16.6
Peru	11.5	16.5	10.5	13.6	20.8	23.2	24.7	21.7	20.4	21.3
Suriname	4.9	7.8	9.4	3.3	5.8	8.4	11.5	13.3	13.3	16.5
Trinidad & Tobago	10.1	7.8	5.8	11.3	5.6	5.8	6.4	7.4	6.2	10.7
Uruguay	11.1	12.1	10.9	9.4	9.1	11.3	13.0	11.3	8.7	...
Venezuela	31.1	18.5	23.6	30.3	25.7	26.9	39.2	26.4	23.0	21.9

[1] Includes Net Lending.
[2] Fiscal year (April - March) used.
[3] Due to changes in methodology and coverage, data from 1989 are not comparable with those of earlier years.

TABLE C-16. TOTAL INVESTMENT

(As a Percent of Total Expenditures)

Country	1988	1989	1990	1991	1992	1993	1994	1995	1996	1997p
Argentina	4.9	3.8	2.2	1.6	1.8	2.0	1.6	1.3	1.1	...
Bahamas	7.5	10.5	5.1	3.4	4.4	5.5	7.2	10.1	7.0	11.3
Barbados	...	...	...	...	...	...	...	...	...	...
Belize[1]	31.8	36.0	40.3	48.0	44.6	32.6	...	...	...	...
Bolivia[2]	15.5	...	...	...	...	...	...	...	...	...
Brazil	3.0	2.4	1.6	2.7	2.0	1.6	...	...	...	...
Chile	10.1	10.1	9.0	10.3	12.0	13.2	13.5	12.7	14.3	13.8
Colombia	2.3	1.9	12.5	13.2	12.4	15.5	15.6	15.6	15.0	16.7
Costa Rica	4.1	3.7	3.9	3.3	3.6	3.5	3.4	4.0	3.0	4.4
Dominican Rep.	...	...	...	...	...	...	...	32.0	32.5	18.0
Ecuador	7.9	4.5	5.2	3.5	4.2	5.6	13.9	11.2	15.2	...
El Salvador	18.0	15.2	8.4	13.2	19.5	18.4	14.4	16.0	16.6	14.8
Guatemala	10.3	10.2	9.7	9.6	10.0	9.3	9.6	13.5	13.8	15.5
Guyana	13.1	16.1	16.5	8.8	12.6	16.5	28.3	29.7	34.1	28.2
Haiti	...	...	...	...	...	...	...	6.7	3.4	12.2
Honduras	14.9	13.9	8.4	12.8	17.6	21.4	17.3	15.5	15.3	11.7
Jamaica	16.3	14.3	9.3	11.3	15.6	10.5	...	...	...	...
Mexico	2.0	2.2	4.2	6.0	6.5	6.4	7.7	5.3	5.9	4.8
Nicaragua	8.0	4.4	2.8	7.8	12.0	9.1	15.3	15.8	19.1	15.0
Panama	2.2	3.7	1.2	3.1	4.1	8.1	12.5	8.3	8.3	12.6
Paraguay	16.5	9.6	9.0	10.1	9.1	10.3	11.9	15.2	13.0	...
Peru	7.8	11.5	9.3	11.4	12.8	13.2	15.4	14.6	13.5	15.5
Suriname	3.5	6.6	7.5	2.2	5.4	8.2	11.5	13.3	13.3	14.0
Trinidad & Tobago	12.2	10.2	8.0	11.9	7.6	7.2	6.7	8.4	7.0	12.8
Uruguay	8.8	9.0	8.8	8.1	7.7	7.8	8.7	7.9	...	...
Venezuela	7.8	2.5	2.8	5.0	5.8	5.2	2.9	2.9	2.0	2.1

[1] Fiscal year (April - March) used.
[2] Due to changes in methodology and coverage, data from 1989 are not comparable with those of earlier years.

TABLE C-17. FINANCIAL INVESTMENT AND NET LENDING

(As a Percent of Total Expenditures)

Country	1988	1989	1990	1991	1992	1993	1994	1995	1996	1997p
Argentina	0.6	0.8	0.5	0.3	0.4	0.4	0.3	0.2	0.1	...
Bahamas	1.0	-0.1	3.4	6.1	3.7	5.4	5.9	3.8	0.3	0.1
Barbados	3.5	2.8	-0.2	0.7	0.5	1.2	2.5	-1.1	0.0	0.9
Belize[1]	-29.0	-0.5	-4.9	-8.6	-11.4	-0.2	...	...	...	...
Bolivia[2]	0.4	...	...	...	...	...	...	...	...	...
Brazil	11.5	9.6	6.5	7.4	5.5	6.0	...	...	...	...
Chile	5.7	4.0	3.8	4.3	5.4	4.7	5.3	4.3	4.0	4.4
Colombia	2.0	3.3	1.1	8.0	13.8	3.8	1.3	...	0.3	...
Costa Rica	0.0	0.0	0.0	0.0	0.0	0.0	0.0	0.0	0.0	0.0
Dominican Rep.	3.9	1.6	0.8	0.6	0.3	0.5	1.1	1.1	0.9	0.4
Ecuador	0.0	0.1	1.1	0.0	0.0	0.1	5.2	4.9	3.0	...
El Salvador	1.4	2.1	-0.4	5.0	3.1	1.2	0.8	1.7	0.0	-1.7
Guatemala	1.9	2.2	2.2	2.3	1.2	4.4	4.2	3.8	3.1	4.9
Guyana	0.0	0.0	0.0	0.0	0.0	0.0	...	...	...	...
Haiti	...	...	...	...	...	...	...	...	...	...
Honduras	1.8	0.9	1.4	2.7	1.1	1.3	4.1	6.7	-2.8	-0.7
Jamaica	2.6	1.7	4.7	1.6	3.2	1.9	...	...	...	...
Mexico	0.2	0.3	0.0	0.0	0.0	0.0	...	0.7	0.4	0.1
Nicaragua	0.0	0.0	0.0	3.4	0.8	0.9	2.1	3.1	0.0	0.1
Panama	0.3	0.2	0.2	0.1	0.8	0.4	...	...	3.4	-1.8
Paraguay	2.2	2.2	0.8	0.9	2.6	1.0	1.7	3.1	2.3	...
Peru	...	...	...	...	...	...	...	...	...	...
Suriname	1.4	1.2	1.9	1.1	0.4	0.1	...	...	...	2.5
Trinidad & Tobago	-2.2	-2.4	-2.2	-0.6	-2.0	-1.4	-0.3	-1.1	-0.8	-2.1
Uruguay	...	...	...	...	...	...	...	...	...	...
Venezuela	9.5	8.3	11.8	12.4	10.3	10.2	17.6	7.1	7.2	4.3

[1] Fiscal year (April - March) used.
[2] Due to changes in methodology and coverage, data from 1989 are not comparable with those of earlier years.

GOVERNMENT FINANCE NOTES

The statistical tables refer generally to the central government. The data do not cover extrabudgetary revenues and expenditures of the central government, or the transactions of state and local governments, decentralized agencies or other entities comprising the general government, except for Chile, where the data reflect the general government concept. The data for Argentina refer to "National Administration" and include decentralized agencies in addition to central government.

Total Revenues:

Include current and capital revenues.

Current Revenue: Includes all non-repayable receipts raised by the government in the form of tax and non-tax revenue, but excludes the sale of fixed government capital assets. Current revenue excludes the proceeds from government borrowings and from the issuance of government bonds and the sale of other financial assets.

Tax Revenue — Direct Taxes:

Income Taxes: Include taxes imposed on the actual or presumptive income and profits of individuals and corporations in the form of dividends, rents, royalties, interest, wages, pensions, and other income; and on capital gains on land, financial securities, equity or other assets.

Property Taxes: Include taxes on the use or ownership of wealth and tangible property such as real estate holdings, land, and other fixed assets. Included also are betterment levies and special levies on improvements of immovable property.

Other Direct Taxes: Include taxes on inheritances, gifts and property transfers.

Tax Revenue — Indirect Taxes:

Production and Sales Taxes: Include all general sales, value-added and turnover taxes, and all other taxes and duties levied on the production, extraction, sale, leasing or delivery of goods and rendering of services.

International Trade Taxes: Include all taxes on international trade and commercial transactions in the form of both specific and ad-valorem import and export duties raised for purposes of revenue mobilization and for protectionism. Also included are taxes that are levied on foreign exchange transactions.

Other Indirect Taxes: Include revenue from fiscal monopolies, business and professional licenses, motor vehicle registrations, poll and stamp taxes, and excise duties.

Non-Tax Revenue: Comprises noncompulsory current revenue arising from government ownership of property, enterprises, financial assets, land or intangible holdings, in the form of dividends, interest, rents, royalties and entrepreneurial income. Also included are administrative fees, charges, fines and forfeits levied by the government.

Capital Revenue: Includes sales of fixed assets, stocks (strategic materials, stabilization stocks, grains), land and intangible assets.

Total Expenditures and Net Lending:

Include all payments by the government in the form of current and capital expenditures and financial investment and net lending, but exclude amortization payments on domestic and external government debt.

Current Expenditures: Include expenditures for goods and services, interest payments and transfers and subsidies:

Goods and Services: Include wages and salaries to government employees and the purchases of goods and services for the operation of the administration other than fixed assets and land.

Interest Payments: Include domestic and external interest payments on government debt outstanding in the form of bonds and other financial liabilities.

Current Transfers: Include transfers and subsidies intended to support the current expenditures of state and local governments, decentralized agencies, and public enterprises.

Capital Expenditures: Comprises fixed investment, capital transfers and financial investment and net lending:

Fixed Investment: Includes government outlays for investment in capital equipment, public works, and construction and the acquisition of any other fixed assets for nonmilitary productive purposes. Also included is the purchase of inventories and of land, subsoil deposits, and nonfinancial intangible assets such as patents, copyrights, and trademarks.

Capital Transfers: Include unrequited transfers with the purpose of permitting the acquisition of fixed assets by the beneficiary, compensation for damages or destruction of fixed assets or capital gains. Includes transfers for the construction of bridges, highways, hospitals, schools and other buildings. However, transfers for military construction or the purchase of military equipment are classified as current transfers. Also included is the amortization by the government of debts contracted by third parties, only if the government does not assume the debt. Includes transfers to those enterprises that have accumulated large losses in various years or suffered losses beyond their control. The nonreimbursable unrequited transfers of irregular character for both parties to the transaction are also considered as capital transfers.

Financial Investment and Net Lending: This category comprises government transactions in financial claims undertaken for purposes of public policy rather than for management of government liquidity. It covers government net loans to, and the acquisition of financial assets issued by other government levels, financial and nonfinancial public enterprises and government participation in the equity capital and debt of private enterprises. Net lending to financial institutions includes the provision of funds for their capitalization and the financing of any government lending activity considered to be part of the financial sector.

Current Savings:

Represent current revenue less current expenditures. By disbursing only part of its current receipts for current expenditures, the government generates a current account surplus available for the financing of real investment, financial investment and capital transfers, thereby contributing to domestic capital formation.

Surplus (+) or Deficit (-):

Total revenues plus grants less total expenditures and net lending.

Source:

Official statistics of member countries and IDB estimates. All calculations use current values in local currency.

TABLE D-1. BALANCE OF PAYMENTS SUMMARY[1]

(Millions of U.S. Dollars)

Item	1988	1989	1990	1991	1992	1993	1994	1995	1996	1997p
Current Account Balance	-9,830	-8,047	-1,542	-17,798	-33,990	-44,878	-49,377	-34,232	-37,116	-63,428
Trade Balance	25,019	29,526	30,510	12,087	-5,733	-9,574	-14,505	577	2,197	-16,970
Exports of Goods (fob)	115,365	128,037	141,099	141,500	150,720	164,568	191,433	232,532	259,437	287,955
Imports of Goods (fob)	90,346	98,511	110,590	129,413	156,453	174,143	205,940	231,956	257,240	304,924
Service Balance	-5,625	-4,382	-6,582	-7,715	-9,060	-11,286	-10,204	-9,436	-11,807	-13,621
Transportation	-4,559	-4,654	-5,136	-6,743	-7,419	-8,976	-9,131	-10,047	-10,580	-13,281
Travel	2,094	3,311	2,235	2,088	1,403	1,875	2,839	5,037	4,342	4,405
Other Services	-3,158	-3,039	-3,681	-3,060	-3,050	-4,194	-3,913	-4,245	-4,406	-4,353
Addendum: Freight and Insurance	-3,441	-3,522	-4,209	-5,819	-6,741	-9,023	-9,838	-10,314	...	...
Income Balance	-35,597	-40,020	-35,565	-32,817	-31,434	-35,634	-37,716	-40,746	-42,902	-48,508
Compensation of Employees	530	614	623	545	657	63	133	-16	-16	-409
Investment Income	-36,032	-40,531	-36,079	-33,252	-32,088	-35,742	-37,863	-40,683	-43,055	...
Current Transfers Balance	6,372	6,829	10,097	10,647	12,237	11,615	13,047	15,373	14,914	15,671
General Government	1,864	2,017	3,203	2,335	2,004	1,451	1,510	1,764	1,720	1,451
Other Sectors	4,508	4,812	6,893	8,312	10,232	9,847	11,295	13,275	12,693	7,138
Capital and Financial Account Balance[a]	5,093	5,698	16,808	34,639	56,171	68,669	49,056	61,970	63,745	77,875
Capital Account Balance	35	-16	11	268	326	322	1,128	2,013	5,424	...
Financial Account Balance	5,058	5,714	16,797	34,371	55,846	68,347	47,928	59,958	58,321	77,354
Direct Investment	8,036	7,307	7,029	11,382	13,760	12,125	25,235	27,687	37,285	55,251
Abroad	-309	-748	-1,061	-1,349	-742	-2,059	-2,909	-2,891	-1,622	-3,588
In Reporter	8,339	8,046	8,083	12,705	14,493	13,916	27,754	30,026	38,012	52,900
Portfolio Investment	4,323	1,843	11,354	16,909	36,123	70,412	65,976	4,891	33,313	27,583
Assets	1,273	-544	-9,825	-9,087	1,039	-3,870	-4,494	-1,005	...	...
Liabilities	3,050	2,387	21,179	25,995	35,081	74,227	70,420	5,910	...	...
Other Investment	-7,301	-3,436	-1,586	6,080	5,963	-14,190	-43,283	27,379	-12,276	-5,480
Assets	8,293	3,443	-5,278	1,818	-2,002	-8,943	-28,083	-17,362	...	...
Liabilities	-15,639	-6,959	3,534	4,129	7,965	-5,830	-15,172	44,023	...	...
Change in Reserves (- Increase)	6,835	-2,424	-15,123	-17,973	-22,612	-21,744	4,160	-23,606	-27,015	-15,107
Errors and Omissions	-2,080	4,800	-99	1,175	492	-2,046	-3,842	-4,132	387	659

[1] The totals in this table are those shown for Latin America in the following Appendix D tables. Totals are incomplete for some countries because of unavailable data. Furthermore, countries may provide estimates for aggregates but not their components. Therefore, components do not always correspond with the tables.[a] Includes Errors and Omissions for El Salvador (1995-97), Jamaica (1996-97), and Panama (1997).

TABLE D-2. CURRENT ACCOUNT BALANCE

(Millions of U.S. Dollars)

Country	1988	1989	1990	1991	1992	1993	1994	1995	1996	1997p
Argentina	-1,572.0	-1,305.0	4,552.0	-647.0	-5,462.0	-7,672.0	-10,118.0	-2,768.0	-3,787.0	-10,119.0
Bahamas	-66.5	-84.2	-36.6	-179.8	35.8	48.7	-42.2	-145.9	-263.3	-462.1
Barbados	48.0	28.0	-7.9	-23.5	143.4	70.0	132.3	90.2	104.4	58.4
Belize	-2.6	-19.0	15.4	-25.8	-28.6	-48.5	-40.1	-2.8	-2.3	-42.1
Bolivia	-324.9	-291.7	-219.8	-283.9	-561.2	-538.9	-87.8	-315.5	-364.1	-662.7
Brazil	4,156.0	1,002.0	-3,823.0	-1,450.0	6,089.0	20.0	-1,153.0	-18,136.0	-24,800.0	-33,482.0
Chile	-231.0	-689.0	-487.0	-99.0	-956.0	-2,547.0	-1,587.0	-1,403.0	-3,742.0	-4,062.0
Colombia	-216.0	-201.0	542.0	2,349.0	901.0	-2,102.0	-3,113.0	-4,101.0	-4,754.0	-4,968.5
Costa Rica	-178.5	-414.9	-424.0	-75.2	-370.4	-620.2	-233.6	-143.0	-125.2	-422.0
Dominican Rep.	-18.9	-327.3	-279.6	-157.3	-707.9	-421.4	-226.6	-101.1	-238.6	-224.9
Ecuador	-680.0	-715.0	-360.0	-708.0	-122.0	-678.0	-681.0	-735.0	111.0	-743.0
El Salvador	25.8	-194.4	-151.7	-167.5	-109.0	-77.2	-18.1	-261.5	-169.0	95.9
Guatemala	-414.0	-367.1	-212.9	-183.7	-705.9	-701.7	-625.3	-572.0	-451.5	-660.6
Guyana	-93.6	-113.3	-149.6	-119.0	-138.5	-140.2	-124.9	-134.8	-50.0	-68.4
Haiti	-40.4	-62.7	-21.9	-56.1	7.9	-16.6	4.0	-38.0	-73.5	-85.8
Honduras	-110.8	-170.3	-51.4	-172.4	-258.0	-327.2	-345.7	-179.7	-190.1	-94.9
Jamaica	47.5	-282.4	-312.1	-240.1	28.5	-184.0	16.9	-245.2	-238.4	-403.5
Mexico	-2,374.0	-5,825.0	-7,451.0	-14,888.0	-24,442.0	-23,400.0	-29,662.0	-1,576.0	-1,923.0	-7,226.8
Nicaragua	-715.4	-361.7	-305.2	-264.2	-769.0	-604.3	-644.5	-490.0	-419.3	-649.0
Panama	721.7	111.6	208.4	-212.4	-270.0	-143.4	22.3	-343.0	-60.3	-249.9
Paraguay	-210.2	255.6	-172.3	-324.1	-600.1	-412.6	-566.6	-500.5	-637.4	-669.4
Peru	-1,819.0	-570.0	-1,384.0	-1,510.0	-2,101.0	-2,302.0	-2,662.0	-4,298.0	-3,605.0	-3,414.0
Suriname	114.3	293.5	66.8	-133.4	25.4	44.0	58.6	72.9	9.6	5.5
Trinidad & Tobago	-88.6	-38.5	459.0	-4.7	138.9	113.1	217.8	293.8	-37.4	-554.8
Uruguay	22.1	133.5	185.9	42.4	-8.8	-243.8	-438.3	-212.5	-233.4	-321.1
Venezuela	-5,809.0	2,161.0	8,279.0	1,736.0	-3,749.0	-1,993.0	2,541.0	2,014.0	8,824.0	5,999.0
Latin America	**-9,830.0**	**-8,047.3**	**-1,541.5**	**-17,797.7**	**-33,989.5**	**-44,878.2**	**-49,376.8**	**-34,231.6**	**-37,115.8**	**-63,427.8**

TABLE D-3. TRADE BALANCE (FOB)

(Millions of U.S. Dollars)

Country	1988	1989	1990	1991	1992	1993	1994	1995	1996	1997p
Argentina	4,242.0	5,709.0	8,628.0	4,419.0	-1,450.0	-2,426.0	-4,238.0	2,238.0	1,622.0	-3,195.0
Bahamas[1,2]	-672.1	-910.8	-796.5	-816.9	-767.7	-738.0	-815.3	-931.3	-1,014.1	-1,038.2
Barbados[2]	-338.9	-416.4	-408.7	-416.1	-277.8	-326.7	-354.8	-445.7	-456.2	-600.6
Belize	-41.8	-64.1	-59.2	-97.5	-103.9	-118.5	-75.4	-67.6	-54.2	-80.7
Bolivia	-48.4	-6.0	55.2	-43.9	-432.4	-396.2	-30.0	-182.3	-236.1	-491.0
Brazil	19,168.0	16,112.0	10,747.0	10,578.0	15,239.0	14,329.0	10,861.0	-3,157.0	-5,539.0	-8,372.0
Chile	2,210.0	1,484.0	1,283.0	1,484.0	722.0	-990.0	732.0	1,368.0	-1,094.0	-1,296.0
Colombia	827.0	1,474.0	1,971.0	2,959.0	1,234.0	-1,657.0	-2,292.0	-2,699.0	-2,133.0	-2,392.3
Costa Rica	-97.9	-238.6	-442.5	-199.5	-471.8	-760.8	-605.8	-473.5	-413.6	-714.4
Dominican Rep.[3]	-718.3	-1,039.4	-1,058.3	-1,070.5	-1,611.8	-1,540.4	-1,541.9	-1,492.2	-1,531.9	-1,806.4
Ecuador	622.0	662.0	1,009.0	643.0	1,018.0	592.0	561.0	354.0	1,220.1	598.0
El Salvador[4]	-355.9	-662.7	-665.6	-704.6	-962.3	-1,034.9	-1,155.3	-1,444.0	-1,242.9	-1,107.5
Guatemala	-339.9	-358.3	-216.6	-443.0	-1,044.1	-1,020.8	-996.5	-875.1	-643.4	-940.1
Guyana	18.6	11.6	-22.9	17.2	-61.0	-68.3	-40.6	-40.8	-5.0	-24.4
Haiti	-103.5	-111.0	-176.8	-246.6	-138.5	-185.0	-83.8	-379.9	-351.1	-319.5
Honduras[3]	-34.0	-44.5	-11.8	-71.9	-150.9	-231.0	-257.4	-110.7	-132.7	-125.4
Jamaica[2]	-356.9	-589.8	-502.1	-391.6	-424.6	-815.1	-513.8	-813.2	-1,263.1	-1,780.9
Mexico[5]	2,611.0	405.0	-881.0	-7,279.0	-15,934.0	-13,481.0	-18,464.0	7,089.0	6,531.0	623.6
Nicaragua	-482.6	-228.6	-237.3	-419.9	-547.7	-392.4	-417.5	-334.8	-359.7	-741.8
Panama[6]	156.8	-123.9	-157.7	-399.6	-375.5	-334.2	-250.5	-575.0	-629.8	-562.6
Paraguay	-159.1	164.1	-253.5	-746.8	-869.1	-892.0	-1,270.0	-1,440.8	-1,428.9	-1,393.7
Peru	-134.0	1,246.0	399.0	-189.0	-341.0	-607.0	-997.0	-2,170.0	-2,000.0	-1,814.0
Suriname	212.3	389.7	163.3	-2.0	122.1	84.4	99.3	123.0	8.0	30.7
Trinidad & Tobago	405.3	505.5	1,012.5	564.2	695.7	547.2	741.1	587.7	275.7	-294.4
Uruguay	292.3	462.8	426.0	61.0	-121.8	-386.7	-706.0	-563.0	-686.9	-723.1
Venezuela	-1,863.0	5,694.0	10,706.0	4,900.0	1,322.0	3,275.0	7,606.0	7,013.0	13,756.0	11,592.0
Latin America	**25,019.0**	**29,525.6**	**30,509.5**	**12,087.0**	**-5,733.1**	**-9,574.4**	**-14,505.2**	**576.8**	**2,197.2**	**-16,969.7**

[1] Includes goods for processing in Free Trade Zone.
[2] Include goods procured in ports by carriers.
[3] Include goods for processing from 1993.
[4] Include goods for processing from 1995.
[5] Includes goods for processing.
[6] Includes activity within the Colón Free Zone.

TABLE D-4. EXPORTS OF GOODS (FOB)

(Millions of U.S. Dollars)

Country	1988	1989	1990	1991	1992	1993	1994	1995	1996	1997p
Argentina	9,134.0	9,573.0	12,354.0	11,978.0	12,235.0	13,117.0	15,839.0	20,964.0	23,811.0	25,223.0
Bahamas[1,2]	310.8	221.0	283.5	229.4	216.6	192.2	198.5	225.4	273.2	295.0
Barbados[2]	179.4	187.3	218.9	206.6	189.8	187.6	189.8	245.4	286.7	240.4
Belize	119.4	124.4	129.2	126.1	140.6	132.0	156.5	164.3	171.1	176.5
Bolivia	542.5	723.5	830.8	760.3	608.4	715.5	985.1	1,041.4	1,132.0	1,151.7
Brazil	33,773.0	34,375.0	31,408.0	31,619.0	35,793.0	39,630.0	44,102.0	46,506.0	47,747.0	52,986.0
Chile	7,054.0	8,079.0	8,372.0	8,942.0	10,007.0	9,198.0	11,604.0	16,025.0	15,405.0	16,923.0
Colombia	5,343.0	6,031.0	7,079.0	7,507.0	7,263.0	7,429.0	8,748.0	10,222.0	10,651.0	11,648.5
Costa Rica	1,180.7	1,333.4	1,354.2	1,498.1	1,739.1	1,866.8	2,122.0	2,480.2	2,743.6	2,953.8
Dominican Rep.[3]	889.7	924.4	734.5	658.3	562.5	3,114.0	3,361.5	3,652.8	4,195.3	4,801.8
Ecuador	2,205.0	2,354.0	2,724.0	2,851.0	3,101.0	3,066.0	3,843.0	4,411.0	4,900.0	5,264.0
El Salvador[4]	610.6	557.5	643.9	586.8	598.1	731.5	1,252.2	1,652.1	1,789.2	2,415.9
Guatemala	1,073.3	1,126.1	1,211.4	1,230.0	1,283.7	1,363.2	1,550.1	2,157.5	2,236.9	2,602.6
Guyana	214.6	204.7	203.9	239.0	381.7	415.5	463.4	495.7	575.0	594.0
Haiti	180.4	148.3	265.8	202.0	75.6	81.6	57.4	137.3	147.5	192.7
Honduras[3]	889.4	911.2	895.2	840.6	839.3	1,001.9	1,141.4	1,460.4	1,626.2	1,839.0
Jamaica[2]	898.4	1,028.9	1,190.6	1,196.7	1,116.5	1,105.4	1,551.0	1,792.7	1,379.4	1,361.2
Mexico[5]	30,692.0	35,171.0	40,711.0	42,687.0	46,196.0	51,885.0	60,882.0	79,542.0	96,000.0	110,431.4
Nicaragua	235.7	318.7	332.4	268.1	223.1	267.0	363.7	530.2	673.5	708.6
Panama[6]	2,505.9	2,742.1	3,346.2	4,191.8	5,104.2	5,416.9	6,044.3	6,104.0	5,888.6	6,934.9
Paraguay	871.0	1,180.0	1,382.3	1,120.8	1,081.5	1,827.0	2,281.7	3,030.4	2,766.7	2,643.4
Peru	2,731.0	3,533.0	3,321.0	3,406.0	3,661.0	3,516.0	4,598.0	5,591.0	5,897.0	6,754.0
Suriname	639.7	980.3	831.6	617.5	608.6	298.3	293.6	415.6	434.3	538.1
Trinidad & Tobago	1,469.5	1,550.8	1,960.1	1,774.5	1,691.4	1,500.1	1,777.6	2,456.1	2,565.2	2,528.6
Uruguay	1,404.5	1,599.0	1,692.9	1,604.7	1,801.4	1,731.6	1,917.6	2,147.6	2,448.5	2,780.5
Venezuela	10,217.0	13,059.0	17,623.0	15,159.0	14,202.0	14,779.0	16,110.0	19,082.0	23,693.0	23,966.0
Latin America	**115,364.5**	**128,036.6**	**141,099.4**	**141,500.3**	**150,720.1**	**164,568.1**	**191,433.4**	**232,532.1**	**259,436.9**	**287,954.6**

[1] Includes goods for processing in Free Trade Zone.
[2] Include goods procured in ports by carriers.
[3] Include goods for processing from 1993.
[4] Include goods for processing from 1995.
[5] Includes goods for processing.
[6] Includes activity within the Colón Free Zone.

TABLE D-5. IMPORTS OF GOODS (FOB)

(Millions of U.S. Dollars)

Country	1988	1989	1990	1991	1992	1993	1994	1995	1996	1997p
Argentina	4,892.0	3,864.0	3,726.0	7,559.0	13,685.0	15,543.0	20,077.0	18,726.0	22,189.0	28,418.0
Bahamas[1,2]	982.9	1,131.8	1,080.0	1,046.3	984.3	930.2	1,013.8	1,156.7	1,287.3	1,333.2
Barbados	518.4	603.7	627.6	622.7	467.7	514.3	544.6	691.2	742.9	841.0
Belize	161.2	188.5	188.4	223.6	244.5	250.5	231.8	231.9	225.3	257.2
Bolivia	590.9	729.5	775.6	804.2	1,040.8	1,111.7	1,015.1	1,223.7	1,368.1	1,642.7
Brazil	14,605.0	18,263.0	20,661.0	21,041.0	20,554.0	25,301.0	33,241.0	49,663.0	53,286.0	61,358.0
Chile	4,844.0	6,595.0	7,089.0	7,458.0	9,285.0	10,188.0	10,872.0	14,657.0	16,499.0	18,219.0
Colombia	4,516.0	4,557.0	5,108.0	4,548.0	6,029.0	9,086.0	11,040.0	12,921.0	12,784.0	14,040.8
Costa Rica	1,278.6	1,572.0	1,796.7	1,697.6	2,210.9	2,627.6	2,727.8	2,953.7	3,157.2	3,668.2
Dominican Rep.[3]	1,608.0	1,963.8	1,792.8	1,728.8	2,174.3	4,654.4	4,903.4	5,145.0	5,727.2	6,608.2
Ecuador	1,583.0	1,692.0	1,715.0	2,208.0	2,083.0	2,474.0	3,282.0	4,057.0	3,680.0	4,666.0
El Salvador[4]	966.5	1,220.2	1,309.5	1,291.4	1,560.5	1,766.4	2,407.4	3,096.1	3,032.1	3,523.4
Guatemala	1,413.2	1,484.4	1,428.0	1,673.0	2,327.8	2,384.0	2,546.6	3,032.6	2,880.3	3,542.7
Guyana	196.0	193.1	226.8	221.8	442.7	483.8	504.0	536.5	580.0	618.4
Haiti	283.9	259.3	442.6	448.6	214.1	266.6	141.2	517.2	498.6	512.2
Honduras	923.4	955.7	907.0	912.5	990.2	1,232.9	1,398.8	1,571.1	1,758.9	1,964.4
Jamaica[2]	1,255.3	1,618.7	1,692.7	1,588.3	1,541.1	1,920.5	2,064.8	2,605.9	2,642.5	3,142.1
Mexico[5]	28,081.0	34,766.0	41,592.0	49,966.0	62,130.0	65,366.0	79,346.0	72,453.0	89,469.0	109,807.8
Nicaragua	718.3	547.3	569.7	688.0	770.8	659.4	781.2	865.0	1,033.2	1,450.4
Panama[6]	2,349.1	2,866.0	3,503.9	4,591.4	5,479.7	5,751.1	6,294.8	6,679.0	6,518.4	7,497.5
Paraguay	1,030.1	1,015.9	1,635.8	1,867.6	1,950.6	2,719.0	3,551.7	4,471.2	4,195.6	4,037.1
Peru	2,865.0	2,287.0	2,922.0	3,595.0	4,002.0	4,123.0	5,596.0	7,761.0	7,897.0	8,568.0
Suriname	427.4	590.6	668.3	619.5	486.5	213.9	194.3	292.6	426.3	507.4
Trinidad & Tobago	1,064.2	1,045.2	947.6	1,210.3	995.6	952.9	1,036.6	1,868.5	2,289.5	2,823.0
Uruguay	1,112.2	1,136.2	1,266.9	1,543.7	1,923.2	2,118.3	2,623.6	2,710.6	3,135.4	3,503.6
Venezuela	12,080.0	7,365.0	6,917.0	10,259.0	12,880.0	11,504.0	8,504.0	12,069.0	9,937.0	12,374.0
Latin America	**90,345.6**	**98,510.9**	**110,589.9**	**129,413.3**	**156,453.3**	**174,142.5**	**205,939.5**	**231,955.5**	**257,239.8**	**304,924.3**

[1] Includes goods for processing in Free Trade Zone.
[2] Include goods procured in ports by carriers.
[3] Include goods for processing from 1993.
[4] Include goods for processing from 1995.
[5] Includes goods for processing.
[6] Includes activity within the Colón Free Zone.

TABLE D-6. SERVICE BALANCE

(Millions of U.S. Dollars)

Country	1988	1989	1990	1991	1992	1993	1994	1995	1996	1997p
Argentina	-687.0	-600.0	-674.0	-1,599.0	-2,257.0	-2,730.0	-2,941.0	-2,222.0	-2,495.0	-3,069.0
Bahamas	784.0	952.3	927.1	804.9	874.1	891.3	883.4	903.2	862.4	697.0
Barbados	405.9	465.6	403.7	398.9	409.7	416.9	492.5	550.1	573.1	687.5
Belize	21.1	23.4	55.4	54.5	61.0	58.0	33.2	47.6	46.8	32.8
Bolivia	-126.5	-154.9	-164.7	-154.2	-146.4	-140.3	-124.5	-151.7	-172.0	-211.7
Brazil	-3,023.0	-2,785.0	-3,761.0	-3,891.0	-3,342.0	-5,590.0	-5,346.0	-7,495.0	-8,984.0	-11,195.0
Chile	-690.0	-460.0	-230.0	31.0	-177.0	-223.0	-150.0	-351.0	-354.0	-314.0
Colombia	-262.0	-274.0	-150.0	-219.0	-45.0	199.0	623.0	184.0	-227.0	-38.3
Costa Rica	6.6	1.9	59.3	156.6	130.7	222.9	334.9	362.8	316.8	358.3
Dominican Rep.	616.4	576.4	656.8	719.4	793.5	788.7	974.1	1,058.5	1,208.6	1,429.5
Ecuador	-166.0	-110.0	-112.0	-148.0	-113.0	-143.0	-163.0	-118.0	-91.0	-385.0
El Salvador	-13.4	-41.1	14.6	-12.0	12.4	24.2	-56.7	-137.0	-90.1	-72.8
Guatemala	-122.1	-79.2	-27.6	102.4	88.7	74.3	52.6	-29.0	-100.7	-73.1
Guyana	-37.9	-43.8	-46.3	-48.2	-34.0	-32.8	-40.2	-38.4	-41.8	-48.8
Haiti	-102.6	-100.4	-19.8	-25.7	3.3	5.6	-57.2	-180.4	-174.2	-193.2
Honduras	-81.1	-80.8	-82.5	-51.7	-41.2	-85.1	-87.5	-67.6	-74.7	-48.9
Jamaica	217.7	155.3	329.1	321.8	389.6	437.2	367.2	353.5	...	908.2
Mexico	-197.0	-672.0	-2,229.0	-2,090.0	-2,684.0	-2,529.0	-2,721.0	64.0	82.0	420.0
Nicaragua	-100.7	-97.2	-52.5	-66.0	-62.1	-56.4	-56.9	-101.6	-116.4	-79.5
Panama	544.5	406.3	409.2	348.9	294.2	298.2	310.6	402.5	525.3	480.9
Paraguay	-4.9	91.4	39.9	356.7	283.7	473.8	739.6	942.4	843.0	781.8
Peru	-333.0	-307.0	-365.0	-413.0	-575.0	-575.0	-502.0	-773.0	-679.0	-739.0
Suriname	-95.7	-119.6	-134.3	-134.6	-135.7	-55.1	-40.9	-57.8	-124.7	-127.8
Trinidad & Tobago	-182.7	-158.9	-150.6	-129.1	-109.1	-112.9	-111.5	100.7	235.5	242.6
Uruguay	32.8	11.6	73.1	173.7	271.5	281.9	469.1	501.5	559.6	528.6
Venezuela	-2,028.0	-982.0	-1,351.0	-2,202.0	-2,951.0	-3,185.0	-3,086.0	-3,184.0	-3,335.0	-3,592.0
Latin America[1]	**-5,624.6**	**-4,381.7**	**-6,582.1**	**-7,714.7**	**-9,060.1**	**-11,285.6**	**-10,204.2**	**-9,435.7**	**-11,806.5**	**-13,620.9**

[1] Latin American aggregate excludes Jamaica (1996).

TABLE D-7. SERVICE TRANSACTIONS: TRANSPORTATION BALANCE

(Millions of U.S. Dollars)

Country	1988	1989	1990	1991	1992	1993	1994	1995	1996	1997p
Argentina	43.0	155.0	219.0	-161.0	-460.0	-841.0	-1,075.0	-969.0	-1,142.0	-1,555.0
Bahamas	-102.1	-97.2	-78.5	-76.0	-67.3	-73.4	-65.0	-81.8	-115.4	-132.3
Barbados	-77.0	-90.8	-89.1	-86.9	-69.2	-77.4	-82.9	-100.4	-106.0	...
Belize	-14.2	-15.9	-14.0	-22.1	-23.0	-24.7	-26.7	-32.3	-31.5	-34.1
Bolivia	-91.7	-123.9	-131.9	-120.8	-113.5	-117.9	-119.0	-133.1	-143.0	-169.7
Brazil	-1,040.0	-1,452.0	-1,643.0	-1,655.0	-1,360.0	-2,417.0	-2,100.0	-3,200.0	-3,480.0	-6,514.0
Chile	-298.0	-344.0	-225.0	-262.0	-310.0	-382.0	-157.0	-532.0	-575.0	-589.0
Colombia	-87.0	-110.0	-104.0	-53.0	25.0	181.0	193.0	278.0	258.0	...
Costa Rica	-89.2	-112.0	-127.5	-118.1	-143.2	-192.5	-180.2	-200.3	-237.8	-293.8
Dominican Rep.	-118.2	-150.5	-113.0	-108.3	-159.9	-11.9	-11.4	-10.6	-16.3	-11.9
Ecuador	-94.0	-66.0	-72.0	-133.0	-124.0	-150.0	-170.0	-137.0	-76.0	-276.0
El Salvador	-5.7	-20.4	-57.1	-81.0	-106.0	-113.0	-134.3	-211.2	-171.1	-180.6
Guatemala	-135.8	-139.6	-125.7	-159.7	-183.7	-197.2	-216.1	-224.9	-224.5	-260.1
Guyana	-10.9	-6.1	-6.8	-2.5	-39.4	-37.3	-36.4	-35.7	-37.8	-41.4
Haiti	-80.9	-77.6	-25.5	-30.8	-21.5	-16.8	-44.9	...	...	...
Honduras	-57.1	-58.7	-54.3	-51.7	-55.6	-95.2	-118.0	-140.3	-151.1	...
Jamaica	-92.7	-171.2	-143.3	-166.4	-178.9	-224.3	-188.7	-241.7	...	...
Mexico	-792.0	-1,266.0	-1,619.0	-1,952.0	-2,245.0	-2,388.0	-3,220.0	-2,259.0	-2,766.0	-1,226.4
Nicaragua	-67.1	-43.6	-45.2	-29.6	-65.0	-52.8	-62.2	-65.2	-72.1	-53.3
Panama	282.6	172.7	144.3	64.9	-23.3	-25.0	-37.9	17.6	119.9	89.9
Paraguay	-150.7	-136.9	-184.7	-187.6	-208.6	-328.4	-320.4	-441.5	-438.0	-433.4
Peru	-168.0	-95.0	-154.0	-297.0	-292.0	-333.0	-424.0	-567.0	-504.0	-537.0
Suriname	-49.3	-58.3	-62.6	-55.2	-49.4	-30.5	-21.8	-36.5	-31.4	-37.4
Trinidad & Tobago	-58.0	-90.9	-74.7	-106.3	-61.9	-44.5	-58.8	99.6	101.7	102.5
Uruguay	-15.1	-0.5	-5.3	-19.5	50.1	-10.3	16.5	22.9	8.9	...
Venezuela	-1,190.0	-255.0	-343.0	-872.0	-1,134.0	-973.0	-470.0	-846.0	-749.0	-1,128.0
Latin America[1]	**-4,559.1**	**-4,654.4**	**-5,135.9**	**-6,742.6**	**-7,419.3**	**-8,976.1**	**-9,131.2**	**-10,047.4**	**-10,579.5**	**-13,281.0**

[1] Latin American aggregate excludes Barbados (1997), Colombia (1997), Haiti (1995-97), Honduras (1997), Jamaica (1996-97), and Uruguay (1997).

TABLE D-8. SERVICE TRANSACTIONS: TRAVEL BALANCE

(Millions of U.S. Dollars)

Country	1988	1989	1990	1991	1992	1993	1994	1995	1996	1997p
Argentina	-341.0	-224.0	-268.0	-957.0	-1,430.0	-1,608.0	-1,636.0	-1,010.0	-1,071.0	-1,094.0
Bahamas	972.3	1,118.9	1,128.0	985.9	1,050.5	1,125.7	1,134.0	1,133.0	1,163.3	1,166.2
Barbados	425.0	490.1	458.9	422.0	428.5	481.1	543.9	597.9	618.5	685.1
Belize	15.5	21.0	31.5	37.9	45.8	48.9	52.7	62.2	66.9	61.2
Bolivia	-2.2	-1.7	-2.1	-0.5	-2.4	0.1	1.3	6.9	10.4	8.7
Brazil	-588.0	474.0	-122.0	-212.0	-319.0	-801.0	-1,212.0	-2,419.0	-3,593.0	-4,377.0
Chile	-243.0	12.0	105.0	270.0	174.0	234.0	318.0	208.0	143.0	176.0
Colombia	-77.0	-159.0	-48.0	-41.0	65.0	61.0	50.0	43.0	3.0	...
Costa Rica	105.3	93.8	129.5	186.2	212.7	317.9	330.5	343.3	359.1	406.9
Dominican Rep.	641.1	570.7	582.1	602.0	682.2	1,118.2	1,274.3	1,389.7	1,592.0	1,888.4
Ecuador	6.0	18.0	13.0	12.0	14.0	40.0	49.0	20.0	62.0	63.0
El Salvador	-19.7	-45.7	15.2	14.0	15.4	17.7	16.0	13.0	13.7	...
Guatemala	-33.1	-14.6	18.3	45.0	83.1	87.4	54.3	71.4	80.9	120.8
Guyana	-5.7	-14.0	-7.5	-15.4	18.7	17.9	11.1	11.5	11.8	11.5
Haiti	39.6	37.2	-3.3	5.2	18.7	12.7	-9.2	...	...	...
Honduras	-9.5	-10.0	-8.5	-6.2	-6.4	5.0	15.0	50.1	55.0	83.6
Jamaica	431.8	490.4	637.7	703.5	776.5	862.6	842.4	874.5	979.7	932.4
Mexico	847.0	574.0	7.0	147.0	-23.0	605.0	1,026.0	3,008.0	3,545.0	3,902.5
Nicaragua	3.6	3.2	-2.5	-11.4	-6.9	10.2	10.1	9.5	-5.8	14.8
Panama	77.8	74.5	73.2	94.5	94.9	103.1	139.0	182.8	207.3	213.3
Paraguay	54.8	52.2	24.9	365.6	337.7	412.4	523.1	774.3	645.5	558.7
Peru	30.0	-16.0	-79.0	-39.0	-100.0	-54.0	65.0	131.0	281.0	320.0
Suriname	-6.8	-10.0	-20.9	-27.4	-16.7	5.1	8.1	17.8	6.1	6.4
Trinidad & Tobago	-76.6	-34.1	-27.6	-9.2	-3.8	-25.4	-3.0	8.1	34.7	34.5
Uruguay	64.3	61.4	126.8	232.8	277.0	318.1	398.0	374.9	524.7	495.2
Venezuela	-218.0	-251.0	-527.0	-717.0	-984.0	-1,521.0	-1,163.0	-865.0	-1,392.0	-1,273.0
Latin America[1]	**2,093.5**	**3,311.3**	**2,234.7**	**2,087.5**	**1,402.5**	**1,874.7**	**2,838.6**	**5,036.9**	**4,341.8**	**4,405.2**

[1] Latin American aggregate excludes Colombia (1997), El Salvador (1997), and Haiti (1995-97).

TABLE D-9. SERVICE TRANSACTIONS: OTHER SERVICES BALANCE

(Millions of U.S. Dollars)

Country	1988	1989	1990	1991	1992	1993	1994	1995	1996	1997p
Argentina	-389.0	-531.0	-625.0	-481.0	-367.0	-281.0	-230.0	-243.0	-282.0	-420.0
Bahamas	-86.2	-69.4	-122.4	-105.0	-109.1	-161.0	-185.6	-148.0	-185.5	-336.9
Barbados	58.0	66.4	33.9	63.9	50.4	13.2	31.5	52.6	60.6	...
Belize	19.8	18.3	37.9	38.7	38.2	33.8	7.2	17.7	11.4	5.7
Bolivia	-32.6	-29.3	-30.7	-32.9	-30.5	-22.5	-6.8	-25.6	-39.4	-50.7
Brazil	-1,395.0	-1,807.0	-1,996.0	-2,024.0	-1,663.0	-2,372.0	-2,034.0	-1,876.0	-1,911.0	-304.0
Chile	-149.0	-128.0	-110.0	23.0	-41.0	-75.0	-311.0	-27.0	78.0	99.0
Colombia	-98.0	-5.0	2.0	-125.0	-135.0	-43.0	380.0	-137.0	-488.0	...
Costa Rica	-9.5	20.1	57.3	88.5	61.2	97.5	184.6	219.8	195.5	245.2
Dominican Rep.	93.5	156.2	187.6	225.7	271.2	-317.6	-288.8	-320.6	-367.1	-447.0
Ecuador	-78.0	-62.0	-53.0	-27.0	-3.0	-33.0	-42.0	-1.0	-77.0	-172.0
El Salvador	12.1	25.0	56.5	55.1	102.9	119.5	61.6	61.2	67.3	107.6
Guatemala	46.8	75.0	79.8	217.1	189.3	184.1	214.4	124.5	42.9	66.2
Guyana	-21.3	-23.7	-32.0	-30.3	-13.2	-13.4	-14.8	-14.2	-6.8	-9.3
Haiti	-61.4	-60.1	9.0	-0.1	...	...	-3.1	...	...	...
Honduras	-14.5	-12.1	-19.7	6.2	20.8	5.1	15.5	22.6	21.4	...
Jamaica	-121.4	-163.9	-165.3	-215.3	-208.0	-201.1	-286.5	-279.3	...	-24.2
Mexico	-252.0	20.0	-617.0	-285.0	-416.0	-746.0	-528.0	-685.0	-697.0	-2,256.2
Nicaragua	-37.2	-56.8	-4.8	-25.0	9.8	-13.8	-4.8	-45.9	-38.5	-41.0
Panama	184.1	159.1	191.7	189.5	222.6	220.1	209.5	202.1	198.1	177.7
Paraguay	91.0	176.1	199.7	178.7	154.6	389.8	536.9	609.6	635.5	656.5
Peru	-193.0	-196.0	-132.0	-78.0	-184.0	-188.0	-143.0	-337.0	-456.0	-522.0
Suriname	-39.6	-51.4	-50.7	-52.0	-69.6	-29.7	-27.3	-39.1	-99.4	-96.8
Trinidad & Tobago	-48.1	-33.9	-48.4	-13.6	-43.4	-43.0	-49.7	-7.0	99.0	105.6
Uruguay	-16.3	-49.3	-48.4	-39.6	-55.6	-25.8	54.6	103.7	26.0	54.2
Venezuela	-621.0	-476.0	-481.0	-613.0	-833.0	-691.0	-1,453.0	-1,473.0	-1,194.0	-1,191.0
Latin America[1]	**-3,157.8**	**-3,038.7**	**-3,681.0**	**-3,060.4**	**-3,050.4**	**-4,193.8**	**-3,912.6**	**-4,244.9**	**-4,406.0**	**-4,353.4**

[1] Latin American aggregate excludes Barbados (1997), Colombia (1997), Haiti (1992-93; 1995-97), Honduras (1997), and Jamaica (1996).

TABLE D-10. SERVICE TRANSACTIONS: FREIGHT AND INSURANCE

(Millions of U.S. Dollars)

Country	1988	1989	1990	1991	1992	1993	1994	1995	1996	1997p
Argentina	137.0	193.0	142.0	-224.0	-518.0	-585.0	-846.0	-818.0	-974.0	-1,267.0
Bahamas	-75.9	-103.2	-97.4	-99.6	-98.0	-115.4	-141.7	-153.7	-158.6	-163.9
Barbados	-63.3	-56.9	-75.4	-77.7	-54.3	-81.5	-102.9	-118.7	-113.2	...
Belize	-20.3	-23.7	-23.2	-27.6	-30.2	-30.9	-32.6	-32.9	...	...
Bolivia	-102.3	-130.2	-138.1	-127.4	-115.8	-117.0	-121.5	-140.0	...	...
Brazil	394.0	71.0	-72.0	-230.0	-152.0	-998.0	-411.0	-1,122.0	...	-2,866.0
Chile	8.0	-64.0	140.0	49.0	139.0	32.0	9.0	-240.0	-214.0	-297.0
Colombia	-246.0	-171.0	-86.0	-126.0	-174.0	-277.0	-248.0	-462.0	-557.0	...
Costa Rica	-146.0	-176.2	-194.5	-153.9	-242.7	-291.4	-302.9	-334.4	-314.1	-378.6
Dominican Rep.	-148.9	-187.9	-156.3	-157.2	-216.1	-503.5	-502.4	-532.7	-522.3	-581.4
Ecuador	-29.0	5.0	...	-31.0	-30.0	-66.0	-74.0	-79.0	-61.0	-276.0
El Salvador	-73.8	-94.1	-95.7	-115.5	-145.8	-152.0	-179.2	...	...	...
Guatemala	-148.2	-157.7	-135.3	-171.0	-197.9	-222.1	-241.5	-261.4	-264.0	...
Guyana	...	...	...	...	-4.4	-4.8	-5.0	-5.4	-9.0	-9.6
Haiti	-52.6	-51.6	5.4	4.0	1.4	1.6	-31.4	...	...	...
Honduras	-84.9	-87.0	-85.4	-85.3	-92.9	-108.4	-122.8	-136.2	-153.4	-171.4
Jamaica	-201.6	-260.1	-251.8	-250.4	-249.4	-321.6	-352.2	-473.8	...	...
Mexico	-862.0	-1,184.0	-1,664.0	-1,725.0	-2,050.0	-2,577.0	-3,830.0	-2,601.0	-3,068.0	...
Nicaragua	-75.1	-49.1	-51.0	-41.6	-62.8	-49.1	-58.3	-62.3	-69.2	-48.3
Panama	-170.9	-256.7	-377.5	-506.5	-558.9	-634.6	-691.5	-703.6	-628.0	-624.7
Paraguay	-150.6	-139.6	-209.1	-251.5	-271.4	-329.0	-294.7	-407.4	-410.7	-393.0
Peru	-66.0	-9.0	-151.0	-292.0	-305.0	-371.0	-472.0	-625.0	-589.0	-628.0
Suriname	-38.2	-42.4	-39.8	-29.6	-36.0	-22.9	-14.4	-25.6	...	...
Trinidad & Tobago	-124.2	-154.6	-161.8	-232.1	-212.2	-191.9	-164.3	-24.8	...	18.0
Uruguay	-20.7	-24.3	-8.1	20.3	44.2	22.0	77.8	46.6	-17.2	-20.8
Venezuela	-1,079.0	-368.0	-423.0	-937.0	-1,108.0	-1,028.0	-684.0	-1,001.0	-925.0	-1,137.0
Latin America[1]	**-3,440.5**	**-3,522.3**	**-4,209.0**	**-5,818.6**	**-6,741.2**	**-9,022.5**	**-9,837.5**	**-10,314.3**	...	...

[1] Latin American aggregate excludes Ecuador (1990), El Salvador (1995), Guyana (1988-91), and Haiti (1995).

TABLE D-11. INCOME BALANCE

(Millions of U.S. Dollars)

Country	1988	1989	1990	1991	1992	1993	1994	1995	1996	1997p
Argentina	-5,127.0	-6,422.0	-4,400.0	-4,260.0	-2,416.0	-2,927.0	-3,259.0	-3,216.0	-3,248.0	-4,205.0
Bahamas	-166.9	-131.6	-172.8	-179.0	-82.6	-128.4	-137.6	-135.7	-148.8	-160.2
Barbados	-35.5	-25.8	-45.7	-39.5	-28.9	-41.0	-40.7	-47.7	-52.2	-59.2
Belize	-7.7	-9.4	-10.2	-10.8	-16.1	-17.5	-25.3	-23.0	-26.0	-23.8
Bolivia	-285.3	-280.7	-269.5	-268.3	-225.0	-239.3	-199.3	-226.1	-206.2	-212.2
Brazil	-12,080.0	-12,546.0	-11,608.0	-9,651.0	-7,997.0	-10,322.0	-9,091.0	-11,105.0	-12,723.0	-16,091.0
Chile	-1,932.0	-1,940.0	-1,737.0	-1,926.0	-1,881.0	-1,655.0	-2,499.0	-2,730.0	-2,794.0	-2,979.0
Colombia	-1,745.0	-2,299.0	-2,305.0	-2,089.0	-2,022.0	-1,782.0	-2,307.0	-2,265.0	-2,925.0	-3,129.6
Costa Rica	-342.6	-369.6	-232.7	-173.9	-202.6	-225.4	-128.4	-185.8	-168.0	-201.5
Dominican Rep.	-270.6	-248.7	-248.7	-192.7	-321.4	-552.6	-623.1	-659.4	-1,062.5	-1,193.3
Ecuador	-1,233.0	-1,364.0	-1,364.0	-1,313.0	-1,147.0	-1,257.0	-1,224.0	-1,202.0	-1,308.0	-1,347.0
El Salvador	-105.5	-101.3	-131.7	-120.8	-97.2	-111.6	-94.6	-70.0	-90.5	-87.2
Guatemala	-176.3	-179.4	-195.7	-102.8	-141.0	-118.4	-130.0	-159.1	-229.9	-181.4
Guyana	-93.8	-102.7	-108.7	-109.0	-96.6	-101.8	-106.1	-117.7	-53.9	-59.2
Haiti	-27.1	-25.6	-18.2	-18.0	-11.9	-10.6	-11.2	-30.6	-10.7	-13.6
Honduras	-231.3	-237.6	-236.8	-246.1	-282.0	-229.4	-211.7	-265.4	-259.4	-232.6
Jamaica	-335.2	-350.1	-430.0	-438.8	-293.9	-195.9	-294.1	-320.1	...	-219.3
Mexico	-7,043.0	-8,101.0	-8,316.0	-8,265.0	-9,209.0	-11,030.0	-12,259.0	-12,689.0	-13,067.0	-13,400.4
Nicaragua	-262.1	-204.8	-217.0	-363.3	-494.8	-429.1	-465.5	-358.6	-300.3	-194.5
Panama	-87.9	-266.5	-262.4	-384.1	-392.7	-310.5	-186.7	-324.7	-107.5	-331.6
Paraguay	-81.3	-23.4	-14.3	-6.3	-48.6	-94.7	-67.7	-74.3	-90.9	-106.9
Peru	-1,515.0	-1,685.0	-1,733.0	-1,367.0	-1,632.0	-1,615.0	-1,800.0	-1,997.0	-1,573.0	-1,497.0
Suriname	-15.1	-11.3	-15.2	-20.0	-13.3	-6.2	-3.8	-2.6	2.8	-0.2
Trinidad & Tobago	-302.0	-377.6	-396.8	-442.1	-448.1	-325.8	-412.1	-390.1	-536.0	-498.0
Uruguay	-324.3	-348.9	-321.3	-232.4	-187.1	-192.4	-242.6	-227.0	-188.6	-207.8
Venezuela	-1,771.0	-2,368.0	-774.0	-598.0	-1,746.0	-1,715.0	-1,896.0	-1,924.0	-1,735.0	-1,877.0
Latin America[1]	**-35,596.5**	**-40,020.0**	**-35,564.7**	**-32,816.9**	**-31,433.8**	**-35,633.6**	**-37,715.5**	**-40,745.9**	**-42,901.6**	**-48,508.5**

[1] Latin American aggregate excludes Jamaica (1996).

TABLE D-12. INVESTMENT INCOME BALANCE

(Millions of U.S. Dollars)

Country	1988	1989	1990	1991	1992	1993	1994	1995	1996	1997p
Argentina	-5,127.0	-6,422.0	-4,400.0	-4,260.0	-2,416.0	-2,927.0	-3,259.0	-3,216.0	-3,248.0	-4,205.0
Bahamas	-149.6	-110.8	-138.3	-132.0	-58.0	-105.4	-112.6	-107.9	-119.7	-129.1
Barbados	-43.7	-34.4	-56.8	-56.7	-39.9	-52.4	-47.9	-55.8	-61.2	...
Belize	-6.2	-7.9	-8.4	-9.3	-15.0	-16.2	-20.0	-21.5	-24.0	-21.1
Bolivia	-284.7	-276.1	-264.9	-263.6	-220.3	-234.3	-193.6	-222.5	-204.4	-223.5
Brazil	-12,084.0	-12,547.0	-11,613.0	-9,652.0	-8,002.0	-10,210.0	-8,960.0	-10,948.0	-12,660.0	-16,137.0
Chile	-1,918.0	-1,923.0	-1,730.0	-1,926.0	-1,881.0	-1,655.0	-2,499.0	-2,730.0	-2,794.0	-2,979.0
Colombia	-1,742.0	-2,291.0	-2,269.0	-1,999.0	-1,953.0	-1,711.0	-2,231.0	-2,142.0	-2,727.0	...
Costa Rica	-351.7	-379.6	-244.7	-187.3	-216.8	-241.4	-138.4	-193.5	-186.5	-220.8
Dominican Rep.	-270.6	-248.7	-248.7	-192.7	-321.4	-558.1	-633.6	-675.0	-1,080.2	-1,209.1
Ecuador	-1,047.0	-1,190.0	-1,209.0	-1,115.0	-947.0	-925.0	-1,000.0	-936.0	-1,038.0	-1,067.0
El Salvador	-118.1	-106.9	-137.7	-126.7	-103.9	-116.7	-99.6	...	...	...
Guatemala	-177.0	-191.4	-204.4	-139.9	-178.5	-151.7	-148.7	-159.1	-229.9	-203.1
Guyana	...	...	...	...	-93.9	-92.7	-97.6	-108.7	-44.9	-41.9
Haiti	-27.1	-25.6	-18.2	-18.0	-11.9	-10.6	-11.2	...	...	...
Honduras	-243.1	-251.2	-249.7	-276.7	-334.0	-41.1	-3.6	-34.3	-41.0	-41.5
Jamaica	-407.4	-435.4	-517.1	-478.9	-348.2	-240.2	-335.5	-366.6	-209.0	...
Mexico	-7,585.0	-8,681.0	-8,922.0	-8,881.0	-9,839.0	-11,677.0	-12,906.0	-13,384.0	-13,792.0	...
Nicaragua	-262.1	-204.8	-217.0	-363.3	-494.8	-429.1	-465.5	-358.6	-300.3	-194.5
Panama	-170.6	-354.8	-354.4	-478.0	-481.7	-402.5	-281.6	-420.4	-185.1	-426.0
Paraguay	-105.0	-62.5	-48.1	-48.7	-112.5	-94.7	-67.7	-74.3	-90.9	-106.9
Peru	-1,515.0	-1,685.0	-1,733.0	-1,367.0	-1,632.0	-1,615.0	-1,800.0	-1,997.0	-1,573.0	-1,497.0
Suriname	-12.2	-9.6	-13.0	-16.9	-10.4	-4.6	-2.8	-1.4	4.2	0.9
Trinidad & Tobago	-297.9	-375.7	-394.8	-439.3	-444.3	-324.3	-410.7	-388.7	-536.0	-498.0
Uruguay	-324.3	-348.9	-321.3	-232.4	-187.1	-192.4	-242.6	-227.0	-188.6	...
Venezuela	-1,763.0	-2,368.0	-765.0	-592.0	-1,745.0	-1,714.0	-1,895.0	-1,915.0	-1,725.0	-1,865.0
Latin America[1]	**-36,032.3**	**-40,531.3**	**-36,078.5**	**-33,252.4**	**-32,087.6**	**-35,742.4**	**-37,863.2**	**-40,683.3**	**-43,054.5**	...

[1] Latin American aggregate excludes El Salvador (1995-96), Guyana (1988-91), Haiti (1995-96).

TABLE D-13. CURRENT TRANSFERS BALANCE

(*Millions of* U.S. *Dollars*)

Country	1988	1989	1990	1991	1992	1993	1994	1995	1996	1997p
Argentina	...	8.0	998.0	793.0	661.0	411.0	320.0	432.0	334.0	350.0
Bahamas	-11.5	5.9	5.6	11.2	12.0	23.8	27.3	17.9	37.2	39.3
Barbados	16.6	4.7	42.7	33.2	40.4	20.8	35.3	33.6	39.8	30.6
Belize	25.8	31.1	29.4	28.0	30.4	29.5	27.5	40.2	31.1	29.6
Bolivia	135.3	149.9	159.2	182.5	242.6	236.9	266.0	244.6	250.2	252.2
Brazil	91.0	221.0	799.0	1,514.0	2,189.0	1,603.0	2,423.0	3,621.0	2,446.0	2,176.0
Chile	181.0	227.0	197.0	312.0	380.0	321.0	330.0	310.0	500.0	527.0
Colombia	964.0	898.0	1,026.0	1,698.0	1,734.0	1,138.0	862.0	679.0	532.0	591.7
Costa Rica	255.4	191.4	191.9	141.6	173.3	143.1	165.7	153.5	139.6	135.6
Dominican Rep.	353.6	384.4	370.6	386.5	431.8	882.9	964.3	992.0	1,147.2	1,345.3
Ecuador	97.0	97.0	107.0	110.0	120.0	130.0	145.0	231.0	290.0	391.0
El Salvador	500.5	610.7	631.0	669.9	938.2	1,045.0	1,288.5	1,389.5	1,254.5	1,363.4
Guatemala	224.3	249.8	227.0	259.7	390.5	363.2	448.6	491.2	522.5	534.0
Guyana	19.5	21.6	28.3	21.0	53.0	62.6	61.9	62.1	50.7	64.0
Haiti	192.9	174.3	192.9	234.2	155.0	173.4	156.2	552.9	462.5	440.5
Honduras	235.6	192.6	279.7	197.3	216.1	218.3	210.9	264.0	276.7	312.0
Jamaica	521.9	502.2	290.9	268.5	357.4	389.8	457.6	534.6	542.3	688.5
Mexico	2,255.0	2,543.0	3,975.0	2,746.0	3,385.0	3,640.0	3,782.0	3,960.0	4,531.0	5,130.0
Nicaragua	130.0	168.9	201.6	585.0	335.6	273.6	295.4	305.0	357.1	366.8
Panama	108.3	95.7	219.3	222.4	204.0	203.1	148.9	154.2	151.7	163.4
Paraguay	35.1	23.5	55.6	72.3	33.9	100.3	31.5	72.2	39.4	49.4
Peru	163.0	176.0	316.0	459.0	446.0	495.0	637.0	642.0	647.0	636.0
Suriname	12.8	34.7	53.0	23.2	52.3	20.9	4.0	10.3	123.5	102.8
Trinidad & Tobago	-9.2	-7.5	-6.2	2.4	0.4	4.7	0.3	-4.5	-12.5	-5.0
Uruguay	21.3	8.0	8.1	40.1	28.6	53.4	41.2	76.0	82.5	81.2
Venezuela	-147.0	-183.0	-302.0	-364.0	-374.0	-368.0	-83.0	109.0	138.0	-124.0
Latin America	**6,372.2**	**6,828.9**	**10,096.6**	**10,647.0**	**12,236.5**	**11,615.3**	**13,047.1**	**15,373.3**	**14,914.0**	**15,671.3**

TABLE D-14. CAPITAL AND FINANCIAL ACCOUNT BALANCE, EXCLUDING RESERVES[1]

(*Millions of* U.S. *Dollars*)

Country	1988	1989	1990	1991	1992	1993	1994	1995	1996	1997p
Argentina	3,625.0	-272.0	-2,145.0	3,028.0	8,363.0	12,149.0	10,674.0	2,707.0	7,570.0	13,176.0
Bahamas	70.2	72.2	59.1	167.4	-6.8	-0.1	55.2	92.1	156.7	396.1
Barbados	27.1	-34.4	40.8	20.9	-32.1	-0.5	-11.0	-79.8	-7.0	-17.6
Belize	24.3	21.3	22.1	21.8	22.4	32.8	3.6	1.4	37.3	27.4
Bolivia	287.4	305.3	255.0	261.5	569.7	462.2	417.2	607.1	610.8	949.9
Brazil	-2,080.0	710.0	4,594.0	229.0	9,974.0	9,504.0	8,810.0	29,609.0	32,492.0	26,739.0
Chile	1,108.0	1,268.0	2,658.0	753.0	2,928.0	2,737.0	5,064.0	2,091.0	5,383.0	7,405.0
Colombia	939.0	478.0	-2.0	-777.0	183.0	2,702.0	2,783.0	4,662.0	6,786.0	5,542.0
Costa Rica	142.0	318.2	183.4	391.4	345.3	261.6	-81.0	202.7	109.8	505.0
Dominican Rep.	42.2	310.9	351.3	-33.6	202.3	677.1	501.2	488.6	430.3	564.2
Ecuador	629.0	719.0	345.0	622.0	337.0	1,237.0	1,154.0	1,838.0	1,449.0	1,520.0
El Salvador	51.3	163.6	16.9	-28.1	135.0	98.9	83.9	408.1	333.9	266.7
Guatemala	305.8	371.4	134.9	651.7	572.4	737.0	696.2	550.9	722.2	857.6
Guyana	50.9	88.2	164.5	158.6	193.4	186.3	163.0	122.8	111.0	63.4
Haiti	24.8	69.5	29.2	33.2	-3.0	-1.6	21.1	127.7	80.8	92.8
Honduras	202.3	306.2	220.4	132.3	373.6	293.2	279.8	304.4	304.3	329.3
Jamaica	-26.7	232.5	348.0	207.6	223.6	227.3	301.2	153.9	509.7	251.4
Mexico	-1,155.0	1,863.0	9,484.0	25,320.0	26,467.0	32,585.0	14,587.0	15,472.0	3,331.0	14,220.8
Nicaragua	707.4	495.0	447.1	288.7	709.2	396.8	664.9	433.0	415.1	288.6
Panama	18.5	172.6	283.4	-269.0	-296.1	-20.5	134.8	626.5	-9.4	531.2
Paraguay	-156.3	-19.8	29.2	151.0	-204.5	180.7	363.9	251.2	494.7	344.8
Peru	1,338.0	979.0	1,812.0	1,294.0	2,238.0	1,737.0	5,462.0	4,681.0	4,500.0	4,816.0
Suriname	-120.3	-311.4	-31.7	56.0	-92.3	-72.6	-84.3	-30.2	38.1	90.2
Trinidad & Tobago	40.0	151.5	-149.3	-69.2	-190.7	-41.9	-110.5	-335.0	176.4	323.3
Uruguay	178.1	-74.1	-181.4	-397.7	-43.3	213.6	526.6	411.9	199.5	669.7
Venezuela	-1,180.0	-2,686.0	-2,161.0	2,425.0	3,203.0	2,388.0	-3,404.0	-3,427.0	-2,480.0	-2,078.0
Latin America	**5,093.0**	**5,697.7**	**16,807.9**	**34,638.5**	**56,171.1**	**68,669.3**	**49,055.8**	**61,970.3**	**63,745.2**	**77,874.9**

[1] Includes Errors and Omissions for El Salvador (1995-97), Jamaica (1996-97), and Panama (1997).

TABLE D-15. CAPITAL ACCOUNT BALANCE

(Millions of U.S. Dollars)

Country	1988	1989	1990	1991	1992	1993	1994	1995	1996	1997p
Argentina	...	...	...	...	...	...	...	...	...	...
Bahamas	-3.0	-16.6	-7.7	-5.6	-9.8	-9.4	-11.6	-12.5	-24.4	-12.9
Barbados	...	...	...	...	...	...	20.3	...	0.2	...
Belize	...	...	...	...	...	...	...	-2.6	-2.2	-3.4
Bolivia	49.0	6.4	7.4	0.5	0.6	1.0	1.2	2.0	40.4	25.3
Brazil	3.0	23.0	35.0	42.0	54.0	81.0	173.0	352.0	453.0	44.0
Chile	...	...	...	...	...	...	...	...	...	...
Colombia	...	...	...	...	...	...	...	...	28.1	...
Costa Rica	...	...	...	...	...	77.0	659.5	68.0	72.0	144.5
Dominican Rep.	...	...	...	...	...	...	43.0	...	7.0	138.0
Ecuador	...	...	...	...	...	...	...	...	...	...
El Salvador	...	...	...	...	...	...	...	61.6	65.0	78.0
Guatemala	...	...	...	...	...	...	...	...	...	...
Guyana	...	...	...	...	81.7	65.7	16.4	10.1	524.0	...
Haiti	...	...	...	...	...	...	...	...	...	...
Honduras	20.0	26.0	41.5	45.0	52.8	54.0	31.9	14.2	...	4.1
Jamaica	-15.4	-15.0	-15.9	-15.7	-17.6	-12.9	14.7	37.1	...	...
Mexico	...	...	...	...	...	...	...	...	...	...
Nicaragua	...	...	...	259.4	53.0	147.7	141.5	1,452.7	4,208.1	103.7
Panama	...	...	...	...	130.0	...	...	...	...	...
Paraguay	0.1	0.4	...	...	...	...	...	...	...	...
Peru	4.0	-20.0	-25.0	-40.0	3.0	-71.0	45.0	42.0	66.0	...
Suriname	-2.7	-2.8	-5.0	-1.9	-5.7	0.5	-0.2	...	...	...
Trinidad & Tobago	-20.4	-17.2	-19.2	-16.1	-16.5	-11.5	-6.4	-11.9	-13.0	...
Uruguay	...	...	...	...	...	...	...	...	...	...
Venezuela	...	...	...	...	...	...	...	...	...	...
Latin America	**34.6**	**-15.8**	**11.1**	**267.6**	**325.5**	**322.1**	**1,128.3**	**2,012.7**	**5,424.2**	**...**

TABLE D-16. CAPITAL TRANSFERS BALANCE

(Millions of U.S. Dollars)

Country	1988	1989	1990	1991	1992	1993	1994	1995	1996	1997p
Argentina	...	...	...	...	...	...	...	...	...	...
Bahamas	-3.0	-16.6	-7.7	-5.6	-9.8	-9.4	-11.6	-12.5	-24.4	-12.9
Barbados	...	...	...	...	...	...	20.3	...	0.2	...
Belize	...	...	...	...	...	...	...	-2.6	-2.2	-3.4
Bolivia	49.0	6.4	7.4	0.5	0.6	1.0	1.2	2.0	40.4	25.3
Brazil	3.0	23.0	35.0	42.0	54.0	81.0	173.0	352.0	453.0	44.0
Chile	...	...	...	...	...	...	...	...	...	...
Colombia	...	...	...	...	...	...	...	...	28.1	...
Costa Rica	...	...	...	...	...	...	...	...	...	...
Dominican Rep.	...	...	...	...	...	...	43.0	...	7.0	138.0
Ecuador	...	...	...	...	...	...	...	...	...	...
El Salvador	...	...	...	...	...	...	...	61.6	65.0	78.0
Guatemala	...	...	...	...	...	...	...	...	...	...
Guyana	...	...	...	...	81.7	65.7	16.4	10.1	524.0	...
Haiti	...	...	...	...	...	...	...	...	...	...
Honduras	20.0	26.0	41.5	45.0	52.8	54.0	31.9	14.2	...	4.1
Jamaica	-15.4	-15.0	-15.9	-15.7	-17.6	-12.9	14.7	37.1	...	...
Mexico	...	...	...	...	...	...	...	...	...	...
Nicaragua	...	...	...	259.4	53.0	147.7	141.5	1,452.7	4,208.1	103.7
Panama	...	...	...	...	130.0	...	...	...	...	...
Paraguay	0.1	0.4	...	...	...	...	...	...	...	...
Peru	4.0	-20.0	-25.0	-40.0	3.0	-71.0	45.0	42.0	66.0	...
Suriname	-2.7	-2.8	-5.0	-1.9	-5.7	0.5	-0.2	...	...	...
Trinidad & Tobago	-20.4	-17.2	-19.2	-16.1	-16.5	-11.5	-6.4	-11.9	-13.0	...
Uruguay	...	...	...	...	...	...	...	...	...	...
Venezuela	...	...	...	...	...	...	...	...	...	...
Latin America	**34.6**	**-15.8**	**11.1**	**267.6**	**325.5**	**245.1**	**468.8**	**1,944.7**	**5,352.2**	**...**

TABLE D-17. FINANCIAL ACCOUNT BALANCE

(Millions of U.S. Dollars)

Country	1988	1989	1990	1991	1992	1993	1994	1995	1996	1997p
Argentina	3,625.0	-272.0	-2,145.0	3,028.0	8,363.0	12,149.0	10,674.0	2,707.0	7,570.0	13,176.0
Bahamas	73.2	88.8	66.8	173.0	3.0	9.3	66.8	104.6	181.1	409.0
Barbados	27.1	-34.4	40.8	20.9	-32.1	-0.5	-31.3	-79.8	-7.2	-17.6
Belize	24.3	21.3	22.1	21.8	22.4	32.8	3.6	4.0	39.5	30.8
Bolivia	238.4	298.9	247.6	261.0	569.1	461.2	416.0	605.1	570.4	924.6
Brazil	-2,083.0	687.0	4,559.0	187.0	9,920.0	9,423.0	8,637.0	29,257.0	32,039.0	26,695.0
Chile	1,108.0	1,268.0	2,658.0	753.0	2,928.0	2,737.0	5,064.0	2,091.0	5,383.0	7,405.0
Colombia	939.0	478.0	-2.0	-777.0	183.0	2,702.0	2,783.0	4,662.0	6,786.0	5,542.0
Costa Rica	142.0	318.2	183.4	391.4	345.3	261.6	-81.0	202.7	81.7	505.0
Dominican Rep.	42.2	310.9	351.3	-33.6	202.3	600.1	-158.3	420.6	358.3	419.7
Ecuador	629.0	719.0	345.0	622.0	337.0	1,237.0	1,111.0	1,838.0	1,442.0	1,382.0
El Salvador	51.3	163.6	16.9	-28.1	135.0	98.9	83.9	408.1	333.9	266.7
Guatemala	305.8	371.4	134.9	651.7	572.4	737.0	696.2	489.3	657.2	779.6
Guyana	50.9	88.2	164.5	158.6	111.7	120.6	146.6	112.7	-413.0	63.4
Haiti	24.8	69.5	29.2	33.2	-3.0	-1.6	21.1	127.7	80.8	92.8
Honduras	182.3	280.2	178.9	87.3	320.8	239.2	247.9	290.2	304.3	325.2
Jamaica	-11.3	247.5	363.9	223.3	241.2	240.2	286.5	116.8	509.7	251.4
Mexico	-1,155.0	1,863.0	9,484.0	25,320.0	26,467.0	32,585.0	14,587.0	15,472.0	3,331.0	14,220.8
Nicaragua	707.4	495.0	447.1	29.3	656.2	249.1	523.4	-1,019.7	-3,793.0	184.9
Panama	18.5	172.6	283.4	-269.0	-426.1	-20.5	134.8	626.5	-9.4	531.2
Paraguay	-156.4	-20.2	29.2	151.0	-204.5	180.7	363.9	251.2	494.7	344.8
Peru	1,334.0	999.0	1,837.0	1,334.0	2,235.0	1,808.0	5,417.0	4,639.0	4,434.0	4,816.0
Suriname	-117.6	-308.6	-26.7	57.9	-86.6	-73.1	-84.1	-30.2	38.1	90.2
Trinidad & Tobago	60.4	168.7	-130.1	-53.1	-174.2	-30.4	-104.1	-323.1	189.4	323.3
Uruguay	178.1	-74.1	-181.4	-397.7	-43.3	213.6	526.6	411.9	199.5	669.7
Venezuela	-1,180.0	-2,686.0	-2,161.0	2,425.0	3,203.0	2,388.0	-3,404.0	-3,427.0	-2,480.0	-2,078.0
Latin America	**5,058.4**	**5,713.5**	**16,796.8**	**34,370.9**	**55,845.6**	**68,347.2**	**47,927.5**	**59,957.6**	**58,321.0**	**77,353.6**

TABLE D-18. FINANCIAL ACCOUNT: DIRECT INVESTMENT

(Millions of U.S. Dollars)

Country	1988	1989	1990	1991	1992	1993	1994	1995	1996	1997p
Argentina	1,147.0	1,028.0	1,836.0	2,439.0	4,019.0	3,262.0	2,982.0	4,628.0	4,885.0	6,298.0
Bahamas	36.7	25.0	-17.2	...	7.4	27.0	23.5	106.7	88.1	209.6
Barbados	10.6	5.4	9.8	6.1	13.6	6.8	11.9	8.5	9.8	...
Belize	14.0	18.6	17.2	13.6	15.6	9.2	15.4	20.8	16.6	11.9
Bolivia	30.4	35.0	65.9	93.7	120.1	121.6	128.0	372.3	472.0	608.2
Brazil	2,629.0	608.0	324.0	89.0	1,924.0	801.0	2,035.0	3,475.0	9,519.0	18,601.0
Chile	952.0	1,277.0	653.0	696.0	540.0	600.0	1,673.0	2,220.0	3,561.0	3,468.0
Colombia	159.0	547.0	484.0	433.0	679.0	719.0	1,515.0	2,033.0	3,254.0	5,303.3
Costa Rica	121.4	95.2	160.4	172.8	221.6	244.4	292.9	390.0	421.9	446.2
Dominican Rep.	106.1	110.0	132.8	145.0	179.7	214.0	347.5	389.8	357.9	405.2
Ecuador	155.0	160.0	126.0	160.0	178.0	469.0	531.0	470.0	447.0	577.0
El Salvador	17.0	14.4	1.9	25.2	15.3	16.4	...	38.0	...	...
Guatemala	329.7	76.2	47.6	90.7	94.1	142.5	65.2	75.2	76.9	82.3
Guyana	6.2	9.2	6.5	23.5	146.6	69.5	106.7	74.4	53.0	47.5
Haiti	10.1	9.4	8.0	13.6	...	...	...	7.4	4.1	5.0
Honduras	48.3	51.0	43.5	52.1	47.6	52.1	41.5	69.4	90.0	121.5
Jamaica	-12.0	57.1	137.9	133.2	142.4	77.9	116.8	166.7	...	...
Mexico	2,879.0	3,174.0	2,634.0	4,762.0	4,393.0	4,389.0	10,972.0	9,526.0	7,619.0	11,500.0
Nicaragua	...	...	...	...	15.0	38.8	40.0	70.4	85.0	162.0
Panama	-595.1	51.5	131.9	41.2	138.7	155.7	353.6	178.9	237.6	...
Paraguay	8.4	12.8	76.3	83.5	136.6	119.2	124.1	163.7	297.6	215.0
Peru	26.0	59.0	41.0	-7.0	136.0	670.0	3,083.0	2,083.0	3,571.0	2,005.0
Suriname	-171.0	-299.7	-76.8	18.5	-54.3	-46.6	-30.2	-21.3	54.2	56.0
Trinidad & Tobago	62.9	148.9	109.4	169.3	177.9	379.2	516.2	298.9	400.0	782.0
Uruguay	44.5	...	...	...	...	101.5	154.5	156.6	168.9	...
Venezuela	21.0	34.0	76.0	1,728.0	473.0	-514.0	136.0	686.0	1,595.0	4,346.0
Latin America[1]	**8,036.2**	**7,307.0**	**7,029.1**	**11,382.0**	**13,759.9**	**12,125.2**	**25,234.6**	**27,687.4**	**37,284.6**	**55,250.7**

[1] Latin American aggregate excludes Barbados (1997), El Salvador (1994; 1996-97), Haiti (1992-94), Jamaica (1996-97), Nicaragua (1988-91; 1997), Panama (1997) and Uruguay (1989-92; 1997).

TABLE D-19. FINANCIAL ACCOUNT: PORTFOLIO INVESTMENT

(Millions of U.S. Dollars)

Country	1988	1989	1990	1991	1992	1993	1994	1995	1996	1997p
Argentina	-656.0	2,618.0	-1,309.0	483.0	910.0	28,304.0	4,537.0	5,173.0	10,868.0	10,448.0
Bahamas	...	...	...	...	...	...	...	...	...	...
Barbados	42.5	-4.2	-25.2	-2.8	-11.9	-8.4	46.9	37.4	25.9	...
Belize	...	...	...	...	0.2	7.0	6.1	3.7	10.1	10.1
Bolivia	...	...	...	...	...	...	...	...	5.0	-53.0
Brazil	176.0	-421.0	512.0	3,808.0	14,466.0	12,322.0	51,135.0	9,745.0	...	10,330.0
Chile	-8.0	83.0	361.0	187.0	457.0	730.0	908.0	35.0	1,098.0	2,370.0
Colombia	...	179.0	-4.0	86.0	126.0	498.0	584.0	-170.0	1,656.0	-136.0
Costa Rica	-6.0	-13.2	-28.2	-13.0	-16.9	-5.1	-1.2	-24.4	-21.5	-24.3
Dominican Rep.	...	...	...	...	...	51.0	-31.4	-17.0	-12.7	-14.6
Ecuador	...	...	...	...	...	...	...	...	...	...
El Salvador	...	...	...	...	...	...	...	68.5	71.5	111.0
Guatemala	-220.6	-24.8	-16.6	74.9	11.7	85.4	-4.0	-16.3	-16.0	-22.0
Guyana	...	...	...	...	2.8	3.6	15.8	3.2	...	...
Haiti	...	...	...	...	...	...	...	...	...	...
Honduras	-0.2	0.1	0.1	0.1	0.1	...	...	...	...	...
Jamaica	...	...	...	...	...	...	...	...	...	...
Mexico	2,677.0	298.0	-3,985.0	12,138.0	19,206.0	28,355.0	7,415.0	-10,377.0	14,697.0	3,600.0
Nicaragua	...	...	...	...	...	...	...	...	...	...
Panama	2,154.2	-468.1	-235.8	-246.7	-117.4	-809.3	373.3	313.6	3,642.7	...
Paraguay	...	...	...	...	...	...	...	...	...	...
Peru	...	...	...	...	...	228.0	572.0	145.0	341.0	348.0
Suriname	...	...	0.9	-4.1	2.6	...	...	...	...	...
Trinidad & Tobago	...	...	...	...	...	...	...	8.8	9.9	-10.0
Uruguay	164.2	129.8	107.8	47.4	83.4	29.3	158.1	288.8	179.9	...
Venezuela	...	-534.0	15,976.0	351.0	1,003.0	621.0	261.0	-326.0	758.0	626.0
Latin America	**4,323.1**	**1,842.6**	**11,354.0**	**16,908.8**	**36,122.6**	**70,411.5**	**65,975.6**	**4,891.3**	**33,312.8**	**27,583.2**

TABLE D-20. FINANCIAL ACCOUNT: OTHER INVESTMENT

(Millions of U.S. Dollars)

Country	1988	1989	1990	1991	1992	1993	1994	1995	1996	1997p
Argentina	3,134.0	-3,918.0	-2,672.0	106.0	3,434.0	-19,417.0	3,155.0	-7,094.0	-8,183.0	-3,570.0
Bahamas	36.5	63.8	84.0	173.0	-4.4	-17.7	43.3	-2.1	93.0	199.4
Barbados	-26.0	-35.6	56.2	17.6	-33.8	1.1	-90.1	-125.7	-42.9	-17.6
Belize	10.3	2.7	4.9	8.2	6.6	16.6	-17.9	-20.5	12.8	8.8
Bolivia	208.0	263.9	181.7	167.3	449.0	339.6	288.0	232.8	93.4	369.4
Brazil	-4,888.0	500.0	3,723.0	-3,710.0	-6,470.0	-3,700.0	-44,533.0	16,037.0	22,520.0	-2,236.0
Chile	164.0	-92.0	1,644.0	-130.0	1,931.0	1,407.0	2,483.0	-164.0	724.0	1,567.0
Colombia	780.0	-248.0	-482.0	-1,296.0	-622.0	1,485.0	684.0	2,799.0	1,876.0	374.7
Costa Rica	26.6	236.2	51.2	231.6	140.6	22.3	-372.7	-162.9	-318.7	83.1
Dominican Rep.	-63.9	200.9	218.5	-178.6	22.6	335.1	-474.4	47.8	13.1	29.1
Ecuador	474.0	559.0	219.0	462.0	159.0	768.0	580.0	1,368.0	995.0	805.0
El Salvador	34.3	149.2	15.0	-53.3	119.7	82.5	83.9	301.6	262.4	155.7
Guatemala	196.7	320.0	103.9	486.1	466.6	509.1	635.0	430.4	596.3	719.3
Guyana	44.7	79.0	158.0	135.1	-37.7	47.5	24.1	35.1	-466.0	15.9
Haiti	14.7	60.1	21.2	19.6	-3.0	-1.6	21.1	120.3	76.7	87.8
Honduras	134.2	229.1	135.3	35.1	273.1	187.1	206.4	220.8	214.3	203.7
Jamaica	0.7	190.4	226.0	90.1	98.8	162.3	169.7	-49.9	509.7	251.4
Mexico	-6,711.0	-1,609.0	10,835.0	8,420.0	2,868.0	-159.0	-3,800.0	16,323.0	-18,985.0	-879.2
Nicaragua	707.4	495.0	447.1	29.3	641.2	210.3	483.4	-1,090.1	-3,878.0	22.9
Panama	-1,540.6	589.2	387.3	-63.5	-447.4	633.1	-592.1	134.0	-3,889.7	531.2
Paraguay	-1,64.8	-33.0	-47.1	67.5	-341.1	61.5	239.8	87.5	197.1	129.8
Peru	1,308.0	940.0	1,796.0	1,341.0	2,099.0	910.0	1,762.0	2,411.0	522.0	2,463.0
Suriname	53.4	-8.9	49.2	43.5	-34.9	-26.5	-53.9	-8.9	-16.1	34.2
Trinidad & Tobago	-2.5	19.8	-239.5	-222.4	-352.1	-409.6	-620.3	-630.8	-220.5	-448.7
Uruguay	-30.6	-203.9	-289.2	-445.1	-126.7	82.8	214.0	-33.5	-149.3	669.7
Venezuela	-1,201.0	-2,186.0	-18,213.0	346.0	1,727.0	2,281.0	-3,801.0	-3,787.0	-4,833.0	-7,050.0
Latin America	**-7,300.9**	**-3,436.1**	**-1,586.3**	**6,080.1**	**5,963.1**	**-14,189.5**	**-43,282.7**	**27,378.9**	**-12,276.4**	**-5,480.4**

TABLE D-21. CHANGE IN RESERVES (- INCREASE)

(*Millions of U.S. Dollars*)

Country	1988	1989	1990	1991	1992	1993	1994	1995	1996	1997p
Argentina	-1,888.0	1,826.0	-3,121.0	-2,040.0	-3,106.0	-4,512.0	-541.0	49.0	-3,775.0	-3,082.0
Bahamas	0.7	25.2	-11.7	-12.6	28.0	-18.6	-9.1	2.9	7.6	-56.5
Barbados	-27.6	48.9	42.3	40.8	-80.3	-21.0	-58.9	-23.5	-60.6	-15.0
Belize	-18.7	-11.3	-12.5	16.8	-0.1	14.2	3.6	-3.1	-20.9	-0.9
Bolivia	12.8	57.3	-5.0	-8.4	-41.2	-81.7	-170.7	-152.3	-292.9	-142.4
Brazil	-1,250.0	-893.0	-474.0	369.0	-14,670.0	-8,709.0	-7,215.0	-12,920.0	-8,665.0	7,871.0
Chile	-756.0	-548.0	-2,122.0	-1,049.0	-2,344.0	-169.0	-2,917.0	-740.0	-1,107.0	-3,184.0
Colombia	-193.0	-434.0	-610.0	-1,763.0	-1,274.0	-464.0	-153.0	-351.0	-1,598.0	16.0
Costa Rica	-188.0	-112.3	197.2	-416.1	-176.8	59.6	65.5	-154.1	75.8	-127.9
Dominican Rep.	-58.9	90.0	49.0	-357.4	-63.5	-156.0	386.6	-131.0	15.2	-39.5
Ecuador	26.0	-118.0	-195.0	-78.0	-22.0	-490.0	-453.0	233.0	-245.0	-235.0
El Salvador	30.1	-110.0	-164.6	70.0	-91.6	-112.0	-113.0	-146.6	-164.9	-362.6
Guatemala	110.6	-59.0	41.8	-551.3	51.6	-120.5	-47.3	157.3	-199.0	-287.0
Guyana	32.2	29.5	-18.1	-40.5	-67.1	-57.1	-21.8	0.8	-63.0	16.0
Haiti	1.2	3.9	39.0	-20.0	-11.3	-19.1	12.8	-175.6	48.6	-34.2
Honduras	21.6	28.9	-20.1	-66.9	-92.0	105.3	-17.2	-136.4	-174.3	-295.1
Jamaica	25.2	39.9	-65.3	52.9	-192.2	-92.9	-331.0	55.3	-271.3	152.1
Mexico	6,721.0	-542.0	-3,261.0	-8,154.0	-1,173.0	-6,057.0	18,398.0	-9,648.0	-1,805.0	-10,494.0
Nicaragua	-43.9	-78.6	7.3	-41.7	-0.5	79.4	-84.6	-3.1	-37.9	-173.2
Panama	5.5	-47.9	-355.7	-148.4	116.2	-93.0	-104.7	-77.2	-237.7	-281.3
Paraguay	168.2	-145.2	-219.3	-298.9	346.9	-86.2	-327.8	-47.7	44.3	215.3
Peru	149.0	-242.0	-212.0	-899.0	-554.0	-667.0	-3,068.0	-950.0	-1,877.0	-1,635.0
Suriname	9.2	0.2	-18.3	78.3	21.5	-12.7	-34.3	-96.6	21.4	-31.4
Trinidad & Tobago	27.4	-158.5	-197.7	102.7	124.4	-29.4	-113.6	-40.1	-219.0	-155.8
Uruguay	46.8	3.2	-40.2	-113.5	-186.2	-178.6	-98.5	-218.0	-118.6	-321.1
Venezuela	3,872.0	-1,077.0	-4,376.0	-2,645.0	845.0	144.0	1,173.0	1,910.0	-6,296.0	-2,424.0
Latin America	**6,835.4**	**-2,423.8**	**-15,122.9**	**-17,973.2**	**-22,612.2**	**-21,744.3**	**4,160.0**	**-23,606.0**	**-27,015.2**	**-15,107.5**

TABLE D-22. ERRORS AND OMISSIONS[1]

(*Millions of U.S. Dollars*)

Country	1988	1989	1990	1991	1992	1993	1994	1995	1996	1997p
Argentina	-165.0	-249.0	715.0	-341.0	205.0	35.0	-16.0	12.0	-8.0	25.0
Bahamas	-4.4	-13.2	-10.8	25.0	-49.6	-30.0	-3.9	50.9	99.0	122.5
Barbados	-47.6	-42.5	-75.1	-38.2	-31.1	-48.5	-62.3	13.2	-36.8	-25.8
Belize	-2.9	9.1	-25.0	-12.8	6.3	1.5	32.8	4.5	-14.1	15.6
Bolivia	24.7	-70.9	-30.3	30.9	32.7	158.5	-158.6	-139.3	46.2	-144.8
Brazil	-827.0	-819.0	-296.0	852.0	-1,393.0	-815.0	-442.0	1,447.0	973.0	-1,128.0
Chile	-121.0	-31.0	-49.0	394.0	372.0	-21.0	-560.0	52.0	-534.0	-159.0
Colombia	-530.0	157.0	70.0	191.0	191.0	-135.0	482.0	-210.0	-434.0	-589.5
Costa Rica	224.6	208.9	43.4	99.9	201.9	299.0	249.1	94.4	-60.4	44.9
Dominican Rep.	35.6	-73.6	-120.7	548.3	569.0	-99.7	-661.2	-256.5	-206.9	-299.8
Ecuador	25.0	114.0	210.0	164.0	-192.0	-69.0	-20.0	-1,336.0	-1,315.0	-542.0
El Salvador	-107.1	140.9	299.4	125.6	65.6	90.3	47.3	0.0	0.0	0.0
Guatemala	-2.4	54.7	36.2	83.3	81.8	85.2	-23.6	-136.2	-71.7	90.0
Guyana	10.5	-4.4	3.2	0.9	12.2	11.0	-16.3	11.2	2.0	-11.0
Haiti	14.3	-10.7	-46.3	42.9	6.4	37.3	-37.9	85.9	-55.9	27.2
Honduras	-93.1	-138.9	-107.4	152.0	29.2	-71.3	83.1	11.7	60.1	60.7
Jamaica	-46.0	10.0	29.3	-20.4	-59.9	49.7	12.9	36.1	0.0	0.0
Mexico	-3,193.0	4,504.0	1,228.0	-2,278.0	-852.0	-3,128.0	-3,323.0	-4,248.0	398.0	3,500.0
Nicaragua	51.9	-54.7	-149.2	17.2	60.2	128.1	64.2	60.1	42.1	533.6
Panama	-745.7	-236.3	-136.1	629.9	449.9	256.9	-52.5	-206.3	307.5	0.0
Paraguay	198.3	-90.6	362.4	472.0	457.7	318.1	530.5	297.0	98.4	109.3
Peru	332.0	-167.0	-215.0	1,114.0	417.0	1,232.0	267.0	567.0	982.0	233.0
Suriname	-3.2	17.7	-16.8	-0.9	45.4	41.3	60.0	53.9	-69.1	-64.3
Trinidad & Tobago	21.1	45.4	-112.0	-29.0	-72.6	-41.8	6.3	81.4	80.0	387.3
Uruguay	-247.0	-62.6	35.7	468.8	238.3	208.7	10.2	18.6	152.5	-27.5
Venezuela	3,117.0	1,603.0	-1,742.0	-1,516.0	-299.0	-539.0	-310.0	-497.0	-48.0	-1,498.0
Latin America	**-2,080.4**	**4,800.3**	**-99.1**	**1,175.4**	**492.4**	**-2,045.7**	**-3,841.9**	**-4,132.4**	**386.9**	**659.4**

[1] Included in Capital and Financial Account Balance for El Salvador (1995-97), Jamaica (1996-97), and Panama (1997).

BALANCE OF PAYMENTS NOTES

The concepts and definitions underlying the Balance of Payments statistics are described in the IMF Balance of Payments Manual, Fifth Edition (1993). For analytical purposes, the tables follow a summarized uniform presentation of the balance of payments for the Latin American countries.

Current Account Balance:

This account is the sum of the trade, services (factor services), income (non-factor services), and current transfers balances.

Trade Balance: Records the difference between merchandise exports and imports, both expressed as "free on board" (f.o.b.) values.

Exports of Goods (f.o.b.): Merchandise exports (includes goods for processing, e.g., maquiladora exports; repairs on goods; goods procured in ports by carriers; and non-monetary gold).

Imports of Goods (f.o.b.): Merchandise imports (includes goods for processing, e.g., maquiladora imports; repairs on goods; goods procured in ports by carriers; and non-monetary gold).

Service Balance: This is the net result of receipts and payments under the categories of transportation, travel and other services.

Service Transactions — Transportation Balance: Most transportation services (e.g., freight transportation by sea and air).

Service Transactions — Travel Balance: Includes all receipts for goods and services provided to foreigners visiting the reporting country (credit), and all payments for goods and services provided by foreigners to the residents of the reporting country traveling abroad (debit).

Service Transactions — Other Services Balance: Refers to receipts and payments of the following items: property income; insurance services; communications services; construction services; management fees; financial services; computer and information services; royalties; and other business services related to merchandise transactions and other trade-related services, operational leasing, miscellaneous business, professional and technical services, and personal, cultural and recreational services.

Service Transactions — Freight and Insurance: An addendum item taken from Transport and Other Services, respectively. Covers net transactions in connection with all forms of transportation used for international shipments, including ocean and inland waterway shipping, air, rail and road transportation. Also includes insurance claims paid by foreigners to residents (credit) and by residents to foreigners (debit) with respect to international shipments.

Income Balance: The entries in this account cover net accrued income derived from holdings of external financial assets by residents, and from accrued liabilities to non-residents, respectively; includes income in arrears. These holdings constitute approximately all non-factor services, and are composed of two elements: (1) Investment Income which includes Direct Investment, Portfolio Investment and Other Investment

Income; and (2) Compensation of Employees—domestic workers working for foreign firms and expenditure of foreign workers in the home country, usually workers employed by residents other than the government of the home country.

Investment Income Balance: The total of (1) Direct Investment Income which is income derived from dividends on shares and profits of enterprises; (2) Portfolio Investment Income which is income derived from interest and dividends on bonds, securities, and other equity and debt instruments; and (3) Other Investment Income which is income derived from interest on loans and deposits. The credits of Investment Income are income received by residents of the reporting country from assets invested abroad; the debits are income paid to non-residents on their assets invested in the reporting country.

Current Transfers Balance: Refers to receipts and payments without a quid pro quo. They may be in cash or in kind and include (1) general government transfers between the home government and all non-residents, and all current international cooperation between governments and international organizations (such as inter-governmental grants, withholding taxes on interest and dividends, and pensions); and (2) other sectors (mainly private transfer payments), especially workers' remittances (transfers by migrants employed in-country—credit, and from migrants employed abroad—debit).

Capital and Financial Account Balance (excludes Reserves):

Transactions likely to result in a change in the stock of assets of one or other of the parties, but do not directly affect the level of disposable income, or influence the current consumption of goods and services. This is the net result of capital inflows and outflows of the Capital Account Balance and the Financial Account Balance. Capital movements in the following categories are entered on a net basis.

Capital Account Balance: Sum of Capital Transfers and the acquisition or disposal of assets which are non-produced and non-financial (e.g., tangible assets such as embassy-negotiated land transactions, and intangible assets, such as patents or franchises, which may be needed for the production of foods and services but which themselves have not been produced).

Capital Transfers Balance: Consists of the transfer of ownership of a fixed asset or the forgiveness of a liability by a creditor when no counterpart is received in return (e.g., debt forgiveness); or a transfer of cash when it is linked to, or conditional upon, the acquisition or disposal of a fixed asset (e.g., migrants' transfers: contra-entries to flows of goods and changes in financial items that arise from the migration of individuals from one economy to another).

Financial Account Balance (excludes Reserves): All transactions associated with changes in legal ownership of the foreign financial assets and liabilities of an economy; all public and private investment capital transactions. An increase in liabilities or a fall in assets is recorded with a positive sign, while a decrease in liabilities or an increase in assets is recorded with a negative sign. This item is the sum of Direct Investment Balance, Portfolio Investment Balance, and Other Investment Balance.

Financial Account — Direct Investment Balance: The flow of international capital where the investor (either foreign or domestic) seeks to have an effective voice in the management of an enterprise located in a foreign economy. In addition to branches and subsidiaries, ownership of 10% or more of the voting stock of an enterprise is considered as direct investment.

Financial Account — Portfolio Investment Balance: Transactions which usually are in the form of long-term corporate bonds or debentures which provide the holder with a guaranteed income. Includes holdings of less than 10% of the voting stock of an enterprise, and does not confer on the holders an 'effective voice' in the management of an enterprise. Includes equity securities (instruments and records acknowledging claims to the residual values of incorporated enterprises), and debt securities (bonds, debentures, notes, money market instruments and financial derivatives that usually do not extend to actual delivery and are utilized for hedging of risk, investment and trading purposes).

Financial Account — Other Investment Balance: A residual category composed of transactions not covered under direct or portfolio investment.

Change in Reserves (a minus sign signifies an increase):

Foreign assets available to the authorities for financing or regulating a payments imbalance. The change in the holdings of such items reflects the responses to the aggregate deficit or surplus accruing as a result of autonomous transactions. Shows the change in the net position in actual assets and liabilities available to an economy's monetary authorities to use in meeting balance of payments needs. Thus, this category includes changes in monetary gold; Special Drawing Rights (SDRs) in the International Monetary Fund (IMF); reserve position in the IMF; foreign exchange assets; and other assets.

Errors and Omissions:

This item, estimated as a residual, is an offset to the overstatement or understatement of the recorded components in the Balance of Payments. Positive net errors and omissions suggest that the debit entries have been overestimated, or that the credits have been underestimated. Hence, if the balance of those components is a credit, the item for net errors and omissions will be shown as a debit of equal value, and vice versa.

Sources:

The historical data are from the International Monetary Fund Balance of Payments magnetic tapes, various dates. The source for the latest year(s) is IDB estimates based on official information in the countries.

TABLE E-1. DISBURSED TOTAL EXTERNAL DEBT OUTSTANDING[1]

(Millions of U.S. Dollars)

Country	1988	1989	1990	1991	1992	1993	1994	1995	1996	1997p
Argentina	56,610.1	59,615.2	54,671.7	56,778.1	59,268.8	70,575.0	77,433.5	83,536.1	93,840.7	...
Bahamas	171.3	221.0	266.2	412.4	440.4	453.3	413.7	394.3	360.8	...
Barbados	696.3	641.7	682.8	651.7	609.3	569.7	614.5	596.7	581.2	...
Belize	139.3	144.4	153.2	170.1	186.7	196.6	198.2	255.5	282.7	...
Bolivia	4,793.2	4,082.4	4,268.7	4,046.4	4,224.1	4,293.0	4,836.8	5,244.2	5,147.9	...
Brazil	117,215.6	111,344.2	111,087.9	110,405.3	124,449.5	136,610.1	149,857.0	158,903.2	177,608.1	...
Chile	19,581.9	18,032.3	19,227.2	17,946.9	19,133.7	20,636.9	24,728.4	25,567.8	27,410.5	...
Colombia	17,015.0	16,883.0	17,193.8	17,181.4	17,266.2	18,926.7	21,929.1	25,045.9	28,859.0	...
Costa Rica	4,250.7	4,204.4	3,678.3	3,952.8	3,905.9	3,830.4	3,867.7	3,761.9	3,427.6	...
Dominican Rep.	3,756.6	3,799.7	3,866.0	4,202.7	4,269.4	4,327.7	4,095.3	4,220.8	4,082.3	...
Ecuador	9,945.6	10,246.1	10,586.9	10,575.9	10,234.7	11,819.9	12,725.7	13,977.4	14,409.5	...
El Salvador	1,987.6	2,058.3	2,141.6	2,175.6	2,248.4	2,005.6	2,187.2	2,586.8	2,891.4	...
Guatemala	2,532.0	2,516.9	2,866.0	2,869.9	2,813.5	3,106.9	3,328.9	3,568.8	3,681.1	...
Guyana	1,756.1	1,532.5	1,882.3	1,911.0	1,844.8	1,917.0	1,974.7	1,970.1	1,555.9	...
Haiti	803.6	790.4	865.3	744.3	764.1	772.7	683.0	805.4	896.2	...
Honduras	3,170.7	3,213.7	3,634.4	3,321.1	3,558.9	3,984.1	4,368.2	4,513.9	4,397.4	...
Jamaica	4,490.2	4,435.9	4,546.2	4,282.5	4,126.7	3,975.0	4,208.4	4,166.3	3,943.6	...
Mexico	99,215.7	93,840.6	104,442.1	114,067.4	112,265.0	131,572.3	140,006.1	166,104.1	157,124.6	...
Nicaragua	7,615.5	8,307.4	9,019.6	9,610.8	9,750.2	9,826.1	10,107.9	8,889.3	5,453.9	...
Panama	5,733.3	5,654.9	5,660.1	5,533.7	5,280.9	5,363.5	5,528.6	5,537.1	6,941.4	...
Paraguay	2,257.6	2,303.9	1,989.0	1,944.7	1,602.2	1,567.3	1,954.7	2,219.9	2,130.7	...
Peru	15,268.3	15,304.6	16,330.7	18,281.5	18,541.4	19,480.7	22,075.4	26,244.0	28,955.4	...
Suriname	96.6	117.7	125.5	194.2	204.9	206.1	198.1	197.2	178.0	...
Trinidad & Tobago	2,098.4	2,137.8	2,511.1	2,488.0	2,452.7	2,240.0	2,493.2	2,730.6	2,232.8	...
Uruguay	3,820.8	4,448.6	4,415.1	4,191.2	4,573.5	4,850.7	5,077.3	5,317.3	5,898.8	...
Venezuela	34,734.9	32,371.3	33,170.4	34,121.6	37,701.8	37,349.8	36,559.8	35,537.0	35,048.2	...
Latin America	**419,756.9**	**408,248.9**	**419,282.1**	**432,061.2**	**451,717.7**	**500,457.1**	**541,451.4**	**591,891.6**	**617,339.7**	...

[1] Sum of Long-Term and Short-Term External Debt and Use of IMF credit.

TABLE E-2. DISBURSED TOTAL EXTERNAL DEBT OUTSTANDING: LONG-TERM

(Millions of U.S. Dollars)

Country	1988	1989	1990	1991	1992	1993	1994	1995	1996	1997p
Argentina	49,346.3	53,632.3	48,705.5	49,374.0	49,854.9	58,403.3	66,052.3	67,235.2	75,348.1	...
Bahamas	171.3	221.0	266.2	412.4	440.4	453.3	413.7	394.3	360.8	...
Barbados	528.9	479.9	504.2	482.7	400.6	348.1	370.7	369.6	381.7	...
Belize	127.1	136.7	147.6	159.9	176.5	179.6	184.2	220.3	252.2	...
Bolivia	4,339.2	3,625.6	3,863.7	3,671.4	3,809.8	3,879.1	4,307.2	4,690.0	4,523.4	...
Brazil	103,559.8	94,095.7	94,342.4	93,372.8	103,852.1	112,903.5	119,619.9	129,069.6	143,540.5	...
Chile	16,057.6	13,789.2	14,688.7	14,790.4	15,180.8	16,031.0	17,999.2	18,612.8	20,421.0	...
Colombia	15,406.0	15,269.0	15,783.8	15,449.8	14,726.3	15,289.3	17,448.1	19,502.7	22,975.3	...
Costa Rica	3,863.3	3,849.0	3,367.0	3,595.4	3,508.9	3,410.4	3,445.5	3,339.8	3,082.0	...
Dominican Rep.	3,378.9	3,424.2	3,518.2	3,839.5	3,802.4	3,842.6	3,647.7	3,659.7	3,519.9	...
Ecuador	9,147.0	9,585.2	10,030.3	10,093.5	9,931.6	10,215.3	10,776.6	12,504.0	12,754.9	...
El Salvador	1,742.9	1,868.0	1,938.4	2,079.4	2,159.7	1,904.0	2,002.2	2,064.4	2,298.3	...
Guatemala	2,244.6	2,240.9	2,592.6	2,599.1	2,506.7	2,665.9	2,889.9	2,976.8	2,886.5	...
Guyana	994.6	1,261.0	1,757.4	1,760.2	1,673.1	1,731.4	1,787.2	1,781.9	1,370.1	...
Haiti	685.2	688.1	750.7	620.7	638.0	647.9	635.0	751.1	836.1	...
Honduras	2,859.0	2,951.2	3,492.2	3,170.7	3,322.0	3,739.4	4,002.0	4,095.9	3,981.2	...
Jamaica	3,774.4	3,785.5	3,967.5	3,736.6	3,593.6	3,486.0	3,514.8	3,536.0	3,305.7	...
Mexico	86,532.2	80,088.0	81,808.8	85,444.6	81,780.4	90,527.7	96,823.4	112,975.5	113,777.8	...
Nicaragua	6,950.5	7,589.4	8,280.4	9,152.6	9,311.3	9,440.1	9,760.8	8,540.5	5,122.4	...
Panama	4,005.2	3,935.3	3,988.0	3,918.1	3,771.2	3,799.4	3,930.4	3,913.6	5,210.6	...
Paraguay	2,119.6	2,120.9	1,731.0	1,703.7	1,384.2	1,306.5	1,374.7	1,443.9	1,398.2	...
Peru	12,718.1	12,995.4	13,959.0	15,656.7	15,804.7	16,946.0	18,851.2	20,213.7	21,792.7	...
Suriname	...	...	...	...	...	...	...	...	...	...
Trinidad & Tobago	1,856.9	1,806.1	2,054.7	1,976.1	1,973.4	1,957.6	2,079.0	2,031.6	1,948.9	...
Uruguay	3,036.8	3,112.7	3,113.8	2,928.2	3,177.3	3,438.5	3,814.6	3,960.2	4,231.6	...
Venezuela	29,463.9	29,089.2	28,158.7	28,588.6	29,627.5	30,177.3	30,478.2	30,507.7	30,266.1	...
Latin America	**364,909.3**	**351,639.5**	**352,810.8**	**358,577.1**	**366,407.4**	**396,723.2**	**426,208.5**	**458,390.8**	**485,586.0**	...

TABLE E-3. DISBURSED TOTAL EXTERNAL DEBT OUTSTANDING: SHORT-TERM[1]

(Millions of U.S. Dollars)

Country	1988	1989	1990	1991	1992	1993	1994	1995	1996	1997p
Argentina	3,586.0	2,883.0	2,883.0	4,921.0	7,100.0	8,652.0	7,170.0	10,170.0	12,200.0	...
Bahamas	...	...	...	...	...	...	...	...	...	...
Barbados	157.0	157.5	177.9	169.0	158.0	171.0	190.0	190.0	190.1	...
Belize	4.4	4.4	5.2	10.2	10.2	17.0	14.0	35.2	30.5	...
Bolivia	245.0	205.0	148.0	130.2	165.2	193.4	266.0	286.4	348.4	...
Brazil	10,322.7	14,826.0	14,925.0	15,795.0	19,798.0	23,403.0	30,051.0	29,692.0	34,000.0	...
Chile	2,202.0	2,973.0	3,382.0	2,199.0	3,231.0	4,130.0	6,438.0	6,955.0	6,989.5	...
Colombia	1,609.0	1,614.0	1,410.0	1,731.6	2,539.9	3,637.4	4,481.0	5,543.2	5,883.7	...
Costa Rica	316.0	320.0	300.0	274.4	315.5	338.6	355.8	397.8	344.9	...
Dominican Rep.	160.0	253.0	276.0	274.0	344.0	299.0	258.0	401.4	466.8	...
Ecuador	394.0	336.0	292.0	300.0	203.3	1,533.5	1,751.0	1,299.9	1,509.6	...
El Salvador	234.0	185.0	203.0	96.2	88.7	101.6	185.0	522.4	593.1	...
Guatemala	199.4	203.0	206.8	206.8	276.0	441.0	439.0	592.0	794.6	...
Guyana	651.5	165.2	12.0	1.4	3.7	9.0	9.0	16.4	17.4	...
Haiti	71.0	61.0	77.0	91.0	91.0	91.0	13.0	25.6	35.2	...
Honduras	275.0	227.1	110.0	116.7	125.0	126.6	257.0	319.4	358.3	...
Jamaica	233.0	267.0	222.0	154.5	176.0	153.6	375.9	389.9	476.5	...
Mexico	7,879.0	8,662.0	16,082.0	21,857.0	24,535.0	36,257.4	39,322.6	37,300.4	30,068.0	...
Nicaragua	665.0	718.0	739.2	433.8	415.5	362.6	296.1	309.5	302.7	...
Panama	1,400.0	1,400.0	1,400.0	1,400.0	1,400.0	1,451.0	1,465.0	1,513.0	1,600.0	...
Paraguay	138.0	183.0	258.0	241.0	218.0	260.8	580.0	776.0	732.5	...
Peru	1,749.0	1,551.0	1,617.0	1,919.0	2,106.0	1,651.9	2,286.0	5,075.0	6,238.5	...
Suriname	...	...	...	...	...	...	...	...	...	...
Trinidad & Tobago	127.0	127.0	127.0	127.0	197.0	127.5	323.0	648.8	260.2	...
Uruguay	475.0	1,134.4	1,200.6	1,205.2	1,343.8	1,373.9	1,232.8	1,336.3	1,658.6	...
Venezuela	5,271.0	2,284.0	2,000.0	2,284.0	5,128.0	4,493.0	3,439.0	2,790.7	2,585.7	...
Latin America	**38,364.0**	**40,739.6**	**48,053.7**	**55,938.0**	**69,968.8**	**89,275.8**	**101,198.2**	**106,586.3**	**107,684.8**	**...**

[1] Includes Arrears on Long-Term Debt.

TABLE E-4. DISBURSED TOTAL EXTERNAL DEBT OUTSTANDING: USE OF IMF CREDIT

(Millions of U.S. Dollars)

Country	1988	1989	1990	1991	1992	1993	1994	1995	1996	1997p
Argentina	3,677.8	3,099.9	3,083.2	2,483.1	2,313.9	3,519.7	4,211.2	6,130.9	6,292.6	...
Bahamas	...	...	...	...	...	...	...	...	...	...
Barbados	10.4	4.3	0.7	0.0	50.7	50.6	53.8	37.1	9.4	...
Belize	7.8	3.3	0.4	0.0	0.0	0.0	0.0	0.0	0.0	...
Bolivia	209.0	251.8	257.0	244.8	249.1	220.5	263.6	267.8	276.1	...
Brazil	3,333.1	2,422.5	1,820.5	1,237.5	799.4	303.6	186.1	141.6	67.6	...
Chile	1,322.3	1,270.1	1,156.5	957.5	721.9	475.9	291.2	0.0	0.0	...
Colombia	0.0	0.0	0.0	0.0	0.0	0.0	0.0	0.0	0.0	...
Costa Rica	71.4	35.4	11.3	83.0	81.5	81.4	66.4	24.3	0.7	...
Dominican Rep.	217.7	122.5	71.8	89.2	123.0	186.1	189.6	159.7	95.6	...
Ecuador	404.6	324.9	264.6	182.4	99.8	71.1	198.1	173.5	145.0	...
El Salvador	10.7	5.3	0.2	0.0	0.0	0.0	0.0	0.0	0.0	...
Guatemala	88.0	73.0	66.6	64.0	30.8	0.0	0.0	0.0	0.0	...
Guyana	110.0	106.3	112.9	149.4	168.0	176.6	178.5	171.8	168.4	...
Haiti	47.4	41.3	37.6	32.6	35.1	33.8	35.0	28.7	24.9	...
Honduras	36.7	35.4	32.2	33.7	111.9	118.1	109.2	98.6	57.9	...
Jamaica	482.8	383.4	356.7	391.4	357.1	335.4	317.7	240.4	161.4	...
Mexico	4,804.5	5,090.6	6,551.3	6,765.8	5,949.6	4,787.2	3,860.1	15,828.2	13,278.8	...
Nicaragua	0.0	0.0	0.0	24.4	23.4	23.4	51.0	39.3	28.8	...
Panama	328.1	319.6	272.1	215.6	109.7	113.1	133.2	110.5	130.8	...
Paraguay	0.0	0.0	0.0	0.0	0.0	0.0	0.0	0.0	0.0	...
Peru	801.2	758.2	754.7	705.8	630.7	882.8	938.2	955.3	924.2	...
Suriname	...	...	...	...	...	...	...	...	...	...
Trinidad & Tobago	114.5	204.7	329.4	384.9	282.3	154.9	91.2	50.2	23.7	...
Uruguay	309.0	201.5	100.7	57.8	52.4	38.3	29.9	20.8	8.6	...
Venezuela	0.0	998.1	3,011.7	3,249.0	2,946.3	2,679.5	2,642.6	2,238.6	2,196.4	...
Latin America	**16,387.0**	**15,752.1**	**18,292.1**	**17,351.9**	**15,136.6**	**14,252.0**	**13,846.6**	**26,717.3**	**23,890.9**	**...**

TABLE E-5. DISBURSED EXTERNAL PUBLIC DEBT OUTSTANDING: LONG-TERM

(Millions of U.S. Dollars)

Country	1988	1989	1990	1991	1992	1993	1994	1995	1996	1997p
Argentina	47,546.3	51,832.3	46,905.5	47,574.0	47,610.9	52,033.9	55,832.3	55,970.2	62,391.8	...
Bahamas	171.3	221.0	266.2	412.4	440.4	453.3	413.7	394.3	360.8	...
Barbados	528.9	479.9	504.2	482.7	400.6	348.1	370.7	369.6	381.7	...
Belize	119.3	129.0	136.5	151.0	170.1	176.0	182.7	220.3	252.2	...
Bolivia	4,139.2	3,425.6	3,687.2	3,529.4	3,669.5	3,694.7	4,116.7	4,450.9	4,238.4	...
Brazil	92,045.7	88,088.2	87,671.4	85,535.9	90,672.3	91,987.7	94,919.3	97,183.0	94,587.2	...
Chile	13,696.4	10,865.5	10,426.1	10,070.5	9,577.5	8,867.4	8,994.9	7,183.9	4,889.8	...
Colombia	13,846.0	13,989.0	14,670.8	14,468.8	13,476.3	13,242.9	14,357.6	13,949.6	14,813.6	...
Costa Rica	3,546.7	3,545.3	3,063.0	3,291.6	3,175.1	3,130.4	3,217.5	3,125.6	2,889.0	...
Dominican Rep.	3,261.3	3,319.6	3,419.4	3,756.7	3,736.4	3,792.1	3,612.5	3,640.4	3,514.7	...
Ecuador	9,027.7	9,427.0	9,866.7	9,951.0	9,831.4	9,974.3	10,552.2	12,064.0	12,434.9	...
El Salvador	1,687.7	1,828.7	1,912.6	2,058.3	2,148.0	1,896.0	1,994.2	2,059.8	2,296.7	...
Guatemala	2,131.6	2,118.1	2,465.7	2,472.2	2,365.6	2,483.2	2,729.2	2,834.8	2,765.5	...
Guyana	994.6	1,261.0	1,757.4	1,760.2	1,673.1	1,731.4	1,787.2	1,781.9	1,370.1	...
Haiti	685.2	688.1	750.7	620.7	638.0	647.9	635.0	751.1	836.1	...
Honduras	2,757.7	2,867.2	3,425.8	3,095.9	3,231.8	3,651.0	3,901.9	3,982.3	3,855.1	...
Jamaica	3,723.5	3,743.5	3,933.9	3,708.8	3,565.8	3,457.8	3,436.8	3,408.0	3,182.7	...
Mexico	80,601.2	76,117.0	75,973.8	77,824.6	71,105.4	74,989.2	79,334.7	94,388.1	93,437.8	...
Nicaragua	6,950.5	7,589.4	8,280.4	9,152.6	9,311.3	9,440.1	9,760.8	8,540.5	5,122.4	...
Panama	4,005.2	3,935.3	3,988.0	3,918.1	3,771.2	3,799.4	3,930.4	3,913.6	5,135.6	...
Paraguay	2,091.2	2,093.5	1,711.9	1,683.4	1,363.2	1,280.8	1,356.9	1,427.1	1,377.2	...
Peru	12,332.1	12,611.4	13,629.0	15,438.7	15,576.7	16,382.0	17,678.2	18,925.7	20,414.7	...
Suriname	...	...	...	...	...	...	...	...	...	...
Trinidad & Tobago	1,856.9	1,806.1	1,781.6	1,749.9	1,787.7	1,807.5	1,961.3	1,941.2	1,870.9	...
Uruguay	2,950.6	3,007.8	3,044.9	2,899.7	3,142.6	3,371.5	3,752.4	3,832.9	4,097.1	...
Venezuela	25,180.9	25,166.2	24,508.7	24,938.6	25,829.5	26,855.3	28,041.8	28,494.3	28,452.1	...
Latin America	**335,877.7**	**330,155.7**	**327,781.4**	**330,545.7**	**328,270.4**	**339,493.9**	**356,870.9**	**374,833.1**	**374,968.1**	**...**

TABLE E-6. DISBURSED MULTILATERAL PUBLIC DEBT OUTSTANDING

(As a Percent of Total Debt)

Country	1988	1989	1990	1991	1992	1993	1994	1995	1996	1997p
Argentina	7.1	7.3	9.2	9.5	8.5	10.1	10.0	11.3	10.5	...
Bahamas	...	...	...	...	...	...	...	...	...	...
Barbados	24.0	25.7	26.5	27.5	28.2	28.8	26.5	27.4	33.2	...
Belize	29.8	35.9	37.7	35.7	34.2	32.0	35.8	35.1	31.8	...
Bolivia	26.9	35.2	37.2	42.4	43.3	46.5	47.0	49.1	51.1	...
Brazil	9.7	10.0	10.3	10.0	8.1	6.9	6.3	5.9	5.3	...
Chile	17.3	19.7	21.5	24.0	22.6	21.0	17.7	11.2	7.6	...
Colombia	33.0	33.5	35.5	35.8	34.0	29.9	24.6	21.2	16.5	...
Costa Rica	24.7	25.5	31.0	29.9	30.2	31.8	33.9	35.8	37.5	...
Dominican Rep.	19.8	20.6	22.2	21.0	20.3	20.5	22.9	24.5	25.0	...
Ecuador	19.5	19.2	20.1	21.1	22.0	20.1	20.3	21.4	20.2	...
El Salvador	36.6	37.8	36.7	38.5	41.0	52.6	57.2	52.4	53.7	...
Guatemala	35.2	36.2	35.8	34.6	32.9	28.1	29.6	28.1	28.1	...
Guyana	20.4	24.0	24.8	27.7	29.1	29.9	30.8	32.4	43.0	...
Haiti	53.8	56.9	56.5	68.3	68.3	66.7	76.7	75.8	77.1	...
Honduras	42.9	46.2	43.5	49.9	50.6	49.0	47.2	47.9	48.2	...
Jamaica	24.1	24.6	25.7	27.6	27.1	29.0	28.1	29.2	28.0	...
Mexico	10.4	11.5	13.7	13.6	13.8	12.2	12.2	11.2	11.3	...
Nicaragua	11.4	10.6	10.3	9.8	11.1	11.3	13.0	16.4	28.4	...
Panama	17.7	17.6	18.0	17.3	13.1	11.7	10.7	11.2	9.8	...
Paraguay	34.4	31.8	36.8	37.0	43.2	43.8	36.3	35.0	37.8	...
Peru	13.4	13.3	13.5	10.3	11.2	14.1	14.4	14.2	12.4	...
Suriname	...	...	...	...	...	...	...	...	...	...
Trinidad & Tobago	3.2	3.2	4.1	6.3	8.5	13.1	16.0	19.3	25.7	...
Uruguay	14.8	14.1	15.8	20.5	21.3	22.5	24.0	23.7	20.4	...
Venezuela	0.9	1.7	4.9	6.5	7.2	7.7	8.6	9.3	8.0	...
Latin America	**12.0**	**12.7**	**14.3**	**14.4**	**13.6**	**13.0**	**12.7**	**12.3**	**11.4**	**...**

TABLE E-7. SERVICE PAYMENTS ON THE TOTAL EXTERNAL DEBT[1]

(Millions of U.S. Dollars)

Country	1988	1989	1990	1991	1992	1993	1994	1995	1996	1997p
Argentina	5,023.1	5,060.4	6,161.0	5,544.6	5,003.1	6,556.4	8,174.8	9,692.0	14,021.2	...
Bahamas	67.5	56.1	45.2	73.2	78.7	81.9	95.4	85.3	93.5	...
Barbados	94.1	101.9	140.6	148.9	112.6	112.9	89.1	118.7	101.1	...
Belize	26.3	18.1	20.0	19.5	19.4	21.2	30.1	37.7	44.3	...
Bolivia	543.2	332.0	442.4	347.8	287.8	334.1	347.4	371.3	412.5	...
Brazil	16,842.6	14,122.4	8,168.8	8,337.1	8,666.1	11,242.9	16,212.4	22,366.1	25,091.2	...
Chile	2,147.5	2,667.8	2,771.7	3,882.5	2,693.4	2,841.9	2,932.8	5,151.7	6,270.4	...
Colombia	3,342.7	3,905.0	4,093.5	3,754.9	4,008.1	3,706.6	5,570.0	4,344.9	5,400.7	...
Costa Rica	403.5	345.4	521.2	443.0	542.5	551.8	503.7	646.7	637.8	...
Dominican Rep.	339.7	322.3	232.0	266.3	345.8	375.1	544.9	409.1	445.2	...
Ecuador	1,058.6	1,047.4	1,112.2	1,106.0	1,077.9	920.5	1,000.1	1,863.2	1,314.0	...
El Salvador	203.1	219.6	207.8	354.1	241.0	293.9	339.4	283.2	314.4	...
Guatemala	372.7	303.2	213.6	288.6	536.9	305.9	308.4	347.0	353.2	...
Guyana	66.3	377.9	295.5	106.9	101.6	92.3	97.0	109.0	104.6	...
Haiti	67.2	62.5	32.8	26.7	5.3	4.9	79.3	93.8	26.4	...
Honduras	394.0	190.2	506.0	307.3	377.0	360.7	432.6	553.4	563.9	...
Jamaica	735.4	642.5	706.3	759.3	681.2	563.9	596.6	672.9	682.2	...
Mexico	15,473.0	15,563.3	11,315.5	13,545.0	20,812.5	24,218.1	21,942.6	28,909.4	48,017.9	...
Nicaragua	20.5	11.3	15.8	672.6	124.7	186.7	273.9	287.8	227.9	...
Panama	28.1	13.3	345.1	335.5	965.9	281.9	385.7	374.3	954.0	...
Paraguay	381.4	149.9	324.9	275.3	648.8	285.6	255.7	288.3	283.3	...
Peru	347.1	604.5	475.3	1,151.5	1,003.4	3,211.9	1,141.9	1,239.7	2,931.5	...
Suriname	...	...	...	...	...	...	45.2	41.0	40.0	...
Trinidad & Tobago	383.0	247.1	449.1	427.8	576.5	701.1	544.6	416.7	861.2	...
Uruguay	890.4	659.9	986.7	805.9	524.4	586.6	676.9	865.5	664.5	...
Venezuela	5,551.5	6,817.8	5,273.7	3,321.4	3,331.4	4,579.9	4,744.9	5,515.6	4,711.2	...
Latin America[2]	**54,802.5**	**53,841.8**	**44,856.7**	**46,301.7**	**52,766.0**	**62,418.7**	**67,365.4**	**85,084.3**	**114,568.1**	**...**

[1] Includes Interest and Amortization Payments.
[2] For 1988-1993, Latin American total excludes Suriname.

TABLE E-8. SERVICE PAYMENTS ON THE TOTAL EXTERNAL DEBT: INTEREST

(Millions of U.S. Dollars)

Country	1988	1989	1990	1991	1992	1993	1994	1995	1996	1997p
Argentina	3,103.4	2,129.3	2,717.1	2,926.8	2,825.4	3,300.9	4,110.4	5,358.3	5,904.3	...
Bahamas	...	...	...	...	...	...	...	...	...	...
Barbados	44.8	48.0	48.6	46.0	42.7	40.9	40.7	41.7	39.7	...
Belize	5.4	7.3	7.1	6.4	6.6	6.9	8.2	11.4	12.8	...
Bolivia	121.4	125.9	144.1	138.1	120.9	139.4	159.7	172.7	182.4	...
Brazil	12,629.8	5,215.1	2,256.4	3,527.8	3,830.4	4,431.2	6,631.1	10,846.1	10,636.5	...
Chile	1,262.1	1,636.3	1,792.0	1,555.8	1,340.2	1,120.5	1,240.8	1,486.9	1,593.5	...
Colombia	1,539.6	1,762.0	1,700.8	1,555.6	1,394.0	1,302.1	1,677.9	1,998.0	2,036.0	...
Costa Rica	228.6	169.6	206.3	233.4	239.7	209.1	215.4	250.3	215.4	...
Dominican Rep.	181.9	120.9	85.9	105.9	148.9	147.3	209.4	174.9	198.4	...
Ecuador	372.4	494.2	473.6	503.9	420.4	403.5	491.7	665.8	669.2	...
El Salvador	78.5	69.1	84.1	81.4	84.0	121.9	98.2	122.9	136.7	...
Guatemala	125.8	131.7	111.6	131.9	173.6	115.4	126.7	152.3	159.7	...
Guyana	54.7	58.6	120.2	53.0	48.9	41.5	36.4	34.9	32.0	...
Haiti	17.4	17.1	14.7	16.1	4.9	4.5	0.8	31.7	13.1	...
Honduras	158.0	72.1	177.7	160.0	173.8	150.8	178.3	217.0	173.5	...
Jamaica	251.0	230.2	260.0	239.9	211.9	203.8	216.0	233.2	228.2	...
Mexico	8,712.2	9,310.4	7,303.7	8,186.1	7,538.0	8,101.2	9,236.9	11,208.3	11,721.5	...
Nicaragua	11.6	4.8	11.4	200.2	64.5	69.3	104.4	85.3	87.5	...
Panama	12.9	5.0	224.0	206.8	363.5	136.3	220.5	201.8	490.7	...
Paraguay	133.0	74.5	90.0	106.7	246.1	88.2	96.0	129.2	106.7	...
Peru	218.6	238.3	246.5	524.5	464.4	1,137.7	541.5	720.7	1,704.7	...
Suriname	...	...	...	...	...	...	...	...	...	...
Trinidad & Tobago	161.1	179.9	216.3	212.6	180.2	144.3	155.2	175.7	193.6	...
Uruguay	353.8	368.7	428.1	255.1	262.5	262.7	304.0	379.1	367.2	...
Venezuela	3,122.7	3,086.3	3,242.2	2,424.6	2,137.2	2,161.7	2,117.6	2,402.9	2,141.0	...
Latin America	**32,900.7**	**25,555.3**	**21,962.4**	**23,398.6**	**22,322.7**	**23,841.1**	**28,217.8**	**37,101.1**	**39,044.3**	**...**

TABLE E-9. SERVICE PAYMENTS ON THE TOTAL EXTERNAL DEBT: AMORTIZATION

(*Millions of* U.S. *Dollars*)

Country	1988	1989	1990	1991	1992	1993	1994	1995	1996	1997p
Argentina	1,919.7	2,931.1	3,443.9	2,617.8	2,177.7	3,255.5	4,064.4	4,333.7	8,116.9	...
Bahamas	...	...	...	...	...	...	...	...	...	...
Barbados	49.3	53.9	92.0	102.9	69.9	72.0	48.4	77.0	61.4	...
Belize	20.9	10.8	12.9	13.1	12.8	14.3	21.9	26.3	31.5	...
Bolivia	421.8	206.1	298.3	209.7	166.9	194.7	187.7	198.6	230.1	...
Brazil	4,212.8	8,907.3	5,912.4	4,809.3	4,835.7	6,811.7	9,581.3	11,520.0	14,454.7	...
Chile	885.4	1,031.5	979.7	2,326.7	1,353.2	1,721.4	1,692.0	3,664.8	4,676.9	...
Colombia	1,803.1	2,143.0	2,392.7	2,199.3	2,614.1	2,404.5	3,892.1	2,346.9	3,364.7	...
Costa Rica	174.9	175.8	314.9	209.6	302.8	342.7	288.3	396.4	422.4	...
Dominican Rep.	157.8	201.4	146.1	160.4	196.9	227.8	335.5	234.2	246.8	...
Ecuador	686.2	553.2	638.6	602.1	657.5	517.0	508.4	1,197.4	644.8	...
El Salvador	124.6	150.5	123.7	272.7	157.0	172.0	241.2	160.3	177.7	...
Guatemala	246.9	171.5	102.0	156.7	363.3	190.5	181.7	194.7	193.5	...
Guyana	11.6	319.3	175.3	53.9	52.7	50.8	60.6	74.1	72.6	...
Haiti	49.8	45.4	18.1	10.6	0.4	0.4	78.5	62.1	13.3	...
Honduras	236.0	118.1	328.3	147.3	203.2	209.9	254.3	336.4	390.4	...
Jamaica	484.4	412.3	446.3	519.4	469.3	360.1	380.6	439.7	454.0	...
Mexico	6,760.8	6,252.9	4,011.8	5,358.9	13,274.5	16,116.9	12,705.7	17,701.1	36,296.4	...
Nicaragua	8.9	6.5	4.4	472.4	60.2	117.4	169.5	202.5	140.4	...
Panama	15.2	8.3	121.1	128.7	602.4	145.6	165.2	172.5	463.3	...
Paraguay	248.4	75.4	234.9	168.6	402.7	197.4	159.7	159.1	176.6	...
Peru	128.5	366.2	228.8	627.0	539.0	2,074.2	600.4	519.0	1,226.8	...
Suriname	...	...	...	...	...	...	...	...	...	...
Trinidad & Tobago	221.9	67.2	232.8	215.2	396.3	556.8	389.4	241.0	667.6	...
Uruguay	536.6	291.2	558.6	550.8	261.9	323.9	372.9	486.4	297.3	...
Venezuela	2,428.8	3,731.5	2,031.5	896.8	1,194.2	2,418.2	2,627.3	3,112.7	2,570.2	...
Latin America	**21,834.3**	**28,230.4**	**22,849.1**	**22,829.9**	**30,364.6**	**38,495.7**	**39,007.0**	**47,856.9**	**75,390.3**	...

TABLE E-10. TOTAL EXTERNAL DEBT TO GROSS DOMESTIC PRODUCT

(In *Percent*)

Country	1988	1989	1990	1991	1992	1993	1994	1995	1996	1997p
Argentina	44.9	77.8	38.7	29.9	25.9	27.4	27.5	29.8	31.7	...
Bahamas	6.6	7.4	8.5	13.3	14.0	13.9	12.2	11.3	9.6	...
Barbados	44.9	37.4	39.7	38.4	38.4	34.5	35.4	32.0	29.1	...
Belize	44.2	39.8	38.1	39.4	38.9	37.4	36.5	43.6	46.7	...
Bolivia	104.3	86.6	87.7	75.7	74.8	74.9	80.9	78.1	71.5	...
Brazil	38.0	26.9	24.0	18.3	31.1	31.2	27.4	22.6	22.9	...
Chile	81.1	63.9	63.2	52.2	44.8	45.2	47.4	38.0	38.1	...
Colombia	43.4	42.7	42.7	41.7	39.1	37.2	32.0	31.1	33.7	...
Costa Rica	92.1	80.5	64.4	70.1	58.0	50.9	46.5	41.7	38.0	...
Dominican Rep.	69.9	56.8	54.7	55.4	48.4	45.0	39.6	35.8	31.0	...
Ecuador	99.3	104.3	99.1	90.0	80.9	82.6	76.6	77.9	75.7	...
El Salvador	40.6	36.2	40.2	40.9	37.7	28.9	27.0	27.2	27.8	...
Guatemala	32.3	29.9	37.5	30.5	26.9	27.3	25.6	24.4	23.3	...
Guyana	424.4	402.9	475.0	567.6	500.5	421.9	364.9	317.3	221.6	...
Haiti	...	...	43.5	33.7	41.4	49.6	40.5	41.5	41.8	...
Honduras	68.5	62.2	119.2	108.2	104.1	113.6	127.3	113.9	107.6	...
Jamaica	126.7	108.9	107.0	114.7	123.1	94.3	99.8	81.5	66.8	...
Mexico	54.1	42.1	39.7	36.3	30.8	32.7	33.2	57.9	46.9	...
Nicaragua	1,176.6	842.1	406.0	552.5	528.4	499.0	546.0	465.8	273.8	...
Panama	117.6	115.7	106.5	94.7	79.5	74.0	71.5	70.0	84.3	...
Paraguay	37.4	52.8	37.8	31.1	24.9	22.8	25.0	24.7	22.1	...
Peru	40.2	35.5	45.2	42.9	44.3	48.4	44.3	44.5	47.5	...
Suriname	27.3	33.7	39.7	53.4	60.6	101.6	63.7	47.0	31.1	...
Trinidad & Tobago	46.7	49.5	49.5	46.9	45.1	48.9	50.4	51.4	39.4	...
Uruguay	50.4	55.7	52.8	41.7	38.6	35.1	31.2	29.5	30.8	...
Venezuela	57.5	75.6	68.3	63.8	62.4	62.2	62.6	46.0	49.9	...
Latin America	**49.1**	**43.1**	**37.9**	**31.6**	**35.3**	**35.7**	**33.9**	**35.1**	**33.7**	...

TABLE E-11. DEBT SERVICE RATIO[1]

(In Percent)

Country	1988	1989	1990	1991	1992	1993	1994	1995	1996	1997p
Argentina	45.1	43.0	41.6	38.5	34.1	42.1	44.3	40.7	51.9	...
Bahamas	4.3	3.3	2.5	4.6	4.9	5.0	5.6	4.8	5.1	...
Barbados	12.1	11.5	16.1	18.1	13.9	12.9	8.9	10.2	8.1	...
Belize	13.6	8.6	8.2	7.8	6.9	7.5	10.8	12.6	14.4	...
Bolivia	81.0	38.3	45.3	37.9	37.2	37.3	28.6	30.0	31.3	...
Brazil	46.7	37.7	23.2	23.9	21.7	25.8	33.1	42.5	46.2	...
Chile	26.4	27.8	27.1	35.1	21.8	24.3	20.3	26.8	33.4	...
Colombia	49.5	53.3	47.2	41.3	43.3	37.3	46.1	31.6	37.2	...
Costa Rica	25.0	18.9	26.5	20.2	21.0	19.0	15.2	17.1	15.5	...
Dominican Rep.	17.8	16.4	12.7	14.3	18.1	8.1	10.7	7.4	7.1	...
Ecuador	40.0	36.5	34.1	32.5	29.0	24.8	21.8	35.4	22.9	...
El Salvador	21.6	24.2	21.4	39.4	24.7	25.8	20.7	13.9	14.3	...
Guatemala	29.4	21.3	13.6	17.1	28.3	15.1	13.7	12.3	12.6	...
Guyana	25.2	150.5	117.6	36.5	20.8	17.4	16.6	17.3	14.7	...
Haiti	24.4	26.4	10.3	10.3	4.6	4.2	123.7	38.9	10.3	...
Honduras	38.4	17.9	49.0	30.3	36.2	29.7	31.6	31.9	29.4	...
Jamaica	43.7	33.7	31.9	34.7	30.7	23.8	21.1	21.2	...	...
Mexico	42.1	36.7	23.2	26.3	37.5	39.4	30.8	32.4	44.9	...
Nicaragua	7.5	3.3	4.0	198.8	40.3	50.8	57.6	44.5	28.3	...
Panama	0.8	0.4	7.8	6.2	15.3	4.2	5.2	4.9	12.8	...
Paraguay	32.7	9.5	17.3	13.6	34.0	9.6	7.0	6.0	6.4	...
Peru	9.7	13.8	11.5	27.2	22.3	73.8	20.2	18.4	40.3	...
Suriname	...	...	...	...	...	...	12.3	7.9	7.6	...
Trinidad & Tobago	22.0	13.5	19.6	19.6	26.9	37.8	25.9	14.9	28.4	...
Uruguay	50.8	32.5	45.7	36.6	19.9	21.3	20.8	24.7	17.3	...
Venezuela	50.2	48.7	28.0	20.3	21.5	28.4	26.8	26.6	18.7	...
Latin America	**40.1**	**35.3**	**26.5**	**27.1**	**28.8**	**31.3**	**29.1**	**30.8**	**37.6**	...

[1] Debt Service to Exports of Goods and (Non-Factor) Services.

EXTERNAL DEBT NOTES

Unless otherwise specified, the concept used in the tables is disbursed debt (i.e., the credit effectively used by the country).

Principal repayments and interest payments are recorded on a "cash" basis. The difference with the Balance of Payments approach of what was "due" is equal to the amount due but fallen in arrears and/or the payment of old arrears and/or the part which has been rescheduled.

Total External Debt:

The sum of long- and short-term external debt and the use of International Monetary Fund (IMF) credit:

Long-term Debt: Debt with an original or extended maturity of more than one year, repayable in foreign currency, goods or services. This is divided into public or publicly guaranteed debt and private non-guaranteed debt:

Public or Publicly Guaranteed: includes all external long-term debt contracted directly by public bodies or by private entities with a guarantee of payment by any of the following public institutions: central governments or their departments; political subdivisions (such as states, provinces, departments or municipalities); central banks; autonomous institutions (such as corporations, development banks, railways, utilities, etc.) where (a) the budget of the institution is subject to the approval of the government of the reporting country; or where (b) the government owns more than 50 percent of the voting stock or more than half of the members of the Board of Directors are government representatives; or where (c) in the case of default the state would become liable for the debt of the institution.

Consequently, long-term public or publicly guaranteed debt excludes: obligations with a maturity of less than one year; loans contracted with the option of repayment in local currency; the debt of the private sector without the guarantee of the public sector; the "purchases" and "repurchases" operations with the International Monetary Fund and the "swap" transactions between central banks.

Private Non-guaranteed: is the external obligation of a private resident of the country with a non-resident that is not guaranteed by a public institution of that country.

Short-term Debt: Debt with an original maturity of one year or less. It could be public or private, but there is no available data for this distinction.

Use of IMF Credit: Net credit (purchases, repurchases and charges) transactions with respect to all uses of IMF resources, excluding those resulting from drawings in the reserve tranche and the IMF Trust Fund. The use of IMF credit is a special item and is not included in either short- or long-term debt.

Data are also presented on a regional level, by types of credits and creditors. For this purpose, the latter are defined as follows:

Suppliers: include credits from manufacturers, exporters or other suppliers of goods to finance the purchase of their products;

Private Banks: consist of credits extended by commercial banks, whether their ownership is private or public, as well as credits from private financial institutions other than commercial banks;

Bond Issues: consist of securities offered to the general public, which are traded in the stock exchanges, as well as securities privately placed with a limited number of investors, usually banking institutions, that could trade them on the stock exchanges at a later date;

Other: consists of debts that arise from a settlement for compensation to foreigners for property owned by them, which has been acquired by the public authorities by means of expropriation or by common consent and other unclassified debt;

Official Multilateral: includes loans and credits extended by international, regional or subregional financial organizations, such as the World Bank, the International Development Association, the Inter-American Development Bank (IDB) and the Central American Bank for Economic Integration. However, this category does not include the loans made out of the funds administered by the IDB on behalf of a government. Loans from the Canadian Fund, for example, are registered with the Canadian Government as official bilateral loans; and

Official Bilateral: includes direct loans from governments or public entities, and government loans administered by the IDB as explained above.

Sources:

The World Bank Debtor Reporting System (DRS) is the source for most of the data in the tables, supplemented where necessary by IDB estimates using official information from the countries.

TABLE F-1. MARKET EXCHANGE RATES[1]

(Local Currency per U.S. Dollar)

Country	1988	1989	1990	1991	1992	1993	1994	1995	1996	1997p
Argentina[2]	-	-	0.5	1.0	1.0	1.0	1.0	1.0	1.0	1.0
Bahamas	1.0	1.0	1.0	1.0	1.0	1.0	1.0	1.0	1.0	1.0
Barbados	2.0	2.0	2.0	2.0	2.0	2.0	2.0	2.0	2.0	2.0
Belize	2.0	2.0	2.0	2.0	2.0	2.0	2.0	2.0	2.0	2.0
Bolivia	2.4	2.7	3.2	3.6	3.9	4.3	4.6	4.8	5.1	5.3
Brazil[2]	-	-	-	-	-	-	0.6	0.9	1.0	1.1
Chile	245.0	267.0	304.9	349.2	362.6	404.2	420.2	396.8	412.3	419.3
Colombia[3]	299.2	382.6	502.3	633.1	759.3	863.1	844.8	912.8	1,036.7	1,143.1
Costa Rica	75.8	81.5	91.6	122.4	134.5	142.2	157.1	179.7	207.7	232.6
Dominican Rep.	6.1	6.3	8.5	12.7	12.8	12.7	13.2	13.6	13.8	14.3
Ecuador	301.6	526.4	767.8	1,046.3	1,534.0	1,919.1	2,196.7	2,564.5	3,189.5	3,998.3
El Salvador	5.0	5.0	6.8	8.0	8.4	8.7	8.7	8.8	8.8	8.8
Guatemala	2.6	2.8	4.5	5.0	5.2	5.6	5.8	5.8	6.0	6.1
Guyana	10.0	27.2	39.5	111.8	125.0	126.7	138.3	142.0	140.4	142.4
Haiti[4]	6.0	6.6	7.5	7.7	9.1	12.4	14.7	14.5	16.1	16.2
Honduras	2.0	2.0	4.1	5.3	5.5	6.5	8.4	9.5	11.7	13.0
Jamaica	5.5	5.7	7.2	12.1	23.0	24.9	33.1	35.1	37.1	35.4
Mexico	2.3	2.5	2.8	3.0	3.1	3.1	3.4	6.4	7.6	7.9
Nicaragua[2]	-	-	0.1	4.3	5.0	5.6	6.7	7.5	8.4	9.4
Panama	1.0	1.0	1.0	1.0	1.0	1.0	1.0	1.0	1.0	1.0
Paraguay	550.0	1,056.2	1,229.8	1,325.2	1,500.3	1,744.4	1,911.5	1,970.4	2,062.8	2,191.1
Peru[2]	-	-	0.2	0.8	1.2	2.0	2.2	2.3	2.5	2.7
Suriname[5]	6.6	7.8	9.8	10.2	14.8	51.2	208.5	457.1	404.9	408.7
Trinidad & Tobago	3.8	4.3	4.3	4.3	4.3	5.4	5.9	5.9	6.0	6.3
Uruguay	0.4	0.6	1.2	2.0	3.0	3.9	5.1	6.3	8.0	9.4
Venezuela	14.5	34.7	46.9	56.8	68.4	90.8	148.5	176.8	417.3	488.6

Sources: Official statistics, IDB estimates and International Monetary Fund, International Financial Statistics, various issues.
[1] Period average. [2] (-) Indicates that the exchange rate is less than half of a significant digit, given the magnitude of the depreciations experienced.
[3] Refers to annual average until 1990; representative market rate from 1991. [4] Reference rate for 1988-1997.
[5] Average exchange rate, taking into account parallel rate.

TABLE F-2. AVERAGE ANNUAL GROWTH OF CONSUMER PRICES

(In Percent)

Country	1988	1989	1990	1991	1992	1993	1994	1995	1996	1997p
Argentina	348.3	3,084.6	2,315.5	171.7	24.9	10.6	4.2	3.4	0.2	0.5
Bahamas	4.5	5.3	4.7	7.1	5.8	2.6	1.5	2.0	1.4	0.5
Barbados	4.9	6.1	3.1	6.3	6.0	1.2	0.1	1.8	2.4	7.7
Belize	5.4	0.0	3.0	2.3	2.3	1.4	2.6	2.8	6.4	1.1
Bolivia	15.9	15.2	17.1	21.4	12.1	8.5	7.9	10.2	12.4	4.7
Brazil	690.0	1,289.0	2,937.7	440.9	1,008.7	2,148.5	2,668.6	84.4	18.2	7.5
Chile	15.0	16.2	26.6	22.0	15.6	12.1	12.0	7.9	7.3	6.3
Colombia	28.0	25.9	29.2	30.4	27.0	22.6	23.8	21.0	20.2	17.7
Costa Rica	20.8	16.5	19.0	28.7	21.8	9.8	13.5	23.2	17.5	13.2
Dominican Rep.	58.4	40.6	50.4	47.1	4.2	5.3	8.2	12.5	5.4	8.3
Ecuador	58.1	75.7	48.6	48.8	54.4	45.0	27.4	22.9	24.4	30.7
El Salvador	19.9	17.5	24.1	14.4	11.2	18.6	10.6	10.1	9.7	4.5
Guatemala	10.9	11.3	41.2	33.2	10.0	11.9	10.9	8.4	11.1	9.2
Guyana	39.9	89.7	63.6	101.5	28.2	10.0	16.1	8.1	4.5	4.2
Haiti	4.1	7.9	20.4	18.2	17.9	18.9	37.4	30.2	20.5	16.1
Honduras	4.5	9.9	23.3	34.0	8.7	10.8	21.7	29.5	23.8	20.2
Jamaica	8.8	17.2	29.8	80.2	40.2	30.1	26.8	25.6	15.8	9.2
Mexico	114.2	20.1	26.6	22.7	15.5	9.7	6.9	35.0	34.4	20.6
Nicaragua	10,215.2	4,770.3	7,485.2	2,742.3	20.3	20.4	7.8	11.0	11.6	10.0
Panama	0.4	0.1	0.8	1.3	1.8	0.5	1.3	0.9	1.3	1.2
Paraguay	22.5	26.6	38.1	24.2	15.2	18.2	20.5	13.4	9.8	7.0
Peru	660.0	3,321.1	7,592.3	409.5	73.5	48.6	23.7	11.1	11.5	8.6
Suriname	7.3	0.7	21.8	26.0	43.7	143.5	368.5	235.6	-0.7	7.1
Trinidad & Tobago	7.7	11.4	11.1	3.8	6.5	10.8	8.8	5.2	3.4	3.7
Uruguay	62.3	80.5	112.3	102.0	68.4	54.1	44.7	42.2	28.3	19.8
Venezuela	29.3	84.7	40.6	34.2	31.4	38.1	60.8	59.9	99.9	50.0
Latin America	**271.2**	**464.7**	**661.7**	**160.5**	**190.0**	**268.7**	**294.4**	**44.1**	**21.7**	**12.2**

Sources: Official statistics, IDB estimates and International Monetary Fund, International Financial Statistics, various issues.

TABLE F-3. REAL EFFECTIVE EXCHANGE RATE

(Index 1990=100)

Country	1988	1989	1990	1991	1992	1993	1994	1995	1996	1997p
Argentina	130.3	148.7	100.0	73.4	64.6	59.0	58.1	57.7	...	...
Bahamas	99.0	97.1	100.0	96.9	94.4	92.4	96.2	99.6	99.0	96.9
Barbados	101.3	97.8	100.0	98.2	95.4	94.5	93.1	91.7	90.3	89.0
Belize	92.8	94.2	100.0	98.7	100.8	98.5	103.2	105.6	100.3	97.3
Bolivia	81.3	84.6	100.0	95.7	97.7	99.5	107.2	110.9	104.9	100.8
Brazil	142.4	116.0	100.0	126.2	138.3	122.4	102.7	90.5	89.1	85.0
Chile	99.2	96.9	100.0	97.2	92.0	100.5	88.5	83.7	80.8	73.9
Colombia	85.0	88.2	100.0	97.2	89.4	84.6	75.6	74.5	69.5	62.1
Costa Rica	101.8	98.1	100.0	109.6	107.5	109.2	111.8	106.9	110.5	110.0
Dominican Rep.	119.7	99.0	100.0	99.0	98.5	94.5	91.0	88.6	85.0	82.7
Ecuador	105.4	91.1	100.0	94.2	94.0	80.6	75.9	77.3	77.7	72.4
El Salvador	88.0	89.2	100.0	97.3	96.3	87.5	83.2	77.3	72.7	71.3
Guatemala	79.8	82.6	100.0	85.0	80.5	79.3	75.8	77.0	73.6	66.1
Guyana	56.4	71.4	100.0	116.7	106.1	97.3	97.6	96.9	89.7	90.2
Haiti	87.6	89.5	100.0	129.7	131.3	124.7	124.7	125.0	92.3	85.0
Honduras	68.8	64.0	100.0	108.9	109.0	114.5	120.2	108.0	109.0	100.7
Jamaica	95.5	89.2	100.0	111.1	127.8	111.8	95.0	94.6	70.9	128.9
Mexico	109.6	100.2	100.0	90.9	85.6	80.5	85.7	115.0	105.8	91.2
Nicaragua	91.3	149.2	100.0	104.5	107.2	110.2	118.1	116.9	114.9	115.0
Panama	90.6	94.6	100.0	102.7	105.1	108.2	112.3	115.8	116.2	116.2
Paraguay	78.4	102.5	100.0	88.4	91.3	91.0	88.8	88.0	84.2	80.6
Peru	212.6	120.2	100.0	80.8	78.9	91.2	84.1	82.1	79.9	78.2
Suriname	68.6	85.1	100.0	84.7	88.1	120.5	110.6	81.4	73.5	66.0
Trinidad & Tobago	100.9	102.2	100.0	99.6	97.6	108.3	117.2	119.6	117.4	118.4
Uruguay	96.5	92.2	100.0	86.9	81.3	69.1	65.3	63.6	62.3	59.3
Venezuela	75.6	88.8	100.0	93.0	89.6	85.5	89.5	71.6	84.8	64.7

Sources: Official statistics, IDB estimates and International Monetary Fund, *International Financial Statistics*, various issues.

TABLE F-4. TERMS OF TRADE

(Index 1990=100 *except where noted*)

Country	1988	1989	1990	1991	1992	1993	1994	1995	1996	1997p
Argentina	97.9	96.6	100.0	101.7	109.0	109.4	108.3	109.4	119.0	120.3
Bahamas	...	...	...	...	...	...	...	...	...	...
Barbados	...	...	...	...	...	...	...	...	...	...
Belize	...	...	100.0	98.0	94.7	96.6	97.7	97.5	96.2	95.7
Bolivia	110.5	94.5	100.0	92.6	70.4	71.2	84.1	74.7	66.9	67.9
Brazil	114.8	106.1	100.0	104.9	103.4	107.3	113.9	113.8	111.8	118.2
Chile	103.8	103.3	100.0	102.3	101.3	92.2	101.7	115.2	95.6	101.1
Colombia	103.6	102.6	100.0	106.8	108.6	105.0	120.2	122.5	123.4	132.5
Costa Rica	104.8	103.1	100.0	104.0	105.8	104.7	107.1	108.2	107.8	114.4
Dominican Rep.	137.1	131.1	100.0	114.6	107.2	105.2	110.8	123.3	118.5	123.3
Ecuador	93.4	100.8	100.0	88.4	89.5	77.9	81.2	79.7	86.9	91.4
El Salvador	85.5	82.3	100.0	98.5	98.6	97.1	131.4	138.0	134.5	149.7
Guatemala	98.8	97.6	100.0	104.3	103.8	97.7	112.6	115.6	109.4	117.3
Guyana[1]	109.8	97.4	100.0	128.7	125.6	103.2	101.8	74.9	110.4	110.1
Haiti	113.5	86.8	100.0	84.1	79.9	80.7	80.8	85.7	80.7	87.5
Honduras	105.3	101.0	100.0	105.2	99.2	103.0	114.0	115.4	111.9	123.9
Jamaica[1]	92.3	89.2	86.0	83.0	79.6	78.5	78.4	83.4	89.4	...
Mexico	85.6	92.7	100.0	100.5	105.6	105.7	105.7	105.7	105.7	104.0
Nicaragua	113.4	103.8	100.0	92.7	67.9	78.6	90.9	104.8	96.8	104.2
Panama	101.1	100.5	100.0	95.6	97.5	98.6	99.1	93.8	94.4	99.7
Paraguay	91.1	95.5	100.0	99.5	98.6	103.5	108.1	111.1	109.8	113.1
Peru	96.8	94.1	100.0	96.1	95.1	92.1	93.9	94.7	94.2	100.5
Suriname[1]	84.7	122.0	99.1	84.1	77.0	75.0	83.2	91.1	81.4	83.9
Trinidad & Tobago[1]	68.5	66.5	71.1	71.6	69.6	72.5	88.2	98.9	88.3	90.0
Uruguay	102.9	105.5	100.0	99.6	104.3	94.3	95.3	101.4	98.5	102.0
Venezuela	72.2	91.0	100.0	82.6	79.4	74.0	74.8	77.6	92.1	90.2

[1] Index 1980 = 100.

TABLE F-5. ANNUAL GROWTH OF TOTAL: DOMESTIC CREDIT[1]

(Annual Growth Rates)

Country	1988	1989	1990	1991	1992	1993	1994	1995	1996	1997p
Argentina	...	...	...	84.0	23.2	20.5	10.8	5.3	6.5	15.2
Bahamas	12.3	13.5	20.5	5.5	4.5	15.7	8.5	9.6	7.8	22.8
Barbados	12.1	8.4	11.0	7.3	0.4	2.2	1.5	3.4	7.9	14.3
Belize	-9.7	0.4	5.9	38.4	23.3	14.4	7.4	16.6	-0.7	15.8
Bolivia	51.4	65.3	48.3	31.4	45.1	52.6	22.4	-2.2	14.0	22.3
Brazil	...	...	900.0	420.0	1,351.9	2,666.2	864.3	17.3	25.3	15.3
Chile	12.3	11.4	20.3	14.1	19.9	24.3	8.9	22.4	16.4	14.3
Colombia	42.6	...	...	6.8	32.9	50.0	54.1	36.2	25.3	42.0
Costa Rica	15.5	7.6	20.7	10.8	24.0	23.8	16.3	8.5	83.7	33.8
Dominican Rep.	28.8	33.1	23.6	15.2	23.2	15.7	30.4	21.6	30.1	26.5
Ecuador	80.5	10.2	14.7	80.5	47.2	257.6	36.5	-22.0	33.5	54.8
El Salvador	9.9	19.2	7.4	20.6	32.1	12.2	28.3	19.7	16.3	20.4
Guatemala	8.0	12.1	20.0	6.6	28.5	8.2	35.2	27.2	13.8	12.2
Guyana	60.7	127.8	34.5	102.4	47.6	1.3	1.2	12.9	-14.5	-7.4
Haiti	7.5	15.7	-1.3	4.0	16.8	14.7	23.5	22.2	12.8	27.3
Honduras	13.0	12.2	1.9	4.3	10.9	18.4	27.1	9.1	25.3	33.9
Jamaica	2.9	8.7	-5.1	0.6	56.5	70.9	31.1	61.1	29.3	42.2
Mexico	66.9	46.5	42.3	36.6	21.8	12.7	31.5	22.8	2.6	0.9
Nicaragua	...	...	25,400.0	1,332.5	510.8	15.5	9.0	1.1	-9.0	19.0
Panama	-15.5	-0.7	-12.4	9.0	20.6	15.7	12.5	11.1	15.3	9.4
Paraguay	28.3	25.7	37.2	58.8	108.8	30.3	13.6	7.7	14.6	27.1
Peru	...	1,600.0	5,711.8	157.5	97.7	77.9	7.2	46.3	22.5	73.6
Suriname	22.9	16.8	3.5	23.3	17.2	37.8	24.3	37.0	202.9	...
Trinidad & Tobago	3.5	4.0	0.8	10.7	2.3	-1.4	-13.0	20.3	16.0	18.2
Uruguay	78.4	75.0	92.5	50.6	65.7	43.3	42.2	45.8	31.0	...
Venezuela	51.9	19.7	65.3	11.6	41.5	26.8	95.3	70.5	18.9	36.4

Sources: Official statistics, IDB estimates and International Monetary Fund, International Financial Statistics, various issues.
[1] At end of period.

TABLE F-6. ANNUAL GROWTH OF NOMINAL MONEY SUPPLY[1]

(Annual Growth Rates)

Country	1988	1989	1990	1991	1992	1993	1994	1995	1996	1997p
Argentina	500.0	4,450.0	1,023.8	148.6	49.0	33.0	8.2	1.6	14.6	12.7
Bahamas	9.1	1.6	14.3	7.0	3.8	0.4	9.1	6.8	0.5	15.7
Barbados	12.4	-12.5	14.6	-5.9	1.5	-5.1	8.3	-17.0	46.4	-3.2
Belize	-3.0	22.1	6.1	11.6	6.8	7.9	5.7	7.8	5.5	1.3
Bolivia	35.3	2.4	39.4	45.1	32.9	30.0	29.3	21.1	21.7	19.5
Brazil	...	...	...	400.0	960.0	2,000.0	2,194.7	25.7	29.5	22.1
Chile	46.5	17.2	23.3	44.8	26.3	21.2	16.2	22.2	16.2	20.2
Colombia	25.7	...	...	31.7	44.3	27.7	27.4	23.5	23.4	17.2
Costa Rica	53.3	-2.0	3.9	20.0	37.2	7.0	37.9	-6.0	16.9	54.3
Dominican Rep.	55.9	24.3	41.2	24.5	16.9	22.7	1.4	17.1	29.8	19.3
Ecuador	52.7	43.8	65.9	46.7	48.4	63.7	32.5	2.7	28.9	30.0
El Salvador	7.9	13.4	22.4	18.1	29.5	17.2	5.2	15.8	12.9	-2.1
Guatemala	14.4	20.7	33.0	18.6	9.1	20.4	40.1	9.9	13.5	29.9
Guyana	54.8	33.9	54.5	65.5	31.5	32.0	10.4	16.7	14.5	10.0
Haiti	-22.1	61.1	-12.6	7.0	27.8	22.7	31.8	31.6	-13.1	10.2
Honduras	11.9	20.0	23.6	11.1	22.5	11.9	36.1	21.7	29.4	41.0
Jamaica	53.0	-8.5	27.4	94.7	71.3	26.2	25.7	38.0	14.4	2.8
Mexico	67.8	37.3	63.1	123.9	15.1	17.7	1.1	3.5	36.9	32.2
Nicaragua	...	...	5,200.0	1,330.2	11.5	-4.7	36.3	13.2	33.3	32.0
Panama	-31.3	1.0	41.0	28.7	14.8	10.8	13.5	1.3	3.3	18.3
Paraguay	35.5	31.7	28.3	32.4	22.5	16.5	30.0	28.2	-2.3	10.3
Peru	...	900.0	6,970.0	127.3	76.9	52.6	28.9	34.2	19.7	64.3
Suriname	24.5	11.3	4.0	28.2	11.6	87.6	245.6	178.2	-2.0	...
Trinidad & Tobago	-13.6	13.7	20.8	13.4	-7.7	16.3	19.5	4.7	-6.1	21.1
Uruguay	64.4	72.5	101.0	98.4	69.0	57.7	39.4	33.7	25.5	...
Venezuela	18.7	15.6	58.4	28.4	7.6	11.2	140.1	39.4	145.0	66.9

Sources: Official statistics, IDB estimates and International Monetary Fund, International Financial Statistics, various issues.
[1] M1 at end of period.

TABLE F-7. TOTAL RESERVES MINUS MONETARY GOLD

(Millions of U.S. Dollars)

Country	1988	1989	1990	1991	1992	1993	1994	1995	1996	1997p
Argentina	3,363.0	1,463.0	4,592.0	6,005.0	9,990.0	13,791.0	14,327.0	14,288.0	18,104.0	22,320.0
Bahamas	172.0	146.8	158.2	181.3	155.3	172.3	176.6	179.2	171.4	227.1
Barbados	135.5	109.5	117.5	87.3	140.0	150.5	195.8	219.1	289.7	264.9
Belize	51.7	59.9	69.8	53.0	52.9	38.8	34.5	37.6	58.4	59.4
Bolivia	105.8	204.9	166.8	106.4	181.8	223.4	451.0	660.0	955.0	1,086.6
Brazil	6,972.0	7,535.0	7,441.0	8,033.0	22,521.0	30,604.0	37,070.0	49,708.0	58,323.0	50,827.0
Chile	3,160.5	3,628.6	6,068.5	7,041.3	9,167.7	9,640.3	13,087.6	14,139.8	14,833.2	17,305.8
Colombia	3,248.0	3,616.0	4,212.0	6,029.0	7,389.0	7,552.0	7,750.0	8,102.0	9,597.0	9,507.0
Costa Rica	668.0	742.6	520.6	919.8	1,018.7	1,024.0	893.2	1,046.6	1,000.2	1,261.8
Dominican Rep.	254.0	164.0	61.6	441.9	499.8	651.2	252.1	365.6	350.3	391.0
Ecuador	397.6	540.4	838.5	924.3	868.2	1,379.9	1,844.2	1,627.6	1,858.5	2,092.8
El Salvador	161.6	265.9	414.8	287.2	422.1	536.2	649.4	758.3	936.9	1,307.9
Guatemala	201.2	306.0	282.0	807.3	765.2	867.8	863.1	702.0	869.7	1,111.1
Guyana	4.0	13.4	28.7	124.4	188.1	247.5	247.1	268.9	329.7	315.5
Haiti	13.0	12.6	3.2	17.3	...	...	30.9	105.8	107.9	77.1
Honduras	50.0	21.1	40.4	104.9	197.5	97.2	171.0	261.5	249.2	580.4
Jamaica	147.2	107.5	168.2	106.1	324.1	417.0	735.9	681.3	880.0	682.1
Mexico	5,279.0	6,329.0	9,863.0	17,726.0	18,942.0	25,110.0	6,278.0	16,847.0	19,433.0	28,797.0
Nicaragua	38.1	115.8	106.6	134.1	130.5	55.0	141.0	136.2	197.3	377.9
Panama	72.2	119.4	343.5	499.1	504.4	597.4	704.3	781.4	866.5	1,147.8
Paraguay	323.7	432.6	661.4	962.1	561.5	631.2	1,016.4	1,026.6	869.1	694.7
Peru	511.0	808.4	1,039.8	2,443.0	2,849.0	3,407.9	6,992.4	8,221.7	10,578.3	10,982.2
Suriname	12.6	9.3	21.1	1.1	17.3	17.7	39.7	132.9	96.3	109.1
Trinidad & Tobago	127.1	246.5	492.0	338.6	172.2	206.3	352.4	358.2	543.9	706.1
Uruguay	532.0	501.3	523.5	335.8	509.4	758.4	968.6	1,150.1	1,251.0	1,556.4
Venezuela	3,092.0	4,106.0	8,321.0	10,666.0	9,562.0	9,216.0	8,067.0	6,283.0	11,788.0	14,378.0
Latin America	**29,092.7**	**31,605.3**	**46,555.7**	**64,375.4**	**87,129.6**	**107,392.8**	**103,339.3**	**128,088.5**	**154,537.5**	**168,166.7**

Sources: Official statistics, IDB estimates and International Monetary Fund, International Financial Statistics, various issues.

TABLE F-8. GOLD (NATIONAL VALUATION)

(Millions of U.S. Dollars)

Country	1988	1989	1990	1991	1992	1993	1994	1995	1996	1997p
Argentina	1,421.0	1,421.0	1,421.0	1,430.0	1,446.0	1,672.0	1,651.0	1,679.0	1,611.0	120.0
Bahamas	...	...	...	...	...	...	...	...	...	...
Barbados	3.9	3.1	0.0	0.0	0.0	0.0	0.0	0.0	0.0	0.0
Belize	...	...	...	...	...	...	...	...	...	...
Bolivia	37.8	37.8	37.8	37.8	37.8	39.6	37.7	37.7	39.6	39.6
Brazil	1,144.0	1,194.0	1,735.0	731.0	747.0	1,107.0	1,418.0	1,767.0	1,381.0	903.0
Chile	679.4	592.0	641.5	596.9	574.0	612.0	652.0	642.8	637.4	533.0
Colombia	468.0	249.0	248.0	323.0	172.0	119.0	112.0	119.0	94.0	104.0
Costa Rica	...	...	...	...	96.0	...	...	...	...	...
Dominican Rep.	7.6	7.5	6.8	6.5	6.1	6.9	6.8	6.8	6.7	5.5
Ecuador	165.7	165.7	165.7	165.7	165.7	165.6	165.6	166.6	166.6	166.7
El Salvador	19.8	19.8	19.8	19.8	19.8	19.8	19.8	19.8	19.8	19.8
Guatemala	22.1	22.9	8.8	8.8	5.1	8.8	8.8	8.9	8.9	9.0
Guyana	...	...	...	...	...	...	...	...	...	...
Haiti	...	...	...	...	...	...	...	...	...	...
Honduras	1.1	1.1	1.1	7.8	7.8	8.5	8.3	8.4	8.0	6.4
Jamaica	...	...	...	...	...	...	...	...	...	...
Mexico	...	...	...	...	...	...	...	...	...	...
Nicaragua	...	...	...	...	...	...	...	...	...	...
Panama	0.0	0.0	0.0	0.0	0.0	0.0	0.0	0.0	0.0	0.0
Paraguay	14.3	14.0	14.0	12.8	11.6	13.7	13.4	13.5	12.9	10.1
Peru	587.1	671.6	728.9	556.5	515.6	434.0	362.9	366.6	349.7	272.0
Suriname	20.4	19.8	18.7	17.7	16.2	841.7	14.3	41.3	58.2	...
Trinidad & Tobago	2.0	2.0	2.0	2.0	2.0	1.4	1.4	1.4	1.3	1.3
Uruguay	969.8	855.4	736.9	640.4	541.2	453.6	497.4	525.4	672.1	650.8
Venezuela	3,439.0	3,439.0	3,439.0	3,439.0	3,439.0	3,440.0	3,440.0	3,440.0	3,440.0	3,440.0
Latin America[1]	**9,003.0**	**8,715.6**	**9,224.9**	**7,995.7**	**7,802.9**	**8,943.5**	**8,409.4**	**8,844.3**	**8,507.2**	**6,281.2**

Sources: Official statistics, IDB estimates and International Monetary Fund, International Financial Statistics, various issues.
[1] For 1997, Latin American aggregate excludes Suriname.

TABLE F-9. TOTAL RESERVES

(*Millions of* U.S. *Dollars*)

Country	1988	1989	1990	1991	1992	1993	1994	1995	1996	1997p
Argentina	4,784.0	2,884.0	6,013.0	7,435.0	11,436.0	15,463.0	15,978.0	15,967.0	19,715.0	22,440.0
Bahamas	172.0	146.8	158.2	181.3	155.3	172.3	176.6	179.2	171.4	227.1
Barbados	139.4	112.6	117.5	87.3	140.0	150.5	195.8	219.1	289.7	264.9
Belize	51.7	59.9	69.8	53.0	52.9	38.8	34.5	37.6	58.4	59.4
Bolivia	143.6	242.7	204.6	144.2	219.6	263.0	488.7	697.7	994.6	1,126.2
Brazil	8,116.0	8,729.0	9,176.0	8,764.0	23,268.0	31,711.0	38,488.0	51,475.0	59,704.0	51,730.0
Chile	3,839.9	4,220.6	6,710.0	7,638.2	9,741.7	10,252.3	13,739.6	14,782.6	15,470.6	17,838.8
Colombia	3,716.0	3,865.0	4,460.0	6,352.0	7,561.0	7,671.0	7,862.0	8,221.0	9,691.0	9,611.0
Costa Rica	668.0	742.6	520.6	919.8	1,114.6	1,024.0	893.2	1,046.6	1,000.2	1,261.8
Dominican Rep.	261.6	171.5	68.4	448.4	505.9	658.1	258.9	372.4	357.0	396.5
Ecuador	563.3	706.1	1,004.2	1,090.0	1,033.9	1,545.5	2,009.8	1,794.2	2,025.1	2,259.5
El Salvador	181.4	285.7	434.6	307.0	441.9	556.0	669.2	778.1	956.7	1,327.7
Guatemala	223.3	328.9	290.8	816.1	770.3	876.6	871.9	710.9	878.6	1,120.1
Guyana	4.0	13.4	28.7	124.4	188.1	247.5	247.1	268.9	329.7	315.5
Haiti	13.0	12.6	3.2	17.3	...	...	30.9	105.8	107.9	77.1
Honduras	51.1	22.2	41.5	112.7	205.2	105.6	179.3	269.9	257.2	586.8
Jamaica	147.2	107.5	168.2	106.1	324.1	417.0	735.9	681.3	880.0	682.1
Mexico	5,279.0	6,329.0	9,863.0	17,726.0	18,942.0	25,110.0	6,278.0	16,847.0	19,433.0	28,797.0
Nicaragua	38.1	115.8	106.6	134.1	130.5	55.0	141.0	136.2	197.3	377.9
Panama	72.2	119.4	343.5	499.1	504.4	597.4	704.3	781.4	866.5	1,147.8
Paraguay	338.0	446.5	675.4	974.9	573.1	644.9	1,029.8	1,040.1	882.0	704.8
Peru	1,098.1	1,480.0	1,768.7	2,999.5	3,364.6	3,841.9	7,355.3	8,588.3	10,928.0	11,254.2
Suriname	33.0	29.0	39.7	18.8	33.5	859.4	54.0	174.3	154.5	109.1
Trinidad & Tobago	129.1	248.5	494.0	340.6	174.2	207.7	353.8	359.6	545.2	707.4
Uruguay	1,501.8	1,356.7	1,260.4	976.2	1,050.6	1,212.0	1,466.0	1,675.5	1,923.1	2,207.2
Venezuela	6,531.0	7,545.0	11,760.0	14,105.0	13,001.0	12,656.0	11,507.0	9,723.0	15,228.0	17,818.0
Latin America	**38,095.7**	**40,320.9**	**55,780.6**	**72,371.0**	**94,932.5**	**116,336.4**	**111,748.7**	**136,932.7**	**163,044.7**	**174,447.9**

Sources: Official statistics, IDB estimates and International Monetary Fund, *International Financial Statistics*, various issues.

ARGENTINA
Statistical Profile[1]

	1988	1989	1990	1991	1992	1993	1994	1995	1996	1997p
Real Gross Domestic Product (GDP)[2]					(Average Annual Growth Rates)					
Total GDP	-2.0	-7.0	-1.3	10.5	10.3	6.3	8.5	-4.6	4.3	8.4
Agriculture, Forestry and Fishing	8.3	-8.6	8.4	4.3	-1.0	3.1	3.6	2.3	1.6	0.5
Manufacturing	-4.5	-7.6	-2.3	9.9	10.2	5.1	6.2	-7.0	5.2	10.2
Construction	-2.9	-24.5	-16.1	25.4	16.9	11.2	15.2	-10.9	1.1	20.8
Non-Financial Public Sector[3]					(As a Percent of Current GDP)					
Current Revenue	22.1	24.0	20.4	20.3	20.9	19.4	17.8	17.1	15.6	17.2
Current Expenditures	24.8	25.2	20.9	20.8	20.3	17.2	16.9	16.9	16.4	17.6
Current Saving	-2.7	-1.2	-0.5	-0.5	0.6	2.3	1.0	0.2	-0.8	-0.4
Capital Expenditures[4]	4.2	3.1	1.4	1.0	0.8	1.5	1.4	1.1	1.2	1.2
Overall Balance (- Deficit)	-6.0	-3.8	-1.5	-0.5	0.6	1.1	-0.1	-0.5	-1.8	-1.4
Domestic Financing	0.2	1.4	-0.1	-0.6	-0.4	-0.6	...	...	...	...
Money and Credit[5]					(As a Percent of Current GDP)					
Domestic Credit	18.9	13.6	21.1	20.9	20.4	22.0	23.5	24.4	24.7	25.4
Public Sector	10.4	7.5	12.1	10.7	7.8	6.9	6.8	6.7	7.5	7.3
Private Sector	8.6	6.1	9.0	10.2	12.6	15.1	16.7	17.8	17.2	18.1
Money Supply (M1)	2.2	0.9	1.9	2.8	4.2	4.7	5.2	5.3	5.9	6.0
Interest Rate[6]	372.0	1,7236.0	1,517.9	61.7	16.8	11.3	8.1	11.9	7.4	7.8
Prices and Salaries					(Average Annual Growth Rates)					
Consumer Prices	348.3	3,084.6	2,315.5	171.7	24.9	10.6	4.2	3.4	0.2	0.5
Real Wages[7]	-5.5	0.1	-8.9	-11.2	-5.0	-1.6	0.7	-1.2	-2.0	1.0
Exchange Rates					(Pesos per Dollar)					
Market Rate[8]	-	0.04	0.49	0.95	0.99	1.00	1.00	1.00	1.00	1.00
					(Index 1990 = 100)					
Real Effective[9]	130.3	148.7	100.0	73.4	64.6	59.0	58.1	57.7	...	...
					(Index 1990 = 100)					
Terms of Trade	97.9	96.6	100.0	101.7	109.0	109.4	108.3	109.4	119.0	120.3
Balance of Payments					(Millions of Dollars)					
Current Account Balance	-1,572.0	-1,305.0	4,552.0	-647.0	-5,462.0	-7,672.0	-10,118.0	-2,768.0	-3,787.0	-10,119.0
Trade Balance	4,242.0	5,709.0	8,628.0	4,419.0	-1,450.0	-2,426.0	-4,238.0	2,238.0	1,622.0	-3,195.0
Exports of Goods (FOB)	9,134.0	9,573.0	12,354.0	11,978.0	12,235.0	13,117.0	15,839.0	20,964.0	23,811.0	25,223.0
Imports of Goods (FOB)	4,892.0	3,864.0	3,726.0	7,559.0	13,685.0	15,543.0	20,077.0	18,726.0	22,189.0	28,418.0
Service Balance	-687.0	-600.0	-674.0	-1,599.0	-2,257.0	-2,730.0	-2,941.0	-2,222.0	-2,495.0	-3,069.0
Income Balance	-5,127.0	-6,422.0	-4,400.0	-4,260.0	-2,416.0	-2,927.0	-3,259.0	-3,216.0	-3,248.0	-4,205.0
Current Transfers	...	8.0	998.0	793.0	661.0	411.0	320.0	432.0	334.0	350.0
Capital and Financial Account Balance	3,625.0	-272.0	-2,145.0	3,028.0	8,363.0	12,149.0	10,674.0	2,707.0	7,570.0	13,176.0
Capital Account Balance	...	...	...	...	...	...	...	...	...	...
Capital Transfers	...	...	...	...	...	...	...	...	...	...
Financial Account Balance	3,625.0	-272.0	-2,145.0	3,028.0	8,363.0	12,149.0	10,674.0	2,707.0	7,570.0	13,176.0
Direct Investment	1,147.0	1,028.0	1,836.0	2,439.0	4,019.0	3,262.0	2,982.0	4,628.0	4,885.0	6,298.0
Portfolio Investment	-656.0	2,618.0	-1,309.0	483.0	910.0	28,304.0	4,537.0	5,173.0	10,868.0	10,448.0
Other Investment	3,134.0	-3,918.0	-2,672.0	106.0	3,434.0	-19,417.0	3,155.0	-7,094.0	-8,183.0	-3,570.0
Change in Reserves (- Increase)	-1,888.0	1,826.0	-3,121.0	-2,040.0	-3,106.0	-4,512.0	-541.0	49.0	-3,775.0	-3,082.0
Errors and Omissions	-165.0	-249.0	715.0	-341.0	205.0	35.0	-16.0	12.0	-8.0	25.0
Total External Debt					(Millions of Dollars)					
Disbursed Debt	56,610.1	59,615.2	54,671.7	56,778.1	59,268.8	70,575.0	77,433.5	83,536.1	93,840.7	109,000.0
Debt Service Actually Paid	5,023.1	5,060.4	6,161.0	5,544.6	5,003.1	6,556.4	8,174.8	9,692.0	14,021.2	12,000.0
					(In Percent)					
Interest Payments Due/Exports of Goods and Non-Factor Services	42.0	51.2	38.0	36.1	11.8	13.4	11.1	10.3	9.7	9.3

[1] *Source:* IDB Statistics and Quantitative Analysis Unit and Regional Operations Department.
[2] At market prices.
[3] Corresponds to the National Non-Financial Public Sector, excluding the provinces.
[4] Includes net lending.
[5] Mid-year values.

[6] Average-nominal rate offered on 30-day time deposits.
[7] In Manufacturing.
[8] (-) Indicates that the exchange rate is less than half of a significant digit, given the magnitude of the depreciation experienced.
[9] Trade-weighted calculated using the period average nominal exchange rate.

BAHAMAS
Statistical Profile[1]

	1988	1989	1990	1991	1992	1993	1994	1995	1996	1997p
Real Gross Domestic Product (GDP)[2]					(Average Annual Growth Rates)					
Total GDP	2.3	2.0	-0.4	-2.7	-2.0	1.7	0.9	0.3	4.2	3.5
Agriculture, Forestry and Fishing	...	...	...	...	...	...	...	...	...	...
Manufacturing	...	...	...	...	...	...	...	...	...	...
Construction	...	...	...	...	...	...	...	...	...	...
Central Government					(As a Percent of Current GDP)					
Current Revenue	16.8	15.2	15.9	15.9	17.0	16.5	18.0	18.5	18.5	18.6
Current Expenditures	16.9	15.8	15.7	16.9	16.3	15.1	16.0	16.8	17.4	17.7
Current Saving	-0.2	-0.6	0.2	-1.1	0.6	1.5	1.9	1.7	1.1	0.8
Capital Expenditure[3]	3.2	3.5	2.6	3.2	2.9	2.1	2.7	3.0	1.6	3.0
Overall Balance (- Deficit)	-3.4	-4.1	-2.4	-4.3	-2.2	-0.7	-0.7	-1.1	-0.5	-2.1
Domestic Financing	3.8	4.3	3.9	4.0	...	...	...	...	...	...
Money and Credit[4]					(As a Percent of Current GDP)					
Domestic Credit	39.0	37.1	44.3	48.9	49.6	50.9	56.8	60.4	60.7	70.6
Public Sector	6.6	8.3	10.7	12.0	12.6	13.0	13.5	12.5	12.0	12.2
Private Sector	32.4	28.8	33.6	36.8	37.0	38.0	43.3	47.8	48.7	58.3
Money Supply (M1)	10.3	9.6	10.0	11.3	11.7	11.9	11.8	12.6	11.8	12.5
Interest Rate[5]	6.0	6.5	6.6	6.9	6.1	5.2	4.3	4.2	5.1	5.3
Prices and Salaries					(Average Annual Growth Rates)					
Consumer Prices	4.5	5.3	4.7	7.1	5.8	2.6	1.5	2.0	1.4	0.5
Real Wages	...	...	...	...	...	...	...	...	...	...
Exchange Rates					(Bahamas Dollars per Dollar)					
Market Rate	1.00	1.00	1.00	1.00	1.00	1.00	1.00	1.00	1.00	1.00
					(Index 1990 = 100)					
Real Effective[6]	99.0	97.1	100.0	96.9	94.4	92.4	96.2	99.6	99.0	96.9
					(Index 1980 = 100)					
Terms of Trade	...	...	...	...	...	...	...	...	...	...
Balance of Payments					(Millions of Dollars)					
Current Account Balance	-66.5	-84.2	-36.6	-179.8	35.8	48.7	-42.2	-145.9	-263.3	-462.1
Trade Balance[7]	-672.1	-910.8	-796.5	-816.9	-767.7	-738.0	-815.3	-931.3	-1,014.1	-1,038.2
Exports of Goods (FOB)[7]	310.8	221.0	283.5	229.4	216.6	192.2	198.5	225.4	273.2	295.0
Imports of Goods (FOB)[7]	982.9	1,131.8	1,080.0	1,046.3	984.3	930.2	1,013.8	1,156.7	1,287.3	1,333.2
Service Balance	784.0	952.3	927.1	804.9	874.1	891.3	883.4	903.2	862.4	697.0
Income Balance	-166.9	-131.6	-172.8	-179.0	-82.6	-128.4	-137.6	-135.7	-148.8	-160.2
Current Transfers	-11.5	5.9	5.6	11.2	12.0	23.8	27.3	17.9	37.2	39.3
Capital and Financial Account										
Balance	70.2	72.2	59.1	167.4	-6.8	-0.1	55.2	92.1	156.7	396.1
Capital Account Balance	-3.0	-16.6	-7.7	-5.6	-9.8	-9.4	-11.6	-12.5	-24.4	-12.9
Capital Transfers	-3.0	-16.6	-7.7	-5.6	-9.8	-9.4	-11.6	-12.5	-24.4	-12.9
Financial Account Balance	73.2	88.8	66.8	173.0	3.0	9.3	66.8	104.6	181.1	409.0
Direct Investment	36.7	25.0	-17.2	...	7.4	27.0	23.5	106.7	88.1	209.6
Portfolio Investment	...	...	...	...	...	...	...	...	...	...
Other Investment	36.5	63.8	84.0	173.0	-4.4	-17.7	43.3	-2.1	93.0	199.4
Change in Reserves (- Increase)	0.7	25.2	-11.7	-12.6	28.0	-18.6	-9.1	2.9	7.6	-56.5
Errors and Omissions	-4.4	-13.2	-10.8	25.0	-49.6	-30.0	-3.9	50.9	99.0	122.5
Total External Debt					(Millions of Dollars)					
Disbursed Debt	171.3	221.0	266.2	412.4	440.4	453.3	413.7	394.3	360.8	398.0
Debt Service Actually Paid	67.5	56.1	45.2	73.2	78.7	81.9	95.4	85.3	93.5	94.0
					(In Percent)					
Interest Payments Due/Exports of Goods and Non-Factor Services	10.4	20.5	20.8	20.8	10.0	13.2	10.2	10.4	11.0	12.4

[1] Source: IDB Statistics and Quantitative Analysis Unit and Regional Operations Department.
[2] At market prices.
[3] Includes net lending.
[4] Mid-year values.

[5] Average of nominal rates quoted by commercial banks for 3-month time deposits.
[6] Trade-weighted calculated using the period average nominal exchange rate.
[7] Include goods procured in ports by carriers.

BARBADOS
Statistical Profile[1]

	1988	1989	1990	1991	1992	1993	1994	1995	1996	1997p
Real Gross Domestic Product (GDP)[2]					(Average Annual Growth Rates)					
Total GDP	3.5	3.6	-3.3	-3.9	-5.8	0.8	4.0	2.9	5.0	4.0
Agriculture, Forestry and Fishing	-5.9	-9.0	7.2	-3.4	-9.7	-4.5	-0.6	0.0	17.3	2.9
Manufacturing	6.7	5.4	-2.7	-4.7	-9.4	-2.8	6.8	7.9	0.1	2.7
Construction	9.0	8.1	-10.2	-7.5	-8.3	2.2	3.5	7.1	4.5	4.8
Tourism	10.5	10.1	-9.8	-5.4	-1.9	4.0	9.4	1.0	6.7	8.6
Central Government					(As a Percent of Current GDP)					
Current Revenue	28.9	29.2	27.3	30.4	31.4	31.5	30.0	31.0	29.7	32.7
Current Expenditures	24.4	24.7	27.9	27.5	30.8	28.4	27.7	27.6	28.8	27.8
Current Saving	4.5	4.5	-0.6	3.0	0.6	3.1	2.3	3.3	0.9	4.9
Capital Expenditures[3]	6.7	6.7	6.9	4.8	3.1	3.2	4.3	2.6	4.5	6.7
Overall Balance (- Deficit)[4]	-2.3	-2.2	-7.5	-1.9	-2.5	0.0	-1.9	0.9	-3.6	-1.8
Domestic Financing	...	...	...	...	...	...	...	...	...	...
Money and Credit[5]					(As a Percent of Current GDP)					
Domestic Credit	45.2	43.6	52.8	54.9	60.7	58.1	57.3	56.3	57.1	54.8
Public Sector	12.5	11.0	18.9	19.3	23.4	22.5	19.2	15.9	17.4	17.6
Private Sector	32.7	32.7	34.0	35.6	37.3	35.5	38.1	40.3	39.7	37.2
Money Supply (M1)	18.5	15.0	18.2	16.2	19.2	18.9	22.9	24.1	26.0	25.6
Interest Rate[6]	9.3	11.5	10.6	14.8	10.9	8.9	9.1	9.9	9.9	9.5
Prices and Salaries					(Average Annual Growth Rates)					
Consumer Prices	4.9	6.1	3.1	6.3	6.0	1.2	0.1	1.8	2.4	7.7
Real Wages	2.4	-3.3	1.7	-2.1	-7.4	0.4	-2.2	-1.1	...	...
Exchange Rates					(Barbados Dollars per Dollar)					
Market Rate	2.00	2.00	2.00	2.00	2.00	2.00	2.00	2.00	2.00	2.00
					(Index 1990 = 100)					
Real Effective[7]	101.3	97.8	100.0	98.2	95.4	94.5	93.1	91.7	90.3	89.0
					(Index 1980 = 100)					
Terms of Trade	...	...	...	...	...	...	...	...	...	...
Balance of Payments					(Millions of Dollars)					
Current Account Balance	48.0	28.0	-7.9	-23.5	143.4	70.0	132.3	90.2	104.4	58.4
Trade Balance[8]	-338.9	-416.4	-408.7	-416.1	-277.8	-326.7	-354.8	-445.7	-456.2	-600.6
Exports of Goods (FOB)[8]	179.4	187.3	218.9	206.6	189.8	187.6	189.8	245.4	286.7	240.4
Imports of Goods (FOB)	518.4	603.7	627.6	622.7	467.7	514.3	544.6	691.2	742.9	841.0
Service Balance	405.9	465.6	403.7	398.9	409.7	416.9	492.5	550.1	573.1	687.5
Income Balance	-35.5	-25.8	-45.7	-39.5	-28.9	-41.0	-40.7	-47.7	-52.2	-59.2
Current Transfers	16.6	4.7	42.7	33.2	40.4	20.8	35.3	33.6	39.8	30.6
Capital and Financial Account										
Balance	27.1	-34.4	40.8	20.9	-32.1	-0.5	-11.0	-79.8	-7.0	-17.6
Capital Account Balance	...	...	...	...	...	...	20.3	...	0.2	...
Capital Transfers	...	...	...	...	...	...	20.3	...	0.2	...
Financial Account Balance	27.1	-34.4	40.8	20.9	-32.1	-0.5	-31.3	-79.8	-7.2	-17.6
Direct Investment	10.6	5.4	9.8	6.1	13.6	6.8	11.9	8.5	9.8	...
Portfolio Investment	42.5	-4.2	-25.2	-2.8	-11.9	-8.4	46.9	37.4	25.9	...
Other Investment	-26.0	-35.6	56.2	17.6	-33.8	1.1	-90.1	-125.7	-42.9	-17.6
Change in Reserves (- Increase)	-27.6	48.9	42.3	40.8	-80.3	-21.0	-58.9	-23.5	-60.6	-15.0
Errors and Omissions	-47.6	-42.5	-75.1	-38.2	-31.1	-48.5	-62.3	13.2	-36.8	-25.8
Total External Debt					(Millions of Dollars)					
Disbursed Debt	696.3	641.7	682.8	651.7	609.3	569.7	614.5	596.7	581.2	...
Debt Service Actually Paid	94.1	101.9	140.6	148.9	112.6	112.9	89.1	118.7	101.1	...
					(In Percent)					
Interest Payments Due/Exports of Goods and Non-Factor Services	0.3	0.2	0.4	0.3	0.2	7.7	...	...	...	...

[1] Source: IDB Statistics and Quantitative Analysis Unit and Regional Operations Department.
[2] At factor cost.
[3] Includes net lending.
[4] Central Bank of Barbados (CBB) Basis.

[5] End of period values except for 1997, which represents end of June values.
[6] Average prime lending rate.
[7] Trade-weighted calculated using the period average nominal exchange rate.
[8] Include goods procured in ports by carriers.

BELIZE
Statistical Profile[1]

	1988	1989	1990	1991	1992	1993	1994	1995	1996	1997p
Real Gross Domestic Product (GDP)[2]					(Average Annual Growth Rates)					
Total GDP	6.3	13.2	10.3	3.1	9.5	4.3	1.5	3.8	1.4	4.4
Agriculture, Forestry and Fishing	0.2	6.0	11.8	3.9	15.1	0.1	2.9	5.6	7.2	12.2
Manufacturing	-0.6	11.0	10.2	-0.2	7.6	4.7	4.8	4.4	0.3	2.7
Construction	8.9	28.4	10.1	7.7	12.1	14.3	-20.5	-0.4	-8.2	-5.4
Central Government[3]					(As a Percent of Current GDP)					
Current Revenue	25.5	26.1	26.1	24.8	25.2	23.8	24.4	22.1	23.4	22.8
Current Expenditures	18.3	17.4	16.8	17.5	19.5	20.9	21.9	22.7	21.2	20.2
Current Saving	7.3	8.6	9.3	7.3	5.7	2.9	2.6	-0.6	2.2	2.6
Capital Expenditure[4]	0.5	10.3	10.3	12.3	10.5	11.0	10.9	4.1	6.3	6.8
Overall Balance (- Deficit)	7.1	-0.8	0.7	-3.2	-3.4	-6.7	-7.4	-3.5	-2.0	-1.6
Domestic Financing	...	...	...	...	...	4.0	4.5	3.2	-0.8	1.3
Money and Credit[5]					(As a Percent of Current GDP)					
Domestic Credit	32.2	28.5	24.9	27.6	32.3	37.7	40.3	43.3	45.8	48.1
Public Sector	5.9	-1.2	-4.8	-5.4	-3.2	2.2	5.2	7.9	9.2	6.2
Private Sector	26.3	29.7	29.8	33.0	35.5	35.4	35.1	35.4	36.7	41.9
Money Supply (M1)	15.0	13.3	12.6	14.6	13.7	14.1	14.2	13.8	14.2	14.0
Interest Rate[6]	5.7	6.0	6.3	6.4	6.0	6.0	6.1	7.2	6.2	6.7
Prices and Salaries					(Average Annual Growth Rates)					
Consumer Prices	5.4	0.0	3.0	2.3	2.3	1.4	2.6	2.8	6.4	1.1
Real Wages	...	...	...	...	...	...	...	...	...	...
Exchange Rates					(Belize Dollars per Dollar)					
Market Rate	2.00	2.00	2.00	2.00	2.00	2.00	2.00	2.00	2.00	2.00
					(Index 1990 = 100)					
Real Effective[7]	92.8	94.2	100.0	98.7	100.8	98.5	103.2	105.6	100.3	97.3
					(Index 1990 = 100)					
Terms of Trade	...	...	100.0	98.0	94.7	96.6	97.7	97.5	96.2	95.7
Balance of Payments					(Millions of Dollars)					
Current Account Balance	-2.6	-19.0	15.4	-25.8	-28.6	-48.5	-40.1	-2.8	-2.3	-42.1
Trade Balance	-41.8	-64.1	-59.2	-97.5	-103.9	-118.5	-75.4	-67.6	-54.2	-80.7
Exports of Goods (FOB)	119.4	124.4	129.2	126.1	140.6	132.0	156.5	164.3	171.1	176.5
Imports of Goods (FOB)	161.2	188.5	188.4	223.6	244.5	250.5	231.8	231.9	225.3	257.2
Service Balance	21.1	23.4	55.4	54.5	61.0	58.0	33.2	47.6	46.8	32.8
Income Balance	-7.7	-9.4	-10.2	-10.8	-16.1	-17.5	-25.3	-23.0	-26.0	-23.8
Current Transfers	25.8	31.1	29.4	28.0	30.4	29.5	27.5	40.2	31.1	29.6
Capital and Financial Account										
Balance	24.3	21.3	22.1	21.8	22.4	32.8	3.6	1.4	37.3	27.4
Capital Account Balance	...	...	...	...	...	...	...	-2.6	-2.2	-3.4
Capital Transfers	...	...	...	...	...	...	...	-2.6	-2.2	-3.4
Financial Account Balance	24.3	21.3	22.1	21.8	22.4	32.8	3.6	4.0	39.5	30.8
Direct Investment	14.0	18.6	17.2	13.6	15.6	9.2	15.4	20.8	16.6	11.9
Portfolio Investment	...	...	...	...	0.2	7.0	6.1	3.7	10.1	10.1
Other Investment	10.3	2.7	4.9	8.2	6.6	16.6	-17.9	-20.5	12.8	8.8
Change in Reserves (- Increase)	-18.7	-11.3	-12.5	16.8	-0.1	14.2	3.6	-3.1	-20.9	-0.9
Errors and Omissions	-2.9	9.1	-25.0	-12.8	6.3	1.5	32.8	4.5	-14.1	15.6
Total External Debt					(Millions of Dollars)					
Disbursed Debt	139.3	144.4	153.2	170.1	186.6	196.6	198.2	255.5	282.7	232.7
Debt Service Actually Paid	26.3	18.1	20.0	19.5	19.4	21.2	30.1	37.7	44.3	30.7
					(In Percent)					
Interest Payments Due/Exports of Goods and Non-Factor Services	2.8	4.2	2.8	2.2	2.0	2.2	3.5	3.8	3.7	3.5

[1] Source: IDB Statistics and Quantitative Analysis Unit and Regional Operations Department.
[2] At factor cost.
[3] Fiscal Year (April-March) used.
[4] Includes net lending.
[5] Mid-year values.
[6] Weighted nominal average deposit rate.
[7] Trade-weighted calculated using the period average nominal exchange rate.

BOLIVIA
Statistical Profile[1]

	1988	1989	1990	1991	1992	1993	1994	1995	1996	1997p
Real Gross Domestic Product (GDP)[2]					(Average Annual Growth Rates)					
Total GDP	3.0	3.8	4.6	5.3	1.6	4.3	4.7	4.7	4.1	4.2
Agriculture, Forestry and Fishing	2.4	-1.5	4.6	9.9	-4.2	4.1	6.7	1.4	3.6	4.9
Mining and Quarrying	19.9	14.5	7.6	2.2	1.3	5.9	3.4	7.3	-1.0	-0.3
Manufacturing	5.4	5.0	7.8	4.8	0.1	4.1	5.4	6.8	3.9	4.2
Construction	14.5	5.8	2.5	6.0	11.2	5.8	1.2	6.0	10.3	7.5
Non-Financial Public Sector					(As a Percent of Current GDP)					
Current Revenue	23.2	24.1	29.6	30.9	30.9	30.0	32.9	33.1	31.5	32.4
Current Expenditures	22.1	22.8	27.4	27.9	27.9	28.4	30.3	29.4	27.2	29.5
Current Saving	1.1	1.2	2.2	3.0	3.0	1.5	2.6	3.7	4.3	2.8
Capital Expenditures[3]	7.3	7.6	8.9	9.3	10.7	9.8	9.8	8.8	9.2	8.1
Overall Balance (- Deficit)	-5.3	-5.0	-4.7	-4.5	-4.8	-6.5	-4.0	-2.1	-2.1	-3.7
Domestic Financing	1.2	3.1	2.1	1.1	0.7	1.1	1.4	-0.0	-0.7	0.8
Money and Credit[4]					(As a Percent of Current GDP)					
Domestic Credit	12.1	17.5	26.5	30.0	34.2	51.1	60.3	55.9	51.2	53.0
Public Sector[5]	-0.4	2.5	4.3	5.1	4.0	11.8	12.6	5.3	1.8	1.9
Private Sector	12.5	15.0	22.2	25.0	30.2	39.3	47.7	50.6	49.4	51.1
Money Supply (M1)	4.3	4.6	5.3	6.3	7.8	9.2	10.3	11.2	11.8	13.3
Interest Rate[6]	15.8	16.1	14.4	11.4	11.7	10.2	9.6	10.3	...	...
Prices and Salaries					(Average Annual Growth Rates)					
Consumer Prices	15.9	15.2	17.1	21.4	12.1	8.5	7.9	10.2	12.4	4.7
Real Wages[7]	23.9	8.6	2.4	-6.6	4.0	6.7	7.9	1.1	-1.0	...
Exchange Rates					(Bolivianos per Dollar)					
Market Rate	2.35	2.69	3.17	3.58	3.90	4.27	4.62	4.80	5.07	5.25
					(Index 1990 = 100)					
Real Effective[8]	81.3	84.6	100.0	95.7	97.7	99.5	107.2	110.9	104.9	100.8
					(Index 1990 = 100)					
Terms of Trade	110.5	94.5	100.0	92.6	70.4	71.2	84.1	74.7	66.9	67.9
Balance of Payments					(Millions of Dollars)					
Current Account Balance	-324.9	-291.7	-219.8	-283.9	-561.2	-538.9	-87.8	-315.5	-364.1	-662.7
Trade Balance	-48.4	-6.0	55.2	-43.9	-432.4	-396.2	-30.0	-182.3	-236.1	-491.0
Exports of Goods (FOB)	542.5	723.5	830.8	760.3	608.4	715.5	985.1	1,041.4	1,132.0	1,151.7
Imports of Goods (FOB)	590.9	729.5	775.6	804.2	1,040.8	1,111.7	1,015.1	1,223.7	1,368.1	1,642.7
Service Balance	-126.5	-154.9	-164.7	-154.2	-146.4	-140.3	-124.5	-151.7	-172.0	-211.7
Income Balance	-285.3	-280.7	-269.5	-268.3	-225.0	-239.3	-199.3	-226.1	-206.2	-212.2
Current Transfers	135.3	149.9	159.2	182.5	242.6	236.9	266.0	244.6	250.2	252.2
Capital and Financial Account										
Balance	287.4	305.3	255.0	261.5	569.7	462.2	417.2	607.1	610.8	949.9
Capital Account Balance	49.0	6.4	7.4	0.5	0.6	1.0	1.2	2.0	40.4	25.3
Capital Transfers	49.0	6.4	7.4	0.5	0.6	1.0	1.2	2.0	40.4	25.3
Financial Account Balance	238.4	298.9	247.6	261.0	569.1	461.2	416.0	605.1	570.4	924.6
Direct Investment	30.4	35.0	65.9	93.7	120.1	121.6	128.0	372.3	472.0	608.2
Portfolio Investment	...	...	...	...	...	...	...	...	5.0	-53.0
Other Investment	208.0	263.9	181.7	167.3	449.0	339.6	288.0	232.8	93.4	369.4
Change in Reserves (- Increase)	12.8	57.3	-5.0	-8.4	-41.2	-81.7	-170.7	-152.3	-292.9	-142.4
Errors and Omissions	24.7	-70.9	-30.3	30.9	32.7	158.5	-158.6	-139.3	46.2	-144.8
Total External Debt					(Millions of Dollars)					
Disbursed Debt	4,793.2	4,082.4	4,268.7	4,046.4	4,224.1	4,293.0	4,836.8	5,244.2	5,147.9	4,504.0
Debt Service Actually Paid	543.2	332.0	442.4	347.8	287.8	334.1	347.4	371.3	412.5	372.0
					(In Percent)					
Interest Payments Due/Exports of Goods and Non-Factor Services	44.0	32.7	27.1	29.2	27.9	24.1	15.0	18.0	...	...

[1] *Source*: IDB Statistics and Quantitative Analysis Unit and Regional Operations Department.
[2] At market prices.
[3] Includes net lending.
[4] Mid-year values.

[5] Decrease between 1994-1995, due mainly to methodological change in January 1995.
[6] Average nominal time deposit rate.
[7] 1996 value through September.
[8] Trade-weighted calculated using the period average nominal exchange rate.

BRAZIL
Statistical Profile[1]

	1988	1989	1990	1991	1992	1993	1994	1995	1996	1997p
Real Gross Domestic Product (GDP)[2]					(Average Annual Growth Rates)					
Total GDP	-0.1	3.2	-4.2	0.3	-0.8	4.2	6.0	4.2	3.0	3.0
Agriculture, Forestry and Fishing	0.8	2.9	-3.7	2.8	5.4	-1.2	7.5	5.9	3.1	...
Manufacturing	-3.4	2.9	-9.5	-2.4	-4.1	7.9	8.0	1.6	0.8	...
Construction	-3.1	3.1	-9.7	-3.5	-6.6	4.9	5.8	0.1	5.5	...
Wholesale and Retail Trade	-2.7	2.7	-7.0	-0.8	-2.4	7.0	5.9	7.4	5.1	...
Non-Financial Public Sector					(As a Percent of Current GDP)					
Borrowing Requirements	56.6	89.9	30.2	23.3	43.1	59.0	45.5	7.2	5.9	5.9
Operational Balance (-Deficit)[3]	-5.1	-7.4	1.4	1.4	-2.2	0.3	1.4	-4.9	-3.8	-4.1
Money and Credit[4]					(As a Percent of Current GDP)					
Domestic Credit	34.0	14.1	34.8	31.5	29.2	24.1	43.8	32.7	37.6	35.9
Public Sector	26.7	...	17.4	19.9	15.9	12.2	14.3	4.2	10.2	10.7
Private Sector	7.3	14.1	17.4	11.6	13.3	11.9	29.5	28.6	27.4	25.2
Money Supply (M1)	2.4	1.4	8.7	3.3	2.0	1.2	2.6	3.2	4.0	4.8
Interest Rate[5]	955.6	2,622.9	1,412.1	558.0	1,547.6	3,019.3	1,327.5	53.3	24.7	24.6
Prices and Salaries					(Average Annual Growth Rates)					
Consumer Prices	690.0	1,289.0	2,937.7	440.9	1,008.7	2,148.5	2,668.6	84.4	18.2	7.5
Real Wages	-1.6	30.6	-42.7	14.9	5.3	-1.4	-16.0	8.5	7.0	2.5
Exchange Rates					(Reals per Dollar)					
Market Rate[6]	-	-	-	-	-	0.03	0.64	0.92	1.01	1.08
					(Index 1990 = 100)					
Real Effective[7]	142.4	116.0	100.0	126.2	138.3	122.4	102.7	90.5	89.1	85.0
					(Index 1990 = 100)					
Terms of Trade	114.8	106.1	100.0	104.9	103.4	107.3	113.9	113.8	111.8	118.2
Balance of Payments					(Millions of Dollars)					
Current Account Balance	4,156.0	1,002.0	-3,823.0	-1,450.0	6,089.0	20.0	-1,153.0	-18,136.0	-24,800.0	-33,482.0
Trade Balance	19,168.0	16,112.0	10,747.0	10,578.0	15,239.0	14,329.0	10,861.0	-3,157.0	-5,539.0	-8,372.0
Exports of Goods (FOB)	33,773.0	34,375.0	31,408.0	31,619.0	35,793.0	39,630.0	44,102.0	46,506.0	47,747.0	52,986.0
Imports of Goods (FOB)	14,605.0	18,263.0	20,661.0	21,041.0	20,554.0	25,301.0	33,241.0	49,663.0	53,286.0	61,358.0
Service Balance	-3,023.0	-2,785.0	-3,761.0	-3,891.0	-3,342.0	-5,590.0	-5,346.0	-7,495.0	-8,984.0	-11,195.0
Income Balance	-12,080.0	-12,546.0	-11,608.0	-9,651.0	-7,997.0	-10,322.0	-9,091.0	-11,105.0	-12,723.0	-16,091.0
Current Transfers	91.0	221.0	799.0	1,514.0	2,189.0	1,603.0	2,423.0	3,621.0	2,446.0	2,176.0
Capital and Financial Account Balance	-2,080.0	710.0	4,594.0	229.0	9,974.0	9,504.0	8,810.0	29,609.0	32,492.0	26,739.0
Capital Account Balance	3.0	23.0	35.0	42.0	54.0	81.0	173.0	352.0	453.0	44.0
Capital Transfers	3.0	23.0	35.0	42.0	54.0	81.0	173.0	352.0	453.0	44.0
Financial Account Balance	-2,083.0	687.0	4,559.0	187.0	9,920.0	9,423.0	8,637.0	29,257.0	32,039.0	26,695.0
Direct Investment	2,629.0	608.0	324.0	89.0	1,924.0	801.0	2,035.0	3,475.0	9,519.0	18,601.0
Portfolio Investment	176.0	-421.0	512.0	3,808.0	14,466.0	12,322.0	51,135.0	9,745.0	...	10,330.0
Other Investment	-4,888.0	500.0	3,723.0	-3,710.0	-6,470.0	-3,700.0	-44,533.0	16,037.0	22,520.0	-2,236.0
Change in Reserves (- Increase)	-1,250.0	-893.0	-474.0	369.0	-1,4670.0	-8,709.0	-7,215.0	-12,920.0	-8,665.0	7,871.0
Errors and Omissions	-827.0	-819.0	-296.0	852.0	-1,393.0	-815.0	-442.0	1,447.0	973.0	-1,128.0
Total External Debt					(Millions of Dollars)					
Disbursed Debt	117,215.6	111,344.2	111,087.9	110,405.3	124,449.5	136,610.1	149,857.0	158,903.2	177,608.1	...
Debt Service Actually Paid	16,842.6	14,122.4	8,168.8	8,337.1	8,666.1	11,242.9	16,212.4	22,366.1	25,091.2	...
					(In Percent)					
Interest Payments Due/Exports of Goods and Non-Factor Services	29.4	29.2	30.9	27.2	20.8	18.0	16.6	12.6	23.5	24.1

[1] *Source*: IDB Statistics and Quantitative Analysis Unit and Regional Operations Department.
[2] GDP at market prices, Sector of Origin at factor cost.
[3] Excludes monetary and exchange correction.
[4] Mid-year values.

[5] Annualized nominal monthly overnight market rate.
[6] (-) Indicates that the exchange rate is less than half of a significant digit, given the magnitude of the depreciations experienced.
[7] Trade-weighted calculated using the period average nominal exchange rate.

CHILE
Statistical Profile[1]

	1988	1989	1990	1991	1992	1993	1994	1995	1996	1997p
Real Gross Domestic Product (GDP)[2]					(Average Annual Growth Rates)					
Total GDP	7.3	10.6	3.7	8.0	12.3	7.0	5.7	10.6	7.4	7.1
Agriculture, Forestry and Fishing	11.5	6.2	9.1	2.4	12.2	2.9	7.5	6.9	3.9	-0.2
Mining and Quarrying	7.8	7.8	0.9	12.4	-1.4	-0.2	8.9	9.3	13.0	8.1
Manufacturing	8.8	11.0	1.0	5.3	11.4	7.3	4.1	7.5	3.5	4.4
Construction	8.6	11.1	10.0	-1.5	13.6	23.5	-1.1	9.9	9.0	6.8
General Government[3]					(As a Percent of Current GDP)					
Current Revenue	31.4	29.6	25.7	27.1	26.3	25.8	25.5	26.2	25.5	25.6
Current Expenditures	21.0	20.7	19.3	20.6	19.2	19.4	18.9	18.5	18.4	18.8
Current Saving	10.4	8.9	6.4	6.5	7.1	6.4	6.6	7.6	7.1	6.8
Capital Expenditures[4]	7.1	4.2	5.2	4.5	4.4	4.5	4.7	4.2	4.7	4.7
Overall Balance (- Deficit)	3.6	5.0	1.4	2.2	2.8	2.0	2.0	3.5	2.5	2.2
Domestic Financing	-5.8	-5.8	-1.3	-0.9	-0.4	-0.2	-0.2	-0.4	-1.1	-0.5
Money and Credit[5]					(As a Percent of Current GDP)					
Domestic Credit	76.4	68.8	65.3	54.5	50.5	54.1	53.9	48.2	54.6	54.9
Public Sector	28.3	23.7	23.4	17.1	12.5	10.8	9.7	5.0	4.5	3.7
Private Sector	48.1	45.0	41.9	37.4	38.0	43.3	44.2	43.2	50.1	51.3
Money Supply (M1)	6.3	6.3	6.1	6.4	7.2	6.8	6.6	7.0	7.2	7.9
Interest Rate[6]	15.1	27.7	40.3	22.3	18.3	18.2	15.1	13.7	13.5	12.3
Prices and Salaries					(Average Annual Growth Rates)					
Consumer Prices	15.0	16.2	26.6	22.0	15.6	12.1	12.0	7.9	7.3	6.3
Real Wages	6.5	1.9	1.8	4.9	4.5	3.5	4.5	4.1	4.5	3.0
Exchange Rates					(Pesos per Dollar)					
Market Rate	245.01	266.95	304.90	349.22	362.58	404.17	420.18	396.77	412.27	419.30
					(Index 1990 = 100)					
Real Effective[7]	99.2	96.9	100.0	97.2	92.0	100.5	88.5	83.7	80.8	73.9
					(Index 1990 = 100)					
Terms of Trade	103.8	103.3	100.0	102.3	101.3	92.2	101.7	115.2	95.6	101.1
Balance of Payments					(Millions of Dollars)					
Current Account Balance	-231.0	-689.0	-487.0	-99.0	-956.0	-2,547.0	-1,587.0	-1,403.0	-3,742.0	-4,062.0
Trade Balance	2,210.0	1,484.0	1,283.0	1,484.0	722.0	-990.0	732.0	1,368.0	-1,094.0	-1,296.0
Exports of Goods (FOB)	7,054.0	8,079.0	8,372.0	8,942.0	10,007.0	9,198.0	11,604.0	16,025.0	15,405.0	16,923.0
Imports of Goods (FOB)	4,844.0	6,595.0	7,089.0	7,458.0	9,285.0	10,188.0	10,872.0	14,657.0	16,499.0	18,219.0
Service Balance	-690.0	-460.0	-230.0	31.0	-177.0	-223.0	-150.0	-351.0	-354.0	-314.0
Income Balance	-1,932.0	-1,940.0	-1,737.0	-1,926.0	-1,881.0	-1,655.0	-2,499.0	-2,730.0	-2,794.0	-2,979.0
Current Transfers	181.0	227.0	197.0	312.0	380.0	321.0	330.0	310.0	500.0	527.0
Capital and Financial Account Balance	1,108.0	1,268.0	2,658.0	753.0	2,928.0	2,737.0	5,064.0	2,091.0	5,383.0	7,405.0
Capital Account Balance	...	...	...	...	...	...	...	...	...	...
Capital Transfers	...	...	...	...	...	...	...	...	...	...
Financial Account Balance	1,108.0	1,268.0	2,658.0	753.0	2,928.0	2,737.0	5,064.0	2,091.0	5,383.0	7,405.0
Direct Investment	952.0	1,277.0	653.0	696.0	540.0	600.0	1,673.0	2,220.0	3,561.0	3,468.0
Portfolio Investment	-8.0	83.0	361.0	187.0	457.0	730.0	908.0	35.0	1,098.0	2,370.0
Other Investment	164.0	-92.0	1,644.0	-130.0	1,931.0	1,407.0	2,483.0	-164.0	724.0	1,567.0
Change in Reserves (- Increase)	-756.0	-548.0	-2,122.0	-1,049.0	-2,344.0	-169.0	-2,917.0	-740.0	-1,107.0	-3,184.0
Errors and Omissions	-121.0	-31.0	-49.0	394.0	372.0	-21.0	-560.0	52.0	-534.0	-159.0
Total External Debt					(Millions of Dollars)					
Disbursed Debt	19,581.9	18,032.3	19,227.2	17,946.9	19,133.7	20,636.9	24,728.4	25,567.8	27,410.5	28,617.7
Debt Service Actually Paid	2,147.5	2,667.8	2,771.7	3,882.5	2,693.4	2,841.9	2,932.8	5,151.7	6,270.4	4,070.0
					(In Percent)					
Interest Payments Due/Exports of Goods and Non-Factor Services	22.0	18.5	17.9	14.7	11.4	10.3	8.2	7.3	7.0	6.7

[1] Source: IDB Statistics and Quantitative Analysis Unit and Regional Operations Department.
[2] GDP at market prices, Sector of Origin at factor cost.
[3] Central government, decentralized entities and municipalities.
[4] Includes net lending.
[5] Mid-year values.
[6] Weighted average rate offered by banks on nominal deposits of 30 to 89 days.
[7] Trade-weighted calculated using the period average nominal exchange rate.

COLOMBIA
Statistical Profile[1]

	1988	1989	1990	1991	1992	1993	1994	1995	1996	1997p
Real Gross Domestic Product (GDP)[2]					(Average Annual Growth Rates)					
Total GDP	4.1	3.4	4.3	2.0	4.0	5.4	5.8	5.4	2.0	3.2
Agriculture, Forestry and Fishing	2.8	4.3	5.8	4.2	-1.8	3.2	0.9	5.2	0.2	0.2
Mining and Quarrying	4.5	11.6	5.9	-0.6	-3.9	-1.7	1.6	17.8	7.7	3.3
Manufacturing	1.9	5.6	4.2	0.8	4.5	1.6	1.6	1.0	-2.7	2.5
Construction	13.2	-8.1	-13.1	0.2	7.3	18.2	19.2	5.2	-0.5	0.4
Wholesale and Retail Trade	5.0	1.8	2.8	0.4	2.6	9.1	6.1	5.2	-0.3	3.9
Non-Financial Public Sector					(As a Percent of Current GDP)					
Current Revenue	21.6	22.4	23.6	25.2	25.5	27.1	27.4	30.9	32.6	32.5
Current Expenditures	16.2	16.3	16.8	18.2	18.7	19.0	20.2	23.6	24.3	25.4
Current Saving	5.4	6.1	6.8	7.0	6.8	8.1	7.2	7.3	8.3	7.1
Capital Expenditures[3]	7.4	7.9	7.2	6.9	8.7	9.4	7.7	8.7	12.5	13.5
Overall Balance (- Deficit)[4]	-2.1	-1.9	-0.3	0.2	-0.2	0.2	2.7	-0.5	-1.0	-0.1
Domestic Financing	0.9	1.1	0.8	0.9	0.2	-0.4	1.3	...	...	...
Money and Credit[5]					(As a Percent of Current GDP)					
Domestic Credit	20.4	...	20.5	16.9	14.7	15.1	16.9	20.5	22.5	22.9
Public Sector	5.9	...	...	...	0.6	-0.6	0.3	0.8	1.2	1.6
Private Sector	14.5	...	20.5	16.9	14.0	15.6	16.6	19.8	21.3	21.3
Money Supply (M1)	8.9	9.0	8.5	8.3	9.6	9.4	8.8	8.6	8.6	8.7
Interest Rate[6]	33.5	33.7	36.4	37.2	26.7	25.8	29.4	32.3	31.1	24.5
Prices and Salaries					(Average Annual Growth Rates)					
Consumer Prices	28.0	25.9	29.2	30.4	27.0	22.6	23.8	21.0	20.2	17.7
Real Wages[7]	-0.5	1.9	0.4	-1.8	2.3	6.2	2.6	3.1	2.8	3.9
Exchange Rates					(Pesos per Dollar)					
Market Rate[8]	299.17	382.57	502.26	633.05	759.28	863.06	844.84	912.83	1,036.69	1,143.12
					(Index 1990 = 100)					
Real Effective[9]	85.0	88.2	100.0	97.2	89.4	84.6	75.6	74.5	69.5	62.1
					(Index 1990 = 100)					
Terms of Trade	103.6	102.6	100.0	106.8	108.6	105.0	120.2	122.5	123.4	132.5
Balance of Payments					(Millions of Dollars)					
Current Account Balance	-216.0	-201.0	542.0	2,349.0	901.0	-2,102.0	-3,113.0	-4,101.0	-4,754.0	-4,968.5
Trade Balance	827.0	1,474.0	1,971.0	2,959.0	1,234.0	-1,657.0	-2,292.0	-2,699.0	-2,133.0	-2,392.3
Exports of Goods (FOB)	5,343.0	6,031.0	7,079.0	7,507.0	7,263.0	7,429.0	8,748.0	10,222.0	10,651.0	11,648.5
Imports of Goods (FOB)	4,516.0	4,557.0	5,108.0	4,548.0	6,029.0	9,086.0	11,040.0	12,921.0	12,784.0	14,040.8
Service Balance	-262.0	-274.0	-150.0	-219.0	-45.0	199.0	623.0	184.0	-227.0	-38.3
Income Balance	-1,745.0	-2,299.0	-2,305.0	-2,089.0	-2,022.0	-1,782.0	-2,307.0	-2,265.0	-2,925.0	-3,129.6
Current Transfers	964.0	898.0	1,026.0	1,698.0	1,734.0	1,138.0	862.0	679.0	532.0	591.7
Capital and Financial Account Balance	939.0	478.0	-2.0	-777.0	183.0	2,702.0	2,783.0	4,662.0	6,786.0	5,542.0
Capital Account Balance	...	...	...	...	...	...	...	...	...	...
Capital Transfers	...	...	...	...	...	...	...	...	...	...
Financial Account Balance	939.0	478.0	-2.0	-777.0	183.0	2,702.0	2,783.0	4,662.0	6,786.0	5,542.0
Direct Investment	159.0	547.0	484.0	433.0	679.0	719.0	1,515.0	2,033.0	3,254.0	5,303.3
Portfolio Investment	...	179.0	-4.0	86.0	126.0	498.0	584.0	-170.0	1,656.0	-136.0
Other Investment	780.0	-248.0	-482.0	-1,296.0	-622.0	1,485.0	684.0	2,799.0	1,876.0	374.7
Change in Reserves (- Increase)	-193.0	-434.0	-610.0	-1,763.0	-1,274.0	-464.0	-153.0	-351.0	-1,598.0	16.0
Errors and Omissions	-530.0	157.0	70.0	191.0	191.0	-135.0	482.0	-210.0	-434.0	-589.5
Total External Debt					(Millions of Dollars)					
Disbursed Debt	17,015.0	16,883.0	17,193.8	17,181.4	17,266.2	18,926.7	21,929.1	25,045.9	28,859.0	...
Debt Service Actually Paid	3,342.7	3,905.0	4,093.5	3,754.9	4,008.1	3,706.6	5,570.0	4,344.9	5,400.7	...
					(In Percent)					
Interest Payments Due/Exports of Goods and Non-Factor Services	20.7	21.7	19.0	16.4	14.6	12.3	12.9	13.7	13.7	14.6

[1] Source: IDB Statistics and Quantitative Analysis Unit and Regional Operations Department.
[2] At market prices.
[3] Includes net lending.
[4] Includes privatization receipts.
[5] Mid-year values.

[6] Weighted average nominal deposit rate paid by commercial banks, financial corporations, and commercial finance companies on all certificates of deposit.
[7] In Industry, excluding the coffee-husking process. For 1997 January-October.
[8] Refers to annual average until 1990; representative market rate from 1991-1995.
[9] Trade-weighted calculated using the period average nominal exchange rate.

COSTA RICA
Statistical Profile[1]

	1988	1989	1990	1991	1992	1993	1994	1995	1996	1997p
Real Gross Domestic Product (GDP)[2]					(Average Annual Growth Rates)					
Total GDP	3.4	5.7	3.6	2.3	7.7	6.3	4.5	2.4	-0.6	3.2
Agriculture, Forestry and Fishing	4.6	7.4	2.5	6.3	4.0	2.4	3.0	4.0	-0.4	-0.7
Manufacturing	2.2	3.4	2.6	2.1	10.3	6.4	3.5	3.6	-4.1	4.5
Construction	0.0	12.4	-2.3	-7.5	2.6	16.5	6.2	-8.3	-9.7	16.3
Non-Financial Public Sector					(As a Percent of Current GDP)					
Current Revenue	28.2	27.4	27.8	27.6	28.2	28.4	26.1	28.6	26.1	28.0
Current Expenditures	24.2	26.1	26.6	23.8	22.2	22.4	26.6	25.9	27.4	25.7
Current Saving	4.0	1.3	1.1	3.8	6.0	6.0	-0.6	2.7	-1.3	2.3
Capital Expenditures[3]	5.3	6.3	5.2	4.1	5.3	5.4	6.0	4.9	3.3	3.7
Overall Balance (- Deficit)	-0.3	-2.9	-2.9	-0.1	0.7	0.6	-6.6	-2.0	-4.5	-1.4
Domestic Financing	0.7	2.0	2.6	-1.6	-1.1	0.5	5.7	3.0	...	...
Money and Credit[4]					(As a Percent of Current GDP)					
Domestic Credit	32.3	28.8	28.0	25.6	19.5	22.0	22.3	18.2	21.8	31.8
Public Sector	15.2	12.9	13.1	11.9	7.8	6.0	5.8	5.6	6.3	15.0
Private Sector	17.0	15.9	14.9	13.7	11.7	16.0	16.5	12.6	15.5	16.7
Money Supply (M1)	10.8	11.8	12.4	8.4	8.6	8.3	7.4	7.4	7.7	8.6
Interest Rate[5]	15.2	15.6	21.2	27.3	15.8	16.9	17.7	23.9	16.1	17.0
Prices and Salaries					(Average Annual Growth Rates)					
Consumer Prices	20.8	16.5	19.0	28.7	21.8	9.8	13.5	23.2	17.5	13.2
Real Wages	-1.4	4.1	2.4	-2.4	0.8	8.7	1.9	-2.1	1.9	3.7
Exchange Rates					(Colones per Dollar)					
Market Rate	75.81	81.50	91.58	122.43	134.51	142.17	157.07	179.73	207.69	232.60
					(Index 1990 = 100)					
Real Effective[6]	101.8	98.1	100.0	109.6	107.5	109.2	111.8	106.9	110.5	110.0
					(Index 1990 = 100)					
Terms of Trade	104.8	103.1	100.0	104.0	105.8	104.7	107.1	108.2	107.8	114.4
Balance of Payments					(Millions of Dollars)					
Current Account Balance	-178.5	-414.9	-424.0	-75.2	-370.4	-620.2	-233.6	-143.0	-125.2	-422.0
Trade Balance	-97.9	-238.6	-442.5	-199.5	-471.8	-760.8	-605.8	-473.5	-413.6	-714.4
Exports of Goods (FOB)	1,180.7	1,333.4	1,354.2	1,498.1	1,739.1	1,866.8	2,122.0	2,480.2	2,743.6	2,953.8
Imports of Goods (FOB)	1,278.6	1,572.0	1,796.7	1,697.6	2,210.9	2,627.6	2,727.8	2,953.7	3,157.2	3,668.2
Service Balance	6.6	1.9	59.3	156.6	130.7	222.9	334.9	362.8	316.8	358.3
Income Balance	-342.6	-369.6	-232.7	-173.9	-202.6	-225.4	-128.4	-185.8	-168.0	-201.5
Current Transfers	255.4	191.4	191.9	141.6	173.3	143.1	165.7	153.5	139.6	135.6
Capital and Financial Account										
Balance	142.0	318.2	183.4	391.4	345.3	261.6	-81.0	202.7	109.8	505.0
Capital Account Balance	...	...	...	...	...	...	...	...	28.1	...
Capital Transfers	...	...	...	...	...	...	...	...	28.1	...
Financial Account Balance	142.0	318.2	183.4	391.4	345.3	261.6	-81.0	202.7	81.7	505.0
Direct Investment	121.4	95.2	160.4	172.8	221.6	244.4	292.9	390.0	421.9	446.2
Portfolio Investment	-6.0	-13.2	-28.2	-13.0	-16.9	-5.1	-1.2	-24.4	-21.5	-24.3
Other Investment	26.6	236.2	51.2	231.6	140.6	22.3	-372.7	-162.9	-318.7	83.1
Change in Reserves (- Increase)	-188.0	-112.3	197.2	-416.1	-176.8	59.6	65.5	-154.1	75.8	-127.9
Errors and Omissions	224.6	208.9	43.4	99.9	201.9	299.0	249.1	94.4	-60.4	44.9
Total External Debt					(Millions of Dollars)					
Disbursed Debt	4,250.7	4,204.4	3,678.3	3,952.8	3,905.9	3,830.4	3,867.7	3,761.9	3,427.6	3,410.3
Debt Service Actually Paid	403.5	345.4	521.2	443.0	542.5	551.8	503.7	646.7	637.8	635.0
					(In Percent)					
Interest Payments Due/Exports of Goods and Non-Factor Services	22.1	23.7	15.5	10.1	8.7	8.1	6.4	6.2	5.6	5.5

[1] *Source*: IDB Statistics and Quantitative Analysis Unit and Regional Operations Department.
[2] At market prices. Mining and Quarrying included in Manufacturing.
[3] Includes net lending.
[4] Mid-year values.

[5] Average official bank rate for nominal time deposits of more than 30 days and less than 90 days. Beginning 1991, average rate offered by state-owned commercial banks on time deposits of one month.
[6] Trade-weighted calculated using the period average nominal exchange rate.

DOMINICAN REPUBLIC
Statistical Profile[1]

	1988	1989	1990	1991	1992	1993	1994	1995	1996	1997p
Real Gross Domestic Product (GDP)[2]					(Average Annual Growth Rates)					
Total GDP	2.2	4.4	-5.5	1.0	8.0	3.0	4.3	4.8	7.3	8.2
Agriculture, Forestry and Fishing	-1.3	2.3	-8.6	4.2	6.0	0.7	-1.8	6.0	9.5	3.4
Mining and Quarrying	-7.0	-0.6	-11.8	-5.9	-17.5	-36.0	88.2	9.4	2.4	3.1
Manufacturing	-0.7	4.6	-4.3	2.6	12.2	2.0	2.9	-0.7	3.7	7.9
Construction	3.2	13.2	-6.9	-12.5	24.4	10.1	6.6	5.7	13.0	17.1
Central Government					(As a Percent of Current GDP)					
Current Revenue	14.9	15.7	12.5	13.6	15.3	15.9	15.1	15.0	14.1	15.9
Current Expenditures	8.0	6.7	6.5	5.5	6.0	8.2	7.7	7.9	8.2	11.2
Current Saving	7.0	9.0	6.0	8.2	9.4	7.7	7.4	7.1	5.9	4.7
Capital Expenditures[3]	7.5	8.6	6.0	5.3	6.5	8.1	8.6	6.6	6.4	4.2
Overall Balance (- Deficit)	-0.0	0.7	0.5	3.6	3.8	0.5	-0.1	1.2	0.1	1.0
Domestic Financing	-0.3	0.9	-0.1	-3.9	-1.9	-0.3	0.3	-0.1	0.9	0.2
Money and Credit[4]					(As a Percent of Current GDP)					
Domestic Credit	18.0	22.2	18.9	11.3	13.2	15.1	17.1	17.0	20.4	19.7
Public Sector	4.7	6.0	4.3	0.9	0.4	-0.6	0.3	1.0	2.4	1.9
Private Sector	13.3	16.2	14.6	10.4	12.7	15.7	16.9	16.0	18.0	17.8
Money Supply (M1)	10.3	10.3	10.2	7.5	8.7	9.2	9.5	8.5	9.8	9.7
Interest Rate	...	...	...	...	...	27.2	29.9	30.0	23.7	21.0
Prices and Salaries					(Average Annual Growth Rates)					
Consumer Prices	58.4	40.6	50.4	47.1	4.2	5.3	8.2	12.5	5.4	8.3
Real Wages	4.0	-11.0	-4.6	6.0	15.0	5.0	-12.5	9.9	5.2	...
Exchange Rates					(Pesos per Dollar)					
Market Rate	6.11	6.34	8.53	12.69	12.77	12.68	13.16	13.60	13.77	14.27
					(Index 1990 = 100)					
Real Effective[5]	119.7	99.0	100.0	99.0	98.5	94.5	91.0	88.6	85.0	82.7
					(Index 1990 = 100)					
Terms of Trade	137.1	131.1	100.0	114.6	107.2	105.2	110.8	123.3	118.5	123.3
Balance of Payments[6]					(Millions of Dollars)					
Current Account Balance	-18.9	-327.3	-279.6	-157.3	-707.9	-421.4	-226.6	-101.1	-238.6	-224.9
Trade Balance[7]	-718.3	-1,039.4	-1,058.3	-1,070.5	-1,611.8	-1,540.4	-1,541.9	-1,492.2	-1,531.9	-1,806.4
Exports of Goods (FOB)[7]	889.7	924.4	734.5	658.3	562.5	3,114.0	3,361.5	3,652.8	4,195.3	4,801.8
Imports of Goods (FOB)[7]	1,608.0	1,963.8	1,792.8	1,728.8	2,174.3	4,654.4	4,903.4	5,145.0	5,727.2	6,608.2
Service Balance	616.4	576.4	656.8	719.4	793.5	788.7	974.1	1,058.5	1,208.6	1,429.5
Income Balance	-270.6	-248.7	-248.7	-192.7	-321.4	-552.6	-623.1	-659.4	-1,062.5	-1,193.3
Current Transfers	353.6	384.4	370.6	386.5	431.8	882.9	964.3	992.0	1,147.2	1,345.3
Capital and Financial Account										
Balance	42.2	310.9	351.3	-33.6	202.3	677.1	501.2	488.6	430.3	564.2
Capital Account Balance	...	...	...	...	...	77.0	659.5	68.0	72.0	144.5
Capital Transfers	...	...	...	...	...	...	...	...	...	...
Financial Account Balance	42.2	310.9	351.3	-33.6	202.3	600.1	-158.3	420.6	358.3	419.7
Direct Investment	106.1	110.0	132.8	145.0	179.7	214.0	347.5	389.8	357.9	405.2
Portfolio Investment	...	...	...	...	...	51.0	-31.4	-17.0	-12.7	-14.6
Other Investment	-63.9	200.9	218.5	-178.6	22.6	335.1	-474.4	47.8	13.1	29.1
Change in Reserves (- Increase)	-58.9	90.0	49.0	-357.4	-63.5	-156.0	386.6	-131.0	15.2	-39.5
Errors and Omissions	35.6	-73.6	-120.7	548.3	569.0	-99.7	-661.2	-256.5	-206.9	-299.8
Total External Debt					(Millions of Dollars)					
Disbursed Debt	3,756.6	3,799.7	3,866.0	4,202.7	4,269.4	4,327.7	4,095.3	4,220.8	4,082.3	3,927.0
Debt Service Actually Paid	339.7	322.3	232.0	266.3	345.8	375.1	544.9	409.1	445.2	506.0
					(In Percent)					
Interest Payments Due/Exports of Goods and Non-Factor Services	14.7	11.8	13.4	8.6	9.1	5.9	4.7	4.9	3.8	3.0

---

[1] Source: IDB Statistics and Quantitative Analysis Unit and Regional Operations Department.
[2] At market prices.
[3] Includes net lending.
[4] Mid-year values.

[5] Trade-weighted calculated using the period average nominal exchange rate.
[6] From 1993 the methodology for compiling the balance of payments statistics was adjusted to conform with the guidelines of the IMF Balance of Payments Manual 5th Edition.
[7] Includes Goods for Processing from 1993.

ECUADOR
Statistical Profile[1]

	1988	1989	1990	1991	1992	1993	1994	1995	1996	1997p
Real Gross Domestic Product (GDP)[2]	(Average Annual Growth Rates)									
Total GDP	10.5	0.3	3.0	5.0	3.6	2.0	4.3	2.3	2.0	3.3
Agriculture, Forestry and Fishing	7.7	2.8	6.1	5.9	3.4	-1.7	3.9	3.2	3.5	3.1
Mining and Quarrying	115.8	-9.7	-0.9	8.4	5.8	11.0	10.6	3.8	-1.9	4.6
Manufacturing	2.0	-5.0	0.7	3.2	3.6	2.5	4.4	2.2	3.3	3.2
Construction	-14.1	4.0	-14.9	-1.1	-0.3	-4.3	5.3	-1.4	2.5	2.0
Non-Financial Public Sector	(As a Percent of Current GDP)									
Current Revenue	21.5	26.2	27.1	25.4	25.8	26.1	24.4	25.5	24.4	23.2
Current Expenditures	21.4	20.1	19.5	18.5	19.6	19.1	17.3	20.1	19.7	19.5
Current Saving	0.1	6.1	7.6	6.9	6.2	7.0	7.1	5.5	4.6	3.7
Capital Expenditures[3]	6.0	7.5	7.5	7.9	7.9	7.4	6.5	6.6	7.6	6.2
Overall Balance (- Deficit)	-5.9	-1.4	0.1	-1.0	-1.7	-0.4	0.6	-1.1	-3.0	-2.5
Domestic Financing	2.8	-2.9	-3.6	-1.0	0.5	-3.3	0.1	1.2	0.3	...
Money and Credit[4]	(As a Percent of Current GDP)									
Domestic Credit	21.1	19.2	15.6	14.1	14.0	13.5	37.0	20.2	23.5	23.2
Public Sector	4.8	8.0	4.6	3.1	2.4	1.0	19.4	-2.4	-1.5	-2.8
Private Sector	16.9	11.9	10.9	11.0	11.6	12.5	17.6	22.5	25.0	26.0
Money Supply (M1)	8.9	7.8	7.4	8.2	6.9	8.4	8.9	8.2	6.8	7.0
Interest Rate[5]	...	40.2	43.5	41.5	46.8	32.0	33.6	43.3	42.7	30.3
Prices and Salaries	(Average Annual Growth Rates)									
Consumer Prices	58.1	75.7	48.6	48.8	54.4	45.0	27.4	22.9	24.4	30.7
Real Wages	-16.0	-21.6	-9.3	-13.0	0.1	14.9	15.8	18.6	9.7	-3.5
Exchange Rates	(Sucres per Dollar)									
Market Rate	301.61	526.35	767.75	1,046.25	1,533.96	1,919.10	2,196.73	2,564.49	3,189.47	3,998.27
	(Index 1990 = 100)									
Real Effective[6]	105.4	91.1	100.0	94.2	94.0	80.6	75.9	77.3	77.7	72.4
	(Index 1990 = 100)									
Terms of Trade	93.4	100.8	100.0	88.4	89.5	77.9	81.2	79.7	86.9	91.4
Balance of Payments	(Millions of Dollars)									
Current Account Balance	-680.0	-715.0	-360.0	-708.0	-122.0	-678.0	-681.0	-735.0	111.0	-743.0
Trade Balance	622.0	662.0	1,009.0	643.0	1,018.0	592.0	561.0	354.0	1,220.0	598.0
Exports of Goods (FOB)	2,205.0	2,354.0	2,724.0	2,851.0	3,101.0	3,066.0	3,843.0	4,411.0	4,900.0	5,264.0
Imports of Goods (FOB)	1,583.0	1,692.0	1,715.0	2,208.0	2,083.0	2,474.0	3,282.0	4,057.0	3,680.0	4,666.0
Service Balance	-166.0	-110.0	-112.0	-148.0	-113.0	-143.0	-163.0	-118.0	-91.0	-385.0
Income Balance	-1,233.0	-1,364.0	-1,364.0	-1,313.0	-1,147.0	-1,257.0	-1,224.0	-1,202.0	-1,308.0	-1,347.0
Current Transfers	97.0	97.0	107.0	110.0	120.0	130.0	145.0	231.0	290.0	391.0
Capital and Financial Account Balance	629.0	719.0	345.0	622.0	337.0	1,237.0	1,154.0	1,838.0	1,449.0	1,520.0
Capital Account Balance	...	...	...	...	...	...	43.0	...	7.0	138.0
Capital Transfers	...	...	...	...	...	...	43.0	...	7.0	138.0
Financial Account Balance	629.0	719.0	345.0	622.0	337.0	1,237.0	1,111.0	1,838.0	1,442.0	1,382.0
Direct Investment	155.0	160.0	126.0	160.0	178.0	469.0	531.0	470.0	447.0	577.0
Portfolio Investment	...	...	...	...	...	...	...	...	...	...
Other Investment	474.0	559.0	219.0	462.0	159.0	768.0	580.0	1,368.0	995.0	805.0
Change in Reserves (- Increase)	26.0	-118.0	-195.0	-78.0	-22.0	-490.0	-453.0	233.0	-245.0	-235.0
Errors and Omissions	25.0	114.0	210.0	164.0	-192.0	-69.0	-20.0	-1,336.0	-1,315.0	-542.0
Total External Debt	(Millions of Dollars)									
Disbursed Debt	9,945.6	10,246.1	10,586.9	10,575.9	10,234.7	11,819.9	12,725.7	13,977.4	14,409.5	15,099.0
Debt Service Actually Paid	1,058.6	1,047.4	1,112.2	1,106.0	1,077.9	920.5	1,000.1	1,863.2	1,314.0	4,984.0
	(In Percent)									
Interest Payments Due/Exports of Goods and Non-Factor Services	35.2	37.9	34.0	29.9	22.8	21.7	19.0	15.7	15.9	16.1

[1] *Source:* IDB Statistics and Quantitative Analysis Unit and Regional Operations Department.
[2] At market prices.
[3] Includes net lending.

[4] Mid-year values.
[5] Average of nominal free market rates offered by deposit money banks on 30 to 89-day time deposits. Beginning 1992, weighted average.
[6] Trade-weighted calculated using the period average nominal exchange rate.

EL SALVADOR
Statistical Profile[1]

	1988	1989	1990	1991	1992	1993	1994	1995	1996	1997p
Real Gross Domestic Product (GDP)[2]					(Average Annual Growth Rates)					
Total GDP	1.9	1.0	4.8	3.6	7.5	7.4	6.1	6.4	2.1	4.0
Agriculture, Forestry and Fishing	-1.0	-0.6	6.5	-0.3	8.0	-2.6	-2.4	4.5	2.0	-0.3
Mining and Quarrying	7.2	3.7	-0.7	9.4	5.2	10.6	10.9	6.7	4.0	5.0
Manufacturing	3.4	2.7	4.9	5.9	9.9	-1.5	7.4	6.9	1.6	8.2
Construction	7.8	3.6	-12.8	10.3	6.5	3.6	11.5	6.1	2.4	6.0
Non-Financial Public Sector					(As a Percent of Current GDP)					
Current Revenue	13.5	11.6	12.4	14.0	14.1	14.4	16.0	17.1	17.3	15.5
Current Expenditures	14.0	13.4	12.8	14.8	13.9	13.6	14.0	13.9	15.5	13.9
Current Saving	-0.6	-1.8	-0.4	-0.8	0.2	0.8	2.0	3.2	1.8	1.6
Capital Expenditures[3]	4.3	4.9	2.5	4.1	6.7	4.6	4.3	4.2	4.4	3.7
Overall Balance (- Deficit)	-2.9	-4.7	-0.4	-2.8	-4.6	-1.6	-0.6	-0.1	-2.4	-1.8
Domestic Financing	1.7	2.9	-1.1	0.8	0.7	-0.3	-1.5	-1.2	0.0	-0.3
Money and Credit[4]					(As a Percent of Current GDP)					
Domestic Credit	34.1	33.6	31.1	28.6	30.3	28.5	30.7	34.4	36.4	41.5
Public Sector	6.7	7.2	8.6	8.9	9.1	8.7	6.5	4.7	4.6	3.6
Private Sector	27.4	26.4	22.5	19.7	21.1	19.8	24.2	29.7	31.8	37.9
Money Supply (M1)	10.2	9.8	9.1	8.5	10.2	9.9	9.8	9.3	9.6	9.0
Interest Rate[5]	15.0	16.2	18.0	16.1	11.5	15.3	13.6	14.4	14.0	11.8
Prices and Salaries					(Average Annual Growth Rates)					
Consumer Prices	19.9	17.5	24.1	14.4	11.2	18.6	10.6	10.1	9.7	4.5
Real Wages[6]	-9.8	-4.7	-5.6	-7.4	-1.1	-5.3	1.2	-0.5	-6.9	...
Exchange Rates					(Colones per Dollar)					
Market Rate	5.00	5.00	6.85	8.02	8.36	8.70	8.73	8.75	8.76	8.76
					(Index 1990 = 100)					
Real Effective[7]	88.0	89.2	100.0	97.3	96.3	87.5	83.2	77.3	72.7	71.3
					(Index 1990 = 100)					
Terms of Trade	85.5	82.3	100.0	98.5	98.6	97.1	131.4	138.0	134.5	149.7
Balance of Payments					(Millions of Dollars)					
Current Account Balance	25.8	-194.4	-151.7	-167.5	-109.0	-77.2	-18.1	-261.5	-169.0	95.9
Trade Balance[8]	-355.9	-662.7	-665.6	-704.6	-962.3	-1,034.9	-1,155.3	-1,444.0	-1,242.9	-1,107.5
Exports of Goods (FOB)[8]	610.6	557.5	643.9	586.8	598.1	731.5	1,252.2	1,652.1	1,789.2	2,415.9
Imports of Goods (FOB)[8]	966.5	1,220.2	1,309.5	1,291.4	1,560.5	1,766.4	2,407.4	3,096.1	3,032.1	3,523.4
Service Balance	-13.4	-41.1	14.6	-12.0	12.4	24.2	-56.7	-137.0	-90.1	-72.8
Income Balance	-105.5	-101.3	-131.7	-120.8	-97.2	-111.6	-94.6	-70.0	-90.5	-87.2
Current Transfers	500.5	610.7	631.0	669.9	938.2	1,045.0	1,288.5	1,389.5	1,254.5	1,363.4
Capital and Financial Account Balance[9]	51.3	163.6	16.9	-28.1	135.0	98.9	83.9	408.1	333.9	266.7
Capital Account Balance	...	...	...	...	...	...	...	...	...	...
Capital Transfers	...	...	...	...	...	...	...	...	...	...
Financial Account Balance	51.3	163.6	16.9	-28.1	135.0	98.9	83.9	408.1	333.9	266.7
Direct Investment	17.0	14.4	1.9	25.2	15.3	16.4	...	38.0	...	...
Portfolio Investment	...	...	...	...	...	...	...	68.5	71.5	111.0
Other Investment	34.3	149.2	15.0	-53.3	119.7	82.5	83.9	301.6	262.4	155.7
Change in Reserves (- Increase)	30.1	-110.0	-164.6	70.0	-91.6	-112.0	-113.0	-146.6	-164.9	-362.6
Errors and Omissions	-107.1	140.9	299.4	125.6	65.6	90.3	47.3	0.0	0.0	0.0
Total External Debt					(Millions of Dollars)					
Disbursed Debt	1,987.6	2,058.3	2,141.6	2,175.6	2,248.4	2,005.6	2,187.2	2,586.8	2,891.4	2,679.7
Debt Service Actually Paid	203.1	219.6	207.8	354.1	241.0	293.9	339.4	283.2	314.4	886.6
					(In Percent)					
Interest Payments Due/ Exports of Goods and Non-Factor Services	9.5	8.9	13.1	12.6	10.5	10.3	6.3	5.9	6.1	6.0

[1] Source: IDB Statistics and Quantitative Analysis Unit and Regional Operations Department.
[2] At market prices.
[3] Includes net lending.
[4] Mid-year values.

[5] Rate offered by banks and savings and loans associations on nominal time deposits of 180 days.
[6] For formal private sector employment only.
[7] Trade-weighted calculated using the period average nominal exchange rate.
[8] Include Goods for Processing beginning from 1995.
[9] Includes Errors and Omissions for 1995-1997.

GUATEMALA
Statistical Profile[1]

	1988	1989	1990	1991	1992	1993	1994	1995	1996	1997p
Real Gross Domestic Product (GDP)[2]					(Average Annual Growth Rates)					
Total GDP	3.9	3.9	3.1	3.7	4.8	3.9	4.0	4.9	3.0	4.1
Agriculture, Forestry and Fishing	4.5	3.1	4.1	3.1	3.0	2.1	2.5	3.5	2.6	2.8
Mining and Quarrying	2.6	3.5	-5.2	8.4	30.2	10.8	3.8	14.3	23.9	26.9
Manufacturing	2.2	2.3	2.2	2.4	3.3	2.9	3.0	3.2	1.9	2.5
Construction	15.7	7.8	-7.9	1.4	25.5	-3.0	-0.2	8.9	0.8	5.5
Central Government					(As a Percent of Current GDP)					
Current Revenue	10.1	9.5	8.1	9.1	10.6	9.1	7.6	8.6	9.2	9.5
Current Expenditures	10.4	10.1	8.5	7.6	7.8	7.4	6.8	6.7	6.7	6.8
Current Saving	-0.2	-0.6	-0.3	1.5	2.9	1.7	0.8	1.9	2.5	2.7
Capital Expenditures[3]	2.5	3.1	1.7	1.5	2.9	3.1	2.3	2.7	2.6	3.9
Overall Balance (- Deficit)	-1.7	-2.9	-1.8	0.0	0.5	-1.3	-1.4	-0.7	-0.1	-1.1
Domestic Financing	1.5	2.4	1.5	0.9	0.1	1.3	-0.4	0.3	-0.2	0.0
Money and Credit[4]					(As a Percent of Current GDP)					
Domestic Credit	18.2	18.3	15.1	10.5	10.8	12.0	11.4	13.3	15.1	14.7
Public Sector	3.6	4.1	3.3	0.8	0.8	1.1	0.8	-0.6	-0.3	-0.0
Private Sector	14.6	14.2	11.8	9.7	10.0	11.0	10.5	13.9	15.3	14.7
Money Supply (M1)	8.1	7.7	7.3	6.0	6.3	6.4	7.2	8.2	7.5	8.3
Interest Rate[5]	15.2	16.0	23.3	34.1	19.6	24.7	22.7	20.5	22.7	18.9
Prices and Salaries					(Average Annual Growth Rates)					
Consumer Prices	10.9	11.3	41.2	33.2	10.0	11.9	10.9	8.4	11.1	9.2
Real Wages	5.2	6.5	-14.8	-6.3	16.3	10.8	7.2	12.0	-0.9	1.0
Exchange Rates					(Quetzales per Dollar)					
Market Rate	2.62	2.82	4.49	5.03	5.17	5.64	5.75	5.81	6.05	6.07
					(Index 1990 = 100)					
Real Effective[6]	79.8	82.6	100.0	85.0	80.5	79.3	75.8	77.0	73.6	66.1
					(Index 1990 = 100)					
Terms of Trade	98.8	97.6	100.0	104.3	103.8	97.7	112.6	115.6	109.4	117.3
Balance of Payments					(Millions of Dollars)					
Current Account Balance	-414.0	-367.1	-212.9	-183.7	-705.9	-701.7	-625.3	-572.0	-451.5	-660.6
Trade Balance	-339.9	-358.3	-216.6	-443.0	-1,044.1	-1,020.8	-996.5	-875.1	-643.4	-940.1
Exports of Goods (FOB)	1,073.3	1,126.1	1,211.4	1,230.0	1,283.7	1,363.2	1,550.1	2,157.5	2,236.9	2,602.6
Imports of Goods (FOB)	1,413.2	1,484.4	1,428.0	1,673.0	2,327.8	2,384.0	2,546.6	3,032.6	2,880.3	3,542.7
Service Balance	-122.1	-79.2	-27.6	102.4	88.7	74.3	52.6	-29.0	-100.7	-73.1
Income Balance	-176.3	-179.4	-195.7	-102.8	-141.0	-118.4	-130.0	-159.1	-229.9	-181.4
Current Transfers	224.3	249.8	227.0	259.7	390.5	363.2	448.6	491.2	522.5	534.0
Capital and Financial Account										
Balance	305.8	371.4	134.9	651.7	572.4	737.0	696.2	550.9	722.2	857.6
Capital Account Balance	...	...	...	...	...	...	...	61.6	65.0	78.0
Capital Transfers	...	...	...	...	...	...	...	61.6	65.0	78.0
Financial Account Balance	305.8	371.4	134.9	651.7	572.4	737.0	696.2	489.3	657.2	779.6
Direct Investment	329.7	76.2	47.6	90.7	94.1	142.5	65.2	75.2	76.9	82.3
Portfolio Investment	-220.6	-24.8	-16.6	74.9	11.7	85.4	-4.0	-16.3	-16.0	-22.0
Other Investment	196.7	320.0	103.9	486.1	466.6	509.1	635.0	430.4	596.3	719.3
Change in Reserves (- Increase)	110.6	-59.0	41.8	-551.3	51.6	-120.5	-47.3	157.3	-199.0	-287.0
Errors and Omissions	-2.4	54.7	36.2	83.3	81.8	85.2	-23.6	-136.2	-71.7	90.0
Total External Debt					(Millions of Dollars)					
Disbursed Debt	2,532.0	2,516.9	2,866.0	2,869.9	2,813.5	3,106.9	3,328.9	3,568.8	3,681.1	3,741.0
Debt Service Actually Paid	372.7	303.2	213.6	288.6	536.9	305.9	308.4	347.0	353.2	322.8
					(In Percent)					
Interest Payments Due/Exports of Goods and Non-Factor Services	13.9	11.3	11.2	7.1	8.8	6.2	5.9	3.9	5.0	4.7

[1] Source: IDB Statistics and Quantitative Analysis Unit and Regional Operations Department.
[2] At market prices.
[3] Includes net lending.
[4] Mid-year values.
[5] Maximum nominal commercial bank lending rate through 1991. Beginning 1992, weighted average nominal commercial bank lending rate.
[6] Trade-weighted calculated using the period average nominal exchange rate.

GUYANA
Statistical Profile[1]

	1988	1989	1990	1991	1992	1993	1994	1995	1996	1997p
Real Gross Domestic Product (GDP)[2]					(Average Annual Growth Rates)					
Total GDP	-6.0	-4.9	-3.0	6.0	7.8	8.2	8.5	5.0	7.9	6.2
Agriculture, Forestry and Fishing	-13.7	-2.9	-13.8	12.4	24.3	6.2	11.8	7.1	6.3	1.5
Mining and Quarrying	-4.5	-26.1	18.0	21.3	-11.5	49.0	6.6	-11.4	15.2	15.0
Manufacturing	-5.5	-7.4	-13.1	10.5	19.3	3.5	5.9	12.7	8.2	7.7
Construction	-4.7	-2.0	2.1	2.0	2.0	3.5	20.0	9.7	14.0	13.1
Central Government					(As a Percent of Current GDP)					
Current Revenue	41.6	31.1	34.1	31.4	38.6	37.8	31.6	33.5	34.8	31.9
Current Expenditures	51.9	35.9	48.7	48.8	50.1	35.9	26.2	27.0	23.9	27.9
Current Saving	-10.3	-4.9	-14.6	-17.4	-11.5	1.9	5.4	6.4	10.8	4.0
Capital Expenditures[3]	22.9	12.1	21.1	11.5	9.5	12.5	14.3	13.1	15.9	13.5
Overall Balance (- Deficit)	-31.6	-7.0	-21.7	-24.3	-17.4	-6.9	-1.5	-3.3	-1.9	-4.6
Domestic Financing	33.4	24.7	4.7	0.6	2.6	-11.2	-2.2	8.3	-3.3	-7.8
Money and Credit[4]					(As a Percent of Current GDP)					
Domestic Credit	278.9	138.1	90.7	27.4	24.5	16.4	5.1	5.8	14.4	19.5
Public Sector	248.9	118.5	78.1	19.7	14.6	8.5	-6.6	-11.4	-11.8	-16.6
Private Sector	30.0	19.6	12.7	7.7	9.9	7.9	11.7	17.2	26.2	36.1
Money Supply (M1)	33.2	22.5	14.8	11.2	13.2	13.7	13.4	13.1	12.5	14.2
Interest Rate[5]	12.2	15.8	29.2	29.5	22.5	12.3	11.4	12.9	10.7	8.6
Prices and Salaries					(Average Annual Growth Rates)					
Consumer Prices	39.9	89.7	63.6	101.5	28.2	10.0	16.1	8.1	4.5	4.2
Real Wages	...	...	0.0	0.0	0.0	5.6	15.9	7.7	7.1	6.2
Exchange Rates					(Guyana Dollars per Dollar)					
Market Rate	10.00	27.16	39.53	111.81	125.00	126.73	138.29	141.99	140.38	142.40
					(Index 1990 = 100)					
Real Effective[6]	56.4	71.4	100.0	116.7	106.1	97.3	97.6	96.9	89.7	90.2
					(Index 1980 = 100)					
Terms of Trade	109.8	97.4	100.0	128.7	125.6	103.2	101.8	74.9	110.4	110.1
Balance of Payments					(Millions of Dollars)					
Current Account Balance	-93.6	-113.3	-149.6	-119.0	-138.5	-140.2	-124.9	-134.8	-50.0	-68.4
Trade Balance	18.6	11.6	-22.9	17.2	-61.0	-68.3	-40.6	-40.8	-5.0	-24.4
Exports of Goods (FOB)	214.6	204.7	203.9	239.0	381.7	415.5	463.4	495.7	575.0	594.0
Imports of Goods (FOB)	196.0	193.1	226.8	221.8	442.7	483.8	504.0	536.5	580.0	618.4
Service Balance	-37.9	-43.8	-46.3	-48.2	-34.0	-32.8	-40.2	-38.4	-41.8	-48.8
Income Balance	-93.8	-102.7	-108.7	-109.0	-96.6	-101.8	-106.1	-117.7	-53.9	-59.2
Current Transfers	19.5	21.6	28.3	21.0	53.0	62.6	61.9	62.1	50.7	64.0
Capital and Financial Account										
Balance	50.9	88.2	164.5	158.6	193.4	186.3	163.0	122.8	111.0	63.4
Capital Account Balance	...	...	...	...	81.7	65.7	16.4	10.1	524.0	...
Capital Transfers	...	...	...	...	81.7	65.7	16.4	10.1	524.0	...
Financial Account Balance	50.9	88.2	164.5	158.6	111.7	120.6	146.6	112.7	-413.0	63.4
Direct Investment	6.2	9.2	6.5	23.5	146.6	69.5	106.7	74.4	53.0	47.5
Portfolio Investment	...	...	...	...	2.8	3.6	15.8	3.2	...	...
Other Investment	44.7	79.0	158.0	135.1	-37.7	47.5	24.1	35.1	-466.0	15.9
Change in Reserves (- Increase)	32.2	29.5	-18.1	-40.5	-67.1	-57.1	-21.8	0.8	-63.0	16.0
Errors and Omissions	10.5	-4.4	3.2	0.9	12.2	11.0	-16.3	11.2	2.0	-11.0
Total External Debt					(Millions of Dollars)					
Disbursed Debt	1,756.1	1,532.5	1,882.3	1,911.0	1,844.8	1,917.0	1,974.7	1,970.1	1,555.9	1,569.0
Debt Service Actually Paid	66.3	377.9	295.5	106.9	101.6	92.3	97.0	109.0	104.6	128.0
					(In Percent)					
Interest Payments Due/Exports of Goods and Non-Factor Services ..	32.3	37.3	40.5	34.1	4.9	6.8	6.7	8.0	7.7	7.3

[1] *Source:* IDB Statistics and Quantitative Analysis Unit and Regional Operations Department.
[2] At factor cost.
[3] Includes net lending.

[4] Mid-year values.
[5] Rate on 3-month nominal deposits at commercial banks.
[6] Trade-weighted calculated using the period average nominal exchange rate.

HAITI
Statistical Profile[1]

	1988	1989	1990	1991	1992	1993	1994	1995	1996	1997p
Real Gross Domestic Product (GDP)[2]					(Average Annual Growth Rates)					
Total GDP	-1.5	-1.5	-3.0	-3.0	-14.8	-2.6	-10.6	4.4	2.7	1.1
Agriculture, Forestry and Fishing	-1.3	-1.1	-3.7	-0.1	-1.1	-2.6	-1.7	-10.1	-0.3	-2.5
Manufacturing	-2.6	-2.1	-7.0	-17.7	-21.5	-0.8	-33.3	9.6	3.0	0.8
Construction	1.0	3.1	-9.1	3.5	-54.0	-3.5	-25.0	31.4	17.2	11.5
Non-Financial Public Sector[3]					(As a Percent of Current GDP)					
Current Revenue	...	...	7.3	7.6	5.5	5.5	3.2	8.0	9.2	11.4
Current Expenditures	...	...	8.8	8.7	8.4	9.8	7.1	13.7	11.5	12.3
Current Saving	...	...	-1.5	-1.1	-2.8	-4.3	-3.9	-5.7	-2.3	-0.9
Capital Expenditures[4]	...	...	5.1	4.5	0.4	1.0	0.4	1.0	0.4	1.7
Overall Balance (- Deficit)	...	...	-6.2	-5.0	-2.3	-3.0	-3.0	-8.3	-2.7	-0.7
Domestic Financing	...	...	1.6	0.7	2.0	2.0	3.0	-0.2	2.4	-0.3
Money and Credit[5]					(As a Percent of Current GDP)					
Domestic Credit	...	...	31.3	30.1	37.6	42.9	33.5	27.4	26.4	25.9
Public Sector	...	...	19.4	18.2	23.8	27.0	21.7	14.1	13.7	10.8
Private Sector	...	...	11.9	11.9	13.7	15.9	10.8	13.3	12.7	15.1
Money Supply (M1)	...	...	14.0	13.6	16.8	19.3	17.7	15.0	12.3	11.5
Interest Rate[6]	...	...	10.2	10.2	6.0	5.7	5.2	6.2	5.5	5.5
Prices and Salaries					(Average Annual Growth Rates)					
Consumer Prices	4.1	7.9	20.4	18.2	17.9	18.9	37.4	30.2	20.5	16.1
Real Wages	-2.7	-9.9	-17.0	-15.4	-15.2	-16.0	-27.2	84.3	-17.1	-13.9
Exchange Rates					(Gourdes per Dollar)					
Market Rate	6.00	6.60	7.50	7.70	9.10	12.40	14.70	14.51	16.13	16.23
					(Index 1990 = 100)					
Real Effective[7]	87.6	89.5	100.0	129.7	131.3	124.7	124.7	125.0	92.3	85.0
					(Index 1990 = 100)					
Terms of Trade	113.5	86.8	100.0	84.1	79.9	80.7	80.8	85.7	80.7	87.5
Balance of Payments[8]					(Millions of Dollars)					
Current Account Balance	-40.4	-62.7	-21.9	-56.1	7.9	-16.6	4.0	-38.0	-73.5	-85.8
Trade Balance	-103.5	-111.0	-176.8	-246.6	-138.5	-185.0	-83.8	-379.9	-351.1	-319.5
Exports of Goods (FOB)	180.4	148.3	265.8	202.0	75.6	81.6	57.4	137.3	147.5	192.7
Imports of Goods (FOB)	283.9	259.3	442.6	448.6	214.1	266.6	141.2	517.2	498.6	512.2
Service Balance	-102.6	-100.4	-19.8	-25.7	3.3	5.6	-57.2	-180.4	-174.2	-193.2
Income Balance	-27.1	-25.6	-18.2	-18.0	-11.9	-10.6	-11.2	-30.6	-10.7	-13.6
Current Transfers	192.9	174.3	192.9	234.2	155.0	173.4	156.2	552.9	462.5	440.5
Capital and Financial Account Balance	24.8	69.5	29.2	33.2	-3.0	-1.6	21.1	127.7	80.8	92.8
Capital Account Balance	...	...	...	...	...	...	...	...	...	...
Capital Transfers	...	...	...	...	...	...	...	...	...	...
Financial Account Balance	24.8	69.5	29.2	33.2	-3.0	-1.6	21.1	127.7	80.8	92.8
Direct Investment	10.1	9.4	8.0	13.6	...	...	...	7.4	4.1	5.0
Portfolio Investment	...	...	...	...	...	...	...	...	...	...
Other Investment	14.7	60.1	21.2	19.6	-3.0	-1.6	21.1	120.3	76.7	87.8
Change in Reserves (- Increase)	1.2	3.9	39.0	-20.0	-11.3	-19.1	12.8	-175.6	48.6	-34.2
Errors and Omissions	14.3	-10.7	-46.3	42.9	6.4	37.3	-37.9	85.9	-55.9	27.2
Total External Debt					(Millions of Dollars)					
Disbursed Debt	803.6	790.4	865.3	744.3	764.1	772.7	683.0	805.4	896.2	1,028.1
Debt Service Actually Paid	67.2	62.5	32.8	26.7	5.3	4.9	79.3	93.8	26.4	32.3
					(In Percent)					
Interest Payments Due/Exports of Goods and Non-Factor Services	8.3	9.5	7.9	7.7	11.3	10.7	17.5	12.7	4.2	4.7

[1] Source: IDB Statistics and Quantitative Analysis Unit and Regional Operations Department.
[2] At market prices.
[3] Central Government for 1995-1997.
[4] Includes net lending.

[5] Mid-year values.
[6] Six-month nominal deposit rate (December of each year).
[7] Trade-weighted calculated using the period average nominal exchange rate.
[8] Fiscal year ending September 30.

HONDURAS
Statistical Profile[1]

	1988	1989	1990	1991	1992	1993	1994	1995	1996	1997p
Real Gross Domestic Product (GDP)[2]					(Average Annual Growth Rates)					
Total GDP	4.6	4.3	0.1	3.3	5.6	6.2	-1.4	4.3	3.7	4.9
Agriculture, Forestry and Fishing	-0.5	10.0	1.1	6.1	3.6	-0.6	0.9	8.8	2.5	3.2
Mining and Quarrying	35.3	13.0	-7.7	4.2	10.7	3.6	-3.5	15.7	7.3	4.9
Manufacturing	5.0	3.8	0.7	1.7	6.1	6.3	-1.8	5.5	4.6	6.1
Construction	14.7	14.7	-9.9	-2.8	34.0	21.1	-18.0	0.7	-4.2	-7.4
Non-Financial Public Sector					(As a Percent of Current GDP)					
Current Revenue	25.1	24.6	27.3	29.7	29.3	27.3	26.7	30.6	29.1	31.7
Current Expenditures[3]	24.6	25.1	25.8	23.1	22.1	23.4	22.6	24.7	25.0	24.9
Current Saving	0.5	-0.4	1.5	6.6	7.2	3.8	4.1	5.8	4.0	6.8
Capital Expenditures[4]	7.2	7.2	7.5	9.1	11.6	14.5	10.7	9.4	8.1	7.9
Overall Balance (- Deficit)	-6.6	-7.4	-5.9	-2.2	-3.7	-10.0	-6.0	-3.0	-3.4	-1.5
Domestic Financing	2.5	5.3	-0.6	-4.3	-1.8	2.5	2.3	0.1	-1.0	...
Money and Credit[5]					(As a Percent of Current GDP)					
Domestic Credit	41.7	40.8	39.6	28.2	25.9	26.9	25.3	22.7	20.6	19.1
Public Sector	12.2	12.7	12.8	5.7	3.3	3.6	3.7	1.7	0.6	-2.0
Private Sector	29.4	28.1	26.8	22.5	22.7	23.3	21.7	21.0	20.0	21.1
Money Supply (M1)	11.5	11.1	12.4	10.3	10.7	10.6	10.0	10.8	10.1	11.2
Interest Rate[6]	15.3	15.3	17.5	22.0	21.5	22.0	25.0	28.4	30.0	33.1
Prices and Salaries					(Average Annual Growth Rates)					
Consumer Prices	4.5	9.9	23.3	34.0	8.7	10.8	21.7	29.5	23.8	20.2
Real Wages[7]	-4.4	-9.0	16.8	0.1	13.3	1.8	-10.0	-2.0	-1.0	7.5
Exchange Rates					(Lempiras per Dollar)					
Market Rate	2.00	2.00	4.11	5.32	5.50	6.47	8.41	9.47	11.71	13.00
					(Index 1990 = 100)					
Real Effective[8]	68.8	64.0	100.0	108.9	109.0	114.5	120.2	108.0	109.0	100.7
					(Index 1990 = 100)					
Terms of Trade	105.3	101.0	100.0	105.2	99.2	103.0	114.0	115.4	111.9	123.9
Balance of Payments					(Millions of Dollars)					
Current Account Balance	-110.8	-170.3	-51.4	-172.4	-258.0	-327.2	-345.7	-179.7	-190.1	-94.9
Trade Balance[9]	-34.0	-44.5	-11.8	-71.9	-150.9	-231.0	-257.4	-110.7	-132.7	-125.4
Exports of Goods (FOB)[9]	889.4	911.2	895.2	840.6	839.3	1,001.9	1,141.4	1,460.4	1,626.2	1,839.0
Imports of Goods (FOB)	923.4	955.7	907.0	912.5	990.2	1,232.9	1,398.8	1,571.1	1,758.9	1,964.4
Service Balance	-81.1	-80.8	-82.5	-51.7	-41.2	-85.1	-87.5	-67.6	-74.7	-48.9
Income Balance	-231.3	-237.6	-236.8	-246.1	-282.0	-229.4	-211.7	-265.4	-259.4	-232.6
Current Transfers	235.6	192.6	279.7	197.3	216.1	218.3	210.9	264.0	276.7	312.0
Capital and Financial Account										
Balance	202.3	306.2	220.4	132.3	373.6	293.2	279.8	304.4	304.3	329.3
Capital Account Balance	20.0	26.0	41.5	45.0	52.8	54.0	31.9	14.2	...	4.1
Capital Transfers	20.0	26.0	41.5	45.0	52.8	54.0	31.9	14.2	...	4.1
Financial Account Balance	182.3	280.2	178.9	87.3	320.8	239.2	247.9	290.2	304.3	325.2
Direct Investment	48.3	51.0	43.5	52.1	47.6	52.1	41.5	69.4	90.0	121.5
Portfolio Investment	-0.2	0.1	0.1	0.1	0.1	...	...	...	...	...
Other Investment	134.2	229.1	135.3	35.1	273.1	187.1	206.4	220.8	214.3	203.7
Change in Reserves (- Increase)	21.6	28.9	-20.1	-66.9	-92.0	105.3	-17.2	-136.4	-174.3	-295.1
Errors and Omissions	-93.1	-138.9	-107.4	152.0	29.2	-71.3	83.1	11.7	60.1	60.7
Total External Debt					(Millions of Dollars)					
Disbursed Debt	3,170.7	3,213.7	3,634.4	3,321.1	3,558.9	3,984.1	4,368.2	4,513.9	4,397.4	...
Debt Service Actually Paid	394.0	190.2	506.0	307.3	377.0	360.7	432.6	553.4	563.9	...
					(In Percent)					
Interest Payments Due/Exports of Goods and Non-Factor Services	17.6	17.6	18.0	21.1	25.9	15.5	15.2	13.3	11.4	8.7

[1] Source: IDB Statistics and Quantitative Analysis Unit and Regional Operations Department.
[2] GDP at market prices. Sector of Origin at factor cost.
[3] On a cash basis.
[4] Includes net lending.

[5] Mid-year values.
[6] Weighted nominal lending rate.
[7] Minimum wages.
[8] Trade-weighted calculated using the period average nominal exchange rate.
[9] Includes Goods for Processing from 1993.

JAMAICA
Statistical Profile[1]

	1988	1989	1990	1991	1992	1993	1994	1995	1996	1997p
Real Gross Domestic Product (GDP)[2]					(Average Annual Growth Rates)					
Total GDP	2.9	6.8	5.5	0.7	1.5	1.4	1.1	0.5	-1.7	-1.4
Agriculture, Forestry and Fishing	-3.4	-9.1	11.5	-0.2	12.9	10.1	7.4	2.2	3.3	-9.8
Mining and Quarrying	-4.5	35.6	22.8	5.7	-2.5	0.3	6.9	-6.8	7.5	...
Manufacturing	5.4	7.5	3.9	-7.5	1.6	-1.9	0.3	-1.2	-3.1	-4.0
Construction	14.8	18.0	1.6	0.6	0.4	-0.5	-6.3	7.2	-5.4	5.5
Central Government[3]					(As a Percent of Current GDP)					
Current Revenue	28.5	29.9	27.6	28.8	28.7	31.4	32.0	34.5	33.0	32.0
Current Expenditures	26.2	25.8	22.7	22.7	21.4	24.7	26.0	27.1	34.6	32.7
Current Saving	2.3	4.1	4.9	6.1	7.3	6.7	6.0	7.4	-1.6	-0.7
Capital Expenditures[4]	8.8	6.4	4.2	5.1	5.3	4.5	4.0	6.7	7.4	6.1
Overall Balance (- Deficit)	-1.5	-0.2	3.0	4.4	4.2	3.5	3.6	1.9	-8.1	-6.1
Domestic Financing	-0.6	-2.8	-5.1	-8.2	-3.4	-4.3	...	...	...	...
Money and Credit[5]					(As a Percent of Current GDP)					
Domestic Credit	32.5	26.5	24.2	14.9	9.3	11.1	14.6	18.0	17.4	28.3
Public Sector	6.2	-2.3	-2.6	-6.6	-6.4	-6.3	-6.5	-3.1	-3.8	6.0
Private Sector	26.3	28.9	26.7	21.5	15.7	17.4	21.1	21.1	21.2	22.3
Money Supply (M1)	13.6	11.2	11.0	11.1	12.4	13.9	14.0	12.6	12.3	13.0
Interest Rate[6]	14.3	20.2	24.5	27.5	23.0	39.8	34.0	26.2	20.0	15.5
Prices and Salaries					(Average Annual Growth Rates)					
Consumer Prices	8.8	17.2	29.8	80.2	40.2	30.1	26.8	25.6	15.8	9.2
Real Wages	...	...	...	...	...	...	...	...	...	...
Exchange Rates					(Jamaica Dollars per Dollar)					
Market Rate	5.49	5.74	7.18	12.12	22.96	24.95	33.11	35.14	37.12	35.40
					(Index 1990 = 100)					
Real Effective[7]	95.5	89.2	100.0	111.1	127.8	111.8	95.0	94.6	70.9	128.9
					(Index 1980 = 100)					
Terms of Trade	92.3	89.2	86.0	83.0	79.5	78.5	78.4	83.4	89.4	...
Balance of Payments					(Millions of Dollars)					
Current Account Balance	47.5	-282.4	-312.1	-240.1	28.5	-184.0	16.9	-245.2	-238.4	-403.5
Trade Balance[8]	-356.9	-589.8	-502.1	-391.6	-424.6	-815.1	-513.8	-813.2	-1,263.0	-1,780.9
Exports of Goods (FOB)[8]	898.4	1,028.9	1,190.6	1,196.7	1,116.5	1,105.4	1,551.0	1,792.7	1,379.4	1,361.2
Imports of Goods (FOB)[8]	1,255.3	1,618.7	1,692.7	1,588.3	1,541.1	1,920.5	2,064.8	2,605.9	2,642.4	3,142.1
Service Balance	217.7	155.3	329.1	321.8	389.6	437.2	367.2	353.5	...	908.2
Income Balance	-335.2	-350.1	-430.0	-438.8	-293.9	-195.9	-294.1	-320.1	...	-219.3
Current Transfers	521.9	502.2	290.9	268.5	357.4	389.8	457.6	534.6	542.3	688.5
Capital and Financial Account Balance[9]	-26.7	232.5	348.0	207.6	223.6	227.3	301.2	153.9	509.7	251.4
Capital Account Balance	-15.4	-15.0	-15.9	-15.7	-17.6	-12.9	14.7	37.1	...	...
Capital Transfers	-15.4	-15.0	-15.9	-15.7	-17.6	-12.9	14.7	37.1	...	...
Financial Account Balance	-11.3	247.5	363.9	223.3	241.2	240.2	286.5	116.8	509.7	251.4
Direct Investment	-12.0	57.1	137.9	133.2	142.4	77.9	116.8	166.7	...	...
Portfolio Investment	...	...	...	...	...	...	...	...	...	...
Other Investment	0.7	190.4	226.0	90.1	98.8	162.3	169.7	-49.9	509.7	251.4
Change in Reserves (- Increase)	25.2	39.9	-65.3	52.9	-192.2	-92.9	-331.0	55.3	-271.3	152.1
Errors and Omissions	-46.0	10.0	29.3	-20.4	-59.9	49.7	12.9	36.1	0.0	0.0
Total External Debt					(Millions of Dollars)					
Disbursed Debt	4,490.2	4,435.9	4,546.2	4,282.5	4,126.7	3,975.0	4,208.4	4,166.3	3,943.6	4,030.7
Debt Service Actually Paid	735.4	642.5	706.3	759.3	681.2	563.9	596.6	672.9	682.2	644.6
					(In Percent)					
Interest Payments Due/Exports of Goods and Non-Factor Services	18.3	17.8	15.5	15.2	13.9	12.7	9.5	8.7	...	...

[1] *Source*: IDB Statistics and Quantitative Analysis Unit and Regional Operations Department.
[2] At market prices.
[3] Fiscal year ending March 31.
[4] Includes net lending.
[5] Mid-year values.
[6] Weighted nominal deposit rate.
[7] Trade-weighted calculated using the period average nominal exchange rate.
[8] Include goods procured in ports by carriers.
[9] Includes Errors and Omissions for 1996 and 1997.

MEXICO
Statistical Profile[1]

	1988	1989	1990	1991	1992	1993	1994	1995	1996	1997p
Real Gross Domestic Product (GDP)[2]	(Average Annual Growth Rates)									
Total GDP	1.3	3.3	4.5	3.6	2.8	0.7	4.5	-6.2	5.1	7.0
Agriculture, Forestry and Fishing	-3.8	-2.3	5.9	1.0	-1.0	1.4	0.9	1.0	1.2	1.4
Mining and Quarrying	0.4	-0.6	2.8	0.8	1.8	0.9	2.5	-2.7	8.3	4.3
Manufacturing	3.2	7.2	6.1	4.0	2.3	-0.8	4.1	-4.8	10.9	9.8
Construction	-0.4	2.1	7.0	2.4	7.8	2.8	8.4	-23.5	11.4	10.2
Non-Financial Public Sector	(As a Percent of Current GDP)									
Current Revenue	28.5	27.2	27.5	24.3	23.8	23.4	22.9	23.0	22.8	22.6
Current Expenditures	33.0	28.1	25.1	20.4	18.6	19.1	19.4	19.7	19.5	19.9
Current Saving	-4.5	-0.9	2.4	3.8	5.1	4.3	3.5	3.3	3.3	2.7
Capital Expenditures[3]	4.2	3.7	4.6	4.1	3.6	3.0	3.7	3.1	3.5	3.3
Overall Balance (- Deficit)	-11.7	-5.2	-3.6	1.6	3.1	0.7	-0.1	0.0	-0.1	-0.7
Domestic Financing[4]	13.2	5.7	2.5	-1.3	-2.9	-0.2	0.4	-5.3	-0.4	1.5
Money and Credit[5]	(As a Percent of Current GDP)									
Domestic Credit	20.7	23.7	26.2	28.7	31.7	33.2	38.0	39.3	27.9	22.0
Public Sector	12.7	12.8	11.6	9.0	5.8	1.5	1.0	0.5	-0.5	-1.3
Private Sector	8.0	11.0	14.6	19.7	25.9	31.7	37.1	38.8	28.4	23.3
Money Supply (M1)	4.2	3.8	4.2	5.3	9.1	9.7	9.3	6.2	6.3	6.8
Interest Rate[6]	68.2	44.9	34.8	19.3	15.7	14.9	13.9	48.6	31.0	19.0
Prices and Salaries	(Average Annual Growth Rates)									
Consumer Prices	114.2	20.1	26.6	22.7	15.5	9.7	6.9	35.0	34.4	20.6
Real Wages[7]	-1.3	9.0	2.9	6.5	8.8	7.1	4.1	-14.8	-8.0	0.5
Exchange Rates	(New Pesos per Dollar)									
Market Rate	2.27	2.46	2.81	3.02	3.09	3.12	3.38	6.42	7.60	7.91
	(Index 1990 = 100)									
Real Effective[8]	109.6	100.2	100.0	90.9	85.6	80.5	85.7	115.0	105.8	91.2
	(Index 1990 = 100)									
Terms of Trade	85.6	92.7	100.0	100.5	105.6	105.7	105.7	105.7	105.7	104.0
Balance of Payments	(Millions of Dollars)									
Current Account Balance	-2,374.0	-5,825.0	-7,451.0	-14,888.0	-24,442.0	-23,400.0	-29,662.0	-1,576.0	-1,923.0	-7,226.8
Trade Balance[9]	2,611.0	405.0	-881.0	-7,279.0	-15,934.0	-13,481.0	-18,464.0	7,089.0	6,531.0	623.6
Exports of Goods (FOB)[9]	30,692.0	35,171.0	40,711.0	42,687.0	46,196.0	51,885.0	60,882.0	79,542.0	96,000.0	110,431.4
Imports of Goods (FOB)[9]	28,081.0	34,766.0	41,592.0	49,966.0	62,130.0	65,366.0	79,346.0	72,453.0	89,469.0	109,807.8
Service Balance	-197.0	-672.0	-2,229.0	-2,090.0	-2,684.0	-2,529.0	-2,721.0	64.0	82.0	420.0
Income Balance	-7,043.0	-8,101.0	-8,316.0	-8,265.0	-9,209.0	-11,030.0	-12,259.0	-12,689.0	-13,067.0	-13,400.4
Current Transfers	2,255.0	2,543.0	3,975.0	2,746.0	3,385.0	3,640.0	3,782.0	3,960.0	4,531.0	5,130.0
Capital and Financial Account Balance	-1,155.0	1,863.0	9,484.0	25,320.0	26,467.0	32,585.0	14,587.0	15,472.0	3,331.0	14,220.8
Capital Account Balance	...	...	...	...	...	...	...	...	...	...
Capital Transfers	...	...	...	...	...	...	...	...	...	...
Financial Account Balance	-1,155.0	1,863.0	9,484.0	25,320.0	26,467.0	32,585.0	14,587.0	15,472.0	3,331.0	14,220.8
Direct Investment	2,879.0	3,174.0	2,634.0	4,762.0	4,393.0	4,389.0	10,972.0	9,526.0	7,619.0	11,500.0
Portfolio Investment	2,677.0	298.0	-3,985.0	12,138.0	19,206.0	28,355.0	7,415.0	-10,377.0	14,697.0	3,600.0
Other Investment	-6,711.0	-1,609.0	10,835.0	8,420.0	2,868.0	-159.0	-3,800.0	16,323.0	-18,985.0	-879.2
Change in Reserves (- Increase)	6,721.0	-542.0	-3,261.0	-8,154.0	-1,173.0	-6,057.0	18,398.0	-9,648.0	-1,805.0	-10,494.0
Errors and Omissions	-3,193.0	4,504.0	1,228.0	-2,278.0	-852.0	-3,128.0	-3,323.0	-4,248.0	398.0	3,500.0
Total External Debt	(Millions of Dollars)									
Disbursed Debt	99,215.7	93,840.6	104,442.1	114,067.4	112,265.0	131,572.3	140,006.1	166,104.1	157,124.6	174,120.0
Debt Service Actually Paid	15,473.0	15,563.3	11,315.5	13,545.0	20,812.5	24,218.1	21,942.6	28,909.4	48,017.9	25,700.0
	(In Percent)									
Interest Payments Due/Exports of Goods and Non-Factor Services	23.6	22.0	19.0	18.0	17.5	18.3	8.9	8.9	7.4	10.9

[1] Source: IDB Statistics and Quantitative Analysis Unit and Regional Operations Department.
[2] At market prices.
[3] Includes net lending.
[4] Includes deficit of non-controlled public sector and financial intermediaries.
[5] Mid-year values.
[6] Nominal average yield on one-month treasury bills, calculated from the weighted average rate of discount on daily transactions among dealers.
[7] Wages, salaries and benefits in Manufacturing.
[8] Trade-weighted calculated using the period average nominal exchange rate.
[9] Include Goods for Processing.

NICARAGUA
Statistical Profile[1]

	1988	1989	1990	1991	1992	1993	1994	1995	1996	1997p
Real Gross Domestic Product (GDP)[2]					(Average Annual Growth Rates)					
Total GDP	-12.4	-1.7	0.0	-0.2	0.4	-0.4	3.3	4.3	4.5	5.0
Agriculture, Forestry and Fishing	-10.2	9.2	0.2	-3.9	3.1	1.8	10.8	5.1	6.6	8.5
Mining and Quarrying	-8.7	41.0	-22.1	-1.4	17.1	2.7	-10.1	30.2	31.0	23.1
Manufacturing	-25.3	-1.9	-1.5	6.4	-5.1	0.0	1.0	2.8	2.4	3.1
Construction	-7.0	-15.0	-5.9	-8.1	8.3	1.5	17.8	17.5	16.5	9.0
Non-Financial Public Sector					(As a Percent of Current GDP)					
Current Revenue	21.6	27.5	17.6	24.3	27.7	28.4	28.7	30.0	30.3	33.0
Current Expenditures	40.0	29.4	35.7	26.8	26.3	25.2	26.4	27.6	28.4	28.4
Current Saving	-18.4	-1.9	-18.1	-2.5	1.4	3.2	2.4	2.5	1.8	4.6
Capital Expenditures[3]	9.6	6.2	2.3	5.5	9.9	12.4	15.0	15.4	17.4	13.3
Overall Balance (- Deficit)	-27.4	-4.5	-18.4	4.1	-3.4	-0.2	-5.9	-6.4	-6.8	-3.5
Domestic Financing	25.0	-0.2	10.3	-4.5	-6.8	-1.2	-2.3	2.1	0.2	0.8
Money and Credit[4]					(As a Percent of Current GDP)					
Domestic Credit	6.5	9.4	8.2	39.4	36.1	37.7	38.1	35.5	37.3	42.4
Public Sector[5]	1.2	-1.0	3.6	10.1	3.5	2.8	6.4	6.4	6.8	7.9
Private Sector	5.3	10.4	4.6	29.3	32.6	34.9	31.7	29.1	30.5	34.5
Money Supply (M1)	4.5	4.4	1.7	7.5	8.4	7.4	6.8	7.2	7.4	9.1
Interest Rate[6]	...	1,585.9	9.5	11.6	12.0	11.6	11.7	11.1	12.3	12.6
Prices and Salaries					(Average Annual Growth Rates)					
Consumer Prices	10,215.2	4,770.3	7,485.2	2,742.3	20.3	20.4	7.8	11.0	11.6	10.0
Real Wages	-42.6	35.6	64.9	-4.5	11.4	-6.4	-0.1	1.9	-1.7	-2.0
Exchange Rates					(Gold Córdobas per Dollar)					
Market Rate[7]	-	-	0.14	4.27	5.00	5.62	6.72	7.55	8.44	9.45
					(Index 1990 = 100)					
Real Effective[8]	91.3	149.2	100.0	104.5	107.2	110.2	118.1	116.9	114.9	115.0
					(Index 1990 = 100)					
Terms of Trade	113.4	103.8	100.0	92.7	67.9	78.6	90.9	104.8	96.8	104.2
Balance of Payments					(Millions of Dollars)					
Current Account Balance	-715.4	-361.7	-305.2	-264.2	-769.0	-604.3	-644.5	-490.0	-419.3	-649.0
Trade Balance	-482.6	-228.6	-237.3	-419.9	-547.7	-392.4	-417.5	-334.8	-359.7	-741.8
Exports of Goods (FOB)	235.7	318.7	332.4	268.1	223.1	267.0	363.7	530.2	673.5	708.6
Imports of Goods (FOB)	718.3	547.3	569.7	688.0	770.8	659.4	781.2	865.0	1,033.2	1,450.4
Service Balance	-100.7	-97.2	-52.5	-66.0	-62.1	-56.4	-56.9	-101.6	-116.4	-79.5
Income Balance	-262.1	-204.8	-217.0	-363.3	-494.8	-429.1	-465.5	-358.6	-300.3	-194.5
Current Transfers	130.0	168.9	201.6	585.0	335.6	273.6	295.4	305.0	357.1	366.8
Capital and Financial Account Balance	707.4	495.0	447.1	288.7	709.2	396.8	664.9	433.0	415.1	288.6
Capital Account Balance	...	...	...	259.4	53.0	147.7	141.5	1,452.7	4,208.1	103.7
Capital Transfers	...	...	...	259.4	53.0	147.7	141.5	1,452.7	4,208.1	103.7
Financial Account Balance	707.4	495.0	447.1	29.3	656.2	249.1	523.4	-1,019.7	-3,793.0	184.9
Direct Investment	...	...	...	...	15.0	38.8	40.0	70.4	85.0	162.0
Portfolio Investment	...	...	...	...	...	...	...	...	...	...
Other Investment	707.4	495.0	447.1	29.3	641.2	210.3	483.4	-1,090.1	-3,878.0	22.9
Change in Reserves (- Increase)	-43.9	-78.6	7.3	-41.7	-0.5	79.4	-84.6	-3.1	-37.9	-173.2
Errors and Omissions	51.9	-54.7	-149.2	17.2	60.2	128.1	64.2	60.1	42.1	533.6
Total External Debt					(Millions of Dollars)					
Disbursed Debt	7,615.5	8,307.4	9,019.6	9,610.8	9,750.2	9,826.1	10,107.9	8,889.3	5,453.9	5,985.8
Debt Service Actually Paid	20.5	11.3	15.8	672.6	124.7	186.7	273.9	287.8	227.9	340.0
					(In Percent)					
Interest Payments Due/Exports of Goods and Non-Factor Services	96.7	62.1	58.3	110.3	158.5	115.6	97.1	54.2	35.9	21.5

[1] Source: IDB Statistics and Quantitative Analysis Unit and Regional Operations Department.
[2] At market prices.
[3] Includes net lending.
[4] Mid-year values.

[5] Includes Area de Propiedad del Pueblo (APP).
[6] Average rate offered by commercial banks on one-month nominal deposits.
[7] (-) Indicates that the exchange rate is less than half of a significant digit, given the magnitude of the depreciation experienced.
[8] Trade-weighted calculated using the period average nominal exchange rate.

PANAMA
Statistical Profile[1]

	1988	1989	1990	1991	1992	1993	1994	1995	1996	1997p
Real Gross Domestic Product (GDP)[2]					(Average Annual Growth Rates)					
Total GDP	-13.4	1.6	8.1	9.4	8.2	5.5	2.9	1.8	2.4	4.2
Agriculture, Forestry and Fishing	-6.4	5.6	1.5	1.1	4.4	0.0	2.7	3.2	0.7	-1.4
Manufacturing	-22.5	1.3	13.8	10.5	9.2	6.3	4.3	0.2	0.7	3.4
Construction	-52.8	-40.3	17.9	131.9	36.7	40.5	2.2	4.1	-4.1	4.8
Transportation and Communications	-8.0	-2.6	2.9	2.4	3.8	-3.2	4.4	9.4	2.7	4.3
Non-Financial Public Sector					(As a Percent of Current GDP)					
Current Revenue	21.7	22.2	26.7	28.4	29.2	28.1	28.2	28.9	27.8	28.0
Current Expenditures	30.4	31.7	28.7	27.8	25.1	25.8	24.7	25.6	23.7	25.2
Current Saving	-8.7	-9.6	-1.9	0.6	4.0	2.3	3.4	3.3	4.1	2.7
Capital Expenditures[3]	1.2	1.1	0.7	2.1	3.1	4.0	3.4	3.4	3.8	5.0
Overall Balance (- Deficit)	-10.0	-10.7	-2.5	-1.2	1.4	-1.4	0.3	0.2	0.4	-0.6
Domestic Financing	-0.3	1.7	-4.3	-1.3	-1.7	-0.8	-1.9	-2.8	1.4	-2.1
Money and Credit[4]					(As a Percent of Current GDP)					
Domestic Credit	70.9	64.5	49.6	49.1	52.9	55.0	59.8	66.6	66.4	70.8
Public Sector	13.6	13.4	4.7	2.1	-0.5	-5.0	-5.2	-8.4	-9.9	-9.6
Private Sector	57.3	51.1	44.9	47.0	53.4	60.0	65.0	75.0	76.2	80.4
Money Supply (M1)	6.2	5.3	6.5	6.9	7.9	8.4	8.9	8.8	8.8	9.4
Interest Rate[5]	7.5	8.5	8.4	7.7	5.7	5.9	6.1	7.2	7.2	7.1
Prices and Salaries					(Average Annual Growth Rates)					
Consumer Prices	0.4	0.1	0.8	1.3	1.8	0.5	1.3	0.9	1.3	1.2
Real Wages	0.3	0.0	0.9	0.3	1.3	4.1	...	...	...	...
Exchange Rates					(Balboas per Dollar)					
Market Rate	1.00	1.00	1.00	1.00	1.00	1.00	1.00	1.00	1.00	1.00
					(Index 1990 = 100)					
Real Effective[6]	90.6	94.6	100.0	102.7	105.1	108.2	112.3	115.8	116.2	116.2
					(Index 1990 = 100)					
Terms of Trade	101.1	100.5	100.0	95.6	97.5	98.6	99.1	93.8	94.4	99.7
Balance of Payments					(Millions of Dollars)					
Current Account Balance	721.7	111.6	208.4	-212.4	-270.0	-143.4	22.3	-343.0	-60.3	-249.9
Trade Balance[7]	156.8	-123.9	-157.7	-399.6	-375.5	-334.2	-250.5	-575.0	-629.8	-562.6
Exports of Goods (FOB)[7]	2,505.9	2,742.1	3,346.2	4,191.8	5,104.2	5,416.9	6,044.3	6,104.0	5,888.6	6,934.9
Imports of Goods (FOB)[7]	2,349.1	2,866.0	3,503.9	4,591.4	5,479.7	5,751.1	6,294.8	6,679.0	6,518.4	7,497.5
Service Balance	544.5	406.3	409.2	348.9	294.2	298.2	310.6	402.5	525.3	480.9
Income Balance	-87.9	-266.5	-262.4	-384.1	-392.7	-310.5	-186.7	-324.7	-107.5	-331.6
Current Transfers	108.3	95.7	219.3	222.4	204.0	203.1	148.9	154.2	151.7	163.4
Capital and Financial Account Balance[8]	18.5	172.6	283.4	-269.0	-296.1	-20.5	134.8	626.5	-9.4	531.2
Capital Account Balance	...	...	...	...	130.0	...	...	...	...	...
Capital Transfers	...	...	...	...	130.0	...	...	...	...	...
Financial Account Balance	18.5	172.6	283.4	-269.0	-426.1	-20.5	134.8	626.5	-9.4	531.2
Direct Investment	-595.1	51.5	131.9	41.2	138.7	155.7	353.6	178.9	237.6	...
Portfolio Investment	2,154.2	-468.1	-235.8	-246.7	-117.4	-809.3	373.3	313.6	3,642.7	...
Other Investment	-1,540.6	589.2	387.3	-63.5	-447.4	633.1	-592.1	134.0	-3,889.7	531.2
Change in Reserves (- Increase)	5.5	-47.9	-355.7	-148.4	116.2	-93.0	-104.7	-77.2	-237.7	-281.3
Errors and Omissions	-745.7	-236.3	-136.1	629.9	449.9	256.9	-52.5	-206.3	307.5	0.0
Total External Debt					(Millions of Dollars)					
Disbursed Debt	5,733.3	5,654.9	5,660.1	5,533.7	5,280.9	5,363.5	5,528.6	5,537.1	6,941.4	5,083.0
Debt Service Actually Paid	28.1	13.3	345.1	335.5	965.9	281.9	385.7	374.3	954.0	1,745.4
					(In Percent)					
Interest Payments Due/ Exports of Goods and Non-Factor Services ..	31.3	30.5	27.0	22.9	19.1	15.6	15.0	21.6	15.6	17.9

[1] Source: IDB Statistics and Quantitative Analysis Unit and Regional Operations Department.
[2] At market prices.
[3] Includes net lending.
[4] Mid-year values.

[5] Average rate offered by deposit money banks on 6-month time deposits. Beginning December 1992, weighted average rate.
[6] Trade-weighted calculated using the period average nominal exchange rate.
[7] Include activity within the Colón Free Zone.
[8] Includes Errors and Omissions for 1997.

PARAGUAY
Statistical Profile[1]

	1988	1989	1990	1991	1992	1993	1994	1995	1996	1997p
Real Gross Domestic Product (GDP)[2]					(Average Annual Growth Rates)					
Total GDP	6.4	5.8	3.1	2.5	1.8	4.1	3.1	4.7	1.3	2.6
Agriculture, Forestry and Fishing	12.1	7.7	2.2	-0.6	0.1	5.6	-0.6	8.1	1.3	4.1
Manufacturing	5.8	5.9	2.5	1.1	0.4	2.0	1.5	3.0	-2.2	1.0
Construction	2.6	2.5	-0.9	3.0	5.0	2.7	3.6	4.0	3.0	3.1
Wholesale and Retail Trade	4.1	4.7	3.6	4.4	0.6	3.8	4.3	1.6	-1.0	1.5
Central Government					(As a Percent of Current GDP)					
Current Revenue	8.0	11.4	12.4	11.8	13.3	12.2	14.5	15.3	14.7	13.1
Current Expenditures	5.3	6.7	6.1	5.7	11.3	11.0	11.3	12.1	12.7	11.0
Current Saving	2.6	4.7	6.2	6.1	2.1	1.1	3.2	3.3	2.0	2.2
Capital Expenditure[3]	1.3	0.9	1.1	1.6	2.4	2.0	2.5	3.9	3.1	2.2
Overall Balance (- Deficit)	1.4	3.8	5.2	4.5	-0.2	-0.8	1.0	-0.3	-0.8	0.2
Domestic Financing	-1.2	-3.7	-4.5	-5.8	0.0	0.3	-1.1	-0.4	0.4	...
Money and Credit[4]					(As a Percent of Current GDP)					
Domestic Credit	11.5	10.8	11.0	9.6	15.1	22.8	20.9	19.7	20.1	22.7
Public Sector	3.0	1.0	0.6	-1.9	-0.3	6.1	3.5	-0.2	-0.5	-0.9
Private Sector	8.6	9.9	10.4	11.5	15.4	16.7	17.4	19.9	20.6	23.6
Money Supply (M1)	9.0	8.9	6.9	7.6	7.6	7.4	7.3	7.9	8.1	7.9
Interest Rate[5]	14.0	14.0	12.0	12.0	10.4	10.6	12.0	12.5	11.9	9.7
Prices and Salaries					(Average Annual Growth Rates)					
Consumer Prices	22.5	26.6	38.1	24.2	15.2	18.2	20.5	13.4	9.8	7.0
Real Wages	13.4	0.7	-3.7	-4.8	-8.8	-3.9	2.7	6.9	2.5	...
Exchange Rates					(Guaranies per Dollar)					
Market Rate	550.00	1,056.22	1,229.81	1,325.18	1,500.26	1,744.35	1,911.54	1,970.40	2,062.78	2,191.05
					(Index 1990 = 100)					
Real Effective[6]	78.4	102.5	100.0	88.4	91.3	91.0	88.8	88.0	84.2	80.6
					(Index 1990 = 100)					
Terms of Trade	91.1	95.5	100.0	99.5	98.6	103.5	108.1	111.1	109.8	113.1
Balance of Payments					(Millions of Dollars)					
Current Account Balance	-210.2	255.6	-172.3	-324.1	-600.1	-412.6	-566.6	-500.5	-637.4	-669.4
Trade Balance	-159.1	164.1	-253.5	-746.8	-869.1	-892.0	-1,270.0	-1,440.8	-1,428.9	-1,393.7
Exports of Goods (FOB)	871.0	1,180.0	1,382.3	1,120.8	1,081.5	1,827.0	2,281.7	3,030.4	2,766.7	2,643.4
Imports of Goods (FOB)	1,030.1	1,015.9	1,635.8	1,867.6	1,950.6	2,719.0	3,551.7	4,471.2	4,195.6	4,037.1
Service Balance	-4.9	91.4	39.9	356.7	283.7	473.8	739.6	942.4	843.0	781.8
Income Balance	-81.3	-23.4	-14.3	-6.3	-48.6	-94.7	-67.7	-74.3	-90.9	-106.9
Current Transfers	35.1	23.5	55.6	72.3	33.9	100.3	31.5	72.2	39.4	49.4
Capital and Financial Account										
Balance	-156.3	-19.8	29.2	151.0	-204.5	180.7	363.9	251.2	494.7	344.8
Capital Account Balance	0.1	0.4	...	...	...	...	...	...	...	...
Capital Transfers	0.1	0.4	...	...	...	...	...	...	...	...
Financial Account Balance	-156.4	-20.2	29.2	151.0	-204.5	180.7	363.9	251.2	494.7	344.8
Direct Investment	8.4	12.8	76.3	83.5	136.6	119.2	124.1	163.7	297.6	215.0
Portfolio Investment	...	...	...	...	...	...	...	...	...	...
Other Investment	-164.8	-33.0	-47.1	67.5	-341.1	61.5	239.8	87.5	197.1	129.8
Change in Reserves (- Increase)	168.2	-145.2	-219.3	-298.9	346.9	-86.2	-327.8	-47.7	44.3	215.3
Errors and Omissions	198.3	-90.6	362.4	472.0	457.7	318.1	530.5	297.0	98.4	109.3
Total External Debt					(Millions of Dollars)					
Disbursed Debt	2,257.6	2,303.9	1,989.0	1,944.7	1,602.2	1,567.3	1,954.7	2,219.9	2,130.7	...
Debt Service Actually Paid	381.4	149.9	324.9	275.3	648.8	285.6	255.7	288.3	283.3	...
					(In Percent)					
Interest Payments Due/Exports of Goods and Non-Factor Services ..	11.8	7.1	5.3	4.7	8.3	3.2	2.2	1.8	2.1	2.4

[1] Source: IDB Statistics and Quantitative Analysis Unit and Regional Operations Department.
[2] At market prices.
[3] Includes net lending.

[4] Mid-year values.
[5] Short-term nominal deposit rate.
[6] Trade-weighted calculated using the period average nominal exchange rate.

PERU
Statistical Profile[1]

	1988	1989	1990	1991	1992	1993	1994	1995	1996	1997p
Real Gross Domestic Product (GDP)[2]	(Average Annual Growth Rates)									
Total GDP	-8.3	-11.7	-5.4	2.8	-1.4	6.4	13.1	7.2	2.6	7.4
Agriculture, Forestry and Fishing	7.9	-4.8	-6.4	1.9	-6.1	10.4	15.3	4.9	5.7	3.6
Mining and Quarrying	-15.0	-4.9	-8.7	2.2	-2.6	8.2	4.4	2.2	2.6	5.8
Manufacturing	-11.2	-15.7	-5.8	6.2	-2.4	4.8	15.8	4.5	2.7	6.5
Construction	-6.8	-14.7	3.2	1.7	4.3	14.4	32.1	17.2	-4.6	21.3
Non-Financial Public Sector	(As a Percent of Current GDP)									
Current Revenue	10.9	9.0	10.0	10.3	11.3	13.3	14.9	...	...	...
Current Expenditures	15.7	14.3	11.8	9.0	9.8	10.5	11.3	...	...	...
Current Saving	-4.7	-5.3	-1.8	1.2	1.5	2.8	3.6	2.1	3.4	4.5
Capital Expenditures[3]	3.7	4.4	2.8	2.8	3.5	4.5	5.1	5.0	4.8	4.6
Overall Balance (- Deficit)	-8.1	-8.5	-4.5	-1.5	-1.7	-1.3	3.1	-1.3	2.4	0.8
Domestic Financing	4.1	4.9	2.0	-0.6	0.8	-0.3	-4.2	-1.0	-3.1	-0.3
Money and Credit[4]	(As a Percent of Current GDP)									
Domestic Credit	3.6	3.5	1.6	5.6	6.3	8.8	7.2	8.5	11.8	14.1
Public Sector	1.4	1.4	0.8	2.0	0.7	0.8	-2.6	-3.5	-4.2	-4.7
Private Sector	2.2	2.1	0.8	3.5	5.5	7.9	9.8	12.1	16.0	18.8
Money Supply (M1)	3.0	2.2	0.7	3.5	3.8	4.4	4.2	4.8	5.3	7.5
Interest Rate[5]	161.8	1,135.6	2,439.6	170.5	59.7	44.1	22.3	16.0	15.4	15.0
Prices and Salaries	(Average Annual Growth Rates)									
Consumer Prices	660.0	3,321.1	7,592.3	409.5	73.5	48.6	23.7	11.1	11.5	8.6
Real Wages	-23.6	-46.7	-14.4	15.2	-3.6	-0.8	14.9	-8.4	-4.5	0.4
Exchange Rates	(New Soles per Dollar)									
Market Rate[6]	-	-	0.19	0.77	1.25	1.99	2.19	2.25	2.45	2.66
	(Index 1990 = 100)									
Real Effective[7]	212.6	120.2	100.0	80.8	78.9	91.2	84.1	82.1	79.9	78.2
	(Index 1990 = 100)									
Terms of Trade	96.8	94.1	100.0	96.1	95.1	92.1	93.9	94.7	94.2	100.5
Balance of Payments	(Millions of Dollars)									
Current Account Balance	-1,819.0	-570.0	-1,384.0	-1,510.0	-2,101.0	-2,302.0	-2,662.0	-4,298.0	-3,605.0	-3,414.0
Trade Balance	-134.0	1,246.0	399.0	-189.0	-341.0	-607.0	-997.0	-2,170.0	-2,000.0	-1,814.0
Exports of Goods (FOB)	2,731.0	3,533.0	3,321.0	3,406.0	3,661.0	3,516.0	4,598.0	5,591.0	5,897.0	6,754.0
Imports of Goods (FOB)	2,865.0	2,287.0	2,922.0	3,595.0	4,002.0	4,123.0	5,596.0	7,761.0	7,897.0	8,568.0
Service Balance	-333.0	-307.0	-365.0	-413.0	-575.0	-575.0	-502.0	-773.0	-679.0	-739.0
Income Balance	-1,515.0	-1,685.0	-1,733.0	-1,367.0	-1,632.0	-1,615.0	-1,800.0	-1,997.0	-1,573.0	-1,497.0
Current Transfers	163.0	176.0	316.0	459.0	446.0	495.0	637.0	642.0	647.0	636.0
Capital and Financial Account Balance	1,338.0	979.0	1,812.0	1,294.0	2,238.0	1,737.0	5,462.0	4,681.0	4,500.0	4,816.0
Capital Account Balance	4.0	-20.0	-25.0	-40.0	3.0	-71.0	45.0	42.0	66.0	...
Capital Transfers	4.0	-20.0	-25.0	-40.0	3.0	-71.0	45.0	42.0	66.0	...
Financial Account Balance	1,334.0	999.0	1,837.0	1,334.0	2,235.0	1,808.0	5,417.0	4,639.0	4,434.0	4,816.0
Direct Investment	26.0	59.0	41.0	-7.0	136.0	670.0	3,083.0	2,083.0	3,571.0	2,005.0
Portfolio Investment	...	...	...	...	...	228.0	572.0	145.0	341.0	348.0
Other Investment	1,308.0	940.0	1,796.0	1,341.0	2,099.0	910.0	1,762.0	2,411.0	522.0	2,463.0
Change in Reserves (- Increase)	149.0	-242.0	-212.0	-899.0	-554.0	-667.0	-3,068.0	-950.0	-1,877.0	-1,635.0
Errors and Omissions	332.0	-167.0	-215.0	1,114.0	417.0	1,232.0	267.0	567.0	982.0	233.0
Total External Debt	(Millions of Dollars)									
Disbursed Debt	15,268.3	15,304.6	16,330.7	18,281.5	18,541.4	19,480.7	22,075.4	26,244.0	28,955.4	27,520.0
Debt Service Actually Paid	347.1	604.5	475.3	1,151.5	1,003.4	3,211.9	1,141.9	1,239.7	2,931.5	...
	(In Percent)									
Interest Payments Due/Exports of Goods and Non-Factor Services	44.8	42.6	46.4	36.7	37.3	38.9	34.4	33.0	25.4	19.5

[1] Source: IDB Statistics and Quantitative Analysis Unit and Regional Operations Department.
[2] At market prices.
[3] Includes net lending.
[4] Mid-year values.

[5] Average rate offered by commercial banks on 31- to 179-day nominal time deposits; converted to percent per annum by compounding monthly interest rates.
[6] (-) Indicates that the exchange rate is less than half of a significant digit, given the magnitude of the depreciations experienced.
[7] Trade-weighted calculated using the period average nominal exchange rate.

SURINAME
Statistical Profile[1]

	1988	1989	1990	1991	1992	1993	1994	1995	1996	1997p
Real Gross Domestic Product (GDP)[2]					(Average Annual Growth Rates)					
Total GDP	9.4	4.7	0.3	2.8	-10.7	-12.5	-2.4	6.7	6.9	4.7
Agriculture, Forestry and Fishing	-0.5	-2.4	0.9	16.8	0.4	-2.0	-8.4	-3.4	-4.1	-3.2
Mining and Quarrying	43.8	6.6	-1.9	1.4	5.5	9.1	19.1	3.5	7.7	16.0
Manufacturing	11.9	1.5	0.9	-3.2	-11.4	-16.1	1.9	-0.9	6.6	0.5
Construction	-1.7	-10.3	-13.7	-2.2	18.9	-27.1	-38.2	131.8	18.4	-1.3
Central Government					(As a Percent of Current GDP)					
Current Revenue	29.3	31.2	31.5	27.2	22.8	12.6	19.0	34.7	34.4	30.8
Current Expenditures	49.0	44.8	37.8	44.9	37.6	39.0	25.7	38.5	45.6	38.0
Current Saving	-19.7	-13.5	-6.3	-17.8	-14.8	-26.4	-6.7	-3.8	-11.2	-7.2
Capital Expenditures[3]	2.5	3.8	3.9	1.5	2.3	3.6	3.3	5.9	7.0	7.5
Overall Balance (- Deficit)	-21.3	-14.0	-6.3	-17.4	-8.7	-9.4	4.1	4.6	0.5	-4.0
Domestic Financing	20.9	16.7	2.2	18.9	8.7	8.5	-2.2	-5.8	1.9	3.7
Money and Credit[4]					(As a Percent of Current GDP)					
Domestic Credit	137.1	142.0	126.8	126.5	115.4	66.2	13.7	5.9	10.0	21.0
Public Sector	101.8	102.8	86.2	84.2	73.3	39.6	7.4	-0.5	-3.8	-0.3
Private Sector	35.3	39.2	40.6	42.3	42.0	26.6	6.3	6.4	13.8	21.3
Money Supply (M1)	74.2	75.3	69.8	67.7	59.1	37.1	14.5	18.6	25.0	22.9
Interest Rate[5]	8.8	8.6	8.8	9.2	9.2	11.7	32.2	39.9	35.2	34.6
Prices and Salaries					(Average Annual Growth Rates)					
Consumer Prices	7.3	0.7	21.8	26.0	43.7	143.5	368.5	235.6	-0.7	7.1
Real Wages	-5.4	9.4	-16.7	-4.6	-14.4	-33.9	12.3	22.0	85.4	33.6
Exchange Rates					(Guilders per Dollar)					
Market Rate[6]	6.56	7.77	9.76	10.23	14.80	51.23	208.50	457.14	404.87	408.66
					(Index 1990 = 100)					
Real Effective[7]	68.6	85.1	100.0	84.7	88.1	120.5	110.6	81.4	73.5	66.0
					(Index 1980 = 100)					
Terms of Trade	84.7	122.0	99.1	84.1	77.0	75.0	83.2	91.1	81.4	83.9
Balance of Payments					(Millions of Dollars)					
Current Account Balance	114.3	293.5	66.8	-133.4	25.4	44.0	58.6	72.9	9.6	5.5
Trade Balance	212.3	389.7	163.3	-2.0	122.1	84.4	99.3	123.0	8.0	30.7
Exports of Goods (FOB)	639.7	980.3	831.6	617.5	608.6	298.3	293.6	415.6	434.3	538.1
Imports of Goods (FOB)	427.4	590.6	668.3	619.5	486.5	213.9	194.3	292.6	426.3	507.4
Service Balance	-95.7	-119.6	-134.3	-134.6	-135.7	-55.1	-40.9	-57.8	-124.7	-127.8
Income Balance	-15.1	-11.3	-15.2	-20.0	-13.3	-6.2	-3.8	-2.6	2.8	-0.2
Current Transfers	12.8	34.7	53.0	23.2	52.3	20.9	4.0	10.3	123.5	102.8
Capital and Financial Account										
Balance	-120.3	-311.4	-31.7	56.0	-92.3	-72.6	-84.3	-30.2	38.1	90.2
Capital Account Balance	-2.7	-2.8	-5.0	-1.9	-5.7	0.5	-0.2	...	...	...
Capital Transfers	-2.7	-2.8	-5.0	-1.9	-5.7	0.5	-0.2	...	...	...
Financial Account Balance	-117.6	-308.6	-26.7	57.9	-86.6	-73.1	-84.1	-30.2	38.1	90.2
Direct Investment	-171.0	-299.7	-76.8	18.5	-54.3	-46.6	-30.2	-21.3	54.2	56.0
Portfolio Investment	...	...	0.9	-4.1	2.6	...	...	...	...	...
Other Investment	53.4	-8.9	49.2	43.5	-34.9	-26.5	-53.9	-8.9	-16.1	34.2
Change in Reserves (- Increase)	9.2	0.2	-18.3	78.3	21.5	-12.7	-34.3	-96.6	21.4	-31.4
Errors and Omissions	-3.2	17.7	-16.8	-0.9	45.4	41.3	60.0	53.9	-69.1	-64.3
Total External Debt					(Millions of Dollars)					
Disbursed Debt	96.6	117.7	125.5	194.2	204.9	206.1	198.1	197.2	178.0	187.1
Debt Service Actually Paid	...	...	...	...	...	...	45.1	41.0	40.0	...
					(In Percent)					
Interest Payments Due/Exports of Goods and Non-Factor Services ..	0.7	0.6	1.6	2.0	1.5	1.3	1.0	...	...	...

[1] *Source*: IDB Statistics and Quantitative Analysis Unit and Regional Operations Department.
[2] GDP at market prices. Sector of Origin at factor cost.
[3] Includes net lending.

[4] Mid-year values.
[5] Weighted average commercial bank lending rate.
[6] Average exchange rate taking into account parallel rate.
[7] Trade-weighted calculated using the period average nominal exchange rate.

TRINIDAD AND TOBAGO
Statistical Profile[1]

	1988	1989	1990	1991	1992	1993	1994	1995	1996	1997p
Real Gross Domestic Product (GDP)[2]					(Average Annual Growth Rates)					
Total GDP	-3.9	-0.8	1.5	2.7	-1.6	-1.5	3.6	2.4	3.1	3.9
Agriculture, Forestry and Fishing	-2.8	6.0	17.0	3.0	-1.1	8.4	0.8	-2.8	3.8	-0.9
Mining and Quarrying	-2.6	-1.2	0.6	-3.1	-5.0	-9.0	6.1	0.2	-1.7	-4.0
Manufacturing	0.7	5.1	2.7	8.4	2.6	-3.1	6.6	3.7	6.0	7.0
Construction	-2.5	-8.2	2.2	11.7	-5.0	-4.3	13.5	7.9	5.3	9.4
Central Government					(As a Percent of Current GDP)					
Current Revenue	28.6	26.3	25.7	29.9	26.3	27.4	25.6	26.8	28.1	25.4
Current Expenditures	30.9	28.3	25.8	26.8	27.5	26.1	24.2	24.8	25.9	24.0
Current Saving	-2.3	-2.0	-0.1	3.1	-1.2	1.4	1.4	2.0	2.2	1.4
Capital Expenditures[3]	3.4	2.4	1.6	3.4	1.6	1.6	1.6	2.0	1.7	2.9
Overall Balance (- Deficit)	-5.7	-4.2	-1.2	-0.2	-2.8	-0.2	-0.0	0.2	0.5	0.7
Domestic Financing	5.8	5.0	3.3	1.9	3.6	-1.9	-1.1	2.4	-0.5	1.5
Money and Credit[4]					(As a Percent of Current GDP)					
Domestic Credit	53.5	52.2	44.6	43.2	47.8	48.6	38.0	32.2	35.9	38.6
Public Sector	19.0	18.9	15.7	11.7	15.9	16.5	11.6	7.4	7.9	3.0
Private Sector	34.5	33.4	28.9	31.4	31.9	32.1	26.4	24.9	28.1	35.5
Money Supply (M1)	11.0	11.0	10.4	11.2	11.4	12.1	10.7	11.2	11.0	11.4
Interest Rate[5]	12.1	12.0	11.7	11.8	12.8	13.1	13.9	13.4	14.2	13.8
Prices and Salaries					(Average Annual Growth Rates)					
Consumer Prices	7.7	11.4	11.1	3.8	6.5	10.8	8.8	5.2	3.4	3.7
Real Wages	-6.8	-12.8	-9.2	-0.7	-1.6	-6.9	-7.6	-3.2	-0.8	-0.8
Exchange Rates					(Trinidad and Tobago Dollars per Dollar)					
Market Rate	3.84	4.25	4.25	4.25	4.25	5.35	5.92	5.95	6.01	6.25
					(Index 1990 = 100)					
Real Effective[6]	100.9	102.2	100.0	99.6	97.6	108.3	117.2	119.6	117.4	118.4
					(Index 1980 = 100)					
Terms of Trade	68.5	66.5	71.1	71.6	69.6	72.5	88.2	98.9	88.3	90.0
Balance of Payments					(Millions of Dollars)					
Current Account Balance	-88.6	-38.5	459.0	-4.7	138.9	113.1	217.8	293.8	-37.4	-554.8
Trade Balance	405.3	505.5	1,012.5	564.2	695.7	547.2	741.1	587.7	275.7	-294.4
Exports of Goods (FOB)	1,469.5	1,550.8	1,960.1	1,774.5	1,691.4	1,500.1	1,777.6	2,456.1	2,565.2	2,528.6
Imports of Goods (FOB)	1,064.2	1,045.2	947.6	1,210.3	995.6	952.9	1,036.6	1,868.5	2,289.5	2,823.0
Service Balance	-182.7	-158.9	-150.6	-129.1	-109.1	-112.9	-111.5	100.7	235.5	242.6
Income Balance	-302.0	-377.6	-396.8	-442.1	-448.1	-325.8	-412.1	-390.1	-536.0	-498.0
Current Transfers	-9.2	-7.5	-6.2	2.4	0.4	4.7	0.3	-4.5	-12.5	-5.0
Capital and Financial Account Balance	40.0	151.5	-149.3	-69.2	-190.7	-41.9	-110.5	-335.0	176.4	323.3
Capital Account Balance	-20.4	-17.2	-19.2	-16.1	-16.5	-11.5	-6.4	-11.9	-13.0	...
Capital Transfers	-20.4	-17.2	-19.2	-16.1	-16.5	-11.5	-6.4	-11.9	-13.0	...
Financial Account Balance	60.4	168.7	-130.1	-53.1	-174.2	-30.4	-104.1	-323.1	189.4	323.3
Direct Investment	62.9	148.9	109.4	169.3	177.9	379.2	516.2	298.9	400.0	782.0
Portfolio Investment	...	...	...	...	...	...	...	8.8	9.9	-10.0
Other Investment	-2.5	19.8	-239.5	-222.4	-352.1	-409.6	-620.3	-630.8	-220.5	-448.7
Change in Reserves (- Increase)	27.4	-158.5	-197.7	102.7	124.4	-29.4	-113.6	-40.1	-219.0	-155.8
Errors and Omissions	21.1	45.4	-112.0	-29.0	-72.6	-41.8	6.3	81.4	80.0	387.3
Total External Debt					(Millions of Dollars)					
Disbursed Debt	2,098.4	2,137.8	2,511.1	2,488.0	2,452.7	2,240.0	2,493.2	2,730.6	2,232.8	2,661.0
Debt Service Actually Paid	383.0	247.1	449.1	427.8	576.5	701.1	544.6	416.7	861.2	600.0
					(In Percent)					
Interest Payments Due/Exports of Goods and Non-Factor Services	10.8	12.7	10.4	11.6	10.4	11.4	9.4	10.0	4.7	...

[1] Source: IDB Statistics and Quantitative Analysis Unit and Regional Operations Department.
[2] At market prices.
[3] Includes net lending.
[4] Mid-year values.
[5] Weighted average lending rates.
[6] Trade-weighted calculated using the period average nominal exchange rate.

URUGUAY
Statistical Profile[1]

	1988	1989	1990	1991	1992	1993	1994	1995	1996	1997p
Real Gross Domestic Product (GDP)[2]					(Average Annual Growth Rates)					
Total GDP	-0.0	1.3	0.9	3.2	7.9	3.0	6.3	-1.8	5.3	5.1
Agriculture, Forestry and Fishing	-1.6	3.5	0.3	2.2	12.1	-3.7	9.2	3.1	8.5	-1.2
Manufacturing	-0.9	-0.2	-1.5	-0.5	1.5	-9.0	4.0	-2.8	4.0	5.8
Construction	6.7	2.2	-14.5	10.1	15.7	20.5	1.4	-15.8	4.2	2.9
Wholesale and Retail Trade	-1.6	-0.9	0.2	8.4	13.5	16.7	10.0	-9.3	5.6	8.2
Non-Financial Public Sector					(As a Percent of Current GDP)					
Current Revenue	24.9	23.8	28.9	31.1	31.7	30.8	30.5	30.0	30.4	30.8
Current Expenditures	22.6	23.5	24.5	25.7	26.4	26.9	27.3	26.9	27.6	27.7
Current Saving	2.3	0.3	4.4	5.3	5.3	3.9	3.2	3.1	2.9	3.1
Capital Expenditures[3]	4.2	3.8	4.0	4.1	3.9	4.7	5.7	4.2	3.9	4.1
Overall Balance (- Deficit)	-1.9	-3.5	0.4	1.3	1.4	-0.8	-2.5	-1.1	-1.0	-1.0
Domestic Financing	-1.3	-4.0	-2.0	-2.5	-2.5	...	...	...	...	...
Money and Credit[4]					(As a Percent of Current GDP)					
Domestic Credit	47.6	47.1	46.0	34.1	29.0	31.9	28.9	30.6	32.8	35.0
Public Sector	12.2	11.6	13.5	8.4	5.7	7.3	5.5	5.6	4.9	5.3
Private Sector	35.4	35.5	32.5	25.7	23.3	24.6	23.4	25.0	27.9	29.7
Money Supply (M1)	6.0	5.1	4.9	4.7	5.4	6.1	5.2	5.2	5.2	5.3
Interest Rate[5]	67.8	84.7	97.8	75.2	54.5	39.4	37.0	38.2	28.1	...
Prices and Salaries					(Average Annual Growth Rates)					
Consumer Prices	62.3	80.5	112.3	102.0	68.4	54.1	44.7	42.2	28.3	19.8
Real Wages	1.5	-0.4	-7.3	3.8	2.2	4.8	0.9	-2.9	0.6	0.2
Exchange Rates					(Pesos per Dollar)					
Market Rate	0.36	0.61	1.17	2.02	3.03	3.95	5.05	6.35	7.97	9.44
					(Index 1990 = 100)					
Real Effective[6]	96.5	92.2	100.0	86.9	81.3	69.1	65.3	63.6	62.3	59.3
					(Index 1990 = 100)					
Terms of Trade	102.9	105.5	100.0	99.6	104.3	94.3	95.3	101.4	98.5	102.0
Balance of Payments					(Millions of Dollars)					
Current Account Balance	22.1	133.5	185.9	42.4	-8.8	-243.8	-438.3	-212.5	-233.4	-321.1
Trade Balance	292.3	462.8	426.0	61.0	-121.8	-386.7	-706.0	-563.0	-686.9	-723.1
Exports of Goods (FOB)	1,404.5	1,599.0	1,692.9	1,604.7	1,801.4	1,731.6	1,917.6	2,147.6	2,448.5	2,780.5
Imports of Goods (FOB)	1,112.2	1,136.2	1,266.9	1,543.7	1,923.2	2,118.3	2,623.6	2,710.6	3,135.4	3,503.6
Service Balance	32.8	11.6	73.1	173.7	271.5	281.9	469.1	501.5	559.6	528.6
Income Balance	-324.3	-348.9	-321.3	-232.4	-187.1	-192.4	-242.6	-227.0	-188.6	-207.8
Current Transfers	21.3	8.0	8.1	40.1	28.6	53.4	41.2	76.0	82.5	81.2
Capital and Financial Account Balance	178.1	-74.1	-181.4	-397.7	-43.3	213.6	526.6	411.9	199.5	669.7
Capital Account Balance	...	...	...	...	...	...	...	...	...	...
Capital Transfers	...	...	...	...	...	...	...	...	...	...
Financial Account Balance	178.1	-74.1	-181.4	-397.7	-43.3	213.6	526.6	411.9	199.5	669.7
Direct Investment	44.5	...	...	...	...	101.5	154.5	156.6	168.9	...
Portfolio Investment	164.2	129.8	107.8	47.4	83.4	29.3	158.1	288.8	179.9	...
Other Investment	-30.6	-203.9	-289.2	-445.1	-126.7	82.8	214.0	-33.5	-149.3	669.7
Change in Reserves (- Increase)	46.8	3.2	-40.2	-113.5	-186.2	-178.6	-98.5	-218.0	-118.6	-321.1
Errors and Omissions	-247.0	-62.6	35.7	468.8	238.3	208.7	10.2	18.6	152.5	-27.5
Total External Debt					(Millions of Dollars)					
Disbursed Debt	3,820.8	4,448.6	4,415.1	4,191.2	4,573.5	4,850.7	5,077.3	5,317.3	5,898.8	...
Debt Service Actually Paid	890.4	659.9	986.7	805.9	524.4	586.6	676.9	865.5	664.5	...
					(In Percent)					
Interest Payments Due/Exports of Goods and Non-Factor Services	18.8	20.9	21.2	16.2	11.8	11.0	12.1	12.8	11.9	...

[1] Source: IDB Statistics and Quantitative Analysis Unit and Regional Operations Department.
[2] At market prices.
[3] Includes net lending.
[4] Mid-year values.
[5] Rates on 1-6 month domestic currency fixed nominal deposits at deposit money banks; average rate for 5 most representative private banks at end of month.
[6] Trade-weighted calculated using the period average nominal exchange rate.

VENEZUELA
Statistical Profile[1]

	1988	1989	1990	1991	1992	1993	1994	1995	1996	1997p
Real Gross Domestic Product (GDP)[2]					(Average Annual Growth Rates)					
Total GDP	6.2	-7.8	6.9	9.7	6.1	0.3	-2.3	3.7	-0.4	5.1
Agriculture, Forestry and Fishing	4.6	-5.1	-1.5	2.4	2.1	3.0	-1.1	-0.5	1.9	2.7
Petroleum	4.1	0.0	17.9	9.5	1.4	9.0	5.5	6.0	8.4	8.9
Manufacturing	6.9	-11.8	6.0	9.7	2.5	-1.0	-2.4	7.9	-2.6	4.1
Construction	7.9	-27.0	7.8	30.9	34.6	-5.5	-17.4	-5.0	1.9	12.6
Non-Financial Public Sector[3]					(As a Percent of Current GDP)					
Current Revenue	23.8	29.4	32.9	29.5	24.2	25.7	27.7	25.8	34.4	28.4
Current Expenditures	18.0	18.4	20.1	18.0	17.7	15.9	16.3	17.3	16.0	17.4
Current Saving	5.8	11.1	12.7	11.5	6.5	9.9	11.4	8.5	18.4	11.0
Capital Expenditures[4]	14.4	12.3	12.7	15.3	12.5	11.3	25.3	15.8	12.1	12.5
Overall Balance (- Deficit)	-8.5	-1.2	0.1	-3.5	-5.9	-1.3	-13.8	-7.3	6.8	2.3
Domestic Financing	...	...	...	...	...	...	...	...	...	...
Money and Credit[5]					(As a Percent of Current GDP)					
Domestic Credit	30.6	24.1	18.5	27.6	22.8	21.2	30.4	19.6	16.3	11.9
Public Sector	1.0	1.2	2.5	10.6	6.4	6.7	8.1	7.1	7.0	0.2
Private Sector	29.7	22.9	16.0	17.0	16.5	14.5	22.3	12.5	9.2	11.7
Money Supply (M1)	13.5	9.3	7.0	8.7	8.4	6.1	7.2	8.2	5.4	8.0
Interest Rate[6]	8.9	33.1	29.1	31.3	35.6	53.9	39.0	25.1	26.3	23.2
Prices and Salaries					(Average Annual Growth Rates)					
Consumer Prices	29.3	84.7	40.6	34.2	31.4	38.1	60.8	59.9	99.9	50.0
Real Wages	-8.8	-15.8	-7.9	-8.2	3.8	-6.8	-11.0	-7.0	...	13.0
Exchange Rates					(Bolivares per Dollar)					
Market Rate	14.50	34.68	46.90	56.82	68.38	90.83	148.50	176.84	417.33	488.63
					(Index 1990 = 100)					
Real Effective[7]	75.6	88.8	100.0	93.0	89.6	85.5	89.5	71.6	84.8	64.7
					(Index 1990 = 100)					
Terms of Trade	72.2	91.0	100.0	82.6	79.4	74.0	74.8	77.6	92.1	90.2
Balance of Payments					(Millions of Dollars)					
Current Account Balance	-5,809.0	2,161.0	8,279.0	1,736.0	-3,749.0	-1,993.0	2,541.0	2,014.0	8,824.0	5,999.0
Trade Balance	-1,863.0	5,694.0	10,706.0	4,900.0	1,322.0	3,275.0	7,606.0	7,013.0	13,756.0	11,592.0
Exports of Goods (FOB)	10,217.0	13,059.0	17,623.0	15,159.0	14,202.0	14,779.0	16,110.0	19,082.0	23,693.0	23,966.0
Imports of Goods (FOB)	12,080.0	7,365.0	6,917.0	10,259.0	12,880.0	11,504.0	8,504.0	12,069.0	9,937.0	12,374.0
Service Balance	-2,028.0	-982.0	-1,351.0	-2,202.0	-2,951.0	-3,185.0	-3,086.0	-3,184.0	-3,335.0	-3,592.0
Income Balance	-1,771.0	-2,368.0	-774.0	-598.0	-1,746.0	-1,715.0	-1,896.0	-1,924.0	-1,735.0	-1,877.0
Current Transfers	-147.0	-183.0	-302.0	-364.0	-374.0	-368.0	-83.0	109.0	138.0	-124.0
Capital and Financial Account Balance	-1,180.0	-2,686.0	-2,161.0	2,425.0	3,203.0	2,388.0	-3,404.0	-3,427.0	-2,480.0	-2,078.0
Capital Account Balance	...	...	...	...	...	...	...	...	...	...
Capital Transfers	...	...	...	...	...	...	...	...	...	...
Financial Account Balance	-1,180.0	-2,686.0	-2,161.0	2,425.0	3,203.0	2,388.0	-3,404.0	-3,427.0	-2,480.0	-2,078.0
Direct Investment	21.0	34.0	76.0	1,728.0	473.0	-514.0	136.0	686.0	1,595.0	4,346.0
Portfolio Investment	...	-534.0	15,976.0	351.0	1,003.0	621.0	261.0	-326.0	758.0	626.0
Other Investment	-1,201.0	-2,186.0	-18,213.0	346.0	1,727.0	2,281.0	-3,801.0	-3,787.0	-4,833.0	-7,050.0
Change in Reserves (- Increase)	3,872.0	-1,077.0	-4,376.0	-2,645.0	845.0	144.0	1,173.0	1,910.0	-6,296.0	-2,424.0
Errors and Omissions	3,117.0	1,603.0	-1,742.0	-1,516.0	-299.0	-539.0	-310.0	-497.0	-48.0	-1,498.0
Total External Debt					(Millions of Dollars)					
Disbursed Debt	34,734.9	32,371.3	33,170.4	34,121.6	37,701.8	37,349.8	36,559.8	35,537.0	35,048.2	32,000.0
Debt Service Actually Paid	5,551.5	6,817.8	5,273.7	3,321.4	3,331.4	4,579.9	4,744.9	5,515.6	4,711.2	9,800.0
					(In Percent)					
Interest Payments Due/Exports of Goods and Non-Factor Services	29.0	24.9	16.3	7.1	10.4	10.1	9.1	8.5	5.5	4.5

[1] Source: IDB Statistics and Quantitative Analysis Unit and Regional Operations Department.
[2] At market prices.
[3] On a cash basis.
[4] Includes net lending.
[5] Mid-year values.
[6] Nominal average annual time deposit rate.
[7] Trade-weighted calculated using the period average nominal exchange rate.

SOURCES OF THE STATISTICAL PROFILES

Real Gross Domestic Product:

Argentina: Ministerio de Economía y Obras y Servicios Públicos, Secretaría de Programación Económica.

Bahamas: IDB estimates based on information furnished by the Department of Statistics and the Central Bank of the Bahamas.

Barbados: Barbados Statistical Service and the Central Bank of Barbados.

Belize: Central Statistical Office, Ministry of Finance.

Bolivia: Instituto Nacional de Estadística, Departamento de Cuentas Nacionales.

Brazil: Fundação Instituto Brasileiro de Geografía e Estatística, Departamento de Contas Nacionais.

Chile: Banco Central de Chile, Departamento de Cuentas Nacionales.

Colombia: Departamento Administrativo Nacional de Estadística.

Costa Rica: Banco Central de Costa Rica, Departamento de Contabilidad Social.

Dominican Republic: Banco Central de la República Dominicana, División de Cuentas Nacionales.

Ecuador: Banco Central del Ecuador, Subgerencia de Cuentas Nacionales.

El Salvador: Banco Central de Reserva de El Salvador, Departamento de Cuentas Económicas.

Guatemala: Banco de Guatemala, Departamento de Estudios Económicos.

Guyana: Statistical Bureau and Bank of Guyana.

Haiti: Institut Haïtien de Statistiques et d'Informatique, Banque de la République d'Haïti and International Monetary Fund estimates.

Honduras: Banco Central de Honduras, Departamento de Estudios Económicos.

Jamaica: Statistical Institute of Jamaica.

Mexico: Instituto Nacional de Estadística, Geografía e Informática.

Nicaragua: Banco Central de Nicaragua, Gerencia de Estudios Económicos.

Panama: Contraloría General de la República, Dirección de Estadística y Censo.

Paraguay: Banco Central del Paraguay, Departamento de Cuentas Nacionales y Mercado Interno.

Peru: Instituto Nacional de Estadística and Banco Central de Reserva del Perú.

Suriname: Algemeem Bureau Voor de Statistiek and IDB estimates.

Trinidad and Tobago: Central Statistical Office of Trinidad and Tobago.

Uruguay: Banco Central del Uruguay, Departamento de Estadísticas Económicas.

Venezuela: Banco Central de Venezuela, Departamento de Cuentas Nacionales.

Non-Financial Public Sector:

Argentina: Ministerio de Economía y Obras y Servicios Públicos and Secretaría de Hacienda.

Bolivia: Banco Central de Bolivia, Gerencia de Estudios Económicos and Ministerio de Finanzas.

Brazil: Banco Central do Brasil, Departamento Econômico.

Colombia: Departamento Nacional de Planeación.

Costa Rica: Ministerio de Hacienda, Autoridad Presupuestaria.

Ecuador: Ministerio de Finanzas, Banco Central del Ecuador and International Monetary Fund estimates.

El Salvador: Ministerio de Hacienda and Banco Central de Reserva de El Salvador.

Haiti: Ministère de l'Economie et des Finances and International Monetary Fund.

Honduras: Banco Central de Honduras, Departamento de Estudios Económicos and International Monetary Fund.

Mexico: Dirección General de Planeación Hacendaria. Secretaría de Hacienda y Crédito Público.

Nicaragua: Ministerio de Finanzas y Banco Central de Nicaragua.

Panama: Contraloría General de la República, Ministerio de Planificación y Política Económica, International Monetary Fund and IDB estimates.

Peru: Banco Central de Reserva del Perú and Ministerio de Economía.

Uruguay: Banco Central del Uruguay.

Venezuela: Banco Central de Venezuela and International Monetary Fund.

Central Government:

Bahamas: Central Bank of the Bahamas, *Quarterly Statistical Digest*.

Barbados: Central Government of Barbados and Ministry of Finance.

Belize: Ministry of Finance.

Chile: Contraloría General de la República, División de Contabilidad.

Dominican Republic: Tesorería Nacional, Contraloría General de la República and Banco Central de la República Dominicana.

Guatemala: Ministerio de Finanzas.

Guyana: Ministry of Finance and Bank of Guyana.

Jamaica: Ministry of Finance, Fiscal Policy Management Unit.

Paraguay: Ministerio de Finanzas.

Suriname: International Monetary Fund based on data furnished by the Ministerie van Financiën en Planning and Planbureau.

Trinidad and Tobago: Central Statistical Office of Trinidad and Tobago and the Ministry of Finance and the Economy.

Money and Credit (mid-year observations)

International Monetary Fund, *International Financial Statistics* and the following national sources:

Brazil: Domestic Credit: Banco Central do Brasil, Departamento Econômico.

Ecuador: International Monetary Fund, *International Financial Statistics* and IDB estimates based on information furnished by the Banco Central del Ecuador.

Guyana: Bank of Guyana.

Haiti: Banque de la République d'Haïti.

Nicaragua: Banco Central de Nicaragua (annual average).

Peru: Banco Central de Reserva del Perú.

Suriname: Centrale Bank van Suriname.

Prices:

Consumer Prices: International Monetary Fund, *International Financial Statistics*.

Real Wages:

Argentina:	Fundación de Investigaciones Económicas Latinoamericanas.
Barbados:	Central Bank of Barbados.
Brazil:	Fundação Getúlio Vargas, Conjuntura Econômica.
Chile:	Banco Central de Chile, *Boletín Mensual*, various issues.
Colombia:	Departamento Administrativo Nacional de Estadística, Encuesta mensual manufacturera.
Costa Rica:	Banco Central de Costa Rica, Departamento de Contabilidad Social based on information furnished by the Caja Costarricense del Seguro Social.
Dominican Republic:	Oficina Nacional de Planeación.
Ecuador:	Consejo Nacional de Desarrollo (CONADE) and Banco Central del Ecuador.
El Salvador:	Instituto Salvadoreño del Seguro Social.
Guatemala:	Instituto Guatemalteco de Seguridad Social and Banco de Guatemala, Sección de Cuentas Nacionales.
Haiti:	Ministère des Affaires Sociales, and the Institut Haïtien de Statistiques et d'Informatique.
Honduras:	Banco Central de Honduras, Departamento de Estudios Económicos.
Mexico:	Banco de México.
Nicaragua:	IDB estimates based on data furnished by Ministerio de Trabajo.
Panama:	Contraloría General de la República, Dirección de Estadística y Censo, and IDB estimates.
Paraguay:	Banco Central del Paraguay.
Peru:	Banco Central de Reserva del Perú.
Suriname:	Algemeem Bureau Voor de Statistiek and IDB estimates.
Trinidad and Tobago:	Central Statistical Office of Trinidad and Tobago.
Uruguay:	Dirección General de Estudios y Censos, *Boletín Mensual*.
Venezuela:	Oficina Central de Coordinación y Planificación (CORDIPLAN), Dirección de Planificación de Empleo, Producción y Precios.

Market Exchange Rates:

International Monetary Fund, *International Financial Statistics* and the following national sources:

Haiti:	Banque de la République d'Haïti.

Real Effective Exchange Rates:

IDB estimates based on data from the International Monetary Fund, *International Financial Statistics*, and the following national sources:

Guatemala:	Banco de Guatemala, Departamento de Estudios Económicos.
Mexico:	Banco de México, Dirección de Operaciones Internacionales.
Peru:	Banco Central de Reserva del Perú.

Terms of Trade:

ECLAC, *Balance preliminar de la economía de América Latina y el Caribe*, various issues, and IDB estimates for Guyana, Jamaica, Suriname and Trinidad and Tobago.

Balance of Payments:

International Monetary Fund, *Balance of Payments Statistics* (magnetic tapes) and the following national sources:

Argentina:	Ministerio de Economía.
Bahamas:	Central Bank of the Bahamas.
Barbados:	Central Bank of Barbados.
Belize:	Central Bank of Belize.
Bolivia:	Banco Central de Bolivia.
Brazil:	Banco Central do Brasil.
Chile:	Banco Central de Chile.
Colombia:	Banco de la República, Subgerencia de Estudios Económicos.
Costa Rica:	Banco Central de Costa Rica.
Dominican Republic:	Banco Central de la República Dominicana, División de Balanza de Pagos.
Ecuador:	Banco Central del Ecuador, Subgerencia de Balanza de Pagos.
El Salvador:	Banco Central de Reserva de El Salvador.
Guatemala:	Banco de Guatemala, Departamento de Estudios Económicos.
Guyana:	Ministry of Finance.
Haiti:	Banque de la République d'Haïti.
Honduras:	Banco Central de Honduras.
Jamaica:	Bank of Jamaica.
Mexico:	Banco de México.
Nicaragua:	Banco Central de Nicaragua.
Paraguay:	Banco Central del Paraguay.
Peru:	Banco Central de Reserva del Perú.
Suriname:	Centrale Bank van Suriname.
Trinidad and Tobago:	Central Bank of Trinidad and Tobago.
Uruguay:	Banco Central del Uruguay.
Venezuela:	Banco Central de Venezuela.

External Debt:

World Bank, *World Debt Tables* (magnetic tapes) and the following national sources:

Bahamas:	Treasury Accounts, Treasury Statistical Printout and Quarterly Reports from Public Corporations, and estimates.
Suriname:	IDB estimates based on information from the Centrale Bank van Suriname.
All countries:	Interest Payments Due/Exports of Goods and Non-Factor Services: Ibidem and see also Balance of Payments above.

Interest Rates:

International Monetary Fund, *International Financial Statistics*, and the following national sources:

Barbados:	Central Bank of Barbados.
Belize:	Central Bank of Belize.
Bolivia:	Banco Central de Bolivia.
Brazil:	Fundação Getúlio Vargas, Conjuntura Econômica.
Guatemala:	Banco de Guatemala.
Haiti:	Banque de la République d'Haïti.
Honduras:	Banco Central de Honduras.
Jamaica:	Bank of Jamaica.
Paraguay:	Banco Central del Paraguay.
Suriname:	Centrale Bank van Suriname and IDB estimates.
Trinidad and Tobago:	Central Bank of Trinidad and Tobago.